Edexcel
Religious Studies
for AS

Peter Cole
Richard Gray
Consultant: Arthur Giles

HODDER
EDUCATION

Dedication

For Nicola, Jack, Ethan, Elizabeth and Anna Gray and also for my godson Edward Szymczyk

Acknowledgements

There are many people we have to thank. First of all, we are indebted to our very patient, encouraging and inspiring editors Jane Tyler, Joan Miller and Rob Bircher, who have managed us through some very busy periods and tight deadlines. Thanks go to Garth Ratcliffe, who has spent many a long evening correcting and suggesting improvements to the text. Also, special thanks to our consultant, Arthur Giles from Edexcel, for his sharp insight and honest comments on many drafts. Finally, appreciation for Margaret Gray and June Rowley in supporting the Gray family once again throughout another project – your love and support has been immense!

This material has been endorsed by Edexcel and offers high-quality support for the delivery of Edexcel qualifications.

Edexcel endorsement does not mean that this material is essential to achieve any Edexcel qualification, nor does it mean that this is the only suitable material available to support any Edexcel qualification. No endorsed material will be used verbatim in setting any Edexcel examination and any resource lists produced by Edexcel shall include this and any other appropriate texts. While this material has been through an Edexcel quality-assurance process, all responsibility for content remains with the publisher. Copies of the official specifications for all Edexcel qualifications may be found on the Edexcel website: www.edexcel.org.uk.

Although every effort has been made to ensure that website addresses are correct at the time of going to press, Hodder Education cannot be held responsible for the content of any website mentioned in this book. It is sometimes possible to find a relocated web page by typing in the address of the home page for a website in the URL window of your browser.

Hachette UK's policy is to use papers that are natural, renewable and recyclable products and made from wood grown in sustainable forests. The logging and manufacturing processes are expected to conform to the environmental regulations of the country of origin.

Orders: please contact Bookpoint Ltd, 130 Milton Park, Abingdon, Oxon OX14 4SB. Telephone: (44) 01235 827720. Fax: (44) 01235 400454. Lines are open 9.00–5.00, Monday to Saturday, with a 24-hour message answering service. Visit our website at www.hoddereducation.co.uk

First published in 2009 by
Hodder Education,
An Hachette UK Company
338 Euston Road
London NW1 3BH

Impression number   5 4 3 2 1
Year   2013 2012 2011 2010 2009

Cover photo © Design Pics/Imagestate
Illustrations by Beehive Illustration (Jim Eldridge) and Ken Vail Graphic Design
Typeset in Bembo 11pt by Ken Vail Graphic Design, Cambridge www.kvgd.com
Index by Indexing Specialists (UK) Ltd
Printed in Italy

A catalogue record for this title is available from the British Library
ISBN: 978 0340 957806

CONTENTS

INTRODUCTION	**1**

UNIT 1 – FOUNDATIONS	**11**

AREA A: PHILOSOPHY OF RELIGION | 11
1A The design argument | 11
1B The cosmological argument | 23
1C A critical analysis of the issues | 32
2A The problems of evil and suffering and possible solutions | 43
2B Definitions and some philosophical problems of miracles | 54
2C A critical analysis of the issues | 65

AREA B: ETHICS | 70
1A The relationship between religion and morality | 70
1B Utilitarianism and situation ethics | 79
1C A critical analysis of the issues | 91
2A Issues of war and peace | 96
2B Sexual ethics | 102
2C A critical analysis of the issues | 112

AREA C: BUDDHISM | 115
1A The historical, social and religious context for Buddhism | 115
1B The life and work of the Buddha and his significance for Buddhists | 124
1C Influence of society on the Buddha and his teachings | 133
2A The three refuges, meaning and significance | 137
2B Types and purposes of meditation, their context and application | 149
2C An evaluation of the significance of Buddhist teaching and practice | 158

AREA F: ISLAM | 162
1A The life and work of Muhammad in its historical, religious and social background | 162
1B The significance of Muhammad for Muslims | 173
1C A critical analysis of the issues | 184
2A The six beliefs – meaning and significance for belief and practice | 188

2B The five pillars – meaning and significance for belief and practice 198
2C A critical analysis of the issues in teaching and practice 215

AREA I: NEW TESTAMENT – LUKE'S GOSPEL 219
1A Jesus' moral teachings 219
1B The meaning and significance of the miracles 233
1C A critical analysis of the issues 241
2A Prayer, praise and the Sabbath 246
2B The nature and demands of discipleship 255
2C A critical analysis of the issues 263

AREA I: NEW TESTAMENT – THE FOURTH GOSPEL 266
1A The 'I am' sayings 266
1B The meaning and significance of the miracles 277
1C A critical analysis of the issues 287
2A Women 292
2B The nature and demands of discipleship 299
2C A critical analysis of the issues 310

UNIT 2 INVESTIGATIONS 313

INTRODUCTION 313
Area A: The study of religion 321
Area B: The study of philosophy of religion 340
Area C: The study of ethics 353
Area D: The study of world religions (Buddhism) 367
Area D: The study of world religions (Islam) 379
Area F: The study of the New Testament 394

GLOSSARY 410

INDEX 416

INTRODUCTION

The aim and approach of the book

- This is a book for both teachers and students of religious studies (RS).
- It is a source book of information and is a key tool for completing the AS course.
- The approach is skills-based and focuses on how to develop the key areas of expertise outlined by the Edexcel specification.
- The content covers the core nature of the AS course, including the specification details, the assessment objectives, the levels of attainment and how each of these interacts with the others.
- This book is a complete AS-level package for the selected areas from Unit 1 (Foundations) and Unit 2 (Investigations).

In addition, this book has been written with two specific aims in mind.

- The course content required by the specification is sharply focused and delivers all the essential facts and relevant material without compromising on quality.
- The focus is always on using the book to develop the examination skills required for success and to encourage an 'assessment for learning' approach.

In covering the most popular aspects of the Edexcel specification, the book offers a range of curriculum areas. Although only two key areas (units) are studied for examination purposes, this may appeal for the following reasons.

- Some schools may want to offer more than one combination of topics, for example, because they have several groups and more than one teacher.
- Diversity may be offered within a small group, creating more individualised study.
- It may give RS teachers the confidence to extend their specialism, given the nature of the comprehensive support offered by the book, for example, to deliver a topic they have not covered before.
- In the light of a synoptic element at A2 and the new QCA-driven emphasis on stretch and challenge, it may be advantageous to dip into related elements from other units for general synoptic work, or to provide distinct and discernible extension activities for students who are more able.
- It is interesting to compare the units and further consolidate skills.

> This book uses the BCE and CE date system:
> - BCE stands for Before the Common Era and is the equivalent of BC
> - CE stands for the Common Era and is the equivalent of AD.

How this book aids success at AS level

1 The difficulties at AS level

The basic problem with AS-level examinations is that many students do not apply what they know effectively. Students can be well instructed in the topics covered, but may not understand the precise demands of the skills specified in the assessment objectives. They have the *what* (the content) but not the *how* (application to a specific focus or question). For example, in the case of assessment objective 1 (AO1) and 'select and demonstrate', the facts are often there in a student's answer but the way in which they are presented does not demonstrate clear knowledge and understanding.

Examiners' reports always indicate that the problem is not *what* the students know but *how* they are answering the questions. Essentially, it is about students 'using and applying their knowledge' to demonstrate the necessary understanding through 'application and analysis of that knowledge'.

This is even more likely to be the case with assessment objective 2 (AO2). There are currently very few books offering organised AO2 material. The ideas of 'problems with...' or 'criticisms of...' are sometimes presented either as questions throughout a text or as a section at the end. Thus, what might require an AO2 response is reduced to an AO1 list of views rather than requiring a questioning approach, demonstrating a process of reasoning. The unfortunate result is that responses do not always reflect students' actual knowledge and understanding.

The problems become self-perpetuating because many resources have been purely content-based. This means there is a risk that students who depend on such resources will be trained and encouraged to reiterate the facts, with little appreciation of the context or application of the assessment objectives.

More recently, text books have started to use tasks or suggestions for work. However, it is still often left to the individual teacher to bridge the gap between knowledge and skills by designing a course that effectively rewrites the content and integrates a focus on skills. Even here, there is a risk of the assessment objectives being separated from the factual knowledge rather than being integral to the learning process. The assessment criteria should not be bolt-on, add-on or out-of-the-blue tasks at the end; instead, they should be driving the learning throughout the course.

2 The solution: a skills-based approach

All teachers know that the solution is to focus on skills. The problem is how to achieve this in the classroom. How do teachers help students build up their knowledge base while simultaneously training them to develop the skills expected? This is not a new problem.

The approach of this book is to integrate skills with the content. It takes a holistic approach towards assessment objectives and content; it advocates learning the content, not in isolation but in relation to the skills and assessment objectives. To reiterate, this book is intended as a skills-based resource.

Questions at AS level are separated into AO1 and AO2 and this is supported within the book, with a clear AO2 section within every unit. This book is grounded firmly in QCA *Assessment for learning* (AfL) principles.

What is assessment for learning?

Assessment for learning involves:

- effective planning of teaching and learning
- focus on how students learn
- learner motivation
- emphasis on progress and achievement rather than failure
- a shared understanding of the criteria by which students are assessed.

> 66 **KEY QUOTE**
>
> *Much of what teachers and learners do in classrooms can be described as assessment. That is, tasks and questions prompt learners to demonstrate their knowledge, understanding and skills. What learners say and do is then observed and interpreted, and judgements are made about how learning can be improved. These assessment processes are an essential part of everyday classroom practice and involve both teachers and learners in reflection, dialogue and decision-making.*
>
> **(Qualifications and Curriculum Alliance QCA)** 99

Effective assessment for learning occurs all the time in the classroom. This book, then, adopts this approach, using features that effectively promote and relate to AfL principles in the following ways.

QCA AfL principles	Related features in this book
sharing learning goals with students	• Reflection and assessment sections that serve to consolidate • Assessment objectives (AOs) clearly stated, together with levels of response (see end of this section) • Sharp focus on the precise materials to be selected and evaluated at the start of each section • Examination tips that focus on AOs • Outcomes for tasks related to AOs • Exemplar answers, materials clearly related to levels of response, descriptors
helping students know and recognise the standards to aim for	• Clear and regular reminders throughout the book • Levels of response and descriptors used to measure activities, for example, in planning answers and reviewing answers • Examination tips that remind students of specific skills in the AOs
providing feedback that helps students to identify how to improve	• Reflection and assessment activities to promote this • Use of the suggested template for effective feedback between teachers and students • Use of the template in self-assessment • Peer assessment activities and self-assessment
believing that every student can improve in comparison with previous achievements	• The reflection and assessment tasks are deliberately progressive and refined to see a clearly staged improvement and development in performance • Clear targets on written feedback grid
both the teacher and students reviewing and reflecting on students' performance and progress	• Clear reflection and assessment sections at the end of each part of the unit of study • Feedback grid that also encourages discussion (research demonstrates that oral feedback is most effective)
students learning self-assessment techniques to discover areas in which they need to improve	• Use of feedback grid • Activities that test gaps in learning and provide students with ownership of their work • Suggestions for further or independent tasks and further consolidation of learning
motivation and self-esteem, crucial for effective learning and progress, can be increased by effective assessment techniques	• Focus on celebrating achievement and recognising strengths upon which to build • A constant and constructive emphasis on how to improve the quality of answers and on meeting the high standards set by AS

66 **KEY QUOTE**

Assessment for learning involves using assessment in the classroom to raise students' achievement. It is based on the idea that students will improve most if they understand the aim of their learning, where they are in relation to this aim and how they can achieve the aim (or close the gap in their knowledge).

(QCA) 99

How to use this book

1 The features

Students need to be informed and guided in order to plan their learning. They should be given opportunities to:

- pinpoint their own strengths and be clear about how to develop through the levels of attainment
- be clear and constructive about their own weaknesses and how these might be addressed in relation to the levels of attainment
- improve their work through reflection, redrafting and dialogue with peers and teachers.

The features of this book directly relate to and indicate the skills developed in relation to the assessment objectives and, more specifically, to the levels of attainment.

Icon	Feature	Skills developed
	Key words	AO1, selection of key terms, understanding correct terminology
	Key quotes	AO1, selection of appropriate and relevant material
	Key ideas	AO1, selection and presentation to demonstrate understanding
	Key people, profiles, dates	AO1, contextual information to support AO1 understanding
?	Key questions	AO2, encouraging dialogue, argument, questioning, debate
	Exam tips	AO1 and AO2, specific focus on individual skills within these objectives, for example, selecting appropriate material and using evidence, correct terminology
	Tasks	AO1 and AO2, interacting and engaging with the specification content, recognising a variety of learning styles to consolidate learning and to stretch and challenge
	Pictures with related tasks	Stimulus for further research, independent thinking to stretch and challenge and further contextualise AO1 material and AO2 issues
	Summary diagrams	To visualise learning and encourage the use of thought-process diagrams in summarising key points and questions as a basis for planning examination answers
	Reflection and assessment	A consolidation of specification content and a focused practice of both AO1 and AO2 skills incorporating specific examination-style tasks
	Suggestions for further activities incorporating AfL principles for improvement	A specific focus on activities that encourage the use of peer- and self-assessment for the purpose of effective feedback

2 The division between AO1 and AO2

As highlighted earlier, in relation to AO2, each topic in the book has a separate section to exemplify the examination question. The inference is that, at AS level, AO2 is dealt with separately from AO1. However, it would be dangerous to think of it in isolation. It is clearly linked to aspects of AO1, almost an extension of the 'learning from ...' aspect at Key Stage 3 and Key Stage 4.

The presentation of AO2 material in the book is in keeping with both examination formats found in Foundations and Investigations. A benefit of this approach is that it can assist with the critical analysis of topics. In many books this aspect is either not available or it is not organised clearly for the student to recognise.

To see how this works in practice, consider each unit and each area. Sometimes the two parts of AO1 in the Foundations Unit may be linked in the evaluation as, for example, in Foundations Area C, *Buddhism*, Topic 1, Part 1C. Alternatively, the AO2 work may be focused on a preceding part, as with Foundations Area A, *Philosophy*, Topic 2, Part 2C. This is due to the fact that the two AO1 parts are not linked but provide opportunities for further development of another part for AO2 through the *Suggestions for further application of skills*. Indeed, readers may decide to go straight to the AO2 section that is relevant to the AO1 material after studying a discrete AO1 section, according to preference.

Nonetheless, it is important that – right from the start of the course – students are made familiar with the format of an examination paper and the nature of a question with its composite AO1 and AO2. A discussion about both assessment weighting and the breakdown of marks is also vital, especially since the marks awarded for Foundations and Investigations are very different. In addition to this, the papers are of different lengths and the expectations in the extended writing pieces are reflected in there being five levels in AO1 for Investigations, rather than four. Once again, this difference in weighting and marks at AS level is reflected in the book's format and indicated clearly in the Reflection and assessment content. In general, considering the weighting of assessment objectives, AO2 represents substantially less than the AO1.

3 Feedback and dialogue

In terms of AfL, the dialogue that is deemed essential to enable students to make progress is called feedback by QCA. A strong feature of this book is the wealth of opportunities for students to practise the skills required for examination success. In this they are supported by feedback, analysis and comparison, targeting areas for development in relation to the AOs and levels of attainment. Such a process, however, needs to be effective and not simply mechanical.

Further, QCA indicates that the characteristics of effective feedback include these features.

- It confirms that students are on the right track – it is positive and constructive.
- It stimulates correction or improvement of a piece of work.
- It acts as scaffolding, providing students with support in using their knowledge.
- It offers regular and constructive comment on progress over a number of attempts.
- It is oral as well as written.
- It develops in students the skills to ask for help.

If this is achieved, then '...a culture of success is promoted in which every student can make achievements by building on their previous performance.'

> 66 **KEY QUOTE**
>
> *Research has shown that students will achieve more if they are fully engaged in their own learning process. This means that if students know what they need to learn and why, and then actively assess their understanding, gaps in their own knowledge and areas they need to work on, they will achieve more than if they sit passively in a classroom working through exercises with no real comprehension either of the learning intention of the exercise or of why it might be important.*
>
> (QCA) 99

The following ideas may help in using feedback.

- Peer-assessment can be effective because students can clarify their own ideas while marking other students' work.
- Once students understand how to assess their current knowledge, and the gaps in it, they will have a clearer idea of how they can help themselves to progress.
- Teachers and students can set targets relating to specific goals tailored to the level descriptors and assessment objectives. The students will then be empowered to guide their own learning, with the teacher providing support and guidance.
- Student analysis of work that both does and does not meet the assessment criteria can help them to understand what was required from a task and to determine the next steps they might need to take to improve the quality of that work.
- Looking at different styles of writing and answering questions can also help students understand the different approaches they could have taken to the task.

In using this approach to feedback it is useful to have some kind of support in the form of consistent procedure. The grid below is intended to provide this. When applying and using the following grid as scaffolding, students will need to:

- reflect on their own work
- be encouraged to admit problems without risk to self-esteem
- be given time to work problems out.

4 Feedback grid or scaffolding

Specification area – unit and part	Foundations Area C, *Buddhism*, Topic 1, Part 1A: The historical, sociological and religious context for Buddhism
Question	'Examine...' (AO1) or 'Consider...' (AO2)
General comments on the answer – what was achieved	Teacher feedback
Strengths	Refer to *general* descriptors from levels of response
Level awarded and reasons (AO1) and/or (AO2)	Refer to *specific* aspects of the level descriptors
Areas for development – identifying any learning gaps in knowledge, understanding or evaluation	Refer to *specific* aspects of the level descriptors (usually taken from the *levels above*, or also using aspects of that same level awarded that need development)
Target for improvement (agreed in discussion with teacher, peer or through self-reflection)	A *focused* and *achievable* target to enable improvement Refer to the above areas for development and indicate three ways, *with examples*, of how this can be achieved
Overall mark out of 21 (AO1) and out of 9 (AO2) Estimated grade	

The structure of the book

This book is divided into two sections that mirror the Edexcel Specification for AS.

For the areas selected from the Foundations Unit that are covered by this book, the content is comprehensive and deals with all aspects of the Specification content. It is skills-based and has clear Assessment and reflection sections in order to consolidate the information and develop the skills necessary for examination success.

The Investigations Unit is more selective due to the nature of this unique unit. The content is more of an overview based upon **one** area that has been selected. The material serves as a stimulus for further 'Investigation'. This unit is also skills-based but the instructions and guidance are very comprehensive, geared towards support for more independent learning but still with an ultimate focus of preparing students for an extended essay under examination conditions.

The checklists you will need

This section is a vital point of reference throughout the course. It is the tool by which everything is measured.

1 Summary of knowledge and understanding and skills, Edexcel advanced subsidiary and advanced GCE specification (specification page 12)

The specification requires students, within the chosen areas of study, to acquire knowledge and understanding of:

- the key concepts (for example, religious beliefs, teachings, doctrines, principles, ideas and theories), including how these are expressed in texts, writings and/or other forms and practices
- major issues and questions (for example, issues of commonality and diversity, the role of dialogue, methods of study, relevance to contemporary society)
- the contribution of significant people, traditions or movements
- religious language and terminology

and to develop the following skills:

- to reflect on, select and deploy specified knowledge
- to identify, investigate and analyse questions and issues arising from the course of study
- to interpret and evaluate religious concepts, issues, ideas, the relevance of arguments and the views of scholars
- to use appropriate language and terminology in context
- to communicate, using reasoned arguments substantiated by evidence.

Reference will be made to assessment objectives (AO1 and AO2) throughout and to the levels of attainment. Students will need to refer to the descriptors listed below at regular intervals.

2 Assessment objective 1 for Foundations (Unit 1) and Investigations (Unit 2)

a) AO1 Demonstrate knowledge and understanding

Assessment objective 1
Select and demonstrate clearly relevant knowledge and understanding through the use of evidence, examples and correct language and terminology appropriate to the course of study.

It is important to note the following points.

- The Foundations Unit examines candidates by means of three (shorter) essays to be written in 105 minutes in total. The maximum mark for AO1 is 21 for each essay. There are four levels.

- The Investigations Unit examines candidates by means of one (extended) essay to be written in 75 minutes. The maximum mark for AO1 is 35 for this essay. There are five levels.
- The assessment objective descriptor for AO1 is the same for each unit but the level descriptors are discrete for each unit and each set of descriptors has sub-levels.

b) AO1 level descriptor marks for the Foundations Unit

These are taken from the Edexcel specification and the sample assessment materials.

Level 1: **1–5 marks**	**A limited range of isolated facts which are accurate and relevant, but unstructured; a generalised presentation with mainly random and unorganised detail; imprecisely expressed.**
Low level 1: **1 mark**	minimal accuracy or relevance in factual detail; no coherent organisation; very broad and unfocused generalisations; unclear as a response to the task, but not worthless
Mid level 1: **2–3 marks**	a mixture of accurate and relevant information with unrelated factual detail and inaccurate information; some relevant but unfocused generalisations; recognisable as a response to the task
High level 1: **4–5 marks**	some accurate and relevant information; an attempt to organise this within a structure; some broad but relevant generalisations with occasional detail; a valid response to the task, but lacking clarity or focus
Level 2: **6–10 marks**	**Mainly relevant and accurate information presented within a structure which shows a basic awareness of the issue raised, and expressed with a sufficient degree of accuracy to make the meaning clear.**
Low level 2: **6 marks**	most information presented is relevant to the task and accurate; limited in scope; organised sufficiently to show an implicit awareness of the issue; expressed with limited clarity
Mid level 2: **7–8 marks**	relevant and accurate information organised to show some awareness of the issue raised; with sufficient scope to show recognition of the breadth of the task; expressed simply and with some clarity
High level 2: **9–10 marks**	a simple structure in which appropriate information is organised; leading to a clear though basic awareness of the issue raised; expressed clearly
Level 3: **11–15 marks**	**A range of accurate and relevant knowledge, presented within a recognisable and generally coherent structure, selecting significant features for emphasis and clarity, and dealing at a basic level with some key ideas and concepts; expressed clearly and accurately, using some technical terms.**
Low level 3: **11 marks**	sufficient accurate and relevant knowledge to show a sound awareness of the issue; information organised to present a clear structure; some key features identified; reference to some key ideas and concepts; expressed clearly, using technical terms occasionally
Mid level 3: **12–13 marks**	breadth of accurate and relevant knowledge; organised and presented in a clear structure; significant features identified with some elaboration; showing understanding of some key ideas and concepts; expressed clearly and accurately, using technical terms
High level 3: **14–15 marks**	a good range and/or detail of appropriate knowledge; presented in a mainly coherent structure; significant features explained for emphasis and clarity; showing basic but clear knowledge of some key ideas and concepts; expressed clearly and accurately, using technical terms appropriately
Level 4: **16–21 marks**	**A coherent and well-structured account of the subject matter, with accurate and relevant detail, clearly identifying the most important features; using evidence to explain key ideas; expressed accurately and fluently, using a range of technical vocabulary.**
Low level 4: **16–17 marks**	accurate, relevant and detailed knowledge of the subject matter at a broad range or in sufficient depth; emphasis on significant features; using evidence to show general understanding of the key ideas; expressed clearly, using technical language appropriately
Mid level 4: **18–19 marks**	accurate, relevant and detailed knowledge of the subject matter at a wide range or in significant depth; emphasis on the most important features; using well-chosen evidence to support understanding of key ideas and concepts; expressed clearly and accurately, using technical language widely
High level 4: **20–21 marks**	accurate, relevant and detailed knowledge used concisely to present a coherent and well-structured response to the task at a wide range or considerable depth; selecting the most important features for emphasis and clarity; using evidence to explain the key ideas; expressed cogently using technical language

c) AO1 level descriptor marks for the Investigations Unit

Level 1: 1–6 marks	**Uncritical and descriptive presentation of mainly random information about the topic investigated, demonstrating a minimal ability to identify and select material relevant to the task; communicated within a largely simplistic and unstructured framework.**
Low level 1: 1–2 marks	minimal accurate or relevant factual information; no obvious organisation; unfocused and simple generalisations; unclear as a response to the task, but not worthless
Mid level 1: 3–4 marks	mixture of accurate and relevant factual information with inaccurate or unrelated material; some relevant but unfocused generalisations; limited but discernible structure; a recognisable attempt to respond to the task
High level 1: 5–6 marks	some relevant and mainly accurate information; an attempt to organise this within a structure; some broad but relevant generalisations; a valid response to the task but lacking clarity or focus
Level 2: 7–13 marks	**Some relevant and partially structured knowledge of the topic investigated, presented within a limited framework which shows an awareness of some of its significant features, with a general link to the task, expressed with sufficient accuracy to make the meaning clear.**
Low level 2: 7–8 marks	most factual information accurate and relevant to the task; limited in scope; organised sufficiently to show implicit awareness of issue; expressed with limited clarity
Mid level 2: 9–10 marks	generally accurate and relevant information; limited appreciation of the scope of the task; sufficiently organised to show partial awareness of the issue; expressed simply and with some clarity
High level 2: 11–13 marks	accurate and relevant information, demonstrating basic knowledge of the task; organised sufficiently to identify some significant features; with general links to the task; expressed simply and clearly
Level 3: 14–20 marks	**Presentation of a selection of relevant material, which reflects some understanding of the significant features of the topic investigated; linked directly to the issue(s) raised in the task; with some use of specialised religious language in appropriate contexts.**
Low level 3: 14–15 marks	sufficient accurate and relevant knowledge to show a sound awareness of the issue; organised within a generally clear structure; some key features/ideas/concepts identified but not elaborated; expressed clearly with occasional use of technical terms
Mid level 3: 16–17 marks	breadth of accurate and relevant knowledge; organised and presented in a clear structure; significant features/ideas/concepts identified with basic elaboration; expressed clearly and accurately, using some technical terms
High level 3: 18–20 marks	good range of, and/or detailed, appropriate knowledge; significant features described and elaborated for emphasis and clarity; linked directly to the issues raised in the task; expressed clearly and accurately, using appropriate technical terms
Level 4: 21–27 marks	**Presentation of a good range of well-selected material from the topic investigated, to show a coherent understanding of its significant features within the context of the issue(s) raised in the task, highlighting some key concepts and supported by the use of appropriate evidence and/or examples; topic explored using defined and relevant religious terms further reflecting an understanding of the topic.**
Low level 4: 21–22 marks	a range of accurate and suitably selected knowledge of the subject matter; a basic understanding of some significant features; selected key ideas/concepts elaborated by reference to evidence and/or examples; expressed clearly, using a range of technical terms
Mid level 4: 23–24 marks	a range of accurate and well-selected knowledge; some understanding of the key issues of the task; key ideas/concepts explained by reference to evidence and/or examples; clearly expressed, using a range of technical terms in context
High level 4: 25–27 marks	a substantial range of accurate and well-selected knowledge; organised to demonstrate a thorough understanding of the key issues of the task; explanation of key ideas/concepts supported by evidence and examples; wide use of technical terms further demonstrates overall understanding of the issue

Level 5: 28–35 marks	**Presentation of a wide range of selected, relevant factual knowledge and understanding of the topic investigated; offering some analysis of issues raised by the topic, using a variety of sources, examples and/or illustrations; structured around, and showing clear understanding of, the main theme(s) or concept(s) of the task; both topic and task explored with the proficient use of religious language.**
Low level 5: 28–29 marks	well-selected wide-ranging knowledge used to show clear understanding of the topic; key ideas/themes/concepts explained by reference to evidence and examples; evidence of an attempt to offer a basic analysis of some issues raised by the topic; typically by reference to appropriate sources; the whole explored with proficient use of religious language
Mid level 5: 30–32 marks	clear and thorough understanding of the topic; demonstrated through carefully selected knowledge of the issues raised; well-structured in depth or broad response to the task; some analysis of the main ideas/themes/concepts; examples/arguments/sources deployed to give emphasis and clarity; expressed coherently with a wide deployment of religious language
High level 5: 33–35 marks	coherent understanding of the task; based on selection of material to demonstrate emphasis and clarity of ideas; careful analysis of key concepts; supported by widely deployed evidence/arguments/sources; well-structured response to the task in breadth or depth; expressed cogently through skilful deployment of religious language

3 Assessment objective 2 for Foundations (Unit 1) and Investigations (Unit 2)

a) AO2 Analysis, evaluation and application

Assessment objective 2

Critically evaluate and justify a point of view through the use of evidence and reasoned argument.

It is important to note the following points.

● The Foundations Unit examines candidates by means of three (shorter) essays to be written in 105 minutes. The maximum mark for AO2 is 9 for each essay. There are four levels.

● The Investigations Unit examines candidates by means of one (extended) essay to be written in 75 minutes. The maximum mark for AO2 is 15 for this essay. There are still four levels for this.

b) AO2 level descriptor marks

These are taken from the Edexcel specification and sample assessment material.

Level 1: 1–2 marks (Foundations Unit) 1–3 marks (Investigations Unit)	A mainly descriptive response, at a general level, to the issue(s) raised in the task; leading to a point of view that is logically consistent with the task, supported by reference to a simple argument or unstructured evidence; imprecisely expressed.
Level 2: 3–4 marks (Foundations Unit) 4–7 marks (Investigations Unit)	A response to the task showing a simple but partial awareness of the issue(s) raised, typically supported by some attempt to set out a range of views; a point of view supported by limited but appropriate evidence and/or argument; communicated with a sufficient degree of accuracy to make the meaning clear.
Level 3: 5–6 marks (Foundations Unit) 8–11 marks (Investigations Unit)	An accurate statement of the main issue(s) raised by the task with some attempt to set out reasons for a range of views; a point of view expressed clearly, supported by relevant evidence and argument and deploying some technical language appropriately.
Level 4: 7–9 marks (Foundations Unit) 12–15 marks (Investigations Unit)	An attempt at an evaluation of the issue(s) raised in the task, typically through a careful analysis of alternative views; leading to a clearly expressed viewpoint supported by well-deployed evidence and reasoned argument; expressed accurately, fluently and using a range of technical vocabulary.

FOUNDATIONS
Area A: Philosophy of religion

TOPIC 1: A STUDY OF PHILOSOPHICAL ARGUMENTS ABOUT THE EXISTENCE OF GOD

Part 1A: The design argument

This means I am expected:

to know about the key issues:
- empirical basis
- interpretation of experience
- role of analogy
- cumulative effect of evidence
- notions of 'God'

and to study:
- Aquinas' argument 'from the governance of things'
- Paley's argument by analogy (qua purpose)
- Paley's argument by evidence (qua regularity)
- Tennant's anthropic argument
- Swinburne's probability argument
- challenges to the argument.

In this book the evidence and examples given are relevant and appropriate because this material focuses only on the content for AO1 that is given by the Edexcel specification. The evaluation materials for AO2 will be aimed at helping you 'critically evaluate and justify a point of view through the use of evidence and reasoned argument'.

It would be helpful to write your notes using the headings listed above, as it is from these areas that the examination questions will be derived.

In your studies, remember that you have to bear in mind the **two** basic assessment objectives of:

- Knowledge and Understanding (AO1)
- Evaluation (AO2).

See pages 7–8 in the Introduction to remind yourself of these objectives.

The evaluation material set out in Part 1C (page 32) can be studied either alongside the AO1 material, as you work through this unit, or as a separate unit.

This unit starts by exploring some of the main forms of the design argument for the existence of God. The examination questions will not specify a particular form of the argument so it is acceptable to use any version(s) that are relevant. Questions will be set on key ideas and strengths and weaknesses. The key ideas need to be explained and illustrated, with reference to the different forms of the design argument. Strengths involve outlining and explaining how the argument works. Weaknesses involve outlining and explaining the challenges to the arguments. Evaluation of the strengths and weaknesses of the design argument will be examined in Part 1C.

1 The background to the design argument

 KEY WORD

Teleological: explanation by reference to end, goal or purpose, derived from the Greek *telos*, meaning end, purpose or goal and *logos*, meaning reason

The design argument has been a popular one to support the existence of God. It is often referred to as the **teleological** argument. This word, derived from the Greek words *telos* and *logos*, is an explanation with reference to some purpose or end. Nature is viewed as directed, in order that something beneficial may result.

Key ideas

i) The design argument infers the existence of God from the particular character of the world. There are a number of characteristics of the world upon which the various forms of the design argument focus.

● Order – the nature of the Universe seems ordered and it seems to work to definable rules (laws of nature); for example, the law of gravity. Swinburne's argument involving temporal order is a good example of this form of the design argument, as is the argument by Paley.

● Regularity – the Universe is, to a great extent, predictable because there is order and because it acts in a regular and consistent way; an example is the movement of the planets, which revolve in their predictable orbits. Examples of the form of the design argument that focus on this feature are cited by Aquinas and Paley.

● Purpose – the order and regularity do not seem aimless but, rather, there seems to be some goal or purpose; for example, the parts of the human eye fit together for the purpose of seeing. An example of the form of the design argument that focuses on this feature is cited by Paley.

● Benefit – this goal or purpose seems to be beneficial; for example, the water cycle provides the Earth with water. Examples of the forms of the design argument that focus on this feature are cited by Aquinas and Paley.

● Suitability for life – one of the main benefits that result from this order and regularity is the sustaining of human life; for example, if the Earth were either 5% closer to or 1% further from the Sun, life would not be possible. An example of the form of the design argument that focuses on this feature is cited by Tennant.

● **Aesthetic** value – the Universe exhibits beauty. This feature is aesthetically pleasing to human beings yet, in and of itself, serves no function. This beauty is from the microscopic to the macroscopic level. Examples of the form of the design argument that focus on this feature are cited by Tennant and Swinburne.

 KEY WORD

Aesthetic: appreciation of beauty

ii) Such features are seen as marks of design and so the argument concludes that God must be the source of that design. In other words, the features require some kind of explanation, and that explanation is seen to be 'God'.

iii) The notion of 'God' is different in the various versions of the argument.

● For Aquinas, the emphasis is on regularity and predictability of natural laws that require something intelligent to direct them, and this is God.

● For Paley, the emphasis is more on purpose and order. Things have been arranged in a particular way. It implies that there must be an intelligent designer, God. The **anthropic argument** of Tennant identifies this beneficial order as designed for sustaining human life. This implies that God has human beings as his central focus.

iv) The role of **analogy** is central to Paley's form of the design argument (see below). An analogy identifies a number of common features of two or more things. Paley compared manufactured machines (a watch) with the Universe. A number of common features were identified. By implication, if one of them (the manufactured machine) had another feature, then it is likely that the Universe also shared that feature. For Paley, the implied feature was an intelligent designer.

KEY WORDS

Anthropic argument: the argument that nature is planning in advance for the needs of humans
Analogy: a comparison of two or more things to show how they are similar

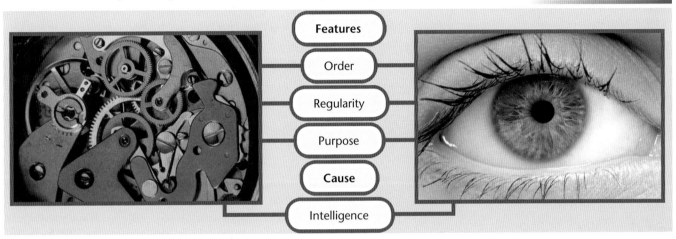

Features
Order
Regularity
Purpose
Cause
Intelligence

v) Any argument that rests on observation must include the key ideas of empirical evidence and interpretation of observation. In other words, evidence is gained from our senses, since we appeal to our experience of the Universe as evidence. This experience of the Universe has to be interpreted. We have to make sense of what we experience.

KEY IDEA

Deductive arguments offer proof while inductive arguments only offer probabilities.

vi) The philosophical methodology of the design argument is an **inductive argument** (see below).

2 Philosophical arguments

a) *The form of the argument – deductive or inductive?*

Consider the following argument.

● If Charles does his homework he will gain a grade A at AS Religious Studies.
● Charles does his homework.
● Therefore Charles gains a grade A at AS Religious Studies.

The form or structure of this argument is such that if both the first statement and the second statement (**premises**) are true then it must follow that the final statement (**conclusion**) must also be true. The conclusion is already contained in the premises. It is *deduced* or *subtracted* from them.

Hence the conclusion must follow. This form of argument is called a **deductive argument**.

KEY WORDS

Induction: a process of reasoning that draws a general conclusion from specific instances
Premise: a statement that forms part of an argument from which a conclusion is drawn
Conclusion: a statement that purports to be drawn from a set of premises
Deduction: a process of reasoning by which the conclusion is shown to follow necessarily from the premises

KEY WORDS

Truth value: whether a statement is actually true or false

A posteriori: after experience, derived from observed facts

A priori: the truth value can be determined without reference to any experience or investigation

TASK

Make up two deductive arguments and two inductive arguments. Think about how you would decide whether they were true.

Objective: To check understanding of the difference between the two types of argument, demonstrating 'key ideas and concepts; expressed clearly and accurately using some technical terms' (level 3 descriptor AO1).

However there is another form of argument.

- If Charles does his homework he will almost certainly gain a grade A at AS Religious Studies.
- Charles gains a grade A at AS Religious Studies.
- Therefore Charles did his homework.

The form or structure of this argument is different. Even if both the first statement and the second statement are true, we cannot be certain about the conclusion. It is just possible that Charles cheated or that the examiner marked the paper wrongly or the wrong mark was put into the computer and sent out by the exam board. In fact there could be a number of alternative explanations.

If the premises are true then the conclusion does **not** have to follow from the premises, though it is consistent with them. In this case the conclusion is not deduced (subtracted) from the premises, but is **inducted** (inferred). The conclusion does not necessarily follow.

This form of argument is an inductive argument.

Hence a deductive argument with true premises offers certainty in proof, whilst an inductive argument with true premises offers only degrees of probability.

b) The truth value of the premise – a priori *or* a posteriori?

Identifying the type of argument – deciding it is deductive or inductive – does not, in itself, prove whether the conclusion is true or false. We must also decide whether the individual premises are true or false. Types of argument merely tell you about the logical connection between the premises and the conclusion. How then do we decide about the **truth value** of the premises?

Consider the following premise.

- Charles gains a grade A at AS Religious Studies.

How do I go about finding out if it is true? I would have to go and check in some way, maybe by looking at a list of published results or asking to see Charles' certificate from the examination board. I cannot assume that Charles has a grade A at AS Religious Studies. I would need to make some kind of investigation. I could only conclude the truth value in the light of some experience, such as seeing the certificate.

If this is the case then the premise is said to be *a posteriori*.

Some premises may be such that their truth value can be decided without reference to experience.

Consider the following premise.

- The circle is square.

I do not need to investigate the truth of whether a circle is square. I know that the premise is false. By definition a circle is round, not square.

Premises such as these are called *a priori*.

3 Various forms of the design argument

a) Aquinas' design argument

Aquinas wrote about his *Five Ways*; the teleological argument was the *Fifth Way*:

> *The Fifth Way is taken from the governance of the world. We see that things that lack knowledge, such as natural bodies, act for an end, and this is evident from their acting always, or nearly always, in the same way, so as to obtain the best result. Hence it is plain that they achieve their end, not fortuitously, but designedly. Now whatever lacks knowledge cannot move towards an end, unless it be directed by some being endowed with knowledge and intelligence; as the arrow is directed by the archer. Therefore some intelligent being exists by whom all natural things are directed to their end; and this being we call God.*

The heart of this argument is that non-intelligent material things are governed by certain laws that direct them to produce beneficial order. This regularity of succession requires an intelligent being to bring it about, namely, God. Aquinas' views about nature included the principle that things develop toward the realisation of ends that are internal to their own natures. Just as an archer must direct an arrow, God must direct nature. Aquinas argued that there cannot be purposefulness without a guiding intelligence. This can be expressed in argument form.

- There are beings without knowledge that act for ends.
- If a being without knowledge acts for an end, then it must be because it is directed by a being with knowledge and intelligence.
- Therefore, there must be a being with knowledge and intelligence – God.

b) Paley's design argument

Paley presented a different approach to teleology. His influential book *Natural Theology: or, Evidences of the Existence and Attributes of the Deity, Collected from the Appearances of Nature*, first published in 1802, expounded the belief that the nature of God could be understood by reference to the natural world, which was God's creation. He likened the workings of biological organisms to machines made by an intelligent being. It reflected the contemporary thinking about a mechanistic Universe. His teleological argument has two parts, as follows.

KEY PERSON

Thomas Aquinas (1225–74)
He argued that all human understanding was ultimately based on what had been revealed by God. However, it was necessary for humans to have rational thought in order to understand God's revelations. He thus combined faith and reason.

In his famous *Five Ways*, he summarised five arguments for the existence of God.

KEY PROFILE: WILLIAM PALEY (1743–1805)
Paley was a clergyman who, in 1782, was appointed Archdeacon of Carlisle. He became well known for his writings on philosophy and Christian apologetics. His 1794 book, *A View of the Evidence of Christianity*, was required reading at Cambridge University until the 20th century. Charles Darwin, in his autobiography wrote:

> *…In order to pass the BA examination, it was, also, necessary to get up Paley's* Evidences of Christianity, *and his* Moral Philosophy… *The logic of this book and as I may add of his* Natural Theology *gave me as much delight as did Euclid.*

Though Paley's material was not particularly original, his clear style made it popular and widely read. David Hume had some years earlier criticised such a form of the teleological argument. However, Hume's writings sold little and so were not well known. It was not until much later that Hume's philosophical writings became popular.

EXAM TIP

Marks are awarded for the demonstration of understanding of arguments, not for irrelevant biographical details. This demonstrates relevant selection and clear understanding through the use of evidence (AO1).

i) Design *qua* purpose

At the time of Paley, the pocket watch was considered a very intricate machine, and people were very impressed by it. Paley used the analogy of the watch to illustrate his argument. It was by no means original but, through Paley, it became well known.

Suppose you were crossing a heath and came across a watch. Paley argued that, even if you had never seen a watch before, you would know that this instrument did not happen by chance but must be the product of an intelligent mind. All the parts fit together and achieve the purpose of telling time. The watch must have had an intelligent and skilled maker, who designed it to do what it does. The watch demands a watchmaker and no entirely naturalistic explanation would be acceptable. Likewise, the way the Universe fits together, for a purpose, demands an intelligent designer. The designer would have to be God.

Paley also supported his argument by giving further examples of complex purposeful design found in nature. For instance, he referred to the eye as being designed for the particular purpose of seeing. Paley regards both the watch and the Universe as teleological systems that require an intelligent mind to bring them into being.

This can be expressed as the following argument.

- There exist in nature many examples of beneficial order.
- Beneficial order is best explained as the result of an intelligent designer.
- Therefore, nature is probably the result of an intelligent designer, God.

Alternatively, the argument may be based on analogy.

- Objects in nature are analogous to manufactured machines.
- Manufactured machines are the result of intelligent design.
- Analogous effects will have analogous causes.
- Therefore, objects in nature are the result of something analogous to intelligent design, namely God.

The analogous argument rests on the idea that similar effects imply similar causes.

Paley was aware of criticisms made against this approach (possibly those made by David Hume). To offset them he claimed that the argument was not weakened if:

- we had never seen a watch before
- we found that the mechanism did not always work perfectly
- there were parts of the machine whose function we did not understand.

ii) Design *qua* regularity

As well as purpose, Paley also argued that the regularity observed in the Universe demanded as explanation an intelligent mind. He used as evidence scientific findings from his own time, from astronomy and from Newton's laws. An instance of this was the way in which the planets obeyed laws in their movements. The whole Universe, and all its parts, seemed ordered and acted in a regular and predictable way, according to fundamental laws. The agent responsible for such order must be God.

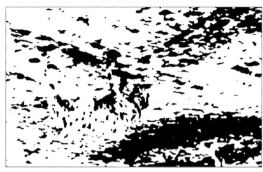

Accident or design?

TASK

Which of the pictures, if either, is designed? How did you decide?
Objective: To appreciate the problem of recognising design.
To consider what an undesigned Universe would look like.
(To find out which, if either, is designed, turn to page 22.)

c) Tennant's design argument

i) The anthropic principle

This argues that nature seems to plan in advance for the needs of animals and humans. This planning cannot be accounted for by physical laws alone since there are innumerable ways in which electrons could run. There must be more than physical laws to account for the improbability of life. It suggests mind or intelligence.

ii) The aesthetic argument

Tennant argued that the Universe is not just beautiful in places; it is saturated with beauty from the microscopic to the macroscopic level. However, beauty has no survival value. It is unnecessary but it still exists.

d) Swinburne's forms of the design argument

i) Order and probability

Swinburne's approach is closer to that of Aquinas than that of Paley. Swinburne acknowledges that the argument from spatial order, used by Paley, is not very persuasive. By spatial order, Swinburne means the complex structures of organisms such as plants and animals. He calls this spatial order 'the regularities of co-presence'. It is not persuasive, because such ordered complexities can be explained by modern science (theory of natural selection, see page 20) and so does not require the introduction of God.

However, Swinburne focuses on temporal order (what he calls 'regularities of succession'). By temporal order he means the laws of nature throughout the Universe. The Universe is orderly, yet it could have been chaotic. Nature seems to conform to a formula. If there is an explanation to account for this, then it cannot be a scientific one because we explain the operation of scientific laws in terms of more general scientific laws. Swinburne concludes:

> So either the orderliness of nature is where all explanation stops, or we must postulate an agent of such great power and knowledge…the simplest such agent…God.

One aspect of Swinburne's argument involves probability. He argued that the occurrence of such order can increase the probability of the existence of God since it is consistent with God's character. God has reason for creating an orderly Universe; order is a part of beauty (which is a better state of affairs than ugliness) and order means that human beings can make predictions about the future, on which they can rely. Hence the occurrence of order supports the likelihood of God existing.

KEY PERSON

Richard Swinburne (b. 1934)
An Oxford professor of philosophy who has devoted himself to promoting arguments for theism.

66 KEY QUOTES

Maybe only if order is there can we know what is there, but that makes what is there no less extraordinary and in need of explanation.
(Swinburne)

Nearly all the things which men are hanged or imprisoned for doing to one another are nature's everyday performances.
(Mill)
99

Remember that Paley actually wrote his design argument *after* Hume had written his challenges. Hume did not therefore ever read Paley's argument. However, Paley's argument, using analogy, was not original to Paley, as there were forms of it circulating in the time of Hume. Paley's version merely popularised it.

TASK

Can you think of some examples of analogies where the effects are the same but the cause is different?

Objective: To understand the weakness of argument by analogy, demonstrating that you are 'selecting the most important features for emphasis and clarity' (high level 4 descriptor AO1).

ii) Beauty

Swinburne argued that God would have reason to make a basically beautiful world. There is no more reason to expect a beautiful world than an ugly one. Hence, if the world is beautiful, that fact would be evidence for God's existence.

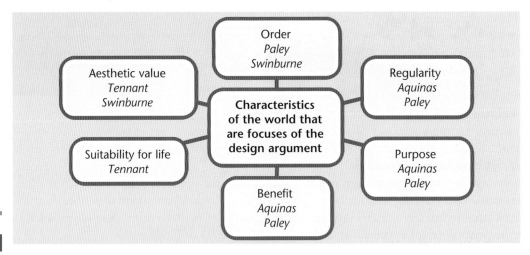

Summary diagram: The key ideas and arguments

4 Challenges to the design argument

a) Hume's criticisms of the design argument

Paley's argument was published in 1802, some 26 years after the death of Hume. In his lifetime Hume had strongly attacked the design argument and many felt that his criticisms, of the form of the same argument that Paley later used, were valid. This criticism occurred in *Dialogues Concerning Natural Religion*, a book that was not published until 1779, three years after Hume had died. Hume had deliberately delayed publication until after his own death because he felt the book was controversial. His criticisms of the argument cover several points, as described below.

i) An unsound analogy

The strength of the argument depends upon the similarity between the items held to be analogous (the machine and the world). The greater the similarity, the stronger the argument; the weaker the similarity, the weaker the argument. But, according to Hume, the two analogies are far apart. Our world is *not* like a machine at all since it is composed of vegetables and animals. It is more organic than it is mechanical.

Neither is it philosophically sound to argue that intelligence is the necessary governing principle behind the world. Hume pointed out that there were lots of alternative governing principles (generation, vegetation, gravity). Why should one of these not be the dominant principle? Indeed, why should different principles not rule over their own natural domains: vegetation in plants, generation in animals, gravity in movements of planets? We cannot project from one limited area to another part or to the whole of nature.

Hume re-emphasised the point that the world did *not* closely resemble something manufactured. If we see a house we conclude with certainty that it had an architect or builder. This is because we have seen it being built. We cannot infer from this that the

Universe bears a similar cause (intelligence) because it does not bear close resemblance to a house. Hume pointed out that a number of people are involved in designing a house so perhaps, by analogy, there could be a team of gods who designed the world.

ii) Similar effects do not necessarily imply similar causes

Hume goes further by questioning whether it is a sound notion that similar effects result necessarily from similar causes. To know that an orderly Universe must arise from intelligence and thought, we would have to have experienced the origin of the world. Why should similar effects not be the result of *different* causes?

iii) Other possible analogies

This has already been hinted at in (i) above. Hume argued that 'the world plainly resembles more an animal or a vegetable than it does a watch or a knitting loom'. In particular, he argued that the world could be compared to a carrot. The relevance of this is that if the analogy is made with the carrot then the mark of design in the world could be caused by something similar to generation or vegetation. The natural world may possess some inner self-regulation and growth. Had Hume lived long enough he may well have joined forces with Darwin. **Darwinism** sees beneficial adaptations explained in non-personal terms by means of natural selection.

KEY WORD

Darwinism: the theory of natural selection to account for changes in nature

Indeed, Hume argued that at its base, intelligence is itself caused by the process of generation. Surely the process of causes continues, since intelligence requires a cause. Hence you end up with an infinite regression of causes.

iv) Analogy makes God more human than divine

The more you press the analogy of the manufactured machine, such as the watch, with the Universe, the more human you have to make God; similar effect implies similar causes. For instance, consider this summary.

- We cannot ascribe infinity to God because, as the cause ought only to be proportional to the effect, the effect is not infinite.
- Likewise, perfection cannot be ascribed to God. It is impossible for us to tell whether this system contains any great faults. Even if the system were perfect, it is not certain whether all the excellences can be ascribed to the workers. For instance, many worlds might have been botched and bungled before this system was made.
- Hume drove his point home by suggesting:

This world is very faulty and imperfect, and was only the first rude essay of some infant deity who afterwards abandoned it, ashamed of his lame performance; it is the work only of some inferior deity and is the object of derision to his superiors; it is the production of old age in some superannuated deity, and ever since his death has run on from the first impulse and active force which he gave it…

v) Analogy leads to a non-moral God

Hume listed some unpleasant features of nature, for example, earthquakes, war and disease, and questioned how the planning and design could be that of a just and good God. Workers have to be judged in proportion to the quality of the work produced! Equally, Hume argued, you cannot attribute to the cause anything more than is sufficient to produce the effect. He claimed that a more plausible hypothesis was that of a God who had no moral character. Alternatively, there could be two forces, one good and one evil.

vi) Other explanations for apparent order

Hume suggested that we cannot be sure that the so-called organised Universe is not the result of some blind, cosmic accident. Indeed any Universe is bound to have the appearance of design. There could be no Universe at all if the parts of it were not mutually adapted to some degree.

b) Mill's criticisms of the design argument

In *Nature and Religion* (1874), **Mill** focused on a criticism that Hume had identified earlier: the occurrence of disorder in the Universe. In particular, Mill argued that in nature various atrocities occur that go unpunished. He concluded from this that such things could not result from an intelligent designer who had the attributes of the Christian God. In other words, Mill saw natural evil as evidence against God as designer. The work of nature that is destructive and random shows that we do not live in a benevolent world designed by a moral God. He draws the parallel with our reaction to human beings who acted in a similar way to nature. We would demand justice. (See more about the problem of evil on page 44.)

KEY PROFILE: JOHN STUART MILL (1806–1873)

Mill is probably best known for his writings on Utilitarianism, which held that one must always act so as to produce the greatest happiness for the greatest number of people, and his defence of free speech and liberty in his book, *On Liberty*. However, he also wrote an influential book in which he argued that evil counted against belief in a designer God. Indeed, the amount of goodness in nature is far outweighed by the amount of suffering.

During his life he served as a member of Parliament and was godfather to Bertrand Russell.

c) Darwin's criticisms of the design argument

With the publication of Darwin's *Origin of Species* (1859), many regarded the teleological argument as no longer convincing. Darwin's theory described a way of understanding the natural world whereby its complex biological functions no longer required an intelligent designer to account for apparent order.

Firstly, Darwin noticed that variations occur in offspring within a species. These are accidental. Secondly, he argued for natural selection that involved the theory of the survival of the fittest. This is the theory that the organisms that are best able to survive, for example, those that find food and avoid predators, pass on their genetic traits. The combination of variation and survival leads eventually to the emergence of organisms that are suited to their environment. They will have the appearance of design but will be the result of evolving by variation and survival. God becomes an unnecessary hypothesis.

Darwin demonstrated that order was not necessarily evidence of purpose and design. Order could result from blind chance.

d) Dawkins' criticisms of the design argument

In our own time, Richard Dawkins joins those who have argued for a naturalistic explanation for the features of the Universe without recourse to the supernatural.

A true watchmaker has foresight; he designs his cogs and springs, and plans their interconnections, with a future purpose in his mind's eye. Natural selection, the blind, unconscious, automatic process which Darwin discovered, and which we now know is the explanation for the existence and apparently purposeful form of all life, has no purpose in mind. It has no mind and no mind's eye. It does not plan for the future. It has no vision, no foresight, no sight at all. If it can be said to play the role of the watchmaker in nature, it is the blind watchmaker.

Another challenge that Dawkins has made involves 'memes'. According to Dawkins, this is an abbreviation of the term 'mimeme'. His theory is that:

Just as genes propagate themselves in the gene pool by leaping from body to body via sperm and eggs, so memes propagate themselves in the meme pool by leaping from brain to brain…

In this way, Dawkins argues for cultural evolution. The 'god-meme' accounts for people's belief in God. It is like a God-virus that infects people.

Hume	Mill	Darwin
An unsound analogy Similar effects do not imply similar causes Other possible analogies God more human than divine Non-moral God Universe accidental	Disorder Natural evil Atrocities in nature go unpunished God not moral	Apparent order not design Naturalistic explanation Survival of fittest Natural selection **Dawkins** Blind watchmaker Memes Cultural evolution

Summary diagram: Criticisms of the design argument

Reflection and assessment

It is vital to bring together the information that has been covered so far and recognise how it can be transformed into effective examination-style revision and answers. The best way to do this is to ask the question: 'How am I going to be assessed on this information?'

The first way is through assessment objective 1 (AO1). For this objective you need to be able to 'select and clearly demonstrate the relevant knowledge and understanding through the use of evidence, examples and correct language and terminology'.

a) Key points

● Use the correct technical language to refer to key ideas and arguments.
● Always relate any examples to the meaning or argument to show understanding of it.

Use the writing frame provided on page 22 to answer this question.

What are the main strengths of the design argument for the existence of God?'   (21 marks)

As you work through each unit in this book, you will find that the amount of support in these sections will gradually be reduced, in order to encourage the development of your independence and the honing of your AO1 skills.

b) Writing frame

We seek explanation in everything. Science works on the basis that everything has an explanation. The design argument uses the same approach when it asks the question: 'Why is the Universe...?'

There are a number of characteristics of the world that the various forms of the design argument focus on. Four of them are...

These four characteristics suggest design because...

The role of analogy is central to Paley's form of the design argument. An analogy is...

Paley's analogy compared the Universe with...

The reason this analogy implies God as designer of Universe is that...

The anthropic argument is...

The aesthetic argument is...

At its basis, there are two ways of looking at the Universe. One way is...

The other way is...

Answer to the task on page 17: The first picture is designed. If you turn it upside down you will see a picture of a Dalmatian dog.

The question asks about the main strengths. This is not evaluative (AO2) since you are not being asked to evaluate the arguments. You are merely asked to state what the arguments are.

c) Suggestion for a further activity

Use the levels and the AO1 descriptors on pages 8–10 to award marks out of 21. Identify strengths and areas for development. Then, as a group, collaborate to create a level 4 answer.

Now construct your own writing frame for this question.

> **What are the key ideas of the design argument for the existence of God?**
>
> (21 marks)

TOPIC 1: A STUDY OF PHILOSOPHICAL ARGUMENTS ABOUT THE EXISTENCE OF GOD

Part 1B: The cosmological argument

> ## This means I am expected:
>
> **to know about the key issues:**
> - Aquinas' argument of the unmoved mover
> - Aquinas' argument of the uncaused causer
> - Aquinas' argument from possibility and necessity
> - Copleston's cosmological argument
>
> **and to study:**
> - weaknesses of the argument identified by Hume
> - weaknesses of the argument identified by Russell.

In this book the evidence and examples given are relevant and appropriate because this material focuses only on the content for AO1 that is given by the Edexcel specification. The evaluation materials for AO2 will be aimed at helping you 'critically evaluate and justify a point of view through the use of evidence and reasoned argument'.

It would be helpful to write your notes using the headings listed above, as it is from these that the examination questions will be derived.

In your studies, remember that you have to bear in mind the **two** basic assessment objectives of:

- Knowledge and Understanding (AO1)
- Evaluation (AO2).

See pages 7–8 in the Introduction to remind yourself of these objectives.

The evaluation material set out in Part 1C (page 32) can be studied either alongside the AO1 material, as you work through this unit, or as a separate unit.

This part of the unit explores some of the main forms of the cosmological argument for the existence of God. No particular form of the argument will be specified in the exam question, but a discussion of the key ideas will require you to refer to some of the forms of the argument. As well as the strengths of these arguments, particular challenges to them will also be examined. Discussion of strengths involves outlining and explaining how the argument works. Discussion of weaknesses involves outlining and explaining the challenges to the arguments. The extent to which those challenges are successful is assessed in Part 1C.

KEY WORD

Cosmology: the scientific study of the origin and nature of the Universe

 KEY PERSON

Gottfried Leibniz (1646–1716)
He contributed to a wealth of subjects including philosophy and mathematics. He invented calculus and discovered the binary system.

 EXAM TIP

When you illustrate a point, make sure that you explain the illustration and, in particular, *how* it does illustrate or support the point you are making. This demonstrates selection of clear, relevant knowledge and understanding through use of example (AO1).

 KEY IDEA

Key concepts of the cosmological argument are:
- movement
- cause and effect
- contingency
- infinite regression
- first cause
- necessary existence.

1 Introduction

The **cosmological** argument attempts to infer the existence of God from the existence of the cosmos or from phenomena within it.

The claim is that the Universe cannot account for its own existence, and so the argument seeks causes that have their culmination in the existence of God. The arguments are inductive and *a posteriori* (see page 14) and so, at best, lead to probabilities rather than proofs.

Key ideas and concepts

i) **Leibniz** said that the great principle of the cosmological argument is that: 'nothing takes place without sufficient reason'. In other words, there must be some sort of explanation, known or unknown, for any positive truth. There must be an explanation of why something is as it is. He defined the principle as:

> *I am granted this important principle, that nothing happens without a sufficient reason why it should be thus and not otherwise.*

To illustrate this, see page 27 for an account of Leibniz's form of the cosmological argument. In essence, all of the cosmological arguments seek explanation as to why there is a Universe rather than nothing.

ii) The various forms of the cosmological arguments are *a posteriori*. In other words, their starting point is some observation or experience of the Universe. The argument is based on experience (of the Universe). This means that the evidence involves an interpretation of that experience.

All forms of the cosmological argument illustrate this.

iii) There are a number of key concepts that occur in the cosmological arguments.
- Movement: perhaps a more helpful word that brings out its meaning is 'change'. This involves change of place, change of size and change of state. **Aquinas'** First Way focuses on this aspect.
- Cause and effect: the underlying concept here is that everything that happens has a cause. Nothing can cause itself for this would mean it preceded itself, and this is impossible. Aquinas' Second Way focuses on this aspect.
- Contingency: this refers to items that need not be, that could have been different. A contingent being is one that has not in itself the complete reason for its existence. The underlying concept here is that of dependency. Aquinas' Third Way focuses on this aspect, as does Copleston's version of the cosmological argument.
- Infinite regression: this is the concept of a causal relationship that has an indefinite number of terms. Every effect has a cause but there is no term that starts the series. All of Aquinas' first three Ways involve this concept.
- First cause: the cosmological arguments seek explanation as to why there is something rather than nothing. Ultimately a starting point for cause and effect is sought as the explanation: in other words, a first cause, that itself is not caused. The cosmological argument does not attempt to prove anything about the first cause or about God, except to argue that such a cause must exist. Examples of this type of cosmological argument are that of Kalaam and Aquinas' Second Way (though there is debate as to whether the chain of causes is in time or in terms of hierarchy).

● Necessary existence: the first cause sees God as a factual necessity, as the causal explanation to the Universe. This means that God is seen as a being who is not dependent on any other for his existence. He is a contingent being who is causeless, and it would not be a logical contradiction if such a being did not actually exist. In contrast, another classic argument for the existence of God, the ontological argument, sees God as a logical necessity, whose non-existence would be a logical contradiction. Examples of this type of cosmological argument include those by Aquinas (Third Way), Leibniz and Copleston.

iv) Philosophical arguments – inductive and *a posteriori*. Check back to page 14 to remind yourself about these concepts.

2 Various forms of the cosmological argument

a) Aquinas' cosmological argument

Thomas Aquinas wrote a compact form of the arguments for God and these have become known as the Five Ways. The first three Ways are varying forms of the cosmological argument.

i) The First Way: the unmoved mover

The First Way is called the *unmoved mover*, the *unchanged changer* or the *prime mover*. It focuses on the idea of change or motion, by which Aquinas means the process by which an object acquires a new form. An object has the potentiality to become something different, so movement (or change) is the actualisation of that potential. For instance, wood is potentially hot but for a piece of wood to become hot it has to be changed by fire. Clearly nothing can be both potential and actual at the same time. There is a transition from one state to the other. Some change or movement takes place. What is

KEY IDEA

Aquinas' argument is about dependency and sustaining, rather than beginnings.

KEY QUESTION

What type of movement did Aquinas mean in the phrase 'the unmoved mover'?

> **KEY PROFILE: THOMAS AQUINAS (1225–74)**
>
> Thomas Aquinas has been a very influential philosopher and theologian who is especially highly regarded by Roman Catholics. He lived at a time when a renewed interest in Aristotle coincided with a view that philosophy could be useful to Christian theology, to demonstrate the reasonableness of faith and also to help explore articles of faith. Hence Aquinas attempted to apply the philosophy of Aristotle to Christianity. The philosophy of Aquinas is often referred to as *Thomism*. He wrote prolifically and in *Summa Theologica*, a book containing over 4000 pages, Aquinas devoted only two pages to his arguments for the existence of God. However their compact form has made them popular, and they have become known as the Five Ways:
>
> ● the unmoved mover (the cosmological argument)
> ● the uncaused causer (the cosmological argument)
> ● possibility and necessity (the cosmological argument)
> ● goodness, truth and nobility (the moral argument)
> ● teleological (the design argument).
>
> Each of his 'proofs' assumes the existence of a God who is uncreated and independent of the Universe. This means that though God is not reliant on the Universe for his existence, the Universe is reliant on God for its existence.

potentially *x* is not actually *x*, yet what *is* actually *x* can only be produced by something that is actually *x*. Whatever is moved (changed) must be moved (changed) by another, which itself was moved (changed). If we trace back far enough we must arrive at a first mover, moved by no other. This first mover must also contain all actuality and no potentiality. According to Aquinas, this is what we understand to be God. Again, this can be expressed in argument form:

- Nothing can move (change) itself.
- Everything that is in motion (change) is moved (changed) by something else.
- Infinite regress of movers (changers) is impossible.
- Therefore there must be a first mover (changer) – God.

Aquinas was not arguing that the Universe necessarily had a beginning. He thought it did, but said that you could not reason that out as it was revealed doctrine. Rather, his emphasis was on dependency. Christian theology has always taught that God sustains the Universe. In other words, if God ceased to exist then the Universe would also cease. There must be an initiator of the change whose continued existence is depended upon. An analogy of this type of causal relationship is of a performance that depends on the continued existence of actors. Such a causal relationship is known as hierarchical.

ii) The Second Way: the uncaused causer

This Second Way focuses on cause and existence. It has a structured argument similar to that of the First Way. Neither argument is original to Aquinas, in that they are both adapted from Aristotle. The argument states that nothing could be the cause of itself. The reason is that it would already have had to exist in order to bring itself into existence. This would be impossible. Therefore, if we trace back far enough, there must be a first cause, caused by no other. According to Aquinas, this is what we understand to be God. Once more, this can be expressed in argument form.

- Nothing can be the cause of itself.
- Infinite regress of causes is impossible.
- Therefore there must be a first cause – God.

Again, Aquinas was arguing for a hierarchical chain of causes rather than a linear chain.

iii) The Third Way: possibility and necessity

For Aquinas, anything that had a property was referred to as a being. The world consists of contingent items, that is, beings that have a possibility of ceasing to exist. In a finite period of time a possibility need not be realised. However, in an infinite period of time all possibilities occur. This means there will have been a time when all **contingent beings** will have ceased to exist. As there are contingent beings existing now, so there must be something non-contingent or necessary. This **necessary being** sustains the existence of contingent beings. According to Aquinas, this necessary being is what we understand to be God. Expressed in argument form:

- Some contingent beings exist.
- If any contingent beings exist, then a necessary being must exist.
- Therefore, a necessary being exists, namely God.

This argument contains the idea that if something is possible, then that possibility must be realised (given infinite time).

EXAM TIP

If you are asked about Aquinas' cosmological argument, remember that he has *three* forms of it. This demonstrates 'accurate and relevant detail' (level 4 descriptor AO1).

KEY IDEA

The difference between the first and second ways:

- In the First Way, the mover (changer) produces the various stages through which changeable things pass, and produces another state of something.
- In the Second Way, the causer produces the existence of the thing.

KEY WORDS

Contingent being: a being that depends upon something else for its existence

Necessary being: a being which, if it exists, cannot not exist

b) The Kalaam cosmological argument

This form of the cosmological argument is Islamic in origin and dates back to about CE850, to a group that belonged to the Islamic Kalaam tradition of philosophy. However, the argument has had a revival in the late twentieth century, mainly through the writings of **William Craig**.

The argument claims that everything that begins to exist has a cause of its existence and since the Universe began to exist, the Universe has a cause of its existence. Behind the entire Universe exists a cause that brought the Universe into being. This cause is God.

c) Leibniz's cosmological argument

Leibniz avoided the problem of infinite regression by reinterpreting the endless series, not of events but of explanations. Even if the Universe has always existed, there is nothing within the Universe to show why it exists. According to Leibniz, everything has a sufficient reason.

The **principle of sufficient reason** states that, in the case of any positive truth, there is some sufficient reason for it: there is some sort of explanation, known or unknown, for everything. The world does not seem to contain within itself the reason for its own existence.

Therefore, if there is a God who stands outside the entire sequence, a God who is eternal and necessary, and thus does not depend upon any further explanation, our system is coherent and we can know the ultimate reason for things. Leibniz therefore argued that God exists since, if we do not know ultimate reasons, we must hold that things are as they are only arbitrarily.

d) Copleston's cosmological argument

i) The radio debate

In 1948 a radio debate was broadcast in which **Frederick Copleston** and **Bertrand Russell** discussed the cosmological argument. Copleston was professor at Heythrop College and strongly supported the argument, while Russell, a British philosopher, opposed it. The form of the cosmological argument that Copleston defended was one based on contingency and the principle of sufficient reason. It was an argument that, in basic form, was originally presented by Leibniz. Key to Copleston's argument was the appeal for explanation.

KEY PERSON

William Craig (b. 1949)
An American philosopher and theologian who has popularised the Kalaam argument.

KEY WORD

Principle of sufficient reason: there is a complete explanation for everything

KEY QUOTE

If one refuses to even sit down at the chessboard and make a move, one cannot, of course, be checkmated.
(Copleston to Russell)

KEY PERSON

Frederick Copleston (1907–94)
Copleston was a Jesuit priest and writer of philosophy. He was also well known for his several radio debates on philosophy. In particular he debated with the atheistic philosophers Bertrand Russell and A. J. Ayer.

One of his great contributions is his nine-volume *History of Philosophy* (1946–75).

KEY PERSON

Bertrand Russell (1872–1970)
A British philosopher, logician and mathematician, he is regarded as one of the founders of analytic philosophy. Russell was well known for his anti-war protests and remained active in public life until his death at the age of 97.

ii) Copleston's argument

The key steps in his argument are as listed below.

- There are at least some beings in the world that do not contain in themselves the reason for their existence.
- The totality of the world is comprised of such objects. There is no world distinct from these objects.
- The explanation for the world must therefore be found externally to it.
- The reason must ultimately be an existent being that contains within itself the reason for its own existence.
- That reason is that it cannot not exist. It is a necessary being – God.

To put it another way, only God, a necessary being, can be the complete explanation for the existence of the Universe that contains contingent items. It is the explanation that requires no further explanation.

3 Challenges to the cosmological argument

a) Hume's criticisms of the cosmological argument

i) Rejection of the idea that we cannot know anything about cause

Hume was an **empiricist**. He viewed experience as the foundation of knowledge. When he came to consider causation, he claimed that we could not experience the actual cause.

Human beings in their imagination make the connection between cause and effect. Two events follow each other and our minds, through habit, make a connection between them. This is what Hume understood by 'cause'.

This demand, that experience is required for knowledge, led Hume to question other aspects of the argument. He argued that because we do not have any direct experience of the creation of Universes, we are unable to make conclusions about the creation of this Universe.

If we use the cosmological argument, we have gone beyond our experiences, which Hume would not allow. We began with familiar concepts of the Universe that come from our regular experiences, and concluded with concepts far beyond human experience, which implies a necessary being.

ii) Rejection of the idea of moving from individual causes to a cause for the totality

Hume rejected the argument that we could make the move from saying that every event in the Universe has a cause to the claim that the Universe has a cause. One cannot move from individual causes to the claim that the totality has a cause.

In fact Hume argued that when the parts are explained the whole is explained.

iii) Rejection of the idea of a beginning to the Universe

Hume questioned whether the Universe had a beginning. He suggested that perhaps it has always existed. In such a case it would be meaningless to ask about a cause.

Modern cosmology does allow for an infinite past history of the Universe since it is consistent with current scientific understanding to have an infinite series of expanding and contracting Universes. This is known as the *oscillating Universe theory*.

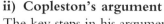

KEY QUOTE

An expanding Universe does not preclude a creator, but it does place limits on when he might have carried out his job!
(Stephen Hawking)

KEY WORD

Empiricist: a person who takes the view that the dominant foundation of knowledge is experience

iv) Rejection of the idea of the Christian God as the necessary being

Hume saw no reason to conclude that, even if the Universe did have a cause, that cause must be the Christian God. The cosmological argument tells us nothing about the attributes of the necessary being. Hume suggested that it could be argued that the cause of the Universe is a committee of gods.

b) Russell's criticisms of the cosmological argument

i) Rejection of the principle of sufficient reason

Russell questioned the claim that there was a reason for everything. In particular, he challenged the view that the Universe required an explanation. Indeed, he went even further and argued that any talk of the cause of the Universe as a whole was meaningless. He argued that '...the Universe is just there, and that's all.' In other words, there was no explanation. It is just a brute fact.

> **TASK**
>
> In the radio debate, Russell supports his view that not everything has a cause, by appealing to science. How might science support this view? How might science support the opposite view, namely that everything does have a cause?
>
> Objectives: To engage in the debate about causes. To appreciate how science can be used both for and against the view. This demonstrates that you are 'using evidence to explain key ideas' (level 4 descriptor AO1).

ii) Rejection of the idea of moving from individual causes to a cause for the totality

Like Hume, Russell rejected the argument that made the move from saying that every event in the Universe has a cause to the claim that the Universe has a cause. One cannot move from individual causes to the claim that the totality has a cause. He used an illustration to demonstrate his argument: To say that every person who exists has a mother does not then imply that the human race must have a mother. Technically this error of logic is known as the **fallacy** of composition. The error is to conclude mistakenly that since the parts have a certain property, the whole likewise has that property.

iii) Rejection of the notion of a necessary being

Russell claimed that the word 'necessary' could not meaningfully be applied to things. To say something is necessary is to claim that it must exist. However, Russell argued that the word 'existence' is not an additional property. The word functions in a different way and merely indicates an instance of something. Therefore he concluded that it was meaningless to use the term 'necessary' when applying it to a thing, as though it were an additional property that the object possessed. There is no relationship between a concept and its actuality (existence).

c) Further criticisims of Aquinas' cosmological argument

There are a number of challenges.

- Some scholars have argued that Aquinas' arguments rest on assumptions that are no longer widely held. Ancient and medieval science thought in terms of a hierarchy of causes, which is different to modern-day thinking. It is an assumption that actual x can only be brought about by what is actual x. For example, two cold objects rubbed together will cause heat.

KEY QUOTES

...the Universe is just there, and that's all.

(Russell)

Every man who exists has a mother... therefore the human race must have a mother, but obviously the human race hasn't a mother – that's a different logical sphere.

(Russell)

...and it raises, of course, the question what one means by existence, and as to this, I think a subject named can never be significantly said to exist but only a subject described.

(Russell)

KEY WORD

Fallacy: unsound reasoning

- Why cannot there be an endless series of causes? In reply, Mackie cites the analogy of a railway train comprising an infinite number of carriages. Each carriage may move the next carriage but ultimately it only makes sense if there is an engine. The problem then becomes one of demonstrating that Aquinas' Three Ways have such a relation of dependence.
- Why cannot there be some contingent items that have lasted through all past time and will show their contingency by perishing at some time in the future?
- If nothing can cause itself, how can God be seen as an uncaused causer?
- Why must there be a single termination? Why must the regression lead to one first cause? Independent happenings might lead back to causes that are independent of each other. Therefore there would not be a single first cause but a plurality of first causes.
- Why cannot the different forms of the Three Ways lead to a different God for each? Why should it lead to God as understood in the Christian concept? Indeed, why should God not be the originator and now no longer exist? After all, a mother causes a child but then dies.
- The argument begins with this world and concludes with concepts of which we have no experience such as the uncaused and infinity.
- The Universe is not contingent: matter or energy in the Universe is eternal. Particular objects come and go but the matter of which they are composed is for ever and exists necessarily. It could not have failed to exist. There is not a reason, it is just brute fact. Thus the great ultimates of the Universe are about matter, not about a metaphysical being called God.

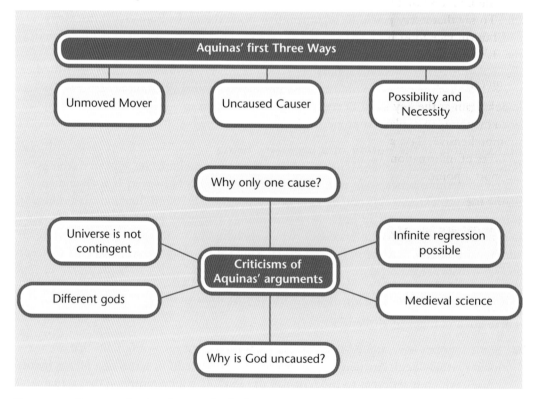

Summary diagram: Aquinas' cosmological argument

Reflection and assessment

It is vital to bring together the information that has been covered so far and recognise how it can be transformed into effective examination-style revision and answers. The best way to do this is to ask the question: 'How am I going to be assessed on this information?'

Look back to pages 8–10 in the Introduction to review the level descriptors for AO1. There is a description of the character and features for each level. The examination is marked with reference to levels.

The following points, which are not in any particular order, are some of the key points in answer to this question.

Examine the challenges to the cosmological argument. (21 marks)

- One cannot move from individual causes to the claim that the totality has a cause.
- The Universe has a plurality of causes.
- A mother causes a child and then dies.
- Every event has a cause.
- The cosmological argument commits the fallacy of composition.
- Three ways implies three different gods.
- The Universe has always existed.
- Only God, a necessary being, can be the complete explanation for the existence of the Universe that contains contingent items.
- To say that every person who exists has a mother does not then imply that the human race must have a mother.
- It's a brute fact.

Suggestion for further application of skills

Look again at the key ideas of the cosmological argument (page 24). Make a list of six key points to explain them. With a partner, add further points to make it more comprehensive. Try, as well, to find relevant quotes from scholars or texts or further sources of information, to add at suitable places to use as examples or illustrations or to support a point.

Now use your lists to develop an answer to this question.

What are the key ideas of the cosmological argument? (21 marks)

TASK

Use the key points opposite as a basis for a writing frame to answer the question:

Examine the challenges to the cosmological argument. (21 marks)

Add one other challenge. Where necessary, expand your answer so you explain rather than just make statements.

Objective: To practise good 'selection of clearly relevant knowledge, identifying the most important features, expressed accurately and fluently (level 4 descriptor AO1).

FOUNDATIONS
Area A: Philosophy of religion

TOPIC 1: A STUDY OF PHILOSOPHICAL ARGUMENTS ABOUT THE EXISTENCE OF GOD

Part 1C: A critical analysis of the issues

This means I am expected:

to analyse and critically evaluate:
- the strengths and weaknesses of the design argument
- the strengths and weaknesses of the cosmological argument.

? KEY QUESTIONS
- Does everything have an explanation?
- Do all the arguments lead to the *same* God?
- Is God the same God as the Christian God?
- Could the cosmological constants have been different?
- Does the claim to uniqueness mean that we are unable to investigate it?

1 Challenges to the strengths of the design argument

Evaluating the strengths of the design and cosmological arguments demands more than simply outlining and explaining how the arguments work. It is about assessing and weighing up those arguments, asking such questions as: 'Are those strengths convincing?' and 'To what extent are the strengths successful?'

The strengths themselves are discussed in Part 1A (pages 14–18). Some possible responses that challenge the success are covered below.

a) Not a proof

The design arguments tend to be expressed as inductive arguments and so are about probabilities rather than deductive proofs.

b) An undesigned Universe

Linguistic philosophy has focused on the issue of whether statements are meaningful. One claim is that a meaningful statement is one for which we know what would disprove it. Hence, until we can say what the world would have to be like for it *not* to have been designed, we cannot conclude that the world *is* designed.

c) God is not an external being

Others would argue that God is not an additional being but rather a word used to describe a sense of ultimate meaning for life. God is not an object. God represents what is most important to us.

However, all the traditional arguments for the existence of God assume that the word 'God' is defined as relating to some kind of supreme being. To define God as other than an objective entity alters the whole subject of debate and makes it meaningless.

If one wanted to argue in support of the design argument, then an added line of argument might be to show how the challenges to the argument are flawed and so fail. If this is so, then the design argument remains persuasive.

2 Evaluating the weaknesses of the design argument

Again, the weaknesses of the design argument can be found in Part 1A (pages 18–21). Evaluation involves some kind of assessment of those weaknesses. Some possible responses follow.

a) It gives an explanation

We seek an explanation of everything else, so why not of the Universe? The design argument answers the question: 'Why is the Universe the way it is?' Science works on the basis that everything has an explanation. That is what scientific enquiry assumes is the case. This brings into sharp contrast the two ways of looking at the Universe; either it is accidental or it is deliberate and purposeful.

b) It fits in with the other arguments for God's existence

Although the design argument, by itself, does not lead to a fully defined God of the Christian understanding, it can be seen as an important part of a cumulative argument. When all the arguments for the existence of God are taken together, they all point to the same conclusion – God. Taken together, they fill out the attributes of the necessary being.

c) Recent scientific findings support it

When the anthropic argument was first debated there was little scientific evidence to support it. The argument spoke for the most part only in generalities, for example, 'the fitness of the inorganic to minister to life'. Few, if any, specific examples could be given.

However, recent science has shown how finely balanced the Universe is. For instance, it has identified what are called 'cosmological constants', such as the gravitational constant, the speed of light, the basic properties of elementary particles and the **Planck constant**. All these constants could have been different and are, in most cases, causally unrelated to each other but must fall within a very narrow range, if life is to be possible. If any had changed even by a small amount then life as we understand it would not exist. This strongly supports the view that the Universe is not an accident but has a design.

d) New approach of 'intelligent design'

i) What is meant by intelligent design (ID)?
This view argues that an intelligence is necessary to explain the complex, information-rich structures of biology and that this intelligence is empirically detectable.

ii) What is the evidence for intelligent design?
There are three main thrusts.

- **Irreducible complexities**
  Irreducible complexity means that all the parts of a system must be in place at once for the system to work. The different parts could not have arisen separately or at different times by a process of gradual change such as evolution. It is claimed that many examples of biochemical systems reflect irreducible complexity. The originator of this approach is **Michael Behe**.
- **Specified complexities**
  This argues that design is implied any time that two criteria are satisfied: namely complexity and specification. Behe argued that we should infer intelligent design when we see what he calls 'specified complexity'. By this, he means that we detect

KEY QUOTE

As we look out into the Universe and identify the many accidents of physics and astronomy that have worked to our benefit, it almost seems as if the Universe must in some sense have known that we were coming.

(Dyson)

KEY WORD

Planck constant: used in quantum mechanics to describe the sizes of quanta

KEY PERSON

Michael Behe (b. 1952) Professor of biochemistry, who framed the concept of irreducible complexity.

KEY QUESTION

Is intelligent design scientific?

KEY WORD

Irreducible complexity: when all parts of the system must be in place in order for the system to work. The removal of any one of the parts causes the system to stop functioning

TASK

Express the design argument, using the analogy of a work of art and the Universe. List its strengths and weaknesses as an argument.

Objectives: To help understand analogous arguments and how they function, demonstrating that you are 'using evidence to explain key ideas' (level 4 descriptor AO1).

intelligent design in events that are highly improbable (thus complex) and that also correspond to some independently given pattern (thus specified). Some structures can be explained in terms of natural laws that do not necessarily point to design. For instance, we cannot conclude that, on the basis of scientific evidence, natural selection was designed. It may have been, but it is not necessarily so. However, ID claims that other structures show obvious design. These are the structures that have the characteristic of irreducible complexities that perform a specified task.

An illustration that might help to explain this idea is the example of placing seaweed on a sandy beach in order to make it appear that the seaweed has been thrown up on the beach by the tide. If you had seen me place the seaweed on the beach you would have known it was not there by chance. But you cannot deduce this just by seeing the seaweed lying on the beach. The fact it had been placed there is not obvious. However, if you placed the seaweed in such a way to spell out the phrase 'Welcome to Worthing', then such an arrangement would point to design. The claim is that specified complexities are of this second type of arrangement.

- **Evidence not theory**
  Supporters of the ID theory claim that the debate is about evidence. So are there any examples of **irreducible complex** systems? It is claimed that ID as a scientific theory is a more adequate scientific explanation of the biological evidence than is the theory of evolution. Intelligent design is not creationism. It does not say anything about the nature of the source of design, though it could be seen as pointing towards theism.

Another aspect of evaluating the weaknesses is to consider the counter arguments to challenges made against the argument.

e) The challenges by Hume fail

i) An unsound analogy

There appears to be purpose in nature and the functionality of the watch displays purpose, so supporters of the argument would claim it was a sound analogy. Purpose shouts for an explanation.

Even in the case of a vegetable (which Hume suggests), it could be argued that the vegetable shows features of design, so who or what designed the vegetable?

It seems unreasonable of Hume to say that no questions can be asked about the origin of things that are unique. Scientists try to account for things that are unique and the Universe shares many characteristics with its parts.

ii) Similar effects do not necessarily imply similar causes

The obvious cause of beneficial order, purpose and regularity is intelligence. There would have to be good reasons why this should not be the case and why an alternative should be considered.

iii) Other possible analogies

Supporters of Paley have in fact offered other analogies. For example, instead of a machine they propose a work of art. This would allow the idea of beauty also to be a common feature. We evaluate works of art in a different way from how we evaluate mechanical efficiency. Beauty is not just about efficiency. This analogy has the added attraction of embracing a rather wasteful process such as evolution.

iv) Analogy makes God more human than divine

It could be argued that making God more human is actually contrary to the analogical argument. It is a non-explanation to appeal to a material God as explanation for the material order in the Universe, since the material God already possesses this order.

Given that the argument is analogical, it does not demand a direct relationship between human designers and God.

Finally, the claim that the analogy leads us to suppose a whole community of gods can be challenged on the basis of **Ockham's razor**. This principle of reasoning assumes that entities are not to be multiplied beyond necessity.

KEY IDEA

Ockham's razor is the philosophical principle that states that entities should not be multiplied beyond necessity. The name derives from the idea of 'shaving off' those entities that are not needed. This principle is also extended to recommend, where there are multiple theories, selecting the simplest theory – the one that introduces fewest assumptions and fewest entities.

v) Analogy leads to a non-moral God

The design argument is part of a cumulative argument and does not claim to demonstrate all the attributes of God in each argument. Supporters would point challengers toward the moral argument for the existence of God, on page 25. See also the section on the problem of evil, on page 44.

vi) Other explanations for apparent order

People claimed that the fact that they find order is hardly surprising. What else could they find? Swinburne has challenged the argument of those who maintain that, unless the Universe was an orderly place, people would not be around to comment on its existence.

He deals with this position by pointing out that the existence of an observer has no bearing on the probability of the occurrence of the events being observed. If a series of highly improbable events give rise to an observer who can note this improbability, they are nonetheless improbable. He uses an illustration to make his point clear.

> *Suppose that a madman kidnaps a victim and shuts him in a room with a card-shuffling machine. The machine shuffles ten decks of cards simultaneously and then draws a card from each deck and exhibits simultaneously the ten cards. The kidnapper tells the victim that he will shortly set the machine to work and it will exhibit its first draw, but that unless the draw consists of an ace of hearts from each deck, the machine will simultaneously set off an explosion which will kill the victim, in consequence of which he will not see which cards the machine drew. The machine is then set to work, and to the amazement and relief of the victim the machine exhibits an ace of hearts drawn from each deck. The victim thinks that this extraordinary fact needs an explanation in terms of the machine having been rigged in some way. But the kidnapper, who now reappears, casts doubt on this suggestion. 'It is hardly surprising,' he says, 'that the machine draws only aces of hearts. You could not possibly see anything else. For you would not be here to see anything at all, if any other cards had been drawn.' But of course the victim is right and the kidnapper is wrong. There is indeed something extraordinary in need of explanation in ten aces of hearts being drawn. The fact that this peculiar order is a necessary condition of the draw being perceived at all makes what is perceived no less extraordinary and*

TASK

In groups, discuss whether the watch analogy refers to the parts of the Universe or the whole Universe. What problems does each raise about 'purpose'?

Objective: To understand Paley's analogy and its problems, demonstrating that you are 'clearly identifying the most important features' (level 4 descriptor AO1).

? KEY QUESTIONS

- Is God the God of Christianity?
- Does the Universe have to be ordered?

66 KEY QUOTE

The teleologist's starting point is not that we perceive order rather than disorder, but that order rather than disorder is there.
(Swinburne)

99

in need of explanation. The teleologist's starting-point is not that we perceive order rather than disorder, but that order rather than disorder is there. Maybe only if order is there can we know what is there, but that makes what is there no less extraordinary and in need of explanation.

f) The challenges by Mill fail

Many challenge Mill's claim, which seems to equate nature's crimes with the crimes of the human race. The difference is one of intention. Nature does not act with intention in the way that human beings do. This seems to be a flaw in Mill's argument.

There is a problem about what we mean by the word 'disorder'. What is disorder to some is order to others. The use of the word is subjective. Added to this, even if there were agreed disorder, this disorder may be part of God's greater plan; see the section on the problem of evil, page 44.

g) The challenges by Darwin fail

Without doubt, the theory of natural selection has been regarded as a major challenge to the design argument. However, various responses have been made in reply.

- Evolution is only a theory and not proven. The theory is seen as wrong.
- There is a jump in moving from a description of how natural selection operates upon existence to the assumption that natural selection also provides the explanation for that existence. As Tennant said: 'The survival of the fittest presupposes the arrival of the fit.'
- There can be no origin of species without a mechanism that is itself teleological. This system needs an explanation. Natural selection cannot give it. The explanation is God. God is the designer of the process of natural selection.
- Most regard the evolution debate as religiously inconclusive. There are both religious and non-religious scholars who accept the theory of evolution. It is neither necessarily atheistic nor necessarily theistic. It is more agnostic.
- Swinburne felt that natural selection could explain spatial order (complex structures of things such as plants and animals). Instead he focused on temporal order (what he calls 'regularities of succession'). By temporal order he meant the laws of nature throughout the Universe. The Universe is orderly, yet it could have been chaotic. Nature seems to conform to a formula. If there is an explanation to account for this, then it cannot be a scientific one because we explain the operation of scientific laws in terms of more general scientific laws. The best explanation and by far the simplest is a personal explanation rather than scientific laws – God.

h) The challenges by Dawkins fail

A major critic of Dawkins is the theologian Alister McGrath. He makes a number of points about the theory of memes.

- Rejecting the whole idea of cultural Darwinism, that the development of culture and the history of ideas can be accounted for by the idea of memes, McGrath points out that culture and ideas are deliberate, intentional and planned, which is contrary to the theory about memes.
- There seems no evidential support for memes. It can be abandoned without difficulty. The concept is so vague that there is no means by which it can be verified or falsified.

● If the belief in God is explained by memes, then why cannot atheism be explained in the same way? Indeed, all beliefs are subject to the same criticism, including belief in memes!

Again, if one wanted to argue against the design argument, then an added line of argument might be to show how the strengths of the argument are flawed and so fail. If this is so, then the design argument is weakened; see section 1, page 32.

? KEY QUESTION

Are there such things as irreducible complexities?

3 Possible conclusions

When assessing the issues that arise from the design argument, it is important to reflect upon the arguments previously discussed and arrive at some appropriate conclusion.

It may be that you accept none of these listed here, or just one of them, or you may have a different conclusion that is not listed. However, what is important is the way that you have arrived at your conclusion – the reasoning process.

From the preceding discussions, here are some possible conclusions you could draw.

1 The design argument is successful and proves the existence of God. There are a variety of design arguments. It could be that one particular form of the argument is regarded as successful or it could be the general approach shared by them all.

2 The design argument does not prove that God exists. However, it is persuasive, especially when considered alongside the other arguments for the existence of God. It forms part of the cumulative case for the existence of God.

3 The design argument fails to prove the existence of God. This could refer to one particular form of the argument. The fact that one argument fails does not prove that all forms of the design argument fail.

4 The Universe is inexplicable. It has no explanation and it does not need one. It just is.

5 The success or failure of the design argument is still being debated. The argument remains a live issue in philosophical circles and no agreed conclusion has yet been reached.

6 The whole idea of trying to demonstrate that God exists is nonsensical. It is to misunderstand the meaning of the word 'God'. God is not an object or a thing. It is a word used to encapsulate that which is most important to us.

66 KEY QUOTE

...far from being the 'terminus' of the quest for intelligibility and explanation in the Universe, God is the terminal illness of reason.

(Atkins)

99

? KEY QUESTIONS

● Would any world, whatever its form, appear to have been designed?

● If everything has a cause, what caused God?

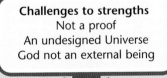

Challenges to strengths
Not a proof
An undesigned Universe
God not an external being

Challenges to weaknesses
Hume's challenges fail
Mill's challenges fail
Darwin's challenges fail
Dawkins' challenges fail
Gives an explanation
Recent scientific findings
support the design argument

Summary diagram: Evaluating strengths and weaknesses of the design argument

✏ TASK

'God is part of the Universe.'
List some points that support this view and list some points that oppose such a view.
Objective: To understand the issues of God's relationship to the Universe, demonstrating that you are using 'a careful analysis of alternative views' (level 4 descriptor AO2).

4 Evaluating the strengths of the cosmological argument

As was identified earlier (page 32), evaluating the strengths of the design and cosmological argument is more than stating what the strengths are. It is about assessing and weighing up those strengths. It involves asking such questions as: 'Are those strengths convincing?' and 'To what extent are the strengths successful?'

The strengths themselves are discussed in Part 1B (pages 24–8). Possible responses that challenge the success are covered below.

a) Not a proof

The design arguments tend to be expressed as inductive arguments and so are about probabilities rather than deductive proof.

b) The problem of 'infinity'

Many argue that to treat infinity as though it were a number is to misunderstand the word. Infinity is a concept. Hence it is meaningless to speak of 'adding more moments of time'.

c) The Universe is not contingent

The Universe is matter and energy and is eternal. Particular objects come into and go out of existence, but the matter of which they are composed lasts for ever and exists necessarily. It could not have failed to exist. There is no reason – it is just brute fact. Thus, the great ultimates of the Universe are about matter, not about a metaphysical being called God.

d) God is not an external being

Others would argue that God is not an additional being but rather a word used to describe a sense of ultimate meaning to life. God is not an object. God represents what is most important to us.

However, all the traditional arguments for the existence of God assume that the word 'God' is defined as describing some kind of supreme being. To define God as other than an objective entity alters the whole subject of debate and makes it meaningless.

5 Evaluating the weaknesses of the cosmological argument

Again, the challenges to the cosmological argument can be found in Part 1B (pages 28–30). Evaluation involves some kind of assessing of those challenges. Some possible responses are discussed below.

a) The challenges by Hume fail

Hume's view concerning causes has come under criticism. He claimed that our minds make the connection of cause when one event constantly follows another. However, even when one event follows another, we distinguish between the ideas both of cause and coincidence. This suggests they are different things. Night and day are two events that constantly follow one another but we would not claim that one causes the other. Sometimes two events are regarded as causally related yet do not always follow one after the other. For instance, we reason that staring at a computer screen sometimes causes headaches!

Hume argued that perhaps the Universe never had a beginning. For criticism of this, see sections c) and d) on page 39.

TASK

What is meant by 'the Universe'? Is it possible to envisage the total absence of matter and space? Give reasons. So, could there have been nothing at all or did the Universe have to exist?

Objective: To develop deeper understanding of the complexities of the cosmological argument. This demonstrates that you are using 'well deployed evidence and reasoned argument' (level 4 descriptor AO2).

b) The challenges by Russell fail

Philosopher's challenge the claim by Russell that a 'necessary being' is a meaningless term. Some claim that there can be a relationship between a concept and its actuality (existence). Take, for example, 'round squares'. These cannot exist. A concept leads to a non-existence. Therefore the two processes of concept and actuality are related.

? KEY QUESTION

Does everything have an explanation?

6 Further evaluation of the weaknesses of the cosmological argument

a) It gives an explanation

We seek an explanation for everything else, so why not for the Universe? Indeed, science works on the basis that everything has an explanation. That is what scientific enquiry assumes is the case. It brings into sharp contrast the two ways of looking at the Universe. Either it is inexplicable or it is intelligible. If there is an explanation, it is possible that it could be contained in 'God'.

b) It fits in with the ontological argument

The ontological argument explored the idea of a necessary being. The cosmological argument leads to the idea of a necessary being. Although the cosmological argument, by itself, does not lead to a fully defined God in the Christian sense, it can be seen as an important element of a cumulative argument. When all the arguments for the existence of God are taken together, they all point to the same conclusion – God. Taken together, they fill out the attributes of the necessary being.

? KEY QUESTIONS

- Is the necessary being God?
- Is God the same God as the Christian God?
- Did the Universe have a beginning or has it always existed?
- Is a Universe with no beginning, possible?

c) Science supports the view that the Universe had a beginning

Modern cosmology suggests that the **Big Bang theory** implies a finite past history of the Universe. Support for such a theory includes the evidence that the Universe is expanding, which suggests that it had a starting point.

KEY WORD

Big Bang theory: the theory of an expanding Universe that began as an infinitely dense and hot medium at some finite time in the past; the initial instant is called the Big Bang

d) Philosophy supports the view that the Universe had a beginning

If the Universe had no beginning, then an actual infinite number of past moments of the Universe's history have elapsed, and they are being added to as time goes on. But one cannot add to an infinite number of things. For instance, if you had an infinite number of dogs, then you cannot add to that number of dogs by introducing another dog. Likewise, if there has elapsed an infinite number of past moments of the Universe, then this number cannot be added to either. Yet the Universe continues to exist. Moments continue to be added. This implies that the Universe had a beginning. Furthermore, if the Universe had no beginning, then an infinity of years will have been passed, which is impossible.

e) Not a contradiction

It is not a contradiction to argue that everything needs a cause except God. Aquinas did not see God as just another thing, like everything else in the Universe. God is not one more in a line of causes. God is of a totally different order and not subject to the same conditions as the Universe.

66 KEY QUOTE

An event is 'fully explained when we have cited the agent, his intention that the event occur, and his basic powers' that include his ability to bring about events of that sort.

(Swinburne)

99

7 Possible conclusions

When assessing the issues that arise from the cosmological argument, it is important to reflect upon the arguments previously discussed and arrive at some appropriate conclusion.

It may be that you accept none of these listed here, or just one of them, or you may have a different conclusion that is not listed. However, what is important is the way that you have arrived at your conclusion – the reasoning process.

From the preceding discussions, here are some possible conclusions you could draw.

1   The cosmological argument is successful and proves the existence of God. There are a variety of arguments that are covered by the heading 'cosmological'. It could be one particular form of the argument that is regarded as successful or it could be the general approach shared by all the arguments.

2   The cosmological argument does not prove that God exists. However, it is persuasive, especially when considered alongside the other arguments for the existence of God. It forms part of the cumulative case for the existence of God.

3   The cosmological argument fails to prove the existence of God. This could refer to one particular form of the argument. The fact that one argument fails does not prove that all forms of the cosmological argument fail. (Although other forms of the argument are not required to be studied in detail, it would be useful to be aware that other formulations exist, such as the **Kaalam argument**.)

4   The Universe is a brute fact. No explanation is required.

5   The success or failure of the cosmological argument is still being debated. The argument remains a live issue in philosophical circles and no agreed conclusion has yet been reached.

6   The whole concept of trying to demonstrate that God exists is nonsensical. It is to misunderstand the meaning of the word 'God'. God is not an object or a thing. It is a word used to convey that which is most important to us.

 **KEY WORD**

Kaalam argument: an argument that claims that everything that begins to exist has a cause of its existence, and since the Universe began to exist, the Universe has a cause of its existence. Transcending the entire Universe there exists a cause which brought the Universe into being. This cause is God.

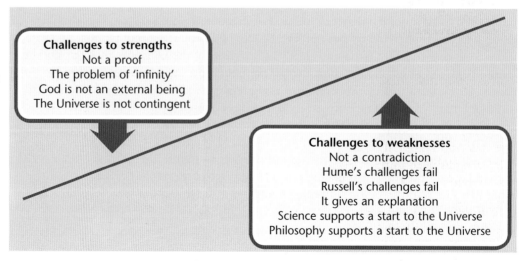

Challenges to strengths
Not a proof
The problem of 'infinity'
God is not an external being
The Universe is not contingent

Challenges to weaknesses
Not a contradiction
Hume's challenges fail
Russell's challenges fail
It gives an explanation
Science supports a start to the Universe
Philosophy supports a start to the Universe

Summary diagram: Evaluating the strengths and weaknesses of the cosmological argument

Reflection and assessment

Look back to page 10 in the Introduction to review the level descriptors for AO2. There is a description of the character and features for each level. The exam is marked with reference to levels.

Look at the following sample answer – a response to this question.

> **Comment on the strengths of the cosmological argument.** (9 marks)

As this is a second part of a question (AO2), the first part of the question (AO1) would have been about the cosmological argument itself. If so, there will be no need to repeat the argument since it will already have been given.

This needs expanding to make clear why it is common sense.

Need to make clear how this is consistent with the cosmological argument. It is not the job of the examiner to work it out.

Needs relating more clearly to the argument. Also the ending is abrupt and needs some sort of conclusion about the weight of the strengths.

The cosmological argument by Aquinas consists of the first three Ways of his Five Ways. Aquinas lived in Italy and was a prolific writer. His dates are 1225 to 1274. He attempted to apply the philosophy of Aristotle to Christianity. His First Way involved the unmoved mover. The Second Way involved the uncaused causer and the Third Way centred on the need for a necessary being to sustain the existence of contingent beings.

The argument seems common sense. It provides an explanation. That is one of its strengths. The Big Bang supports the idea of the Universe having a starting point and this is consistent with the cosmological argument. The picture it gives of God is one of a necessary being and this is consistent with, and adds to the other arguments for God. Together they give a more complete picture. This is another of its strengths.

However, the argument is not a proof and that is its weakness. It merely shows the possibility/probability of God's existence. It does not prove that God exists. Therefore, as an argument to prove that God exists, it fails. Indeed, claiming that everything requires an explanation is an actual weakness of the argument rather than a strength, since therefore God himself/herself must also require an explanation.

Besides questioning the claims of the strengths of the argument, the argument itself is prone to a number of weaknesses. For instance, the whole idea of causation has been challenged by David Hume.

This is not relevant. Need to focus on the question slant.

Further comment is needed to clarify.

Good to link back to focus of question.

Again, this needs further explanation.

Good that the answer has developed on from just stating the strengths to the evaluative element and showing an understanding of the strengths.

This is a good further development that points to a weakness that challenges the strengths.

a) So what does it score?

In the exam the answer will be marked according to levels (see the Introduction, page 10).

Certainly there is some basic reasoning. The candidate clearly has an understanding of the main cosmological arguments by Aquinas and some of their strengths. However, the strengths need further development and justification in order to clarify 'why' they are strengths.

The candidate has gone beyond merely supporting the argument and has made some attempt to evaluate those strengths. In doing so they have challenged the strengths and made a very brief reference to a weakness. However, the points are not developed and the material is limited in its range.

TASK

Using this answer as a framework, and the comments, write a level 4 answer.

Objective: To identify the weaknesses of a lower level 3 answer and be able to differentiate it from a higher level.

This would score level 3 (a point of view expressed clearly, supported by relevant evidence and argument and deploying some technical language appropriately, supported by limited but appropriate evidence – AO2 level descriptor).

b) Suggestion for further application of skills

Look at an essay that you have recently completed.

1 Underline in green what could have been omitted or is repeated.

2 Underline in blue any evaluation words.

3 Underline in red key phrases.

4 Referring to the level descriptors, consider the reasons for the level awarded for your essay.

5 Use the level descriptors to identify how the essay could be improved.

TOPIC 2: A STUDY OF SELECTED PROBLEMS IN THE PHILOSOPHY OF RELIGION

Part 2A: The problems of evil and suffering and possible solutions

---

This means I am expected:

to know about the key emphases:

- the nature of the problem of evil and suffering
- moral and non-moral evil
- some attempts at solutions to the problems.

In this book the evidence and examples given are relevant and appropriate because this material focuses only on the content for AO1 that is given by the Edexcel specification. The evaluation materials for AO2 will be aimed at helping you 'critically evaluate and justify a point of view through the use of evidence and reasoned argument'.

It would be helpful to write your notes using the headings listed above, as it is from these areas that the examination questions will be derived.

In your studies, remember that you have to bear in mind the **two** basic assessment objectives of:

- Knowledge and Understanding (AO1)
- Evaluation (AO2).

See pages 7–8 in the Introduction to remind yourself of these objectives.

The evaluation material set out in Part 2C (page 65) can be studied either alongside the AO1 material, as you work through this unit, or as a separate unit.

This part of the topic explores the problem of evil and suffering, identifying the different aspects of the problem and considering the main solutions offered. This is followed by an examination of the strengths and weaknesses of these various solutions (theodices). Note that the specification uses the word 'solution' rather than 'theodicy'. This choice of word is deliberate, so that some candidates (especially those studying a world religion) could address the problem of evil from the perspective, for example, of a Buddhist or apply some Hindu approaches to the problem of suffering. In this book, the classic Christian solutions, for example, Augustinian and Irenaean, will be studied. Evaluation of the strengths and weaknesses of the solutions will be examined in Part 2C.

1 The nature of the problem of evil

a) The logical problem

The so-called 'problem of evil' was first formulated by the Greek philosopher Epicurus (342–270BCE) and has been restated in various forms down the centuries, especially by Augustine (CE354–430) in his *Confessions*. If we accept that God is both all-powerful and good, then the assumption is that a good God would eliminate evil as far as he is able. Why does the God who has the power to eliminate all evil not do so? God has the means (power) and the motivation (love, goodness) to eliminate evil but chooses not to.

When put in its simplest **argument** form, it is seen as essentially a logical problem, expressed by means of three premises and a conclusion.

- God is all powerful.
- God is all good.
- God opposes evil.
- Therefore evil does not exist in the world.

A theist would agree with the premises, yet most would not agree with the conclusion. In other words, they would admit that evil did exist. But the question they have to answer is: 'What prevents a good and all-powerful God from eliminating all evil?' Trying to resolve this problem is not at all easy, especially when you bear in mind the following points.

- God's omnipotence includes God's omniscience, a God who can do anything but does not always know what is the best way of doing it, might be said to be less than all-powerful.
- God cannot do the logically impossible, for example, make square circles. Neither can he do what is inconsistent with his nature.
- God being all good implies that he opposes evil and will wish to remove it.

The problem is really only a problem for the believer in God, since if there is no God there is no problem.

b) Moral and natural evil

The illustration of evil is an important aspect of unpacking the problem since different types of evil raise different philosophical issues. It is usual to divide evil into:

- moral, in which responsible actions cause suffering or harm, for example, murder, stealing or lying
- natural, in which events cause suffering but over which human beings have little or no control, such as earthquakes and diseases. At various times certain events have been used as classic illustrations of natural evil. At one stage it was the Lisbon earthquake of 1755, but in the present day it is the tsunami of 2004, or Aids and cancer.

Some make further groupings such as physical, which refers to pain itself and mental anguish, and metaphysical, which refers to imperfection and contingency as a feature of the cosmos.

TASK

The photograph shows part of the tsunami of December 2004. Explain why such an event is an example of natural evil. List the similarities *and* the differences between natural and moral evil.

Objective: To understand the perceived differences between natural and moral evil. This demonstrates that you are using 'accurate, relevant and detailed knowledge of the subject matter' (level 4 descriptor AO1).

Are natural disasters God's fault?

The problem of suffering has a slightly different emphasis. It focuses on the *experience* of the evil. It raises different questions because of the experience. It deals with the problem on a more personal level, asking: 'How does the individual respond to suffering?' The questions that are raised here are more of the form: Why me? Why now? Why this particular form? Why this intensity? Why this length? They are questions that struggle to find purpose and explanation in what is being experienced.

Quite clearly, rather academic and cold discussions about the philosophical problems of evil are often inappropriate for someone battling with their own personal pain and grief.

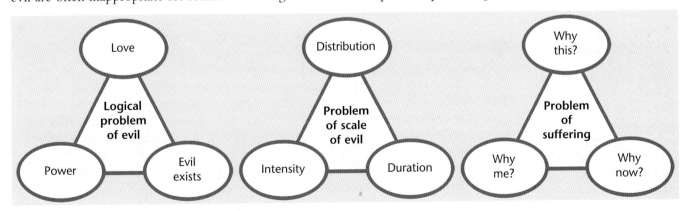

Summary diagram: The problem of evil

2 The classical solutions (theodicies)

Many have argued that there is a contradiction between belief in a God and the existence of evil. However, it does not seem logically contradictory, since it is not the same thing as saying: 'There is a God and there is no God,' (which would be a straight contradiction). A **theodicy** is an attempt at a solution of the problem of evil that seeks to show how God is justified in allowing evil.

In Western philosophy there have been two main theodicies, those of **Irenaeus** and **Augustine**.

a) Irenaeus' theodicy (soul-making)

In the writings of Irenaeus appears the idea that human beings were not created perfect but are developing towards perfection. Irenaeus made a distinction between the 'image' and the 'likeness' of God (Genesis 1:26). Adam had the form of God but not the content of God. Adam and Eve were expelled from the Garden of Eden because they were immature and needed to develop: they were to grow into the likeness (content) of God. They were the raw material for a further stage of God's creative work.

The fall of humanity is seen as an inevitable part of its growing up and maturing. This maturing takes place as free persons make decisions about their lives and the world in which God has placed them and so the emphasis in this theodicy is on **soul-making**.

How far Irenaeus intended to take these ideas we simply do not know, but in recent times **John Hick** developed a full theodicy, taking as his starting point the ideas of Irenaeus. Hick sees the first phase of God making humankind in his image as the culmination of the evolutionary process, whereby a creature has evolved who has the possibility of existing in conscious fellowship with God. The second phase involves a being who makes moral responsible choices in real-life situations. It is a necessary pilgrimage within the life of each individual.

An essential part of this theodicy is that this process is worthwhile because of the eventual outcome. If the process is not completed in this life, then Hick argued that there is another life in another realm to which we go, until the process is complete. In other words, all will eventually succeed.

 KEY PROFILE: IRENAEUS (CE130–202)

Irenaeus is thought to have been a Greek from Smyrna (modern-day Izmir in Turkey). He was raised in a Christian family and became the second bishop of Lyon. Almost all of his writings were directed against Gnosticism, which he considered a heresy. Gnosticism preached a hidden wisdom or knowledge that was only given to a select group. This knowledge was necessary for salvation or escape from this world.

One of his most influential arguments concerns the concept that human beings were created in a form that was not thoroughly developed. This theory later influenced eastern theology and was used by John Hick for his modern soul-making theodicy.

Irenaeus is referred to as an Early Church Father. This is the term used of the early and influential theologians and writers in the Christian Church, particularly those of the first five centuries of Christian history. It does not generally include the New Testament authors.

KEY WORD

Theodicy: a justification of the righteousness of God, given the existence of evil, from the Greek *theos* meaning 'God' and *dike* meaning 'righteous'

KEY QUOTE

And God said: 'Let us make humankind in our image, after our likeness.'
(Genesis 1:26 NRSV)

**KEY WORD**

Soul-making: the presence of evil helps people to grow and develop

KEY PERSON

John Hick (b. 1922)
English theologian and philosopher. Hick has been influential in popularising a soul-making theodicy. He has also argued for religious pluralism. Hick has developed his theodicy in his book *Evil and the God of love* from his understanding of Irenaeus.

KEY PROFILE: AUGUSTINE (CE354–430)

Augustine was Bishop of Hippo and is regarded as the first major Christian philosopher. He was distinctive in that he thought through philosophical issues in the light of his faith and his understanding of the Bible. His various approaches on the issue of the problem of evil can be found mainly in *The City of God* and in his autobiography *The Confessions*.

b) Augustine's theodicy (soul-deciding)

Augustine did not have a fully worked-out theodicy, as such. He approached the issue of the problem of evil from a variety of angles and these general ideas have been the basis of a number of Augustinian-type theodicies, which reflect the traditional Christian approach. His main themes are listed below.

- Creation is good.
- Humans beings were created perfect.
- Human beings have free will.
- Human beings used their free will to turn away from God (the Fall).
- God makes possible repentance and salvation.

The emphasis is soul-deciding, in that those who do not turn back to God are condemned to hell.

This approach to the problem of evil is seen more as a soul-deciding theodicy, since our response to evil and God's rescue plan of salvation (belief in Jesus and his death for us) determines what happens to us when we die.

3 Some modern solutions (theodicies)

a) Protest theodicy

In the aftermath of the Holocaust there has been a development of a **protest theodicy**. Given God's omnipotence, events in history, such as the Holocaust, demonstrate that such a wasteful God cannot be totally benevolent. In the foreword to his play, *The trial of God*, **Wiesel** recounts an occasion in Auschwitz when he saw three rabbis put God on trial; they found him guilty and then went off to pray. It is this sort of tension that this theodicy advocates. In a sense it is not a new response since it follows the pattern set by Abraham, Moses and Job, all of whom contended with God. The Psalms are full of protest to God; for example, see Psalm 90. Nevertheless, the response is not despair but a defiance of God, reminding him of his promises and a risky hope for the future.

b) Free will defence theodicy

Free will is implicit in the classical theodicies. It is argued that the evil that exists in the world is due to humanity's misuse of the gift of free will. God wished to create a world in which rational agents (human beings) could decide freely to love and obey God.

Richard Swinburne has addressed the problem of the sheer quantity of evil, which many feel is unnecessarily large. He points out that a genuinely free person must be allowed to harm herself and others. God could intervene to stop her or let her learn from the consequences. However, the latter is more in keeping with the exercise of moral freedom. What of free choice to bring about death? Swinburne argues that death is

 EXAM TIP

Remember that most questions will not require a full account of the theodicy. Select those aspects of the theodicy that are relevant to the particular focus of the question. This demonstrates selection skills (AO1).

 KEY WORD

Protest theodicy: theodicy that protests against God and puts him on trial

 KEY PERSON

Elie Wiesel (b. 1928) A holocaust survivor and author of *Night*, which described experiences in a concentration camp.

good, in that it brings an end to suffering. It would surely be immoral for God to allow humans to have unlimited power to do harm. Also, actions matter more when there is a limited life. Death makes possible the ultimate sacrifice, it makes possible fortitude in the face of absolute disaster. When it comes to the Holocaust he says: 'the less God allows men to bring about large scale horrors, the less the freedom and responsibility he gives them'. In other words, we can make real choices.

c) Process theodicy

The starting point of **process theodicy** is to question the view that God is omnipotent and the assumption that he is capable of destroying evil. Its main proponents are A.N. Whitehead and David Griffin. The problem of evil is removed by redefining the meaning of omnipotence. It is a reaction against the classical Christian theodicies in which God seems unaffected by our suffering, even immune to it, and this world and its experiences are seen as relatively unimportant. The emphasis in salvation on escaping from this realm is said to illustrate this view.

In contrast, process theodicy stresses this life and maintains that the most real thing about a person is the series of experiences that make up the process of their life here and now. God is seen as intimately involved with this world and its suffering. Indeed, God is called a 'co-sufferer'. The different understanding of God's omnipotence derives from process theodicy's view that creation was not *ex nihilo* (out of nothing). Rather, creation was the achievement of order out of a pre-existing chaos. This limits God's power since these pre-existing materials are not totally subject to God's will. Hence God is depicted not as a powerful, almighty despot but rather as someone who creates by persuasion and lures things into being. God is in time, and both affects and is affected by the world. He even depends on his creatures to shape the course of his own experiences. Such a God cannot control finite beings, but can only set them goals that he then has to persuade them to actualise. Evil occurs when such goals are not realised. Natural evil is also explained. For instance, in *Encountering Evil*, Griffin states:

> *If cancerous cells have developed in your body, God cannot lure them to leave voluntarily.*
>
> (Davis)

4 How the theodicies address...

a) The origins of evil

The actual origin of evil is part of the problem of evil. If God created or caused all things then clearly he is the originator of evil. The fact that God is all-powerful and so all-knowing also raises problems about our free will and hence responsibility for doing evil.

In both Irenaean and Augustinian theodicy, the origin of evil is traced back to the Fall, as described in Genesis 3. However, for Irenaeus, it is seen as a necessary part of the growing and maturing process.

In contrast, Augustine sees it as a falling from perfection that can only be reversed by accepting God's rescue plan of salvation through Jesus.

As God is the author of everything in the created Universe, it follows that evil is not a substance, otherwise it would mean that God created it, which Augustine rejects. Thus, for Augustine, evil is a **privation**. For instance, sickness is a real physical lack of good health. Evil cannot exist in its own right. Evil happens when something renounces its proper role in the divine scheme and ceases to be what it is meant to be. Hence, moral evil is the privation of right order in the human will.

Our rebellion against God has affected all of creation and distorted it, so that our environment is not as God intended it (Romans 8:22). In addition, Augustine saw natural evil caused by fallen angels who, by their free decisions, wreak havoc.

Process theodicy sees evil occurring when God sets goals that he fails to persuade us to actualise. Evil is discord, good is harmony. God offers the best possibility for each occasion as it creates itself, but humans are free to ignore his attempt at persuasion.

TASK

Read William Blake's poems, *The Lamb* and *The Tyger*. What do you think these poems say about the problem of evil?

Objective: To appreciate some of the problems that evil poses in relation to God's existence. This demonstrates that you are using 'detailed knowledge of the subject matter at a wide range or in significant depth' (level 4 descriptor AO1).

> 66 **KEY QUOTE**
>
> *We know that the whole of creation has been groaning as in the pains of childbirth right up to the present time.*
>
> **(Romans 8:22)**
>
> 99

The Lamb

Little Lamb, who made thee?
Dost thou know who made thee?
Gave thee life, and bid thee feed,
By the stream and o'er the mead;
Gave thee clothing of delight,
Softest clothing, woolly, bright;
Gave thee such a tender voice,
Making all the vales rejoice?
Little Lamb, who made thee?
Dost thou know who made thee?

Little Lamb, I'll tell thee,
Little Lamb, I'll tell thee.
He is called by thy name,
For he calls himself a Lamb.
He is meek, and he is mild;
He became a little child.
I a child, and thou a lamb,
We are called by his name.
Little Lamb, God bless thee!
Little Lamb, God bless thee!

The Tyger

Tyger! Tyger! burning bright
In the forests of the night,
What immortal hand or eye
Could frame thy fearful symmetry?

In what distant deeps or skies
Burnt the fire of thine eyes?
On what wings dare he aspire?
What the hand dare sieze the fire?

And what shoulder, & what art.
Could twist the sinews of thy heart?
And when thy heart began to beat,
What dread hand? & what dread feet?

What the hammer? what the chain?
In what furnace was thy brain?
What the anvil? what dread grasp
Dare its deadly terrors clasp?

When the stars threw down their spears,
And watered heaven with their tears,
Did he smile his work to see?
Did he who made the Lamb make thee?

Tyger! Tyger! burning bright
In the forests of the night,
What immortal hand or eye
Dare frame thy fearful symmetry?

The Lamb and *The Tyger*, by William Blake

b) God's responsibility for the existence of evil

For Irenaeus, the existence of evil is positive and God is responsible for it. The justification is that evil leads to a greater good. It is the means by which human beings progress and mature. It is through suffering that character and virtues are often developed. Some moral goods, for example, courage, compassion, forgiveness, are responses to evils and hence could not exist without them. Sometimes these are referred to as **second-order goods**.

KEY WORD

Second-order good: a moral good that is a response to evil

The moral goods are those that result from alleviating, resisting and overcoming evil and involve intelligent and informed responses to evils. This could be seen as a necessary part of the soul-making process. In *Evil and the God of Love*, Hick comments that the value of this world is:

> …to be judged, not primarily by the quantity of pleasure and pain occurring in it at any particular moment, but by its fitness for its primary purpose, the purpose of soul-making.

In contrast, the Augustinian theodicy sees evil as something negative and an unwelcome intruder. Evil spoils the perfect world that God created. The death of Jesus is seen as the ultimate solution to evil. In some way, through that event, evil is overcome. The Bible claims that linking your life with God starts putting evil into reverse, so that in heaven pain and suffering will be totally absent.

Process theodicy identifies God's responsibility, to the extent that he urged creation forward in the evolutionary process, aware that he was not able fully to control it. However, as part of the Universe, God, like everything else, suffers when evil occurs.

c) The role of free will

In the Irenaean theodicy, the existence of evil gives people freedom to come to God. God deliberately creates a world in which it is not immediately and overwhelmingly evident that there is a God. This is called an **epistemic distance**. Thus, the world is ambiguous and it could be reasoned that there is no God just as strongly as that there is a God. Human goodness that has come about through the making of free and responsible moral choices, in situations of difficulty and temptation, is more valuable than goodness that has been created ready-made.

KEY WORD

Epistemic distance: distance from knowledge of God – God is hidden and so this allows human beings to choose freely

Equally, if human beings had been created in the direct presence of God they could have no genuine freedom. Hence the need for the epistemic distance that evil provides. It is best that free beings freely choose to love God.

For Augustine, free will plays a vital role in understanding the existence of evil in the world. It is deemed better to have free will than to have no free will. Indeed, moral beings require free will if there is to be any meaning to the word 'moral'. However, with that freedom comes the capability of actualising evil. It is free will, enacted wrongly, that spoils God's perfect creation. God foresaw humankind's fall 'from the foundation of the world' and planned their redemption through Christ.

Process theodicy clearly has free will as a core aspect, since the universal process in its continuous creativity is free to ignore the persuasive attempts by God to direct it.

EXAM TIP

It is important not to mix up the two classic theodicies. Although they have some similarities, remember that the Augustinian is *from* perfection whereas the Irenaean is *to* perfection. Even for level 1 at AS level, AO1 requires 'facts which are accurate'.

5 Strengths and weaknesses of Irenaean theodicy (soul-making)

a) Strengths

- This theodicy seems consistent with modern thinking about origins of life.
- The focus on seeing Earth as a suitable environment for making free choices seems to remove blame from God for creating evil. A paradise environment would have led to a non-moral world. No second-order goods could have been developed; see page 50.
- All evil is justified since all ultimately achieve the goal of heaven.

b) Weaknesses

- If the end result is guaranteed by God, what is the point of the pilgrimage? Indeed, if there is universal salvation then do we have free will to refuse to mature?
- Does the end justify the means? The suffering experienced, for example, at Auschwitz, cannot justify the ultimate joy. In the Holocaust, people were ruined and destroyed more than made or perfected. It is hard to see how this fits God's design and human progress.
- Could not the greater goods be gained without such evil and suffering?
- As a Christian theodicy, it seems to make the **atonement** superfluous and unnecessary.
- A number of criticisms involve suggestions of better ways to achieve this process. For example, why did the natural environment have to be created through a long, slow, pain-filled evolutionary process? Why could an omnipotent God not do it in 'the twinkling of an eye'? Equally, if we go on to another life to reach maturity, then why did God not simply make our earthly spans longer, so we could reach the Celestial City on Earth, or at least get closer? Indeed, is there any evidence for other lives?

KEY WORD

Atonement: the reconciliation of human beings with God through the sacrificial death of Christ

6 Strengths and weaknesses of Augustinian theodicy (soul-deciding)

a) Strengths

- It is attractive to those who accept the authority of Scripture, as the Genesis account is central to Augustine's argument.
- The view that evil is not a substance and therefore not created by God seems to free God from responsibility for evil.
- Augustine seems to account successfully for the occurrence of natural evil.

b) Weaknesses

- Many scientists reject the picture of a fall of humanity from perfection. Rather they suggest an evolutionary development.
- If human beings began by being perfect, then even though they are free to sin they need not do so. If they do sin, then they were not flawless to start with and so God must share the responsibility of their fall. (Note that Augustine argues that some angels were predestined to fall. If this view is not accepted then how did angels fall, given that they were perfect?) Surely in a perfect world they would have no reason to sin?
- It is hard to clear God from responsibility for evil since he chose to create a being whom he foresaw would do evil.
- The existence of hell is not consistent with an all-loving God. Hell seems contrary to a loving and good God.
- Augustine's view of evil as a privation is challenged. It is not sufficient to say that it is a lack or absence. Many would argue that it is a real entity.
- If everything depends on God for its existence, then God must be causally involved in free human actions. Do we have free will?

EXAM TIP

Exam questions are based around words that tell you what to do in your answer. For AO1 they are:
- Compare…
- Describe…
- Examine…
- Give an account of…
- How…
- Identify…
- Illustrate…
- In what ways…
- Outline…
- Select…
- What…?

7 Strengths and weaknesses of process theodicy

a) Strengths

- Fits in with modern evolutionary theories.
- God is not distant or disinterested, He is a co-sufferer.
- It uses Biblical understanding of chaos prior to creation (Genesis 1:1).

b) Weaknesses

KEY WORD

Classical theism: the belief in a personal deity, creator of everything that exists and who is distinct from that creation

- A radical departure from the God of **classical theism**. It is questioned whether this is God in any normal meaning of the word.
- There is no guarantee that good will ultimately overcome evil.
- It is not clear that there is any sense of a life after death. Some process theologians speak in terms of existing in the memory of God.
- It raises questions as to whether such a God is worthy of worship.
- It seems elitist since very few gain, and then the gain may be for this life only.

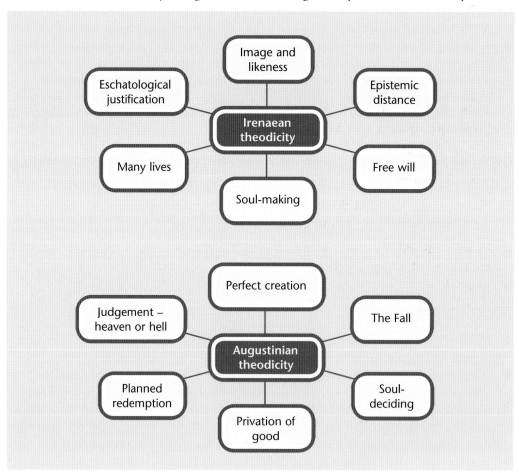

Summary diagram: The theodicies – Irenaean and Augustinian

Reflection and assessment

It is now time to channel the information you have considered in a more focused way. In order to do this, once again you need to ask yourself the question: 'How am I going to be assessed on my use of this information?'

Look back to pages 8–10 in the Introduction to review the levels of response descriptors for AO1.

Look at the following notes for a sample basic answer, which is a response to this question.

What is meant by the problem of evil? (21 marks)

The *basic* answer might deal with the question by:

● stating the basic problem that a good and powerful God should stop evil, yet evil exists
● giving some basic indication of evil in terms of natural or moral evil.

Indicate how a *developed* answer would deal with the question, by adding two or three more bullet points.

Now go on to develop this answer to indicate how a *higher* answer (level 4) would deal with the question, by adding further bullet points. Don't forget to keep the bullet points focused on the question.

Suggestion for further application of skills

Create a plan for this question.

Examine one solution that attempts to understand the responsibility or otherwise of God for the existence of evil in the world. (21 marks)

Then write up your answer under timed conditions. Working in a group, compare your answers. Photocopy the best answers and, still as a group, consider what makes them good.

Use this time of reflection to revisit your own work and improve it by redrafting it.

FOUNDATIONS

Area A: Philosophy of religion

TOPIC 2: A STUDY OF SELECTED PROBLEMS IN THE PHILOSOPHY OF RELIGION

Part 2B: Definitions and some philosophical problems of miracles

---

This means I am expected:

to know about the key emphases:
- different definitions of miracles
- the main features of those definitions

and to study:
- reasons to believe in miracles
- problems of believing in miracles.

In this book the evidence and examples given are relevant and appropriate because this material focuses only on the content for AO1 that is given by the Edexcel specification. The evaluation materials for AO2 will be aimed at helping you 'critically evaluate and justify a point of view through the use of evidence and reasoned argument'.

It would be helpful to write your notes using the headings listed above, as it is from these areas that the examination questions will be derived.

In your studies, remember that you have to bear in mind the **two** basic assessment objectives of:

- Knowledge and Understanding (AO1)
- Evaluation (AO2).

See pages 7–8 in the Introduction to remind yourself of these objectives.

The evaluation material set out in Part 2C (page 65) can be studied either alongside the AO1 material, as you work through this unit, or as a separate unit.

This part of the unit explores the topic of miracles. This will involve the concepts of miracles, reasons to believe in miracles and the philosophical problems, especially with reference to Hume. The philosophical problems will be examined and evaluated in Part 2C.

1 Definitions of miracles

a) Miracles as interventions

This classic understanding of a miracle focuses on the interventionist approach. A miracle involves some intervention by God, without which the event would not have taken place. The intervention is usually seen in terms of the breaking of a **law of nature**.

KEY WORD

Law of nature: a generalisation based on regular happenings within nature

Aquinas defined miracles, saying:

Those things must properly be called miraculous which are done by divine power apart from the order generally followed in things.

He was one of the earliest philosophers to attempt to define a miracle.

He distinguished between three kinds of miracle:

- events in which something is done by God which nature could never do, for example, the Sun going back on its course across the sky
- events in which God does something which nature can do, but not in this order, for example, someone living after death
- events that occur when God does what is usually done by the working of nature, but without the operation of the principles of nature, for example, someone being instantly cured of an illness that usually takes much longer to cure.

In all three events God is active.

Probably the best-known expression of this understanding of miracles is by David Hume.

A law of nature tells us how bodies must behave under certain circumstances when not interfered with. A miracle occurs when the world is not left to itself, when something distinct from the natural order as a whole intrudes into it, such as God.

An example of this would be the raising of a person from the dead. It breaks our regular experience of the law of nature and demands an intervention by God or some supernatural power.

b) Miracles as having religious significance

Many think miracles need to hold some deeper religious significance than just breaking laws of nature. This view was supported by Swinburne.

Certainly the Judaeo-Christian tradition supports this understanding, by which miracles are seen as signs from God. The word 'sign' is used in John's Gospel to refer to Jesus' miracles, which always seem to point to something beyond the actual event. The Gospel miracles were not seen as an end in themselves (see Luke 10:13).

c) Miracles as interpretations

Ray Holland presents a completely different point of view on defining miracles. His most often quoted illustration is of the child caught between the rail tracks, with a train fast approaching out of sight of the boy. The mother could see both the boy on the tracks and the train approaching. She realised that the boy would be hit by the train as there was too little distance for it to stop, once the driver saw the boy. However, the train suddenly started to slow down, even though the driver could not see the boy ahead. The train eventually stopped about a metre away from the boy, leaving him therefore unharmed. The mother looking on saw it as a miracle. She still said it was a miracle, even when she was later told that the reason for the train stopping was that the driver, who suffered a heart condition, had had a heavy meal and passed out, causing the automatic braking system to come into play and so stop the train.

> **KEY QUOTE**
>
> *A miracle...is a transgression of a law of nature by a particular volition of the Deity or by the interposition of some invisible agent.*
>
> (Hume)

> **KEY QUOTES**
>
> *If a god intervened in the natural order to make a feather land here rather than there for no deep ultimate purpose, or to upset a child's box of toys just for spite, these events would not naturally be described as miracles.*
>
> (Swinburne)
>
> *Woe to you, Korazin! Woe to you, Bethsaida! For if the miracles that were performed in you had been performed in Tyre and Sidon, they would have repented long ago, sitting in sackcloth and ashes.*
>
> (Luke 10:13)

Evidence of the miraculous? Who stopped the train?

A miracle can only be spoken about against a religious background. It will only make sense if the mother is religious or open to religion. In Holland's 'train' illustration the mother thanks God. A non-religious person would describe the event as just a piece of extraordinary luck. But to the religious person, whether it breaks the laws of nature or not, it is seen as a miracle.

Holland claimed that an event that has an explanation within natural laws can, nevertheless, be considered a miracle if it is taken religiously as a sign. Holland refers to this as a 'contingency miracle'. The presence of religious significance is sufficient, according to Holland, for a certain event to be called a miracle. Reading Holland's account (*The Miraculous: American Philosophical Quarterly 2*, 1965), it is not clear whether he was arguing that God actually intervened. On balance, it seems that Holland wants us to think that it was divine providence that the driver fainted at that particular moment. William Craig discusses how theologians have identified different types of divine providence, in particular the type that Holland may be expressing in his train illustration:

> *…as Paul and Silas lie bound in prison for preaching the Gospel, an earthquake occurs, springing the prison doors and unfastening their fetters…God can providentially order the world so that the natural causes of such events are, as it were, ready and waiting to produce such events at the propitious time, perhaps in answer to prayers which God knew would be offered.*

For an **anti-realist** a miraculous event is an event that is a disclosure. It is not about a real action undertaken by a supernatural being. It is an interpretation of an ordinary event. The event makes sense within the form of life of the religious believer and involves no 'real' actions of a God.

This contrasts with Swinburne's understanding of miracles. He, too, emphasised interpretation in that there had to be religious significance in the event. However, he argued that the word 'miracle' applied to such events in which God did intervene. If God had not intervened, the event would not have occurred. He clearly argued for a supernatural intervention. However, he regarded Hume's description of 'violations of laws of nature' as misleading and instead used the phrase 'counter instances to a law of nature'.

Swinburne also disagreed with Holland's understanding of miracles. Swinburne claimed that miracles are objective events and they are miracles whether or not a person interprets them in this way. It seems that Holland's understanding of miracles does not require such an intervention and only if the person interpreted them as a miracle could the event be called a miracle.

This view that miracles could be applied to natural events rather than supernatural, since the criterion was one of interpretation by the person, had already been aired from the time of the **Enlightenment**. Whereas biblical scholars such as Reimarus (1694–1768) had argued that the Gospel-writers had distorted the accounts about Jesus or gave the miracles natural explanations (Jesus walking on a sandbank, not on water), Strauss (1808–74) introduced the idea of 'myth'. He did not challenge the Gospel-writers' integrity but interpreted miracles in the light of first-century Palestinian culture, which Strauss saw as dominated by a mythical world view. He did not regard miracles as actual historical events. **Bultmann** developed this view, arguing that the mythological world view portrayed in the New Testament was unintelligible and unacceptable. As far as miracles were concerned, they needed to be reinterpreted and their spiritual truths made clear.

 **KEY WORD**

Enlightenment: an eighteenth-century philosophical movement that stressed the importance of reason

 KEY PERSON

Rudolf Bultmann (1884–1976)
A theologian who denied that there could be miracles. He interpreted the supernatural elements of the Gospels (demythologising).

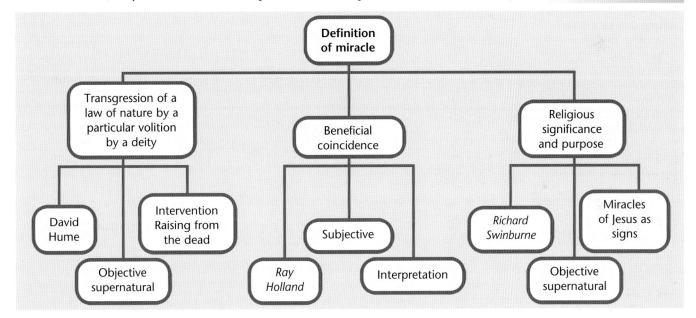

Summary diagram: Definitions of 'miracle'

2 Reasons to believe in miracles

The issue concerning philosophical reasons and evidence to believe in miracles will depend much on which concept of miracles one is using.

a) Miracles as supernatural events

If the definition being considered is 'miracles as interventions', then reasons to believe may be viewed in several ways.

i) Consistent with the nature of God

Hume's definition of miracles involved the idea of a God who intervenes in the laws of nature. If a person believes in God then, in this interventionist understanding, they are more likely to believe that miracles can happen. God is seen as the supreme being of the Universe.

KEY PERSON

John Polkinghorne (b. 1930) Professor of Mathematical Physics at Cambridge University until he resigned his chair and became an Anglican priest, he argues that science and religion both address aspects of the same reality.

TASK

Explain the reasons people give to support the claim that 'laws of nature can be broken'.

Objective: To enable you to understand the concept of 'laws of nature' and highlight some clear arguments to support Hume's definition. This demonstrates 'selecting the most important features for emphasis and clarity' (level 4 descriptor AO1).

❝ KEY QUOTES

Touch me and see; a ghost does not have flesh and bones, as you see I have.

(Luke 24:39)

…that he was buried, that he was raised on the third day according to the Scriptures, and that he appeared to Peter, and then to the Twelve. After that, he appeared to more than five hundred of the brothers at the same time, most of whom are still living…

(1 Corinthians 15:5–6)

❞

He is creator and sustainer of the Universe and all things depend upon him for their continued existence. He has created the Universe for a purpose and he is wholly good.

The Bible suggests that God reveals himself to his people through miracles, through events in which he suspends the laws of nature. He does this to accomplish the divine purpose for the Universe. Part of that purpose is to reveal himself and make himself known.

Swinburne argues that we should expect miracles, given that we expect revelation, since because God needs to communicate with his creatures, he needs to authenticate his revelation.

ii) Not contrary to science

Scientists who believe in a God who performs miracles seem to see no contradiction between this belief and scientific understanding. Science is concerned with observation and explanation. There is no entity called 'science' that can authoritatively rule whether miracles can or cannot happen. Science is neutral.

Amongst the most recent defenders of miracles are the philosopher Richard Swinburne and the physicist–theologian **John Polkinghorne**. Both argue that science does not prove that miracles are impossible or self-contradictory. In addition, Swinburne, in *The Concept of Miracle*, argues the case that evidence for a non-repeatable happening, which breaks the law of nature, is acceptable historical evidence. This dismisses Hume's claim that the law of nature must always be the stronger evidence (see page 61). The fact that God is the cause of the extraordinary event is strengthened if the event occurs in answer to a prayer and if it is an act consistent with the nature of God. In *The Concept of Miracle*, Swinburne also attacks the argument that when a law of nature appears to be broken it is either because we are mistaken or that we are not yet aware of the true law.

We have, to some extent, good evidence about what are laws of nature, and some of them are so well established and account for so much data that any modification of them which we could suggest to account for the odd counter instance would be so clumsy and ad hoc as to upset the whole structure of science

(Swinburne)

Indeed, it has been said that to salvage the law of nature requires just too many *ad hoc* adjustments. For example, the law of nature that people die and stay dead may be amended by the clause: 'Except when the person's name begins with the letter J, he claims to be God and founds a major western religion.'

Such an approach for maintaining that laws of nature are never transgressed seems unreasonable.

iii) Accounts of miracles

In many accounts of miracles there are appeals to witnesses, for instance, more than 70 miracle cures at Lourdes have been ratified by the Vatican.

The most important miracle in the New Testament (the Resurrection) is given considerable coverage (in the Gospels, the Book of Acts and in 1 Corinthians 15). The importance of eye-witnesses is strongly emphasised and a large number of eye-witnesses are cited. If God is outside time and the Universe, it may not be surprising that his entry and exit into this world in human form are by means of miraculous events.

Pilgrims at Lourdes

TASK

Research the evidence for miracles that have been claimed to have happened at Lourdes. Do you think the tests, to check whether a miracle had occurred, were stringent enough?
Objective: To demonstrate 'relevant detail' and 'evidence' for points made in an answer (level 4 descriptor AO1).

> **66 KEY QUOTE**
>
> *This salvation, which was first announced by the Lord, was confirmed to us by those who heard him. God also testified to it by signs, wonders and various miracles...*
>
> **(Hebrews 2:3–4)**
>
> **99**

b) Miracles as natural events, interpreted

If the definition of miracles is 'having a religious significance' or 'beneficial coincidences', then the events could be consistent with our everyday experience of the world and do not require a violation of a law of nature. If we assign a religious significance, then it would imply that we had a belief in God.

Belief in miracles is strengthened if the event occurs in answer to a prayer and is consistent with the nature of God.

3 Problems of believing in miracles

Again, it is important to identify which concept of miracle is under discussion. This is because different definitions of a miracle can give rise to very different conclusions when applied to an issue.

If we accept Holland's interpretative understanding of miracles, then they occur whenever anyone interprets an event as such. Therefore, most philosophical debate has centred on Hume's concept of miracle.

Problems raised by Hume's definition

i) **Coherency of the term 'laws of nature'**
●   This problem arises out of our understanding of the laws of nature. If laws of nature are generalisations formulated retrospectively to cover what has happened, then there

KEY IDEA

Problem of believing, if using Hume's definition:
● coherency of term 'laws of nature'
● nature of God
● testimony.

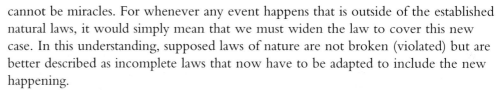

cannot be miracles. For whenever any event happens that is outside of the established natural laws, it would simply mean that we must widen the law to cover this new case. In this understanding, supposed laws of nature are not broken (violated) but are better described as incomplete laws that now have to be adapted to include the new happening.

- Is it coherent to talk about laws of nature at all? If nature is to some extent random, as modern science may suggest, then we can never know whether some law has been broken or whether things are happening in a natural but random way, as opposed to a natural but ordered way.
- The description of 'violating' a law of nature seems inappropriate. Laws of nature merely describe what will occur, given a particular set of initial conditions. When those conditions are changed in some way, then the 'law' does not apply. When a miracle occurs, the initial conditions are different, since God's special activity is now a new, added condition. Hence the 'law' has not been violated.

ii) Nature of God

- To say that God intervenes in the working of the Universe seems to imply a view of God as spectator of events. It suggests that an agent moves in where he had not been before. This seems contrary to classical theism where God is seen as sustainer and preserver of the Universe.
- If God is considered to be outside time, then maybe it is incoherent to propose that a timeless God enters time and space and acts since, at that moment, God would be limited to a time frame.

KEY IDEA

Hume's empiricism:

As an empiricist, Hume believed that all questions of truth had to be based on experience, which therefore involves an enquiry about evidence. Given that a wise person 'proportions' their belief to the evidence, and that laws of nature have been established and supported over a period of many hundreds of years, then it will always be more reasonable to believe that the law of nature has held and has not been broken, than to believe testimony claiming that the law of nature has been broken. In particular, he noted that there were no equivalents in modern-day events that compared to the recorded miraculous events in the Bible. Hence he focused on testimony of others in the distant past. He concluded, in *An Enquiry Concerning Human Understanding* (1777), that their testimony could never outweigh our present-day experience of the regularity of nature.

iii) Problem of testimony

Although Hume's chapter on miracles in his book *Enquiry Concerning Human Understanding* is scarcely 20 pages long, it is regarded as a major contribution to the debate. He wrote his famous chapter on miracles to demonstrate that no one could use the argument of miracles to demonstrate the truth of Christianity or religion in general.

He stated that our evidence for the truth of the Christian religion is less than the evidence of our senses. This is because the authors of the Bible had, at best, the evidence of their senses. However, as the account of those events has been passed down, its reliability in transmission lessens. The testimony is weighed against our experiences. Weaker evidence cannot defeat stronger evidence.

A wise man therefore proportions his belief to the evidence, as follows.

- Where the experience has been constant then this constitutes a full proof.
- Where it has been variable then it is a case of weighing the proportionate probability (deducting the smaller from the greater to see the force of the superior evidence).
- Where the belief is about miracles then, Hume argued, a difficulty arose. This was because a miracle is a violation of the laws of nature that have been established by firm and unalterable experience. In other words, there must have been a uniform experience against such an event for it to be called a miracle. In such a case, even the most impressive testimony would merely balance the counter-evidence provided by the improbability of the miracle. Only testimony so strong that its falsehood would itself be more miraculous than the alleged miracle would convince Hume of a miracle.

What Hume is involved in is an exercise in probability. Which is more likely: that a miracle occurred or that a witness is either lying or mistaken? People lying or being mistaken is common; exceptional events are, by definition, rare. The probability is therefore against the miracle occurring.

The balance of probability swings in favour of the miracle having occurred when the chance of the people reporting the miracle lying or being mistaken is as inconceivable as was the miracle occurring in the first place. Therefore one needs criteria by which to establish the virtual impossibility that the witnesses are lying or mistaken. This is what he does in Part 2 of his essay.

It is important to stress, again, that, as an empiricist, Hume does not deny the possibility of miracles as such. However, in Part 2 of his essay, Hume demonstrates that such testimony required can *never* be forthcoming, and so miracles cannot be shown to have happened.

Therefore, Hume himself concluded that testimony could never outweigh our present-day experience of the regularity of nature. He argued that no testimony is sufficient to establish a miracle unless the testimony be of such a kind that its falsehood would be more miraculous than the fact which it endeavoured to establish.

In particular, he highlighted several reasons why testimony was unlikely to be true. He argued that a miraculous event has never been proven to be true, using the following statements.

- No miracle has a sufficient number of witnesses. What is required is a quantity of educated, trustworthy witnesses to a public event; for example, people who would have a lot to lose if they were found to be lying.
- People are prone to look for marvels and wonders. We all like ghost stories and recount them, even when we don't believe them.
- The sources of miracle stories are from ignorant people. This seems to refer partly to uneducated Galilean peasants, as in the Gospels. The miracle stories acquired authority without critical or rational inquiry.
- The writers had a vested interest and so there was bias. This was particularly the case if a miracle was being used to establish a religion, as in the case, for example, of the Resurrection.
- Religious traditions counteract each other. This last argument is different from the other four. Unreliability here does not derive from that of the witnesses but rather that evidence is further contradicted by other witnesses. If an Islamic miracle supports Islam and so discredits Christianity as a true religion then, equally, any claim of a Christian miracle will likewise discredit Islam. Hence, evidence for one is evidence against the other and vice versa. This seems to undermine the evidence.

KEY IDEA

Many philosophers are uncertain whether or not Hume actually denied the possibility of miracles. If he did, then it would seem contrary to the empiricist position, which was the basis of all his philosophy. For a good discussion on this see Palmer, *The Question of God* (2001), pages 182–3.

KEY IDEA

Many scholars argue that Hume presents an *a priori* argument in Part 1 of his essay, and in Part 2 he presents an *a posteriori* argument. Other scholars debate whether an empiricist could have an *a priori* argument, given empiricists argue that knowledge derives from experience.

66 KEY QUOTE

…that no testimony is sufficient to establish a miracle, unless the testimony be of such a kind, that its falsehood would be more miraculous, than the fact, which it endeavours to establish.

(Hume)

99

Hence Hume's conclusion is that it was more rational to distrust the testimony about a miracle than to believe that the law of nature had been broken.

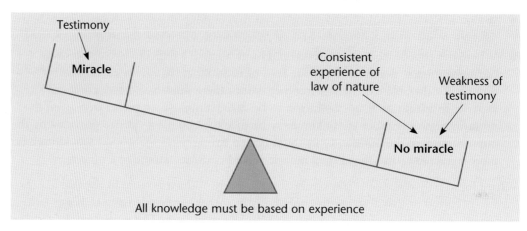

Testimony

Miracle

Consistent experience of law of nature

Weakness of testimony

No miracle

All knowledge must be based on experience

Hume: A wise man proportions his belief to the evidence

iv) A trivial act

The acceptance that God can intervene and that God is good does raise questions about the problem of evil and of a moral God. If God is all good and all powerful, then why are there so few miracles? Why doesn't God address the problems of the world more directly by means of miracles? What are we to make of a God who stands by and watches as millions of people are led to gas chambers, yet who seemingly intervenes to heal an individual? Surely such a God would not be worthy of worship. **Maurice Wiles** expressed this tension in his book, *God's Action in the World* (1986):

> *Miracles must by definition be relatively infrequent or else the whole idea of laws of nature... would be undermined, and ordered life as we know it would be an impossibility. Yet even so it would seem strange that no miraculous intervention prevented Auschwitz or Hiroshima, while the purposes apparently forwarded by some of the miracles acclaimed in traditional Christian faith seem trivial by comparison.*

A God who acts in such a trivial way is, according to Wiles, a God not worthy of worship. This implies miracles do not happen if belief in a traditional God is to be maintained.

v) No explanation is not the same as 'the explanation is God'

The basis of a miracle is that no explanation can be found as the cause of the event. Gareth Moore argued that the fact that no cause can be found is not the same as demonstrating the cause is God. He also challenged the idea that God 'performs' miracles. He felt this was language relevant to a person, and God is not a person.

KEY PERSON

Maurice Wiles (1923–2005)
He rejected the possibility that God directly intervenes in the world and therefore rejected the existence of miracles. He argued that either God acts arbitrarily (and is therefore not worthy of worship) or that God does not intervene at all.

Reflection and assessment

It is now time to bring together the information and channel this into a more focused appraisal. In order to do this, once again, you need to ask yourself the question, 'How am I going to be assessed on this information?'

Look back to pages 8–10 in the Introduction to review the level descriptors for AO1. There is a description of the character and features for each level. The exam is marked with reference to levels.

Look at the following sample answer, which is a response to this essay question.

Examine the statement 'Miracles can happen', referring to two definitions of 'miracle' in your answer. (21 marks)

One definition of a miracle is from David Hume – 'a miracle is a transgression of a natural law by violation of a Deity.' That is that events occur which do not work harmoniously with the natural laws of the world. This is certainly true – things do happen which cannot be explained by our natural laws – for example, a person being cured of cancer when they have not received treatment. There are many cases of this. In this sense the statement 'miracles can happen' has to be seen as true.

Another definition of miracle which we can see at work in the world today is that of a coincidence of a beneficial nature. For example, if a boy was on the train tracks and a train was coming towards him and the driver, through an unrelated event stopped the train, then it could be seen as a miracle. The mother looking on thanks God as she sees the child is safe and unharmed. It is she who identifies the event as miraculous even when she later finds out that the driver stopped for other reasons than because he saw the child on the line. The explanation that it was by natural causes does not diminish the miraculous element. In such an instance, it can be agreed that miracles can happen.

The phrase 'natural laws' needs explaining.

It is not sufficient justification to merely say it is 'true'.

Need to show clearly how it is an example of the definition.

Confusion with the word 'volition' meaning 'by a free act of will'. The candidate, however, does understand the definition and this is probably just a writing error that would have been corrected if they had checked the answer with a read through before the end of the exam.

Justification should include such things as – consistent with nature of God; not contrary to science and possible reference to an actual account of a miracle.

TASK

Have a look at a recent piece of work you or another member of your group has completed. Refer to the level descriptors on pages 8–10 and try to do your own comments analysis. Aim to make comments that focus on improvements towards level 4.

Objective: To improve a piece of work and transform it into a level 4 response so that it demonstrates 'a well structured response to a task...selecting the most important features...using evidence to explain key ideas' (higher level 4 descriptor AO1).

a) So what does it score?

In the exam, the answer will be marked according to levels. Refer back to pages 8–10 of the Introduction to remind yourself about the level descriptors.

The two definitions are clearly identified and an illustration is given of each, though this is not fully expanded and there is no explanation to exemplify the definition. There is some development of the basic statement of the definition.

The focus of the question is in applying each of the two definitions to argue that miracles can happen. Clearly, different arguments apply to the two definitions.

The answer does have that focus and there is some attempt, though limited, to explain and develop the points.

A level 1 answer would be a 'limited range of isolated facts...unstructured'. Clearly this answer is not in that level.

A level 2 answer would be 'accurate and relevant information within structure which shows a basic awareness of the issue...'. The answer is mostly accurate and relevant. However, the answer also has a number of arguments to support the focus claim which moves it beyond 'basic awareness'. Hence it is a level 3 answer. It is at the lowest end of the level 3 range, rather than the top end. It does not show breadth or a good range and/or detail of appropriate knowledge.

b) Suggestion for further application of skills

Use the points identified above to redraft the answer on the previous page. Copy it to obtain a text version, then delete material as appropriate, expand on the points that are undeveloped and add in other possible points that could have been included.

You can do this in pairs, groups or individually, but it is important to discuss and compare possible answers. You could even start afresh, listing important points, then create a writing frame and complete the answer as a class.

This will help to improve a lower level 3 response and transform it into a level 4, so that it demonstrates 'accurate, relevant and detailed knowledge...to present a well-structured response to a task...selecting the most important features...using evidence to explain key ideas...expressed cogently, using technical language'.

TOPIC 2: A STUDY OF SELECTED PROBLEMS IN THE PHILOSOPHY OF RELIGION

Part 2C: A critical analysis of the issues

> **This means I am expected:**
>
> **to analyse and critically evaluate:**
> - the strengths and weaknesses of the attempts at solutions to the problem of evil
> - the problems of miracles.

1 What problem were the solutions trying to address?

When evaluating solutions (theodicies), it is important to recognise the different audiences to whom the writings on the problem of evil are addressed, since they are written for different purposes and to achieve different results. Hence, in assessing an argument, it seems unfair to dismiss it as saying nothing about some issues, given that it was actually attempting to address another issue, and unacceptable therefore to conclude that what it says is worthless.

Possibly most discussions on the problem of evil have been aimed at the atheist; attempts have been made to show that evil is not logically incompatible with the existence of God. Such attempts include Swinburne's 'free-will defence', which concentrates particularly on the problem of the *amount* of evil. In contrast, others focus on the moral issue, assuming God exists but remaining unsure whether anyone can trust such a God. Such a stance is found in protest theodicy. Yet another audience consists of believing theists who want to understand why God allows evil. The classic theodicies fit this category.

? KEY QUESTIONS
- In what ways are the two theodicies similar?
- In what ways are the two theodicies different?

2 Evaluating the strengths and weaknesses of Augustinian theodicy

Remember that you can address the problem of evil from the perspective, for example, of a Buddhist or interpret some Hindu approaches to the problem of suffering. In Part 2A the classic Christian solutions were studied, from the Augustinian and Irenaean stances. Therefore, it is these that will now be evaluated to illustrate the AO2 skill.

Evaluating the strengths and weaknesses of the Augustinian theodicy involves more than stating what the strengths and weaknesses are. It is about assessing and weighing up those strengths and weaknesses, asking such questions as: 'Are those strengths convincing?' and 'Do the strengths carry weight?'

The strengths and weaknesses themselves are discussed in Part 2A (pages 51–53). Possible responses might include the following.

- The question of why God did not create free beings who could not sin can be answered by the argument that it is logically impossible for God to create another

? KEY QUESTION

How is natural evil explained?

EXAM TIP

Make sure that you explain how your criticism actually does weaken the argument. Avoid just stating a criticism and leaving it to the examiner to work out why it is valid. Equally, if the argument has a strength then explain what makes it a strength. This demonstrates justifying a point of view (AO2).

KEY QUESTION

Can there be morality without freedom?

KEY WORD

Counter-argument: an argument that tries to refute another argument

being who, by necessity, freely performs only those actions that are good. For God to cause such creatures only to do right and never to do wrong would be a contradiction of the idea of their free choice; they would simply not be free beings. Others have argued along different lines, pointing out that, even if it is logically possible, not everything logically possible is actually achievable. Love cannot be programmed. The fact that heaven is pictured as a place containing people who never sin suggests that perhaps God could have created such beings on Earth. However, people will be in heaven by their own choice. They will have chosen to forgo the opportunity to sin.

- Many see 'love' as the key to answering the criticism that God should not have created beings whom he knew would commit evil. God wishes to enter into loving relations with his creatures. But genuine love is an expression of the free commitment of both parties. Love between God and his creatures is therefore possible only if the creatures are free: that is, if they are able to reject his love as well as respond to it. Without freedom, we could not share in God's goodness because we could not freely love him. Nevertheless, the creation of free creatures involved the risk that persons would misuse their freedom and reject the good, and this is what happened. God could have chosen to make a world without free creatures in it. This would mean that the creatures would be robots and, therefore, it would be a non-moral world. It may be physically better but it cannot be regarded as morally better, since it is non-moral.

- The centrality of Genesis 1–3 to the theodicy weakens the argument, as the literal interpretation of Genesis seems contrary to modern thinking about origins.

- Many of the weaknesses listed on page 51 do not seem, to many critics, to have satisfactory counter-arguments.

3 Evaluating the strengths and weaknesses of Irenaean theodicy

Possible responses are listed below.

- The criticism that, as a Christian theodicy, it seems to make the atonement superfluous and unnecessary can be answered by the **counter-argument** that Jesus is an example, to show us one who has the content of God. Perhaps a more Christian approach would be to see the theodicy more in terms of 'faith-making' than 'soul-making'.

- Many voice unease about what appears to be a lack of fairness in the workings of the theodicy. For instance, is it just that all achieve the goal of heaven? It makes God the author of evil and suffering, and this suffering often seems disproportionate and unfair.

- Many of the criticisms listed on page 51 do not seem, to many critics, to have satisfactory counter-arguments.

4 Possible conclusions about the problem of evil

When assessing the issues that arise from the problem of evil, it is important to reflect upon the arguments previously discussed and arrive at some appropriate conclusion.

It may be that you accept none of these listed here, or just one of them, or you may have a different conclusion that is not listed. However, what is important is the way that you have arrived at your conclusion – the reasoning process.

From the preceding discussions, here are some possible conclusions you could draw.

1 There are no adequate solutions to the problem of evil.

2 There is a solution to the problem of evil, but it points to a God who is either not all-powerful or not all-loving.

3 The Augustinian theodicy is an adequate answer to the problem of evil.

4 The Irenaean theodicy is an adequate answer to the problem of evil.

5 There are other theodicies, such as process theodicy, that offer a more satisfactory solution to the problem of evil.

5 Evaluation: considering a defence against the empirical and moral problems raised by belief in miracles as a violation of the laws of nature

- Many regard Hume's criteria for testimony as being too stringent. If applied consistently to all past occurrences, the writing of any history would seem impossible.
- Hume writes as if all believers were either deceivers or deceived. He fails to take into account the possibility that some people, including religious people, are by nature, sceptics.
- Testimony is not the only evidence for miracles. Physical effects could be seen: for instance, a healed withered arm. Also, such things as X-rays may provide evidence of a 'before and after' situation.
- Some advocates of one religion will now often allow that a number of other religions have at least some elements of truth and may even have partial divine authority. Therefore, miracles could occur in other religions.
- Even if Hume is correct about the self-cancelling, it would not follow that the evidence for all miracles would be invalidated, for the evidence for the miracles of one religion might be much more impressive than the evidence for miracles in another.
- Swinburne argues that it is rational to believe that a miracle has occurred, while allowing the possibility that evidence might turn up later to show that we are mistaken.
- Wiles' argument, that God is not worthy of worship, because of the trivial way he is said to intervene, depends on prior beliefs about the nature of God. If there is other evidence that God is all loving, then God may have reasons for acting as he does. For further discussion see page 50.

6 Evaluation: considering the problems associated with advocating the possibility of miracles as a violation of the laws of nature

- All religions do not recognise the truth claims about miracles made by other religions; the exclusive nature of a religion being considered the only way means that miracles are self-cancelling.
- There is a growing awareness concerning the role of the mind in the healing process. Therefore it is very difficult to decide whether a healing miracle is indeed a miracle at all, because it now becomes consistent with and not a violation of the processes of nature.

? KEY QUESTIONS
- Is all evil justified?
- Did the death of Jesus achieve anything? Or did he die needlessly?

→ EXAM TIP

Do not just give a list of criticisms like some shopping list. It is far better to discuss and develop 3–4 criticisms, explaining and responding to them, than to give a list of 7–8. This demonstrates a process of reasoning and a sustained argument (AO2). The key trigger words for AO2 are:

- Comment on…
- Consider…
- How far…
- To what extent…
- Why…?

❝ KEY QUOTE

'We may be mistaken' is a knife which cuts both ways – we may be mistaken in believing that an event is not a divine intervention when really it is, as well as the other way around.
(Swinburne)
❞

● Wiles' objections to miracles on moral grounds do raise several crucial questions about the nature of God. If we accept miracles, does this mean that we also accept an inconsistent, unfair, unjust and trivial God? Does belief in miracles create a new 'monster' God?

7 Possible conclusions about miracles

When assessing the issues that arise from miracles, it is important to reflect upon the arguments previously discussed and arrive at some appropriate conclusion.

It may be that you accept none of these listed here, or just one of them, or you may have a different conclusion that is not listed. However, what is important is the way that you have arrived at your conclusion – the reasoning process.

From the preceding discussions, here are some possible conclusions you could draw.

1 Miracles (supernatural) happen and there are convincing reasons to believe that they do.

2 Miracles (supernatural) happen but the evidence is weak.

3 Miracles (supernatural) may or may not happen. We cannot know.

4 Miracles (supernatural) cannot happen. The concept is incoherent.

5 Miracles (natural) happen. It depends on the person interpreting the event.

Problems
Religions are exclusive
Awareness of the role of the mind
Do we create a 'monster' God?

Defences
Testimony demands are too stringent
Testimony is not the only evidence for miracles
Miracles can occur in other religions
Belief in miracles can be rational
Other evidence for God as all-loving

Summary diagram: Problems of believing in miracles

Reflection and assessment

It is now time to channel the information you have considered in a more focused way. In order to do this, once again you need to ask yourself the question: 'How am I going to be assessed on my use of this information?'

Look back to page 10 to review the levels of response descriptors for AO2. There is a description of the character and features for each level. The exam is marked by reference to levels.

The following key points, which are not in any particular order, are some key points in answer to this question.

> **Comment on one attempt to answer the problem of evil.**　　　　(9 marks)

The specification does not specify any particular attempts at solutions to the problem of evil. Therefore, no particular solution would be specifically asked for in a question. For the purposes of this reflection and assessment, the Augustinian theodicy has been used.

Use these points to do the task below.

- God foresaw the fall.
- Evil is a privation.
- Not all are saved, so God is not all-loving.
- God is omnipotent, all good and opposes evil. Therefore evil does not exist in the world.
- Augustinian theodicy is soul-deciding.
- Why not make us flawless and perfect, so we would not fall?

TASK

Use the key points above as a basis for a writing frame to answer this question.

> **Comment on one attempt to answer the problem of evil.**　　　　(9 marks)

The list is deliberately basic. At this stage you should be able to identify the fact that it contains the general issues but does not have the detail of development. You will need to add this detail. Do not forget to add relevant quotes and questions at suitable places. The final product should show 'an attempt at evaluation of the issue raised, through a careful analysis of alternative views, leading to a clearly expressed viewpoint supported by well-deployed evidence and reasoned argument' (AO2 level 4 descriptor).

Objective: Exam practice.

Suggestion for further application of skills

Read again the possible conclusions about miracles. In a group, design a flow chart that clearly provides the evidence for each conclusion.

FOUNDATIONS
Area B: Ethics

TOPIC 1: A STUDY OF ETHICAL CONCEPTS

Part 1A: The relationship between religion and morality

This means I am expected:

to know about the key issues:
- reasons for the independence of morality from religion

and to study:
- what is an ethical theory?
- grouping ethical theories
- what is applied ethics?
- the Euthyphro dilemma
- divine command theory
- conflicting religious moralities
- inconsistencies within a religion
- further considerations of religious morality.

In this book the evidence and examples given are relevant and appropriate because this material focuses only on the content for AO1 that is given by the Edexcel specification. The evaluation materials for AO2 will be aimed at helping you 'critically evaluate and justify a point of view through the use of evidence and reasoned argument'.

It would be helpful to write your notes using the headings listed above, as it is from these areas that the examination questions will be derived.

In your studies, remember that you have to bear in mind the **two** basic assessment objectives of:

- Knowledge and Understanding (AO1)
- Evaluation (AO2).

See pages 7–8 in the Introduction to remind yourself of these objectives.

The evaluation material set out in Part 1C (page 91) can be studied either alongside the AO1 material, as you work through this unit, or as a separate unit.

This part of the unit explores some of the main ideas behind ethics and considers the relationship between religious ideas and moral behaviour. The guidance notes from the Specification have been used to highlight key areas for study.

1 What is an ethical theory?

a) Ethics versus morals

In current usage there is a tendency to treat the two terms **ethics** and **morals** as interchangeable. However, their origins each indicate a different focus. The study of ethics examines the guiding principles that direct an action. It is a theory or system of moral values. Ethics not only directs a person how to act, if they wish to be morally good, but also sets before that person the obligation of doing good rather than evil.

In contrast, **morality** is the application of these guiding principles, leading to appropriate conduct in particular situations such as war or genetic engineering. In this way, ethics can be seen as the philosophical treatment of morality.

b) Right versus wrong

Suppose a terrorist bursts into a house. He threatens to shoot the son if his father does not give vital information to the terrorist that will lead to the death of the leader of the country. What should the father do? If he refuses, then his son will be shot and he himself may also be killed. Yet, if he gives the information, it is almost certain that the leader of the country, a leader who has achieved great things for the country, will die. His death could result in the outbreak of civil war.

What are the guiding principles that will help the man decide what action to take? How were the guiding principles derived?

This framework of guiding principles is called an ethical theory.

Acting consistently within this framework is acting morally. Sometimes we may choose to act contrary to our framework and so be said to be acting immorally. Disagreements about what is a moral action and what is not show that different people have different sets of guiding principles. Hence, one action may be seen as moral, often referred to as **right**, while others may judge the same action as immoral, or **wrong**.

In ethics, right and wrong generally have stronger meanings than just error or misjudgement. There is often an implied 'going against character' or failing to be the sort of person you should be. There is a standard of which you have fallen short. There is an indication that you have done something that you are obliged *not* to do.

TASK

Identify some of the possible guiding principles that people may use. What do these imply about the sort of character they aim to be?
Objective: To ensure accuracy with ethical ideas and the accurate use of correct terminology (a prerequisite for a level 4 response at AS 'expressed clearly and accurately, using technical language widely', level 4 descriptor AO1).

➡ EXAM TIP

Always point out the variety of ethical ideas. The AO1 descriptor demands for level 4 at least 'accurate, relevant and detailed knowledge of the subject matter at a broad range or in sufficient depth' (low level 4 descriptor).

2 Grouping ethical theories

Philosophers have identified common links between the various ethical theories and have categorised them into groups.

a) Absolutist versus relativist

Absolutists believe that there exists a standard of right and wrong that is fully and totally binding on all human beings. Those who are religious may feel that this absolute standard proceeds from the mind and will of a supreme being. Those who are not religious may believe that the standard simply exists.

Relativists believe that there is no absolute right or wrong. They do not see morality as imposing a binding obligation on human beings to behave in a particular way. They see morality as the response of human communities to issues of how to behave in relation to each other. There are no absolute rules, but there are norms of behaviour that promote goodwill and happiness or some other desirable objective.

A relativist can say that she finds a certain course of action unjust or morally wrong, but it is difficult for her to conclude that someone else should feel that this action was wrong. To the absolutist, a wrong course of action is something that they are under a binding and absolute obligation *not* to do.

Whereas the absolutist would have to say: 'This is wrong for me and for you and for everyone,' the relativist could say: 'This is wrong for me but may be right for you,' which is something the absolutist could never say.

There is some ambiguity in the terms 'absolutist' and 'relativist' in that they are not always mutually exclusive but can overlap; for example, relativist systems may have an absolutist element. Hence, moral relativists might agree on very basic human values, such as respect for property, even though they may interpret this very differently.

b) Subjective versus objective

In ethics, a theory is described as **subjective** if its truth is dependent on the person's view. This is very different from saying that an ethical theory is relativist, since this describes the range of the truth and does not hold true in all situations.

A theory is described as **objective** if its truth is independent of a person's view. Again, this is very different from saying that an ethical theory is absolutist, since this describes the range of the truth and it holds true in all situations.

It seems natural to link subjectivity with relativism, since both terms imply freedom of choice of the individual: nothing is fixed and immovable. However, there is also a sense in which subjectivity can be linked to absolutism. For example, you might conclude that no ethical theory can be absolutist since our values stem from our own feelings and choices.

However, you may also think that some of those feelings and choices are universal to human beings, and so apply to everyone.

This implies that it is not a contradiction to have an ethical theory that is subjectively grounded but holds to absolute values.

 **KEY WORDS**

Absolutist: an ethical system involving rules that are to be followed by all people at all times, in all circumstances
Relativist: an ethical system that has no fixed rules but each action depends on the situation

KEY QUESTIONS

- Can an ethical theory be absolutist and subjective?
- Can an ethical theory be relativist and objective?

KEY WORDS

Subjective: having its source within the mind; a particular point of view; dependent on the subject
Objective: external to the mind; real or true regardless of subject and their point of view

c) Deontological versus teleological

The dilemma of the father facing the terrorist raised questions about the consequences of various actions that could be taken. Indeed, it is often the case that thinking about the consequences of a particular action persuades us whether or not to take that action. Such an approach, that focuses on the consequences, is called a **teleological ethical** theory.

In such theories, the rightness or wrongness of an action is identified by the consequences it produces. If the theory held that the action that best resulted in 'the good of the majority' was the criterion for judging right action, then the right action would be the one that resulted in the most good for the majority. It is the result, not the act itself, that decides the right action to take. This approach is also called **consequentialism**, since it claims that the value of the consequences of our actions is decisive for their moral status as right or wrong.

In **deontological** theories there is a relationship between duty and the morality of human actions. Therefore, deontological ethical theories are concerned with the acts themselves, irrespective of the consequences of those acts. For instance, a deontologist might argue that murder was wrong *whatever* the situation or consequence, and therefore euthanasia was morally wrong.

It is not such things as feelings of happiness, or good for the greatest number, that decide a right action, but rather that certain acts are *intrinsically* right or wrong. These wrong acts go against our duty or obligation.

3 What is applied ethics?

Applied ethics is the term used to describe the debates that arise when ethical issues are considered in practice. The study of applied ethics is complex and difficult because it is the point at which principles are tested in the real world. Applied ethics often involves the conflicting nature of principles and challenges a person to order and prioritise these principles.

> *An ethical dilemma arises when two or more causes of conduct may be justifiable in any given set of circumstances, possibly resulting in diametrically opposed outcomes.*
>
> **(Mason and Laurie)**

A person making an ethical decision is often driven by deeply held convictions. This is especially the case when a **value judgement** is made to decide whether something is right or wrong. Such convictions are influenced by principles, emotions, different situations, a process of reasoning, cultural influences, the immediate environment and even upbringing. These are all issues to consider at a deeper level.

There is no one uniform approach to dealing with ethical issues. It is interesting to see that there are even slightly different perspectives and emphases when it comes to considering ethical issues. For example, in medical ethics the philosophical writer takes a slightly different approach from the medical stance and the approach of the legal scholar is different again. Compare, for example, the works of Singer, Vardy, Grosch and Wilcockson (philosophy) with those of the General Medical Council, the *British Medical Journal* and Hope (medical) and Mason and Laurie (legal).

 KEY WORDS

Teleological ethics: any ethical system that is concerned with consequences of actions; from the Greek, meaning 'end' or 'purpose'

Consequentialism: another name for teleological ethics

Deontological ethics: any ethical system that is concerned with the act itself rather than the consequences of the act; from the Greek, meaning 'obligation' or 'duty'

? KEY QUESTION

What is the difference between deontological and teleological ethics?

 KEY WORDS

Applied ethics: the application of ethical theory to actual problems

Value judgement: an assessment that says more about the values of the person making it than about what is actually being assessed

We are considering matters of life and death. When it comes to these ethical issues, there are some important factors to take into consideration when debating the apparent rights and wrongs.

No one would argue that the act of abortion is a good thing to do *per se*. That is because there are universal principles to which all rational and sane people would agree. One such principle is that killing is not a good thing. However, it is when we ask the question: 'In what situation…?' that the whole area explodes. What about war? What about respecting the rights of another individual? What about protecting another? The list is endless.

It is important to bear in mind that those people that compromise this principle, whether in times of war or in an argument for euthanasia or abortion, are doing so not because they reject the idea that killing is wrong but because they recognise two things:

- the principle that 'killing is wrong…' is an ideal that, when applied to the real world, needs further qualification
- sometimes one has to weigh up and prioritise the application of principles in a real situation where conflicts of ideology arise.

There is, therefore, a clear distinction between theory in itself and that same theory in terms of how it unfolds in practice. The classic case is euthanasia, for which the complexities of situations give rise to a plethora of legal and ethical dilemmas.

Jesus is believed to have said, in response to violence: 'Turn the other cheek.' Mahatma Gandhi interpreted this literally and founded his ideology of passive resistance through non-violence (*ahimsa*) on such a principle. However, there are always limitations and even Gandhi could not make this a legal principle. Turning the other cheek and forgiveness would not be workable principles for society.

Any individual may be inspired and such principles are wonderful for people to follow as a guide. They are, however, directives addressed to the individual, not regulations for society, and only a fool would reject our legal and judicial system for such principles. Why? Ideally, they are splendid but, in practice, regrettably unworkable as enforced rules or laws.

Applied ethics, then, can be seen as the pursuit of standards that can be applied and that work in practice. It is the search for a solution that offers the workability of a principle that recognises the rights of an individual, that respects deeply held values and principles and thus is able to benefit society as a whole.

It is here that things really get interesting as, once again, the principles and their varying application and prioritisation give way to a complexity of debates.

KEY QUOTE

Given that we want to regard a newly born baby as a person, and to forbid the killing of it as murder, it seems arbitrary to distinguish between this and the killing of an unborn child almost at full term, and then the argument can be carried back step by step until immediately after conception.

(Mackie)

➡ **EXAM TIP**

It is important to be able to describe and explain the key facts to do with ethical ideas. However, it is even more important to be able to discuss the implications and questions that the ethical issues raise. This demonstrates both 'a coherent and well-structured response to the task at a wide range or considerable depth' and also that you are 'selecting the most important features for emphasis and clarity; using evidence to explain the key ideas' (top level 4 descriptor A01).

4 The Euthyphro dilemma

Plato wrote a dialogue called *Euthyphro*, in which Euthyphro takes his father to court, charging him with murder. His father failed in care and attention and allowed a worker to die. Socrates is at the court awaiting his own trial, so he engages him in dialogue about moral goodness.

In the dialogue Socrates poses the question that has become known as the Euthyphro dilemma.

Euthyphro: *Well, I should certainly say that what's holy is whatever all the gods approve of, and that its opposite, what all the gods disapprove of, is unholy…*

Socrates: *We'll soon be in a better position to judge, my good chap. Consider the following point: is the holy approved by the gods because it's holy, or is it holy because it's approved?*

(Plato)

Put in a religious context it can be expressed as:

Does God command things because they are good, or are things good because God commands them?

Put more simply:

Does good exist independently, and separate from approval, or does good exist as a consequence of it being approved?

5 Divine command theory

Divine command theory in relation to ethics proposes that God has established eternal, objective principles of morality.

John Robinson summarises this position well in his book, *Honest to God*:

They are the commandments which God gives, the laws which he lays down…They come down direct from heaven, and are eternally valid for human conduct…Certain things are always 'wrong' and 'nothing can make them right', and certain things are always 'sins', whether or not they are judged by differing human societies to be 'crimes'…

Followers of the divine command theory accept that there is an objective standard but the standard is not external to God, but internal.

Morality is grounded in the character of God, who is perfectly good. His commands are rooted in his character. That is not the same thing as saying that 'God' and 'good' are identical. God is not the very same thing as goodness. Goodness is an essential characteristic of God.

If whatever God thinks and does is simply, by definition good, regardless of what it is, then does it make sense to praise God for his goodness?

If God commands things because they are good, then it implies there is a standard of goodness independent of God. In this case, God is no longer the creator of everything. There is a standard of values outside of his control and creativity. Plato's idea of forms would be consistent with the standard of goodness as independent of God.

TASK

Design a flowchart that explains the variety of ethical theories and the issues that arise from their use.
Objective: To gain knowledge and understanding of the significance of the enlightenment illustrating 'accurate and relevant detail, clearly identifying the most important features' (level 4 descriptor AO1).

➡ EXAM TIP

When answering a question on ethical theories, make sure that you focus on the area highlighted in the question. Make sure you pick out the key ideas and explain why they are important in relation to other ethical theories and practical ideas. This means that it is not just a general answer that presents 'a limited range of isolated facts…with mainly random and unorganised detail' or 'information presented within a structure which shows a basic awareness of the issue raised' (level 1 and 2 descriptors AO1). Remember, you are aiming for 'a coherent and well-structured account of the subject matter' (level 4 descriptor AO1).

6 Conflicting religious moralities

There are clear problems when it comes to considering the relationship between religion and morality, as there are very different ethical systems and principles that can be found within the religions of the world.

Look at pages 371 and 381 and investigate the different ideals behind the shari'ah law, compared to the Buddhist precepts. Read on further and consider the application of Christian love that Fletcher uses for situation ethics. Think about the ten commandments and the idea of an absolute set of imperatives, compared to the relative and mixed ideas behind personal karma.

The questions this raise include:

● Which system is right?
● Are these systems compatible?

7 Inconsistencies within a religion

Not only do we have different systems but we also have the problem of identifying a specific religious ethic within a religion, and then the variety of interpretations this may be given.

Once again, turn to page 381 and consider the conflicting interpretations of Shariah found in the different law schools for a classic example.

There are also a variety of understandings and applications of the Buddhist precepts, as is clearly demonstrated by pages 371.

Many conflicts arise between some very respected and virtuous principles. 'Thou shalt not kill' is directly challenged by the principle of agape, when it comes to issues of abortion and euthanasia.

Can Gandhi's use of *ahimsa* as an absolute ever work in a time of war?

8 Further considerations of religious morality

There are specific areas of this book that can be further investigated to pursue the issue of inconsistencies, differences and variety, both within and between religious traditions. Recommended reading to follow this up certainly includes the sections on religious ethics in the Investigations unit (page 353).

In addition, there are the more controversial aspects of conflict, when a small minority group within a religion proposes suspect and dubious interpretations of ethical principles that have been extrapolated clumsily and, one could argue, without thought, from religious texts.

The idea of sacrifice or martyrdom has been promoted in interpreting certain verses from the Qur'an in Islam, the story in Genesis 22 and also the flexible ideal of skilful means in Buddhism (see page 100).

Below are some texts from the Bible. Read them and consider how they may present a problem when establishing ethical principles for Christians to follow.

EXAM TIP

Exam questions are expressed in words that tell you what to do in your answer. For AO1 they are:

● Compare…
● Describe…
● Examine…
● Give an account of…
● How…
● Identify…
● Illustrate…
● In what ways…
● Outline…
● Select…
● What…?

a) Lot – Genesis 19:4–8

4 Before they had gone to bed, all the men from every part of the city of Sodom – both young and old – surrounded the house.

5 They called to Lot, 'Where are the men who came to you tonight? Bring them out to us so that we can have sex with them.'

6 Lot went outside to meet them and shut the door behind him

7 and said, 'No, my friends. Don't do this wicked thing.

8 Look, I have two daughters who have never slept with a man. Let me bring them out to you, and you can do what you like with them.'

b) Joshua 6:20–21

20 When the trumpets sounded, the people shouted, and at the sound of the trumpet, when the people gave a loud shout, the wall collapsed; so every man charged straight in, and they took the city.

21 They devoted the city to the LORD and destroyed with the sword every living thing in it – men and women, young and old, cattle, sheep and donkeys.

c) Ephesians 6:5–6

5 Slaves, obey your earthly masters with respect and fear, and with sincerity of heart, just as you would obey Christ.

6 Obey them not only to win their favour when their eye is on you, but like slaves of Christ, doing the will of God from your heart.

d) Colossians 3:1

1 Masters, provide your slaves with what is right and fair, because you know that you also have a Master in heaven.

> **EXAM TIP**
>
> Do not answer a question on ethical theories by simply 'listing' points. Your answer should always select the key elements and examples, that is, the appropriate information relevant to the question. This demonstrates more personal understanding or 'ownership' of the knowledge; this demonstrates 'significant features explained for emphasis and clarity' which is awarded for higher level answers (level 3 and above descriptor AO1).

Summary diagram: Introduction to the language of ethics

> **EXAM TIP**
>
> Always point out the variety of ethical ideas. The AO1 descriptor demands for level 4 at least 'accurate, relevant and detailed knowledge of the subject matter at a broad range or in sufficient depth' (low level 4 descriptor).

Reflection and assessment (AO1)

It is vital to bring together the information that has been covered so far and recognise how it can be transformed into effective examination-style revision and answers. The best way to do this is to ask the question: 'How am I going to be assessed on this information?'

The first way is through assessment objective 1 (AO1). For this objective you need to be able to 'select and clearly demonstrate the relevant knowledge and understanding through the use of evidence, examples and correct language and terminology appropriate to the course of study' (AO1 descriptor).

Use the writing frame provided below to answer this question.

> **Identify the different approaches people may take for making ethical decisions.** (21 marks)

As you work through each unit in this book, you will find that the amount of support in these sections will gradually be reduced, in order to encourage the development of your independence and the honing of your AO1 skills.

a) Key points

- Use the *correct technical language* to refer to ethical theories.
- Always give *examples* of the terms.
- Always relate any examples to the meaning or argument to show *understanding* of it.

b) Writing frame

An absolutist believes...

An example of an absolutist ethical system is...

This is described as an absolutist ethical system because...

A relativist believes...

An example of a relativist ethical system is...

This is described as a relativist ethical system because...

One difference between the absolutist and relativist approach to ethics is...

Another difference is...

Whereas the absolutist would have to say: 'This is wrong for me and for you and for everyone', the relativist could say...

An understanding of the two terms 'absolutist' and 'relativist' is clearly required before discussing the differences. The best way to explain a term is to use an example as an illustration. However, be aware that you must explain the illustration rather then leave it to the examiner to work out what you mean. The differences then become clearer.

c) Suggestions for further application of skills

Construct your own writing frame for this question.

> **Illustrate the relationship between religion and morality and outline the problems involved in making ethical decisions.** (21 marks)

TOPIC 1: A STUDY OF ETHICAL CONCEPTS

Part 1B: Utilitarianism and situation ethics

> **This means I am expected:**
>
> **to know about the key issues:**
> - the context of utilitarianism
> - key forms of utilitarian theory
> - the context of situation ethics
> - key ideas involved in situation ethics
>
> **and to study:**
> - Bentham's utilitarianism
> - Mill's utilitarianism
> - Singer's utilitarianism
> - Fletcher's situation ethics
> - criticisms of situation ethics by William Barclay.

In this book the evidence and examples given are relevant and appropriate because this material focuses only on the content for AO1 that is given by the Edexcel specification. The evaluation materials for AO2 will be aimed at helping you 'critically evaluate and justify a point of view through the use of evidence and reasoned argument'.

It would be helpful to write your notes using the headings listed above, as it is from these areas that the examination questions will be derived.

In your studies, remember that you have to bear in mind the **two** basic assessment objectives of:

- Knowledge and Understanding (AO1)
- Evaluation (AO2).

See pages 7–8 in the Introduction to remind yourself of these objectives.

The evaluation material set out in Part 1C (page 91) can be studied either alongside the AO1 material, as you work through this unit, or as a separate unit.

This part of the unit explores both ethical theories of utilitarianism and situation ethics.

1 Bentham's utilitarianism

a) Why is it called utilitarianism?

Utilitarianism: an ethical theory that maintains that an action is right if it produces the greatest good for the greatest number; morality of actions is therefore based on consequences for human happiness

Utilitarianism derives its name from utility, which means usefulness. In particular it concerns the usefulness of the results of actions.

Utilitarians argue that everyone should do the most useful thing. The most useful thing is seen as action or actions that result in maximum levels of happiness or pleasure. Therefore, actions that produce the most happiness are seen as good and right actions or moral actions.

Because utilitarianism is concerned about the outcome of an action, it is a consequential and teleological ethical theory (see page 73).

b) Bentham's principle of utility

" KEY QUOTE

Nature has placed mankind under the governance of two sovereign masters, pain and pleasure. It is for them alone to point out what we ought to do, as well as to determine what we shall do.

(Bentham)

"

Bentham is usually accepted as the originator of utilitarianism. As a social reformer he sought to develop an ethical theory that promoted actions that would benefit the majority of people. For him, happiness was the only ethical value. Actions are good or useful if they produce happiness. Bentham argued that as we are motivated by pleasure and pain so we pursue pleasure and avoid pain. This view of happiness being linked to pleasure owes something to an earlier ethical theory called **hedonism**, in which the only thing that is right is pleasure.

Although utilitarianism is a teleological ethical theory, there is a rule or guiding principle underpinning this approach. This guiding principle, known as the **principle of utility**, states that people should act to bring about the greatest balance of good over evil. Bentham expressed this as 'the greatest happiness for the greatest number'.

This is a slightly misleading summary of the principle, since the greatest happiness did not necessarily involve the greatest number of people. The emphasis is more on the action that produces the greatest amount of happiness overall. In other words, what is right is what maximises happiness.

KEY WORDS

Hedonism: an ethical theory that defines what is right in terms of pleasure
Principle of utility: an action is right if it maximises happiness

c) The hedonic calculus

Having established that the measure of happiness is the criterion for a right act, there arises the problem of how to calculate that measurement. For Bentham, happiness consisted of pleasure minus pain.

 KEY PERSON

Jeremy Bentham (1748–1832) The social context of utilitarian theory
As a barrister, Bentham became aware of widespread social injustice. This prompted him to become concerned with issues of public morality. He was instrumental in reforming prisons and advocated that the penalties imposed for crimes should be sufficient to deter but not cause unnecessary suffering. He also advocated such things as censorship and laws governing sexual activity, in an attempt to improve public morality. His guiding principle for public policy was 'the greatest happiness for the greatest number'. He then developed this into a moral philosophy. In 1826, Bentham founded University College. Rather strangely, his embalmed body, wearing his usual clothes, sits in the entrance hall in a glass case! Only his head was replaced by a wax model.

? KEY QUESTIONS

- What is the most useful act?
- What is happiness?

The principle of utility centred on the act delivering the greatest amount of pleasure and the least amount of pain. Bentham's solution to measuring this balance was his hedonic calculus, also called the *pleasure calculus*.

He thought there were seven different elements that should be taken into account when calculating the amount of happiness. They are:

- the intensity of the pleasure – the more intense, the better
- the duration of the pleasure – the longer-lasting, the better
- the certainty of the pleasure – the more certain that pleasure will result, the better
- the fecundity, fertility or fruitfulness of the pleasure, the more chance the pleasure will be repeated or will result in other pleasures, the better
- the propinquity or nearness of the pleasure – the nearer the pleasure is to you, the better
- the purity of the pleasure – the least amount of pain it involves, the better
- the extent of the pleasure – the more people who experience it, the better.

Using these criteria, Bentham argued that it was possible to work out the right course of action in any situation. The balance of pain and pleasure created by one choice of action could be compared with those created by other available choices.

TASK

Design a diagram that links the different elements of Bentham's version of utilitarianism. Begin with the hedonic calculus but remember to place the ideas of the seven elements within the context of Bentham's ideas as a whole.

Objective: To develop ability to demonstrate the inter-relatedness of these teachings and demonstrate 'detailed knowledge of the subject matter at a wide range or in significant depth' (level 4 descriptor AO1) as opposed to simply 'very broad and unfocused generalisations' (level 1 descriptor) or an answer that is 'limited in scope' (level 2 descriptor).

2 Mill's utilitarianism

a) Bentham's approach revisited

The ethical theory of utilitarianism proposed by Bentham soon started to raise some strong criticisms. Not least amongst the critics was his former pupil, John Stuart Mill.

The main criticism against Bentham was that he tried to measure pleasure in quantitative terms. It appeared to allow for some actions to be called right and good when they seemed, to others, to be wrong. For instance, Bentham's approach appeared to conclude that a gang rape would be a right action if the pleasure gained by the group of rapists exceeded that of the pain experienced by the person raped. This also raised questions about the exact nature of pleasure.

As a result, Mill revised Bentham's form of utilitarianism.

b) Mill's alterations to Bentham's utilitarianism

i) The definition of happiness (pleasure)
This equating of happiness with good is a view that can be found in the writings of Aristotle. He referred to it as *eudaimonia*. Aristotle argued that pleasure was not mere gratification but rather includes the idea of well-being, living well, being fulfilled. This is much closer to the view that Mill took.

66 **KEY QUOTE**

By the principle of utility is meant that principle which approves of every action whatsoever, according to the tendency which it appears to have to augment or diminish the happiness of the party whose interest is in question.

(Bentham)

99

➡ **EXAM TIP**

Always remember to point out the historical context and development of utilitarianism in relation to the different versions presented. This ensures that you are 'selecting the most important features for emphasis and clarity' (level 4 descriptor AO1) rather than presenting a descriptive or 'a simple structure' (level 2 descriptor) for your answer.

66 **KEY QUOTES**

It is better to be a human being dissatisfied than a pig satisfied; better to be Socrates dissatisfied than a fool satisfied.

(Mill)

Over himself, over his own body and mind, the individual is sovereign.

(Mill)

99

The theory of utilitarianism affected all of Mill's thinking, possibly because of his home education in his early years. Both his father, James Mill, and Bentham were adherents to the theory. However, Mill deepened the understanding of happiness and advocated a weak rule utilitarianism.

ii) Higher and lower pleasures

Mill distinguished between pleasure that stimulated the mind, which he called higher pleasure, and pleasure that was merely physical or lower pleasure. He claimed that human beings alone could achieve the higher pleasure and it was the higher pleasure that was more satisfying. However, Mill was aware that people often did not choose the higher pleasure in preference to the lower pleasure. He felt that this was because they had not experienced both. Had they done so, they would have known that the higher pleasure was more satisfying than the lower pleasure.

iii) Quantity versus quality

By making a distinction between higher and lower pleasures, Mill moved the calculation of pleasure away from quantity towards quality. No longer was it simply how much pleasure an action caused. Now it was also a matter of the quality of the pleasure.

iv) Universalisability

This is a form of Bentham's principle of utility. Mill wanted to show that what is right and wrong for one person in a situation is right or wrong for all. He argued that:

● happiness is desirable, since we all desire it
● happiness is the only thing desirable as an end, since things are only desirable because they bring about happiness.

Therefore, everyone ought to aim at the happiness of everyone, as increasing the general happiness will increase my happiness.

This argument supports the idea that people should put the interests of the group before their own interests. Bentham's principle of utility had focused much more on the individual and had no concept of protecting the common good.

v) Act versus rule

There are two different forms of utilitarianism – **rule utilitarianism** and **act utilitarianism**. In its strong form, rule utilitarianism claims that an action is right if, and only if, it follows the rules: the rules should never be disobeyed. These rules are universal in nature and, if applied in any situation, would lead to the greatest happiness for the greatest number. They would maximise happiness.

In contrast, act utilitarianism treats each new situation as different from all the others, thus requiring a fresh calculation. The rule utilitarian would notice the similarities between the present case and the previous ones and draw on those previous calculations.

Many would argue that the two types of utilitarianism are not mutually exclusive. For instance, Bentham is said to be an act utilitarian; however, he did not claim that it was necessary to calculate the rightness and wrongness of every act from first principles.

Likewise, Mill is said to be a rule utilitarian; however, it is doubtful whether he advocated the strong form. He viewed the rules more as helpful guidance than obligatory. They were necessary as a means of saving time and addressing the distribution problem.

This view, known as weak rule utilitarianism, states that, on certain occasions, the rules can be disobeyed if a greater amount of happiness will result.

KEY WORDS

Rule utilitarianism: an action can only possibly be right if it follows the rules, which should never be disobeyed

Act utilitarianism: every new situation is different and requires a fresh calculation

3 Singer's utilitarianism

Preference utilitarianism

As for the utilitarianism theories discussed above, **preference utilitarians** claim that the right thing to do is that which produces the best consequences. However, instead of specifying the end to be pursued in terms of pleasure, they define the best consequences in terms of preference. This is based on the questions: 'What outcome do I prefer? What is in the best interests of those concerned?' The principle of utility is still followed, so preference utilitarianism considers the preferences of all sentient beings.

The more preferences satisfied in the world, the better. Peter Singer argues that it is preferences, rather than human life, that we ought to value, and this means that animals fall within our sphere of moral obligations since certain animals show preferences, such as to be with others of the same species and to avoid pain. It also means that killing a person who wanted to be killed could be seen as a morally right action.

4 Fletcher's situation ethics

In 1966 an American episcopal moral theologian, Joseph Fletcher, published a book called *Situation Ethics: The New Morality*.

In it, Fletcher advocated a new approach to Christian ethics and moral decision-making that promoted a compromise between the two extremes of legalism and antinomianism.

This approach, called situationism, was a theological way of meeting a practical need in light of the radical changes of the 20th century. Bishop John Robinson, author of the equally popular *Honest to God*, saw Fletcher's book as the only ethic for 'man come of age', a phrase that was to become very pertinent to the whole debate that surrounded situation ethics.

Situation ethics was simply one concise and well-publicised statement of a trend in Christian ethics that had been growing for decades. It was not something entirely new.

> **KEY WORD**
>
> Preference utilitarianism: an ethical theory that sees actions as right when they allow the greatest number to live according to their own preferences, even if those preferences are not those that will make them experience the most pleasure

> **KEY QUOTE**
>
> *...an action contrary to the preference of any being is, unless this preference is outweighed by contrary preferences, wrong.*
>
> (Singer)

> **KEY QUOTES**
>
> *There is an old joke which serves our purposes. A rich man asked a lovely young woman if she would sleep the night with him. She said, 'No.' He then asked if she would do it for $100 000? She said, 'Yes!' He then asked if she would do it for $10 000. She replied, 'Well, yes, I would.' His next question was, 'How about $500?' Her indignant, 'What do you think I am?' was met by the answer, 'We have already established that. Now we are haggling over the price.'*
>
> (Fletcher)

> *Situation ethics was, as are most books, a product of its times. If we distinguish ethics from morality, the method of situation ethics had such widespread appeal partly because of its close fit with the 'new morality' that had emerged or was emerging. The 'new morality' provided a fertile ground for the book and helped to make it a bestseller. Fletcher tapped into powerful social and cultural undercurrents that were becoming more and more evident.*
>
> (Childress)

KEY IDEA

The development of situation ethics:

- 1928 Durant Drake, published *The New Morality*, calling for a pragmatic approach to ethics.
- 1932 Emil Brunner published his *Divine Imperative*, an influence on Fletcher.
- 1932 Reinhold Niebuhr published *Moral Man and Immoral Society*, another influence on Fletcher.
- 1959 Fletcher himself published a seminal paper on situation ethics in the *Harvard Divinity Bulletin*, promoting the 'new morality'.
- 1963 H. Richard Niebuhr published *The Responsible Self*.
- 1963 Paul Lehmann's *Ethics in a Christian Context* and John Robinson's *Honest to God* were published.
- 1966 saw the final statement in this growing trend when Fletcher published his book *Situation Ethics*.

 KEY WORD

Legalistic: set principles are applied regardless of the context

The 'liberal era' of the 60s was certainly part of the reason for the popularity of situation ethics (post–World War 2 feminism, Vietnam, civil rights, teenager and hippy culture, sexual liberation and rejection of traditional sources of authority), but this was definitely not the reason for its emergence. The theological origins of situation ethics are much more complex than its popular social context may suggest.

The changing moralities and questioning of authority that are usually associated with situation ethics had their origins much earlier in theological circles. Situation ethics found a niche in the growing dissatisfaction of religious followers with the inflexible nature of tradition.

a) What is situation ethics?

The simple-minded use of the notions of 'right and wrong' is one of the chief obstacles to the progress of understanding.

(Whitehead, *Modes of Thought*)

In short, situation ethics proposes the idea that absolute moral principles do not work in reality. 'Do not kill' is applicable only in given circumstances. What about war? Self-defence? Meat-eating? The list is endless. Fletcher argued that to make a meaningful ethical decision, the situation needed to be considered. Deciding to do what is right depends upon the practical application of Christian love (agape). The right decision in one circumstance does not become the blueprint for all other circumstances. Each situation should be considered independently.

Fletcher's approach to ethics was that the use of absolute ethical principles and applying them to real-life situations was simply not Christian.

The best way to understand Fletcher's work is to cite two anecdotes.

- Fletcher quotes a conversation with a taxi driver, in which the taxi driver states: 'There are times when a man has to push his principles aside and do the right thing.'
- Fletcher also quotes from Nash's play. *The Rainmaker*, in which a father says to his son: 'Noah, you're so full of what's right that you can't see what's good.'

The common thread here is that absolute principles of right and good are not really absolute, and there are times when principles are inappropriate to apply to the real world. The author Arthur Miller referred to the strict application of moral principles (legalism) as 'the immorality of morality'.

Fletcher pointed out two things about his new method of moral decision-making:

- his 'new morality' (as it was known) was not really new
- the roots of 'new morality' can be found in 'classical' Christianity.

As Robinson writes:

The 'new morality' is, of course, none other than the old morality, just as the new commandment is the old, yet ever fresh, commandment of love.

In beginning his work, Fletcher argued that there are three possible options for making a moral decision:

- the **legalistic** approach, applying set principles rigidly and without consideration of context

- the **antinomianistic** approaches, tending to champion the freedom of the individual without reference to any rules
- the **situational** approach, considering each situation on its merits before applying the Christian principle of love (agape).

Despite rejecting both legalism and antinomianism as approaches to ethics, he was more dismissive of the former:

> *There can be no 'system' of situation ethics, but only a 'method' of situational or contextual decision-making.*

> *Even though Fletcher rejects both, he appears to fear the tyranny of legalism more than the anarchy of antinomianism.*

> (Childress)

Fletcher's theory does appear to be more in line with freedom from rules and laws that are seen to be artificial. His *Situation Ethics* is based on four working principles and six propositions.

b) The four working principles

i) Pragmatism
The solution to any ethical dilemma has to be practical. This idea was influenced by the philosopher and psychologist William James. Fletcher wrote: 'All are agreed: the good is what works, what is expedient, what gives satisfaction.'

ii) Relativism
Again, influenced by earlier theologians, this is the idea that:

> *…the situationist avoids words such as 'never' and 'perfect' and 'always' and 'complete' as he avoids the plague, as he avoids 'absolutely'.*

> (Fletcher)

However, to be relative, one has to have an object *to which to be relative*, a kind of measurement of its true relativity. Fletcher declared this to be: 'agapeic love: it relativises the absolute, it does not absolute the relative.'

iii) Positivism
This is the view that statements of faith are accepted voluntarily and reason is then used to work within, or work out, one's faith. This is in opposition to the view that reason should be the basis of faith; in terms of Christian ethics this means the voluntary acceptance of the principle of agape. Faith comes first: 'The Christian does not understand God in terms of love; he understands love in terms of God as seen in Christ.'

iv) Personalism
This is the basic understanding that ethics deals primarily with people; it is a concern for people rather than things. It is a concern for the subject rather than the object; the disciple is given the command to love people and not laws or principles:

> *Situation ethics puts people at the centre of concern, not things. Obligation is to persons, not to things; to subjects, not objects. The legalist is a what asker (What does the law say?); the situationist is a who asker (Who is to be helped?)*

> (Fletcher)

This, then, is the basis, but how does it work in practice?

The six propositions:

- Only one 'thing' is intrinsically good; namely, love: nothing else at all.
- The ruling norm of Christian decisions is love: nothing else.
- Love and justice are the same, for justice is love distributed, nothing else.
- Love wills the neighbour's good whether we like him or not.
- Only the end justifies the means, nothing else.
- Love's decisions are made situationally, not prescriptively.

c) The six propositions

Fletcher identifies six statements to serve as basic propositions for the outworking of his ethical theory. These are discussed below.

i) Only one 'thing' is intrinsically good; namely, love: nothing else at all

'There are no values at all; there are only things (material and non-material) which happen to be valued by persons.' Agape, however, is the only one thing that is intrinsically good. 'Only love is objectively valid, only love is universal.'

Fletcher calls it the New Testament's law of love. There is, however, some confusion here; despite love being always 'intrinsically good regardless of the context', Fletcher denies that it is some kind of 'thing' as in a noun, rather, it is an action. He prefers to see love as an active principle – it is a doing thing. 'Love is the only universal. But love is not something we have or are, it is something we do.'

ii) The ruling norm of Christian decisions is love: nothing else

Fletcher argues that religious and moral laws have been given artificial status and understanding. He uses the response of Jesus when accused of breaking Sabbath rules: 'the Sabbath was made for man and not man for the Sabbath'. The laws have become dictator to the person.

Fletcher's argument is that love is the new covenant; it replaces the old laws and he refers to the teachings of both Jesus and Saint Paul for justification: 'They redeemed law from the letter that kills and brought it back to the spirit that gives it life.'

Fletcher does not disrespect the law but argues that the situationist recognises the law for what it is – a distillation of the spirit of love rather than a compendium of the legalistic rules.

Love alone, because, as it were, it has a built in moral compass, enabling it to 'home' in intuitively upon the deepest need of the other, can allow itself to be directed completely by the situation.

(Robinson)

This is the radical simplicity of the Gospel's ethic, even though it can lead situationally to the most complicated, headaching, heartbreaking calculations and gray rather than black or white decisions.

(Fletcher)

iii) Love and justice are the same, for justice is love distributed, nothing else

So what is this love? Fletcher distinguishes agape from other Greek words for love. It is 'giving love'.

If justice is to apportion human beings that to which they are entitled, Fletcher asks what this means in Christian terms. He writes: 'For what is it that is due to our neighbours? It is love that is due – only love. (Owe no man anything except to love.) Love is justice, justice is love.'

iv) Love wills the neighbour's good whether we like him or not

Jesus urged everyone to 'love your enemies'. This is a classical statement of the substance and fibre of Christian love, leading to a radical obligation. Love then becomes, according to Fletcher, 'kenotic or self-emptying'.

> Disinterested love can only mean impartial love, inclusive love, indiscriminate love, love for Tom, Dick and Harry.
>
> (Fletcher)

Pure love, then, according to Fletcher, is indiscriminate in its application.

v) Only the end justifies the means, nothing else

Fletcher rejects the idea that the end should not be used to justify the means (found in traditional Christian thinking) as an 'absurd abstraction'. Ethics is, in principle, teleological.

In other words, Fletcher sees any system that proposes that means are intrinsically good, and therefore absolute, as fundamentally flawed. For instance, in practice, there is 'an unlovely lip service paid to a maxim that the practices in question all obviously contradict'. For example, while on the one hand upholding these as infallible blueprints, the same society can justify war, corporal and capital punishments, surgical mutilations, espionage and 'a whole host of things'.

In this light, there are, according to Fletcher, four factors of judging a situation in ethics:

- What is the desired end?
- What should be the means to achieve it?
- What is the motive in achieving it?
- What would be the consequences?

The clear contradiction in making flexible the 'inflexible maxims' clearly shows that it is the ends that dictate moral behaviour and ethical decisions.

vi) Love's decisions are made situationally, not prescriptively

Fletcher sees it as part of our heritage that we have sought laws to which to become slaves; however, once again this only leads to failure as the principles fail to unfold in practice:

> Nothing in the world causes so much conflict of conscience as the continual, conventional payment of lip service to moral 'laws' that are constantly flouted in practice because they are too petty or too rigid to fit the facts of life.

He calls for an end to the ideology that proposes absurdities:

> For real decision-making, freedom is required, an open-ended approach to situations. Imagine the plight of an obstetrician who believed he must always respirate every baby he delivered, no matter how monstrously deformed.

Fletcher's clear conclusion is that all ethical decisions *must* be situation-based (led, of course, by agape) and *not* principle based.

KEY QUOTES

Justice is the many-sidedness of love.
(Fletcher)

To love Christianly is a matter of attitude, not of feeling. Love is discerning and critical; it is not sentimental.
(Fletcher)

…unless some purpose or end is in view, to justify or sanctify it, any action we take is literally meaningless.
(Fletcher)

The new morality, situation ethics, declares that anything and everything is right or wrong, according to the situation.
(Fletcher)

The moral precepts of Jesus are not intended to be understood legalistically, as prescribing what all Christians must do, whatever the circumstances, and pronouncing certain courses of action universally right and others universally wrong. They are not legislation laying down what love always demands of every one: they are illustrations of what love may at any moment require of anyone.
(Robinson)

5 Criticisms of situation ethics by William Barclay

On 2 February 1956, the study of 'new morality', as advocated by Fletcher and similar theologians, was banned from all Roman Catholic academies and seminaries. However, it was much later that an official critique emerged.

In a book published in 1971, *Ethics in a Permissive Society*, Barclay presented concerns over the theory of situation ethics.

Barclay was in no doubt of the sensitive and intelligent nature of agape. 'Obviously, when we define love like this, love is a highly intelligent thing.' However, it was Barclay's view that there will always be a dispute as to what really is the most loving thing to do, and what this actually means in practice.

Since an accurate understanding of love and its precise outworkings is crucial to Fletcher's approach, Barclay pointed out four initial problems with situation ethics.

1. Barclay accused Fletcher of using the exceptional as a basis to establish his theory: 'It is much easier to agree that extraordinary situations need extraordinary measures than to think that there are no laws for ordinary everyday life.' The examples Fletcher uses to justify situation ethics are so extreme that they account for very few real instances in life.

2. It is human nature to crave for rules, as Fletcher himself indicated:

   There is no doubt that most people do not want to be continually confronted with the necessity of making decisions. They would rather have their decisions made for them; they would rather apply laws and principles to the situation. And it may well be that people are right.

   However, to abandon rules on this dubious basis alone, according to Barclay, is dangerous:

   If love is perfect then freedom is a good thing. But if there is no love, or if there is not enough love, then freedom can become licence, freedom can become selfishness and even cruelty.

3. The problem is, according to Barclay, one of human nature. Barclay referred to Robinson's description of situation ethics as 'the only ethic for man come of age' and responded by arguing: 'This is probably true – but man has not yet come of age.' Humanity as a whole is not mature enough for such a sophisticated philosophy.

   Barclay was uncomfortable with Fletcher's view that nothing is intrinsically good or bad in itself. He allowed that some actions can be seen as morally right, given an extraordinary situation; but this does not necessarily follow that the thing involved is in itself morally good. He went even further to suggest that there are some actions that can never be seen to be morally right, for instance, to encourage a young person to experiment and experience drugs for themselves, knowing that it could lead to addiction. 'The right and the wrong are not so easily eliminated.'

4. Finally, Barclay criticised Fletcher's various examples of allegedly immoral action preventing further immoralities. He did this on the grounds that such actions were not the only possibilities to prevent further immorality and would certainly not guarantee the end intended. Once again, the abnormal or extraordinary appears to be the basis of Fletcher's theory of ethics.

In summary, Barclay recognises the value of a situationist approach in its reminder for people to be more flexible in applying moral rules and laws; however, 'we do well still to remember that there are laws which we break at our peril.' A great lesson from situation ethics, according to Barclay, is that it teaches and encourages sympathy and discourages self-righteousness in approaching ethical dilemmas.

But what did Barclay make of Fletcher's views about the nature and purpose of moral laws? In response to Fletcher's attack on legalism, Barclay clarifies the nature and function, the *raison d'être* of the law:

● it is 'the distillation of experience' that society has found to be beneficial – if this is so 'to discard law is to discard experience' and the valuable wisdom and insight it may bring
● it is 'the rule of reason applied to existing circumstances'
● it is a tool for defining approval and punishment
● it is a deterrent but simultaneously can unleash temptation
● it is for the protection of society
● law concerns itself with public morals and not with private morals. 'In other words, there are many things which are immoral, but which are not illegal.'

In conclusion, Barclay points out that, when we deal with the issue of the relationship between morality and the law, there are three main tensions that all have a bearing on the debate regarding situation ethics:

● the tension between freedom and the law – Fletcher's view is that true morality can only exist with the freedom to choose; Barclay questions the very nature of this freedom and the fact that freedom involves the freedom *not* to choose a course of action as well
● the tension between that which is illegal and that which may be immoral
● the tension between the individual's rights and those of the community:

> *Too much law means the obliteration of the individual; too much individualism means the weakening of the law.*

Overall, Barclay's was a scathing critique of the new morality. His view was that Fletcher's morality was too dangerous for society as a whole. According to Barclay, there are certain moral principles that are absolute and always morally good. However, Barclay did concede that these absolute principles were not always absolute in their application (what is morally right or appropriate), especially in extreme circumstances. Such circumstances, however, are so rare as never to justify questioning the whole fabric of the 'law'.

KEY IDEAS

● To say that nothing has intrinsic value or goodness is dangerous and open to abuse.
● In Fletcher's cited examples, other courses of actions could have been offered; his examples were limited.

TASK

Try to match the elements of Fletcher's ideas to the different criticisms Barclay presents. This will give you a good overall picture. In table form, try listing the principles of Fletcher down one side and the criticisms across the top.

Objective: To differentiate accurately between arguments and counter-arguments involved in situation ethics. This demonstrates both 'a coherent and well-structured response to the task at a wide range or considerable depth' and also that you are 'selecting the most important features for emphasis and clarity; using evidence to explain the key ideas' (top level 4 descriptor A01).

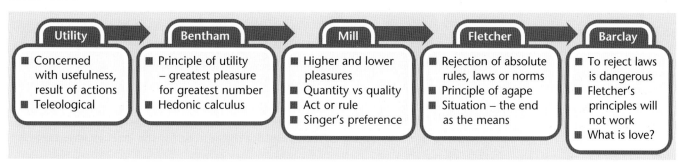

Summary diagram: Utilitaranism and situation ethics

TASK

Connect the comments with the appropriate part of the essay answer. Note that not all the comments are appropriate for this essay answer.

- What do you think about this style of writing? How would you improve it?
- Do you think it is clear which material refers to 'righteous' and which to 'martyr'?
- Do you think the two aspects have been adequately covered? If not, how would you improve the answer?
- Why would this answer not score level 3 or 4?
- Using this structure, now write a level 4 answer.

Objective: To understand the difference between different level answers.

Reflection and assessment (AO1)

It is necessary to bring together the information that has been covered so far and to see how it can be transformed into effective examination-style revision and answers. The best way to do this is to ask the question: 'How am I going to be assessed on this information?'

The first way is through assessment objective 1 (AO1). For this objective you need to be able to 'select and demonstrate clearly relevant knowledge and understanding through the use of evidence, examples and correct language and terminology appropriate to the course of study' (AO1 descriptor).

Look at the following sample answer, which is a response to this question.

Examine the approach of utilitarianism to making ethical decisions.   (21 marks)

> Bentham believes in Utilitarianism. This is to act in a good way to bring happiness to a great number of people. He takes his view from the Principle of Utility which is about the consequences of the situation or action creating more good than pain. To do this he calculates the good (happiness) through his hedonic calculus. Hedonic means pleasure.
>
> The calculation has 7 stages. Three of them are intensity, duration and proximity. These measure happiness and if the happiness is greatest for the greatest number of people then the action is seen as morally right. If a different action would cause more happiness to more people then this action rather then the previous one would be the one considered morally right. The first would be morally wrong.

These are comments that could be applied to the answer. Read through them and then complete the task.

- Spelling errors
- Irrelevant material
- Inaccurate material
- Needs an example to illustrate
- Not enough to demonstrate the point
- No religious references
- Repetition of same point
- Not answered the question
- The illustration needs to be explained as it is not clear why it demonstrates the point.

Suggestion for further application of skills

Look at an essay that you have recently completed.

1 Underline in green what could have been omitted or is repeated.

2 Underline in blue any evaluation words.

3 Underline in red key phrases.

4 Referring to the level descriptors, consider the reasons for the level awarded for your essay.

5 Use the level descriptors to identify how the essay could be improved.

TOPIC 1: A STUDY OF ETHICAL CONCEPTS

Part 1C: A critical analysis of the issues

This means I am expected:

to analyse and critically evaluate:
- the strengths and weaknesses of each theory
- some possible conclusions.

---

1 Strengths of utilitarianism

It has aims that are attractive – happiness and avoidance of pain. It does seem that we are motivated by pleasure and motivated to avoid pain.

It seems straightforward to apply to most situations and concurs with common sense.

It takes into account the consequences of our actions. Looking just at intentions, with no regard to their consequence, seems impersonal. For instance, keeping alive someone who is terminally ill and suffering great pain ignores the consequences for that person.

It considers others and not just the individual. It is concerned with the common good. It takes into account all who are affected by the action. It even goes wider in that it can consider society as a whole. For instance, does allowing abortion have a detrimental effect on society as a whole, in terms of devaluing human life?

2 Weaknesses of utilitarianism

It seems to ignore intentions and an individual's motives. The means by which the greatest good is achieved seems incidental and of no moral relevance. Indeed, it could allow an innocent person to be punished if the consequences resulted in an overall greater happiness, greater than if the person was justly found innocent. In other words, injustice could be seen as the right action, which seems contrary to common sense.

It rejects any theory of moral rights. Rights get in the way of utility.

Because it is concerned with the happiness of the greater number, the happiness of minorities may not be protected.

It is not clear how the hedonic calculus resolves the problem of assessing the quantity of pleasure. For instance, how is it possible to quantify and compare intensity of pleasure with duration of pleasure? Listing elements of pleasure does not resolve the problem of quantifying the pleasure.

Is happiness or pleasure a valid aim? Does it seem rather self-indulgent? Is Mill right when he argues that higher pleasures are better than lower pleasures?

Are there not instances where pain is a good thing?

TASK

Make your own list of questions that you would like to ask about the different ethical theories studied.
Objective: To encourage the use of questions in answers for AO2 that helps to demonstrate more than 'A mainly descriptive response, at a general level' (level 1 descriptor AO2) and aim for 'an attempt at an evaluation of the issue(s) raised in the task' (level 4 descriptor AO2).

KEY QUESTIONS
- Is it possible to quantify pleasure?
- Is discussing philosophy (higher pleasure) more desirable than having sex (lower pleasure)?
- What about the rights of individuals?
- What about the happiness of the minorities?
- Are pleasure and happiness valid aims?
- Are they not rather self-indulgent?
- Is pain always a bad thing?

In deciding whether an action is morally right, it requires the outcomes of the action to be known. However, outcomes may not be accurately predictable.

Indeed, the consequences of our actions persist for an almost indefinite time and may well affect a large number of people. This is certainly true in the case of a war.

To decide what action will produce the greatest good, the alternative actions also have to be considered and their possible outcomes predicted. This seems an impossible task.

Utilitarianism seems too demanding since we ought always to do that which gives greatest good for the greatest number. However, there may always be an act, other than what we choose, that would give greater good.

3 Possible conclusions

When assessing the issues that arise from utilitarianism, it is important to reflect upon the arguments previously discussed and arrive at some appropriate conclusion.

It may be that you accept none of these listed here, or just one of them, or you may have a different conclusion that is not listed. However, what is important is the way that you have arrived at your conclusion – the reasoning process.

From the preceding discussions, here are some possible conclusions you could draw.

1 Utilitarianism is the correct moral theory and so defines all moral action. Other ethical theories are therefore in error.

2 Utilitarianism makes assumptions that may or may not be correct. Whether it is valid or not cannot be determined. However, its strengths outweigh its weaknesses.

3 Utilitarianism makes assumptions that may or may not be correct. Whether it is valid or not cannot be determined. However, its weaknesses outweigh its strengths.

4 Utilitarianism is one ethical system among others and has equal status with them.

5 Utilitarianism is flawed and invalid.

4 Strengths of situation ethics

Fletcher never demanded that an ethical decision should become law; the whole point of situation ethics is against this idea. Therefore issues of right and wrong always remain relative.

Just because something is seen to be appropriate in one case does not mean it is justified in all cases, or that it is right *per se*; love deems it to be fitting and appropriate for the circumstance, it meets the needs of the moment.

Situation ethics does not reject laws but argues that it sees them holistically for what they are, useful tools but not absolute:

> *No principle or rule, other than love, is always reliable.*
>
> (Childress)

> *...the 'agapeic calculus' differs from the 'hedonistic calculus' by substituting human welfare for pleasure.*
>
> (Childress on Fletcher)

> **EXAM TIP**
>
> Exam questions are expressed in words that tell you what to do in your answer. For AO2 they are:
>
> - Comment on...
> - Consider...
> - How far...
> - To what extent...
> - Why...?

? KEY QUESTIONS

- Did Fletcher intend his 'method' to become a system to be considered at a large-scale social level?
- How does situation ethics view the law?
- Can we be so sure about what is right and wrong?
- In the light of changes to morality and society, how can we deny that principles and rules that we have now will not change in the future?

Barclay's criticisms have not stood the test of time and are outdated; for example, page 90 of his book reads: 'Are we quite happy if the law progressively makes what we think wrong easier?' and then goes on to suggest that legalising homosexuality, easing divorce regulations and allowing unmarried students to live together is clearly morally wrong. The 'situationism' of Fletcher has been instrumental in, for example, the Church of England (among others), recognising the injustice of such views being imposed upon society.

Finally, it is with a sense of irony that Barclay's critique of situation ethics ends in a clear recognition of the role of agape in understanding morality:

> *We may well come to the conclusion that one of the great problems of the present situation is to adjust the delicate balance between freedom and the law, and between the individual and society. And the only solution is that a man should discover what it is to love his neighbour as himself.*
>
> **(Barclay)**

5 Weaknesses of situation ethics

Situation ethics is too complex to be of any practical use. It is too intelligent a system and therefore is only for those who are able fully to understand, apply and use the system accurately, appropriately and effectively.

It is not practical for society and a confusion emerges between what is good and what is right. A practical application would cause confusion on a whole scale such as society at large.

Situation ethics seems to deconstruct itself:

> *We cannot say which acts are right or wrong, what we ought to do, until we can say which will probably produce more good than evil, but we cannot say which will probably produce more good than evil until we have some conception of value.*
>
> **(Childress)**

Childress also notes that when Fletcher defines situations, such situations themselves are interpreted by whoever sees them. Then whoever sees them interprets them according to their own values and theories. In addition, agape is sometimes used so broadly by Fletcher that it becomes almost meaningless; any action given the possibility of any present and future context could be ethically justified.

> *Fletcher is not totally consistent in his description of love. One critic charged that the term 'love' runs through the book like a 'greased pig', while others accused him of 'sloppy agape'.*
>
> **(Childress)**

6 Possible conclusions

When assessing the issues that arise from situation ethics, it is important to reflect upon the arguments previously discussed and arrive at some appropriate conclusion.

It may be that you accept none of these listed here, or just one of them, or you may have a different conclusion that is not listed.

? KEY QUESTIONS

- Can only the intelligent 'philosopher' apply situation ethics?
- Is what is appropriate for the individual appropriate for society as a whole?

TASK

Draw a table, using as headings the different ethical theories you have studied. Try to complete the table by putting the appropriate strengths and weaknesses in the boxes. Try having an extra column for conclusions and rank them, giving clear reasons why.

Objective: To summarise the different responses to ethical decision-making. This could serve as a basis for your evidence to include in the mark scheme and notes for answers in the task at the end of this chapter. This meets the AO2 level 4 descriptor criteria of 'a careful analysis of alternative views...supported by well deployed evidence'.

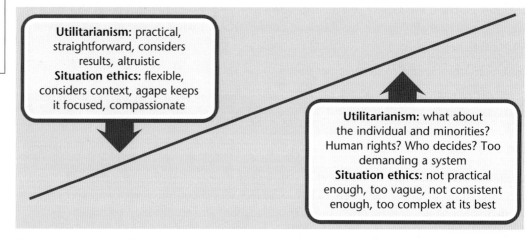

→ EXAM TIP

Always point out both specific and general reasons for the strengths, weaknesses and possible conclusions in evaluating the effectiveness of ethical theories. Include some key questions and make sure that you offer more than one possible conclusion and then give your own, reasoned opinion based upon what you have chosen to write about. This clearly is what a level 4 answer expects: 'a clearly expressed viewpoint supported by well-deployed evidence and reasoned argument' (level 4 descriptor AO2).

However, what is important is the way that you have arrived at your conclusion – the reasoning process.

From the preceding discussions, here are some possible conclusions you could draw.

1 Situation ethics is to be rejected outright as an antinomian system that is disguised and 'sugar-coated' with agape to make it more palatable.

2 People prefer rules. Situation ethics is too vague an approach, too difficult and does not provide the individual enough guidance or clarity.

3 Situation ethics can be accepted with qualifiers and conditions. It can be used alongside a more flexible, legalistic system that recognises the mitigating circumstances behind extreme situations.

4 It is useful in theory for identifying the morally good but not necessarily what is right for society or the individual. If it is applied to society as a whole then there would be antinomianistic chaos.

5 Situation ethics is a tried and tested system. Many of the decisions and changes in society in terms of ethics since the 1960s have been influenced by an element of situationism. It is definitely the ethic for 'man come of age'!

Utilitarianism: practical, straightforward, considers results, altruistic
Situation ethics: flexible, considers context, agape keeps it focused, compassionate

Utilitarianism: what about the individual and minorities? Human rights? Who decides? Too demanding a system
Situation ethics: not practical enough, too vague, not consistent enough, too complex at its best

Summary diagram: Strengths and weaknesses of utilitarianism and situation ethics

Reflection and assessment

TASK

- Look at the suggestions for the basic answer, below. Try to work out how a *developed* answer (top of level 2 to level 3) would deal with the question by adding two or three more bullet points.
- Now go on to develop this answer to indicate how a *higher* answer (level 4) would deal with the question by adding further bullet points. Remember to keep the bullet points centred around the question focus.

Objective: To develop awareness of what will constitute a very good answer by gradually building up a response that is 'an attempt at an evaluation of the issue(s) raised in the task, typically through a careful analysis of alternative views; leading to a clearly expressed viewpoint supported by well-deployed evidence and reasoned argument; expressed accurately, fluently and using a range of technical vocabulary' (level 4 descriptor AO2).

Look back to page 10 in the Introduction to review the levels of response descriptors for AO2. There is a description of the character and features for each level. The exam is marked with reference to levels.

Look at the following notes for a sample basic level 1–2 answer, in response to this question.

Consider the claim that situation ethics is an effective method for making ethical decisions. **(9 marks)**

The *basic* answer might deal with the question by:

- giving a simple description of the 'method'
- presenting a simple explanation of one or two of the strengths
- stating simply a weakness as matter of fact
- stating a personal opinion as a conclusion, without reference to the evidence they present.

Suggestions for further application of skills

Apply the above principles for this question.

Consider the claim that utilitarianism is an effective method for making moral decisions. **(9 marks)**

You can even, later and for revision, go on to develop these into more specific evaluations such as focusing them on responses to particular ethical issues studied later on.

FOUNDATIONS
Area B: Ethics

TOPIC 2: A STUDY OF ETHICAL DILEMMAS

Part 2A: Issues of war and peace

> **This means I am expected:**
>
> **to know about the key emphases:**
> - the just war theory
> - pacifism.
>
> **and to study:**
> - rule of war and the responsibilities involved
> - examples of pacifism
> - attitudes towards pacifism.

This part of the unit explores some of the issues highlighted by war, in particular, the contrasting ideals behind the just war and pacifism.

It would be helpful to write your notes using the headings listed above, as it is from these areas that the examination questions will be derived.

In your studies, remember that you have to bear in mind the **two** basic assessment objectives of:

- Knowledge and Understanding (AO1)
- Evaluation (AO2).

See pages 7–8 in the Introduction to remind yourself of these objectives.

The evaluation material set out in Part 2C (page 112) can be studied either alongside the AO1 material, as you work through this unit, or as a separate unit.

1 War and peace

KEY WORDS

Weapons of mass destruction: weapons capable of killing enormous numbers of people

Genocide: mass killing, unlawful mass murder; the intentional destruction or eradication of an entire racial, political, cultural or religious group

a) Introduction to war and peace

It is a regrettable fact that violence and murder are part of human history. The Old Testament is full of violence; the Mahabharata is based on family feuds and warfare; even the establishment of Islam, the 'religion of peace', was achieved through famous conflicts.

Indeed, it has often been observed that, of all creatures on Earth, the human being is by far the most ferocious and dangerous. For example, humans in recent history have developed **weapons of mass destruction** such as nuclear, biological and chemical weapons. It is interesting to note that, in shifting from medical ethics to war, we move from the idea that humanity is advancing towards improvement in the quality of life worldwide to the appalling fact that, over the last century, humanity is faced with the worst record of **genocide** and cruelty in its history.

b) Key facts about war and peace (the just war and pacifism)

The idea of a **just war** has been debated for centuries. It would be incorrect to identify the just war theory as a single theory. It is more fluid than this. It has developed from simple ideals to a complex range of proposals and even now is still being debated and re-evaluated.

There are three aspects of a just war to consider:

- *jus ad bellum*: the just nature of the reasoning and decision to take part in a war
- *jus in bello*: the just nature of conduct during the war once it begins
- *jus post bellum*: the just nature of how a war is ended.

i) Jus ad bellum

These are rules for state leaders and there are six requirements.

1 Just cause: war has to be for the right reason. The ideas of right reason and just cause cover self-defence, defending others from attack and protecting the innocent.

2 Right intention: even if a just cause can be established, the motive has to be pure. Power, finance, land or revenge are examples of wrong motives.

3 Proper authority and public declaration: the leader must declare war and do so publicly.

4 Last resort: all other diplomatic negotiations must have failed.

5 Probability of success: there must be a reasonable chance of winning.

6 Proportionality: it is only sensible to weigh up the probability that greater good is going to come from the war.

ii) Jus in bello

These responsibilities are directed towards the military.

1 Obey all international laws on weapons prohibition: chemical and biological weapons must not be used.

2 Discrimination and non-combatant immunity: the military must not target civilians.

3 Proportionality: once the end is achieved, no further force is needed.

4 Benevolent quarantine for prisoners of war (POWs): all prisoners are to be given basic rights.

5 No means that are *mala in se*: no methods or weapons that are evil in themselves may be used.

6 No reprisals: this includes the ideas of revenge and retribution.

iii) Jus post bellum

This is a relatively new aspect to the just war tradition. The purpose is to restore peace in a controlled manner. Debated principles include:

- restoring human rights
- distinguishing between innocent civilians, who are to be free from post-war punishment, and those who have incurred penalties
- public agreement and proclamation
- giving war criminals fair trials; this applies both to leaders and any ordinary soldiers
- establishing financial compensation where necessary but so that civilians are not taxed and that the country can restore itself
- giving the country and its inhabitants the opportunity to reform.

KEY WORDS

Just war: a specific concept of how warfare might be justified, typically in accordance with a particular situation or scenario

Jus ad bellum: a set of criteria to be consulted before engaging in war, in order to determine whether entering into war is justifiable

Jus in bello: laws stating acceptable practices while engaged in war, such as the Geneva Convention

Jus post bellum: suggested rules about justice after a war, including peace treaties, reconstruction, war crimes trials and war reparations

TASK

Summarise, in table form, key points for the different aspects of the just war theory. Add an extra column and use it to compare and contrast the ideas.

Objective: To ensure accuracy with reasons and conditions for war and the accurate use of correct terminology (a prerequisite for a level 4 response at AS 'expressed clearly and accurately, using technical language widely', level 4 descriptor AO1).

c) Specific issues and key areas of debate surrounding war and peace

i) Principles

Waging of war contradicts principles such as peace, non-violence, that killing is wrong and that conflicts can be resolved through discussion. Those who support the use of war see the compromise of such principles as necessary, for example, the reasons for a just rebellion against an unjust dictatorship. Essentially, the questions raised focus on whether such principles can be compromised at all and the consequential vagueness that ensues about when and why such compromises are made.

There are two main responses to the idea of war. The first considers war as the lesser evil than the one that allows matters to continue unaddressed.

The other is the line taken by **ethical and religious pacifism**. Examples of people who have consistently refused to support war in any way include the Quakers, **Gandhi** and **Bertrand Russell**.

KEY PEOPLE

Mohandas Karamchand Gandhi (1869–1948)
Also known as the Mahatma (great soul), Gandhi was an inspirational spiritual and political leader in the drive for Indian independence from the British, during the last century. He inspired many people worldwide through his principles of truth and active resistance to evil through non-violent protest. His strong ideas of justice through peaceful means influenced later civil rights leaders and those in the fight for freedom, and are still respected by many today. His birthday is a national holiday in India.

Mohandas Karamchand Gandhi

Bertrand Russell (1872–1970)
A famous British philosopher and mathematician, Russell was renowned for his attitudes towards social reform and pacifism. Russell was critical of war and of the nuclear arms race and, in his early life, was imprisoned for his beliefs.

Bertrand Russell

ii) Life

The main issue, once again, relates to the value, sanctity and quality of life. War devastates. As well as the immediate destruction it causes, the impact of war can be felt for years afterwards. Another consideration is the impact upon individuals affected by the violence and poverty that war brings.

iii) Human rights

Debates about the violation of human rights before, during and after war continue. The rights to life, freedom and protection are the first three that seem to be relevant. The issues of such rights can be seen running through the just war theory and its process of reasoning.

iv) Practical implications

This is the most crucial area of debate and any decision for war must take it into account. Many questions need to be asked, and many arguments debated, about the consequences of war. Death, poverty, discrimination, suffering, disease and financial ruin of a country are all potential areas for consideration. Is there ever a case for justifying such horror? How can we learn from human history? How can war be prevented? How can humanity ensure atrocities such as the Holocaust and the ethnic conflicts in Rwanda and former Yugoslavia will never happen again?

v) The Quaker Peace Testimony

Quakers have always taken a clear stand for peace and campaigned against violence and war. Originally a declaration made in 1660, the Quaker Peace Testimony has become an active expression of Quaker understanding of the nature of how to live in this world.

As a result, Quakers are active in their support, including long-term individual and collective Quaker action as an expression of the peace testimony. Quakers aim to develop and support alternative ways of resolving and engaging in conflicts, campaigning to reduce armaments and changing the conditions and circumstances that lead to war.

Quakers focus on the root causes of war, seeing their stance of non-violence as a challenge to war, violence and injustice. Quakers do not avoid conflict or believe that there should be none. Conflict can be worked through peacefully and resolved. Conflict is met head-on but is tackled by humane and just means.

2 What utilitarianism says about the issue of war and peace

As with most moral issues, the outcomes are difficult to predict with any certainty. This is certainly true of war. The criterion used by utilitarians is 'the greatest happiness for the greatest number'. However, the calculation of happiness seems impossible where a war is involved. One of the key considerations would be the peace that is gained as a result of the war. Put simply: 'Does the end justify the means?' The idea of a just war may be applicable as it is concerned with just causes and the likelihood of success. Preference utilitarianism focuses on the preferences of those involved. This is very difficult to assess, given the complexities of war and the numbers that could be involved.

3 Buddhist attitudes to war

In his book, *An Introduction to Buddhist Ethics*, Peter Harvey spends a great deal of time outlining the Buddhist analysis of the causes of conflict. Indeed, in the Buddhist path much emphasis is placed on preventing conflicts from arising in the first place.

> **KEY IDEA**
>
> The Quaker Peace Testimony:
> We utterly deny all outward wars and strife and fightings with outward weapons, for any end, or under any pretence whatsoever; and this is our testimony to the whole world. The spirit of Christ, by which we are guided, is not changeable, so as once to command us from a thing as evil and again to move unto it; and we do certainly know, and so testify to the world, that the spirit of Christ, which leads us into all Truth, will never move us to fight and war against any man with outward weapons, neither for the kingdom of Christ, nor for the kingdoms of this world.
> (Declaration of Friends to Charles II, 1660)

> **66 KEY QUOTE**
>
> *I have had this Dhamma edict written so that my sons and great-grandsons may not consider making new conquests, or that if military conquests are made, that they be done with forbearance and light punishment, or better still, that they consider making conquest by Dhamma only, for that bears fruit in this world and the next.*
>
> **(Asoka, 13th Rock Edit)**
> 99

Identifying the causes at an early stage can help defuse a potentially awkward situation. The great Buddhist ruler, King Asoka (see Area C, Buddhism) is the ideal convert from the horrors of war. Asoka promoted peace and non-violence at all costs.

The idea of a life as a soldier clearly breaks with the first precept and also the aspect of the eight-fold path that indicates right livelihood. There are, though, several justifications for a Buddhist to be involved with war and it has been argued that there is a history of the just war that has evolved in Buddhism. Typical of this is the association of the Japanese bushido or warriors within Zen Buddhism. Military practices were modelled upon Zen monastic practices to create in the soldier an indifference to death and suffering.

Buddhism's use of skilful means encourages the use of practical judgement in applying moral principles to any situation. For example, the precept against violence is not absolute because it can be suspended in favour of defending another.

In practice, in Buddhism there is certainly a tradition that parallels the Christian and western criteria for a just war. Nonetheless, as within any religious tradition, there remains a group of thinkers who could not justify violence in any shape or form. The Buddhist precepts are deontological in nature and, no matter how the situation is justified through the use of kharmic calculations, emotional pleas through compassion or by the use of skilful means, the cold facts are that violence met with violence only produces more violence.

66 **KEY QUOTE**

Although the Buddha's precepts are unconditional, conflicts between precepts require contextual reasoning that employs utilitarian (maximising compassion and minimising suffering) and virtue ethical (the effects actions have on one's condition) considerations.

(*Journal of Military Ethics*)

99

TASK

Design a flowchart that explains the process of reasoning involved in the responses to war by both utilitarianism and Buddhism.

Objective: To develop knowledge and understanding of the significance of the enlightenment illustrating 'accurate and relevant detail, clearly identifying the most important features' (level 4 descriptor AO1).

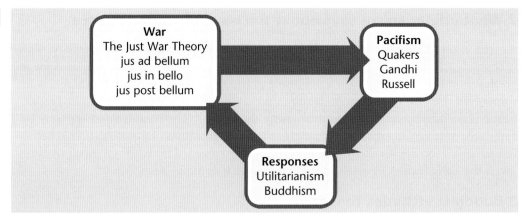

Summary diagram: War and peace and pacifism

Reflection and assessment

Below is an answer given in response to this question.

Outline the principles of a just war and examine its application. (21 marks)

It is not the best response and would probably be awarded level 2. The examiner's comments suggest why.

Needs to give a context for how and why the just war theory developed.

Again, needs to explain how it 'developed' rather than just involve one thinker.

A just war is when a country decides that it has good reason to go to war. It is not just because of land or because they have disagreed with another country. Augustine said it had to be a proper authority that started it and it must be for a genuine reason. Over the years the just war has developed and there are many areas to consider. Many people have added rules and countries now generally agree as to what a just war is. It is usually split into two parts that deal with behaviour during the war but also considering reasons for going to war in the first place.

Reasons are not explored in a systematic manner – disorganised.

This is quite vague and the answer lacks examples of rules or applications to illustrate points made.

TASK

Try rewriting the response shown above, using the following as a plan.

Principles: Reasons for war, conduct and termination
Application: Explain the rules suggested for each principle
Objective: To develop awareness of what will constitute a very good answer by gradually building up a response that demonstrates 'accurate, relevant and detailed knowledge used concisely to present a coherent and well-structured response to the task at a wide range or considerable depth; selecting the most important features for emphasis and clarity; using evidence to explain the key ideas; expressed cogently, using technical language' (high level 4 descriptor AO1).

Suggestions for further application of skills

As a group, divide up the tasks to explain the principles, law and areas for debate for pacifism. In small groups or as individuals, take charge of one area. Spend 15 minutes on this and then swap with another group (or person) for them to add to or rework your initial outline. Keep going as a group until you are satisfied that you have a good enough description to present as an examination answer.

TOPIC 2: A STUDY OF ETHICAL DILEMMAS

Part 2B: Sexual ethics

This means I am expected:

to know about the key emphases:

● the laws surrounding the sexual ethics debate

● religious attitudes towards the sexual ethics debate

and to study:

● laws concerning consent, marriage, divorce and homosexuality

● Christian responses to consent, marriage, divorce and homosexuality

● Muslim responses to consent, marriage, divorce and homosexuality.

In this book the evidence and examples given are relevant and appropriate because this material focuses only on the content for AO1 that is given by the Edexcel specification. The evaluation materials for AO2 will be aimed at helping you 'critically evaluate and justify a point of view through the use of evidence and reasoned argument'.

It would be helpful to write your notes using the headings listed above, as it is from these areas that the examination questions will be derived.

In your studies, remember that you have to bear in mind the **two** basic assessment objectives of:

● Knowledge and Understanding (AO1)
● Evaluation (AO2).

See pages 7–8 in the Introduction to remind yourself of these objectives.

The evaluation material set out in Part 2C (page 112) can be studied either alongside the AO1 material, as you work through this unit, or as a separate unit.

This part of the topic explores some of the main issues involved with sexual ethics.

1 Sexual ethics: facts and issues from a secular, Christian and Muslim perspective, an introduction

It is true that for many societies and for much of history the legitimate expression of sexuality has been controlled by social norms, including the stability of family life… the prohibition of homosexuality, and the use of marriage as a means of forging political, financial or social links between families or even nations.

(Thompson)

66 **KEY QUOTE**

Fifty years ago no one mentioned sex in public; today you cannot avoid it. Sex sells everything from newspapers to cars. Books, magazines and films gain popularity (and profits) because of their sexual content.

(Shannon, 1996)

99

It has been said often in literature that sexual ethics is an issue of power, male dominance and oppression. Throughout history, woman have had lamentably few rights. The restrictive use of marriage as a trading tool, bribe or resolution to a family conflict is all too familiar.

At the same time, though, the picture should not be painted as totally bleak. Heroism, nobility, gentleness and stories of love abound and enrich our cultural heritage. Societies such as that of ancient Greece are testimony to the fact that not all was repressed in terms of sexuality and relationships.

In historical terms it is only relatively recently that the rights and freedoms of individuals have justly been addressed, whether concerning issues of sexual equality or gender equality. There have been long-awaited changes in laws, attitudes and moralities reflected in the thinking of groups such as those advocating gay rights and civil partnership relationships.

Society has changed dramatically over the last century. However, such radical changes do not necessarily take with them the *status quo* of traditional values. It is this issue of sexuality and how we define and work out the practicalities associated with it that is the focus of this section.

What, then, is sexuality? In the west, as Michael Foucault has pointed out, people like to label and categorise sexuality – heterosexual, homosexual, bisexual.

> The controversial philosopher Michael Foucault (1926–84) even argued that the idea of 'sexuality' is a modern invention designed to exercise political power over different members of society.
>
> (Wilcockson)

Foucault argued that sexuality could not and should not be defined in this way. It is too restrictive and repressive. His theory has come to be know as *Queer theory*.

2 The law

a) Age of consent

> The term 'pre-marital sex' can be understood in two ways. It can mean either indiscriminate sexual activity before a person settles to one partner in marriage, or the sexual expression of the love existing between two people who intend to marry (or who are in a long-term relationship).
>
> (Shannon)

The age of consent for heterosexual sex
In England and Wales, the age of consent to any form of sexual activity is 16 for both men and women (in Scotland it is 17 for a woman).

The Sexual Offences Act of 2003 produced a series of laws intended to protect children under 16 from sexual abuse. The Acts did not intend to prosecute mutually agreed teenage sexual activity, unless it involved abuse or exploitation.

There are specific laws to protect children under 13, who cannot legally give their consent to any form of sexual activity. Such laws carry with them severe penalties: the maximum sentence of life imprisonment can be administered for rape, assault by penetration or causing or inciting a child to engage in sexual activity.

> **❝ KEY QUOTE**
>
> *Queer theory suggests that there can be no hard and fast boundaries about what is or is not a legitimate sexual relationship and no institution has the right to impose its views on others; being queer is the freedom to define oneself according to one's nature, whatever that may be.*
>
> **(Wilcockson)** ❞

> **❝ KEY QUOTE**
>
> *Increasingly, people claim that they embark on a sexual relationship as part of the quest for personal fulfilment…Sex is seen in that context – as a pleasure in itself, but also as a way of becoming intimate with the partner, sharing in a way that has an effect on the relationship as a whole.*
>
> **(Thompson)** ❞

b) Marriage

One of two officials may perform a marriage ceremony: either an 'authorised celebrant' (usually, but not always, a minister of religion) or an 'authorised registrar'.

There are both civil and religious ceremonies. Religious venues cannot, by law, accommodate civil marriages but the Marriage Act of 1994 made it possible for alternative venues to be used that are also licensed for officiating the ceremony legally. The marriage register is signed by the couple, two witnesses and the official.

Church of England clergy are obliged to marry people if at least one of them belongs to their parish, even if they are not practising Christians. For a ceremony outside a person's parish, special permission needs to be granted.

Following the Marriage Act of 1753, and up until 1837, the only marriages that were recognised in England and Wales were those conducted by the Church of England, those by Quakers or Jewish marriages. However, the Marriage Act of 1836 changed this by introducing civil marriage and allowing ministers of other faiths to act as registrars. This civil marriage law was superseded by the Marriage Act of 1949.

The ancient Marriage Duty Acts of 1694, 1695 and 1753 were notoriously strict, stipulating:

- that banns or marriage licences must be obtained
- where marriages were allowed to take place
- whom a person was and was not allowed to marry
- at least two witnesses to be present at the marriage ceremony
- a minimum marriageable age.

The legendary flight to Gretna Green was born!

Today, for a civil marriage the banns must be posted for 15 days before the ceremony and they must be read out at least three times, on separate occasions, in the Church of England for Anglican marriages.

Legally, if a person is at least 16 years old then they can marry, although parental permission is sought for anyone below the age of 18. Surprisingly, if no parental permission is given, the marriage can still be validated.

c) Divorce and the law

In England and Wales, the grounds upon which divorce is granted is irretrievable breakdown. In 1996 The Family Law Act was passed that has the potential to make fine changes to the law but these have never come into fruition and may never be brought into effect.

Divorce, then, in England and Wales is based on this idea of the irretrievable breakdown of the marriage; however, proving this is another matter and must be evidenced in at least one of five ways:

- adultery
- unreasonable behaviour
- desertion
- two years' separation with consent
- five years' separation without consent.

The most frequent grounds in English divorce law is unreasonable behaviour, because it is ambiguous and open to wide interpretation, unlike the other four reasons, which are specific. It is no surprise, then, that the speed and relative ease of this form of divorce makes it the most popular choice.

Desertion and separation require lengthy periods of time to establish the evidence (at least two years). A claim of adultery has to be supported by evidence, so is generally avoided for the simplicity of unreasonable behaviour.

d) Homosexuality

There have been several debates as to the reasons for homosexual behaviour. Some see it as a 'condition' still, others have argued that it is socially induced and some have even tried to establish that it is a genetic condition. If we were to take the line of Foucault, then it is interesting to see that the questions concerning homosexuality are no more relevant than those we could ask of any other sexual orientation. Indeed, why does there have to be a specific reason?

Considering that homosexuality has existed as far back in history as we can delve, it is surprising that the laws for treatment of homosexuals and their rights have only been liberalised in the western legal system relatively recently.

During the 1950s, a committee was established to investigate the issues and 'social problems' associated with prostitution and homosexuality; the committee included a judge, a psychiatrist, an academic and various theologians. Their findings, *The Wolfenden Report*, was published in 1957.

The main conclusion of the report concerning homosexuality was that it would be wrong for criminal law to intervene in what they did in the privacy of their own homes and, therefore, consenting adults should be given the freedom to explore their sexuality. The report stated:

> ...unless a deliberate attempt be made by society through the agency of the law to equate the sphere of crime with that of sin, there must remain a realm of private life that is, in brief, not the law's business.

(Wolfenden Report, 1957)

However, it was not until ten years later, under a more liberal-thinking government, that the recommendations actually came into force on 28 July 1967. This was the result of great pressure from several areas of public influence, who felt that homosexual men, in particular, were already the object of ridicule and derision.

Even so, it was still widely held to be a disability or condition that carried with it a burden of shame.

Since this breakthrough in public and government acknowledgement of the rights of homosexuals, there have been several developments in the law.

- 1967: the age of consent set for homosexual males was 21.
- 1994: the Criminal Justice and Public Order Act reduces the age of consent to 18.
- 2000: the Parliament Act was invoked to ensure the passage of the Sexual Offences (Amendment) Act 2000, which made the age of consent 16 (17 in Northern Ireland for girls) for both homosexuals and heterosexuals.

66 **KEY QUOTES**

It is important to understand the distinction between homosexuality and homosexual acts. The condition of homosexuality means that a person, whether a man or a woman, is sexually attracted to persons of the same sex. The exact cause of this are unknown: they may be social, genetic or hormonal but the recognition of its existence is quite recent.

(Shannon)

In 1991, in response to the quest for the gay gene started by Dean Hamer:

By his own admission Hamer concludes that his present research can only locate a cluster or 'linkage' of genes. This suggests that sexuality is something that cannot be pinned down to something as definite as a gene. It is just as likely that there are other social factors as well.

(Wilkcockson)

99

EXAM TIP

Remember to explain each point that you make in your answer to the full. Think carefully about each sentence and how it relates to the question and the previous sentence. Aim for at least three clear sentences to explain a concept or idea, giving examples from different sources to support your point. To develop the point, bring in a variety of ways in which the application of this principle is demonstrated and introduce some contrasting scholarly views. This demonstrates that the answer is 'accurate, relevant and detailed knowledge of the subject matter at a wide range or in significant depth' (mid level 4 descriptor AO1) as opposed to the information being simply 'minimal accuracy or relevance in factual detail' (level 1 descriptor AO1) or 'limited in scope' (level 2 descriptor AO1).

- 2003: The Sexual Offences Act completely overhauled the outdated procedures for dealing with sexual offences, including making gross indecency, buggery and sexual activity between more than two men no longer crimes in the United Kingdom.

In summary, the privacy law that was initially seen to be a right and a breakthrough was later seen to have become an admission of disagreement. In order fully to acknowledge the rights of homosexuals, the freedom of expression in public, within the laws of common decency and inoffensiveness afforded to all subjects, needed to be acknowledged.

3 Religious responses: Christianity and Islam

a) Christianity: sex within and outside marriage

Sex is a gift from God. It is an expression of love and responsibility within marriage. A sexual relationship reflects trust, respect, and commitment.

From the Christian perspective, it is generally regarded that sex, used wrongly, can encourage promiscuity, illegitimacy, moral disorder, adultery and a lack of trust in relationships.

In summary, sex should be valued and given dignity within family life or a loving relationship.

Roman Catholic teaching states that sex is a gift from God to be enjoyed. It has both a unitive and procreative function. *Humana Vitae* teaches that these functions are inseparable. Family planning is acceptable but only through natural contraception not artificial contraception.

The view of the Church of England is that sex depends upon the quality of the relationship and that it is reasonable to accept sexual relations, as long as there is trust and commitment, respect and consent.

Despite their differences, both denominations agree that sex outside matrimony, involving adultery, is wrong.

b) Islam: views about sexual relationships

Islam does not approve of sex outside marriage, even within a stable relationship, classing it as promiscuity. Adultery is forbidden. It is seen to be a serious offence, with severe punishments under shari'ah law.

Sex is a gift from Allah and should be enjoyed in a wholesome and pure manner. Marriage is for the production of a family, to continue a family name or lineage. Sex should never cause suffering or be excessive; it is quite natural and not unclean. Indeed, sex is just another aspect of our physical humanity, taken with the spiritual and intellectual. According to Islamic teaching, lack of respect for sexuality can lead to the breakdown of society.

TASK

Design a leaflet that compares the Christian and Muslim attitudes to issues concerning marriage and sexual ethics. Make sure that you highlight the differences and the similarities clearly. You could colour-code your diagram.

Objective: To appreciate an overview of the different religious responses to the issue and to be aware of the key terminology involved. This demonstrates 'well-chosen evidence to support understanding of key ideas and concepts' that is 'expressed clearly and accurately, using technical language widely' (level 4 descriptor AO1).

c) Christianity and marriage

Marriage is a gift from God. It is one of the sacraments in Roman Catholicism, a covenant in Protestantism and a mystical union in the Anglican Church. The Bible teaches marriage as a good way of life, as the family unit promotes social stability.

Marriage is a demonstration of love. It is for companionship; the procreation of children is seen to be a way of completing this union. Marriage avoids illegitimacy and channels sexual instinct into a healthy relationship and gives it meaning.

The importance of the institution of marriage can be seen from the ceremony and its symbolic representations.

- The bride usually wears white as a symbol of chastity.
- The vicar advises the congregation as to the purpose of the gathering, in the presence of God.
- Before the couple takes the vows, they and the congregation are asked if there is any reason why they should not be lawfully married.
- Vows between bride and groom are exchanged and are spoken before God.
- The marriage is affirmed in the statement: 'That which God has joined together let no one separate.'
- Hymns and a brief sermon about love underline the seriousness of marriage.
- Sometimes the eucharist is celebrated.
- Usually a meal of celebration follows.
- The ceremony can last anything between one and two hours.

d) Islam and marriage

The first thing to note is that arranged weddings are not a Muslim tradition but are a cultural phenomenon. For example, Indian Christians will have arranged marriages.

Despite this, marriages tend to be arranged by parents although there is more flexibility today. Indeed, many Muslims prefer the term 'guided marriage'.

According to tradition, suitable partners are selected by the parents. As has already been implied, the bride and groom do have a certain amount of freedom in choosing their partners. There are usually 'introduction parties'; however, the couple are not allowed to be alone together before marriage.

Marriage is seen to be for life. While polygamy is allowed it is not often practised; UK law does not allow it. As in Christianity, marriage is seen to promote stability and social order, serve to unite the wider family and community (ummah) and provide a secure environment for children.

Again, as with Christianity, the importance of marriage in Islam is underlined in the ceremony.

- The father of the bride must give permission in public.
- The religious ceremony, called the Aqd Nikah, takes place either in the bride's house or at a mosque.
- The fourth chapter of the Qur'an, entitled 'The Woman', and extracts from the Hadith are read by the legal official (qadi) who may also be an official registrar.
- Three copies of a written contract are also distributed (to the husband, the wife and the official) but there is also a spoken one. However, this contract is between the groom and the bride's male guardian, not husband and wife.

EXAM TIP

When answering a question on sexual ethics, make sure that you focus on the area highlighted in the question. Make sure you pick out the key issues and explain why they are important in relation to the key religious teachings. Comment on any legalities that may contrast to the religious views. This means that it is not just a general answer that presents 'a limited range of isolated facts… with mainly random and unorganised detail' or 'information presented within a structure which shows a basic awareness of the issue raise' (level 1 and 2 descriptors A01). Remember, we are aiming for 'a coherent and well-structured account of the subject matter' (level 4 descriptor A01).

- A dowry (mahr) is demanded from the husband to the wife, according to the Qur'an, and this belongs to the wife and can never be accessed by the husband. (Because of controversy, this element is not always present.)
- The ceremony must be performed by a male, usually the imam.
- Rings are exchanged but the man's ring must not be made of gold.
- A feast of dates follows the ceremony but the main celebrations are held the following day.

e) Christianity and divorce

For Roman Catholics, marriage is a sacred contract. The ceremony is a sacrament and involves mass. The vows are witnessed by God and, partly, made to God. Marriage cannot be annulled unless:

- the intent of the married couple was not really clear
- the judgement of one or the other was impaired
- they cannot carry out marital duties
- the marriage is not consummated
- they have not given consent freely.

Special cases have to go to the Vatican, for the Pope to consider them individually and, if appropriate, to declare that the marriage is annulled. Unless an annulment is granted, the couple are still considered as married in the eyes of the Church, even though they may be legally divorced.

Divorced couples who have not had their marriage annulled are not able to marry again in church or to receive communion, 'but must not consider themselves separated from the Church' according to Roman Catholic teaching.

TASK

Design a diagram to summarise the possible reasons for divorce in Christianity. Try to link the reasons to any religious principles that have been highlighted when considering the purpose of marriage.
Objective: To develop ability to demonstrate the inter-relatedness of these teachings and demonstrate 'detailed knowledge of the subject matter at a wide range or in significant depth' (level 4 descriptor AO1) as opposed to simply 'very broad and unfocused generalisations' (level 1 descriptor) or an answer that is 'limited in scope' (level 2 descriptor).

The Church of England does not regard marriage as an official sacrament; however, the sacredness of the ceremony is underlined by the fact that God is present: 'we are gathered here today in the presence of God to witness...'. It is a very serious commitment. Ideally it is for life.

Jesus appears to have taken a very strict stance on divorce and remarriage; the only grounds for divorce is adultery (Matthew 5:31–2). However, Jesus taught love and forgiveness in response to conflict and moral problems.

In 1 Corinthians 7:10ff Paul follows the teaching of Jesus, and adds that an unbelieving spouse can choose to divorce the believer but not the other way around.

In Old Testament times, as Deuteronomy 24:1 testifies, divorce was easy and not really a moral dilemma; the husband simply needed to write his wife a bill of divorce and send her out of his house. However, as this text demonstrates, remarriage was possible but not to the same partner.

The Church of England encourages marriage counselling and reconciliation, but allows divorce as a last resort.

Remarriage in an Anglican Church is allowed but is dependent on the discretion of the individual clergy. Some Protestant Churches allow their ministers to decide for themselves what is appropriate in each situation. In Methodist, Baptist and Quaker denominations, for example, they act according to their conscience.

f) Islam and divorce

Islam does not forbid divorce but neither does it condone it. It is accepted as a weakness of human nature, highly discouraged but accepted as a last resort.

Divorce can be mutual, initiated by the wife due to a grievance or (only on proof of immorality) by the husband. A wife may divorce her husband if:

- he cannot maintain her
- there is abuse
- he is impotent
- he is insane
- he has a repulsive disease
- there is desertion
- he suffers imprisonment
- there is deception or concealment of important information.

Strict conditions, however, must be met:

- persons should be sane, conscious and under no pressure
- it must be clear to all
- persons should not divorce in anger or under the influence of alcohol or drugs.

There is a waiting period (iddah) of three months for the benefit of the woman, who can live under her husband's maintenance and be treated well before divorce and official separation take place.

According to shari'ah law, custody of the children is usually given to the father.

Unlike Christianity, in which there is no obvious preference, Islam encourages remarriage.

> **KEY QUOTE**
>
> *...the most detestable act that God permits is divorce.*
>
> **(Hadith)**

TASK

Design a diagram to summarise the possible reasons for divorce in Islam. Try to link the reasons to any religious principles that have been highlighted when considering the purpose of marriage.

Objective: To develop ability to demonstrate the inter-relatedness of these teachings and demonstrate 'detailed knowledge of the subject matter at a wide range or in significant depth' (level 4 descriptor AO1) as opposed to simply 'very broad and unfocused generalisations' (level 1 descriptor) or an answer that is 'limited in scope' (level 2 descriptor).

g) Christianity and homosexuality

There is no doubt that homosexuality is a divisive issue in Christianity. The religion encompasses all views and even has openly homosexual clergy, including bishops. The Church was divided by the appointment of its first openly gay bishop, Gene Robinson, in 2003.

Recently, the first gay 'marriage' was carried out in an Anglican church between two priests. They exchanged vows at the church of St Bartholomew the Great in the City of London. Before this, in line with the conditions for remarriage, clergy, through personal choice and preference, could perform blessings.

> **KEY QUOTES**
>
> *...it is pointless condemning someone for being homosexual: it is a condition that is not arrived at by choice.*
>
> *...the homosexual, whether he or she indulges in homosexual acts or not, is a person loved by God and for whom Christ died.*
>
> **(Shannon)**

66 KEY QUOTES

If a man lies with a man as one lies with a woman, both of them have done what is detestable. They must be put to death; their blood will be on their own heads.

(Leviticus 20:13)

For this reason a man will leave his father and mother and be united to his wife, and they will become one flesh.

(Genesis 2:24)

In the same way the men also abandoned natural relations with women and were inflamed with lust for one another. Men committed indecent acts with other men, and received in themselves the due penalty for their perversion.

(Romans 1:27)

99

66 KEY QUOTE

And Lot, when he said to his people, 'Do ye approach an abomination which no one in all the world ever anticipated you in? Verily, ye approach men with lust rather than women – nay, ye are a people who exceed.' But his people's answer only was to say, 'Turn them out of your village, verily, they are a people who pretend to purity.' But we saved him and his people, except his wife, who was of those who lingered; and we rained down upon them a rain;...see then how was the end of the sinners!

(Sura 7:80–84)

99

KEY IDEA

As a mark of respect to the prophet, it is customary to write 'peace be upon him' or the abbreviated form, PBUH, after his name. In this section, this custom has been applied on the first mention of his name within each part.

Reactions were mixed: *The Sunday Telegraph* quoted the Archbishop of Uganda, the Most Rev Henry Orombi, as saying:

The leadership tried to deny that this would happen, but now the truth is out. Our respect for the Church of England will erode unless we see a return to traditional teaching.

Under Church of England guidance, gay clergy can enter a civil partnership if they provide reassurance that they will abstain from sex. Couples who ask a priest to bless their union must be dealt with 'pastorally and sensitively' on an individual basis.

Anglican bishops hold widely varying views on sexuality, due to the ambiguity in interpreting ancient passages from the Bible, and there has been no compromise or middle ground.

h) Islam and homosexuality

There is no debate in Islam concerning homosexuality. Traditions and scriptures condemn it. Accordingly:

Though love is the basis of all relationships, Islam forbids homosexual and lesbian relations. Islam views such relations as unnatural and a deviation from the norm.

(ibn Ally)

There is no compromise. Several parts of the Qur'an are seen to refer to gay and lesbian behaviour.

Officially, there are seen to be five references concerning specifically same-sex relationships. It is interesting to note that four are about the same story concerning Lot and this has also caused much debate and controversy within Christian theological circles in response to the issue.

The Hadiths (collections of sayings of Muhammad (PBUH)) are more graphic and explicit, condemning homosexuality. Although they carry authority, they are always secondary to the one divine source, the Qur'an.

Traditionalist orthodox Muslims consider the Hadith literature as the authentic sayings of Muhammad. Many liberal Muslims doubt the authenticity of at least some of them. Indeed, no sahabi (companion) of Muhammad could quote a saying or decision of Muhammad relating to this question.

Passages often cited from the Hadiths include:

- *When a man mounts another man, the throne of God shakes.*
- *Kill the one that is doing it and also kill the one that it is being done to.*
- *Sihaq (lesbian sexual activity) of women is zina (illegitimate sexual intercourse) among them.*

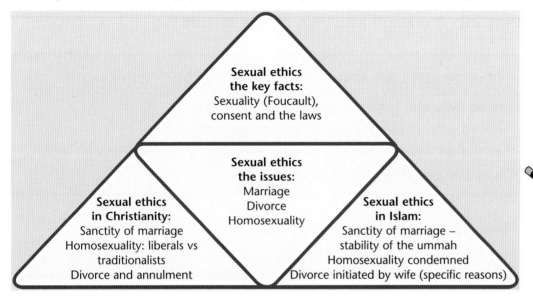

Summary diagram: Sexual ethics

Reflection and assessment

It is vital to bring together the information that has been covered so far and recognise how it can be transformed into effective examination-style revision and answers. The best way to do this is to ask the question: 'How am I going to be assessed on this information?'

Read the following question and complete the task in the margin,

> **Outline the different views concerning sexual behaviour as dictated by religious belief.** (21 marks)

Suggestions for further application of skills

Now complete the same task, applying the same instructions, for this question.

> **Examine religious beliefs concerning marriage and divorce.** (21 marks)

Remember that the focus is religious beliefs on marriage and covers ideals such as purpose, the relevance of, sex within and beyond matrimony and also issues of divorce.

Read pages 106–10 that deal with this issue before attempting this task.

TASK

From what you have learned so far about levels of response, create a list of points to go in a developed-level answer. Improve this further for a higher-level answer. You can then create writing frames and fully drafted answers for each.

Objective: To develop awareness of what will constitute a very good answer by gradually building up a response that is 'accurate, relevant and detailed knowledge used concisely to present a coherent and well-structured response to the task at a wide range or considerable depth; selecting the most important features for emphasis and clarity; using evidence to explain the key ideas; expressed cogently using technical language' (high level 4 descriptor AO1).

TOPIC 2: A STUDY OF ETHICAL DILEMMAS

Part 2C: A critical analysis of the issues

This means I am expected:

to analyse and critically evaluate:
- the different issues and questions raised by war
- the different issues and questions raised by sexual ethics
- some possible lines of argument.

TASK

Make your own list of questions that you would like to ask about the different issues involved in sexual ethics.
Objective: To encourage the use of questions in answers for AO2 that helps to demonstrate more than 'a mainly descriptive response, at a general level' (level 1 descriptor AO2) and aim for 'an attempt at an evaluation of the issue(s) raised in the task' (level 4 descriptor AO2).

1 Introduction

When critically evaluating the ethical issues studied, it is always useful to identify the strengths and weaknesses of each of the arguments that are put forward.

Generally, this involves highlighting the crucial points that support an issue and those that challenge it. The next stage is to decide which arguments are effective and which can be challenged. However, in terms of standardised strengths and weaknesses, there is little that can be written here because of the subjective nature of argument.

Remember that what one person views as a strength of an argument may well be seen as a weakness by another. Therefore, no official judgements are made here regarding the quality of the points put forward. That is for you to decide, after study, reflection and debate.

Each topic is presented with one or two points that support and one or two that challenge an issue. It is anticipated that you will use these as a base for further thought, analysis and argument.

2 War: the issues

a) Support

- War is an absolutely necessary evil. It is not entered into lightly and with close monitoring it is a means of protection and righting wrongs in the world.
- War is controlled (just war). We have advanced from the primitive approaches to conflict. War today is much more effective.
- We have to consider the reality of the situation and not just the ideals. The ideal is to have peace at all costs; the reality is that, due to aggressors, there is sometimes cause for self-defence and self-preservation.
- War saves lives in the long run and alleviates suffering. It frees the oppressed and is a step towards a world in which peace can be established in real terms.

b) Reject

- War is totally against the principles of rights to life and freedom. It is destructive and the 'good' at the end can never justify the catastrophic means used.
- History demonstrates the evils of war and, even to this day, we have not learned sufficiently to justify its continuance.
- The ideal of just war does not work and it is open to interpretation.
- Guidelines to a just war are vague and do not work in practice.

An eye for an eye just makes the whole world blind.

(Gandhi)

- Very simply, two wrongs do not make a right. Non-violence and pacifism can work.

3 Sexual ethics: the issues

a) Support for more freedom in sexual ethics

- There should be clear support for further freedom in sexuality issues. Human rights, not religious ideals, should be the deciding factor.
- There should be further change in the laws to accommodate human rights and freedoms.
- Issues such as homosexuality are clearly legal, they have been decriminalised.
- There is still debate over sexuality and sexual orientation – what is sexuality? Queer theory challenges traditional assumptions.
- There is a clear popularity of civil partnership and decline in choosing marriage to express relationships. This is compounded by the dramatic recent increase in divorce rates.

b) Campaign for restriction of freedom in sexual ethics

- The age of consent is too low.
- The issues concerning marriage, civil partnership and cohabitation are to do with changes and the laxity in the application of the law and the relative ease of getting divorced.
- Homosexuality – if it is considered morally wrong, should homosexual behaviour and expression only be allowed in private?
- Does homosexuality threaten stability of society, rights and freedoms of others?
- Consent issues are based entirely on whether one is rationally able to consent and do not take into account any long-term harmful psychological effects that may develop.

> **EXAM TIP**
>
> Always point out both specific and general reasons for the different responses to sexual ethics. Include some key questions and make sure that you offer more than one possible conclusion and then give your own, reasoned opinion, based upon what you have chosen to write about. This clearly is what a level 4 answer expects: 'a clearly expressed viewpoint supported by well-deployed evidence and reasoned argument' (level 4 descriptor AO2).

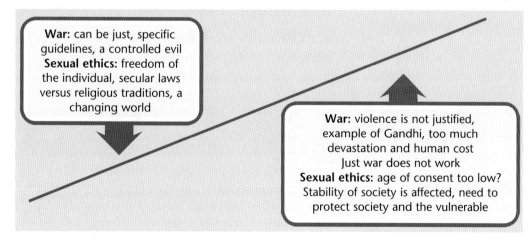

War: can be just, specific guidelines, a controlled evil
Sexual ethics: freedom of the individual, secular laws versus religious traditions, a changing world

War: violence is not justified, example of Gandhi, too much devastation and human cost
Just war does not work
Sexual ethics: age of consent too low? Stability of society is affected, need to protect society and the vulnerable

Summary diagram: Ethical dilemmas

Draw a table with the headings:
- **Religious views**   • **Other religious views**   • **The law**   • **My conclusion**

Try to complete the table by putting the appropriate evidence from the text on sexual ethics (using both AO1 and AO2 sections) into the relevant box.

Objective: To evaluate the different responses and to serve as a basis for your evidence to include in the writing frame at the end of this chapter. This meets the AO2 level 4 descriptor criteria of 'a careful analysis of alternative views...supported by well-deployed evidence'.

Reflection and assessment (AO2)

It is now time to channel the information you have considered in a more focused way. In order to do this, once again you need to ask yourself the question: 'How am I going to be assessed on my use of this information?'

The second way of being assessed is through assessment objective AO2. For this objective you need to be able to 'sustain a critical line of argument and justify a point of view'.

As you work through each unit in this book, you will find that the amount of support in these sections will gradually be reduced, in order to encourage the development of your independence and the honing of your AO2 skills.

Try using the writing frame provided below to help you answer this question.

> **Comment on the view that the just war is an effective means of solving conflicts.**
>
> (9 marks)

a) Writing frame

The issue for debate here is...

There are different ways of looking at this and many key questions to ask such as...

The just war theory involves a variety of thinkers, religious ideas, traditions and practices. We need to look at how people have reacted and used these principles throughout history.

Some ideas, however, are still debated today...

Despite this, another point of view would be that there is clarity to the just war and an argument for its necessity...

In light of all this, it could be argued that...

Nevertheless, it is my view that...

and I base this argument on the following reasons...

b) Suggestion for further application of skills

After completing the question, use the levels and AO2 descriptors to award marks out of 9. Identify strengths and areas for development in each answer. Now, as a group, collaborate to create an ideal answer that demonstrates an answer that displays 'some attempt to set out reasons for a range of views; a point of view expressed clearly, supported by relevant evidence' (level 3 descriptor AO2). Discuss what could make this answer show 'a careful analysis of alternative views; leading to a clearly expressed viewpoint supported by well-deployed evidence and reasoned argument' (level 4 descriptor AO2).

TOPIC 1: KEY ISSUES IN THE STUDY OF BUDDHISM

Part 1A: The historical, social and religious context for Buddhism

---

This means I am expected:

to know about the key issues:

- the life and work of the Buddha in its historical, religious and social context
- his significance for Buddhists

and to study:

- the Buddha and his immediate Indian context
- India at the time of the Buddha
- the identity of Hindusim
- Brahminism
- range of Samana groups such as Jains, Ajivakas, Materialists and Skeptics
- Siddhartha Gotama and Buddhist ideals.

In this book the evidence and examples given are relevant and appropriate because this material focuses only on the content for AO1 that is given by the Edexcel specification. The evaluation materials for AO2 will be aimed at helping you 'critically evaluate and justify a point of view through the use of evidence and reasoned argument'.

It would be helpful to write your notes using the headings listed above, as it is from these areas that the examination questions will be derived.

In your studies, remember that you have to bear in mind the **two** basic assessment objectives of:

- Knowledge and Understanding (AO1)
- Evaluation (AO2).

See pages 7–8 in the Introduction to remind yourself of these objectives.

The evaluation material set out in Part 1C (page 133) can be studied either alongside the AO1 material, as you work through this unit, or as a separate unit.

The study of Buddhism begins with the religious, social and historical context of the life and work of the **Buddha**, which has a wide range of implications for study. If you search on the internet for Indian religious life and belief at the time of the Buddha you will find a wealth of material. Such a vast task is clearly too challenging for AS level. It is important, therefore, to stay close to the unit content listed above.

 **KEY WORD**

Buddha: enlightened one; one who possesses insight into ultimate and perfect wisdom

KEY WORDS

Brahminism: religion based upon priestly practices and sacrifice
Vedas: written holy books
Brahmin: priest

KEY IDEA

Brahminism principles included:
- ritual and sacrifice
- Brahman and atman
- karma
- meditation.

KEY WORDS

Brahman: universal soul
Atman: individual soul
Samsara: cycle of life, death and reincarnation

1 The background to Buddhism

India at the time of the Buddha was very different from the India we know today. Modern India has a complex mixture of religious traditions with very different world-views. Within these world-views is a wide variety of cultural and regional differences that produce a diversity of religious expression.

At the time of the Buddha (c480–400BCE), the religious and philosophical ideas were no less complicated. Although Christianity, Islam and Sikhism were not yet founded, there were other religions and philosophies, some of which still exist in their original forms today. There would have been much questioning and debate, both within and between these philosophical and religious groups.

2 Hindu beliefs and practices

a) Brahminism

One particular expression of Hinduism from the time of the Buddha is often called **Brahminism**. Siddhartha Gotama, the Buddha, was born some time around 480BCE in the north-east of India, in the area surrounding the Ganges basin. Siddhartha was a member of a wealthy family, sometimes referred to as the local royalty, and would have been very familiar with the religious ideas of Brahminism.

b) What did Brahminism teach and how was it practised?

Brahminism was based on both written holy books (**Vedas**) and complicated rituals. These holy books were used to guide and give instructions for the performance of sacrificial rites that involved animals, and where the role of the **Brahmin** was vital. It was believed that prayers offered during the performance of the sacrifice satisfied the gods, so achieving the rituals' underlying purpose of retaining order in the Universe.

In early Indian religion, it was broadly assumed that there were three levels of existence, namely:

- the physical
- the spiritual
- the phonic (sound).

The physical level was represented by the sacrifice, the spiritual by the role of the priest and the phonic by the chanting of a prayer. It was believed that such a combination had the power needed to influence the Universe and maintain order.

Meditation was also a feature of Brahminism. At first, meditation was a preparation for the sacrifice. As Brahminism developed, meditation became a substitute for the sacrifice and was used as a means of mental focus or internalisation. The idea of the **Brahman**, the universal spirit, and the **atman**, the individual soul, became dominant in Indian thought, as did the notion of a continual round or cycle of reincarnations, known as **samsara**. The goal of practising religion was to advance through complex rituals and through meditation to achieve liberation from this round of reincarnation. It was believed that the soul then became united with the Brahman.

Finally, in Brahminism, there is the basic idea of **karma**, which was developed in later Indian thought. Although early Brahminism taught that religious ritual was the only means of achieving spiritual influence, it later embraced the idea that actions or karma beyond the sacrifice affected the reincarnation of the individual soul.

3 Other religious groups

a) Samana groups

As in any major religious tradition, there is always a wide variety of teaching and practice. At the time of the Buddha, these variations were fairly small. Some people, however, rejected Brahmanism completely. Those who did this were known as **Samanas**. They formed groups of wandering holy men or philosophers who were trying to find answers to ultimate questions. There are several examples of different types of Samana, including Jains, Ajivakas, Materialists and Skeptics. A summary of their beliefs and practices will help gain some insight into the Buddha's cultural and religious environment.

What did the Samanas believe and how did they practise?

Samanas rejected Brahminism because they disliked the social elitism of the Brahmins and the idea of ritual sacrifice. They were similar to the wandering holy persons of modern-day India. Like them, they cut all family ties and were dependent upon the general public for their food. Samanas were usually **ascetic** and practised very advanced forms of meditation, taking little sleep and very little food. It is often stated that Buddhism was originally a Samana movement, as the Buddha himself became a wandering holy man.

b) Jainism

Vardhamana the Mahavira or Great Hero was the first person to practise Jainism as an official philosophy and is often acknowledged as its founder.

Jains wearing breathing masks to avoid unintentionally harming airborne creatures

 KEY WORD

Karma: actions, good or bad, bring consequences and affect future lives

 KEY WORDS

Samana: a group of wandering holy men or philosophers who were trying to find answers to ultimate questions
Ascetic: living a very disciplined lifestyle

KEY IDEA

Samana movements:
- rejected Brahminism
- followed ascetic practices
- practised advanced meditation.

 KEY IDEA

Jains believe:
- in jiva (life essence) instead of atman (soul)
- karma imprisons the jiva
- jiva is released through severe discipline and meditation
- the goal is to get rid of the effects of karma.

What did the Jains teach and how did they practise?

Jain teaching accepted reincarnation and the idea of samsara but disagreed with traditional views on escaping the cycle of samsara. Crucial to this difference was its notion of karma.

Instead of the atman or soul, Jains believed in the existence of a life-essence called **jiva**. This is like an internal spark, energy or essence that runs through all living and non-living matter. The jiva is encased by karma that accumulates and leads to further reincarnation. The aim of the Jain practitioner is to free the jiva from the cycle of samsara in two ways:

- by following a very disciplined lifestyle involving **yoga** and very severe practices guided by the principle of **ahimsa** or non-violence towards any living being
- by wiping out any possible new karma, through a policy of non-action, and to wait for all previous karmic effects to take their course and die away.

c) Ajivakas

Makkhali Gosala was the famous leader associated with this Samana movement, although there are other leaders identified in the Buddhist writings.

What did the Ajivakas teach and how did they practise?

Gosala's major disagreement with other religious groups of the time was his outright rejection of the idea of karma. Instead, he replaced it with the idea of **niyati** or destiny. Every soul has its own, uniquely prescribed path that is already set out. Even the number of reincarnations has already been calculated. Therefore, the idea of karma becomes redundant.

In practice, the Ajivakas were similar to the Jains in that they also lived a life of strict discipline, even to the extreme of self-harming and starvation.

d) Materialists

The Buddhist writings identify two more influential groups that need to be considered briefly. The first of these were the Materialists.

What did the Materialists teach and how did they practise?

The Materialists, along with the other Samanas, rejected Brahminism. They did this not only because of dogmatic differences but because Materialists were **empiricists** and they rejected any ideas that were based upon non-empirical evidence. They regarded religious ritual as unreliable because they believed that its outcomes could not be tested. The ideas that they rejected included karma, reincarnation and the concept of a soul.

The main practice of a Materialist was to celebrate life and, although this can be done in many ways, they were generally encouraged to follow a noble and moral path.

e) Skeptics

Another group of Samanas was the Skeptics or 'eel-wrigglers', as Harvey describes them.

What did the Skeptics teach and how did they practise?

The Skeptics did not have any particular teaching or practice. Instead, they constantly weighed things up and seemed reluctant to reach conclusions. Despite arguing against the views and theories of others they remained 'devil's advocates' at all times, without commitment to any particular position.

4 Siddhartha Gotama and Buddhist ideals

The Buddha's teachings and practices shared common areas with those of all his immediate contemporaries. There were also some ideas that were shared with only certain groups, some that were taken from other teachings and modified, some that were rejected outright and new ideas that he developed himself.

TASK

Try to match the things the Buddha accepted, refined and rejected to the religious groups described on pages 117–18. This will give you a good overall picture. List, in table form, the religious groups down one side and the ideas across the top.

Objective: to differentiate accurately the Buddha's different responses to his immediate context. This demonstrates both 'a coherent and well-structured response to the task at a wide range or considerable depth' and also that you are 'selecting the most important features for emphasis and clarity; using evidence to explain the key ideas' (top level 4 descriptor AO1.)

a) What the Buddha accepted

- Samsara: the Buddha accepted the notion of an endless cycle of existences and also the possibility of **moksha**, which was escape from this cycle.
- Meditation: in keeping with all religious traditions of the time, the Buddha taught that realisation of truth was through meditation. However, he did not feel that extreme physical meditation worked and he rejected the idea of a personal union with an absolute power.
- Gods and goddesses: while the Buddha accepted the cosmology or theory of the Universe of the day, he felt that deities were still subject to samsara and therefore ignorant and in need of nirvana or **enlightenment**, which is ultimate wisdom. The concept of a supreme deity or creator God was not rejected outright, but it would be true to say that it was irrelevant to early Buddhism.

b) What the Buddha refined or modified

- Reincarnation: the Buddha taught **rebirth** and not reincarnation. Reincarnation requires some kind of soul or entity that is constant but simply takes on a different form. The Buddha did not accept the existence of such an elusive entity but favoured a passing on of energies from one form to another.
- Karma: the concept of karma was refined or even redefined to include thoughts as well as actions. According to Gombrich, karma became more precise and internalised.
- **Nirvana**: the Buddha accepted that escape from the cycle of samsara was possible. However, the Buddha's concept of nirvana superseded this. Some have described the Buddhist notion of nirvana as truly **ineffable**, it was impossible to put into words.

c) What the Buddha rejected

The Buddha firmly rejected belief in the atman and Brahman, jiva and niyati, the idea that we all have a permanent, eternal entity within us, whether it be a force, power or soul.

d) What was new about the Buddha's teaching?

Instead of accepting the idea of a soul, the Buddha observed that things were **anatta** or not-self, and that we could not identify any one thing within ourselves that we could call 'me'. This, as we shall later see, has far-reaching implications for the rest of Buddhist teaching.

EXAM TIP

It is important to be able to describe and explain the religious ideas at the time of the Buddha. However, it is even more important to be able to show how this influenced the Buddha. This means that you are both 'clearly identifying the most important features' and 'using evidence to explain key ideas; expressed accurately and fluently' (level 4 descriptor AO1).

KEY WORDS

Moksha: escape from the cycle of rebirth
Enlightenment: ultimate wisdom

KEY WORDS

Rebirth: the transfer of energies from one form to another
Nirvana (Pali: nibbana): enlightenment
Ineffable: indefinable, defying expression or description

KEY WORD

Anatta: the Buddhist observation that there is no 'soul'

5 Challenges to the traditional caste system

This was a developed urban culture. Mohenjo-daro and Harappa, separated by some 40 miles, were two of this civilisation's most important cities and housed some 40,000 inhabitants who enjoyed a high standard of living.
(Gavin Flood)

The Indus Valley Civilisation is supported by:
- archaeological evidence of a highly advanced society
- evidence of religious and social organisation.

Aryan: invader from the West of India referred to by their 'pale skins'

In order to look at the traditional caste system it is important to understand its origins in both the Indus Valley Civilisation and the subsequent Aryan Invasion.

a) The influence of the Indus Valley Civilisation c3000–1500BCE

Archaeological excavation uncovering the extent and structure of the Indus Valley civilisation

There is evidence of an advanced civilisation in the Indus Valley and Ganges basin, about 1000 years before the time of the Buddha. Two main cities, Mohenjo-daro and Harappa, which are famous archaeological discoveries of the last century, provide enough evidence to suggest the presence of a primitive water system, possibly including drainage and sewerage, and also baths, stone buildings and artefacts of religious significance. It is probable that these sites had a major influence on the surrounding areas, an impact that lasted through to the time of the Buddha (c480BCE) in terms of the continuity of religious practice, social structure and economy.

The civilisation seems to have come to an end a considerable time before the Aryan invasion; nevertheless, it is at least a possibility that some of the beliefs of these people lingered on in popular form, with elements eventually being absorbed into Hinduism alongside those inherited from the Vedas.
(Brockington)

b) The influence of the Aryan invasion

An invasion from the West began in around 1500BCE, just as the Indus Valley Civilisation was declining. The **Aryans**, as they were called, brought with them a society based heavily upon strict religious structures under the control of a priestly Brahmin group.

The religious writings of these invaders include the earliest of Hindu scriptures, the Vedas, and these are often associated with a class system that has, over the years, increased in complexity and developed into what is referred to as the jati (birth) or caste system in India today. Although it is now officially illegal to discriminate on grounds of caste or birth, at the time of the Buddha a basic caste system was in place.

Modern Hindus describe their **dharma** or faith in two ways:

- as the eternal way of life that is based on ethical principles such as truth and non-violence
- as a way of life based on social groupings and stages in life.

In Hinduism, dhamma has several levels of meaning. It can represent the law. It is mostly understood as social duty, but also can be used generally to mean teaching. An individual's personal duty is to follow the family code of religious and social practice. It is determined by their social classification and also their birth or the caste to which the family belongs. The Buddha was part of this social system.

At the time of the Buddha, Indian society had inherited this ancient culture of social order but was undergoing major expansion and change. In the area of India where the Buddha taught, there were 16 regions or countries, each of which was a developing urban centre.

> At the heart of these states appeared true urban centres where there had been none before. These swelling cities contained the kings' courts, and to the courts and cities were drawn the makings of an urban life: merchants and craftsmen with new skills, soldiers and labourers, conquered lords to render tribute, the displaced, the foreigners, the opportunists.
>
> (Carrithers)

c) The caste system and challenges to it

It is in the Hindu scripture known as the Rig-Veda that we find details of the caste system. Basically, the system comprises four social categories:

- Brahmin or priest
- Kshatriya or warrior
- Vaisya or business person, merchant, professional, skilled worker
- Shudra or labourer, unskilled.

The first three are deemed twice-born because they undergo a second spiritual rebirth when they take the sacred thread ceremony, one of the crucial rites of passage for a Hindu. The unskilled of society, however, are not twice-born and so cannot study the Vedas.

There were also many Indians who were outside the social system and these were known as outcastes or pariahs, translated as untouchables. These were people in a state of permanent spiritual pollution because of their birth and occupation. Gandhi renamed these people harijans, or the children of God, although today they prefer to call themselves dalits or the oppressed, rejecting Gandhi's label as they consider it to be patronising.

At the time of the Buddha, this system would have been both insular and exclusive and it would have been very difficult for people to change their circumstances in life. Gombrich explains the complementary roles of the highest two categories. Warriors were the rulers, responsible for good order in society. To maintain this order, sacrifices were necessary. These were performed by the priests but paid for by the warriors. Priests also depended on the rulers for their material support.

> This pair of complementary roles, patron and functionary, became the model for a wide range of social arrangements in traditional India.
>
> (Gombrich)

KEY WORD

Dharma (Pali: dhamma): basis of faith; the religious doctrine

KEY IDEA

Important features of the Aryan invasion include:
- earliest writings called the Vedas
- the idea of a 'caste' system
- the role of the priest (Brahmin).

KEY QUOTE

Above all the question was, how were the Indians to understand themselves among these unprecedented forms of common life?
(Carrithers)

The Buddha himself is thought to have belonged to the ruling class of warriors, from the Sakya peoples who were based around the Kapilavatthu area of modern-day Nepal.

Although it is not clear exactly what the role and status of women were at the time of the Buddha, it is probable that women had fewer rights than men.

Even though stories about the Buddha often associated him with people from the higher castes, he clearly rejected the idea of a caste system. Stories such as that of Kisa (a woman who had lost her child) and Angulimala (a detestable bandit and murderer) show that the Buddha saw his teachings as challenging the validity of the boundaries established by society.

6 Conflict between the Kshatriya and the Brahmin castes: authority and kingship

> **KEY QUOTE**
>
> *By ideology, of course, the Ksatriya [Kshatriya] ranks second, beneath the Brahmin. Yet he is the man with the real physical power, on whom even the Brahmin depends for his safety and physical welfare. The relations between Brahmin and ksatriya have always been somewhat ambiguous.*
>
> **(Gombrich)**

This social conflict in what had been established for years and the uncomfortable implications it brought with it meant that society in general was ripe for change and already questioning old traditions.

The Brahmins (priests) were at the top of this class system and led the people in the traditions of worship and social order. However, it was always the duty of the Kshatriya (warrior) class to fight for justice and protect the people in practical ways.

Over a period of time, and in the face of poverty, disease and neglect, the Kshatriyas challenged the authority and influence of the Brahmins. Uncomfortable tensions in the relationship between Brahmins and Kshatriyas emerged.

The Buddha, it is claimed, was himself from the Kshatriya class. During the time of the Buddha the tension between Brahmins and Kshatriyas was heightened. The Samana movement had brought a fresh challenge to Brahmins and there is evidence from Hindu writings that even kings were teaching the Brahmins' new religious ideas.

This tension reflected a struggle of minds, and it is no coincidence that the Buddha, as a Kshatriya, rejected the class system and the religious authority of the Brahmins.

> *However, the Sakyas considered themselves to have the effective rank of kings, nobles and warriors in respect of the wider civilisation, and indeed they probably did not recognise, as others did, the ceremonial precedence of Brahmins, priests of high rank.*
>
> **(Carrithers)**

Summary diagram: Social, historical and religious background

Reflection and assessment (AO1)

It is necessary to bring together the information that has been covered so far and to see how it can be transformed into effective examination-style revision and answers. The best way to do this is to ask the question: 'How am I going to be assessed on this information?'

The first way is through assessment objective 1 (AO1). For this objective you need to be able to 'select and demonstrate clearly relevant knowledge and understanding through the use of evidence, examples and correct language and terminology appropriate to the course of study' (descriptor AO1).

As the units in each section of the book develop, the amount of support will be reduced gradually in order to encourage your independence and the perfecting of your AO1 skills.

Try answering this question by using the writing frame below.

> **Outline the features of the religious context prior to the time of the Buddha. Examine their influence on the life of the Buddha.** **(21 marks)**

In answering this question, remember to match the correct teachings and practices to the appropriate groups. Relate these to what Buddha accepted, refined and rejected.

a) Writing frame

At the time of the Buddha there were a variety of religious ideas, traditions and practices. The most common form was...

The term Samana means...

A typical Samana group was the Jains who believed...

The Jains practised...

Another influencial group was the Ajivakas who taught...

The Ajivakas practised...

There were also the Materialists who taught...

Finally, the Skeptics believed ...

The Buddha would have considered all the above views.

Some he accepted, for example...

Others he rejected, for example...

Some he changed or refined slightly, for example...

b) Suggestion for further application of skills

After completing the question, use the levels and AO1 descriptors to award marks out of 21.

Identify strengths and areas for development in each answer. Then, as a group, collaborate to create an ideal answer that demonstrates:

● 'a coherent and well-structured response to the task at a wide range or considerable depth'
● 'selecting the most important features for emphasis and clarity'
● 'using evidence to explain the key ideas' (high level 4 descriptor AO1).

→ **EXAM TIP**

Always point out the variety of religious ideas. The AO1 descriptor demands at least 'accurate, relevant and detailed knowledge of the subject matter at a broad range or in sufficient depth' (low level 4 descriptor AO1).

FOUNDATIONS
Area C: Buddhism

TOPIC 1: KEY ISSUES IN THE STUDY OF BUDDHISM

Part 1B: The life and work of the Buddha and his significance for Buddhists

---

This means I am expected:

to know about the key issues:
● the life and work of the Buddha
● his significance for Buddhists

and to study:
● the birth and background of the Buddha
● the four signs
● ascetic practices
● the Buddha's enlightenment
● the Buddha's teaching: the middle way
● the nature of the Buddha's death.

➡ EXAM TIP

Do not answer a question on the life of the Buddha by simply 'telling a story'. Your answer should always select the key events, that is, the appropriate information relevant to the question. This demonstrates more personal understanding or 'ownership' of the knowledge; this demonstrates 'significant features explained for emphasis and clarity' which is awarded for higher level answers (level 3 and above descriptor AO1).

In this book the evidence and examples given are relevant and appropriate because this material focuses only on the content for AO1 that is given by the Edexcel specification. The evaluation materials for AO2 will be aimed at helping you 'critically evaluate and justify a point of view through the use of evidence and reasoned argument'.

It would be helpful to write your notes using the headings listed above, as it is from these areas that the examination questions will be derived.

In your studies, remember that you have to bear in mind the **two** basic assessment objectives of:

● Knowledge and Understanding (AO1)
● Evaluation (AO2).

See pages 7–8 in the Introduction to remind yourself of these objectives.

The evaluation material set out in Part 1C (page 133) can be studied either alongside the AO1 material, as you work through this unit, or as a separate unit.

The aim of this section is to present key events of the life of the Buddha. There are many stories surrounding the Buddha's birth and upbringing. It is only necessary to consider these briefly in order to be able to establish a context for the key events to be studied.

1 The birth and background of the Buddha

The Buddha was born as Siddhãrtha Gautama (Sanskrit) or Siddhattha Gotama (Pali), the son of a king. His destiny is a theme of the birth narratives and involves the relationship between holy men and the Kshatriya rulers. Seven holy men predicted that he would be a strong ruler, like his father. Another, called Asita, cried from happiness because he recognised him as the Buddha, and a final holy man, Kondanna, predicted that he would become a holy man and pursue the truth. The story continues that, to avoid this happening, the king had to ensure that the prince lived a life of absolute luxury that avoided any unpleasantness. In particular, four things were to be avoided.

2 The four signs

The four things to be avoided are known as the four signs or the four sights.

It was argued that, if the prince was kept away from these four things, then he would not waver from his path as future king and ruler. However, if the prince did encounter these signs, they would serve as a catalyst to stimulate a search for truth that would take Gotama on an alternative path as a wandering holy man.

Up until the age of 29, despite being surrounded by extraordinary levels of luxury and protection, Gotama's life was no more unusual than that of any other prince. He was married to **Yasodhara** at 16 and they lived within their palace grounds in relative calm.

The significant events that brought about change for Gotama, at the age of 29, involve excursions from the palace grounds with his charioteer, **Channa**.

The first sight was an old, weak man, bent over with age. The second sight was another man who had been ravaged by disease, existing as mere skin and bone with the very little strength in his body ebbing away. The third sight was one of grieving relatives carrying the corpse of their beloved on their shoulders in preparation for cremation.

The impact of such experiences was obviously heightened by the sheltered nature of the prince's life. It was his first understanding of the fact that he, like those he saw, was subject to the very same ravaging of time and nature and would ultimately die. This disturbed him and caused great anxiety. Why all this suffering?

Lastly, the sight that provoked the prince most deeply was a wandering holy man, walking calmly and contentedly in pursuit of truth and an answer to life's problems. This man was living a life of purity, in complete detachment from society. From where was his sense of peace derived?

66 KEY QUOTE

To be a renouncer was a young man's, indeed a romantic's, aspiration, and from this point of view the Buddha was but one of many youths who left home, attracted by the challenge of the wandering life.

(Carrithers)

99

On returning to the palace, and hearing the news that Yasodhara had just given birth to a son, **Rahula**, the prince felt even more tied by a new responsibility that bound him to his life as it was.

66 KEY QUOTE

His father provided him with the greatest comforts. He had, so the story tells, three palaces, one for each of the Indian year's three seasons. Lacking nothing of the earthly joys of life, he lived amid song and dance, in luxury and pleasure, knowing nothing of sorrow.

(Piyadassi Thera)

99

 KEY IDEA

The four signs are:
- old age
- sickness
- death
- a wandering holy man

 KEY PEOPLE

Yasodhara: Gotama's wife
Channa: Gotama's charioteer
Rahula: Gotama's son

Despite his family situation and his rich inheritance, the prince immediately sought freedom. He renounced his birthright. Shedding his rich clothes and long hair, he took on the mantle of a wandering holy man, with a simple bowl for food offerings and a single robe, and the thoughts:

> **66 KEY QUOTE**
>
> *Verily, this world has fallen upon trouble – one is born, and grows old, and dies, and falls from one state, and springs up in another. And from the suffering, moreover, no one knows of any way of escape, even from decay and death. O, when shall a way of escape from this suffering be made known – from decay and death?*
>
> (Eliade)

KEY PEOPLE

Alara Kalama: Gotama's first yoga teacher

Uddaka Ramaputta: Gotama's second yoga teacher

Sujata: the woman who revived Gotama with milk-rice

3 Ascetic practices

Gotama sought out two teachers, each renowned for their strict ascetic lifestyle and yogic practice.

The first was **Alara Kalama**, who trained Gotama in yoga. Soon Gotama had attained the same level of experience as his teacher: a state of nothingness. But this did not satisfy Gotama. He felt that desire, passion and attachments were not eradicated and that this method simply ignored them by taking an alternative route. Despite the fact that Kalama asked Gotama to become his teacher, Gotama moved on to find another way.

The second teacher was **Uddaka Ramaputta**. Similarly, mastery of Ramaputta's yoga led not to an awakening of truth or an enlightenment experience, but simply to a plane beyond nothingness referred to as neither perception nor non-perception. Such meditative states were later to become known as false states because they give an impression of awakening or enlightenment but are still far from it.

Whilst Gotama was experimenting with the two schools of yoga, the ascetic lifestyle began to take its toll. He had become so weak and thin that it is alleged that his backbone was visible through his stomach. At this point, after being revived with milk-rice by a woman called **Sujata**, Gotama decided to pursue an alternative lifestyle. Indeed, this was to be his last meal prior to enlightenment.

Carved rock image of meditating Buddha, prior to enlightenment, in Sri Lanka

4 The Buddha's enlightenment

Sitting beneath a Bodhi or Bo tree throughout the night, in a state of deep meditation, Gotama contemplated the nature of existence. Traditional Buddhist writings have vivid accounts of his religious experience that night. All centre around the process of meditation through levels of insight known as **dhyanas** (Pali: jhanas), before explaining how Gotama then encountered the ultimate experience known as nirvana (Pali: nibbana).

The first event was the temptation by the god, **Mara**, who challenged Gotama to abandon his quest. Earlier texts describe Mara encouraging Gotama to seek a more religious path of ceremony and good works in order to strengthen his karma. Gotama simply resisted and Mara vanished. Later texts give more detail, with Mara telling Gotama that no one could bear witness to his good works in previous lives and this one. But Gotama placed his hand to the ground and touched the Earth as a witness to his good works. This is often depicted in art and architecture as the Buddha sitting in a half-lotus (crossed-legged) meditation posture, with one hand in his lap and the other reaching out to touch the Earth as witness.

The second course of events was progression through the four dhyanas or meditative stages, also called absorptions. Each stage has a corresponding experience:

1 first dhyana – unbroken attention to the object of meditation, detached from the world and in a total state of calm

2 second dhyana – thoughts are discarded as detachment becomes more profound and a sense of joy: 'a state free from thought-conception and discursive thinking…which is born of concentration' (Nyanatiloka)

3 third dhyana – a state of equanimity, totally composed and with absolute attentiveness, but still clearly conscious

4 fourth dhyana – 'a state beyond pleasure and pain' (Nyanatiloka), indeed, beyond all sense of joy and thought construction, 'leaving a mind peaceful, tranquil, clear, a sharp tool ready to pierce into reality' (Cush).

There are also four other dhyanas, sometimes referred to as numbers 5–8, but usually they are all grouped under the fourth and are listed as distinct stages within the fourth state. Generally speaking, it is the fourth dhyana that tends to be seen as the most crucial stage.

The fourth dhyana also involves access to **meditative planes** (Carrithers) usually associated with Hindu yoga. Gotama had experienced these planes under his former teachers but was not satisfied. He felt that this was not the answer. At this stage of Gotama's experience, the fourth dhyana gave him further access to three significant insights beyond any that he had experienced before.

● The first was the elevated insight into his many previous lives throughout time.
● After this, he obtained pure observational insight of the plight of other beings tied to the world of rebirth. He had an objective overview of how the world of existence functioned in terms of birth, death and rebirth throughout the Universe.
● Finally, he went through the enlightenment experience, gaining insight into true and perfect wisdom of how the barriers to spiritual truth can be destroyed.

KEY WORD

Dhyanas: stages of meditation through which one passes to reach enlightenment

TASK

Design a flowchart to explain the process of the Buddha's enlightenment and surrounding events.
Objective: To demonstrate knowledge and understanding of the significance of the enlightenment illustrating 'accurate and relevant detail, clearly identifying the most important features' (level 4 descriptor AO1).

KEY PERSON

Mara: god who tempts people

KEY WORD

Meditative planes: specific states of mind, accessed through the fourth dhyana

Nirvana will be discussed later, but for now it can be understood as an experience that provided insight into the way things are in life but, more importantly, how to deal with them.

Gotama had now become the Buddha, the enlightened one or one endowed with wisdom. More accurately, he had achieved **samma-sambodhi**, or perfect enlightenment.

The Buddha had rejected both paths of extreme luxury and asceticism as neither could offer an answer to life's problems.

5 The Buddha's teaching: the middle way

The Buddha's first sermon, known as *The turning of the wheel of truth*, was in the Deer Park of Isipatana. It can be found in the **Dhamma Cakka Pavattana** Sutta (Pali) or Dharma Cakra Pravartana Sutra (Sanskrit). The original text was Pali.

This sermon is dated approximately seven weeks after his enlightenment. It is the first record of his public teaching about his experience. It was also given directly to his five former ascetic companions with whom he had practised such an extreme lifestyle. Indeed, it is said that the Buddha was reluctant to share his new knowledge before meeting up with his former companions. However, it was his former ascetic companions who, amazed at his peaceful countenance, suggested that he break his silence and explain what he had discovered.

He rejected both the life of luxury and the life of extreme asceticism for a more moderate path, which became known as the **middle way**.

For our purposes, it will be enough simply to outline his basic teachings that resulted from his enlightenment experience, as recounted in the Dhamma Cakka Pavattana Sutta.

It is important to point out that the teachings given were not truths in the sense that they were to become doctrine and to be believed. They were truths more in the sense of evident observations of the world around him. It is interesting to see that a recent translation by Harvey refers to the truths as realities, to try to avoid such confusion.

In this way, Buddhism immediately adopts an empirical approach to life. The teachings are a practical tool to use in a personal way, to seek to follow the same path as the Buddha. The best way to explain this is: 'Test, and see for yourself.'

The Buddha outlines the following truths or observations in the Dhamma Cakka Pavattana Sutta.

The two extremes to avoid are:

1 a lifestyle that is driven by sensual pleasure

2 a lifestyle intent on extreme asceticism to the extent of self-mortification.

If a middle way between these two extremes is taken then it will lead to knowledge, peace and the ultimate awakening of nirvana.

The practical way to apply the middle path is by following eight principles, known as the **eight-fold path**: right view, right directed thought, right speech, right action, right livelihood, right effort, right mindfulness and right concentration (see page 151).

There are four concepts that underpin this.

1   The truth of life is that it is a painful experience and full of suffering (**dukkha**). All aspects of life, no matter how pleasurable and attached to them we are, bring dukkha.

2   Craving (greed) and attachment are the cause of this painful experience.

3   The way to stop the suffering involved in life is to eliminate craving and attachment: 'the giving up and relinquishing of it, freedom from it, non-reliance on it.' (Harvey)

4   This is achieved by following the eight-fold path; suffering is eradicated and there is an experience of total freedom and enlightenment (nirvana).

These four principles are known as the **four noble truths**, the four holy truths or, as Harvey suggests, the four realities. In the Dhamma Cakka Pavattana Sutta, the Buddha continued to state how he had achieved the cessation of pain in his own life.

At this point, tradition holds that the holy beings from the heavens witnessed that the rediscovery of dhamma, the truth, in our world had been accomplished:

'At Baranasi, in the Deer Park at Isipatana, the unsurpassed Wheel (of Vision) of the Basic Pattern (of things) has been set in motion by the Blessed One, which cannot be stopped by any renunciant or brahman or mara or brahma or by anyone in the world.'

(Harvey)

After this experience, at which time he was 35 years old, the Buddha went on to deliver a ministry of teaching for a further 45 years. Thousands of people, from all walks of life, were converted to Buddhism, or the middle way, as it was known. His teachings and ministries can be found in the section of Buddhist scriptures known as the Sutta Pitaka (see below).

6 The nature of the Buddha's death

The most famous account of the Buddha's death can be found in the **Sutta Pitaka**, in a book called the **Maha-parinibbana Sutta** (Pali), belonging to the collection of writings from the **Digha Nikaya** 16. The account, originally in Pali, describes the last days of the Buddha before his **parinibbana**, when he passed over to nibbana. The Buddha died at the age of 80. We are interested in the nature of his death, rather than the events preceding it.

There are many theories concerning the specific cause of his death. First of all, it is argued that he predicted his own parinibbana three months earlier. The consensus is that the cause of death was an illness that developed after he ate some contaminated pork.

It is one view that the life story of the Buddha should be read as a teaching aid, it is the way the Buddha coped with his death experience that is of benefit to Buddhist insights.

The Master's parinirvana [parinibbana] is, therefore, the one sorrowful event in the history of Buddhism that turns out in its true meaning, to be really the most blissful.

(Sister Vajira)

The Maha-parinibbana Sutta describes the Buddha's death as taking place while he was in a state of meditation. After this, there were several extraordinary natural events, different emotional and non-emotional responses from the company of followers, a typical Indian funeral with an extraordinary twist and the distribution of the Buddha's remains. A brief summary of the nature of the Buddha's death follows.

 KEY WORDS

Dukkha: suffering
Four noble truths: the four teachings that explain the reality of our world

KEY WORDS

Sutta Pitaka: Second section of the Pali Canon
Maha-parinibbana Sutta: story of the death of the Buddha
Digha Nikaya: Section of the Sutta Pitaka
Parinibbana: passing over into nibanna [nirvana]

EXAM TIP

When answering a question on the life of the Buddha, you must focus on the area highlighted in the question. Make sure you pick out the key events and explain why they are important in relation to the Buddhist teachings. This means that it is not just a general answer that presents 'a limited range of isolated facts...with mainly random and unorganised detail' or 'information presented within a structure which shows a basic awareness of the issue raise' (level 1 and 2 descriptors AO1). Remember, you are aiming for 'a coherent and well-structured account of the subject matter' (level 4 descriptor AO1).

KEY WORD

Stupa: monument built as a memorial to the Buddha and usually containing parts of his remains

TASK

Draw up a lifeline of the Buddha's life, focusing on the cause of the problem he faced, the reaction to the problem and how he solved the problem.
Objective: To show knowledge and understanding of the significance of key events in the life of the Buddha, demonstrating 'evidence to explain key ideas' (level 4 descriptor AO1).

- The Buddha accesses the fourth dhyana and the associated meditative planes of infinite space, infinite consciousness, nothingness and the sphere of neither-perception nor non-perception.
- Ananda, the Buddha's devoted but unenlightened disciple, thinks that the Buddha has passed over at this stage. He is corrected by Anuruddha.
- The Buddha returns through the meditative planes and back through the dhyanas to the first dhyana, only to enter the process once again. When he reached the fourth dhyana the second time he immediately achieved parinibbana, passing over into nibbana.
- At the moment of the Buddha's parinibbana there was thunder and an earthquake.
- Holy beings spoke out and there were speeches given by his followers.
- His followers exhibited two types of reaction. The first was emotional, with demonstrations of grief and acts of remorse. This was from the followers who were not yet free from the attachment of passion. The second, more noble response, was more calm and reflective, with observations that all things are impermanent and so how could it be otherwise? Needless to say, when the local townsfolk of Kusinara were informed, their response was also emotional.
- For six days people paid homage to the Buddha's body with dance, song, music, flower-garlands and perfumes.
- On the seventh day the Buddha's body was prepared for cremation. A procession took the body to the place of cremation.
- A traditional cremation began with a problem over lighting the pyre. It would only light when a respected disciple, Maha Kassapa, had paid respects at the feet of the Buddha and then it did so of its own accord.
- Only the flesh was burned and there was no evidence of ashes at all from his body. The Buddha's bones remained untouched by flame.

The remains of the Buddha were distributed into eight portions and allocated to seven Kshatriya clans and one Brahmin, each of whom built a monument, called a **stupa**, around it as a memorial. The urn itself formed another stupa, and finally the ashes, presumably from the clothes, were the final memorial. These stupas were early places of pilgrimage for Buddhists.

It is evident, then, that the events involved in the actual parinibbana of the Buddha may not be actual, factual accounts but may be more a reminder of who the person of the Buddha was and what he taught in life.

Hagiography or events of religious significance: birth and myths → Four signs (sickness, old age, death, wandering holy man): the fourth stage of life, cutting all ties and following an ascetic way of life based in yoga → Enlightenment and insight into problematic nature of existence: the Deer Park sermon and the four noble truths → The Buddha's parinibbana: mythical materials and the beginnings of early devotion and Buddhology

Summary diagram: Key events in the life of the Buddha

Reflection and assessment (AO1)

It is now time to bring together the information asking the question: 'How am I going to be assessed on this information?'

The exam is marked in terms of levels. There is a description of the character and features for that level. Look back at pages 8–10 in the introduction to see these level descriptions for AO1.

Look at the following sample answer in response to this question.

> **Give an account of the central aspects of the life of the Buddha that are important for Buddhist teaching.** (21 marks)

Through examining the basic understanding of the life of the Buddha it is possible to see how his life did influence his teachings:

EXAM TIP

Exam questions are expressed in words that tell you what to do in your answer. For AO1 they are:

- Compare…
- Describe…
- Examine…
- Give an account of…
- How…
- Identify…
- Illustrate…
- In what ways…
- Outline…
- Select…
- What…?

Quote is not needed as it is not shown how it is relevant to the question. →

'All texts generally agree on the basic story of the Buddha's earthly existence.' (Pye)

This is because many of his experiences reflect his teachings and in particular the teaching of the 'Middle Way' are emphasised by discussing the Buddha as Gotama the prince and Gotama the ascetic. This is emphasised as it is a central doctrine in Buddhism and it would therefore seem logical. The four sights are also important as they not only act as a catalyst for Gotama's religious 'quest' but also raise the fundamental problem of suffering which the Buddha addresses and attempts to eradicate in his teachings.

← *Good point although more explanation of what the 'middle way' is could be given.*

Explain how this served as a 'catalyst' by making the Buddha reflect upon suffering and impermanence. →

It could be argued that the story of the life of the Buddha is only an effective teaching device as the events in his life deal with the principle teachings found in Buddhism and provide a reason why and how they were derived:

'I have conquered all; I know all; and my life is pure. I have left all, and I an free from craving. I myself found the way.' (Dhammapada v.353)

The story of the Buddha's life is important and useful as it encourages people from a variety of backgrounds to follow the Buddhist path, as the Buddha was a symbol of human potential. However, when addressing the question as to what extent his life influenced his teachings, it would be difficult to assess as many would argue that the teachings were formed first so therefore should it be asked whether his teachings influenced his life story?

← *This conclusion does not follow from the above argument. The answer needs more examples of how his life reflects his teaching.*

b) So what would this answer score?

This is where level descriptors are referred to and parts of essays are related to the levels.

In the exam the answer will be marked according to levels (see page 8). There is certainly knowledge and understanding shown in this answer. The writer clearly has an understanding of the key events in the Buddha's life and some understanding of his teaching. So the answer is at least a level 2 (a basic awareness of the issue raised).

However, it is not a well-organised account and it is limited in its explanation and selection of relevant material. For example, it does not explain any of the teachings of the 'middle way' in any detail.

Despite this, there is some signs of understanding in how the answer actually relates the 'middle way' to the Buddha's experience of life.

It does not qualify as a good attempt to address the question ('a coherent and well-structured account of the subject matter, with accurate and relevant detail, clearly identifying the most important features', level 4). However, there is some attempt to answer the question and it therefore scores a level 2.

c) Suggestion for further application of skills

Use the points identified above to redraft this answer. Copy it to obtain a text version, then delete material as appropriate, expand on the points that are undeveloped and add in other possible points that could have been included. You can do this in pairs, groups or individually but it is important to discuss and compare possible answers. You could even start afresh, listing with points, then create a writing frame and complete the answer as a class.

This will help to improve a level 2 response and transform it into a level 4 response so that it demonstrates 'a coherent and well-structured account of the subject matter, with accurate and relevant detail, clearly identifying the most important features' (level 4 descriptor AO1).

FOUNDATIONS
Area C: Buddhism

TOPIC 1: KEY ISSUES IN THE STUDY OF BUDDHISM

Part 1C: Influence of society on the Buddha and his teachings

---

This means I am expected:

to analyse and critically evaluate:

- how the Buddha related to his immediate social and religious background
- how the Buddha reacted against society's influences
- possible conclusions.

---

1 How the Buddha related to his immediate social and religious background

The Buddha was certainly influenced by the social organisation and religious structure that had been established in previous eras and were still operating in his time. The Buddha worked his way through the traditional Indian four stages of life, was part of the social structure, defined by the caste system, as part of the privileged warrior or ruler class. He was familiar enough with Brahminic rites and rituals to be able to reject them in an informed manner.

The Buddha was a beneficiary of all that was best from the Indus Valley Civilisation and the Aryan culture that followed it. He had the benefit of a privileged life with a very rich culture. He did not have to work for a living and had leisure enough to pursue a life of contemplation.

As for the social organisation of his day, the Buddha was brought up as a typical Hindu. The idea of seeking one's own truth was becoming very much part of the religious and philosophical practice at the time. It was almost a social pastime. The Buddha's wealthy background protected him from the experience of poverty, disease and related aspects of human suffering.

The immediate poverty, disease and squalor of some of the less fortunate people around him would naturally have provoked thoughts about social justice and would have influenced his religious and philosophical thinking.

This leads into the complex nature of the religious ideas at the time. Buddhism shares some common ideas with other contemporary religious traditions.

In general terms, it is clear how the Buddha took a very familiar pathway of the time to investigate religious truths. He became an ascetic and cut off all family ties, as the fourth stage of Hindu tradition demands. He sought religious teachers of the day in order to learn advanced meditation practices. In all this there is nothing new.

TASK

Compile a list of questions that you would like to ask about how the Buddha related to or reacted against his immediate historical, social and religious context.

Objective: To encourage the use of questions in answers for AO2 that helps to demonstrate more than 'a mainly descriptive response, at a general level' (level 1 descriptor AO2) and aim for 'an attempt at an evaluation of the issue(s) raised in the task' (level 4 descriptor AO2).

? KEY QUESTIONS

- Was the Buddha simply a product of his religious, social and historical context?
- Was the Buddha really as radical in his views as some may think, or was he really one of many similar thinkers of the time?
- How far did the Buddha's privileged upbringing and social position determine his eventual thirst for answers to the questions of life?
- Is there anything unique about the Buddha's ideas?
- Was the religion established by the Buddha different from ideas at the time?
- Did the Buddha rebel against any of the social and historical conventions of the time?
- If the Buddha was 'original', then which ideas show this?

When we consider such ideas as samsara (the process of living several lives, based on the principle of karma and the acceptance of several levels of existence involving deities) then, once again, we can see that there is much in common with other religious thinking of the time. This gives rise to several key questions.

2 How the Buddha reacted against society's influences

In addition to how the Buddha's teaching reflected the religious teaching of the time, there is another area to consider when assessing the originality of the Buddha's teaching. The way in which the Buddha reacted to his immediate background shows that his teaching is distinct and often unique.

For example, although the Buddha was brought up within a rich historical heritage, he actually rejected this in favour of a society that was looking for change and new answers to old questions. Similarly, the ideal of the extreme practices of the wandering holy man and the stages of life became almost superfluous in his teaching and his establishment of the middle way. More obviously, the Buddha rejected the Vedic religious system in favour of a new, less rigid and more individualistic practice.

Despite being part of it, the Buddha rejected the caste system. He is often depicted in art as the teacher with an open hand. Also, his view of women was atypical and probably socially unacceptable.

As far as the Buddha's religious ideas are concerned, there was something original in anatta, or not-self, that can be found in no other tradition of the time. Additionally, as indicated earlier, the Buddha's originality was characterised by the way in which he refined or changed ideas such as karma and rebirth. The Buddha's practice of meditation was also very different. Again, this provokes key questions.

3 Possible conclusions

TASK

Draw a table like this to show the Buddha's response to his background.

Factor	Buddha responded positively to	Buddha reacted against
Religious		
Social and historical		
Life events		
My conclusion		

Objective: To summarise the Buddha's response to his background. This could serve as a basis for your evidence to include in the writing frame at the end of this chapter. This meets the AO2 level 4 descriptor criteria of 'a careful analysis of alternative views... supported by well-deployed evidence'.

In addressing the key questions of how far the Buddha was a product of his environment, or to what extent the Buddha was a reactionary or even an original thinker, it is important to reflect upon the arguments previously discussed, to draw appropriate conclusions.

You might accept none of those listed below, one of them, some or possibly all – and you may even have your own. However, what matters is the way in which you arrive at your conclusions. Use the arguments from the previous paragraphs to weigh up and balance your thoughts and provide evidence for your decision.

From the previous discussion, here are some possible conclusions.

1 The Buddha shares some of the Indian ideas of the time. These were by no means exclusively Hindu in the usual understanding of the word. They were more typical of the Indic way of life. In this way, the Buddha may have been influenced by religious, social and historical factors but we should not in any way relate these to Hinduism in its strict form.

2 Alternatively, we could say that these common ideas are shared by, and are today identified with, popular Hinduism. In that case, we can clearly argue that the Buddha was influenced by both the history and ideas of Hinduism.

3 Buddhism is original because it not only displays many unique features, it is also very different in its interpretation of some key ideas.

4 The social and historical environment, the mixture of the extremes of pleasure and pain, social injustice and the failure to find a soul all served as a catalyst for the Buddha's response. This response was unique.

5 The unique nature of Buddhism developed later, after the time of the Buddha. Based on the evidence given above, it would have been hard to recognise the Buddha and his teachings as original. The complexity of the ideas and the impact of a changing society make it impossible to distinguish between Buddhism and the ideas of the time.

> **→ EXAM TIP**
>
> Always point out how the Buddha both related to and reacted against his background. Include some key questions and make sure that you offer more than one possible conclusion and then give your own, reasoned opinion, based upon what you have chosen to write about. This clearly is what a level 4 answer expects – 'a clearly expressed viewpoint supported by well-deployed evidence and reasoned argument' (level 4 descriptor AO2).

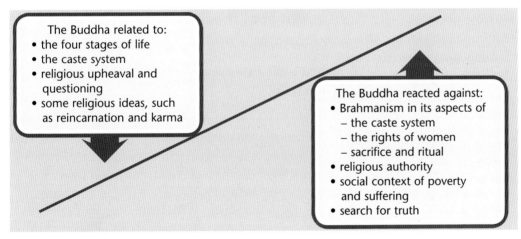

The Buddha related to:
• the four stages of life
• the caste system
• religious upheaval and questioning
• some religious ideas, such as reincarnation and karma

The Buddha reacted against:
• Brahmanism in its aspects of
  – the caste system
  – the rights of women
  – sacrifice and ritual
• religious authority
• social context of poverty and suffering
• search for truth

Summary diagram: How the Buddha reacted to his background

Reflection and assessment (AO2)

It is now time to channel all this information in a more focused way. Again the key question is: 'How am I going to be assessed on my use of this information?'

The second way of being assessed is through assessment objective AO2. For this objective you need to be able to 'critically evaluate and justify a point of view through the use of evidence and reasoned argument'.

a) Exam practice

As the units in each section of the book develop, the amount of support will be reduced gradually in order to encourage your independence and the perfecting of your AO2 skills.

Try using the writing frame provided below to answering this question.

> **To what extent did the religious, social and historical context at the time of the Buddha influence his life and work?** (9 marks)

b) Writing frame

The issue for debate here is...

There are different ways of looking at this and many key questions to ask such as...

At the time of the Buddha there were a variety of religious ideas, traditions and practices. We need to look at how the Buddha reacted to these. For example, it can be argued that he was influenced by certain key ideas from his religious, social and historical context such as...

Some ideas, however, he rejected outright such as...

Despite this influence, another point of view would be that he introduced unique ideas and practices such as...

In light of all this, it could be argued that...

Nevertheless, it is my view that...

and I base this argument on the following reasons...

Suggestion for further application of skills

After completing the question, use the levels and AO descriptors to award marks out of 9. Identify strengths and areas for development in each answer. Then, as a group, collaborate to create an ideal answer that demonstrates at least 'some attempt to set out reasons for a range of views' and 'a point of view expressed clearly, supported by relevant evidence and argument' (level 3 descriptor AO2).

Discuss how this answer could be improved to show 'a careful analysis of alternative views...leading to a clearly expressed viewpoint supported by well-deployed evidence and reasoned argument' (level 4 descriptor AO2).

TOPIC 2: KEY EMPHASES IN TEACHING AND PRACTICE

Part 2A: The three refuges, meaning and significance

This means I am expected:

to know about the key emphases:
- the three refuges
- their meaning and significance

and to study:
- the three refuges
- the Buddha and his status
- the different aspects of dhamma
- the sangha
- the role of the four-fold sangha.

In this book the evidence and examples given are relevant and appropriate because this material focuses only on the content for AO1 that is given by the Edexcel specification. The evaluation materials for AO2 will be aimed at helping you 'critically evaluate and justify a point of view through the use of evidence and reasoned argument'.

It would be helpful to write your notes using the headings listed above, as it is from these areas that the examination questions will be derived.

In your studies, remember that you have to bear in mind the **two** basic assessment objectives of:

- Knowledge and Understanding (AO1)
- Evaluation (AO2).

See pages 7–8 in the Introduction to remind yourself of these objectives.

The evaluation material set out in Part 2C (page 158) can be studied either alongside the AO1 material, as you work through this unit, or as a separate unit.

This section examines some key emphases in Buddhist teaching and practice. It begins with the central focus of Buddhism, namely, the three refuges and takes a look at how these impact upon Buddhist life. Meditation is then examined in terms of the types and purposes while considering their context and application.

KEY WORDS

Sarana: refuge, of which there are three for a Buddhist – Buddha, dhamma and sangha
Sangha: the community of Buddhist monks, nuns and lay people
Ti-ratana: the three jewels, another term for the three refuges

66 **KEY QUOTE**

One of the most remarkable differences between the Pali and the Sanskrit, that is, between the Hinayana and the Mahayana Buddhist literature, is the manner of introducing the characters of persons who take principal parts in the narratives. In the former, sermons are delivered by the Buddha as a rule in such a natural and plain language as to make the reader feel the presence of the teacher...while in the latter generally we have a mysterious, transcendent figure, more celestial than human, surrounded and worshipped by beings of all kinds...
(Suzuki)
99

KEY WORD

Samma-sambuddhasa: the perfectly self-enlightened one

1 The three refuges

a) The meaning of refuge

Although **sarana** is translated directly as refuge, this interpretation needs some consideration. Refuge is associated with a calm, safe environment, away from attack. In a sense, this is true of sarana. It is a place away from the unwholesome nature of the world in its entirety. However, this understanding does not accentuate the positive aspect of refuge. For a Buddhist, the idea of a refuge relates to Buddha, dhamma and **sangha**. It is not a place to hide away and cower from outside attacks. A refuge is a centre of excellence in spiritual terms. It is a place to gain strength, to be rebuilt and refreshed. It is a place to be purified and transformed. This latter understanding is by far the more accurate in terms of Buddhist practice.

The three refuges are also called **ti-ratana** or the three jewels, such is their importance in Buddhism.

b) The inter-relation of the three refuges and how they might be applied in practice

In practice, the most famous application of the refuges is the chant that takes place as part of formal dutiful monastic procedure:

- *Buddham saranam gacchami*
- *Dhammam saranam gacchami*
- *Sangham saranam gacchami.*

Simply translated, this means:

- I go to the Buddha for refuge
- I go to the dhamma for refuge
- I go to the sangha for refuge.

It is a profession of faith. It is a crucial psychological reminder and focus for Buddhist practice. It is seen as an essential mental preparation for meditation and walking the path that the Buddha taught.

There are variations within different traditions of Buddhism in respect of how the words of the chant are both used and understood.

2 The Buddha and his status

The Buddha is seen as a teacher, the awakened or enlightened one. In Theravada, or traditional Buddhism, the Buddha is understood to be a human being and not a divine being. He is a figure whose words offer guidance and who is given respect for what he has achieved.

Buddhists pay devotion to, admire and respect the person of the Buddha; they do not worship him. The life of the Buddha is an example for others to follow. It is an example of how, from the human condition, enlightenment can be realised. The Buddha is a role-model for inspiration. The Buddha was special since he was unique in this world. He is **samma-sambuddhasa**, the perfectly self-enlightened one. The ability to rediscover the dhamma and self-enlightenment is what specifically makes one a Buddha. The Buddha's life illustrates the fundamental teachings of Buddhism.

For example:

- his discovery of a middle way between two extremes of living
- the insight provided by the four sights into the plight of the human condition
- the path away from suffering, the eight-fold path
- the diagnosis of the four noble truths
- the way of mindfulness and meditation.

This can be related to the idea that the life story of the Buddha is not intended to be a factual, historical account, but more a **hagiography** or a religious or spiritual biography, to inform the followers of a particular path.

a) The status of the Buddha

i) Differing attitudes to the Buddha in Theravada and Mahayana Buddhism and the status of the Buddha

In Theravada Buddhism there is generally a rational view of the Buddha. He was human, the samma-sambuddha or self-enlightened one. He is revered for his wisdom and for the role model he provides.

Theravadins take literally his command: 'work out your own salvation with diligence'; they are to take refuge in the dhamma and test it for themselves. There is no dependence upon the Buddha as a vehicle for salvation or enlightenment. Gombrich refers to Theravada as a **soteriology**; it is a personal religious quest, with no god-figure.

Despite this, the human-ness of the Buddha does not mean that **supramundane** powers were not possible. Indeed, the Theravada scriptures reveal a teacher with some remarkable abilities. Some put these incidents, such as the birth narratives, down to legend and dispense with them. Others may explain them in terms of the Buddhist **abhinnas**, supernatural powers developed through high states of meditation. Mahayana Buddhism overtly plays down the historical aspects of the Buddha.

As Suzuki writes:

> …the Buddha in the Mahayana scriptures is not an ordinary human being walking in a sensuous world.

Mahayana Buddhism emphasises the transcendent aspect of Buddha in all his glory. The Buddha was not just human but also has heavenly manifestations and ultimate expressions. In line with this, the idea about the three bodies of the Buddha developed.

KEY WORDS

Hagiography: a spiritual or religious biography
Soteriology: a personal religious quest
Supramundane: paranormal or extraordinary powers
Abhinnas: supra-mundane powers
Bodhisattva: literally, 'a being whose essence is wisdom', generally understood as one who is on the path to enlightenment

The Buddha in his sambhogakaya, surrounded by **bodhisattvas**

KEY WORDS

Trikaya: three bodies
Buddha ksetra: Buddha
field or Universe
Nirmanakaya:
transformation body
Sambhogakaya:
enjoyment body
Dhammakaya: ultimate
body of truth

TASK

Find some examples of different Buddhas and bodhisattvas. Create a brief character profile for each one.
Objective: To demonstrate understanding of the complexity of the ways in which the Buddha is viewed, his status and nature (Buddhology) within Mahayana Buddhism and to show that you are 'selecting the most important features for emphasis and clarity' (level 4 descriptor AO1).

KEY WORD

Pali Canon: the
Buddhist scriptures

ii) The trikaya doctrine

The **trikaya** doctrine is the idea that there are three manifestations, planes of existence or modes of perception from which the Buddha operates. In Mahayana Buddhism there is a multitude of Universes each with its own Buddha, residing in the **Buddha ksetra** (Buddha field) or personal Universe. Gotama Buddha resides in this Universe. Another Universe is in Pure Land Buddhism where Amida Buddha, or Amitabha, resides to welcome those that wish to be reborn there. There are, of course, many more examples.

Each Buddha, then, has trikaya or three bodies of expression:

- **nrmanakaya** or transformation body: a kind of semi-physical body in which a Buddha appears in samsara
- **sambhogakaya** or enjoyment body: a body for the heavenly realms. In this form the Buddha appears to bodhisattvas in his Buddha ksetra, the Buddha Universe
- **dhammakaya** or dhamma body: the ultimate body that is beyond existence. It is also beyond all dualities and conceptions. It neither exists nor does not exist. It is ultimate truth and reality.

The first two bodies are temporal existences whereas the third is the ultimate body. The former two bodies, as all beings, are a partial manifestation of the ultimate dhamma body:

Though they are conceived as three, they are in fact all the manifestations of one Dhammakaya.

(**Suzuki**)

3 The different aspects of the dhamma

The dhamma as a whole is the teaching of the Buddha, later to become the **Pali Canon**. It therefore can refer to the basic teachings as expounded in the Dhamma Cakka Pavattana Sutta or to the whole extent of the Buddhist traditional writings.

The Pali Canon of scriptures consists of three sections, called pitakas, which is literally translated as 'baskets':

- the Vinaya Pitaka, including the rules for discipline in a monastic setting (see page 144)
- the Sutta Pitaka, the writings that describe the teaching in the context of the life of the Buddha
- the Abhidhamma Pitaka, a later philosophical section (the content of which varies according to schools of Buddhism).

a) The development of the written dhamma

Throughout the ministry of the Buddha, there were often points of misunderstanding or conflict among his followers. The Buddha's cousin, Devadatta, was a constant critic of the Buddha and often led splinter groups away from his following. This is not an unfamiliar practice in the Samana tradition. Even the Buddha himself broke away from his teachers to form his own group. Most issues associated with early points of conflict and discussion were addressed by the Buddha personally.

It is no surprise, then, to see that after the death of the Buddha there was immediately dispute. From the description given in the Maha-parinibbana Sutta, the monk Subhadda was recorded to have said that, with the Buddha gone:

…now we shall be able to do as we wish, and what we do not wish, that we shall not do.

(**Vajira and Story**)

It was in response to such attitudes as this that many of the early monks felt that there was a need to gather, with the purpose of consolidating the teachings of the Buddha and also the rules for practising the middle way. A set code of conduct for the sangha could then be established. These decisions were made at gatherings known in Buddhist history as the councils.

b) The three Buddhist councils

There were three very important councils that influenced the course of early Buddhism. No doubt there were many such gatherings throughout this early period but these three are recognised as being the most significant.

1   The first council, led by Kassappa and held in Rajagaha, is believed to have established orally the discipline (for the first part of the Pali Canon) and the teachings of the Buddha (for the second part of the Pali Canon).

2   The second council was where issues of interpreting the Vinaya code were discussed and there was a disagreement between two groups of monks, the Mahasanghikas and the Sthaviravadins.

3   The third council was where the dispute over applying monastic rules continued; a split in the sangha occurred at this point (if it had not done so already at the second council) between the Mahasanghikas and the Sthaviravadins who both went and practised in their separate ways.

By the time of the third council, the content of the code for practising Buddhism was probably finalised. This part of the dhamma is known as the Vinaya.

Much emphasis is given to practising the dhamma. Buddhism is empirical in nature and, in this sense, everyone has to work out their own path.

c) The contents of the Vinaya

Traditionally, the contents of the Vinaya are the 227 **patimokka** or rules that deal with eight types of behaviour for monks and nuns. While they may appear negative, in terms of outlining how to deal with offences, the overall purposes of patimokka are positive and attempt to guide someone back to the right path.

The section of the Vinaya containing the patimokka is specifically directed towards the individual and is known as the **Sutta Vibhanga**.

There is also an additional Bhikkhuni Vibhanga that deals with rules specifically directed towards nuns. Matters covered include:

● offences that require expulsion from the sangha (sex, theft, murder and lying about spiritual achievements)
● rules that require either expiation or confession
● legal matters
● etiquette and general behaviour.

There are, however, two more important aspects of the Vinaya.

The second section is the **Khandhaka**, which deals with overall organisation of the sangha. It is a document of rulings that apply to the collective sangha and covers practical aspects of living as a community under the guidance of the Buddha's teachings. It is

Mahavagga: first section of the Khandhaka
Cullavagga: second section of the Khandhaka
Parivara: the final section of the Vinaya Pitaka that summarises all the Vinaya for the purpose of teaching monks and examinations

 **KEY QUOTE**

It [Vinaya] provides a complete way of life, a rule of conduct, for monks, nuns, novices; the general principles are never lost sight of, and they provide a means of generating a host of detailed, particular prescriptions.'
(Gombrich)

 EXAM TIP

Always remember to point out the historical evidence for the development of Buddhism as a starting point. How do we know of the early practices of the sangha? What evidence do we have of the teachings of the Buddha? This ensures that you are 'selecting the most important features for emphasis and clarity' (level 4 descriptor AO1) rather than presenting a descriptive or 'a simple structure' (level 2 descriptor) for your answer.

split into the **Mahavagga**, dealing with guidance on organisation, and the **Cullavagga**, covering procedures for matters associated with formal discipline. Issues covered include:

- admission to the sangha
- reciting of the patimokka
- residence during the rainy season
- ceremony codes
- dress and diet codes
- sickness
- disagreements
- probation of monks and nuns
- settling legal matters
- accounts of the first and second councils.

The final section of the Vinaya is the **Parivara**. This is a summary and classification of all rules but is arranged so that it can be recited. It is often used for teaching or examination of Buddhist monks and nuns.

 **EXAM TIP**

Always remember to show that you understand the sections of the Vinaya in relation to what they contain. Avoid listing contents in your answer, but be selective. Explain how the different sections are linked to different audiences, with a focus on how to prevent a breach of discipline (patimokka) and not only with how to deal with such breaches by the sangha as a whole (Khandhaka). This demonstrates that you are 'selecting the most important features for emphasis and clarity' and also 'using evidence to explain the key ideas' (level 4 descriptor AO1).

4 The sangha

The sangha is the Buddhist community. The term is used in different ways but, in terms of refuge, it refers to the Buddhist community in its wider sense. The purpose of the sangha as a refuge is for training. This can take place either in a group or within a more formal setting, for example, a monastery.

The aim of the sangha is to follow the path that the Buddha taught and to gain help and assistance from others. It is the gathering of like-minded people for encouragement, each with the common goal of nirvana.

There is a famous parable that the Buddha taught about an elephant that belonged to a king. The elephant was of exceptional character, calm and friendly. However, the king noticed the elephant's character changing. The elephant became irritable, prone to tempers and more difficult. Eventually the problem was identified. A group of criminals was meeting at the elephant's stable. The elephant was clearly picking up characteristics of the people it was spending time with. The criminals were removed and, in time, the elephant rediscovered its old character.

The idea of refuge in the sangha can be compared to this. A person will develop characteristics from those people with whom they interact. The sangha therefore is a place of positive, wholesome activity, with people who will help and not hinder spiritual progress.

5 The role of the four-fold sangha

The four-fold sangha comprises the different categories of members within the Buddhist community. A simple statement of this would be that it includes

- monks (**bhikkhus**)
- nuns (**bhikkhunis**)
- lay-men (**upasakas**)
- lay-women (**upasikas**).

There are more complicated issues, other than gender, in what precisely differentiates a monk from a lay-person, and also the varying degrees of status within each category.

The Edexcel Specification suggests a case study of a monastery in a Buddhist country. The information below is generic for the Theravada tradition of Buddhism and can be related to, or followed up by, reference to countries such as Sri Lanka, Burma, Thailand or even case studies in Britain, such as Ratnagiri and Amaravati.

KEY QUOTE

> *The relations between the sangha and their lay supporters were conceived as reciprocal generosity: the sangha gave the dhamma, the laity gave material support, rather disparagingly termed 'raw flesh'.*
>
> (Gombrich)

a) The status and role of the laity and the relationship between the monastic sangha and the laity

The monastic sangha and the lay community have always had a relationship of interdependence.

The monastery serves the community and, in return, the laity form the economic base of monasticism through alms, land donations, labour and service within the monastery.

At times, the balance has needed to be redressed. For example, in the history of Sri Lanka the king has periodically reclaimed land from the sangha. In general, however, the relationship has been a happy one of willing and mutual-interdependence.

b) The ethical principles and practices for monks and lay people

The major ethical principles for a Buddhist beyond the Vinaya can be found in the five precepts that they take on and adhere to in practice. These are not commandments but serve as vows and form a very powerful and personal vehicle of spiritual motivation. They can be adapted to different levels of commitment, unlike commandments or rules.

For a lay Buddhist there are five such precepts. Each precept is a personal vow to abstain from negative action that is contrary to Buddhist principles.

All Buddhists undertake to refrain from:

1 harming living beings

2 stealing

3 misconduct of the sense-pleasures

KEY WORDS

Bhikkhus: Buddhist monks
Bhikkhunis: Buddhist nuns
Upasakas: lay-men
Upasikas: lay-women

KEY QUOTE

> *It is possible, I think, to identify four particular concerns in the Buddhist monastic rule as set out in Vinaya:*
> *(1) the unity and cohesion of the sangha,*
> *(2) the spiritual life,*
> *(3) the dependence of the sangha upon the wider community, and*
> *(4) the appearance of the sangha in the eyes of that community.'*
> (Gethin)

TASK

Draw a diagram that demonstrates the links between each of the three refuges outlined in this section.

Objective: To demonstrate ability to demonstrate the inter-relatedness of these teachings and demonstrate 'detailed knowledge of the subject matter at a wide range or in significant depth' (level 4 descriptor AO1) as opposed to simply 'very broad and unfocused generalisations' (level 1 descriptor) or an answer that is 'limited in scope' (level 2 descriptor AO1).

Buddhist monks preparing for the alms round

KEY IDEA

The five precepts, by which all Buddhists undertake to refrain from:

1 harming living beings
2 stealing
3 misconduct of the sense-pleasures
4 lying or false speech
5 using intoxicants.

KEY IDEA

Monastic possessions: robes; alms bowl; needle; rosary beads; a razor; a belt; a staff; filter to remove creatures from drinking water. Extras today are for practical reasons and may include: sandals, towel, extra work robes, a shoulder bag, an umbrella, writing materials, books, clock and a picture of a teacher.

KEY WORD

Poverty: living a simple life with basic needs

---

4 lying or false speech

5 using intoxicants.

For a monk and nun there are a further five. They undertake to refrain from:

6 eating after midday

7 dancing, singing, music and shows

8 wearing garlands, scents, cosmetics and adornments

9 laying in luxurious beds

10 accepting gold and silver.

The benefits of the precepts in guiding a person through life on the path of Buddhism are self-evident.

There is complete parity here with the morality of the eight-fold path (Part 2B). In addition, there is correlation with other Buddhist teachings such as karma. As Harvey remarks: 'behaving ethically reduces dukkha and increases happiness for oneself and others'.

6 The monastic sangha: the lifestyle of bhikkhus and bhikkhunis

The effect of the various patimokka and the associated rulings in the Vinaya is that a monk or nun has a very simple lifestyle. The specific purpose of such a lifestyle is to develop that condition in life that most successfully promotes the path of Buddhism.

The purpose of the Vinaya rules was to provide ideal conditions for meditation and renunciation. They try to enforce a complete withdrawal from social life, a separation from its interests and worries, and the rupture of all ties with family or clan. At the same time the insistence on extreme simplicity and frugality was meant to ensure independence, while the giving up of home and all property was intended to foster non-attachment.

(Conze)

Gombrich argues that the monastic life is the 'springboard' for higher, more spiritual attainment. The monastic life is designed to achieve victory over craving and the best way to begin is with a lifestyle that encourages one to be content with very little.

a) Poverty

Conze and Gombrich both refer to the ideals of **poverty** within a monastic lifestyle.

The state of poverty is symbolised by the few possessions a monk is allowed: robes, alms bowl, needle, Buddhist rosary beads, a razor, a belt, a staff and a filter to remove creatures from drinking water. Harvey suggests that, in practice, there are further additions such as sandals, a towel, extra work robes, a shoulder bag, an umbrella, writing materials, books, a clock and a picture of a teacher.

A monk must be homeless, or at least without a permanent shelter. In practice, this is often regarded as a state of mind rather than a pedantic rule. Effectively, a monk will not possess a home.

A monk's bowl is often inaccurately described as a **begging-bowl**. Monks do not beg; instead, they bless the gifts of food that people give. They are providing opportunity for others to make merit by, giving, or **dana**, which is the most significant ethical activity within Buddhism. Giving is the best example of not thinking of self, but of others.

Once again, it is important to remember the purpose of poverty; it is not adopted as a form of punishment, appeasement or a way of building character. The purpose is always to fight the drives of greed, hatred and delusion that cause attachment and suffering. Poverty in this sense is an aid to a better, more spiritually wholesome life.

b) Chastity

The tradition of **chastity** goes back to the fourth stage of a Hindu's life. It encourages total separation from family and dedication to an independent life in pursuit of truth. The Buddha himself entered this stage. Hindus who enter the fourth stage may make an effigy and perform a funeral, as a symbol that they have died and taken on a new life. This is often associated with taking a new name, common in many forms of Buddhism.

The idea of chastity is nothing to do with repression or a view of sex as in some way being contaminated with spiritual ills. It is similar to that of poverty; it is to help the practitioner to become detached from worldly attachments and commitments.

c) Inoffensiveness

The principle of **inoffensiveness** is not a new idea. As observed earlier, the Jains were extreme advocates of **ahimsa** – non-harm, non-violence. It is vital not to generate negative karma by harming others. Moreover, it is also against one of the underlying principles of Buddhism, that of compassion. Because of this principle, many Buddhists are vegetarian.

Monks providing an opportunity for dana (giving)

KEY WORDS

Begging-bowl: a bowl used *not* for begging but for allowing people to display dana by offering food to the monks

Dana: giving, the best example of selflessness

Chastity: freedom from human and emotional attachments

Inoffensiveness: the principle of non-harm to all living beings

Ahimsa: non-violence

TASK

Write a letter to someone who is going to join the sangha. Include an explanation of what rules there are and also what possessions they must bring. Explain why there are such restrictions.

Objective: To demonstrate knowledge and understanding of the restrictions of monastic life but also the reasons for such restrictions. This shows a 'response to the task at … considerable depth' (level 4 descriptor AO1).

An important part of the ideal of inoffensiveness is intention. Although it is impossible to avoid some destruction of micro-creatures in daily life, it is important to minimise that damage. Everyone is fully aware of the potential for this damage and should take care:

> …to diminish the involuntary slaughter, for instance, by being careful about what we tread on when walking in the woods.

> (Conze)

KEY WORDS

Meditation: the specific practice of concentration that the Buddha taught
Study: to remember and preserve the dhamma

d) Meditation and study

A major part of the life of a monk or nun is **meditation**, the practice of concentration taught by the Buddha. Learning how to meditate requires guidance in the traditions of Buddhism from the scriptures, which also need to be maintained, to preserve their teachings.

Monks and nuns **study** scripture, aiming to match the spiritual practice and pursuit of nirvana with the intellectual understanding of how best to go about it. In the history of Buddhism, this balancing act has led to differences in opinion as to how much time should be given to each aspect; however, a healthy Buddhist lifestyle requires a fine balance between study and meditation.

So how does this impact upon daily life in a monastery? In practice, a typical day in a Theravada monastery would involve rising at around 4.30 am.

TASK

Write a diary entry from the perspective of a monk. Imagine a typical day. Describe how you joined the monastery and also how it is run.
Objective: To demonstrate understanding of a typical Buddhist day and the procedures of social etiquette within a monastery. This shows an 'accurate, relevant and detailed knowledge' of the subject (level 4 descriptor AO1).

4.30 am	Study or meditation
6.30 am	Alms-round
7.00 am	Breakfast
8.00 am	Communal chanting
9.00 am	Teaching and instruction
10.30 am	Main meal
11.30 am	Rest period
1.30 pm	Further instruction or ordinations
5.00 pm	Refreshments (drinks only)
5.30 pm	Chores or personal free time
7.00 pm	Communal chanting
8.00 pm	Evening administration, study, further chanting or meditation

e) The relative status of bhikkus and bhikkunis

In order to become ordained as a monk or nun, a Buddhist must complete two stages.

The first is a process called renouncing, in keeping with the Indian tradition of the fourth stage of life. At this point the intention is clearly to become an anagarika or homeless one, going forth (pabbajja) in search of truth. In the early history of Buddhism, many anagarikas were accepted by the Buddha without any formal ordination ceremony.

KEY QUOTE

> *It is the senior monk who is to preside at the patimokkha ceremony and generally has precedence in ecclesiastical affairs. Nuns, on the other hand, were subject not only to their own hierarchy of seniority, but also to monks. They had to receive double ordination, from both nuns and monks, and were always subject to masculine supervision: any nun, no matter how long ordained, ranked below the most junior monk.*
>
> (Gombrich)

Over time, a second, more formal procedure was introduced. This is the official upasampada or ordination. Today, at the first stage of renouncing, the Buddhist becomes a samanera or novice; in Theravada these may be recognised by their white robes. The minimum age for this is seven years although, technically, it is defined as the point at which a child is old enough to scare crows away.

The status of bhikkhu, and the right to wear the orange or brown robe, is achieved through the ordination ceremony. Usually, this is at around the age of 20 and takes place within a sima or monastic boundary. At least five ordained bhikkhus must be present to authenticate it.

Within a monastery there is a definite hierarchy, based purely upon age and gender, although age is based upon the point of ordination, not birth. Junior monks bow to senior monks. Nuns bow to any monks, no matter how junior to them they may be. However, status is considered a mere formality and part of respectful interaction; it is not an indication of worth. Indeed, this would be contrary to Buddhist purposes of cultivating selflessness.

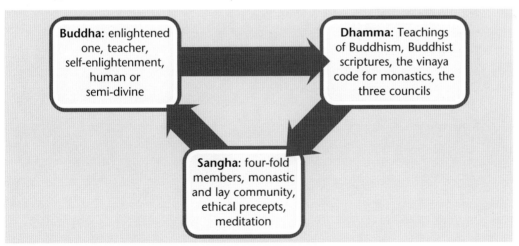

Buddha: enlightened one, teacher, self-enlightenment, human or semi-divine

Dhamma: Teachings of Buddhism, Buddhist scriptures, the vinaya code for monastics, the three councils

Sangha: four-fold members, monastic and lay community, ethical precepts, meditation

Summary diagram: Buddha, dhamma and the sangha

TASK

From what you have learned so far about levels of response, create a list of points appropriate for a developed-level answer. Improve this further for a higher-level answer. You can then create writing frames and fully drafted answers for each.

Objective: Gradually to build up and improve on an answer by reflecting on the Foundations Unit level descriptors 1–4.

Reflection and assessment (AO1)

Bringing together the information that has been covered so far is vital to see how it can be transformed into effective examination-style revision and answers. The best way to do this is to ask the question: 'How am I going to be assessed on this information?'

Read the following question and then complete the task opposite.

> **Examine Buddhist teachings about the three refuges.**   (21 marks)

Suggestion for further application of skills

Look back at pages 141–2, to the discussion about the contents of the Vinaya and a description of how it was compiled. Read the text again, as a class. Without the support of notes or text, try answering this question. Allow about 15 minutes.

> **Describe how the rules for Buddhist monks were compiled and explain the nature of these rules.**   (21 marks)

You should now have a basic answer to develop. In pairs or groups, share answers and select one for development. As before, identify ways in which you could improve this answer and complete your own comments analysis on it. Now write your own answer to the same question, aiming at level 4.

TOPIC 2: KEY EMPHASES IN TEACHING AND PRACTICE

Part 2B: Types and purposes of meditation, their context and application

---

This means I am expected:

to know about the key emphases:

- types and purposes of meditation
- their context and application

and to study:

- the four noble truths
- the eight-fold path
- meditation in the context of the Buddha's teaching
- Buddhist meditation as a discipline
- specific forms of meditation
- the purposes of meditation.

In this book the evidence and examples given are relevant and appropriate because this material focuses only on the content for AO1 that is given by the Edexcel specification. The evaluation materials for AO2 will be aimed at helping you 'critically evaluate and justify a point of view through the use of evidence and reasoned argument'.

It would be helpful to write your notes using the headings listed above, as it is from these areas that the examination questions will be derived.

In your studies, remember that you have to bear in mind the **two** basic assessment objectives of:

- Knowledge and Understanding (AO1)
- Evaluation (AO2).

See pages 7–8 in the Introduction to remind yourself of these objectives.

The evaluation material set out in Part 2C (page 158) can be studied either alongside the AO1 material, as you work through this unit, or as a separate unit.

The Buddha's teaching was, first and foremost, practical. Following an observation that identified the problem in life, the cause and the possibility of a cure, the Buddha proclaimed the solution. This involved following a particular path. The most important aspect of this path is meditation. However, the Buddha's analysis, found in the first three noble truths, and the resulting solution (as outlined in the path to follow in life) were both the result of careful meditation.

This section outlines the Buddha's teaching on meditation. It is within the context of his broader teachings that the study begins. The importance of a meditational approach to life is illustrated in the four noble truths and the eight-fold path, where the significance of the teachings in relation to meditation is drawn out. This is followed by a study of the practice of specific meditation, together with the different types, focusing on considering the purpose or purposes of Buddhist meditation.

1 The four noble truths

The four noble truths were a direct result of meditation. Some would class this a religious experience, others as basic empirical observation. Whatever the case, the four noble truths are essentially a medicinal course and remedy for the problems in life. This is how they are used. They are practical tools for realising nirvana. They are the focus of reflection throughout the process of Buddhist meditation. As well as being the *object of* meditation, the teachings are also *guidance for* meditation.

The crucial aspect of the dhamma, then, is the practical one found in the solution of the fourth noble truth. Arguably, the most important aspect of this path is meditation.

The division of the eight-fold path into wisdom, morality and meditation

The eight-fold path is usually divided into three groupings:

1 wisdom (**prajna**)

2 morality (**sila**)

3 meditation (**dhyana** or sometimes samadhi)

KEY WORDS

Prajna: wisdom associated with the first two sections of the eight-fold path and indicating insight into the reality of existence
Sila: moral teachings associated with the middle section of the eight-fold path
Dhyana: meditation, the last section of the eight-fold path, broadly understood in a variety of ways as a practice that stimulates mental development and concentration; deep state of thought

Wisdom
right view
right thought

Morality
right speech
right action
right livelihood

Meditation
right effort
right mindfulness
right concentration

Summary diagram: The three aspects of the eight-fold path

There is some inconsistency in how the three aspects are presented in relation to the listing of the eight-fold path. Texts generally speak of 'morality, meditation and wisdom'.

Morality, as the first mentioned, reinforces the traditional Indian ideal that in order to practise any form of yoga or meditation one needs to be of good moral character. Indeed, good moral character, as can be seen from an analysis of the eight-fold path, is outward evidence of inner spiritual development.

In addition, the eight-fold path is not chronologically progressive. The numbering and grouping are merely practical ways of preserving dhamma. In practice, all elements of the path are cultivated together and are essential to the ultimate practice of meditation and the development of mindfulness. It is the practice of meditation that unites and integrates the eight aspects of the path.

2 Meditation in the context of the Buddha's teaching (the eight-fold path)

Ariya magga, the noble path

Ariya means either noble or worthy, whereas **magga** means path. Since there are eight aspects to this path, it is known as the noble eight-fold path. In essence, it is the practical way for a Buddhist to address the problem of suffering and aspire to the Buddhist goal of freedom from the influences of the three fires (or defilements) of greed, hatred and delusion.

While there is one specific grouping of three aspects of the path that deals solely with meditation, the eight-fold path, as a whole, is directly related to the practice of creating mindfulness.

Each teaching of the eight-fold path begins with **samma**, meaning right. This refers to a correct, appropriate or effective method. The Buddha demonstrated the right path.

The eight-fold path and the relationship of each aspect to the meditation process can be desribed as follows.

1 Right view (**samma ditthi**) is when a person is aware of the reality of life. The Buddha described this as: 'the understanding of suffering, of the origin of suffering, of the extinction of suffering, and of the path leading to the extinction of suffering' (Thera). It is, however, more than this. It involves a deeper appreciation of the wider implications of these realities in association with other Buddhist teachings. It is true insight. The teachings are reflected upon during meditation.

2 Right thought (**samma sankappa**) or intention is when a person thinks only pure, wholesome and positive thoughts. It is a quality of consciousness that is unimpeded by obstructions. Only pure and positive thoughts are the focus of meditation practice.

3 Right speech (**samma vaca**) involves truth and polite speech. It promotes not only refraining from lying or exaggerating but also avoiding cruelty to others through language. Silence, reflection and the use of chanting to direct speech positively is a feature of meditation.

4 Right action (**samma kammanta**) means that a person will not harm others in any way by violence or theft. This extends to a general awareness of others and encourages dana (giving) as a demonstration of selflessness. Reflection on actions and observation of how a person functions are features of advanced meditation. More basic than this, the traditional path of meditation in Indian thought cannot be pursued without a sound moral basis.

KEY WORDS

Ariya magga: noble path, from ariya, meaning noble or worthy, magga meaning path
Samma: right
Samma ditthi: right view
Samma sankappa: right thought
Samma vaca: right speech
Samma kammanta: right action

KEY QUOTE

That the sequence of the items of the path does not conform to the order of these three categories of practice highlights an understanding of the spiritual life that sees all three aspects of practice as, although progressive, nonetheless interdependent and relevant to each and every stage of Buddhist practice.

(Gethin)

KEY WORDS

Samma ajiva: right livelihood
Samma vayama: right effort
Samma sati: right mindfulness
Samma samadhi: right concentration

5 Right livelihood (**samma ajiva**) means making a living that benefits others and that does not involve any harm. The life of a monk is an ideal lifestyle, one that enables uninterrupted focus on study and meditation.

6 Right effort (**samma vayama**) means a person is determined to avoid unwholesome or evil things. It is linked to the second part of the path, in that this discipline is required to avoid the arising of unwholesome or unskilful states of mind. Meditation is grounded in, and dependent upon, right effort.

7 Right mindfulness (**samma sati**) means to be fully aware of one's motives and reasons for doing something. According to Saddhatissa, this refers to 'gradually extending one's awareness until every action, thought and word is performed in the full light of consciousness'. In meditation, four foundations have developed, from which mindfulness is seen to operate. These include form, feelings and mental constructions.

8 Right concentration (**samma samadhi**) is focusing the mind in meditation. It is complete detachment from the unwholesome states and an immersion into the four absorptions dhyanas, (Pali: jhanas) of meditation. It is the ideal standard set by the Buddha, the middle way between extremes. It is a higher state of awareness and understanding. The monastic life nurtures this and concentration refers directly to Buddhist meditation.

As can be clearly seen, then, meditation is indeed the central focus of all Buddhist teachings. All insight into the true nature of reality and the Buddhist path is a direct consequence of meditation. Without meditation, the teachings would be meaningless.

3 Buddhist meditation as a discipline

Background information

Meditation is an ancient practice that existed long before the time of the Buddha. In essence, it is a deep form of concentration and analysis that explores the processes of the mind and its relationship to the physical world.

A study of meditation can be challenging. A lot of the traditional terminology used for meditation is Sanskrit. However, the types of Buddhist meditation within the Edexcel specification use Pali terms because they are traditionally associated with Theravada Buddhism. Note that Sanskrit terms are used with reference to later Mahayana Buddhist schools; there are also Chinese and Japanese terms for Ch'an and Zen Buddhist meditation.

Several terms are used in a non-literal sense to refer to meditation when, in fact they are more precise than this. For example, dhyana, samadhi and **bhavana** have all been used to refer to meditation in general. As Gethin writes:

> *…it is not entirely clear which Buddhist technical term the English word 'meditation' corresponds to.*

Before undertaking a study of Buddhist meditation, therefore, it would be beneficial to take a brief overview of its historical development. It would also be helpful to review the terminology used.

TASK

Look at the aspects of the eight-fold path. For each aspect, provide a practical example or situation from life to which it applies. Then try to explain this situation, using references to other Buddhist teachings, but in particular how it may be used in meditation.
Objective: To demonstrate how Buddhist teachings are inter-related and to make these connections. This shows an answer that is 'a coherent and well-structured response to the task at…considerable depth' (level 4 descriptor AO1).

KEY WORD

Bhavana: literally 'becoming' but generally translated as mental development

In early history, the first possible evidence for meditation can be found on the famous proto-Shiva amulet discovered at Mohenjo-daro and Harappa. This depicts an ascetic-type person with an animal head, seated in a meditation posture. It is often argued that this is a clear link to the Hinduism of the Upanishad texts and the practice of the **sadhu** or **sannyasin** that exists today.

Whatever the case may be, meditation was a feature of the Buddha's religious background and the Buddha himself was trained by famous Hindu Samana ascetics of the day (see Part 1A). However, it is important to distinguish the term yoga from meditation. The Hindu practice of meditation is often referred to as yoga (from the Sanskrit **yuktah**), literally meaning joined or united. It refers to the idea that a Hindu's soul has escaped the cycle of reincarnation and is no longer born into this world but exists instead in union with the universal spirit Brahman. Since the Buddhist world-view does not acknowledge a soul as such (hence anatta, meaning not-self or no soul), nor does it use the term reincarnation (preferring the term rebirth), then yoga is clearly not a traditional Buddhist practice. Instead, the Buddha went beyond the basic meditational process (referred to as **samatha** in Theravada Buddhism) and created a new type of meditation based on insight, known as **vipassana**. Both samatha and vipassana meditations are discussed in this section.

The whole practice of Buddhist meditation can be summarised with the word 'bhavana'. Literally meaning 'becoming', it suggests the process of mental development and self awareness that a person undergoes throughout its practice.

The aim of meditation is to develop positive mental states in order to open up access to the dhyanas or dhyanas (meditations) or samadhi (concentrations). There are, however, various steps to take and stages through which to progress.

4 Progression in meditation

In order to practise and develop meditation skills and technique, a person needs a teacher. Although it is possible to learn meditation without one, it is much better to have a personal trainer, just as in physical development or learning a musical instrument. The personal experience of others helps the pupil to learn more effectively.

The three stages

i) **Overcoming the five hindrances**
These are:

- sensuous desire
- ill-will
- sloth and torpor
- restlessness and scruples
- sceptical doubt.

ii) **Developing the four brahma viharas**
These are the four sublime or divine abodes, also called the four boundless states:

- loving-kindness
- compassion
- altruistic (or sympathetic) joy
- equanimity.

Anussati: bringing to mind the qualities of the Buddha to aid meditation

Anapanasati: focus on breathing to aid concentration and calm in Buddhist meditation

Kasinas: visual objects for meditation

Asubha: a focus on impurities or ugly things, to aid detachment through meditation

Smriti: to bring before the mind, to recollect, to reflect or remember

Panna: (Pali form of prajna) wisdom or insight

iii) Developing the viharas and eradicating the obstacles presented by the hindrances

The practitioner needs to focus on something (either an aid or quality) such as:

- **anussati** (6–10 recollections)
- **anapanasati** (mindfulness of breathing)
- **kasinas** (10 devices)
- **asubha** (10 uglinesses)

In short, the 40 stages of meditation, as outlined by an ancient Buddhist monk Vasubandhu, form the basis of calm (samatha) meditation practice in the southern tradition of Buddhism. In addition, the seven purifications necessary in order to develop the eight stages of insight (vipassana) combine to make meditation a more holistic experience, conducive to nirvana.

Once this is accomplished it leads to an awareness of the four foundations of mindfulness through sati. Sati means mindfulness and is derived from the Sanskrit **smriti** meaning to recollect or remember.

This leads to concentration (samadhi) and also to wisdom or insight (**panna**). In a sense, the pinnacle of meditation is insight into the truths or realities of the world in which we live. This leads to nirvana, the ultimate expression of truth, enlightenment or meaning in Buddhism.

Depending upon a person's spiritual stage, there are various paths to achieve this. They include:

- equipment
- application
- seeing
- development
- completion.

The paths of equipment and application lead to the initial development of both calm and insight meditation to a proficient standard, possibly as a lay person. The paths of seeing, development and completion are usually associated with the life of the arhat or bodhisattva and represent the stages of perfect insight or wisdom required for nirvana.

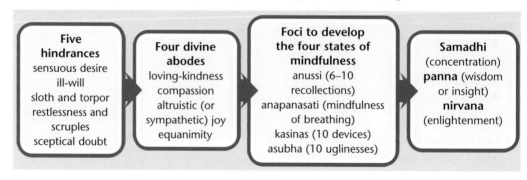

Summary diagram: Meditation processes

5 Specific forms of meditation

a) Samatha (calm) meditation

Samatha meditation requires a comfortable posture (sitting, lotus, half-lotus or even on a chair), with the hands resting in the lap (mudra).

Buddhist monks gathering for communal chanting and meditation

Chanting is usually performed as a warming-up exercise and a preparation for focus. The traditional preparation is usually taking refuge.

The practice of samatha requires thorough observation and involves the use of focus objects for concentration. As mentioned above, there are 40 such objects mentioned in Buddhghosa's Visuddhimagga, including:

- mental images, such as Buddha
- a bodily focus, such as breathing
- physical objects, such as small coloured circles or kasinas.

One of the most popular practices for samatha is anapanasati (mindfulness of breathing). Others include reflecting upon the qualities of the Buddha.

Samatha meditation leads to high mental states of development but it is argued that nirvana, the achievement of cessation, can only be reached in partnership with vipassana meditation.

> It is clear that in developed Buddhist theory the two aspects of Buddhist meditation, calm (samatha) and insight (vipassana), are seen as together forming the basis for the realisation of the Buddhist goal: when calm and insight meditation are brought together (yuga-naddha), the unconditioned (nirvana) may be experienced.
>
> **(Gethin)**

The end result of samatha in itself is a gradual appreciation of calm, concentration or collectedness (samadhi).

TASK

Design a flow diagram that demonstrates the process of meditation. Make sure that you highlight clearly the negative aspects that need to be overcome, the means by which to do this, the positive outcomes and the ultimate goals. You could colour-code your diagram.

Objective: To appreciate an overview of the whole process and purpose of Buddhist meditation and to be aware of the key terminology involved. This demonstrates 'well-chosen evidence to support understanding of key ideas and concepts' that is 'expressed clearly and accurately, using technical language widely' (level 4 descriptor AO1).

b) Vipassana (insight) meditation

The most popular posture or practice for vipassana meditation is 'mindfulness of walking', which is done very slowly, often in an open space such as a field outside a monastery. The practitioner forms a distinct 'path' in the mind and follows it back and forth.

Insight meditation provides an advanced level of mindfulness on its own but generally it is only practised with samatha as its base. Vipassana actually enables the three fires of greed, hatred and delusion to be extinguished and for nirvana to be achieved. It opens the mind rather than remaining focused on a single point, as with samatha.

During vipassana meditation the practitioner observes the arising and passing away of physical, experiential or mental phenomena. The practice generates an awareness of the shared features of phenomena and cultivates a deep appreciation of the three marks of existence.

Vipassana meditation is concerned with reality rather than a particular fixed object but its practice is highly mentally skilled. It cannot be achieved without mastery of the discipline of samatha.

6 The purposes of meditation

The concept of an overall purpose for meditation is misleading since the answer can only be the ultimate experience of enlightenment, an appreciation of reality, of how things really are.

However, the purposes of meditation are multi-layered and at each stage there is meaningful development. There are several aims common to these stages:

- nirvana or satori (enlightenment) as the ultimate goal
- nirodha (to stop suffering, the third noble truth)
- to develop powers of concentration
- to experience the dhyanas and extend the bounds of perception and consciousness
- to achieve insight into a higher truth
- to reduce the effect of suffering.

Indeed, more purposes could be added, such as breaking through the hindrances, eradicating the three fires and so forth. But meditation is wider than monastic Buddhism, even wider than the principles of Buddhism itself. Since Buddhist meditation is grounded in an ancient Indian tradition, it cannot be divorced from the underlying heritage it shares.

The purposes of meditation for a non-Buddhist may be very different; for example, it may be practised purely for health reasons, as it can benefit general health and stability of the body. Meditation is generally for calming, gaining insight and developing loving-kindness, which are altruistic features that are not exclusively Buddhist.

Meditation also has specific physical benefits as it impacts upon mental health, reducing anxiety and stress.

In the light of this it must always be remembered that the spiritual goal of nirvana is often a long-term goal, achievable only after many rebirths.

In the short term, each aspect of meditation may be used as a journey of self-discovery, as it helps an individual to discover who, what and why they are, in being human. In short, it strengthens the spirituality of the individual.

 EXAM TIP

Remember to explain each point that you make in an exam answer to the full. Think carefully about each sentence and how it relates to the question and the previous sentence. Aim for at least three clear sentences to explain a concept or idea, giving examples from different sources to support your point. For development of the point, bring in a variety of ways in which the application of this principle is demonstrated and introduce some contrasting scholarly views.
This demonstrates that the answer shows 'accurate, relevant and detailed knowledge of the subject matter at a wide range or in significant depth' (mid level 4 descriptor AO1) as opposed to the information being simply 'minimal accuracy or relevance in factual detail' (level 1 descriptor AO1) or 'limited in scope' (level 2 descriptor AO1).

Reflection and assessment (AO1)

It is important to bring together the information that has been covered so far, to see how it can be transformed into effective examination-style revision and answers. The best way to do this is to ask the question: 'How am I going to be assessed on this information?'

Look at the following lists of essential, developed and higher points to include in an answer to this question.

Compare ways in which Buddhists practise meditation. (21 marks)

The *essential material* includes the two types and their specific purpose:

Samatha   calm, one-pointedness, concentration

Vipassana   insight, appreciation of reality, how things really are.

The *developed* answer could be drawn from these points:

- several aims common to all types
- nirvana or satori (enlightenment)
- nirodha (to stop suffering, the third noble truth)
- to develop powers of concentration
- to experience the dhyanas and extend the bounds of perception and consciousness
- to achieve insight into a higher truth
- to reduce the effect of suffering.

The *higher-level* response would mention that:

- meditation is wider than Buddhism – monks, lay people and non-Buddhists practise it
- purposes of meditation for a non-Buddhist may be very different, for example, there may be health reasons
- meditation generally is for calming, insight and developing loving-kindness
- meditation has physical benefits and impacts upon mental health, for example, maintaining calm, reducing anxiety or stress
- the spiritual goal of nirvana is a long-term goal, achievable only after many rebirths
- each aspect of meditation helps to discover who, what and why we are
- it strengthens the spirituality of the individual
- it is part of the eight-fold path
- it is practised daily in a monastery
- there are many non-monastic meditation groups.

Suggestion for further application of skills

Now use what you have learned above to create the ideal mark scheme or plan for similar questions that might require you to illustrate the role of meditation in the path taught by the Buddha.

Using the principles developed in the above question and analysis exercise, try doing this under timed conditions. Then use the mark scheme to try some peer assessment. Mark each other's work, identifying strengths and areas for development.

TASK

Using the guidelines of essential, developed and higher as outlined opposite, create a mark scheme for the question: 'Compare ways in which Buddhists practise calm and insight meditation.'
Objective: To demonstrate awareness of what will constitute a very good answer (level 4) by gradually building up a response while referring to the descriptor 'accurate, relevant and detailed knowledge used concisely to present a coherent and well-structured response to the task at a wide range or considerable depth; selecting the most important features for emphasis and clarity; using evidence to explain the key ideas; expressed cogently using technical language' (high level 4 descriptor AO1).

TOPIC 2: KEY EMPHASES IN TEACHING AND PRACTICE

Part 2C: An evaluation of the significance of Buddhist teaching and practice

---

This means I am expected:

to analyse and critically evaluate:

- the different reasons for practising Buddhist meditation
- the role of the three refuges in Buddhist life.

---

1 Buddhist reasons for meditation

There are clearly two types of Buddhist meditation, each with its specific purpose: samatha (calm, focused or 'one-pointed') and vipassana (insight, appreciation of reality).

Within these disciplines there are also immediate aims or purposes to achieve, for example, to develop powers of concentration, to experience the dhyanas and extend the bounds of perception and consciousness, to achieve insight into a higher truth, or to reduce the effect of suffering and so forth. Such aspects could be used as individual reasons rather than single reasons from a more holistic perspective.

Overall, meditation can also be seen as a form of self-development. It could be argued that through the process of meditation one can discover what exactly the 'me' or 'I' that we thought we were actually is; for example, an analysis of the khandhas and the three marks. In this way meditation redefines who we are. Through meditiation, a Buddhist becomes more 'awake'.

All the above arguments could be offered as reasons for Buddhist meditation.

➡ EXAM TIP

Always point out both specific and general reasons for the significance of Buddhist meditation. Include some key questions and make sure that you offer more than one possible conclusion and then give your own, reasoned opinion, based upon what you have chosen to write about. This clearly is what a level 4 answer expects as 'a clearly expressed viewpoint supported by well-deployed evidence and reasoned argument' (level 4 descriptor AO2).

2 General reasons for the practice of meditation

In addition to those discussed above, which are strictly Buddhist reasons, there are certain benefits that meditation can bring, both psychological and emotional, such as encouraging calm or reducing anxiety and stress. Other benefits are physical, for example, bringing general good health.

? KEY QUESTIONS

- Does meditation have a single goal or purpose?
- Which aspect of meditation practice is the most important?
- How can it be that meditation helps a person find out more about themselves when there is, according to Buddhist teaching, 'no-self'?
- Are the psychological and emotional benefits of Buddhist meditation significant for the overall practice of meditation?
- Can a person use Buddhist meditation for general health reasons without being a Buddhist?

These may be important enough reasons in themselves to encourage anyone to practise meditation. Others may see the general benefits as simply by-products of meditation, not in any way linked to the spiritual aspect.

Some may even see health and general well-being as of vital importance, playing a significant role in enabling the effective practice of Buddhist meditation.

3 Possible conclusions

When assessing the issues that arise from Buddhist meditation, it is important to reflect upon the arguments previously discussed and arrive at some appropriate conclusion.

It may be that you accept none of these listed here, or just one of them, or you may have a different conclusion that is not listed. However, what is important is the way that you have arrived at your conclusion – the reasoning process.

From the preceding discussions, here are some possible conclusions you could draw.

1 Nirvana is the only aim for practising Buddhist meditation and all other aspects of meditation are directed towards or lead to this.

2 Buddhist meditation is all about the development of a spiritual self through discovery of what the empirical self really is.

3 Buddhist meditation is complex and has many reasons and purposes that cover general health benefits, as well as specific spiritual stages of development.

4 Buddhist meditation reflects the fact that the Buddhist path is for everyone and has various stages of development that are mirrored by specific purposes and aims along this path.

4 The importance of the three refuges

For a Buddhist, each of the three refuges has significance in several ways. These may overlap, correspond or complement each other.

The table below summarises the areas of significance that a Buddhist may highlight for the three refuges.

	Significance
Buddha	Inspiration: as a figure of aspiration and encouragement Reverence: for the nature of his achievement or his unique status Respect: for the achievement of enlightenment Guidance: as an exemplary Buddhist role-model
Dhamma	Guidance: advice about the Buddhist path Study: an in-depth appreciation of teachings Information: a source of knowledge about the Buddha and his teachings Practice: as a manual for the practical aspects
Sangha	Meditation: practical learning and instruction Practice: the communal aspect of learning alongside others Discussion: analysis and debate Meeting: encouragement of being in the presence of other like-minded individuals Formal training: the monastic emphasis of Buddhism

TASK

Make your own list of questions that you would like to ask about Buddhist meditation.
Objective: To encourage the use of questions in answers for AO2, to help demonstrate more than 'a mainly descriptive response, at a general level' (level 1 descriptor AO2) and aim for 'an attempt at an evaluation of the issue(s) raised in the task' (level 4 descriptor AO2).

TASK

Draw up a table with the headings: 'Buddha', 'Dhamma', 'Sangha'. Down the side put the headings: Basic explanation, Development of detail, Importance, My conclusion. Complete the table by putting the appropriate evidence from the text into the relevant box.
Objective: To summarise the importance of the refuges for Buddhists. This could serve as a basis for your evidence to include in the task 'suggestions for further application of skills' at the end of Part 2C. This meets the criteria of 'a careful analysis of alternative views… supported by well-deployed evidence' (level 4 descriptor AO2).

5 Possible conclusions

When assessing the issues that arise from the three refuges, it is important to reflect upon the arguments previously discussed and arrive at some appropriate conclusion.

It may be that you accept none of these listed here, or just one of them, or you may have a different conclusion that is not listed. However, what is important is the way that you have arrived at your conclusion – the reasoning process.

From the preceding discussions, here are some possible conclusions you could draw.

? KEY QUESTIONS
- How important is the Buddha in following the Buddhist path?
- Is it necessary to focus on the Buddha to achieve enlightenment?
- Is it more important to practise or to study the Buddhist teachings?
- Is it necessary to be part of the sangha in order to follow Buddhism?
- Are the three refuges of equal importance?

1 As long as a person follows the teachings of the Buddha they can achieve enlightenment.

2 Following the teachings alone makes it more difficult to achieve enlightenment.

3 A person needs all three refuges to practise Buddhism.

4 A person need not be a member of a monastery but meeting with the sangha helps.

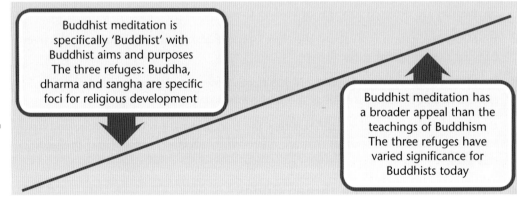

Summary diagram: Buddhist meditation

Reflection and assessment (AO2)

It is important to bring together the information that has been covered so far, to see how it can be transformed into effective examination-style revision and answers. The best way to do this is to ask the question: 'How am I going to be assessed on this information?'

Look back to page 10 in the Introduction to review the level descriptors for AO2. There is a description of the character and features for each level. The exam is marked with reference to levels.

Look at the following notes for a sample basic level 1 answer, which is a response to this question.

> **Comment on the view that 'meditation is too difficult to perfect for an ordinary individual'.** (9 marks)

The *basic-level* answer would deal with the question in the following way.

- State the basic aim of meditation.
- Give some basic information about different ways of practising and their different reasons, aims or purposes.
- Draw a simple conclusion about whether meditation is too difficult to perfect.

There may well be two possible aspects to any answer. The first is specifically Buddhist. The second is that the reasons for meditation for a non-Buddhist may be very different; the best candidates might recognise this.

TASK

Look at the suggestions for a basic answer, above. Try to work out what a developed answer (level 3) would deal with the question by adding two or three more bullet points.

Now go on to develop this answer to indicate what a higher answer (level 4) would deal with the question by adding further bullet points. Don't forget to keep the bullet points centred around the question focus.

Objective: To demonstrate awareness of what will constitute a very good answer by gradually building up a response. Make constant reference to the meaning and application of the AO2 level descriptors in order to see improvement and development.

Suggestion for further application of skills

Now try this technique of building together a level 4 answer with a question such as those below.

> **Consider the importance of meditation for Buddhists.** (9 marks)

> **To what extent is nirvana the sole purpose of Buddhist meditation?** (9 marks)

Try making up a few questions about the types of Buddhist meditation, based on this theme of their relative importance, purpose and goal.

FOUNDATIONS
Area F: Islam

TOPIC 1: KEY ISSUES IN THE STUDY OF ISLAM

Part 1A: The life and work of Muhammad in its historical, religious and social background

---

This means I am expected:

to know about the key issues:

- the life and work of Muhammad in its historical, religious and social context
- his significance for Muslims

and to study:

- the background to Islam
- the historical, geographical and religious background
- political and economic factors
- further religious features of pre-Islamic Arabia
- the environment into which Muhammad was born and Islam was introduced.

In this book the evidence and examples given are relevant and appropriate because this material focuses only on the content for AO1 that is given by the Edexcel specification. The evaluation materials for AO2 will be aimed at helping you 'critically evaluate and justify a point of view through the use of evidence and reasoned argument'.

It would be helpful to write your notes using the headings listed above, as it is from these areas that the examination questions will be derived.

In your studies, remember that you have to bear in mind the **two** basic assessment objectives of:

- Knowledge and Understanding (AO1)
- Evaluation (AO2).

See pages 7–8 in the Introduction to remind yourself of these objectives.

The evaluation material set out in Part 1C (page 184) can be studied either alongside the AO1 material, as you work through this unit, or as a separate unit.

The study of Islam begins with the historical, geographical and religious context of the life and work of Muhammad (PBUH). This has a wide range of implications for study. A search on the internet made for pre-Islamic Arabian culture reveals a wealth of material. Such a vast task is clearly too challenging for AS level. It is important, therefore, to stay close to the unit content listed above.

KEY IDEA

As a mark of respect to the prophet, it is customary to write 'peace be upon him' or the abbreviated form, PBUH, after his name. In this section, this custom has been applied on the first mention of his name within each part.

1 The background to Islam

The era belonging to Muhammad is generally known as **pre-Islamic Arabia**. For Muslims, it is also called **jahiliyya**, which means ignorance. This means for Muslims that **monotheism** and divine law were cast aside as human beings were ruled by other human beings. It was the total opposite of submission to God.

> **66 KEY QUOTE**
>
> *...the 'prehistory' of Islam is a significant conceptual notion...our knowledge of 'prehistory' will remain filtered through the theologically inspired picture of the past provided by the later Muslim sources.*
>
> (Rippin)
> 99

This understanding of pre-Islamic Arabia leads to the issue of the historical reliability of the evidence. What can be known of this time is problematic for historians because of the vested interests that any later writers have in portraying the theological or religious message of Islam. Nonetheless, Islam did not emerge from a vacuum.

This section considers the influencing factors of religion, geography, history and society. It also analyses how far these factors interacted and influenced the emergence of Islam.

2 The historical, geographical and religious background

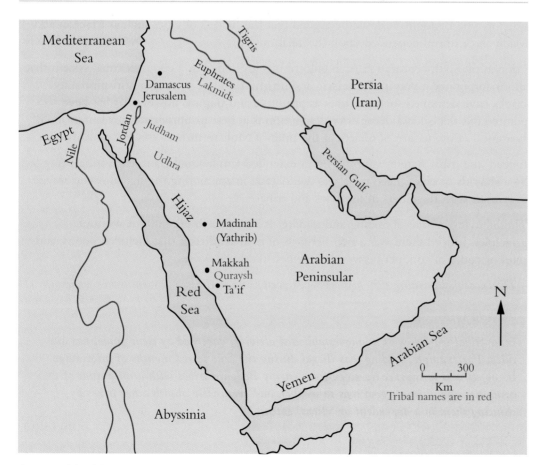

A map of Arabia

KEY WORDS

Pre-Islamic Arabia: the time of Muhammad
Jahiliyya: ignorance, a term used to describe life at the time of Muhammad, referring to pre-Islamic Arabia
Monotheism: belief in only one God

> **66 KEY QUOTE**
>
> *Arabia was considered a god-less region... The intractable steppes of Arabia were a terrifying wilderness, inhabited by a wild race of men to whom the Greeks had given the name 'Sarakenoi', the people who dwell in tents.*
>
> (Armstrong)
> 99

At the time of Muhammad, Arabia covered the area bordering the Persian Gulf, adjacent to the Red Sea and including the Yemen. It was an area of just over one million square miles, equal to 30 per cent of the USA. Its climate was one of temperature extremes and its land area mainly included harsh, dry, sandy desert. The area was mostly uninhabited. Sandstorms were frequent and severe.

> *Those who lived there eked out their existence under the harshest of physical conditions, scorched for most of the year by a relentless sun, which made survival something of an achievement.*
>
> (Turner)

KEY WORDS

Oasis: fertile area of the desert
Hafiz: the fertile area of Arabia including Makkah and Madinah
Makkah: city of Muhammad's birth (some texts use the alternative spelling Mecca)
Madinah: city to which Muhammad fled and established Islam, second most holy city in Islam, originally known as the oasis city of Yathrib (some texts use the alternative spelling Medina)
Bedouin: nomadic peoples of the deserts of Arabia
Polytheistic: worshipping many gods or idols
Animistic: worshipping objects in the belief that they contained spirits
Pagan: a term used to describe a variety of religious traditions at the time of Muhammad
Shaykh: chief or tribal ruler
Oral tradition: the preservation and transmission of 'literature' by the spoken word

The land was populated by some peoples who had fairly established bases, and wandering peoples who mainly occupied the deserts. The more established bases were around **oasis** areas such as the **Hafiz** (central western Arabia), where **Makkah** and **Madinah** (Yathrib) were located.

The origins of the nomads, or **Bedouin** as they came to be called, is unclear. There is a suggestion that they originated from the Yemen, following a severe flood from the burst dam of Ma'rib, and were pushed into the desert areas to survive.

Nevertheless, the nomads gradually infiltrated the desert in the regions known as the 'fertile crescent' and the 'Arabian peninsula'. Farmers settled in the oasis areas and began to trade with the Bedouin, who were obviously more mobile and could deliver goods from areas beyond this. Thus began a very important relationship of inter-dependence. Harvests provided the settlers with a means to trade and buy protection from the fierce, warrior-type Bedouin. It could be argued that the success of cities such as Makkah and Madinah (Yathrib) depended upon this relationship.

Prior to the sixth century CE, Arab culture was grounded in a complex tribal system that also incorporated a very **polytheistic** and **animistic** sense of religion or spirituality. Books have described such practices as primitive and **pagan**; however, it has been pointed out that such a derogatory description is at best inappropriate, revealing lack of awareness of the nature of society at the time of Muhammad.

Indeed, the tribal system was built upon extended families and clans, each tribe being led by a **shaykh** or chief. Each tribe was democratic in appointing the shaykh, who served to consult with the elders of the clans and tribes.

The lifestyle was one of raiding and trading. It was a harsh life but not without principles. Indeed there was a rich heritage of **oral tradition** that included poetry and rules or codes of conduct between the tribes. Ruthven writes:

> *Though without writing, they had developed poetry into a refined and sophisticated art form.*

❝ KEY QUOTE

> *Inter-tribal warfare was a long-established activity, governed by clear guidelines and rules. For example, raiding was illegal during the four sacred months of pilgrimage. Its object was to capture livestock from enemy Bedouin tribes with a minimum of casualties. Its ultimate goal was to weaken and eventually absorb other tribes by reducing them to a dependent or 'client' status.*
>
> (Esposito) ❞

Even the raids had a code of conduct. This sense of principle, or nobility, can be understood in the term **muruwa** or manliness. It encompassed virtue and bravery and was inherited through the blood-line of a tribe. At all times, a tribe's honour was vital.

Likewise, religion mirrored the tribal system, having many different deities represented by objects. They inspired fear and served to deliver protection to individual tribes. Waines writes:

> The gods were consulted on various matters of domestic and other concerns: setting the dates for marriage, confirming the parentage of a child, and the settlement of a quarrel all fell within the purview of the gods' advice, as did seeking the most propitious moment to embark upon a journey.

Here can be seen the early role of the **Ka'aba** stone, a central place in Makkah for pilgrimage and worship of **Allah** and his three daughters.

By the time of Muhammad, the Arabs had begun to engage in trade with surrounding lands. Nomads were being drawn to the cities and there was population growth. This had social implications; issues surrounding the distribution of wealth, poverty, human suffering and social justice were raised.

Surrounding Arabia were three powerful civilisations. The Byzantine (formally Roman) empire to the north was predominantly Christian. The Persian empire to the east was strongly **Zoroastrian**. To the south-west, the Abyssinian empire (NW Africa) adopted a version of Christianity known as **monophysite**. Throughout the empires and in Arabia itself were small influences of Judaism, although none was strong enough to make full communities in Arabia.

3 Political and economic factors

66 KEY QUOTE

> *There is no question that Mecca [Makkah] was out of the way. The natural trade route in the Hijaz lay east of the city…but the city of Mecca was endowed with a special sanctity that went beyond the Ka'ba [Ka'aba] itself, by virtue of the presence of the sanctuary and the gods housed inside…The point is that this trade, modest as it may have been, was wholly dependent on the Ka'ba.*
>
> (Aslan)

The oasis city of Makkah was a stronghold of Arabian culture. It was ideally located to resist invasion. The desert wilderness was clearly an additional line of defence against foreign invasions.

It has been traditionally argued that, geographically, Makkah was ideally suited to trade. It was accessible by two major trade routes: the route to Syria, the Jordan river and the Byzantine empire, known as the **Hijaz road**, and the route to Persia, known as the **Najd road**. Situated by the Red Sea, its potential for trade with north Africa (Abyssinia) was also considerable.

Despite its location, it has been proposed recently that Makkah only attracted trade due to the Ka'aba and its religious significance. This ancient relic, a smooth black stone at the city centre, was surrounded by idols and religious–spiritual artefacts. During a four-month period each year, it drew Arabs from all around, further enhancing trade. Indeed, Waines describes Makkah as being transformed into a 'divine supermarket' during the pilgrimage months.

KEY WORDS

Muruwa: tribal term used to denote manliness or honour
Ka'aba: black stone of religious significance housed in the centre of Makkah (some texts use the alternative spelling Ka'ba)
Allah: the highest form of divinity in pre-Islamic Arabia; also used for the name of the One True God in Islam
Zoroastrian: Persian religion
Monophysite: heretic form of Christianity

66 KEY QUOTE

> *In the sixth century, Mecca [Makkah] was emerging as a new commercial centre with vast new wealth but also with a growing division between rich and poor, challenging the traditional system of Arab tribal values and social security.*
>
> (Esposito)

Quraysh: Muhammad's tribe, dominant in the Makkah area

EXAM TIP

It is important to be able to describe and explain the religious ideas at the time of Muhammad. However, it is even more important to be able to show how they influenced the prophet. This means that what is required is not just a general answer that presents 'a limited range of isolated facts… with mainly random and unorganised detail' or 'information presented within a structure which shows a basic awareness of the issues raised' (level 1 and 2 descriptors AO1). Remember, you are aiming for 'a coherent and well-structured account of the subject matter' (level 4 descriptor AO1).

Makkah was protected from within through an alliance with the Bedouin. In this respect, during the sixth century the **Quraysh** were the dominant and most influential tribe in Makkah and surrounding Arabia. They offered protection and, in return, had a share of the various Makkan businesses, especially during the pilgrimage season when they acted as stewards of all commercial trade. Protection for caravans entering the city also merited a small fee.

Reza Aslan, in his book, *No God But God*, points out that debate surrounds the reasons for Makkah's significance as a trade centre. Past historians have argued that Makkah was the centre of the international trade market, exporting gold, silver and spices from the Yemen and sending them through to the Byzantine empire for a profit. Others, more recently, have suggested that there are 'no tangible signs of amassed capital in pre-Islamic Mecca [Makkah]' and suggest that it is, at the very least, an exaggeration to say that Makkah was the central trading area.

Despite this, Aslan concludes that 'trade, modest as it may have been, was wholly dependent on the Ka'ba [Ka'aba].'

4 Further religious features of pre-Islamic Arabia

It is often the case, historically, that conflicts or interactions between empires have been depicted as religious, caused by conflicting philosophies and beliefs. Pre-Islamic Arabia and the empires surrounding it are no exception.

Armstrong has noted that the Arabs were close to being indifferent to these differences:

The Bedouin Arabs of the Arabia Desert were suspicious of both Judaism and Christianity. The Bedouin Arabs had been intensely proud of their southern Arab neighbours and saw their fall as a catastrophe. They knew that the great powers of Persia and Byzantium were ready to use both faiths as a means of imperial control. In order to avoid the fate of the kingdom of the South, they remained strictly neutral in the struggle between Persia and Byzantium.

(Armstrong)

There was clearly a tension between the different fringes of the empires bordering on Arabia.

In the sixth century, Persia and Christian Byzantium were locked in a debilitating struggle with one another.

(Armstrong)

Arabia was unique, mainly because of its geographical qualities (see earlier). This meant that, in some respects, it was a safe haven. However, when the Persian empire invaded southern Arabia in CE570 it took hold of the area known today as Yemen.

It is important to consider these religious influences in turn and also assess the impact that they had upon their Arab neighbours.

> **KEY QUOTE**
>
> *Bedouins were not actually polytheists, as they have usually been portrayed, but henotheists: those who accept many gods in addition to one central deity…the latter term defines more precisely the religious outlook of the Meccans [Makkans] prior to the advent of Islam.*
>
> (Turner)

a) Jewish

> 66 **KEY QUOTE**
>
> *In sixth-century Arabia, Jewish monotheism was in no way anathema to Arab paganism, which, as mentioned, could easily absorb a cornucopia of disparate religious ideologies. The pagan Arabs would likely have perceived Judaism as just another way of expressing what they considered to be similar religious sentiments.*
>
> (Aslan)
> 99

KEY IDEA

Judaism:
- spread throughout Arabia and beyond
- had no stronghold within Arabia other than Madinah
- existed also in a variant form, based more in superstition
- followed tradition that was linked to the Ka'aba
- included wealthy Jewish tribes in Hijaz.

The presence of Jews in and beyond Arabia can be traced back to the Babylonian exile, 1000 years earlier. Unlike Christianity, Judaism had no empires or cities to speak of, although there were strong Jewish influences in Madinah (Yathrib) in particular. The Jewish peoples in Arabia tended to be scattered groups of settlers rather than established populations.

In Arabia a diluted form of Judaism developed, possibly due to interaction with the Arab culture. This type of Judaism tended to embrace superstitions. For example, they had kohens (priests or soothsayers) that resembled the pagan kahins (poets).

However, the influence was not just one-way; for example, there are strong Jewish overtones linked to stories about the Ka'aba. In addition, the Arab religious heritage before Muhammad tended to trace its descendents back to Abraham.

In terms of economy, the greatest area of influence was the area to the west of Arabia, on the coast known as the Hijaz. Makkah and Madinah were located here and Guillaume comments: 'the Jews dominated the economic life of the Hijaz'. In addition, Guillaume estimates that at least a half of the population of Madinah (Yathrib) were Jewish.

b) Christian

KEY IDEA

Christianity:
- developed the idea of the trinity
- invited some debate and confusion arose over beliefs
- existed in different 'types' or forms.

As one writer comments: 'Arabian Christianity is as old as Christianity itself.' (Guillaume) Despite this, Arabia never officially converted to Christianity, owing to the nature of Arabian paganism (see page 168). Christianity was particularly strong in the Yemen area and influential in the north of Arabia and also Hira in the east. In the Hijaz area there were at least two Christian tribes, the Judham and Udhra.

✏️ **TASK**

In pairs, identify five to ten factors for each of the social, religious and historical factors of key importance at the time of Muhammad. Present them, as a bullet list, to the rest of the group. Following discussion, add two or three more points to each aspect.
Now look at the level 4 descriptor and see how your selection could be described as demonstrating 'a coherent and well-structured response to the task at a wide range or considerable depth' and also shows that you are 'selecting the most important features for emphasis and clarity; using evidence to explain the key ideas' (top level 4 descriptor AO1).
Objective: To summarise, using collaborative learning and peer-assessment to aim for a level 4 answer.

KEY WORD

Trinity: belief in one God in three parts

In the surrounding empires, Christianity was the official religion of Byzantium and Abyssinia. Within the religion itself, there were various controversies, particularly concerning the **trinity**. This debate tended to originate with discussions about the nature of Jesus. The **Nicene Creed** finally established the standard of theology for later **Christology** but, before this, there were variations that can be summarised as:

- Monophysites – those that believed that Jesus had one nature, simultaneously human and divine
- Nestorians – those that believed that Jesus had a dual nature, both human and divine, and that the aspects were individually distinct from each other
- Docetists or Gnostics – those that believed that Jesus only appeared to be human but was really a spiritual body.

One influential tribe of Bedouin, called the Ghassanids, were Christian converts. They actively supported Christian Byzantine missions into Arabia. However, they had a very different understanding of Christianity than their Christian partners and accepted the monophysite version of Christianity.

As a trader, Muhammad was familiar with Christianity although it is not clear to what extent he was actually aware of the intricacies of the Christology debate.

c) Zoroastrian

Another tribe, called the **Lakhmids**, supported the Persian (Sasanian) empire and **Zoroastrianism**. Zarathustra, an ancient teacher, spoke of a heaven and hell, of bodily resurrection (1000 years before Christianity) and also a sense of judgement or day of reckoning. Zoroastrians taught about one Ahura Mazda or 'wise God', who fights evil (which he could not have created). At the time of Muhammad this was a fully developed dualism involving Ohrmaz, the God of Light and Ahrimam, the God of Darkness.

It is not clear how far Zoroastrian influences impacted upon Muhammad but it is probable that he was familiar with their basic beliefs.

d) Pagan

> ❝ **KEY QUOTE**
>
> *The word paganus means a 'rustic villager', or a 'boor', and was originally used…as a term of abuse*
>
> (Aslan) ❞

The word 'pagan', understood as above, is not helpful in terms of appreciating the internal complexities of a system of beliefs and practices. The reason is that it is a word imposed from the outside, an external tag, often accompanied by misunderstanding.

It is therefore important to understand the term 'pagan', when describing pre-Islamic Arabia, in a much more positive manner in terms of its complex and deeply established beliefs and practices, rather than as a superficial label:

> *…paganism is not so much a unified system of beliefs and practices as it is a religious perspective, one that is receptive to a multitude of influences and interpretations.*
>
> (Aslan)

As mentioned earlier, for Muslims jahiliyya refers to a time of ignorance. However, it is important to establish that the term 'ignorance' refers to a lack of insight into divine truth and not to a lack of intelligence or sophistication in doctrine.

So jahiliyya is a direct reference to the lack of submission to the one true God. To wrench it from this context would be misleading. However, there were certain elements of society that demonstrated actions that were seen to be a direct result of this 'ignorance'.

The practical focus of pre-Islamic Paganism in Arabia was the Ka'aba in Makkah, that housed a variety of idols (there were 360 recognised gods in total). As Guillaume comments: 'temples were few and far between' and the only real place of religious gathering around Makkah was the Ka'aba. Once again, this reinforces its popularity as a centre for social interaction and trade.

Of the gods, the most important was Allah and his three daughters **Allat**, **al-Uzza** and **Manat**.

The legends associated with the origins of the Ka'aba all relate to Judaism. It was founded by Adam, rebuilt by Noah and then forgotten, only to be rediscovered by Abraham.

The true associations may, in fact, be astrological, for example, relating to the number of gods mirroring the heavenly bodies or to the movement around the Ka'aba, representing the movement of the heavenly bodies.

Paganism had no real figure of authority such as a priest, and neither did it have religious writings. There were a group of individuals known as kahins. These were more like spiritual poets, who entered trances and revealed messages from the spiritual realm. They could also interpret dreams and often fulfilled the role of giving ethical instruction.

Kahins accessed the divine through the jinn that were believed to dwell in or around things in the world. This idea bordered on **animism** and extended to sacred stones, trees and water sources.

It has been suggested by Max Muller that the Arabs were not really polytheistic but **henotheistic**. This means that they acknowledged many deities but only one supreme overall God (Allah). Recent writers, such as Turner, agree.

There also appears to have been a superficial role for religion and ritual in general as:

It would seem that in general the ordinary Arab sat somewhat lightly on his religious duties.

(Guillaume)

Religion had a practical function, linked to sacrifice and ritual, as opposed to a more deep-rooted theological one.

The final aspect of Arab 'paganism' was the existence of religious people, called hanifs, who lived a very strict lifestyle of moral purity, almost as a reaction to the practices of the day. Hanifism was also strictly monotheistic, in line with Christianity and Judaism. Little more is known of their actual beliefs and practices but Muhammad was aware of their scattered presence in pre-Islamic Arabia.

" **KEY QUOTE**

Especially in Mecca [Makkah] the centre of the Jahiliyyah religious experience, this vibrant pluralistic environment became a breeding ground for bold new ideas and exciting religious experimentation.

(Aslan)

"

KEY WORDS

Al-Allat: one of Allah's daughters, whose name means 'goddess'

Al-Uzza: one of Allah's daughters, whose name means 'mighty'

Al-Manat: one of Allah's daughters, whose name means 'fate'

Animism: belief that a soul or spirit exists in every object, animate or inanimate; from the Latin anima meaning breath or soul

Henotheistic: worshipping a single god while accepting the possible existence of others; a term coined by Max Muller and supported by recent writers such as Turner

TASK

Summarise, in table form, key points for the different religious ideas found in early Arab culture. Add an extra column and use it to compare and contrast the ideas.

Objective: To ensure accuracy with religious ideas and the accurate use of correct terminology, a prerequisite for a level 4 response at AS 'expressed clearly and accurately, using technical language widely' (level 4 descriptor AO1).

5 The environment into which Muhammad was born and Islam was introduced

On the eve of the advent of Islam, historians tell of a city in which the old tribal values had been abandoned, and in which a dog-eat-dog culture had begun to emerge, fuelled by greed and envy.

(Turner)

❞

More needs to be said about the social and moral features of Arabian culture at the time of Muhammad. The strong bonds of tribalism and the moral codes, principles or rules have already been established.

Many books have almost purely negative accounts, from a monotheistic or Muslim perspective of jahiliyya. As has already been discussed, this did not mean that the entirety of pre-Islamic life in Arabia was evil or debased. There were many good qualities of tribal society, such as honour, bravery, hospitality and generosity. As Turner writes:

Yet the old image of the 'uncivilised Bedouin' is most misleading, for in fact desert life was lived to the highest of values.

There were, however, some morally questionable practices and conditions that had arisen, mainly due to the expansion of cities such as Makkah, and the surrounding conflicts between empires. Such issues had been left festering and grew worse with time.

 KEY WORD

Feudal: an environment of retribution and vendetta in the struggle for overall power

While the tribal system promoted the protection of the tribe and individualism was not possible, the consequence of this was the emerging and intensifying **feudal** system. Under such a system life was cheap and there was nothing immoral about killing *per se*: it was only wrong to kill your own tribesmen or their allies.

It followed that each tribe had to avenge the death of any single one of its members by killing somebody in the murderer's tribe. One vendetta bred another; if a tribe felt that revenge had been disproportionate then there was danger of it exploding into full tribal conflict.

In the same way, robbery was not considered immoral unless you stole the goods of kinsmen. Despite this, the food and goods available were distributed equally and fairly among the tribes. Nonetheless, there are clear references to gambling, drunkenness, prostitution and general dishonesty in business.

In such an environment, only the strong could survive and that meant the weak were oppressed and exploited.

➡ EXAM TIP

Always point out the wide variety of influences from the pre-Islamic context and aim to present them, using your own words with quotes to support your points. This demonstrates more personal understanding or 'ownership' of the knowledge with 'significant features explained for emphasis and clarity' which is awarded for higher-level answers (level 3 descriptor and above AO1).

Female infanticide was the normal means of population control. This was because a tribe could only manage to support a given number of women and female babies were more common.

Women, like slaves, were not treated particularly well (unless they were from a family or business of substance) and they had no specific rights, human or legal.

In short, Muhammad was influenced by, and accepted:

- absolute monotheism
- the existing tribal moral codes and social values
- support for the weak in society

and he clearly rejected:

- anything short of absolute monotheism
- immorality
- cruelty and neglect of the weak in society.

TASK

Try to identify positive and negative influences upon Muhammad from the pre-Islamic context. Look at factors such as religious ideas, social systems and morality. Present your answer in table form.

Objective: What is required is not just a general answer that presents 'a limited range of isolated facts...with mainly random and unorganised detail' or 'information presented within a structure which shows a basic awareness of the issue(s) raised' (levels 1 and 2 descriptors AO1). Remember, you are aiming for 'a coherent and well-structured account of the subject matter' (level 4 descriptor AO1).

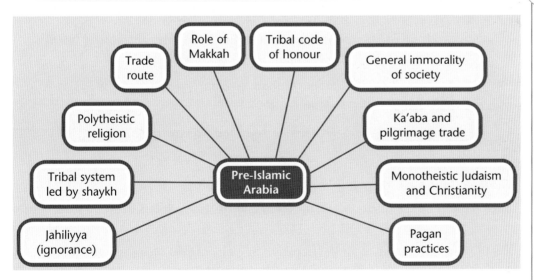

Summary diagram: Pre-Islamic Arabia

Reflection and assessment

It is vital to bring together the information that has been covered so far and recognise how it can be transformed into effective examination-style revision and answers. The best way to do this is to ask: 'How am I going to be assessed on this information?'

The first way is through assessment objective 1 (AO1). For this you need to be able to 'select and clearly demonstrate the relevant knowledge and understanding through the use of evidence, examples and correct language and terminology appropriate to the course of study' (AO1 descriptor).

As you work through each unit in this book, you will find that the amount of support in these sections will gradually be reduced, in order to encourage the development of your independence and the honing of your AO1 skills.

Use the writing frame provided below to answer this question.

> **Examine the environment into which Muhammad was born in pre-Islamic Arabia.** (21 marks)

In answering this question, remember to match the correct teachings and practices to the appropriate groups. Relate these to what Muhammad actually accepted or rejected.

a) Writing frame

At the time of Muhammad there were a variety of religious ideas, social traditions and moral practices. The most common form of religion was paganism...

The term 'pagan' means...

Typical pagan ideas include...

There were also monotheistic groups such as...

Socially, Arabia was based upon a tribal system...

There were also a variety of moral practices...

Muhammad would have interacted and been influenced by all the above.

Some things he clearly accepted, for example...

Others he rejected, for example...

b) Suggestion for further application of skills

After completing the question, use the levels and AO1 descriptors to award marks out of 21.

Identify strengths and areas for development in each answer. Then, as a group, collaborate to create an ideal answer that demonstrates:

- 'a coherent and well-structured response to the task at a wide range or considerable depth'
- 'selecting the most important features for emphasis and clarity'
- 'using evidence to explain the key ideas' (high level 4 descriptor).

FOUNDATIONS
Area F: Islam

TOPIC 1: KEY ISSUES IN THE STUDY OF ISLAM

Part 1B: The significance of Muhammad for Muslims

> **This means I am expected:**
>
> **to know about the key issues:**
> - the life and work of Muhammad in its historical, religious and social context
> - his significance for Muslims
>
> **and to study:**
> - Muhammad in Islam
> - Muhammad's upbringing
> - the night journey
> - the hijra
> - the growth of theocracy and the success of Muhammad's dual role as both prophet and statesman in Madinah
> - the battles and the return to Makkah
> - the implications of the social and political environment.

In this book the evidence and examples given are relevant and appropriate because this material focuses only on the content for AO1 that is given by the Edexcel specification. The evaluation materials for AO2 will be aimed at helping you 'critically evaluate and justify a point of view through the use of evidence and reasoned argument'.

It would be helpful to write your notes using the headings listed above, as it is from these areas that the examination questions will be derived.

In your studies, remember that you have to bear in mind the **two** basic assessment objectives of:

- Knowledge and Understanding (AO1)
- Evaluation (AO2).

See pages 7–8 in the Introduction to remind yourself of these objectives.

The evaluation material set out in Part 1C (page 184) can be studied either alongside the AO1 material, as you work through this unit, or as a separate unit.

EXAM TIP

Do not answer a question on the life of Muhammad by simply 'telling a story'. Your answer should always select the key events, that is, the appropriate information relevant to the question. This demonstrates more personal understanding or 'ownership' of the knowledge; it also demonstrates 'significant features explained for emphasis and clarity' which is awarded for higher-level answers (level 3 and above descriptor AO1).

KEY WORDS

Qur'an: Muslim scripture
Hadith: oral traditions relating to the words and deeds of Muhammad
Hijra: flight of Muhammad from Makkah to Madinah

KEY PEOPLE

Abd Allah: Muhammad's father
Abu Talib: Muhammad's uncle and his protector
Khadijah: Muhammad's wife
Ruqayya: Muhammad's daughter, married Uthman
Fatima: Muhammad's daughter, married Ali
Ali: husband of Fatima; among the first to accept the teachings of Muhammad

1 Muhammad in Islam

Muhammad (PBUH) is beyond doubt the most important figure in Islam. However, there is absolute resistance in Islam to venerating him beyond his status. Muslims believe there can be no other 'greatness' above Allah, which creates something of a paradox. For a Muslim, Muhammad's greatness is due to the way in which Allah is glorified through Muhammad's life, speech, actions and deeds.

The establishment of Islam depends on two crucial aspects: the revelation of the **Qur'an** and the implementation of Islam. The revelations span several years and the implementation is based on people's interpretations of the revelations. The two aspects are intrinsically linked, and together they form a vast area of study. It therefore makes sense to study each aspect as a distinct focus, while at the same time remembering that each aspect informs, expands on and illuminates the other.

This section deals specifically with Muhammad's life and work, both before and after his revelation and, in particular, the way in which Islam became established as a religion. Topic 2 (starting on page 188) will deal more specifically with the Qur'an itself, how it was compiled and the key teachings it contains.

2 Muhammad's upbringing

There is little biographical detail to be found in the Qur'an or the **Hadith**. The earliest recognised biography is by ibn Ishaq (eighth century CE); however, despite this, the general view as expressed by Rippen is that:

The account of the events during Muhammad's life is fairly standardised.

Muhammad was born in Makkah, in or around CE570. The only certain date for Muhammad, close to his birth, is the **hijra** in CE622.

His father, who died before Muhammad was born, was **Abd Allah**, grandson of Abd al-Muttalib (whose descendants have links to the present-day Hashim royal families of Jordan and Iraq). The tribe of Quraysh, into which Muhammad was born, was well established although at the time it was 'a prominent but not dominant group' (Rippin). His family was not wealthy.

His mother died in his early years, after which he was brought up by his kindly grandfather and then later by his uncle **Abu Talib**. Unfortunately, there is little information beyond this about Muhammad's childhood that does not belong to the world of legend.

As a young man, Muhammad was 'physically well-favoured and mentally astute…a serious-minded introvert'. (Ruthven) He found employment trading camels with Damascus. He worked for, and later married, his distant cousin, **Khadijah**, who was a wealthy widow 15 years his senior.

Together, they had two sons and four daughters. Both sons died as infants but of his daughters, **Ruqayya** married Uthman (the third Caliph) and **Fatima** married **Ali**.

Again, during the 15 years between their marriage and the first revelation very little is known and 'Muhammad virtually disappears from the history books' (Turner).

KEY WORDS

Nabi: or navi, the
Hebrew term for
prophet
Rasul: one who is sent

Guillaume draws parallels with the Hebrew prophet in the early narratives about Muhammad. In the tradition of the Hebrew **nabi** or **rasul**, Muhammad experienced inspired divine utterances and visions. He was intensely preoccupied with morality and ideas about God and he had a compulsion to declare God's will.

According to the story, Muhammad's preoccupation with God took him to a mountain cave to meditate. A vision of an angel, Gabriel, followed in which a silk cloth with 'recite' written on it was given to Muhammad. This experience is recounted in the Bloodclot Sura found in the Qur'an. Muhammad thought that he was possessed and was psychologically and emotionally disturbed by the experience. He even contemplated suicide; however, a voice from heaven and a figure standing astride on the horizon convinced him not to do this.

Guillaume describes the immediate period after Muhammad's initial revelation as a 'dark night of the soul', full of doubts and fears. However, Muhammad was encouraged by Khadijah and others close to him. According to Turner, it was between six months and two years before God spoke again to Muhammad. Indeed, it was three years before Muhammad went public in Makkah with the message from God.

The early message delivered by Muhammad to Makkah had several underlying themes. Muhammad called for uncompromising monotheism and so directly challenged and criticised polytheistic practices associated with the ka'aba. Muhammad spoke of judgement and personal responsibility for actions, indirectly condemning many ancestors of the Makkans. Finally, social injustices were challenged that highlighted the corruption in society as a whole.

KEY QUOTE

Some of his biographers have deleted the passages which speak of his doubts and fears; but they are perhaps the most convincing elements in the story.
(Guillaume)

At first, those who converted to follow Muhammad did so in secret.

For three years Muhammad's message spread quietly and privately, and a group of followers formed around him.

(Brown)

Muhammad led his followers in performing habitual daily prayers as a focus of their newfound faith.

Muhammad now worked to revive the great prophets' institution of formal prayer by teaching his household how to stand, bow and prostrate before God and how to interpose certain recitations from the Koran [Qur'an] between the various movements.

(Turner)

It is interesting to note the sociological background of the first converts. Although many were slaves and people of humble origins, it should not be forgotten that Muhammad did have powerful support and protection from influential figures in the early days.

In the beginning his followers were mocked. As his following grew, people in Makkah, especially the leaders and people of wealth and influence, began to feel threatened for a number of reasons.

● The call to serve one God and reject all idols threatened their businesses.
● Their power over the city was under challenge.
● Their popularity as leading figures in the community faltered as Muhammad's grew.
● In general, there was a feeling that Muhammad just wanted the wealth and power of the city for himself.

The initial mockery soon turned to accusations of sorcery and, finally, to accusations that he was stealing his ideas from the Jews and Christians. People were also sceptical about Muhammad's message and authority because they were not accompanied by miraculous signs. Generally, the early period in Makkah was 'a period of constant pinpricks, petty insults, and persecution of those who had no influential patron' and 'something like a boycott of the Muslims was put in force' (Guillaume).

KEY PERSON

Hamza: uncle to Muhammad, who later provided protection for him in the face of persecution

At this stage the protection offered by Abu Talib and by Muhammad's other uncle, **Hamza**, (a famous warrior and hunter) was crucial for his survival.

The persecution from the opposition grew more intense. It is recorded that, feeling the pressure of persecution, Muhammad was tempted, and succumbed, to acknowledging three other deities usually associated with the Ka'aba (the three 'daughters of Allah' associated with pre-Islamic Arabia). However, under reprimand from Gabriel, Muhammad retracted this acknowledgement. The people of Makkah were now angrier than before due to this apparent inconsistency.

After this, Muhammad began to criticise the Ka'aba and the idols more strongly. Influential figures in Makkah started to contemplate a more violent solution to the problem of Muhammad:

> *The Qurayshi leaders' derision quickly grew into more serious opposition when Muhammad began to mock their gods. From that point the leaders of the Quraysh began to plot his destruction.*

> **(Brown)**

Ruthven identifies three reasons why Muhammad's life was threatened.

1 His message contained direct attacks on the private accumulation of wealth.

2 A man claiming to speak directly for God would be unlikely to submit to any purely political authority.

KEY WORD

Day of judgement: the idea of responsibility for one's actions and consequent accountability before God on a final day

3 The idea of a **day of judgement** implied individual resurrection and responsibility and the attacks on idolatry, combined with the idea of their ancestors burning in hell, was too much for the Makkans to bear.

What followed was a more intense period of persecution. The weakest of his followers, such as the slaves, were targeted for persecution, torture and death for their allegiance to Muhammad. Soon, no one who professed his monotheistic message and faith was safe.

TASK

Design a flowchart that explains the process of Muhammad's revelation and his experiences in Makkah.
Objective: To develop knowledge and understanding of the significance of the revelation and the impact of the message on Muhammad's immediate environment; developing knowledge and understanding of the significance of the revelation, illustrating 'accurate and relevant detail, clearly identifying the most important features' (level 4 descriptor AO1).

3 The night journey

Turner describes Muhammad, during this period of heightened persecution, as being 'possibly at his lowest ebb', but it was also in this period that 'Muhammad experienced what was arguably the most intense spiritual experience of his life'.

This experience, known as the **night journey**, describes Muhammad's miraculous ascension into heaven. This is sometimes associated with a visit to Jerusalem, in the dream, because of reference made to the 'farthest mosque'. However, this is debated and writers such as Turner see it as more as 'a metaphor for the highest degree of submission'.

According to the tradition, Muhammad was accompanied by the angel Gabriel and **Buraq**, a winged horse. On his arrival, he met Abraham, Moses and Jesus and led them in prayers. He was tested with a choice of drink: wine, water or milk, and made the wise choice of milk for the 'rightly guided community' of Muslims. Muhammad was given an insight into hell but then taken on a full tour of heaven, ascending through the seven heavenly realms. While he was in the seventh heaven, Muhammad was commanded by Allah to offer 50 daily prayers. Moses sent Muhammad back to Allah to negotiate five:

> *After shuttling several times between Moses and God, Muhammad came away with five obligatory prayers.*
>
> **(Brown)**

During the most difficult period of his life, this experience served to consolidate Muhammad's strength and resolve. Later, when his wife and uncle died, Muhammad left Makkah and attempted to settle in Ta'if but was met with insults and returned to Makkah, where he had to seek alternative protection.

4 The hijra

Muhammad and his followers were in a desperate situation. They feared for their lives. The only solution was to flee secretly to a place beyond the reach of persecution and oppression. Muhammad and his followers fled to the oasis at Yathrib (Madinah).

This is so important an event to Muslims that it marks the beginning of their calendar. It is called the hijra (flight).

Turner refers to the hijra as 'a psychological turning point of inestimable importance' transforming a 'faith minority' into a community and eventually an empire.

> *The emigration to Yathrib [Madinah] occurred slowly and stealthily, with the Companions heading out towards the oasis a few at a time. By the time the Quraysh realised what was happening, only Muhammad, Abu Bakr and Ali were left.*
>
> **(Aslan)**

During the flight, Muhammad spent three days in a cave and was miraculously protected from Qurayshi pursuers.

Tradition tells that Muhammad and Abu Bakr escaped a final murder plot; Abu Bakr and Muhammad left Makkah at night, while Ali remained behind to sleep in Muhammad's bed to foil the plot.

KEY WORDS

Night journey: Muhammad's ascension to heaven

Buraq: winged horse that took Muhammad up to heaven

KEY QUOTE

As well, the account of the ascension stands as a model of Muslim spiritual devotion when interpreted on a metaphorical level as the inner journey leading to the vision of God... The story functions on many different levels, therefore, and is not only a vehicle for flights of popular imagination.

(Rippin)

TASK

Design a chart highlighting the causes of the problems Muhammad faced in Makkah, the reaction to the problem and the ways in which the migration to Madinah solved the problems.

Objective: To develop knowledge and understanding of the significance of key events in the life of Muhammad. This demonstrates both 'a coherent and well-structured response to the task at a wide range or considerable depth' and that you are 'selecting the most important features for emphasis and clarity; using evidence to explain the key ideas' (top level 4 descriptor AO1).

There were many reasons to support Muhammad's final decision to flee from the obvious death threats. In a sense, while the final decision and move were swift, they followed a gradual build-up of threatening events.

We can identify and summarise the key factors that led to the hijra under the headings of push factors and pull factors. Not all reasons for the hijra were negative and there were many attractive factors about Madinah.

Push and pull factors

i) Push factors

These included:

- persecution
- threats on people's lives
- inability to practise Islam freely
- lack of influence and limited spread of Islam
- continued growing opposition from leading Makkans.

There were two more major factors.

- The person and message of Muhammad were seen as a threat to religious beliefs, to trade, to ancestors and to the status of Makkan leaders.
- Attempts to migrate to Ta'f had failed; Muhammad had made converts from Madinah at trade fairs and saw this as a sign from God.

ii) Pull factors

- Muhammad was re-motivated after the Night Journey.
- Madinah was a political as well as a religious ally.
- Madinah offered an environment in which to establish formal practices of Islam.
- Muhammad was valued as an **arbitrator** and offered high rank and status.
- Muhammad believed it to be the will of Allah.

5 The growth of theocracy and the success of Muhammad's dual role as both prophet and statesman in al-Madinah

From the pull factors identified above it is clear that in Madinah Muhammad was able to adopt many different roles and develop new skills beyond those of a simple religious leader.

During his time in Madinah, Muhammad demonstrated 'consummate political skills' (Brown) in changing the **ummah** (followers) from an unpolitical religious group to a complete community that embraced all differences. Indeed, it was Muhammad's aim for the ummah in Madinah 'to build up a self-contained community which would hold together and maintain its position' (Guillaume).

❝ KEY QUOTE

The Medinan [Madinan] community formed a total framework for state, society, and culture. It epitomised the Quranic mandate for Muslims as individuals and a community 'to transform the world itself through action in the world'…It inspired Muhammad to transform a local sheikdom into a transtribal state.

(Esposito)

❞

On his arrival in Madinah, when Muhammad was greeted by its different tribes, he displayed his first piece of political tact. Muhammad needed to find a place for his headquarters. To choose wrongly would have been a disastrous show of favouritism, causing conflicts between the tribes. Instead, he let his camel decide where the first **mosque** was to be built. He announced that wherever the camel sat down would be the site.

On the one hand, this showed brilliant political acumen; on the other, it was almost a humorous irony, for 'the house that would become, after the Ka'ba [Ka'aba], the foremost mosque of Islam… it was here that he organised and directed the affairs of the infant Islamic state' (Ruthven).

Madinan society was riven with internal conflict. The two dominant tribes were the Aws and the Khazraj; there were also three Jewish tribes, the Banu Qurayza, Banu Qaynuqa and Banu al-Nadir. Added to this was a diverse mix of immigrants. While executing his authority, Muhammad demonstrated tact and diplomacy, dealing with great wisdom with tribal and religious differences – a vital skill in such a delicate situation of divisions within the Madinan community.

> *The task facing Muhammad was to unite these disparate elements as justly and judiciously as possible.*
>
> **(Turner)**

Muhammad did this by developing the **Constitution of Madinah**, an agreement that stipulated that:

● there was one Muslim single community (ummah)
● Jewish allies could be considered part of the ummah
● Muhammad was the chief arbitrator in all decisions.

> *This brotherhood bound all Muslims together for offence and defence, guaranteed them the protection of the community…and made God and his prophet the final arbiter in all disputes.*
>
> **(Guillaume)**

Ruthven likens the constitution to a **hilf** or tribal pact. Aslan identifies its controversial nature, since it gave to Muhammad 'unparalleled religious and political authority' and 'sole authority to arbitrate all disputes'. Whatever the case, it was a triumph of political diplomacy that earned widespread respect, allegiance and deference.

It was the success of these political dealings that enabled aspects of Islam as a religion to be established (see page 181). As Ruthven comments: 'The new situation demanded a coherent formula for living as well as the will to put this formula into practice.'

There were still problems with dissemblers, who displayed outward allegiance but schemed behind Muhammad's back. However, Muhammad's influence clearly defused any threat they may have posed. Likewise, there were conflicts with Makkans (see below) but these were dealt with in a different way.

Aslan observes that, despite this, Muhammad's work in Madinah 'became the **paradigm** for the Muslim empires that expanded throughout the Middle East after the Prophet's death, and the standard that every Arab kingdom struggled to meet during the Middle Ages'.

KEY WORDS

Mosque: place of prayer or prostration, sometimes called masjid
Constitution of Madinah: an agreement drawn up by Muhammad in Madinah
Hilf: tribal pact or agreement
Paradigm: model, example

KEY QUOTE

Muhammad accomplished his purpose in the course of three small engagements: the number of combatants in these never exceeded a few thousand, but in importance they rank among the world's decisive battles.

(Guillaume)

6 The battles and the return to Makkah

The ongoing conflicts with the now-distant Makkans meant that Muhammad's newfound authority in Madinah was not without its difficulties. In order to deal with these conflicts Muhammad consolidated his support, then went on the offensive. By taking on its aggressors in what Guillaume refers to as 'among the world's decisive battles', Islam secured its future.

a) Badr

This is probably the most famous and influential of the battles. It was initiated by Muhammad's order to attack a Quraysh caravan during the sacred month, when war was banned. One person was killed and two were arrested. This was indeed: 'a provocation that could not go unanswered' (Turner). However, despite the unusual and possibly uncharacteristic decision made by Muhammad, the Qur'an (The Cow, Sura 2:216–17) puts his actions into perspective and justifies the need for them.

The battle, between 300 Muslims and 1000 Makkans, took place at Badr. Muhammad was successful and some significant and determined opponents were defeated in this conflict. Brown cites sources that witness 'angels fighting alongside Muslims'. Muhammad's great success meant that those in Madinah who were undecided joined Muhammad's cause and the Bedouin affiliated themselves more readily with him.

b) Uhud

The relationship between the ummah and the Jews was uneasy. They had rejected Muhammad as prophet and they also had economic supremacy in the Hijaz. When Muhammad provoked the Jewish tribes, 3000 Quraysh marched toward Madinah in support of the Jewish tribe that had been attacked. The Muslims had been ordered to stay within the stronghold of Madinah, but thoughts of the glory after their success at Badr tempted them to march out to Uhud, one mile from the town.

The Muslims were defeated and had to flee. However, only 70 were killed, 'not the total military disaster that some historians have painted it' (Turner).

What followed was quite remarkable. Curiously, the Quraysh did not follow up their victory. Instead, it was Muhammad who led an army to Makkah the next day and camped outside for several days, lighting a large fire. This open defiance clearly lifted the morale of his men after the loss they had suffered. As Brown writes: 'Badr had taught the Muslims about victory; at Uhud they learned fortitude in the face of defeat.'

c) Al-Khandaq

This is called the 'battle of the ditch'. Further disputes between the Jewish tribes and the Muslims led to a great sense of uncertainty and distrust. Within the Jewish population it was not clear just who was supporting whom. The Makkans gathered some Bedouin allies and marched towards Madinah with an army 10 000 strong.

With the memory of defeat at Uhud still fresh, Muhammad took some Persian advice and dug a ditch around Madinah. This kept the enemy in the open, unable to attack without suffering mass casualties. Muhammad's forces were victorious but 'despite the victory of the Battle of the Ditch, Muhammad still did not feel safe' (Ruthven).

There was now discord among the Makkans, the Bedouin and the Jews. The Jews would not attack for fear of being deserted by the Makkans. All trust between parties had

KEY IDEA

The battles:
- **Badr: first battle in which a minority of Muslims overcame a majority of Makkans, according to tradition, through divine assistance**
- **Uhud: defeat for the Muslims but followed immediately by a period of reflection, determination and defiance**
- **Al-Khandaq: final influential battle that saw victory for Muslims, due to effective battle strategies, and led to the final onslaught and command of Makkah.**

TASK

Design a diagram focusing on the three battles that Muhammad faced, showing the cause, the response and the outcome.

Objective: To develop knowledge and understanding of the significance of key events in the life of Muhammad, demonstrating 'evidence to explain key ideas' (level 4 descriptor AO1).

disappeared. There developed a siege-like situation that soon was defused and the armies returned. The forces were now dispersed enough to be open to attack.

Muhammad attacked straight away and overcame the Jews. He went on gradually to conquer the tribes surrounding Makkah. After this, he agreed the **Treaty of Hudaybiya** which was a ten-year truce. Under the treaty, Muhammad could enter Makkah for pilgrimage, the Bedouin were converted and Islam grew.

Muhammad entered Makkah as a pilgrim. He won the allegiance of important figures, such as General Khalid; his influence beyond Madinah went from strength to strength.

In AH8 the truce was broken when the Makkans attacked a tribe that was under Muslim protection. This enabled Muhammad to complete his takeover of Makkah.

7 The implications of the social and political environment

Makkah and Madinah provided very different environments that influenced how Islam was established and grew. Waines notes how Muhammad behaved differently in each situation:

> *Muhammad in Mecca [Makkah] had acted as a missionary to his pagan kinsmen…The Medinan [Madinan] situation demanded other measures to keep the nascent Muslim community intact, secure from external threat or sabotage from within.*

How Muhammad established Islam as a major force

Muhammad recognised the differences and made the most of the opportunity to manipulate the support that he had in Madinah. Indeed, Ruthven adds that Muhammad was well aware of the 'superficial' allegiance to Islam engendered by the Constitution of Madinah:

> *Many, however, embraced Islam only in a nominal sense while remaining attached to pagan practices. Muhammad understood – as his more zealous followers did not – that it would take several generations to 'Islamise' the new adherents.*

Aslan argues that this attitude of making the best of support and building a community was a typical Arab approach, rather than being specific to Muhammad or Islamic ideas:

> *Despite its ingenuity, Muhammad's community was still an Arab institution based on Arab notions of tribal society. There was simply no alternative model of social organisation in seventh-century Arabia, save for monarchy.*

Aslan continues to argue that, since there are so many similarities between the ummah and traditional tribal society, Muhammad himself saw the ummah as 'a tribe, though a new and radically innovative one'.

Ruthven is more cautious in assigning a 'model' of transference from Arab tribe to Muslim ummah. He suggests that the old model did not work and that it is in the transformation of tribalism that Islam found success:

> *What had once worked well in the desert was becoming unsuited both to the caravan-city and to the oasis. Yet tribalism could not be eliminated overnight, or even abolished altogether.*

Whatever the case, Muhammad's 'radical religious, social and economical reforms' enabled 'a new kind of society, the likes of which had never been seen in Arabia' (Aslan). Turner describes the Madinan state as a 'reworking of society along Islamic precepts, be they moral, ethical or socio-political' but identifies the key loyalty as 'not

KEY WORDS

Treaty of Hudaybiya: ten-year agreement to allow access for Muslims to Makkah during pilgrimage

KEY IDEA

The letters AH are used in the Islam calendar, to signify that it dates from the hijra.

❝ KEY QUOTE

What made the Ummah a unique experiment in social organisation was that in Yathrib [Madinah]… Muhammad finally had the opportunity to implement the reforms he had been preaching to no avail in Mecca [Makkah].

(Aslan)

❞

loyalty to the tribe, as had been the case in pre-Islamic Mecca [Mekkah], but a common belief in one God.'

| Upbringing: the trustworthy, marriage and excellent trader, potential for leadership | The revelations: role of Muhammad as prophet, chosen to be 'seal of the prophets', initial fear, lack of confidence, the message of one God, judgement and morality, support of wife and relatives, bravery to speak out | • The night journey and subsequent hijra to Madinah
• Establishment of Muhammad as religious and political leader | • The battles and the return to Makkah: Battle of Badr, Battle of Uhud, Battle of al-Khandaq
• Establishment of Islamic state |

Summary diagram: Key events in the life of Muhammad

Reflection and assessment (AO1)

It is vital to bring together the information covered so far and recognise how it can be transformed into effective examination style revision and answers. The best way to do this is to ask: 'How am I going to be assessed on this information?'

The first way is through assessment objective 1 (AO1). You need to be able to 'select and clearly demonstrate the relevant knowledge and understanding, through the use of evidence, examples and correct language and terminology'.

Look back to pages 8–10 in the Introduction to review the level descriptors for AO1. There is a description of the character and features for each level. The exam is marked with reference to levels.

Look at the answer below, which is a response to this question.

Give an account of the main reasons for Muhammad to migrate from Makkah to Madinah (Yathrib). (21 marks)

Good to point out variety. → There were many reasons why Muhammad migrated from Makkah to Madinah.

Some were to do with him being pressurised to move, whilst others were to do with — *Good to indicate positive and negative.*

the attractions that Madinah had. The 'push' factors tended to be to do with

Muhammad and his followers being persecuted because the message Muhammad

preached contained direct attacks on the private accumulation of wealth. This

The answer digresses here to detail that is not the focus of the question. → was because monotheism would mean a rejection of idols and therefore trade at

the Ka'aba. The Ka'aba was a very important source of income. It was in the centre

of Makkah and pilgrims went there but also there were thousands of idols being

sold and religious trade was rife. Muhammad could not practise Islam openly and — *Returns here to question.*

there were threats on his life. Islam was not really having the impact Muhammad

would have wanted in Makkah. Muhammad had made converts from Madinah at

trade fairs and saw this as a sign from God. Madinah was therefore offering an

environment in which to establish formal practices of Islam.

a) So what would this answer score?

In the exam the answer will be marked according to levels (see pages 7–8 in the Introduction). We need to refer to level descriptors and relate parts of the essay to the levels.

There is certainly knowledge and understanding shown in this answer. The writer clearly has an understanding of the key reasons for Muhammad's migration, so the answer is at least a level 2 ('mainly relevant and accurate information presented within a structure which shows a basic awareness of the issue raised', level 2 descriptor).

Despite attempting to organise the material into positive and negative reasons, this is never really developed fully as it is limited in its explanation and selection of relevant material. There were other points that could have been included.

i) Push
- A man claiming to speak directly for God would be unlikely to submit to any purely political authority.
- The idea of a Day of Judgement implied individual resurrection and responsibility and the attacks on idolatry, combined with the idea of their ancestors burning in hell, was too much for the Makkans to bear.
- There was continued growing opposition from leading Makkans.
- The person and message of Muhammad were seen as a threat to religious beliefs, to trade, to ancestors and to the status of Makkan leaders.
- Attempts to migrate to Ta'if had failed.

ii) Pull
- He was re-motivated after the night journey.
- Madinah was a political as well as a religious ally.
- Muhammad was desired as an arbitrator and offered high rank and status.
- He believed that it was the will of Allah.

iii) Conclusions
Despite having some understanding, the answer is limited in its selection of knowledge and, together with the digressions, this means that understanding is affected. It cannot be level 3, 'a range of accurate and relevant knowledge, presented within a recognisable and generally coherent structure, selecting significant features for emphasis and clarity' (level 3 descriptor), but must be awarded a middle level 2 as it is 'relevant and accurate information organised to show some awareness of the issue raised; with sufficient scope to show recognition of the breadth of the task; expressed simply and with some clarity' (mid level 2 descriptor, 7–8 marks).

b) Suggestion for further application of skills

Use the points identified above to redraft this answer. Copy it to obtain a text version, then delete material as appropriate, expand on the undeveloped points and add in possible points that could be included. You can do this in pairs, groups or individually but it is important to discuss and compare possible answers. Alternatively start afresh, listing points, create a writing frame and complete the answer as a class.

This will improve a level 2 response and transform it into level 4, demonstrating 'a coherent and well-structured account of the subject matter, with accurate and relevant detail, clearly identifying the most important features' (level 4 descriptor AO1).

TOPIC 1: KEY ISSUES IN THE STUDY OF ISLAM

Part 1C: A critical analysis of the issues

> **This means I am expected:**
>
> **to analyse and critically evaluate:**
> - how Muhammad reacted against society's influences
> - how Muhammad related to his immediate context.

1 How Muhammad reacted against society's influences

a) Theological

? KEY QUESTIONS
- How far can Islam be said to be the original religion?
- Is the idea of one-ness of God unique to Islam?
- How far did Muhammad both simplify and standardise religious practice?
- How far did Muhammad reform society?
- Were the social reforms the purpose of Muhammad's message?
- How far was Muhammad a typical prophet in terms of his obsession with morality?

While Muhammad (PBUH) did not introduce monotheism, it is clear that he reacted against the polytheistic or henotheistic nature of pre-Islamic society.

Muhammad's ideas introduced a sense of community within a religion whereas followers of other religions were in effect merely collections of individuals.

The theme of 'one-ness' seemed to extend from theology to practicality under Muhammad's guidance. This was in contrast to the diverse and complex religious ideas of the day.

b) Social

Muhammad united what was previously a disparate series of feudal systems that had developed as a result of the gradual disintegration of tribal values. He challenged the economic and social inequalities that had been entrenched in the previous systems.

The ideal of the ummah, although considered to mirror Arab tribal values, was certainly not a mirror of the norms of society at the time.

The economical superiority of certain areas of society and the consequent disparities caused through this inequality were challenged and redressed.

TASK

Make your own list of questions that you would like to ask about how Muhammad related to or reacted against his immediate moral, social and religious context.
Objective: To encourage the use of questions in answers for AO2 that helps to demonstrate more than 'a mainly descriptive response, at a general level' (level 1 descriptor AO2) and aim for 'an attempt at an evaluation of the issue(s) raised in the task' (level 4 descriptor AO2).

c) Moral

Muhammad's attitudes towards gambling and alcohol were in stark contrast to those that existed in pre-Islamic Makkah and Arabia.

Muhammad's view of the role and status of women was nothing short of radical.

Protection of the weak was a key theme for Muhammad's new community and it was uncompromising and without the conditions of tribal allegiance.

2 How Muhammad related to his immediate context

a) Theological

Muhammad inherited, and was influenced by, the rich Arab–Jewish heritage of monotheistic values. Indeed, the acceptance of previous prophets and acknowledgement of Jesus made Islam a return to the traditions of old.

The use of the Ka'aba embraced the age-old established traditions and cultural practices of Muhammad's Abrahamaic heritage.

Allah, the name of God, was maintained as the one eternal truth and developed through absolute, uncompromising monotheism. This can be understood in theological terms by the concept of jahiliyya (ignorance of God's guidance), which is how Islam views those who do not follow the Qur'an.

b) Social

Muhammad used traditional Arab ideas and social values in creating the ummah.

Muhammad replaced blood ties and tribal identity with a similar but more universal model of religious affinity and identity.

Muhammad emphasised all that was good and honourable from the ancient tribal codes, particularly the ideas of loyalty and protection, to unite the ummah.

c) Moral

There was a return to the original strict tribal code of honour.

The community embraced influences of moral codes from various monotheistic elements such as Hanifs, Christians and Jews.

The Muslim community upheld the themes of justice and equality.

3 Possible conclusions we can draw from this

When assessing the issues that arise from pre-Islamic Arabia's influence on Muhammad, it is important to reflect upon the arguments previously discussed and arrive at some appropriate conclusion.

It may be that you accept none of these listed here, or just one of them, or you may have a different conclusion that is not listed. However, what is important is the way that you have arrived at your conclusion – the reasoning process.

? KEY QUESTIONS

- How far can Islamic religion be said to be unique?
- Did Muhammad fulfil a religious need in pre-Islamic Arabia?
- What did the term 'ignorance' in its purest sense refer to?
- How far did Muhammad's strong kinship experiences influence his formation of the ummah and Islamic values?
- Were the moral codes that were introduced by Muhammad new?
- Were there any new moral practices that promoted the ideal of Islam?

➡ EXAM TIP

Always point out how Muhammad related *to* and reacted *against* his background. Include some key questions and make sure that you offer more than one possible conclusion and then give your own, reasoned opinion, based upon what you have chosen to write about. Questions allow for a range of views (level 3 and above descriptor AO2) and this clearly is what a level 4 answer expects – 'a clearly expressed viewpoint supported by well-deployed evidence and reasoned argument' (level 4 descriptor AO2).

TASK

Draw a table with the headings 'Relate to' and 'React against' at the top. Down the side put the headings: religious, social and moral, life events, my conclusion. Try to complete the table by putting the appropriate evidence from the text into the relevant box.

Objective: To summarise Muhammad's response to his background. This could serve as a basis for your evidence to include in the writing frame at the end of this chapter. This meets the AO2 level 4 descriptor criteria of 'a careful analysis of alternative views...supported by well-deployed evidence'.

Muhammad is not considered the founder of the new religion of Islam. Like the biblical prophets who came before him, he was a religious reformer. Muhammad said that he did not bring a new message from a new God but called people back to the one true God and to a way of life they had forgotten or deviated from.

(Esposito)

From the preceding discussions, here are some possible conclusions you could draw.

1 Muhammad created an entirely new religion and reacted against his immediate environment. This idea raises problems of association with other elements of history – Islam is, perhaps, at best a new interpretation of old ideas.

2 Muhammad cleverly, and with political motives, put together a composite of existing practice. The problem with this conclusion is that, from the outset, many aspects of later Islam were present, for example, ummah, monotheism and the incorporation of ancient moral codes. This suggests that Muhammad was not driven by politics and ambition, but by the will of Allah and concern for society.

3 Muhammad rediscovered the original religion and returned to its purity. The problem with this idea is that we can't be sure that there actually was a pure religion to be rediscovered.

4 Muhammad delivered the true, final and complete message and religion, correcting all aspects of the past.

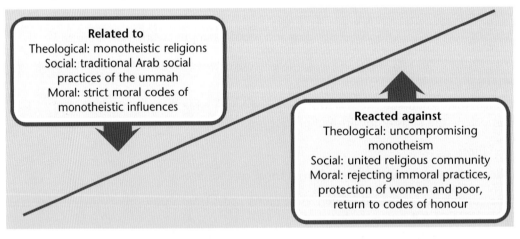

Related to
Theological: monotheistic religions
Social: traditional Arab social practices of the ummah
Moral: strict moral codes of monotheistic influences

Reacted against
Theological: uncompromising monotheism
Social: united religious community
Moral: rejecting immoral practices, protection of women and poor, return to codes of honour

Summary diagram: How Muhammad related to his immediate context

➡ EXAM TIP

Exam questions are expressed in words that tell you what to do in your answer. For AO2 they are:

● Comment on...
● Consider...
● How far...
● To what extent...
● Why...?

Reflection and assessment (AO2)

It is now time to formulate all this information in a more focused way. Again the key question is: 'How am I going to be assessed on my use of this information?'

The second way of being assessed is through assessment objective AO2. You need to be able to 'critically evaluate and justify a point of view through the use of evidence and reasoned argument'.

As the units in each section of the book develop, the amount of support will be reduced gradually in order to encourage your independence and the perfecting of your AO2 skills.

Try using the writing frame below to answer this question.

> **To what extent did the religious, social and historical context at the time of Muhammad have an impact on his mission?** (9 marks)

a) Writing frame

The issue for debate here is...

There are different ways of looking at this and many key questions to ask, such as...

At the time of Muhammad there were a variety of influences. We need to look at how Muhammad reacted to these. For example, it can be argued that he was influenced by certain key ideas from his religious, social and historical context, such as...

Some ideas, however, he rejected outright, such as...

Despite this influence, another point of view would be that he introduced unique ideas and practices, such as...

In this way it could be argued that his message was directed by God and no outside influence could have affected this.

In light of all this, it could be argued that...

Nevertheless, it is my view that...

and I base this argument on the following reasons...

b) Suggestion for further application of skills

After completing the question, use the levels and AO2 descriptors to award marks out of 9. Identify strengths and areas for development in each answer. Then, as a group, collaborate to create an ideal answer that demonstrates at least 'some attempt to set out reasons for a range of views' and 'a point of view expressed clearly, supported by relevant evidence and argument' (level 3 descriptor AO2).

Discuss how this answer could be improved to show 'a careful analysis of alternative views...leading to a clearly expressed viewpoint supported by well-deployed evidence and reasoned argument' (level 4 descriptor AO2).

> ## ➡ EXAM TIP
>
> Look at the levels and create a brief list of essential requirements in order to access a high level of response for an argument at AO2. For example, there needs to be 'an attempt at an evaluation of the issue(s) raised in the task, typically through a careful analysis of alternative views; leading to a clearly expressed viewpoint supported by well-deployed evidence and reasoned argument; expressed accurately, fluently and using a range of technical vocabulary' (level 4 descriptor AO2).

TOPIC 2: KEY EMPHASES IN TEACHING AND PRACTICE

Part 2A: The six beliefs – meaning and significance for belief and practice

➡ **EXAM TIP**

When answering a question on the six beliefs make sure that you focus on the specific area highlighted in the question. Make sure you pick out the key elements of that teaching and explain why it is important for Muslims and how it relates to the other teachings. This means that it is not just a general answer that presents 'a limited range of isolated facts…with mainly random and unorganised detail' or 'information presented within a structure which shows a basic awareness of the issue(s) raised' (level 1 and 2 descriptors A01). Remember, you are aiming for 'a coherent and well-structured account of the subject matter' (level 4 descriptor A01).

This means I am expected:

to know about the key emphasis:

● the six beliefs – meaning and significance for belief and practice

and to study:

● the nature of God (tawhid)
● angels (mala'ika)
● prophethood (nabuwwa or risallah)
● revelation of scriptures
● judgement, life after death (akirah)
● predestination (al-qadr).

In this book the evidence and examples given are relevant and appropriate because this material focuses only on the content for AO1 that is given by the Edexcel specification. The evaluation materials for AO2 will be aimed at helping you 'critically evaluate and justify a point of view through the use of evidence and reasoned argument'.

It would be helpful to write your notes using the headings listed above, as it is from these areas that the examination questions will be derived.

In your studies, remember that you have to bear in mind the **two** basic assessment objectives of:

● Knowledge and Understanding (AO1)
● Evaluation (AO2).

See pages 7–8 in the Introduction to remind yourself of these objectives.

The evaluation material set out in Part 2C (page 215) can be studied either alongside the AO1 material, as you work through this unit, or as a separate unit.

1 The nature of God (tawhid)

Tawhid translates as 'one-ness' and sometimes as 'unity'. God is one, has no partners or equals. He alone is God. This forms the basis of Muslim faith. The opposite of tawhid is **shirk** (associating partners or equals with God), the only unforgivable sin.

⚷ **KEY WORDS**

Tawhid: Muslim teaching of absolute monotheism
Shirk: associating something or someone as being on an equal basis as God

Tawhid is 'uncompromising monotheism' (Turner) and 'the defining doctrine of Islam' (Esposito). It is contained within the first pillar of Islam (the shahadah), 'the declaration of faith' and is what makes a Muslim (one who submits) a Muslim.

Aslan writes of the notion that there is no God but God: 'This deceptively simple statement is not only the basis for all articles of faith in Islam, it is in some ways the sum and total of Islamic theology. This is because the shahadah signifies recognition of an exceedingly complex theological doctrine known as tawhid.'

Although language must be used to express God's attributes, language is merely noises, symbols and metaphors and cannot do justice to the essence of God. Ultimately, God is beyond words and all descriptions.

> *'Allah is greater than anything else, or anything which can possibly be imagined' would be closer to the real meaning of tawheed [tawhid].*
>
> **(Horrie and Chippindale)**

The best depiction of the characteristics of Allah as they run through the Qur'an can be seen in Sura 112:

> *Say, 'He is One God: God the Eternal, the Uncaused Cause of all being. He Begets not, and neither is He begotten; and there is nothing that could be compared with Him.'*

This, in essence, is tawhid.

The concept of tawhid is also demonstrated in the idea of God as sole creator. God the creator is **transcendent** but **immanent** within creation:

> *The Koranic conception of God is as a Creator who is never absent from His creation…he is one who manifests Himself constantly through His creation.*
>
> **(Turner)**

Everything is dependent upon God's creative power. This is the idea of continuous creation. Everything is temporary and needs sustaining through a process of instant creation and re-creation:

> *Thus the Islamic notion of 'continuous creation' holds that God creates and re-creates all things at all times, bringing things into existence, and bringing them back into existence, all within the twinkling of an eye while maintaining the illusion of the permanency of matter.*
>
> **(Turner)**

Anything that casts doubt upon tawhid is considered shirk. While shirk is usually considered as the only unforgivable sin, Islam recognises the distinction between lesser or minor shirk and greater or major shirk. The former can be the unintentional hero-worship of an individual or the worship of materialism. The latter is a deliberate, distinct and clear denial of the unity of Allah. In short, placing any one thing on a par with Allah, whether by virtue of neglect or lack of perspective, is considered shirk.

In practice, this means that by recognising and following the teachings of tawhid, a Muslim becomes a 'true Muslim': that is, one who submits to the greatness of the one true God, Allah. Tawhid, then, is very much a practical tool for idbadah (worship) throughout the whole of life, in and through a Muslim's daily actions.

KEY IDEA

Creation *ex nihilo*: creation out of nothing

KEY QUOTE

Tawhid means that God is One-ness. God is Unity: wholly indivisible, entirely unique, and utterly undefinable. God resembles nothing in either essence or attributes.

(Aslan)

KEY WORDS

Transcendent: having existence outside the universe, usually depicted as an immaterial realm
Immanent: close, immediate

KEY IDEA

God as creator:
- Sole creator
- Created everything
- Has all power
- Made something from nothing
- Created spiritual beings
- Made living things from water
- Always aware of creation
- He is transcendent but also immanent.

As you go through this section, create a table that highlights the information about each of the six beliefs. This will give you a good overall picture. List the different religious beliefs down one side and then expand upon the ideas by adding definitions, further meanings, examples, etc.

Objective: To differentiate accurately between the different teachings and create a structure for a developed answer. This demonstrates both 'a coherent and well-structured response to the task at a wide range or considerable depth' and also that you are 'selecting the most important features for emphasis and clarity; using evidence to explain the key ideas' (top level 4 descriptor AO1).

KEY IDEA

Angels are:
- sexless
- made of light
- without free will
- obedient
- agents for Allah
- not perfect
- invisible and visible
- intermediaries
- messengers.

They:
- have hands and wings
- do not eat.

EXAM TIP

When answering a question on the six beliefs, make sure that you focus on the specific area highlighted in the question. Pick out the key elements of that teaching and explain why it is important for Muslims and how it relates to the other teachings. This means that it is not just a general answer that presents 'a limited range of isolated facts… with mainly random and unorganised detail' or 'information presented within a structure which shows a basic awareness of the issue(s) raised' (level 1 and 2 descriptors AO1). Remember, you are aiming for 'a coherent and well-structured account of the subject matter' (level 4 descriptor AO1).

2 Angels (mala'ika)

Angels are crucial to Islam. The idea of a God who is so perfect and transcendent and yet needs to communicate with humanity and display his immanence is explained through angels.

Angels are made of light. They are sexless and have consciousness but no free will. They are totally obedient but this does not mean that they are perfect. They are beings made for submission to Allah and to fulfil the divine purpose of communicating Allah's message to humanity. They have hands and wings but they do not need to eat.

Colin Turner refers to angels in Islam as mirrors that reflect the divine essence, enabling people to have a glimpse of this reflection and know God:

The angels, then, act as the interface between God and man.

(Turner)

There are several famous angels with specific roles.

- Gabriel (Jibril) is the messenger of Allah.
- Izrail is the angel of death.
- Michael (Mikail) is another messenger of equal standing to Gabriel.

Two recording angels sit on an individual's shoulders and write down every action that this person performs during their life. These are the basis for the book of deeds that is handed to that individual on judgement day and determine whether they enter heaven or live a life of eternal torment in hell.

Angels are part of the invisible realm, although at times they do become visible. The invisible aspect does not mean, however, that they are less real than the visible, physical world. Jinns (spirits) and demons are also mentioned in the Qur'an as being part of the invisible world but they are never mentioned as becoming visible. It is only their actions that are described.

Angels dwell eternally in heaven, constantly praising Allah, until they are required to perform a mission for Allah. While angels have superior status to humans, due to their intermediary roles as trusted servants and agents of God, the example of Iblis (Satan) serves as a reminder that they are neither perfect nor beyond reprimand.

Turner expresses the essence of Islam's relationship with angels: 'Angels are there not because God needs them, but because we need them.'

Belief in angels is essential for Muslims and affects their daily lives. The simple acknowledgement of angels' existence as they record and protect directs a Muslim's thoughts toward heaven and brings awareness of the spiritual. It helps a Muslim to become more God-conscious and serves as a reminder to take care in ensuring their lives are **ibadah**.

3 Prophethood (nabuwwa or risallah)

Prophet means messenger or **warner** *as intellect alone cannot discern the purpose of creation, the nature of the Creator, the path he should tread and the way he should tread it.*

The central function of prophethood, then, is to provide a means whereby God may address man through the channel of human speech.

(Turner)

Muslims believe that prophets bring God's message. They accept the 25 that are named in the Qur'an. Every nation has been sent a prophet. Muslims believe prophets to be sinless because they have been chosen by God.

Muhammad was the **Seal of the prophets** and had been given the final message. There were to be no other prophets to follow Muhammad.

Muhammad is the central figure in Islam. Chosen by God to receive the revelation of the Qur'an, he has been taken by all Muslims to be the ideal man, the perfect embodiment of what it means to be a Muslim.

(Rippin)

Muhammad's initial religious experience was in the cave where he sought refuge and solitude to contemplate life and pray. The experience itself was short but intense. The angel Gabriel was the **intermediary**, who brought Allah's message and told him to read it. The encounter had physical aspects: 'When he explained that he could not read, the angel squeezed him strongly, repeating the request twice, and then recited to him the first two lines of the Qur'an' (Haleem).

Every religious experience that Muhammad had was focused, exact and precise. It was the message from Allah to humankind; it was not specific to Muhammad. Muhammad was the vehicle, a servant who had totally submitted to the Greatness of Allah and was optimally tuned to receive the divine command.

The revelation was in Arabic, 'God's speech' according to Muslims, and was 'a "sign" from Allah, a manifestation of his creative power in the medium of language' (Ruthven). Esposito stresses the unique nature of revelation (**wahy**) in Islam: 'the form and the content, as well as the message and the actual words, of revelation are attributed to an external source, God. Muhammad is merely an instrument or a conduit. He is neither author nor editor of the Qur'an, but God's intermediary.'

Once again, the popular portrait of Muhammad constructs him as an extremely important element in the salvation of his community, someone far more significant than simply the recipient of the revelation of the Qur'an.

(Rippin)

No unprejudiced scholar doubts that legend has been active in the Arabic biographies and traditions, where the prophet is sometimes portrayed as writers think he should have been rather than as he was.

(Guillaume)

Summary of God as guide:
- The Qur'an is the ultimate guide.
- Prophets and messengers have been sent to warn and guide.
- Humanity is constantly being guided.

Muhammad is merely an instrument or a conduit. He is neither author nor editor of the Qur'an, but God's intermediary.

(Esposito)

As Esposito writes: 'God's existence can be known through creation; nature contains pointers or "signs" of God, its creator and sustainer...The verses of revelation are also called signs of God.' The Qur'an, then, is a creation of God through which Muslims can know his revealed will.

Some of Muhammad's revelatory experiences were more public in that they were witnessed by others and recorded.

When he experienced the 'state of revelation', those around him were able to observe his visible, audible, and sensory reactions. His face would become flushed and he would fall silent and appear as if his thoughts were far away, his body would become limp as if he were asleep, a humming sound would be heard about him, and sweat would appear on his face, even on winter days. This state would last for a brief period and as it passed the Prophet would immediately recite new verses of the Qur'an.

(Haleem)

The revelation to Muhammad was gradual, 'piecemeal over a number of years'. Muslims believe this reflects the 'gradual awakening of man to the truth the message contained' (Turner).

For Muslims, Muhammad's actions (**sunnah**) and teachings (hadith) are exemplary, having an essential significance and considerable impact upon their daily lives. This exemplary nature is a direct confirmation of the Islamic understanding of the role of prophethood. The actions of a prophet do not need to be authenticated by miracles:

*A prophet's personality should be able to stand on its own merits. If it can, it needs no **portent**; if it cannot, a portent merely compromises the credibility of the whole narrative by importing the incredible.*

(Guillaume)

Muhammad's character is beyond question and without comparison.

*...the finest of his people in manliness, the best in character...the most kind, truthful, reliable, the furthest removed from filthiness and corrupt morals, through loftiness and nobility, so that he was known among his people as 'the **Trustworthy**'.*

(Ibn Ishaq)

➡️ **EXAM TIP**

Always remember to point out the historical evidence for the development of the Qur'an as a starting point. How do we know of the revelation experience of Muhammad? What evidence do we have of the message of the Qur'an in its early form? This ensures that you are 'selecting the most important features for emphasis and clarity' (level 4 descriptor AO1) rather than presenting a descriptive or 'a simple structure' (level 2 descriptor AO1) for your answer.

4 Revelation of scriptures (Kutubullah)

To say that the Qur'an is the 'holy book' or 'scriptures' of Islam does not do it justice. Muslims accord it unique status, and it could be argued to be unique among the holy books of the religions of the world. What makes it different from other scriptures? What is the essence of its unique nature?

For Muslims, it is impossible to do justice to the greatness of the Qur'an, because of its divine and ineffable nature. It is the **kutubullah**, literally meaning 'the writings, or books, of Allah' but generally understood to be the belief in the infallibility of the Qur'an. Its **I'jaz** (inimitability), based on its literary qualities, has been acknowledged since the 10th century.

Muslims consider that the Qur'an is the complete book of instruction and guidance for humanity. The text itself is seen as inerrant, the word of Allah and the exact copy of a heavenly version.

The Qur'an earns its unique status because:

- it records the actual, **phonic** words of Allah
- it is true, final and a complete message from Allah to humanity
- it has its own style
- it includes the most beautiful poetry
- it is eternal
- it tells the 'miracle' of Islam.

> *The miraculous aspect of the Koran is described by Muslim scholars as its 'I'jaz' or 'inimitability'. The Koran, it, is believed, has no equal: however hard he may try, man will never be able to match the Holy Book in terms of eloquence, beauty or wisdom.*
>
> **(Turner)**

The Qur'an is not organised in a chronological, systematic or thematic way. Haleem describes its stylistic features as one of 'persuasion and dissuasion', which is why it moves from one aspect of Islam to another in the course of one section (**Sura**):

> *The Qur'an may present, in the same sura, material about the unity and grace of God, regulations and laws, stories of earlier prophets and nations and the lessons that can be drawn from these, and descriptions of reward and punishments of the Day of Judgement.*
>
> **(Haleem)**

This all serves to reinforce its unique nature as the complete book of instruction and guidance for humanity.

The need for an understanding of the significance of the Qur'an in the lives of Muslims cannot be overstated. To capture the extent to which this is the case, it is useful to quote David Waines:

> *Scripture lives orally in the Muslim's daily routine to the present day. Parts are included in the daily prayers. It is recited at night in the mosques during the ritual fasting of Ramadan…Every festive or formal event, such as the signing of a wedding contract or the paying of condolences to a deceased's family, will be accompanied by passages recited from the Qur'an. Words from the sacred text are whispered into the ear of a newborn child and at the moment of a person's death.*
>
> **(Waines)**

The Qur'an is used and respected in a Muslim's daily life. It is the 'focal point of the Islamic faith' (Rippin). It plays a major role in:

- devotion – worship and prayer
- legal and social guidance, a guide to living in everyday life; reference may be made to teaching to implement the Muslim religious law
- ritual, at rites of passage
- spiritual inspiration – during fasting it is read through and is a focus for worship

KEY WORDS

Kutubullah: the revelation of the Qur'an, literally meaning 'writings, or books, of Allah'

I'jaz: has no equal, cannot be compared or imitated

Phonic: resonance, sound

Sura: chapter of the Qur'an

66 KEY QUOTES

About the Qur'an

…the very essence of Islam

(Sherif)

The Qur'an is no ordinary book…the Qur'an is a sacred object

(Brown)

For Muslims, the Qur'an is the Book of God. It is the eternal, uncreated, literal word of God sent down from heaven, revealed one final time to the Prophet Muhammad as a guide for humankind.

(Esposito)
99

- spiritual focus and religious experience, used in worship and daily prayer as a means to come closer to God
- prayer – verses are repeated in public prayer to focus on Allah
- moral guidance, as a basis of moral conduct.

In addition:

- it is used as a key reference point for religious, social, moral, political and historical issues
- it is studied at **madrassah**
- Muslims remember the first event of the revelation during **Ramadan** on the night of power (lailat al-qadar).

5 Judgement, life after death (akirah)

The central message of the Qur'an is its teaching about the nature of God. This is partly defined through the way in which God relates to his creation in his role as judge and guide.

God sends messengers (prophets) 'with miracles, clear proof and a Book in its language' (Sherif). God communicates with his creation and offers complete guidance through teachings of justice. He sends glad tidings but also warnings:

*Allah sends **apostles** to guide mankind but it is always Allah that is the guide.*

(Sherif)

From beginning to end of the drama humankind requires his guidance, without which the individual or entire communities would go astray, as indeed has been the case in human experience.

(Waines)

Allah is loving, gracious and forgiving. However, as supreme being, he also has the responsibility of judgement.

Judgement in Islam is linked closely to the idea of **akirah** (judgement day), and to resurrection and the role of angels. It is also related to the teaching about the Mahdi or 'guided one' that appears in both Shi'a and Sunni traditions. According to this teaching, the Mahdi will appear for several years (depending on tradition) before the final day. Belief in the Mahdi is firmer in the Shi'a than in the Sunni tradition, where it is debated and sometimes even rejected.

Whatever the case, on this last day the **mu'min** (believers) will be saved but the **kafir** (unbelievers) will perish in hell. In the Qur'an there are vivid depictions of heaven (Sura 47:15) and hell (Sura 67:7–10).

Judgement day, heaven and hell

According to one source there are no fewer than 67 suras that reference the concept of resurrection of the dead and last or final judgement. The majority of these were from the Makkan period.

i) What Islam and the Qur'an says about judgement day

- It is referred to by many names, including great day, grand news, last day, appointed time, sure reality, doom, reunion, gathering, meeting, judgement, reckoning, torment.

KEY WORDS

Madrassah: classes for children to learn teachings of Islam, usually held at a mosque
Ramadan: holy month of fasting in Islam

KEY WORDS

Apostle: messenger
Akirah: notion of being held accountable for one's deeds before God on a final day of reckoning
Mu'min: believers
Kafir: unbelievers

- It is drawing near or imminent.
- Only Allah knows the appointed time.
- Signs will precede it (the Sun will rise in the west, there will be an eclipse, there will be an antichrist and further apocalyptic events similar to those depicted in Revelation 11–13).
- The last trumpet will announce its arrival.
- All the dead will be raised and every soul tried before Allah.
- All personal records will be revealed and distributed to an individual (right hand for the virtuous, left hand for the doomed).
- Judgement will be pronounced.

ii) Depictions of heaven

- Believers, together with spouse, will be greeted on arrival by 'Guardians of Paradise'.
- Death does not exist.
- There are gardens with fountains and rivers of milk and honey.
- Every fruit a human desires (even out of season) is available.
- There are jewelled couches, raised high.
- The believers will be waited on by youths with goblets of pure wine.
- There will be no idle talk or sinful speech.
- Peacefulness will abound.
- Believers will wear fine silk garments and bracelets of silver.

iii) Depictions of hell

- It will be full of hypocrites, polytheists, sinners, tyrants, immoral peoples, arrogant people.
- The unbelievers will be put in chains.
- The unbelievers will be made deaf, dumb and blind.
- The unbelievers will be guarded by 19 fierce angels
- The unbelievers will be in a furnace fanned by winds.
- Torture will be in full view.
- There will be a bottomless pit with a stream of boiling water.
- Clothes will be made from liquid pitch.
- The skin is branded, consumed by fire and then renewed to experience the pain again.
- Foul foods, decaying, putrid and thorny, will simmer at boiling point in a person's intestines.
- There will be sounds of groaning and wailing constantly.

> **KEY QUOTE**
>
> *According to the principles of justice, punishment is of course awarded where a reprehensible act is committed willfully... Man reaps the result of his deliberate actions.*
>
> **(Turner)**

iv) In summary

The implications and significance for a Muslim of these beliefs cannot be underestimated. It has often been alleged that all Muslims lead their lives in fear and trepidation of Allah and follow the Muslim path through fear. Most Muslims, however, would deny this and say that the threat of Hell has to be balanced with the possibility of Heaven. In this way, a life of submission and worship is finely balanced between awe of Allah, desire to be with Allah and the fear of being separated from Allah.

6 Predestination (al-qadr)

The word for theology in Arabic is kalam, which literally means 'speech' or 'discourse'. There is no real attempt at systematic theology in Islam; rather, there is a fluid set of responses to problems that arise in given socio-historical contexts.

As a result of the idea that Allah had preordained the rule of the Caliphs, and the issues surrounding the early Caliphate, the related debate about predestination arose. Is an all-powerful (omnipotent) God responsible for the actions of everyone because he has knowledge of the future (omniscience)? Does he control humans, or do they have free will?

Some Muslims argued that to allow free will is to limit the omnipotence of God. However, their opponents replied that not to allow free will would make the idea of human accountability on judgement day redundant.

The traditional conclusion is that there is a divinely determined Universe; however, the theology of the Mutazila, who advocate the compatibility of free will and the idea of an all-powerful God, has been popular in modern times.

The position of the Quran is as follows.

KEY IDEA

Summary of God as judge:
- He is the supreme being.
- He is the loving judge.

- Allah reveals signs to humanity through messengers and the Qur'an.
- Recognition of these signs makes a person a believer, rejection makes them an infidel.
- Allah demonstrates clearly what is the 'right path'.
- Those who follow the path are 'rightly guided', those who don't 'go astray'.
- Allah's creation demonstrates the wonders he has performed and continuously does so.
- Gratitude and praise mean salvation.
- 'God leads astray whom he pleases and guides whom he pleases' and simultaneously 'Every soul will be given what it has earned, with no injustice'.

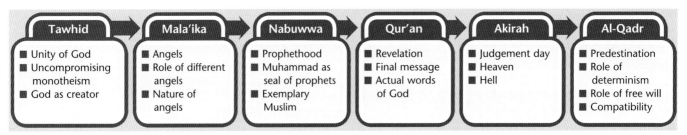

Tawhid	Mala'ika	Nabuwwa	Qur'an	Akirah	Al-Qadr
■ Unity of God ■ Uncompromising monotheism ■ God as creator	■ Angels ■ Role of different angels ■ Nature of angels	■ Prophethood ■ Muhammad as seal of prophets ■ Exemplary Muslim	■ Revelation ■ Final message ■ Actual words of God	■ Judgement day ■ Heaven ■ Hell	■ Predestination ■ Role of determinism ■ Role of free will ■ Compatibility

Summary diagram: The six beliefs

TASK

On small revision cards, create summaries of the key characteristics of God. Support the explanations with quotes from the Qur'an.

Objective: To help appreciate the different aspects of God's nature. To be able to show that you are 'using evidence to explain key ideas; expressed accurately and fluently' through reference to the Qur'anic teachings (level 4 descriptor AO1). This ensures that you are 'selecting the most important features for emphasis and clarity' (level 4 descriptor AO1) rather than presenting a descriptive or 'a simple structure' (level 2 descriptor AO1) for your answer.

Reflection and assessment

It is vital to bring together the information covered so far and recognise how it can be transformed into effective examination-style revision and answers. The best way to do this is to ask yourself: 'How am I going to be assessed on this information?'

The first way is through assessment objective 1 (AO1). You need to be able to 'select and clearly demonstrate the relevant knowledge and understanding through the use of evidence, examples and correct language and terminology'.

Look back to pages 8–10 in the Introduction to review the level descriptors for AO1.

Look at the following sample level 2 answer, which is a response to this question.

> **Describe the manner in which the Qur'an was revealed and explain its unique nature.** (21 marks)

The Qur'an was revealed to Muhammad by an angel while he was in a cave. He was frightened but he also recited what he was told to do. When he told Khadijah his wife, she supported him, as did his close friends. The revelations continued and spoke of warning people to return to the ways of God. They took place over a period of time. In fact it was a while before Muhammad shared them with the people of Makkah. Because the revelations were from God they were in Arabic. This is the word of God and Muslims believe that it is perfect, eternal and poetic. Nothing can be compared to it and it is the final message to humanity. No other book can contain anything like it. Muhammad was just the messenger and had nothing to do with its contents. This is why Muslims have so much respect for it as a book.

TASK

From what you have learned so far about levels of response, create a list of points to go in a developed-level answer to the question above. Improve this further for a higher-level answer. You can then create writing frames and fully drafted answers for each.
What makes the sample answer a level 2 response?
Identify ways in which you could improve this answer. Complete your own comments analysis on this answer.
Now write your own answer to the same question at level 4.
Objectives: To demonstrate 'detailed knowledge of the subject matter at a wide range or in significant depth' (level 4 descriptor AO1) as opposed to simply 'very broad and unfocused generalisations' (level 1 descriptor AO1) or an answer that is 'limited in scope' (level 2 descriptor AO1). Gradually to build up and improve on an answer by reflecting on the Foundations Unit level descriptors 1–4.

Suggestions for further application of skills

Look at pages 192–6, at the discussion of the contents of the Qur'an and describe the way in which it was compiled. Read through the section as a class again. Without support of notes or text, have a quick try at answering this question, allowing about 15 minutes.

> **Describe how the Qur'an was compiled and explain the nature of its contents.** (21 marks)

You should now have a basic answer to develop. In pairs or groups, share answers and select one to use for development. As above, identify ways in which you could improve this answer. Complete your own comments analysis on your answer.

Now write your own answer to the same question, aiming at level 4.

TOPIC 2: KEY EMPHASES IN TEACHING AND PRACTICE

Part 2B: The five pillars – meaning and significance for belief and practice

---

This means I am expected:

to know about the key emphasis:

- the five pillars – meaning and significance for belief and practice

and to study:

- an outline of the five pillars
- the purpose and significance of the pillars
- the practical and theological nature of shahadah
- the practical and theological nature of salah
- the practical and theological nature of saum
- the practical and theological nature of zakat
- the practical and theological nature of hajj
- the effect the observance of the five pillars has on Muslim life and the ummah.

In this book the evidence and examples given are relevant and appropriate because this material focuses only on the content for AO1 that is given by the Edexcel specification. The evaluation materials for AO2 will be aimed at helping you 'critically evaluate and justify a point of view through the use of evidence and reasoned argument'.

It would be helpful to write your notes using the headings listed above, as it is from these areas that the examination questions will be derived.

In your studies, remember that you have to bear in mind the **two** basic assessment objectives of:

- Knowledge and Understanding (AO1)
- Evaluation (AO2).

See pages 7–8 in the Introduction to remind yourself of these objectives.

The evaluation material set out in Part 2C (page 215) can be studied either alongside the AO1 material, as you work through this unit, or as a separate unit.

1 An outline of the five pillars

The five pillars of Islam are the basis of Muslim faith. They are all obligatory (**fard**) acts; they are specific acts of worship that underline the idea of submission.

As has already been discussed, a Muslim is one who submits to Allah. All life, not just these five specific practices, is worship (**ibadah**) to Allah. Indeed, Islam does not differentiate between religious and non-religious actions. Every action should be righteous and a Muslim should be constantly God-conscious.

It is often said that Islam is a complete way of life (**din**). In fact, each of the following pillars is a basis for life in its broadest sense. While aspects of the pillars may be specific to certain times, their underlying influence and impact affect the whole of a Muslim's life.

This can be taken a step further, in that the five pillars are not dogmatic statements of practice imposed upon the religion to drive it and make it work. Rather, they are extracted from the whole of Islamic life and serve as a summary of what Muslims do to become more God-conscious. Some Muslims may even be unaware of the five pillars but are nonetheless devoted practitioners of Islam. For Muslims, a more familiar term for the five pillars would be 'the duties of worship or ibadat' (Waines).

Although there are other elements to the practice of Islam, the five pillars encapsulate the crucial aspects of Muslim practice and, when consistently applied, demonstrate submission.

This section will consider each of the pillars in turn. There is no real hierarchy, despite the first being the central tenet of Islam. The pillars are inter-related and each acts to support the others.

The five pillars of Islam are:

1   **shahadah** (testimony)

2   **salah** (prayer)

3   **saum** (fasting)

4   **zakat** (purification through giving)

5   **hajj** (pilgrimage).

These are simplistic definitions and cannot do justice to the implications of each pillar. Their complexities will be dealt with as each one in turn is studied.

KEY WORDS

Fard: obligatory, compulsory
Ibadah: worship
Din: a complete way of life

KEY WORDS

Shahadah: testimony
Salah: prayer
Saum: fasting
Zakat: purification through giving
Hajj: pilgrimage

➡ EXAM TIP

Remember to explain to the full each point that you make in an exam answer. Think carefully about each sentence and how it relates to the question and to the previous sentence. Aim for at least three clear sentences to explain a concept or idea, giving examples from different sources to support your point. For development of the point, bring in a variety of ways in which the application of this principle is demonstrated and introduce some contrasting scholarly views. This demonstrates 'accurate, relevant and detailed knowledge of the subject matter at a wide range or in significant depth' (mid level 4 descriptor AO1) as opposed to the information being simply 'minimal accuracy or relevance in factual detail' (level 1 descriptor AO1) or 'limited in scope' (level 2 descriptor AO1).

2 The purpose and significance of the pillars

You will need to study references to the five pillars in the Qur'an and Hadith.

It would be a mistake to think of the five pillars as specific teachings established by Allah in the same way as the ten commandments of Judaism, or the four noble truths of Buddhism. The pillars are never presented in a systematic manner and explained in depth. They are simply a reflection of the ideals of Islam. Study of the pillars supports a Muslim's religious instruction and clarifies matters of exposition and spiritual significance. The pillars underpin daily life and existence, and are, in essence, the basis of practice.

The five pillars are mentioned individually in the Qur'an several times, but not collectively. Neither is there a systematic exposition of them collectively in the Hadiths. This is important because it underlines the fact that the message of Islam through the Qur'an and Hadiths is not meant to be a theological statement.

The message of Islam embraces and incorporates all aspects of life. The sporadic and inconsistent dealings with the pillars in the Qur'an and Hadiths reflect perhaps the true spirit of Islam; that all the pillars underpin everyday life and experience.

In terms of clarity, the Qur'an tends to offer the basic understanding of each pillar at both a theological and practical level. The shortest Suras tend not to deal with the pillars other than the first, which conveys the idea of faith in one God and the prophethood of Muhammad (PBUH) (the shahadah). The larger Suras, for example, Sura 2 The Cow, mention each of the pillars, but not as a coherent group, rather as issues in their own right.

The Hadiths are studied for further development and understanding of the Qur'an, often addressing practical implications and situations.

Put simply, the Qur'an provides the basic commandments to enable a Muslim to live correctly and the Hadiths offer guidance on how these commandments may be put into practice.

3 The practical and theological nature of shahadah

Shahadah literally means witness, evidence or testimony. It is derived from 'ash-shadu' (I declare or I bear witness). 'To become a Muslim, one need only make this simple proclamation,' (Esposito).

The Shahadah is as follows.

> There is no God but Allah and Muhammad is the messenger of Allah.
>
> Ash-shadu an la ilaha illallah wa Muhammadar-rasulullah.
>
> By speaking this statement with the intention to become a Muslim, a person does indeed become a Muslim.
>
> (Clark)

Shahadah is the ultimate declaration of faith for Islam. It is more than a creed or statement of belief. It is not just a matter of personal belief; rather, it is a public testimony of truth.

The shahadah is used as a means of recognising conversion. To become a Muslim, a convert must repeat the shahadah twice, with intent, in front of witnesses. In this sense it

...one should not think that prayer, fasts, the payment of alms and the pilgrimage to Mecca are ends in themselves...
(they) are in a sense mnemonic devices: they embody actions, behaviour and ritual performances which are designed to bring about remembrance... of the true state to which he is always expected to aspire.

Why are there five pillars in Islam? Why not six, or ten, or twenty-five? More importantly, why are there any pillars at all?

(Turner)

66 KEY QUOTE

It is the first thing that is whispered into a baby's ears... the utterance that Muslims try to have on their lips at the moment of death.... the formula by which one converts to Islam.

(Elias)

is 'an important psychological mechanism' reflecting a 'transition from one state of being to another…from one way of seeing to another' (Turner).

Although crucial to the act of conversion, speaking the words alone is not in itself sufficient. It is also vital that the convert maintains this state of mind and that a disciplined approach to life follows. The shahadah is often returned to and renewed daily by Muslims, for whom it is a reflection of eternal fact and not simply a belief. Elias states that it 'so perfectly encapsulates the essence of Islamic faith' as a foundation for the other pillars.

It is argued that shahadah brings together all the other four pillars: 'This deceptively simple statement is not only the basis for all articles of faith in Islam, it is in some ways the sum and total of Islamic theology,' (Aslan). It is related to the teaching of the six articles of faith.

1   Tawhid (one-ness, unity of God)

2   Mala'ika (belief in angels)

3   Nabuwwa or risallah (message of God, belief in messengers or prophets)

4   Kutubullah (belief in the infallibility of the Qur'an)

5   Akirah (belief in life after death and judgement)

6   Al-qadr or jabr (belief in predestination).

It is clear, then, that the implications of shahadah run much more deeply for a Muslim than a simple statement of faith would imply.

The shahadah is not merely a part of the act of conversion to Islam. It is there as a constant reminder of the one-ness of God, the crucial role of Muhammad as 'seal of the prophets' and, most importantly, to facilitate consciousness of God's presence in daily life – God-consciousness.

It actually implies an intellectual, emotional and spiritual approach to the world and to everyday life that needs to be nurtured constantly and continuously.

(Turner)

The shahadah puts Allah first, above all else in life as a Muslim. Every Muslim devotee aims to maintain a constant, mindful awareness of this in every aspect and action of daily life.

It involves far more than words; your whole life must back up what has been declared.

(Maqsood)

Part of this 'mindfulness' of God can be seen in the use of the shahadah in the call to prayer five times every day.

4 The practical and theological nature of salah [salat]

Communication with God (salah, or prayer) is a central feature of religion. For Muslims, it is an outward expression of submission at the same time. Prayer is the second pillar of Islam. At any given moment, day or night, any prayers are witnessed by angels. For a Muslim, prayer is obligatory five times a day. 'The Sunnah gives the exact details of how you should offer the salat, but the Koran commands Muslims to "bow down, prostrate yourselves and adore your Sustainer",' (Sultan).

> **KEY QUOTES**
>
> *Acceptance of shahada involves unquestioning acceptance of…articles of faith.*
>
> (Horrie and Chippindale)
>
> *It is incumbent on all Muslims, regardless of whether they are 'born Muslims' or 'converts', to make the shahada part of their mental make-up.*
>
> (Turner)
>
> *More than just a simple declaration, this pillar represents a serious commitment that seeks to transform life and society…by following the divine way, known as the 'straight path'.*
>
> (Sultan)

Key types of prayer:
Tahajjud: night prayers
Nafila: extra prayers beyond the five that are expected
Du'a: personal prayer
Tasbih: use of beads to pray
Wird: personal prayer that follows a set ritual recitation based on the Qur'an.

TASK

Draw a clear diagram to illustrate the actions associated with prayer. Label your diagram and demonstrate with arrows how each of the actions link and are related.
Objective: To develop understanding of the relationship between different aspects of prayer and to be aware of the key terminology involved. This demonstrates 'well-chosen evidence to support understanding of key ideas and concepts' that is 'expressed clearly and accurately, using technical language widely' (level 4 descriptor AO1).

There are many types of prayer but salah (or salat) usually refers to the five prayers established by Muhammad:

Prayer is the pillar of religion; to neglect it is to prepare the downfall of religion.

(Hadith)

The five times of prayers are:

- at daybreak (al-fajr)
- at noon (al-duhr)
- in the afternoon (al-asr)
- at sunset (al-maghreb)
- in the evening (al-isha).

The times of prayer are based on the Sun; however, they are not precisely followed, to 'consciously disassociate Islam from any form of sun worship' (Elias).

66 KEY QUOTE

As such, salat is not prayer in the sense of a personal conversation with God, but rather a ritual obligation which must be fulfilled to reaffirm one's relationship with God.

(Elias)

Despite prayer being necessary, there are exceptions, as Allah is merciful. Young children, travellers and the incapacitated are excused, although, if it is possible and they are capable, they are expected to catch up on missed prayers later.

66 KEY QUOTE

It strengthens the conscience, reaffirms total dependence upon God, and puts worldly concerns within the perspective of death, the last judgment, and the afterlife.

(Esposito)

KEY WORDS

Niyati: destiny
Wudu: ritual washing

Prayer must be performed with intention (**niyati**). Broadly speaking, this means adopting the correct attitude and state of mind as one prostrates before the one true God. Humility and total outpouring of self to God are part and parcel of this act of submission.

Prayer must be performed in a state of purity. In ordinary circumstances, the ritual purification involves ablutions and is known as **wudu**. This minor ablution includes washing the mouth, nose, ears, face and whole head and extends to the arms, hands and finally feet. However, again the actions must be done with intent and reflect respect for Allah, as underlined by a state of absolute purity. 'Wudu literally wakes the soul up from the remembrance of anything other than God,' (Sultan).

Some Muslims perform before wudu before touching the Qur'an.

If a person's state of purity is interrupted and spoiled, for example, by a visit to the lavatory or emissions from the body, such as wind and vomit, wudu has to be repeated.

Wudu becomes invalid if the Muslim visits the toilet, passes wind, burps, falls asleep or bleeds from a wound between the act of washing and praying.
(Horrie and Chippindale)

Wudu at the Bashahi mosque, Lahore, Pakistan

Ghusl or the major ablution is performed after acts of a sexual nature or menstruation. It involves washing under clean, running water. Sometimes ghusl is performed before Friday prayers.

Muslims can pray alone, together or in any place. However, Friday prayers must be performed in a mosque. Muslims are called to prayer by the **muezzin** through the **adhan** that is declared publically from a **minaret** (tower) in the mosque.

During prayer Muslims recite passages from the Qur'an and **takbir** (allahu akbar) in praise of God. They do this facing the direction of the ka'aba, as indicated by the **qiblah**.

The practical features of prayer are known as **rakahs**, sometimes translated as 'movements' or 'units'. Each rakah is a set procedure and involves:

- standing before God to make a statement of intent and recitation involving the **Qiyam**, the very first chapter of the Qur'an (standing before God)
- bowing (**ruku**)
- prostration (**sujud**)
- sitting up to announce (**tashahud** and **salam**) a declaration of faith and greetings of peace.

At the end of prayer, the tashahud or 'bearing witness' is declared. The tashahad gives blessings to all believers and, like the shahadah, declares acceptance of Muhammad as prophet.

Finally, greetings of peace (salam) are offered to the recording angels on both of the worshipper's shoulders.

KEY WORDS

Muezzin: the one who calls prayer from the minaret
Adhan: the official 'call to prayer'
Minaret: tower from which the call to prayer is given
Takbir: God is the greatest
Qiblah: niche in mosque wall indicating the direction of the ka'aba in Makkah
Rakahs: prayer movement
Qiyam: first chapter of the Qur'an
Ruku: bowing
Sujud: prostration
Tashahud and salam: sitting up to announce a declaration of faith and greetings of peace

There are different numbers of rakahs for each part of the day. Midday, late afternoon and late evening prayers have the most (four), whereas morning has two and early evening has three.

This position from the rakah is called sujud, which means prostration

Salat is only one type of prayer. It expresses obedience and submission rather than a description of intimate spiritual experience. Other types of prayer include:

- tahajjud: night prayer, extra prayer during the night
- nafila: extra prayers, before or after the five obligatory ones
- du'a: 'cry' or 'cry of the heart', a personal prayer or period of private devotion
- use of tasbih (subhah): 99 or 33 beads on a string recalling the names of Allah or glory, thanks and God is most great
- wird: ritualised, private prayer concentrating on the recitation of the Qur'an.

There are many reasons for prayer. It may be seen as a pure act of gratitude towards God, thanking him for all his actions. It could also be an acknowledgement of total dependence on God, confirming complete and absolute trust in him.

The whole purpose of prayer is communion with God. Prayer makes a Muslim more God-conscious and hence gradually more spiritually aware. In this respect, prayer can be seen as a form of personal spiritual development and growth. Muslims can perform different aspects of this development and growth through submission and praise, listening to and sharing personal devotion.

Prayer is a reminder of God's greatness. Humans are prone to forget and therefore constantly need waking up to prayer. It is no coincidence that the call to prayer in the morning often includes the phrase 'it is better to pray than to sleep'.

Prayer brings the individual close to God but also brings the community together in closeness and spiritual strength.

The practice of communal prayer on Fridays builds up a (religious) community. It signifies the unity of the ummah and the essential equality therein.

Communal prayer is simultaneously public and private. The barrier (**sutrah**) identifies a worshipper's personal prayer space; it is considered bad manners to pass in front of someone who is praying.

Most of all, prostration in prayer typifies the essence of being a Muslim: submission. A Muslim is 'one who submits' and prayer demonstrates the giving of oneself totally to God. It includes a resignation to the futility of any effort to appease beyond blind obedience, that is, to 'express one's total and utter impotence before One who is omnipotent' (Turner). It is a feeling of total insignificance in face of the almighty; the quintessential numinous experience.

5 The practical and theological nature of saum

Fasting is seen as meritorious act. It is a form of discipline often used by religions to enable followers to enter a more focused period of devotion and contemplation:

Fasting, with its implicit attack on man's animal appetites and carnal cravings, is seen as another way of purifying the self and bringing the recalcitrant soul into line.

(Turner)

KEY QUOTE

Muslim fasting involves deliberately cultivating a peaceful and prayerful attitude of mind, and undergoing the physical discipline of giving up all food, liquid, smoking and sexual intercourse during the hours of first light of dawn to sunset for the entire month.

(Maqsood)

The idea of fasting is not new. It existed before Islam, in other religious traditions, from both east and west.

You who believe, fasting is prescribed for you, as it was prescribed for those before you, so that you may be mindful of God.

(The Cow, Sura 2:183)

Sharing the Judaeo-Christian heritage meant also sharing in its practices. Fasting, however, was made more a priority and, arguably, was placed in its proper context by Muhammad.

Although fasting can be done at any time, it is prescribed during the month of Ramadan between the hours of dawn and dusk. Traditionally, the fast begins when one can distinguish clearly between two strands of black and white cotton: 'Eat and drink until the white thread of dawn becomes distinct from the black,' (The Cow, Sura 2:187).

TASK

Write down situations in life when a Muslim may find it difficult to fast. Try to use a reflection of your own experiences as a basis for this.

Objective: To demonstrate more ownership of the material and deeper understanding through reflection upon the restrictions of fasting but also the principles behind such restrictions. This shows 'significant features explained for emphasis and clarity' which constitutes a higher level answer (level 3 and above descriptor AO1) and also a 'response to the task at…considerable depth' (level 4 descriptor AO1).

KEY WORD

Sutrah: a boundary marking off a personal space for prayer

EXAM TIP

When discussing the five pillars, try to follow the format given here:
1 define the concept in literal terms
2 discuss how this is understood in different ways
3 relate the concept to other aspects of Muslim teachings
4 use quotes only to illustrate a point you are explaining
5 indicate possible problems associated with this concept, including any misunderstandings that may arise.
This is a clear indication of a knowledge and understanding of the significance of the pillars, illustrating 'accurate and relevant detail, clearly identifying the most important features' (level 4 descriptor AO1).

KEY WORDS

Tarawih: extra prayers during Ramadan
I'tikaf: a retreat to focus spiritually during the month of Ramadan

66 **KEY QUOTE**

In Islam the discipline of the Ramadan fast is intended to stimulate reflection on human frailty and dependence on God, focus on spiritual goals and values, and identification with and response to the less fortunate.

(Esposito)

99

TASK

Design a diagram that links the five pillars explained in this section. Label each accordingly and demonstrate their relationship.

Objective: To develop ability to present the inter-relatedness of the pillars and demonstrate 'detailed knowledge of the subject matter at a wide range or in significant depth' (level 4 descriptor AO1) as opposed to simply 'very broad and unfocused generalisations' (level 1 descriptor AO1) or an answer that is 'limited in scope' (level 2 descriptor AO1).

During the hours of fasting nothing, not even water, may enter the mouth. Some Muslims would even go as far as spitting, rather than swallowing saliva, and not cleaning their teeth, to avoid swallowing water. Others will not take oral medications but insist on medical injections.

As discussed above, fasting is to be mindful of God. This is underlined by the fact that, within the month of Ramadan, there are many practices that go beyond the fast. For example, Muslims are expected to say extra prayers (**tarawih**) and many may spend more time reading the Qur'an, even completing it during the month. Some Muslims choose to go on retreat for up to ten days (**i'tikaf**) in order to concentrate more on spiritual matters.

Pregnant women, young children, the elderly, sick and travellers can be excused from fasting, although travellers usually make it up later. As the Qur'an says: 'Fast for a specific number of days, but if one of you is ill, or on a journey, on other days later,' (The Cow, Sura 2:184).

There are disparities over the world in the lengths of time for the fast. This is due to the variations in daylight hours across the globe. This is one of the reasons that 'To describe a typical Ramadan fast day would be impossible, as all communities differ, at least in the detail,' (Turner).

The variation in the length of daylight hours around the globe and the consequent practical differences in demands for Muslims to fast have led to much discussion. It is a fact that 'a Muslim community would not exist within the Arctic Circle without breaking the laws of salat and sawm,' (Horrie and Chippindale). Given this, and the strong sense of community, sharing and equality in Islam it is surprising that the disparity poses no problem. However, Turner cites arguments resulting from discussions about the disparity. One interesting proposal is that, due to the divine wisdom of Islam being based on a lunar calendar, every 33 years the month of fasting will have passed through all seasons for all peoples around the world. It is the bigger picture that triumphs.

Beyond eating, drinking, and smoking, violence and sexual acts are also forbidden. In practice, this includes the thoughts of such acts as well as the deeds. 'Not only is one supposed to refrain from these things but also from thinking about them,' (Elias).

Nonetheless, despite all the forbidden thoughts, actions and the sacrifices, Ramadan is not a negative month. Ramadan is intended to make Muslims mindful of God and should therefore be a happy time. It is a time for joyful discipline and celebration and the mood should not be sombre. It is a time of blessings and for spiritual reward. However, a balance should be kept and the evening breaking of fast is not for gorging. 'The evening is a time of relaxation, visiting, prayer and Quranic recitation,' (Clark). Gorging is not being mindful of God but is making food and drink a priority.

There are spiritual benefits during Ramadan. Muslims offer extra prayers, in an attempt to be more God-conscious. Ramadan is also a time for reflection and empathy with the poor, who are in a constant state of hunger and need. It is also a time to read the Qur'an more. In fact, the most significant night of the year is celebrated for Muslims during Ramadan: 'Ramadan builds up to the "Night of Power (Laylay al-qadr)",' (Horrie and Chippindale). This is when the Qur'an was first revealed to Muhammad.

The fasting lasts for one full month but is broken by **Eid-ul-Fitr**, one of the most famous festivals across the globe. This is a time for celebration, usually with large parties and a meal. Families unite, as does the ummah. At this time, Muslims send cards and give each other gifts. The most significant aspect of Eid-ul-Fitr however, is the gift of money that is given to the poor.

The benefits of fasting in general are well known in terms of detoxification of the body and the stomach is rested; however, in Ramadan there is also a focus on healthy eating.

It is a time of community and togetherness, a time for discipline and submission – it is God's will that Muslims fast. The focus therefore is always on Allah. God comes first and must always take priority in every aspect of life.

Fasting, then, typifies obedience to God's will and it is also following the example of Muhammad and the prophets before him, for example, Jesus.

Overall, Ramadan 'is important as a period of reflection and spiritual discipline, of physical endurance and sharing with others,' (Waines).

According to Horrie and Chippindale, 'Some Muslims, especially in Muslim-minority countries like Britain, practise only a limited form of fasting by giving up something like smoking or eating rich foods.' However, this is the exception rather than the rule, even in Britain today.

The overall benefits of Ramadan can be summarised in:

- the literal and physical application of discipline and obedience
- the reflective and moral aspect of avoiding sins, being more aware of actions and generally becoming more sensitive to the needs of others
- the spiritual aspect of becoming more God-conscious in every aspect of daily life with the result of becoming closer to him.

KEY QUOTE

God alone has the choice of who is to be born rich or poor; therefore all Muslims have a duty towards others.

(Maqsood)

6 The practical and theological nature of zakat

Like fasting, giving is not new to religion. Both Jews and Christians have specific teachings about this act of piety.

In Islam, there are different types of giving. Indeed, there is some debate in books as to how the fourth pillar is defined. The most popular definition refers to charity or alms. However, the true significance of the fourth pillar runs deeper than this. Turner defines it as 'spending for the sake of God' and bases his interpretation on Sura 9:60.

This covers 'not only the donation of money to the poor, but also the giving of one's self – one's time or one's talents perhaps, one's physical skills or one's intellectual powers' (Turner). Given the spirit of prayer and fasting, it is perhaps more appropriate to consider the idea of the fourth pillar in this broader sense.

KEY WORD

Eid ul-Fitr: the celebration at the end of Ramadan

TASK

Have a go at designing cards for a 'game of life' based on the concepts discussed in this section. They need to deal with all five pillars specifically. Include practical examples from life that reflect:
1 **the idea of intention behind an action**
2 **different situations**
3 **different people**
4 **different ways to worship.**
Objective: To move beyond 'a limited range of isolated facts…with mainly random and unorganised detail' or 'information presented within a structure which shows a basic awareness of the issue(s) raised' (level 1 and 2 descriptors AO1) towards a more sophisticated understanding. Remember, you are aiming for 'a coherent and well-structured account of the subject matter' (level 4 descriptor AO1).

The three types of spending or giving are:

- sadaqat: voluntary giving
- zakat: the annual donation of 2.5 per cent of ones wealth that purifies, from the Arabic verb tazakka, to purify
- khums: meaning a fifth, important in Shi'ism today, which originated with the idea of war booty, 20 per cent of which went to Muhammad and his family.

Zakat is usually seen as the spending referred to in the fourth pillar and is 'the cornerstone of social justice in the early Muslim community' (Turner).

It says in the Qur'an:

> *Alms are for the poor and the needy, and (to pay) those employed to administer the funds; for those whose hearts have been (recently) reconciled (to Truth); for those in bondage, and in debt; in the cause of God; and for the wayfarer; (Thus it is) ordained by God, full of knowledge and wisdom.*

(Sura 9:60)

There are many ways of using alms for the poor. Originally, alms were given to orphans, widows, (originally) to free slaves and used to cut the chains of debt, or to support work in the cause of God (and workers). In general, giving serves as a form of Muslim 'social security' as it 'allows wealth to circulate more fairly in society,' (Maqsood).

There is a strong understanding in Islam that the fortunes of humanity are not self-made but God-given. 'In Islam, the true owner of things is not man but God,' (Esposito). All peoples are equal in the eyes of God and therefore the unequal distribution of wealth, as it unfolds in our corrupt and ignorant world, is a clear opportunity for Muslims, especially those who are blessed with wealth, to redress the imbalance.

This means that the mentality of giving imposes a psychological sense of duty as well as direct obedience to the will of Allah. The poor are not beggars, nor do they receive charity as the term is commonly understood: 'Zakat is not charity, but the rightful and legal claim of the poor against the rich,' (Horrie and Chippindale).

In practical terms zakat 'requires an annual contribution of 2.5 per cent of an individual's wealth and assets, not merely a percentage of annual income,' (Esposito). However, although this is directed towards all, as with prayer and fasting, there are certain exceptions: 'If one's "zakatable" property is below a certain minimum (called the **nisab**), a person does not pay zakat,' (Clark).

The idea of giving stems from a time of trade, a time when currency was not simply coin. 'The zakat traditionally could be paid in different forms, either in cash or kind, the latter meaning a proportion of a herd of animals or, for example, of a date crop,' (Waines). Today, money is the most common form of zakat but offerings of land and goods still persist in certain parts of the world.

Beyond the obligatory fourth pillar, as it is literally understood, giving is encouraged at all times. However, giving is often more relevant at special times in the Muslim calendar, such as hajj. Giving provides support for the ummah and gives it its economic base. A Muslim who gives freely is following the example of Muhammad and the first community he established.

The rich also benefit from the opportunity of giving and sharing. As mentioned at the start of this section, it is an opportunity for wealthy Muslims to enact and play their part in realising the will of Allah. The spiritual benefit of this sacrifice far outweighs any sense of ownership or attachment to the material world.

However, the obligatory nature of the fourth pillar and the ideals above lead to strong disapproval in Islam of showing off one's generosity. To reiterate, the opportunity afforded to the wealthy is not self-made but God-given. With this in mind, self-gratification is totally alien to the spirit of the fourth pillar.

EXAM TIP

This section on the five pillars is full of new concepts. In revising, instead of just drawing up a glossary of key words try changing this into a flowchart that links each aspect of the Muslim teachings together. This shows an ability to present the inter-relatedness of the pillars and demonstrates 'detailed knowledge of the subject matter at a wide range or in significant depth' (level 4 descriptor AO1) as opposed to simply 'very broad and unfocused generalisations' (level 1 descriptor AO1) or an answer that is 'limited in scope' (level 2 descriptor AO1).

7 The practical and theological nature of Hajj

At least once in his or her lifetime, every adult Muslim who is physically and financially able is required to make the sacrifice of time, possessions, status, and normal comforts necessary to make this pilgrimage, becoming a pilgrim totally at God's service.

(Esposito)

Hajj is pilgrimage. There is a clear link with the ancient pilgrimage traditions of pre-Islamic Arabia and to the holy site of Makkah at the time of Muhammad. Again, like prayer, fasting and giving, pilgrimage is not restricted to any one time although the minimum requirement is dictated by the fifth pillar.

Hajj takes place during the first two weeks of the 12th month of the Muslim calendar. The non-obligatory (**umra**) version of a pilgrimage can take place at any time.

Hajj must be performed at least once in a Muslim's lifetime. There are certain criteria to meet.

- One must be of good mental health.
- One must be of good physical health.
- One must be able to afford hajj without incurring debt.
- One must be able to provide for dependents while on hajj.
- One must be prepared to sacrifice one's time, possessions, status, and normal comforts in obedience to God's will.

Hajj takes place in Makkah and the focus is the Ka'aba. This is a square building, constructed of grey stone and marble, and stands in the centre of the Great Mosque. It is 12 metres long, 10 metres wide and 15 metres high.

 KEY WORD

Umra: extra, voluntary pilgrimage beyond hajj

KEY QUOTE

To take part in hajj Muslim men must be sane, free from serious physical infirmity and – most importantly – able to provide for their dependants whilst they are away.

(Horrie and Chippindale)

The Ka'aba in Makkah

In the eastern corner of the Ka'aba is the famous black stone (**hajar al-aswad**) that pilgrims come to touch or kiss. It is believed that Hagar and Ishmael (Abraham's wife and son) are buried under the north-west wall. Tradition recounts that it was Abraham who first introduced the rites of hajj, although this pilgrimage had eventually become corrupted. The term hajj is derived from a word meaning circle and refers to the practice of going around the stone.

Hajj itself is not simply a visit to the Ka'aba. The whole process of hajj is much more involved and takes several days to perform. Like the other four pillars, it has a deeper significance than the mere physical act. It is a journey that describes 'the temporary physical movement of the individual from the "this-worldly" to the "other-worldly" while still on earth' (Turner). The **talbiyah** prayer that commemorates God's command to perform hajj marks the beginning of this journey.

The best way to understand hajj is to investigate the route that is taken. Overall, it takes seven days to perform.

TASK

Go through this section again and draw up a table, making notes summarising the key teachings and practices associated with each pillar. Then you can extend your table by comparing it with the one on page 213.

Objective: To consolidate learning and build up a knowledge base with a depth of understanding that can demonstrate 'accurate, relevant and detailed knowledge of the subject matter at a wide range or in significant depth' (mid level 4 descriptor AO1), as opposed to the information being simply 'minimal accuracy or relevance in factual detail' (level 1 descriptor AO1) or 'limited in scope' (level 2 descriptor AO1).

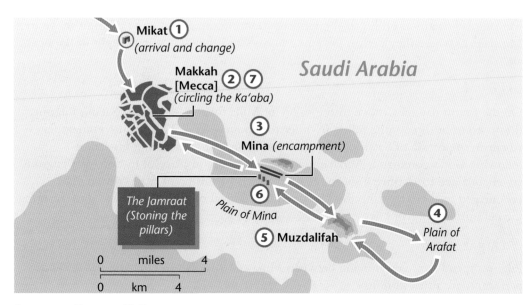

Mikat ① (arrival and change)

Makkah [Mecca] ② ⑦ (circling the Ka'aba)

Saudi Arabia

Mina ③ (encampment)

The Jamraat (Stoning the pillars)

Plain of Mina

⑥

⑤ Muzdalifah

④ Plain of Arafat

0 miles 4

0 km 4

Summary diagram: Hajj

a) Day 1

The first day is a day for preparation: every Muslim must be in a state of **ihram**, that is, to be pure and clean before God. To symbolise this, they wear white clothing. The two simple white sheets symbolise not only purity but also modesty, equality, and obedience. It is symbolic of a physical, mental and spiritual purity. To signify this, every Muslim must abstain from sex, violence and even any thoughts of such sinful action, thinking only of God and goodness.

KEY QUOTE

The journey to Mecca [Makkah] is both physical and metaphorical: physical in the sense that one moves through time and space leaving one's homeland behind; and metaphorical in the sense that one moves upwards, hopefully in an ascension towards God, leaving one's self behind.

(Turner)

b) Day 2

On the second day, the pilgrims enter the Great Mosque and walk seven times round the Ka'aba (**tawaf**). They walk anticlockwise and start from the black stone. This represents the centrality of God in their lives. Every pilgrim offers two rakahs of salat in submission to God. Then they perform **sai** (exertion) by walking between the two hills of **al-Safa** and **al-Marwa**. This emulates the trials and tribulations of Hagar in her search for water for herself and her son Ishmael. At the end of sai, pilgrims take some of the **zamzam** water (a spring that God miraculously caused to appear), which is said to have healing properties. At midday the pilgrims move to Mina for prayers.

c) Day 3

On the third day they travel from Mina, nine miles east to the plain of Arafat. Here they practise **wuquf**, which means standing, and represents a believer standing before the Creator and asking for forgiveness. They listen to a sermon in remembrance of

KEY WORDS

Ihram: a state of purity recognised by ablutions and dress

Tawaf: processing around the Ka'aba

Sai: an effort to move between two hills

Al-Safa and al-Marwa: two hills between which Hagar ran to find water

Zamzam: famous spring of water believed to be discovered by Hagar and provided by God

Wuquf: literally, 'standing' before God

Muhammad's sermon on his final pilgrimage. During the evening the pilgrims move to Muzdalifah, where they perform evening prayers and they stay out all night in the open air.

d) Day 4

KEY WORD

Eid ul-Adha: the celebration at the end of hajj

On the fourth day they move to the valley of Mina for the 'stoning of Satan'. Pilgrims throw stones at three stone pillars in order to renounce evil. This ritual commemorates Abraham's rejection of Satan's suggestion that he should save his son instead of following God's command. Abraham sacrificed a sheep, in place of his son, and pilgrims are encouraged to sacrifice a sheep, goat or camel. At this point male Muslims are encouraged to shave their heads. The three-day festival of **Eid ul-Adha** begins, marking the culmination of hajj.

e) Day 5 and 6

Pilgrims spend two days moving between Mina and Makkah to circle the ka'aba and perform more ritual stonings.

f) Day 7

Pilgrims return to Makkah for the final time.

g) The significant rites that mark the official completion of hajj

These are:

- ihram
- talbiyah prayer ('at your command…without equal…I am here')
- tawaf (circling)
- wuquf (standing).

KEY WORD

Haji: one who has completed hajj

Those who complete hajj are given the honourable title **haji**. The pilgrimage can only be done properly by those with pure intention and without self-interest. It is said that it is better not to do hajj than to do it with wrong intentions and motives. Hajj involves overcoming temptations and distractions. Given the busy nature of hajj today, it has become somewhat commercialised. Some of this can be forgiven, such as the building of better routes, which occurred in response to tragic accidents in which pilgrims were killed in the crush of crowds. However, for Muslims, the pilgrimage should be a return to the essence and source of Islam.

It is this 'perspective' that triumphs when one considers the busy nature of hajj, for example, the sheer practicality of it happening today with stones hitting people and potential crushes at certain points along the way. The Saudi Royal Family have responded by building better routes and any conflicts about hajj being commercialised must be seen within this context.

8 The effect the observance of the five pillars has on Muslim life and the ummah

It has been observed that the pillars are like 'emblems' (Turner) that 'point to deeper truths'. They are simply the core of Islamic practice as all life, in its entirety, is seen as an act of worship (ibadah). However, in consideration of the symbolism and theological significance of the pillars it has been commented that there are 'as many interpretations as there are Muslim scholars' (Turner).

There is a broad consensus on the basic implications that the pillars have for Muslims collectively. This table highlights the ways in which each pillar extends to, and influences, the daily life of a Muslim, but also how each pillar affects the Muslim community (ummah).

Pillar	Impact on daily life	Implications for ummah
Declaring faith (shahadah)	From birth to death a continual renewal Psychological focus daily	Basis of faith and practice for all Muslims Unity of God and believers Declaration common to all Muslims
Prayer (salah)	Extension of salah – different types Dua Al-tarawih (during Ramadan)	Friday prayers
Fasting (saum)	Giving of time Focus on God – becoming more God-conscious	Fasting and giving together *Ramadan unites the Muslim world through the shared experience of fasting, propelling all of its members – theoretically at least – towards the same spiritual goal.* (Turner)
Giving for the sake of God (zakat)	Giving is not just money – it can include time, goods and also can be beyond the minimum of zakat	A strong social and economic base for the community
Pilgrimage (hajj)	A psychological goal The daily spiritual journey recognised as an aspect of hajj	Equality and unity A shared experience Quintessential ummah

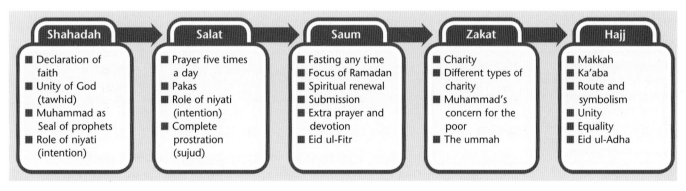

Summary diagram: The five pillars

Study the example of what could be given for *basic*, *developed* and *higher* in the case of the question about salat opposite. Add to this list as a group. Then, in small groups, work out what could be included for *basic*, *developed* and *higher* for a similar question about shahadah. Consider the following question.

Examine Muslim teachings about shahadah. (21 marks)

You could swap ideas between groups in order to finalise your notes. Alternatively, each group could take the *basic*, *developed* and *higher* sections and then discuss your notes.

Objective: To develop awareness of what will constitute a very good answer (level 4) by gradually building up a response while referring to the descriptor 'accurate, relevant and detailed knowledge used concisely to present a coherent and well-structured response to the task at a wide range or considerable depth; selecting the most important features for emphasis and clarity; using evidence to explain the key ideas; expressed cogently using technical language' (high level 4 descriptor AO1).

Reflection and assessment

It is vital to bring together the information that has been covered so far and recognise how it can be transformed into effective examination-style revision and answers. The best way to do this is to ask: 'How am I going to be assessed on this information?'

In the examination you will be assessed by levels of response. Refer to pages 8–10 in the Introduction to check the level descriptors.

Below is an examination-style question about salat. Beneath it are three sets of bullet points under the headings *Basic*, *Developed* and *Higher*. A *basic* answer relates to levels 1 up to the bottom of level 2. The *developed* answer can score level 3, possibly into the lower marks of level 4. The *higher* level scores from the bottom of level 4 up to the maximum marks possible.

Examine Muslim teachings about salat. (21 marks)

Suggestion for further application of skills

Now use what you have learned above to create the ideal mark scheme, or plan for similar questions that might require you to examine teachings of one or more of the other pillars.

Using the principles developed in the above question and analysis exercise, try doing this under timed conditions. Then use the mark scheme to try some peer assessment. Mark each other's work, identifying strengths and areas for development.

Basic

- Prayer five times a day
- Meaning of prayer
- Purpose of prayer

Developed

- A clear discussion of the different types of prayer
- Detail about the rakahs
- Spiritual benefits of prayer

Higher

- A detailed discussion about how prayer affects both an individual and the community (ummah)
- Possible misunderstandings about prayer
- The role of intention
- The purpose of ritual preparations
- A detailed explanation of the meaning of prayer

TOPIC 2: KEY EMPHASES IN TEACHING AND PRACTICE

Part 2C: A critical analysis of the issues in teaching and practice

> **This means I am expected:**
>
> **to analyse and critically evaluate:**
> - the relationship between the five pillars and their relative importance
> - the collective importance.

The idea of the five pillars suggests a very powerful and famous architectural imagery of holding up a building. Pillars work together to support the building's weight in the same way that the five pillars support Islam.

There is clearly strength in unity and this is the idea behind the five pillars. Indeed, this may be the reason that the idea of pillars developed.

However, there is more to the relationship between the five pillars than this. There is also the idea of inter-dependence, for example, the use of the shahadah in prayer, intensive prayer during the month of fasting. All aspects seem to culminate in hajj, which adds force to the view that the pillars are to be seen as a spiritual journey towards their ultimate expression through hajj.

It has been argued that the shahadah is the essence of the rest, that is, the very source of inspiration for practice.

Prayer, fasting and giving for the sake of God are outward expressions of submission (what it is to be Muslim) and obedience to God and worship (ibadah) of him.

Conversion to Islam is demonstrated through shahadah, with intention, before witnesses. It has also been suggested that the cumulative spiritual experience of hajj is like an expression of a lifelong spiritual journey for a Muslim, a return home to spiritual roots.

1 The relationship between the five pillars and their relative importance

What then of the remaining part of a Muslim's life, the so-called nitty-gritty of spiritual practice? Do you have to pray, fast and give to be a Muslim? Are good deeds essential? The answer is clearly: 'Yes!'

Fasting, prayer and giving are obligatory. These three aspects remind a Muslim of God and of others who are in need. Collectively they encourage a Muslim to be more God-conscious, more grateful to God for his mercy and more charitable.

? KEY QUESTIONS
- Can any of the five pillars be truly independent?
- Is one pillar more important than another?
- Are all pillars compulsory?
- How far does one pillar impact upon another?
- Can a Muslim practise fasting without prayer?
- How far do the pillars promote unity?
- In what practical ways do the pillars demonstrate equality?

Fasting, prayer and giving bring both individual and communal benefits. They help a Muslim to rededicate their life and submit to God's power; they are a means to a spiritual recharge and increased preparedness to make more effort to please God.

They bring Muslims closer to, and make them more intimate with, God and encourage them to be more prepared to make sacrifices in putting God first in their lives.

Fasting, prayer and giving encourage humility before God, gratitude for what he has done and compassion towards others. They remind a Muslim to live accountably and to be responsible for their actions and to their Maker.

2 The collective importance

The pillars not only support faith individually, but also serve collectively as an inter-twining tapestry of physical, psychological and spiritual expression in a Muslim's daily life.

Together, fasting, prayer and giving generate a sense of Muslim identity, a commonality of spiritual expression, actively promoting equality as Muslims.

Fasting, prayer and giving keep Muslims on the straight path, being reminded constantly of God`s immanent presence as well as pointing to his ultimate greatness and transcendence.

Fasting, prayer and giving point towards the example set by the prophet. As with the early Muslim community, they promote self-discipline, brotherhood and an awareness of God, and they act as a reminder of the need to submit to God in all aspects of life. Together, fasting, prayer and giving encourage living Islamically.

However, it must always be remembered that fasting, prayer and giving can be completed as rituals, without right intent.

What is most important is intent and God-consciousness in all actions.

Without right intent, fasting, prayer and giving may become hypocritical acts. It is better never to have done the actions in the first place if the intention was not pure.

3 Possible conclusions

What ideas, arguments and conclusions can we draw out of all this? With Islam it may be difficult to find internal contradictions or outright conflicts, due to the tight-knit essence of teachings and the idea of community. This is Islam's great strength as a religion. However, despite this, there are some differences in understanding, in interpreting the significance of the pillars.

When assessing the issues that arise from the importance of the five pillars, it is important to reflect upon the arguments previously discussed and arrive at some appropriate conclusion.

It may be that you accept none of these listed here, or just one of them, or you may have a different conclusion that is not listed. However, what is important is the way that you have arrived at your conclusion – the reasoning process.

From the preceding discussions, here are some possible conclusions you could draw.

1   Shahadah is the only pillar necessary for salvation and is therefore the priority as it encapsulates all that it is to be Muslim.

2 You cannot be a Muslim without good deeds or pure intention in your actions – to say the shahadah once is not enough; it should be a daily acknowledgement as expressed physically through the other pillars.

3 Intention is the ultimate rule for Muslim life and all life, not just the pillars, should be an expression of worship (ibadah) to God.

4 The pillars are not to be seen as separate entities that exist apart from life, because they do indeed penetrate every aspect of daily life.

5 Allah knows the hearts of humans and to argue about issues of relevance and priority is to take a person away from the true message of Islam, which is to be God-conscious and obedient, and submit to his will.

6 Prayer, fasting and zakat are the most important pillars because they are the ultimate expression of shahadah and the outward mark of submission (what it means to be Muslim).

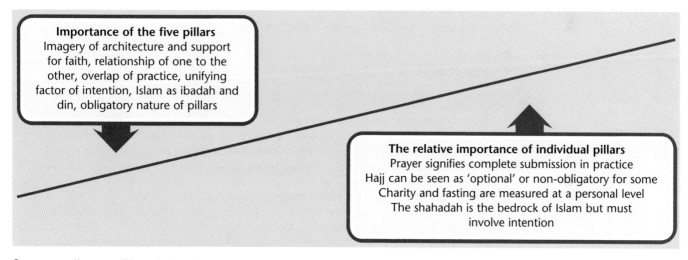

Importance of the five pillars
Imagery of architecture and support for faith, relationship of one to the other, overlap of practice, unifying factor of intention, Islam as ibadah and din, obligatory nature of pillars

The relative importance of individual pillars
Prayer signifies complete submission in practice
Hajj can be seen as 'optional' or non-obligatory for some
Charity and fasting are measured at a personal level
The shahadah is the bedrock of Islam but must involve intention

Summary diagram: The relative importance of the five pillars

Reflection and assessment

Earlier in this topic you considered the assessment objective AO1 which focused on knowledge and understanding. The second way of being assessed is through assessment objective AO2.

For this objective you need to be able to 'critically evaluate and justify a point of view through the use of evidence and reasoned argument'.

The exam is marked with reference to levels. There is a description of the character and features for each level. Look back to page 10 in the Introduction to review the level descriptors for AO2.

Look at the following suggestions for a sample basic level 1–2 answer, which is a response to this question.

How far is prayer the most important practice in Islam? (9 marks)

The *basic* answer would deal with the question by:

- stating the basic definition of prayer and the idea of prostration and submission
- giving some basic evidence or reasoning as to why prayer is vital.

TASK

Look at the notes for a basic answer above. Try to work out how a developed answer (level 2–3) would deal with the question by adding two or three more bullet points. Now go on to develop this answer to indicate how a *higher* answer (level 4) would deal with the question by adding further bullet points. Don't forget to keep the bullet points centred around the question focus.

Objective: To develop awareness of what will constitute a very good answer by gradually building up a response that is 'an attempt at an evaluation of the issue(s) raised in the task, typically through a careful analysis of alternative views; leading to a clearly expressed viewpoint supported by well deployed evidence and reasoned argument; expressed accurately, fluently and using a range of technical vocabulary' (level 4 descriptor AO2).

Suggestions for further application of skills

Now try this technique of building together an ideal answer with one of these questions.

Comment on the view that shahadah is the most important pillar of Islam.
(9 marks)

Comment on the view that fasting is essential if one is a true Muslim.
(9 marks)

Try creating a few questions about the pillars, based around the theme of the relative importance of an individual pillar.

TOPIC 1: KEY ISSUES IN THE STUDY OF THE TEACHINGS OF JESUS CHRIST

Part 1A: Jesus' moral teachings

This means I am expected:

to know about the key issue:

● Jesus' moral teachings

and to study:

● the Gospel setting – the Jewish religion

● the Jewish setting – the religious groups

● the Roman influence

● the sermon on the plain

● teaching on wealth

● teaching about the poor

● teaching about outcasts

● forgiveness.

In this book the evidence and examples given are relevant and appropriate because this material focuses only on the content for AO1 that is given by the Edexcel specification. The evaluation materials for AO2 will be aimed at helping you 'critically evaluate and justify a point of view through the use of evidence and reasoned argument'.

It would be helpful to write your notes using the headings listed above, as it is from these areas that the examination questions will be derived.

In your studies, remember that you have to bear in mind the **two** basic assessment objectives of:

● Knowledge and Understanding (AO1)
● Evaluation (AO2).

See pages 7–8 in the Introduction to remind yourself of these objectives.

The evaluation material set out in Part 1C (page 241) can be studied either alongside the AO1 material, as you work through this unit, or as a separate unit.

This part of the unit explores various aspects and features of Luke's Gospel. Before starting this unit, read through Luke's Gospel. If one is available, watch a DVD of the Gospel.

The exam questions may specify one or more of the areas listed above. You should know the text well enough to be able to explain and illustrate the particular focus of the question from the text. The notes in this section assume you have the text in front of you, as they refer to verse numbers.

This particular part of the unit discusses Jesus' moral teaching in Luke's Gospel, but the first few sections are intended to set the background.

The events recorded in the Gospels are set in a particular place (Palestine) and at a particular time (the first century CE). It is not certain exactly when Jesus was born but most scholars agree that it was towards the end of Herod the Great's reign (4BCE) and Jesus' death is placed roughly between CE29 and CE34.

Jesus lived in a country where the majority of the population were followers of Judaism and were called Jews. Jesus himself was a Jew and followed the religious practises such as attending the synagogue and celebrating the religious festivals.

Therefore, to understand Jesus' teaching and actions fully, it is necessary to understand something of the background – the Jewish religion, the religious groups and the influence of the Romans who were occupying the country at the time of Jesus.

Although no questions will be specifically set on this area, the information here will be relevant to material that will be examined. For instance, in Luke's Gospel Jesus often clashed with the Pharisees over their teaching and beliefs, such as teaching about outcasts and the **Sabbath**. You will need some knowledge of the Pharisees to make sense of these clashes.

Similarly, in John's Gospel, Jesus refers to events in the Torah and makes much use of symbolism from the Jewish festivals. You will need some knowledge of the Jewish religion to make sense of the 'I am' sayings of Jesus, and the signs.

1 The Gospel setting – the Jewish religion

a) The Torah

At the heart of Judaism is the **Torah**. It is not always clear just what the Torah is; it probably refers to the scrolls containing the first five books of the Bible, namely Genesis, Exodus, Leviticus, Numbers and Deuteronomy. The Jews believed that Moses was the author of these writings.

Within these accounts is the story of God's dealings with the Jewish race, of how he brought them out of slavery from Egypt and into the Promised Land of Israel. Specific sections of law contained within these first five books may also be referred to as the Torah. The laws gained their authority from the belief that they had divine origin. They were not seen as negative but, rather, as evidence of God's favour to his chosen people.

b) Covenant

Inseparable from the law was the idea of **covenant**. It is often taken to mean agreement but much more accurate is the idea of God bestowing his favour on the people. The condition for enjoyment of this was obedience. It was not that God required the people's agreement, simply that they could enjoy the results of God's blessings only if they were obedient.

The history of the Jews tells how the people strayed from obedience to God's covenant and suffered the consequences of disobedience. Given the importance of the law, it is

KEY WORD

Sabbath: the seventh day of creation when God rested; in Judaism, it is observed from sundown on Friday to sundown on Saturday

KEY WORDS

Torah: usually refers to the first five books (the law books) of the Bible; the word Torah comes from a root word meaning guidance or instruction, although it is often translated as 'law'
Covenant: agreement, promise; the idea of God bestowing his favour on the people in return for their obedience

easy to see why the religious authorities saw Jesus as a threat to their commitment to God's law in, for example, his attitude towards the Sabbath.

c) The Temple in Jerusalem

The Temple, just as a building, dominated Jerusalem. It also played a major part in the life of the Jews in Palestine. It was considered to be the very dwelling place of God and a sign to the Jews that they were his special people.

The Temple was central to animal sacrifices, which were a major part of the religious rituals.

d) The synagogue

The synagogue was in marked contrast to the Temple. At the synagogue there were no priests and no sacrifices were offered. Prayer and reading the Torah took the place of sacrifices. According to Jewish religious law, men must pray three times a day, ideally in a group of ten or more. The synagogue's primary purpose was to assist this public prayer.

2 The Jewish setting – the religious groups

Jesus lived between two periods where the Jews struggled to gain political freedom. In 165BCE the Jews defeated the Syrians and gained independence in Judea. However, by 63BCE, the Romans had invaded and become the occupying force. An attempt to revolt against the Romans took place in CE66–70, but the outcome was defeat for the Jews and the destruction of Jerusalem and the Temple. It was during this earlier period of independence that various religious groups emerged, in particular, the Pharisees and Sadducees.

a) The Pharisees

i) Their origin

A group arose who wanted to maintain the purity of the Jewish faith and return to the strict keeping of the laws of the Torah. They wanted to separate themselves from the pagan world and, in particular, the effects of Greek and Roman influences. This group became known as the Pharisees. The root of the word is thought to mean 'separated ones'.

ii) Their distinctive ideas

This desire for purity and keeping of the law led them to develop extra laws to make sure people did not break the Torah by accident or through ignorance. This hedging around the law was intended to bring back God's blessing on his chosen people. They regarded the keeping of the Torah as an individual as well as a national duty. The Pharisees themselves were meticulous about the keeping of the law, particularly in matters of ritual purity and tithing. They claimed that the law contained 613 commandments of which 248 were positive and 365 were negative. The hedge they built around them became part of the oral law and gained such authority, since they claimed they had the correct interpretation of the Torah, that it became attributed to Moses. These additions became known as the traditions of the elders and included such things as the list of 39 tasks that could not be done on the Sabbath because they would count as work.

The Pharisees also had distinctive beliefs about the end of the world. They believed in:

- the resurrection of the dead and a world to come
- the soul as being immortal
- angels and demons who surrounded human life and were concerned with human beings

TASK

Carry out some research about the animal sacrifices that were offered at the Temple. Find out about the complex systems they built in order to manage so many sacrifices.

Objective: To appreciate the size, role and importance of the Temple in the life of the people and religion. This demonstrates 'knowledge of the subject matter at a broad range' (level 4 descriptor AO1).

TASK

Use a concordance to research Jesus' attitude towards the Pharisees as recorded in the synoptic Gospels.

Objective: To develop knowledge and understanding of the Pharisees. This demonstrates 'knowledge of the subject matter at a broad range' (level 4 descriptor AO1).

 KEY QUESTIONS

- **Were the Pharisees hypocrites?**
- **Was Jesus unfair to condemn the Pharisees?**
- **Why did the Pharisees see Jesus as a threat?**

- human beings having free choices about whether or not to follow God
- piety being rewarded in the afterlife
- punishment in the afterlife for evildoers
- a day of judgement
- the messiah who would bring in a new age where the righteous would reign.

b) The Sadducees

i) Their origin

The Sadducees formed as a group at about the same time as the Pharisees. They rejected oral tradition and sided more with the ruling class. The origin of their name is unclear, though a popular suggestion is that it derived from Zadok, the name of the chief priest during Solomon's reign. Certainly this would be consistent with the fact that the majority of Sadducees were priests and were centred on Jerusalem around the Temple. They also tended to belong to influential aristocratic families.

ii) Their distinctive ideas

The Sadducees contrasted markedly with the Pharisees. In terms of beliefs, they were very conservative. They:

- only accepted the written Torah and rejected the additions of the oral law and traditions of the elders
- believed that correct worship at the Temple would bring material prosperity
- did not believe in the resurrection of the dead
- did not believe in the later doctrines of the immortality of the soul
- did not believe in rewards or punishments in the afterlife
- did not believe in the doctrines about angels and demons
- believed people had a free choice of good and evil.

3 The Roman influence

TASK

Draw a table with two columns, one headed **Pharisees** and one **Sadducees**. Then list the differences between them. An example is given below.

Pharisees	Sadducees
Believed in resurrection of the dead	Did not believe in resurrection of the dead

Objective: To develop better understanding of the beliefs of the Pharisees and Sadducees. This demonstrates 'knowledge of the subject matter at a broad range' (level 4 descriptor AO1).

TASK

Look at the satellite picture and try to locate where the following places are on it. Jerusalem, Bethlehem, Nazareth, the Dead Sea, the Sea of Galilee

Objective: To develop knowledge of the geography of incidents and events in the Gospels. This demonstrates 'knowledge of the subject matter at a broad range' (level 4 descriptor AO1).

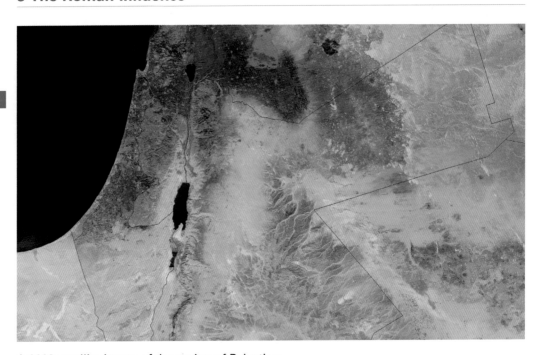

A 2003 satellite image of the region of Palestine

Palestine is about the size of Wales, but was on the main routes from Egypt in the south to Syria and Mesopotamia in the north. As a result of its strategic position, it was much fought over in the power struggles between the major nations of the north and south.

Occupation

In 66–63BCE the Roman general Pompey was engaged in campaigns in the Mediterranean. In 63BCE he took advantage of a dispute between two brothers over the high priest's office and entered Jerusalem. To the horror of the Jews, Pompey entered the Holy of Holies in the Temple, a place where only the High Priest entered and certainly where no Gentile was allowed. Nothing was looted but the Jews never forgave this act of trespass. The Romans occupied and ruled over the area.

By the time of Jesus' birth, Herod the Great was ruling over the Jews from his royal palace in Jerusalem. He began the reconstruction of the Temple, as well as many other building projects. The latter part of his reign was marked by his illness and paranoia. He murdered many of his family, believing they were plotting against him. At his death, the kingdom was split into three areas, in accordance with his will, and divided among three of his remaining sons:

- Archelaus was made ethnarch of Judea, Samaria and Idumea, with a promise that he would be made king if he proved himself a good ruler. However, he was as brutal as his father. After deep unrest amongst the Jews, he was removed by Rome in CE6. A series of regional governors called procurators administered the area. The most well known of these was the sixth one, Pontius Pilate.
- Philip was made tetrarch over the north-eastern part of Herod the Great's kingdom.
- Antipas, the full brother of Archelaus, was made tetrarch of Galilee and Perea.

4 The sermon on the plain

He went down with them and stood on a level plain. A large crowd of his disciples was there and a great number of people from all over Judea;

(Luke 6:17)

The term 'sermon on the plain' comes from Luke's setting of the event. He mentions standing on a level place (6:17). Much of what is in Luke's sermon is also in Matthew's famous 'sermon on the mount'. This close agreement might suggest that they derived from similar sources, though there are also some significant differences.

This is the first occasion on which Jesus has specifically addressed disciples; he speaks to them about the status and demands of discipleship. It is about life in the **Kingdom of God**. It is about the expected character of a follower of Christ.

a) Blessings (6:20–23)

The future tense… emphasises their certainty and not merely their futurity.

(Tasker)

Kingdom of God: God's rule or reign; the idea of kingdom is not necessarily one of territory, but more describing dominion

KEY QUOTE

This is the one I esteem; he who is humble and contrite in spirit and trembles at my word.

(Isaiah 66:2)

EXAM TIP

Do not use a Bible quotation just to repeat what you have just written. You need either to allude to the quotation or to use it to draw out some further comment. This demonstrates 'relevant knowledge and understanding...using evidence to explain the key ideas' (level 4 descriptor AO1).

The root idea of the word 'blessed' is to be approved or to find approval. The four qualities described are approved by God; the promises are for the character described. They have both present and future fulfilment.

i) Blessed are the poor for yours is the Kingdom of God

The reference to the poor has an Old Testament background. The idea of material poverty gradually developed into the idea of humble dependence on God. The poor had no resources so they must rely on God. In other words, they recognised their spiritual bankruptcy. So, right at the start, Luke shows that life in the Kingdom of God requires us to recognise our need for God.

ii) Blessed are you who hunger now for you will be satisfied

Again, this seems to refer to spiritual hunger – hunger for righteousness, as Matthew's Gospel describes it. They hunger after it, in that they cannot get along without it. They are aware of something missing, both morally and spiritually, and only God can give the inward peace that satisfies this hunger.

iii) Blessed are you who weep now, for you will laugh

The weeping is not over loss or grief, but refers to those who are sensitive to evil and suffering, those who feel the pain of the world. The future promise is that, in the Kingdom of God, those tears will become tears of joy and laughter, since evil will have been removed.

iv) Blessed are you when men hate you...because of the Son of Man. Rejoice in that day...

The persecution Jesus refers to is of a particular kind: it is suffering on account of the Son of Man. He points out that they are in good company since that is how the prophets were treated. However, their reward will be in heaven.

b) Woes (6:24–6)

The four woes, only found here in Luke's Gospel, are almost the reversal of the four blessings. In one sense they turn the world the right way up. They highlight the things the world often wants and warns against such desires. Whereas the blessings focused on spiritual qualities, the woes focus on the things that hinder the development of spiritual qualities. The root idea of 'woe' expresses the idea of regret rather than making some kind of threat.

i) Woe to you who are rich, you have already received your comfort

Riches may hinder the development of spiritual qualities, because people rely on riches rather than God.

ii) Woe to you who are well fed now, for you will go hungry

This refers to those who feel they have all they need. They are not even aware of their spiritual bankruptcy. However, there will come a time when they are.

iii) Woe to you who laugh now, for you will mourn and weep

These people may be happy with their present lot in life but they are misguided. Some scholars see it as referring more to the superficiality and the emptiness of riches. In his commentary on Luke's Gospel, Leon Morris states: 'Obviously Jesus is not objecting to laughter as such. But there is a laughter that is the expression of superficiality and it is this shallow merriment that will have to give way to mourning and weeping.'

iv) Woe to you when all men speak well of you, for that is how their fathers treated the false prophets

The false prophets gained approval from the people because they said what the people wanted to hear; they avoided upsetting the *status quo*. True prophets speak uncomfortable words that challenge. Hence, they are persecuted.

c) The Law of Love (6:27–36)

The love being commended here is agape love, or practical love. This love is determined and concerned about the true welfare of others, whoever they are. It requires you to love those who are your enemies and even those who curse and abuse you. Jesus demands that we go further than just refraining from hostile acts. We must do actual good to those who seek to harm us.

Two examples are then given to illustrate this positive action.

1 A personal insult: a sharp backhand slap to the cheek. The action commended by Jesus is to be prepared to take another one rather than retaliate. We must not seek revenge.

2 Over-riding your rights: a cloak is taken. The action commended by Jesus is to give them your tunic. The cloak referred to is the garment recognised in Jewish law as a possession that could not be taken away from you. Therefore Jesus was saying that we should not retaliate even if we have taken from us those things that are ours by rights of law. We must be prepared to abandon our rights.

Verse 31 is known as the Golden rule. The negative form of the rule was well known but Jesus gives the positive form. The emphasis therefore, was not on abstaining and avoiding retaliation, but actually returning a positive act.

The way of the world is to act in a generous way. This is partly for selfish motives – to win friends and influence people. There is less concern for other people's welfare and more concern for self-interest and gain.

Loving our enemies will bring God's approval and our motivation should be our desire to exhibit the same qualities as God, our father.

d) Judging others (6:37–42)

Above, the emphasis was on mercy. This idea continues with the focus on non-judgement. The implication is that if we judge then we shall be judged. However, it is not clear who does the judging. It could refer to the present judgement of people by other people, but most scholars understand that the judgement referred to is by God. The implication is that none of us can survive God's scrutiny, with his perfect justice. God will deal with us in the way in which we have chosen to deal with others, as he looks at us with the eyes of someone who is perfectly just.

Verses 39–42 highlight the importance of acting in the way advocated in the sermon. Jesus is the teacher to follow. It is of no use being led by the blind. Instead we should be led by Jesus. There may also be an implication that we should look to our own moral state before being critical of others. Only when we are self-critical can we be objectively critical of others, and act constructively to help them.

KEY QUOTE

A horrible and shocking thing has happened in the land: The prophets prophesy lies, and the priests rule by their own authority, and my people love it this way.
(Jeremiah 5:31)

KEY QUOTES

It [Jesus' commands on love] takes up and pushes to an extreme the highest demands love might impose in a situation of close community and asks for this to be practised in relation to the enemy.
(Nolland)

If you take your neighbour's cloak as a pledge, return it to him by sunset.
(Exodus 22:26)

KEY IDEA

The negative form of the Golden rule:

What is hateful to you, do not to your neighbour: that is the whole Torah, while the rest is the commentary thereof.
(Hillel)

Hillel lived in Jerusalem during the time of King Herod and the Roman Emperor Augustus. This is therefore pre-Christian. However, Jesus gives the positive form.

e) The two trees (6:43–5)

Having spelt out the moral teaching on love and judgement, Jesus now draws the conclusion that to act in this way requires a true inner goodness of the heart. Right action stems from the right motivation of the inner person.

The first illustration of the tree shows that good fruits can only come from good trees. Each tree is recognised by its fruit.

The second illustration focuses on speech. Here again, outward action reveals the inner heart.

f) The two builders (6:46–9)

Jesus finishes the sermon with an illustration about the importance of not just saying but also doing. He contrasts two types of people: one who hears and does (foundations on rock), and the who hears but does not do (no foundations). The house with foundations that went to the bedrock could withstand calamity in life and withstand the final judgement. The other house with no foundations will be destroyed.

The illustration highlights obedience as the difference between the two buildings.

In the sermon, the moral teaching set out is seen to be distinctive from that of the world. Jesus ends the sermon with a stark choice. On which foundation will we build?

5 Teaching on wealth

a) Introduction

The teaching of Jesus on wealth needs to be contrasted with the response made by Judaism to the social conditions in the time of Jesus. This contrast with the approach of Judaism is discussed in the evaluation section of Part 1C on page 241.

Note that, at the time of Jesus, there was only a very small middle class and the population could be divided into just two groups: the rich and the poor.

The main blocks of teaching in Luke on wealth are to be found in chapters 6, 12 and 16.

b) Jesus' teaching about wealth

i) Possession of wealth is not evil in itself

Although possession of wealth in and of itself is not evil, it has the potential to cause problems. The sermon on the plain (Luke 6), discussed above, highlights some of these problems. Wealth can distract and give false security. It can keep people from God.

ii) Wealth hinders entry into the Kingdom of God

It is this false confidence and security in wealth that can keep people from the Kingdom of God. It is almost as if wealth and possessions become a god themselves and replace the true God. Jesus stated clearly: 'You cannot serve both God and money,' (16:13). Because you cannot give devotion to both, it means that you will love and be devoted to one and hate and despise the other.

A similar point is made in the conversation Jesus had with the rich young ruler (18:18–27). When told to sell everything and give to the poor, the young ruler became very sad because he had great wealth. He was being asked to make a choice between God and money. His reaction suggests that God was not the one he served. Luke records that Jesus looked at the man and said: 'How hard it is for the rich to enter the Kingdom of God. It is easier for a camel to go through the eye of a needle than for a rich man to enter the Kingdom of God,' (18:25). It was thought that wealth was a blessing from God. Hence the reaction of those there: 'Who then can be saved?' If a rich person cannot enter the Kingdom of God, then surely no one can! This illustrates Jesus' revolutionary view about wealth.

Jesus comments: 'A man's life does not consist of the abundance of his possessions,' (12:15) and illustrates this by means of the parable of the Rich Fool (12:16–21). The parable depicts a man who put all his trust and security in wealth. He is described as a fool because he acted as though his wealth enabled him to be assured of his future. The announcement: 'This very night your life will be demanded from you,' (12:20) shows the futility of storing up wealth.

Luke describes the Pharisees as lovers of money (16:14) and Jesus warns that, though people may admire such wealth, this love of money 'is detestable in God's sight,' because God knows what is in the heart.

This self-confidence and self-value based on possession of wealth and seen as praiseworthy in the eyes of the world, is reflected in the parable of the Rich Man and Lazarus (16:19–31). Even in hell, the rich man believes that Lazarus should act as his servant (16:24).

iii) Wealth should be used to help the poor
Is it possible for the rich to be saved? Luke makes clear that wealth can have a positive use. The person Luke chooses to illustrate this proper use of wealth is Zacchaeus, the tax-collector. He records how Zacchaeus gave half of his possessions to the poor (19:8). Jesus responds by saying that salvation had come to that house.

Both the parable of the Rich Fool and the parable of the Rich Man and Lazarus reflect this idea, that the proper use of wealth is to help the poor. The rich fool had stored up wealth for himself rather than giving to the poor. Some verses later, Luke records the saying of Jesus: 'Sell your possessions and give to the poor,' (12:33). Likewise, the rich man had both the means and the opportunity to care for Lazarus when he was outside his house. However, he ignored him and his needs.

The parable of the Shrewd Manager (16:1–9) has as its focus being wise with wealth. Although scholars are divided about how to interpret this parable, many see its meaning as an instruction to Jesus' followers to use their money wisely for spiritual purposes, just as worldly people use their money wisely for material purposes.

iv) Reflection of trust in God
As stated above, to put faith in possessions is to show a lack of trust in God. Conversely, to give freely reflects a trust in God. In chapter 12, Luke includes a section on Jesus' teaching about anxiety and how God cares and provides. The point is made that our attempt to be secure, using only our own resources, is futile, since our real security lies wholly with God. Rather, we should: 'seek his kingdom, and these things will be given to you as well,' (12:31).

> **KEY QUOTES**
>
> *What is highly valued among men is detestable in God's sight.*
> **(Luke 16:15)**
>
> *Father Abraham, have pity on me and send Lazarus to dip the tip of his finger in water and cool my tongue, because I am in agony in this fire.*
> **(Luke 16:24)**

> **KEY QUOTE**
>
> *Renunciation flows out of security, not out of demand. But security is rooted in the knowledge of the Father, not in what is physically present.*
> **(Davids)**

6 Teaching about the poor

TASK

Draw a chart listing, across the top, the four headings of wealth, poor, outcasts, forgiveness. Down the side list the parables of Jesus, found in Luke's Gospel. Then fill in the grid, showing which parables are relevant to the four areas listed.

Objective: To develop well-chosen evidence. This demonstrates that you are 'using evidence to show general understanding of the key ideas' (level 4 descriptor AO1).

a) Introduction

Jesus did not regard poverty as something to be aimed at. Indeed, the picture of the Kingdom of God is one of plenty. Although the term 'the poor' has various meanings, including realising their spiritual need (as in the blessings, see page 224), in this section it refers to the oppressed and the helpless. It should be noted that some of the points made above, concerning the rich by implication, reveal Jesus' teaching about the poor.

b) Jesus' teaching about the poor

i) God's interest in the poor

The Gospels imply that God has a special interest in the oppressed and helpless. Jesus describes his mission as announcing good news to the poor and the oppressed (Luke 4:18–21). In the parable of the Great Banquet (14:15–24) it is the poor, the crippled, the blind and the lame that are invited to the banquet.

ii) Spiritual blessings received

When Jesus was at the Pharisee's house, he told his host that inviting to a banquet those who could not invite you back would bring blessing (14:13). In particular, he named those who should be invited as 'the poor, the crippled, the lame, the blind'. To give them a feast is an act of generosity, because such people could not repay the kindness. Jesus states that there would be repayment at 'the resurrection of the righteous' (14:14).

Generous acts towards the poor show where a person's heart is. As mentioned above (pages 226–7), selling your possessions and giving to the poor is contrasted with concerns for material possessions. What we concentrate on and are interested in reveals what we value most. In this sense, it is our treasure. The heart and the treasure go together. Hence Jesus contrasts earthly and heavenly treasures.

7 Teaching about outcasts

a) Introduction

One of the characteristics of Luke's Gospel is his emphasis on the social outcast. They also feature in Luke's material that is not found in the other Gospels, such as the parable of the Good Samaritan. In Jesus' time, social outcasts would have included such groups as tax-collectors (regarded as traitors since they collected revenue from the occupying forces of Rome), lepers (regarded as unclean), Samaritans (hated by the Jews), shepherds (regarded as irreligious), prostitutes (regarded as sinners) and criminals. (For details about the Samaritans see page 294, in the section on John's Gospel.)

b) Jesus' teaching about outcasts

Linked to Luke's interest in social outcasts is his emphasis on inclusiveness. Luke makes clear that salvation is for all: it is universal. It is available and open to all, including social outcasts and those the religious would regard as automatically excluded. Luke records that the first people to visit Jesus at his birth were shepherds, rather than kings.

The social outcast is often contrasted with those who were regarded as pious and religious. It is the social outcast that Jesus shows is the truly religious. For instance, the incident of the sinner wiping Jesus' feet with her tears is contrasted with the actions of the Pharisee who had invited him to his house for dinner (7:36–50). Likewise, it is the criminal on the cross alongside Jesus who recognises that Jesus is innocent and asks to be remembered when he comes into his kingdom (23:42).

The accounts of people coming to faith include those of social outcasts. They include Zacchaeus, the tax-collector (19:9) and the sinner at the Pharisee's house (7:50).

Jesus also tells parables in which the social outcast is favourably contrasted with the religious person. These include the parable of the Good Samaritan (10:30:37) and the parable of the Pharisee and the Tax-collector (18:9–14). The religious person in the parables often acts without mercy and often lacks humility. In contrast, the social outcast shows mercy, even to an enemy, and shows humility and dependency on God.

8 Forgiveness

a) The parables of the lost

In Luke 15 there are three parables that have a common theme: 'lost'. There is a lost coin (15:3–7), a lost sheep (15:8–10) and a lost son (15:11–32). All three have a similar meaning. They depict a God who seeks the lost and shows great joy when the lost are found and brought back.

God is seen as taking the initiative and searching or, in the case of the lost son, watching out for the son to return home. Hence the three parables share a number of common themes.

i)   The lostness of people

In each of the three parables, something or someone is lost or has strayed away. In each case they left a place that was safe and secure and became cut off. The lost coin may refer to part of a poor woman's savings that she kept secure, or to coins that were strung together as an ornament. The lost sheep left the safety and protection of the rest of the flock. In the final parable, the son left the safety and security of the family. His lostness is vividly described: he fed pigs and 'he longed to fill his stomach with the pods that the pigs were eating, but no one gave him anything' (verse 16). To a Jew, it was degrading to feed pigs. His extreme predicament brought him to his senses. He admits that he has been a fool and prepares himself to admit this to his father. He rehearses what he wants to say, acknowledging that he had sinned both against heaven and against his father (verse 19).

These all give a picture of lostness towards God. This is made clear with the repetition of the words: 'There is joy in heaven over a sinner who repents.' That which was lost to God is found by God.

ii) The searching

Each of the three parables describes the great effort that was put into the search for what was lost.

The coin was lost in the dark, windowless house, so the widow had to light a lamp and do a close search. Luke describes how she swept the house and searched carefully until she found it. She wants the coin so she turns the house upside down.

The shepherd left the 99 sheep and searched until he found the one that was lost. He wants his sheep, so he looks until he finds it.

KEY IDEA

The three parables in Luke 15 share common themes:
- the lostness of people
- the searching
- sharing of the joy of heaven.

When the lost son repents and goes back to seek forgiveness from his father, the father sees him, is filled with compassion and *runs* to meet his son to welcome him back. The father had been looking and waiting for the son.

This reflects the burning desire of God that people come back to him. Luke records that the father (God) saw the son while the son was still a long way off and he ran to meet him. This describes God's preparedness to forgive those who repent. However, God's forgiveness only comes after repentance.

iii) Sharing of the joy in heaven

● **The lost son**

All three parables recount the joy in heaven when that which was lost is found. In the case of the lost son, the father threw his arms around him and kissed him. Before the son could request to be made like one of the hired men, the father ordered the best robes to be put on him, and a ring and sandals. The fatted calf was to be killed and a feast prepared to celebrate the son's return. 'For this son of mine was dead and is alive again; he was lost and is found,' (verse 24).

The parables make clear that God places a high value on human beings. He thinks we are precious. He created us and is concerned about us. The celebration is over something precious that has been reclaimed. We matter to God.

● **The other son**

The context of the telling of the parables is given in verses 1–2. Tax-collectors and sinners were gathered round to listen to Jesus. This message of forgiveness would be clearly relevant to them. However, there were also Pharisees and teachers of the Law present, who were muttering about Jesus welcoming sinners. It is to this group that the reaction of the elder son in the parable is relevant.

The elder son represents the attitude of the religious people who did not want Gentiles and sinners to be included. The elder son could not see what was important – that his brother was saved and welcomed by God. Instead, he was angry and self-righteous. His father affirms: 'all that is mine is yours' (verse 31). Like the Pharisees, he did not realise the extent of his privileges.

The parable showed the respectable religious person that they, like the Father, should rejoice over a sinner restored. Not to do so meant that they did not grasp the nature of God's grace and forgiveness to those who genuinely repent.

b) Other teaching on forgiveness

The story of the paralytic (5:17–26) records Jesus' pronouncement of the forgiveness of sins. This made the religious authorities question who Jesus was, as they acknowledged that only God could forgive sins.

A similar question is raised when Jesus forgives the sins of the woman who anointed him at the Pharisee's house (7:48–9). In this incident, Jesus linked love and gratitude to forgiveness. Because she had been forgiven much, she loved much.

In the sermon on the plain, Jesus taught about not judging. It is the person with a forgiving spirit who is forgiven (6:37).

Forgiveness is also a feature of the Lord's prayer: 'Forgive us our sins, for we also forgive everyone who sins against us,' (11:4). This does not mean that the forgiveness of others is

---

🖉 **TASK**

Compare the story of Jonah (Jonah 3–4) with that of the reaction of the elder son in the parable of the Lost Son.

Objective: To develop understanding of the key ideas. This demonstrates that you can select 'the most important features for emphasis and clarity' (level 4 descriptor AO1).

---

66 **KEY QUOTES**

Do not judge, and you will not be judged. Do not condemn, and you will not be condemned. Forgive, and you will be forgiven.

(Luke 6:37)

If your brother sins, rebuke him, and if he repents, forgive him. If he sins against you seven times in a day, and seven times comes back to you and says, 'I repent', forgive him.

(Luke 17:3–4)

99

the grounds for our forgiveness. Forgiveness is not based on human merit but the grace of God. Rather, it is that we should forgive others because we have been forgiven so much by God. Indeed, our forgiveness of others should have no limits.

Jesus talked about forgiving someone seven times a day (17:3–4). By this he meant that forgiveness should be a part of our character.

On the Cross, Jesus prayed for forgiveness for those who were putting him to death.

The message of repentance and forgiveness is linked to Jesus' death and resurrection in Luke 24:45–7. It is because Jesus died and rose again that forgiveness is possible, and the message of forgiveness can be preached by the disciples.

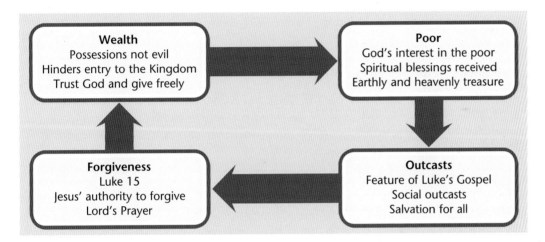

Summary diagram: The teaching of Jesus

Reflection and assessment (AO1)

It is now time to channel the information you have considered in a more focused way. To do this, you need to ask yourself the question: 'How am I going to be assessed on my use of this information?'

The first way is through assessment objective 1 (AO1), for which you need to be able to 'select and clearly demonstrate the relevant knowledge and understanding through the use of evidence, examples and correct language and terminology'.

As you work through each unit in this book, you will find that the amount of support in these sections will gradually be reduced, in order to encourage the development of your independence and the honing of your AO1 skills.

Use the writing frame provided below to answer this question.

Examine Jesus' teaching on forgiveness. (21 marks)

After completing the question, use the levels and AO1 descriptors to award marks out of 21. Identify strengths and areas for development in each answer.

Writing frame

Three parables of the 'lost' that Jesus taught are...

The meaning of the three parables is that there is great joy in heaven...

In one of those parables God is depicted as the Father. The parable shows God's forgiveness by...

The religious authorities questioned Jesus because...

Forgiveness is mentioned in the Lord's Prayer where it says...

By this Jesus meant...

Jesus said that the woman who anointed him at the Pharisees house loved much because...

On the Cross, Jesus displayed forgiveness when he...

Suggestion for further application of skills

Construct your own writing frame for this question.

Illustrate Jesus' teaching about the poor. (21 marks)

Now, as a group, collaborate to create an answer that demonstrates a level 4. Look back at pages 8–10 in the Introduction to check the level descriptors.

FOUNDATIONS
Area I: New Testament – Luke's Gospel

TOPIC 1: KEY ISSUES IN THE STUDY OF THE TEACHINGS OF JESUS CHRIST

Part 1B: The meaning and significance of the miracles

This means I am expected:

to know about the key issue:

● the meaning and significance of the miracles

and to study:

● the meaning and significance of the miracles
● particular miracles in Luke's Gospel.

In this book the evidence and examples given are relevant and appropriate because this material focuses only on the content for AO1 that is given by the Edexcel specification. The evaluation materials for AO2 will be aimed at helping you 'critically evaluate and justify a point of view through the use of evidence and reasoned argument'.

It would be helpful to write your notes using the headings listed above, as it is from these areas that the examination questions will be derived.

In your studies, remember that you have to bear in mind the **two** basic assessment objectives of:

● Knowledge and Understanding (AO1)
● Evaluation (AO2).

See pages 7–8 in the Introduction to remind yourself of these objectives.

The evaluation material set out in Part 1C (page 241) can be studied either alongside the AO1 material, as you work through this unit, or as a separate unit.

This part of the unit discusses miracles in Luke's Gospel. The exam questions may specify one or more of the areas listed above. You should know the text well enough to be able to explain and illustrate the particular focus of the question from the text. The notes in this section assume you have the text in front of you, as they refer to verse numbers.

1 The meaning and significance of the miracles

a) Background to the word 'miracle'

In the Old Testament the Hebrew word for miracle is *oth*. This word is used in the account of the plagues of Egypt, in Exodus 7:3. The word is used not just for an extraordinary event, but often to suggest a happening pointing beyond itself to something further.

> 66 **KEY QUOTE**
>
> *...and though I multiply my miraculous signs and wonders in Egypt, he [Pharaoh] will not listen to you.*
>
> (Exodus 7:3–4) 99

KEY IDEA

The four categories of miracles are:
- healing
- nature
- exorcisms
- raising from the dead.

KEY WORDS

Exorcism: the rite of driving out evil spirits from a person who is believed to be possessed

Messianic Age: the time when the Messiah (the anointed one) would come and bring in an age of peace

KEY IDEA

Messiah is the Hebrew form of the Greek word for 'Christ'. It means 'the anointed one' and refers to one approved by God. Often linked to kings, it later became associated with the hope of an ideal king, the one sent by God to restore Israel.

KEY IDEA

John depicts the death and resurrection of Jesus as the final decisive act of overthrowing the prince of darkness. This could explain why John's Gospel has no exorcisms. He didn't need them. Instead he selects other miracles that reveal the person and work of Jesus.

In the New Testament the Gospel writers used **two** main terms to describe miracles, namely 'mighty works' and 'signs'.

'Mighty works' is used in the synoptic Gospels and emphasises the working and power of God over disease, evil spirits, nature and even death. The use of this term shows that the power and rule of God have interacted with our world; that the Kingdom of God has appeared.

In contrast, John uses the word 'signs'. This is because the miracles he recorded tell the reader about the person and work of Jesus. Hence they were intended to point to something about Jesus that would lead to faith and eternal life.

The 'mighty works' of the synoptic Gospels differ from the miracle stories in John's Gospel in that the synoptic Gospels contain many more miracles. The majority are **exorcisms**. There are none recorded in John's Gospel. The synoptic Gospels emphasise power and the expulsion or conquering of evil.

b) What Luke's Gospel reveals about the meaning of the miracles

Some key texts in Luke suggest the place of miracles in the ministry of Jesus.

i) Signs of the messianic age
- **Luke 4:18f**

  The context is Jesus in the synagogue at Nazareth. The passage he reads is edited from Isaiah 61:1–2 and Isaiah 58:6. Jesus implies that he has been empowered (baptised by the Holy Spirit) to be the figure from Isaiah, who heralds and brings salvation. Jesus was claiming to fulfil the role of the Messiah, the anointed one who would bring in the age of salvation, the **Messianic Age**, the Kingdom of God. Hence the healing ministry was seen as the activity of the Holy Spirit, which was to take place with the coming of the Messianic Age.

- **Luke 7:22f**

  John the Baptist is questioning whether Jesus is the 'coming one'. Most commentators take this title to have links with messianic expectations. John the Baptist is in prison but he sends his disciples to ask Jesus whether he was the Messiah. Jesus' reply picks up the passage from Luke 4, reflecting again the language of Isaiah 61:1. Clearly it is intended to assert that the Messianic Age had arrived. The significance of the miracles is that they are miracles of the New Age.

ii) Evidence that the powers of the New Age were manifested in Jesus
- **Luke 4:36**

  The miracles are included in the Gospels because they belong to a different world-order; they are 'the powers of the coming age' (Hebrews 6:5).

- **Luke 11:20**

  The Gospels show that the powers of the New Age were manifested in Jesus. The forces of evil were being overthrown. The miracles are themselves the message. They are the bringing in of the Kingdom, the defeat of the forces of evil. The miracles are signs that God reigns, he is restoring his Kingdom that was stolen by Satan. Hence the emphasis on exorcisms. Interestingly, Luke selects an exorcism as the first miracle in his Gospel (4:31–37).

iii) Revealing characteristics of the Kingdom

Not only do the miracles announce the arrival of the Kingdom, but their message also parallels Jesus' explicit teaching in many more detailed ways. The miracles parallel the teaching of the parables. Below are some examples to demonstrate this.

- **Luke 10:13**

  People are criticised for not repenting. Because the mighty works are the miracles of the Kingdom, the appropriate response to them is: 'repent and believe the Good News'. The working of miracles is a part of the proclamation of the Kingdom of God, *not* an end in itself.

- **Luke 5:24**

  The context is the healing of the paralytic man who is lowered through the roof. The healing miracles were symbolic demonstrations of God's forgiveness in action.

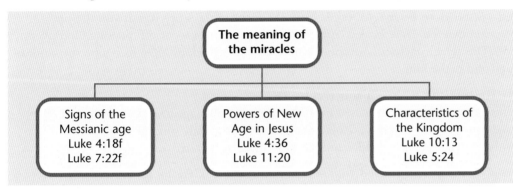

Summary diagram: The meaning of miracles

2 Particular miracles in Luke's Gospel

a) Identifying their meanings

As has been argued above, the miracles are evidence that the Kingdom of God has come and that authority and power are invested in Jesus. It is useful to consider what the miracles teach in terms of the following questions.

i) Where is the Kingdom of God?

There had been an in-breaking with Jesus' life, death and resurrection. Something of the Kingdom life could be experienced now but the Kingdom would not be fully established until Jesus returned in his second coming.

ii) What is the nature of the King?

The Kingdom has a King and the miracles reveal something of his character. He is, for example, compassionate and forgiving.

iii) How do we enter the Kingdom?

The element of faith is a feature of many of the miracle stories.

iv) How should we act in the Kingdom?

This covers both relationship to God and relationship to others. The parables, rather than the miracles, focus on this aspect. The miracle stories should also be used to illustrate the purpose of miracles, as discussed on pages 234–5.

KEY IDEA

The place of miracles in Jesus' ministry:
- signs of the Messianic Age
- powers of this New Age invested in Jesus
- revelation of the characteristics of the kingdom.

EXAM TIP

Good knowledge of the text is vital. However, at AS level you will not be asked to describe the event. The focus will be on its significance or meaning. Therefore, allude to the account by commenting on the aspects and features relevant to the focus of the question. This clearly demonstrates relevant knowledge and understanding and that you are 'clearly identifying the most important features' (level 4 descriptor AO1).

---

66 KEY QUOTE

But if I drive out demons by the finger of God, then the Kingdom of God has come to you.

(Luke 11:20)

99

b) Miracles of healing

i) Healing of the paralytic (5:17–26)

This miracle of the lame man walking reflected the prophecies in Isaiah, which Jesus quoted. The healing miracles were evidence to John the Baptist that the Kingdom had come and that Jesus was the Messiah. They also showed that the powers of the coming Kingdom were manifested in him. He healed with a word of authority and the cure was immediate. In this miracle, Jesus refers to himself as the Son of Man (verse 24) and most scholars take it to be referring to his Messiahship.

KEY QUOTE

When Jesus saw their faith, he said, 'Friend, your sins are forgiven.'
(Luke 5:20)

Faith is highlighted in verse 20. It is not clear if this refers just to the faith of the friends of the paralytic. It seems likely that the paralytic man had faith as well. Faith, along with forgiveness, is the means by which one enters the Kingdom. The healing is total in the sense that it is spiritual (sins forgiven) as well as physical (able to walk).

Jesus is shown to be able to forgive sins; the focus of the story is more on the sin forgiven than the lame healed. After the healing the man went off 'praising God' (verse 25). This is a characteristic of those who enter the Kingdom: they recognise the work of God and praise him.

ii) Raising the widow's son (7:11–17)

This story is about a man raised from the dead. It only appears in Luke's Gospel. The plight of the widow was particularly sad, as it was her only son who had died. She was without protector or provider and her family line had ended.

Jesus is shown to be moved with compassion (verse 13). Again, he showed his power and authority by a command and by immediately bringing the son back to life.

The reaction of the crowd was to recognise this as the work of God and so they praised God. They also recognised Jesus as a great prophet and that God had come to his people.

iii) Jairus' daughter and the bleeding woman (8:40–56)

Another raising of the dead takes place when Jesus raises Jairus' daughter. This miracle shows Jairus as having limited faith. He had faith that Jesus could heal his daughter and he sought Jesus' help. However, when he heard that his daughter had died he thought that it was beyond Jesus' power to do anything more. Jesus focuses on the need for faith and tells Jairus to believe, to 'put your trust in me' (verse 54). As with the previous miracles, Jesus gave a command of authority (verse 54) and the girl was immediately healed (brought back to life).

Many commentators point out the care Jesus shows in this miracle. He was concerned about the girl's practical needs as she recovered. He performed the miracle privately, so that the girl would not be overwhelmed by the people around.

Interposed between two parts of the account is the description of another miracle. It concerned a woman with menorrhagia, which is continuous menstruation. This meant that the woman was regarded as unclean and was not allowed to touch anyone. Luke tells how the woman tried secretly to touch Jesus, using the crush of the crowds to hide her. She thought she could be healed by merely touching Jesus' cloak. In this, she demonstrates that she had considerable faith.

The reference to power going out of Jesus (verse 46) has been variously understood. Some scholars see this as evidence that Jesus lost some of his spiritual energy when he performed miracles. Jesus makes reference to how her faith had healed her (verse 48).

➡ EXAM TIP

When answering a question on miracles, make sure that you focus on the area highlighted in the question. Make sure you illustrate from the text but avoid just recounting the miracle. This avoids writing just a general answer that presents 'a limited range of isolated facts… with mainly random and unorganised detail' or 'information presented within a structure which shows a basic awareness of the issue(s) raised' (level 1 and 2 descriptors AO1). Remember, you are aiming for 'a coherent and well-structured account of the subject matter' (level 4 descriptor AO1).

TASK

Find out what is supposed to have happened to the Ursuline nuns of Loudun in 1633–40.
What is the current view about exorcism in: (a) the Roman Catholic Church (b) The Church of England?
Objective: To have a broader appreciation of the subject that demonstrates 'knowledge of the subject matter at a broad range' (level 4 descriptor AO1).

A woodcut from 1598, showing an exorcism performed on a woman by a priest and his assistant, with a demon emerging from her mouth

c) Miracles over nature

i) Calming the storm (8:22–5)

At first sight it is not obvious how the calming of the storm is linked to the coming of the Kingdom. However, the image of a storm was used in the Old Testament as a metaphor for the evil forces in the world, from which only God could save people (Psalm 69:1–2).

One of the signs of divine power was the ability to control the sea (Psalm 89:9). This action of stilling the storm could be seen as the Kingdom breaking in because Jesus subdued evil forces.

The word used in Mark's Gospel for 'be still' is the same word used in exorcising evil spirits: 'be muzzled'.

The miracle emphasises the need for faith and trust in God. Again, the Psalms made clear that even in bad storms we should not doubt God's power and his concern for us (Psalm 46:1–3). One such illustration is Jesus sleeping peacefully, confident in God's saving power (Psalm 3:24). This is in stark contrast to the lack of faith of the disciples.

This is also a clear revelation of the divine power of Jesus. The Psalms speak of the people calling to waken God when it seemed to them that God was asleep and oblivious of their extreme situation and danger.

A similar action is recorded in the miracle, with the disciples waking Jesus from his peaceful sleep (verse 38). Hence, the miracle revealed who Jesus was. The disciples begin to ask themselves the question: 'Who is this?' (verse 25).

KEY QUOTES

You rule over the surging sea; when its waves mount up, you still them.
(Psalm 89:9)

When you lie down, you will not be afraid; when you lie down, your sleep will be sweet.
(Psalm 3:24)

Awake, O Lord! Why do you sleep? Rouse yourself! Do not reject us for ever. Why do you hide your face and forget our misery and oppression?
(Psalm 44:23–24)

The calming of the storm is miraculous because not only did the wind stop but the sea became calm. Storms are common on the Sea of Galilee but even when the storm stops the water remains rough and choppy for some time after. The disciples realised the miraculous element because they comment that even the sea obeys him.

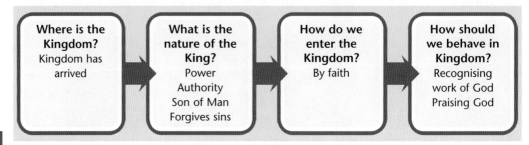

Summary diagram: The healing of the paralytic

TASK

Using the four characteristics of the Kingdom given in the summary diagram, design your own diagrams to show what the other three miracle stories teach.

Objective: To develop understanding of the basic teachings about miracles on the kingdom. This demonstrates the use of 'accurate and relevant detail' in an answer (level 4 descriptor AO1).

Reflection and assessment (AO1)

It is vital to bring together the information covered so far and recognise how it can be transformed into effective examination-style revision and answers. The best way to do this is to ask: 'How am I going to be assessed on this information?'

The first way is through assessment objective 1 (AO1). You need to be able to 'select and clearly demonstrate the relevant knowledge and understanding, through the use of evidence, examples and correct language and terminology'.

Look back to pages 7–8 in the Introduction to review the level descriptors for AO1. There is a description of the character and features for each level. The exam is marked with reference to levels.

Look at the answer opposite, which is a response to this question.

> **Examine the importance for the ministry of Jesus of a healing miracle in Luke's Gospel.**
> **(21 marks)**

a) So what does it score?

In the exam the answer will be marked according to levels (see pages 8–10 in the Introduction). Certainly this candidate has some basic knowledge and understanding. However, important material has been omitted. The candidate has attempted to give a summary of the miracle and then tagged on two or three statements about Jesus. A much more appropriate structure is to have the focus of the question as the heart of the essay, to make the importance for the ministry of Jesus as the focus of each paragraph, and then to allude to aspects of the miracle account that reveal that importance.

At AS level candidates should not be merely 'telling the story'.

This candidate has also been side-tracked into including irrelevant material. As a rough guide, candidates should be gaining a mark every minute (105 minutes and 90 marks available). Clearly the answers are **not** marked on a point-for-point basis, but by levels. However it is a warning that time is short and the assessment objectives stress the need for accurate, relevant knowledge used concisely, selecting the most important features for emphasis and clarity (level 4 descriptor AO1).

This answer would have been awarded high level 1. It has some accurate and relevant information, there is an attempt to organise this within a structure, there are some broad but relevant generalisations, but it lacks focus.

The problem is that, as the response stands, the candidate has left it to the examiner to work out how the importance for the ministry of Jesus is shown by this miracle account. However, it would not take much to develop this essay into a level 4 response.

This is a good start, in that the candidate has immediately identified the miracle story that is going to be discussed. There is no need for a lengthy introduction.

One of the healing miracles that Jesus performed was the healing of the paralytic. As Jesus travelled on his three year ministry he was surrounded by crowds. There were such crowds that some men carrying a paralytic, had to go up onto the roof of the house and lower the man down from the roof in order to ask Jesus to heal him. People had come from every village of Galilee and from Judea and Jerusalem. Amongst those listening to Jesus were the Pharisees and teachers of the Law. The Pharisees developed extra laws to make sure they did not break the law. They were concerned with purity and keeping God's laws. There were 39 things that you could not do on the Sabbath as these things counted as work and you were not allowed to work on the Sabbath. The name Pharisees comes from a word meaning separated ones.

Is this amount of detail relevant? The material needs to be selected to address the focus of the question.

The rest of this paragraph is focusing on material that is not relevant. The word 'Pharisees' has triggered the candidate to write a short paragraph on background but it has not been made relevant to the focus of the question.

Jesus told the paralytic that he had been healed. His sins were forgiven now. Then he told the man to get up and walk. All the people were impressed and praised God.

This is an inaccurate summary. Many important aspects of the miracle account have been omitted.

It was through miracles that Jesus showed who he was. He was the Messiah and the Kingdom had come. He showed he had the power of God. He could heal people. He said faith was needed. Jesus was a miracle worker.

This is not accurate.

These statements have not been explained. The candidate has not indicated how the miracle story shows this about Jesus.

TASK

Use the points identified to redraft the answer on the previous page. Copy it to obtain a text version, then delete material as appropriate, expand on the points that are undeveloped, and add in other possible points that could have been included.

You can do this in pairs, groups or individually but it is important to discuss and compare possible answers if in pairs or groups. You could even start afresh, listing with points. Then you could create a writing frame and complete the answer as a class.

Objective: To improve a level 1–2 response and transform it into a level 3–4 response so that it demonstrates 'a well-structured response... selecting the most important features for emphasis and clarity and using evidence to explain the key issues' (level 4 descriptor AO1).

b) Suggestion for further application of skills

Consider the following question.

> Examine the meaning of miracles in Luke's Gospel.   (21 marks)

As a group, try to create a plan for a level 4 answer. Write this up, under timed conditions, and then compare answers. In your group, discuss which is the best answer and give reasons for your decision.

UNIT 1 FOUNDATIONS
Area I: New Testament – Luke's Gospel

TOPIC 1: KEY ISSUES IN THE STUDY OF THE TEACHINGS OF JESUS CHRIST

Part 1C: A critical analysis of the issues

> **This means I am expected:**
>
> **to analyse and critically evaluate:**
> - the teaching of Jesus compared with that of Judaism at that time
> - the teaching of Jesus contrasted with that of Judaism at that time
> - the purpose of miracles.

1 Judaism at the time of Jesus

? KEY QUESTION

What is Judaism?

The Gospels record the life of Jesus which is set in Palestine in the first century CE. The majority of the population were followers of Judaism, and were referred to as Jews.

Scholars, such as E.P. Saunders and James Dunn, have argued that Judaism, in the centuries either side of the Common Era (CE), exhibited common features and reflect a world of thought that makes it possible to refer to it as common Judaism. Dunn identified four common themes that ran through the wealth of writings produced during this period:

- monotheism – there is only one God
- election – God had chosen the people of Israel alone and given them the Promised Land
- covenant and Torah – the covenant between God and Israel is focused on the keeping of the Torah
- the Temple – the Temple in Jerusalem was at the centre of national worship of God.

The sense of being chosen by God and the various laws and rituals marked the Jews as being different from others.

The keeping of the law was seen as vitally important as a means of earning God's favour. The laws gained their authority from the belief that they had divine origin.

The struggles and difficulties suffered by the Jews were seen by many as a result of their failure to keep the law. Thus, they forfeited God's blessing and protection. The Pharisees argued for a return to the keeping of the strict laws of the Torah. Jesus' understanding of purity was at odds with the thinking of the Pharisees. It was in this area that Jesus came into conflict most with the Pharisees (5:29–32; 11:37–41; 12:1). Other areas of conflict included fasting (5:33–9), keeping the Sabbath (6:1–11), tithing (11:42; 20:20–26) and the interpretation of Scripture (16:18).

(For more details about the Pharisees see pages 221–2.)

2 The teaching of Jesus compared and contrasted with that of Judaism at that time

a) Wealth and the poor

i) Judaism

In Palestine, at the time of Jesus, the poor were generally those who owned no land and were often called the people of the land. They were generally looked down on by the religious, considered as lax in their observance of the law.

Wealth was seen as a blessing of God, although it was recognised that it could lead to greed. A wealthy person could be righteous if they were also generous. The giving of **alms** was a way of becoming righteous in God's sight and so it was a means of gaining merit in the sight of God.

ii) Jesus

Jesus himself would have been identified with the poor, since he was a carpenter who owned no land.

He rejected the link between piety and prosperity. He did not see wealth as a blessing from God. It was seen as something that drew people away from God. The parable of the Sower refers to the world's riches choking the world and making it unfruitful.

Wealth is something that keeps us from God. This is made clear in his statement that it is easier for a camel to go through the eye of a needle, than for a rich man to enter the Kingdom of God. Luke records that one effect of Zacchaeus becoming a follower was that he gave away most of his wealth. Wealth can be surrendered because God can be trusted and relied on. If God cares for the birds, without their having to provide for their own security, and if he clothes the lilies with beauty, then God can be relied on to care for his human children (12:22–31).

However, like Judaism, Jesus taught that there was a right use of wealth. In the parable of the Rich Fool (12:16–21), the man could have given away his surplus to help the poor.

Luke's emphasis on the poor reflects God's special interest in them. This is very different from the view of Judaism at the time. Jesus preached 'good news' to the poor; the people mentioned in Luke's Gospel, who enter the Kingdom, are those who are poor or give away their wealth. For instance, it is the poor who are invited to the banquet (Luke 14:21). Knowing that God will care for us also allows us to give freely and generously. One reason why wealth is seen as a hindrance is that it often leads to a lack of trust in God.

b) Outcasts

There were Jews who either chose or were forced to drop out of respectable society. These people were seen as 'Jews who made themselves Gentiles'. It included people such as tax-collectors (seen as traitors since they worked for the Romans), hired shepherds and prostitutes.

Whereas Judaism saw outcasts (sinners) as people who were disapproved of and to be shunned, Jesus claimed that he came 'not to call the righteous, but sinners'.

Indeed he was always being accused of associating with sinners. Whereas Judaism saw the law as the means of purity, Jesus saw faith and repentance as the means of salvation. However, Jesus still demanded that, as a result, they changed their behaviour.

KEY WORD

Alms: something given to the poor as charity, such as money, clothing or food

KEY QUOTES

Sell your possessions and give to the poor.
(Luke 12:33)

The Spirit of the Lord is on me, because he has anointed me to preach good news to the poor.
(Luke 4:18)

c) Forgiveness

The cause of conflict was not so much one person forgiving another, as that would be recognised in Judaism. It was the fact that Jesus was making statements in God's name. This was not a case of one person forgiving another who had sinned against them. He was announcing forgiveness of sins in a general sense. Such a pronouncement was blasphemous.

Also, Jesus linked God's forgiveness with those who were ready to forgive others. Indeed, the greater the forgiveness, the greater the love. It was because of God's forgiveness that believers were motivated to forgive others. Disciples are called to forgive one another without limit (17:3–4). Jesus also linked repentance and faith to forgiveness.

❝ **KEY QUOTE**

If your brother sins, rebuke him, and if he repents, forgive him. If he sins against you seven times in a day, and seven times comes back to you and says 'I repent', forgive him.
(**Luke 17:3–4**)
❞

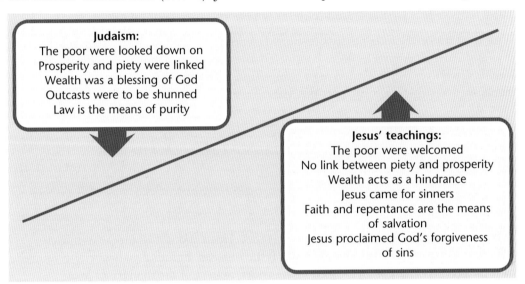

Judaism:
The poor were looked down on
Prosperity and piety were linked
Wealth was a blessing of God
Outcasts were to be shunned
Law is the means of purity

Jesus' teachings:
The poor were welcomed
No link between piety and prosperity
Wealth acts as a hindrance
Jesus came for sinners
Faith and repentance are the means of salvation
Jesus proclaimed God's forgiveness of sins

Summary diagram: A comparison of the attitudes of Judaism and Jesus to wealth and poverty

3 Possible conclusions

When assessing the issues that arise from the comparison of Jesus' teachings with those of Judaism, it is important to reflect upon the arguments previously discussed and arrive at some appropriate conclusion.

It may be that you accept none of these listed here, or just one of them, or you may have a different conclusion that is not listed. However, what is important is the way that you have arrived at your conclusion – the reasoning process.

From the preceding discussions, here are some possible conclusions you could draw.

1 Jesus' teaching was radically different from that of Judaism at that time.

2 Some of Jesus' teaching was different from that of Judaism at that time.

3 There was little or no difference between Jesus' teaching and that of Judaism at that time.

4 We cannot be sure what the teaching of Judaism was at the time of Jesus.

5 We cannot be sure what the teaching of Jesus was.

Was the purpose of the miracles to show that Jesus was divine?

TASK

Compare the account of the healing of the widow's son at Nain (Luke 7:11–17) with 1 Kings 17:8–24. What, if anything, do you conclude from comparing these two accounts?

Objective: To have a broader appreciation of the context of the miracle in terms of biblical criticism. This demonstrates that your answer will have an awareness of 'a careful analysis of alternative views' (level 4 descriptor AO2).

4 The purpose of the miracles

a) Earlier views

Until fairly recently miracles were seen as mere additions to the account of the life and teaching of Jesus. They were seen as stories designed to impress or to call attention to Jesus. In particular they were seen as proof of Jesus' divinity.

With the rise of Biblical criticism, the miracle stories were seen as inventions or creations, with origins that could be traced back to the Old Testament, sayings that were turned into dramatic actions or folk stories and Greek miracle stories attributed to Jesus.

Their purpose was seen as a proof of Jesus' superiority over rival miracle workers.

With their historical authenticity questioned, scholars focused on Jesus as a teacher rather than as divine. The miracles were considered as examples of actions of kindness. The specific references to Jesus' motive of compassion (Mark 1:41; 6:34) were particularly highlighted as evidence to support this view.

66 KEY QUOTE

Filled with compassion, Jesus reached out his hand and touched the man.

(Mark 1:41)

99

b) Recent views

In the mid-twentieth century, a different view developed about the purpose of miracles. Although the rather sceptical attitude towards the miracles' historical authenticity continued, their meaning and purpose were seen in the wider context of the ministry of Jesus.

Mark (1:14) makes clear that the heart of the preaching of Jesus was the message that: 'The time is fulfilled and the Kingdom of God is at hand.' Thus, the miracles are seen to endorse this message of the announcement of the Kingdom of God.

Reflection and assessment (AO2)

Earlier, you considered the assessment objective AO1, which focused on knowledge and understanding. The second way of being assessed is through assessment objective AO2.

Use the writing frame provided below to help you answer this question.

To what extent was Jesus' teaching about wealth different from that of Judaism at that time? (9 marks)

a) Key points

Always point out the case in support of the statement and the case against.

- If appropriate, respond to and assess each point as you proceed through.
- Avoid just listing points.
- Keep relating the material back to the focus of the evaluation.
- Always give a clear weighing up, leading to an appropriate conclusion, even if the conclusion is that both sides of the debate are equally persuasive.
- Remember that the case against can include better alternatives as well as weaknesses of the case in support.

b) Writing frame

> Jesus taught that wealth can be a problem because…
>
> In the parable of the rich young ruler the man of great wealth became sad because…
>
> Jesus replied to the man saying that it was easier for a camel…
>
> By this saying, Jesus was teaching that…
>
> This is in sharp contrast to Judaism, which taught…
>
> According to Jesus, the proper use of wealth was…
>
> A parable that illustrates this teaching is…
>
> Therefore the extent to which Jesus' teaching on wealth differed from that of Judaism is…

This writing frame, although quite basic, does focus on critical analysis and a sustained argument. It is better to deal with three or four criticisms, in some detail, than a longer list with very brief comment. It is important also to make clear in what way your criticism challenges the argument or view.

Use the levels and AO2 descriptors to award your response marks out of 9. Identify strengths and areas for development.

c) Suggestion for further application of skills

Construct your own writing frame for this question.

Comment on the view that the main teaching of the signs is to show that Christianity is the fulfilment of Judaism. (9 marks)

Now, as a group, collaborate to create an answer that demonstrates a level 4. Look back to page 10 in the Introduction to check the level descriptors.

EXAM TIP

Do not feel that you must always reach a conclusion. Not being able to reach a conclusion is an acceptable answer. However, there has to be justification in your answer as to why no one particular conclusion can be fully supported, The AO2 descriptor is 'justify a point of view through the use of evidence and reasoned argument'.

FOUNDATIONS

Area I: New Testament – Luke's Gospel

TOPIC 2: KEY EMPHASES IN THE STUDY OF THE TEACHINGS OF JESUS CHRIST

PART 2A: Prayer, praise and the Sabbath

This means I am expected:

to know about the key emphasis:
- prayer, praise and the Sabbath

and to study:
- Jesus' teaching on prayer
- different examples and purposes of praise
- the Sabbath controversies.

In this book the evidence and examples given are relevant and appropriate because this material focuses only on the content for AO1 that is given by the Edexcel specification. The evaluation materials for AO2 will be aimed at helping you 'critically evaluate and justify a point of view through the use of evidence and reasoned argument'.

It would be helpful to write your notes using the headings listed above, as it is from these areas that the examination questions will be derived.

In your studies, remember that you have to bear in mind the **two** basic assessment objectives of:

- Knowledge and Understanding (AO1)
- Evaluation (AO2).

See pages 7–8 in the Introduction to remind yourself of these objectives.

The evaluation material set out in Part 2C (page 263) can be studied either alongside the AO1 material, as you work through this unit, or as a separate unit.

This part of the unit explores various teachings of Luke's Gospel. You are expected to have a good knowledge and understanding of the meaning and significance of these. You will need to be aware of their context and background, including the Old Testament, and also the views of scholars.

The exam questions may specify one or more of the areas listed above. You should know the text well enough to explain and illustrate the particular focus of the question. The notes in this section assume that you have the text in front of you, as they refer to verse numbers. Evaluation of the issues, especially the comparison and contrasting of the teaching of Jesus with that of Judaism at that time, will be examined in Part 2C.

1 Jesus' teaching on prayer

a) Introduction

Prayer is the act of communicating with God. It can include adoration, confession, thanksgiving and petition. Luke's Gospel recalls times when Jesus prayed to God, his father. Prayer was also a theme about which he gave teaching, as well as providing a model (The Lord's Prayer).

b) Teaching on prayer through Jesus' own example

There are nine occasions where Luke records Jesus praying (3:21; 5:15,16; 6:12; 9:18–22; 9:29; 10:17–21; 11:1; 22:39–46; 23:34, 46). Seven of these prayers are found only in Luke's Gospel.

The subjects of the prayers include Jesus praying for Peter (22:31–2), exhorting the disciples to pray in Gethsemane (22:40), praying for his enemies (23:34) and praying for himself (22:41).

Sometimes Jesus prayed for a short time only, while on other occasions he spent a whole night in prayer (6:12).

c) The Lord's Prayer (11:2–4)

The Lord's Prayer also appears in Matthew's Gospel (6:9–13), though it is longer in form. Some manuscripts of Luke's Gospel have additions that reflect Matthew's version. Most scholars argue that these additions are probably **liturgical** additions and reflect the way that the early Church used the prayer. Alternatively, Jesus could have taught the different forms on different occasions.

Luke's version reads as though the prayer was intended to be used as it stood ('when you pray, say…'). In Matthew's version it seems that the prayer is to be used as a model ('This is how you should pray…').

The structure of the prayer leads through:

● our relationship with God (Father)
● God's concerns and plans (hallowed name/Kingdom come)
● our needs (daily bread/forgiveness/protection from temptation).

Lord's Prayer	Comment
Father	The actual Greek word used for 'Father' is one the Jews would have used (see Part 2C pages 263–4 (box)). However, scholars, such as **Jeremias**, argued that behind Jesus' use of this word is the Aramaic word 'abba'. This is a more intimate word, used in a family situation by a child addressing the parent. For discussion of abba and Jesus' use of the word, see Part 2C page 263–4 (box). The word 'abba' reflects an intimate family relationship between God and the person praying. It focuses on an attitude of dependency and trust in God.

TASK

Using the references opposite, find out the occasions when Jesus prayed. What does this reveal about (a) prayer (b) Jesus?
Objective: To develop the skill of 'using evidence to explain the key ideas' (level 4 descriptor AO1).

KEY WORD

Liturgy: the traditional public worship carried out by a religious group; a particular order of form of worship that is prescribed by a Church

TASK

Compare the version of the Lord's Prayer in Luke with that in Matthew. Can you think why scholars might argue that Luke's version is the one Jesus originally taught?
Objective: To develop the skill of 'using evidence to explain the key ideas' (level 4 descriptor AO1).

KEY PERSON

Joachim Jeremias (1900–79)
Professor of New Testament Studies, his main contribution was shedding light on Jesus' life and teaching through a study of the Jewish background and the Old Testament.

Lord's Prayer	Comment
Hallowed be your name	Names were important in the ancient world. The name of a person summed up their nature and significance. The prayer asks that a proper attitude ('hallowed' means reverenced) is shown to God because of his character and who he is. The believer in God can bring dishonour and shame to the name of God, through their actions and words.
Your Kingdom come	This is a request that God's rule may be effective and his authority seen. There is a sense in which God's rule was present in the lives of believers, but there is also a sense in which it was future and universal, not yet fully established.
Give us each day our daily bread	This is a recognition that God is the provider of our daily needs. The emphasis is on God meeting the needs we actually have, rather than the needs we think we have. It is also a daily request, implying a continuous dependence on God.
Forgive us our sins For we also forgive everyone who sins against us	The emphasis is on our readiness to forgive. Just as God has forgiven us, so we should forgive others. Forgiving others is not a condition of God forgiving us but more a natural response from us, in light of the fact that God has forgiven us.
And lead us not into temptation	This final part of the prayer acknowledges our human weakness. We are tempted and give way easily to temptation. The request is for God to protect us since we are aware of our own weaknesses.

d) Teaching on prayer

i) Ask, seek and knock

Luke 11:9–13 teaches that Jesus' followers should ask, seek and knock, confident that God will respond. The contrast is then made between human fathers and God the Father. If the human father gives good gifts rather than evil gifts to his children, then how much more will God give good things to his children. In particular, the giving of the Holy Spirit is seen as a good gift from God. It is available to those who ask. Hence we can have full confidence and trust in God, knowing that whatever we receive from him will be good.

ii) Persistence

The verbs of asking, seeking and knocking are all in the continuous tense, implying that prayer is habitual. Both the parable of the Friend at Midnight (11:5–8) and the parable of the Unjust Judge (18:1–8) contain similar teaching about persistence. In the one case, the person persists in disturbing his neighbour and not letting him sleep until he gives him the loaves he needs. In the other case, the woman persists in her petitioning to the judge until he is worn down and administers justice. God is contrasted with the sleeping neighbour and the unjust judge. If the neighbour and judge both respond, then how much more will God. God is a willing giver, but the focus in both parables is on the total determination of the characters. They were persistent because what they were asking for was important to them. The teaching is not that persistence will always get its way but it is that God responds when we are serious about relying on his goodness.

KEY IDEA

Some understand this giving of the Holy Spirit to refer to the charismatic gifts that are listed, for instance, in 1 Corinthians 14. Others see it as referring to the general work of the Spirit in a person's life (Romans 8).

iii) Right attitude

The parable of the Pharisee and the Tax-collector focuses on the importance of the right attitude in prayer. The Pharisee, the one usually regarded as religious, is contrasted with the tax-collector, the one usually regarded as irreligious and an outcast. When they went to pray, it was the tax-collector who was justified in the sight of God. He was justified because he had the right attitude. He knew he was a sinner and was humble before God, appealing to God's mercy. The Pharisee was confident about his own self-righteousness but he went away not justified in the sight of God. Whereas he compared himself to other people, the tax-collector compared himself to God and realised God's verdict on him: a sinner.

Jesus also criticised the teachers of the law, accusing them of 'making lengthy prayers for a show' (20:47). They were giving the illusion of being pious. Their prayers had length but no depth. They were empty and worthless because they were pretending to pray in order to impress people.

The parable of the Pharisee and the Tax-collector, depicted in a stained-glass window in St Mary's Church, Banbury

TASK

The picture illustrates the parable of the Pharisee and the Tax-collector. Carry out some research to find out why tax-collectors were regarded as sinners by the religious authorities in Jesus' time.

Objective: To develop 'detailed knowledge... to explain key ideas' (level 4 descriptor AO1).

Joy is the dominant mood in the infancy stories and this mood persists throughout the [Luke's] Gospel.

(Conzelmann)

They were all filled with awe and praised God.

(Luke 7:16)

99

TASK

Read the Song of Hannah (1 Samuel 2:1–10) and list its parallels with the Magnificat.
Objective: To develop understanding of the Old Testament background to the songs of praise that appear in the New Testament. This demonstrates 'detailed knowledge of the subject matter at a broad range' (level 4 descriptor AO1).

TASK

Compare the Benedictus with the Nunc Dimittis (including Simeon's prophecy about Jesus in verses 34–5), listing points they share in common.
Objective: To develop 'accurate, relevant and detailed knowledge of the subject matter' (level 4 descriptor AO1).

2 Different examples and purposes of praise

a) Introduction

Praise is one of the characteristics of Luke's Gospel. It starts (1:14) and ends (24:52) with the theme of joy. Luke's Gospel contains three great songs of praise: the *Magnificat* (1:46f), the *Benedictus* (1:68f) and the *Nunc Dimittis* (2:29f), as well as the song of the angels, called the *Gloria* (2:14). The word 'rejoice' occurs more frequently in this Gospel than any other part of the New Testament. Luke records many instances when people praised God in response to what God had done (for example, 7:16).

There are three main words used by Luke.

i) To glorify

The word originally referred to a quality that was evident in a person but came to refer to honour intended for God. It conveys the idea of God's majesty radiating from his very being. It is used of the shepherds (2:20) and of the blind man who received his sight (18:43).

ii) To praise

This word conveys the giving homage and thanksgiving to God. It is used of the angels (2:13) and of the crowd when Jesus rode into Jerusalem at his triumphal entry (19:37).

iii) To bless

This word conveys adoration and is used of Simeon when he saw the baby Jesus (2:28).

b) The songs of praise

Similar songs of praise can be found in the Old Testament, where they were sung in response to some mighty act of God in the life of that person; one example is Moses and his song (Exodus 15:1–18). The songs in Luke all have the theme of God working out his promises of salvation through Jesus.

i) The *Magnificat* (1:46–55)

The name derives from the Latin text of the first line (*My soul magnifies the Lord*), as do the names of the other songs listed below. This particular song is also known as *Mary's song*. The central message is the fulfilment of the promises of the coming Messiah, who is identified as Jesus and whose mother is Mary. The song proclaims God's greatness and Mary refers to God as her saviour. She praises God for choosing her as the means by which the promises of God's salvation will be fulfilled.

ii) The *Benedictus* (1:68–79)

This is also known as *Zechariah's song* and tells how the promises made to Abraham were now being fulfilled. It would be the task of John the Baptist (Zechariah's son) to prepare the way for the Messiah. The *Magnificat* and the *Benedictus* both have a similar structure, which includes promise, sign of fulfilment and praise for God's compassion.

iii) The *Nunc Dimittis* (2:29–32)

This is also known as *Simeon's song* and also has the three-fold structure of promise (Simeon would see the Messiah), sign of fulfilment (Simeon sees Jesus, through whom God would bring salvation) and praise to God.

iv) The *Gloria* (2:14)

The reference to peace in this song is not so much an absence of war as peace with God (reconciliation).

3 The Sabbath controversies

a) What is the Sabbath?

The Sabbath is the seventh day of the week and is technically celebrated from Friday evening until Saturday evening. It is not Sunday. The Sabbath is a day of rest, in honour of the day God rested after creation. The Jews had strict laws about keeping the Sabbath; Luke's Gospel recounts several occasions when Jesus came into conflict with the authorities over his actions on the Sabbath.

b) Sabbath laws

The law that no work should be done on the Sabbath is in Exodus 20:8–11 and Deuteronomy 5:12–15. The Sabbath was a sign of a covenant relationship with God and so was special. Exodus 31:14 states: 'Anyone who desecrates it must be put to death; whoever does any work on that day must be cut off from his people.'

> **66 KEY QUOTE**
>
> *Six days you shall labour, but on the seventh day you shall rest; even during the ploughing season and harvest you must rest.*
>
> **(Exodus 34:21)** 99

The difficulty arose as to what constituted work. The scribes tried to draw up a list to clarify this, appealing to various Old Testament texts; for instance, sowing and reaping were prohibited on the Sabbath, on the basis of Exodus 34:21.

c) Sabbath controversy

i) The incidents

There are four incidents recorded by Luke, which show Jesus in controversy with the religious authorities over the issue of the keeping of the Sabbath.

- **Reaping and threshing (6:1–5)**
  One Sabbath, as Jesus walked through cornfields, his disciples picked some ears of corn, rubbed them in their hands and ate the grain. In the eyes of the Pharisees, this amounted to reaping and threshing which were considered work, and so were prohibited on the Sabbath.

  Jesus answered by reminding the Pharisees that King David had broken the Sabbath law when he ate bread that was meant for use only in the Temple service. In other words, a person's needs took precedence. Jesus then claimed that he, the Son of Man, was Lord of the Sabbath.

- **Healing a man with a withered hand (6:6–11)**
  Healing was allowed on the Sabbath, if there was danger to life. However, if, by delaying the healing, there would be no danger to the life of the person, then such healing could wait until after the Sabbath. To heal on the Sabbath, in such a situation, would constitute work.

  Clearly, the man with a withered hand was not in danger of his life, so to heal such a person on the Sabbath would be breaking the Sabbath law. Jesus knew their thoughts and so asked them: 'Which is lawful on the Sabbath: to do good or to do evil, to save life or to destroy it?'

> **66 KEY QUOTE**
>
> *Observe the Sabbath day by keeping it holy, as the Lord your God has commanded you. Six days you shall labour and do all your work, but the seventh day is a Sabbath to the Lord your God. On it you shall not do any work...*
>
> **(Deuteronomy 5:12–14)** 99

TASK

What clarifications about the Sabbath law might the following verses imply? Exodus 35:3; Isaiah 58:13; Jeremiah 17:21–2; Amos 8:5

Objective: To develop knowledge and understanding of the origins of the Sabbath laws. This demonstrates 'well-chosen evidence to support understanding of key ideas and concepts' (level 4 descriptor AO1).

Jesus then healed the man's withered hand. The Pharisees and scribes were angry and discussed among themselves what they might do to Jesus.

- **Healing a woman with a bent spine (13:10–17)**
  Without the woman asking for healing, Jesus healed her. The ruler of the synagogue again viewed this healing as work and, therefore, breaking Sabbath law, since there was no urgency to heal at that time and it could have waited. Jesus responded to the reaction of the synagogue ruler by pointing out that the Sabbath allowed people to care for animals. Therefore, how much more was it right to heal someone from an evil illness. Luke records that Jesus' words put his opponents to shame while the people were impressed by all the wonderful things Jesus was doing.

- **Healing a man with dropsy (14:1–6)**
  This healing took place in the house of a Pharisee to which Jesus had been invited for a meal. There was a man who had **dropsy**. Luke comments that they were watching to see if Jesus would heal the man, which implies that the man may have been used in a trap set by Jesus' enemies. Before Jesus acted, he asked whether it was lawful to heal on the Sabbath. The question posed a problem to the Pharisees and experts in the law. The law of Moses did not actually state healing was wrong on the Sabbath. Rather, it was the rabbinical interpretations that argued that healing was work. They remained silent and Jesus then healed the man.

  Jesus then went on to use an illustration showing that they had concern for animals on the Sabbath (they would not leave a animal stuck in a well, they would rescue it, regardless of which day it happened).

ii) **Jesus' teaching**
- **The right use of the Sabbath**
  Jesus replied to those who challenged his breaking of the Sabbath, implying that mercy and compassion and doing good are better guides to right behaviour on the Sabbath than rules defined by legal experts. The rules result in such a rigid code that the whole purpose of the Sabbath is distorted.

  The petty regulations had replaced common sense and mercy. These petty regulations now suggested that healing was work, and that animals were more cared for than human beings.

- **A benefit not a burden**
  The legal experts, with their regulations and interpretations about work, had made the Sabbath a burden. The Sabbath had been instituted by God to be helpful. It had been made for our benefit and joy. However, it had become a yoke.

- **Son of Man is Lord of the Sabbath**
  Scholars are divided as to whether the phrase 'Son of Man' refers to human beings in general or is used as a self-designation by Jesus, possibly referring to the apocalyptic figure in Daniel 7.

  If it refers to human beings, then it would be claiming that man is supreme over the Sabbath. If, however, it is referring to Jesus, then he is making a claim about himself and of his divine status.

KEY WORD

Dropsy: an old term for the swelling of soft tissues due to the accumulation of excess water

EXAM TIP

Do not use a Bible quotation just to repeat what you have written. Either you need to allude to the quotation or you need to use it to draw out some further comment.
This demonstrates relevant knowledge and understanding through the use of evidence and examples (A01).

KEY IDEA

The Son of Man:

This title seems to be a self-designation, since the phrase is only ever applied to Jesus, by Jesus. It occurs 82 times in the Gospels. Commentators tend to divide the occurrences of the term into three types:

- the work of the Son of Man on Earth (Luke 19:10)
- the suffering of the Son of Man (Luke 9:22)
- the future glorification of the Son of Man (Luke 21:27).

The background to this term is thought to be Daniel 7, where Daniel prophesies that a figure would appear as God's agent to gather his people and act as judge. In the Gospels, Jesus seems to avoid the use of 'Messiah' and 'Son of God'. In contrast, he uses the title 'Son of Man' quite freely, in public and on many occasions. Commentators suggest that this was deliberate. The title 'Messiah' had particular connotations, in the public mind, that he wanted to avoid. Calling himself the Son of Man allowed Jesus to fill it with his own meaning. The Daniel context is of a redeemer figure with overtones of supernatural character and origin. However, it is sufficiently ambiguous to allow Jesus to link with it the idea of suffering. Only after the disciples were convinced that he was Messiah could he instruct them in the idea that he would suffer and die and come again in glory.

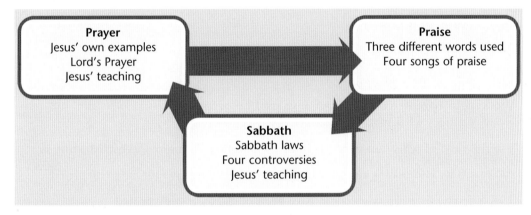

Summary diagram: Prayer, praise and the Sabbath

Reflection and assessment (AO1)

It is vital to bring together the information covered so far and recognise how it can be transformed into effective examination-style revision and answers. The best way to do this is to ask: 'How am I going to be assessed on this information?'

The first way is through assessment objective 1 (AO1). You need to be able to 'select and clearly demonstrate the relevant knowledge and understanding through the use of evidence, examples and correct language and terminology'.

Look back to pages 8–10 in the Introduction to review the level descriptors for AO1.

There is a description of the character and features for each level. The exam is marked with reference to levels.

Look at the following notes for a *basic* level answer, which is a level 1–2 response to this question.

What did Jesus teach about the Sabbath? (21 marks)

The *basic* answer might address the question in the following way.

- State what Sabbath is.
- State that the Pharisees were concerned that no work should be done on the Sabbath.
- Give a brief summary of one event where Jesus came into conflict over the Sabbath.
- Describe Jesus as Lord of the Sabbath.

Now indicate how a *developed* answer (level 3) might deal with the question, by adding two or three more bullet points.

Now go on to develop this answer to indicate how a *higher* answer (level 4) might address this question, by adding further bullet points. Don't forget to keep the bullet points focused on the question.

Suggestion for further application of skills

Create a plan for this question.

Examine the teaching of Jesus on prayer. (21 marks)

Then write up your answer, under timed conditions.

Working in a group, compare your answers. Photocopy the best answers and, still as a group, consider what makes the selected essays good.

Use this time of reflection to revisit your own work and improve it by redrafting it.

Alternatively, you may want to look at an essay that you have recently completed.

1 Underline in green what could have been omitted or was repeated.

2 Underline in blue key terms or technical words.

3 Underline in red any references back to the wording in the question.

4 Referring to the level descriptors, consider the reasons for the level awarded for your essay.

5 Use the level descriptors to identify how the essay could be improved.

TOPIC 2: KEY EMPHASES IN THE STUDY OF THE TEACHINGS OF JESUS CHRIST

Part 2B: The nature and demands of discipleship

This means I am expected:

to know about the key emphasis:

- the nature and demands of discipleship

and to study:

- the meaning of 'discipleship'
- the nature of discipleship
- the demands of discipleship
- the role of key people in the ministry of Jesus
- the Holy Spirit.

In this book the evidence and examples given are relevant and appropriate because this material focuses only on the content for AO1 that is given by the Edexcel specification. The evaluation materials for AO2 will be aimed at helping you 'critically evaluate and justify a point of view through the use of evidence and reasoned argument'.

It would be helpful to write your notes using the headings listed above, as it is from these areas that the examination questions will be derived.

In your studies, remember that you have to bear in mind the **two** basic assessment objectives of:

- Knowledge and Understanding (AO1)
- Evaluation (AO2).

See pages 7–8 in the Introduction to remind yourself of these objectives.

The evaluation material set out in Part 2C (page 263) can be studied either alongside the AO1 material, as you work through this unit, or as a separate unit.

This part of the unit examines the teaching in Luke's Gospel about the nature and the demands of discipleship. The exam questions may specify one or more of the areas listed above. You should know the text sufficiently well to explain and illustrate the particular focus of the question. Indeed, the notes in this section assume you have the text in front of you, as they refer to verse numbers.

In addition, the specification also requires you to study the importance of John the Baptist, the Twelve and the Holy Spirit to the ministry of Jesus.

1 The meaning of discipleship

The word 'disciple' conveys the idea of a follower or student of a great teacher. The New Testament refers to various groups of disciples. There are the disciples of Jesus, of which there was a core of twelve. Luke refers to a large crowd of Jesus' disciples (6:17) and records the sending out not only of the Twelve (9:1–6) but also of seventy-two others (10:1–16). Also mentioned are the disciples of the Pharisees (probably linked to a particular institution), the disciples of John the Baptist and the disciples of Moses (a self-designation by the Pharisees).

The word 'discipleship' highlights the nature of the master–disciple relationship. This section examines the features that mark out the disciple and what demands this relationship makes.

2 The nature of discipleship

The four aspects of discipleship

i) The need to follow

The verb 'to follow', in the sense of following as a disciple, implies a decisive and continuing act of allegiance to Jesus. The first reference to Jesus inviting anyone to follow appears in Simon Peter's calling, and that of James and John, the sons of Zebedee (5:1–11). Luke records how Jesus told them to put down their nets as they sailed into deep water. Simon pointed out that they had caught nothing all night but nonetheless they would do it. To his surprise they suddenly found the nets full of fish, so many fish that the boat was in danger of sinking. Simon seems to have recognised that he was in the presence of someone very holy and became aware of his own sinfulness in comparison. Jesus told him not to be afraid. The response of the disciples was to leave everything and follow Jesus.

In choosing to follow, the disciples committed themselves to certain demands (see pages 257–8). It was not a neutral action. Discipleship caused such a radical change that the external life of each disciple was seen to change.

A similar demand occurred in the calling of Levi (Matthew) the tax-collector (5:27–32). Levi's decision was final, in that he left his job and made his position clear by holding a great celebration for Jesus. Luke states that Levi left everything and followed Jesus.

The radical change of life is also shown in the story of Zacchaeus (19:1–10). He announced that he was going to give half of his possessions to the poor and pay back fourfold if he had cheated anyone.

The parable of the Sower makes clear that true discipleship meant a continuing act of allegiance to Jesus. It was only the seed on good soil that persevered, that produced a crop (8:4–15).

ii) Witness

Another mark of the disciple is the natural desire to tell others. In the call of Simon, Jesus announced: 'from now on you will catch men,' (5:10). The Greek conveys the meaning that the action is continuous. An ongoing ingredient of being a disciple is to make disciples of others. When the Twelve were sent out by Jesus, they were to preach the Gospel (9:6). In the same way, Jesus referred to a harvest (people becoming disciples) when he sent the Seventy (seventy-two) on their mission (10:1–2). Luke is concerned

KEY IDEA

Aspects of discipleship:

- to follow
- to witness
- to have faith
- to love one another.

EXAM TIP

When answering a question on discipleship, you must focus on the area highlighted in the question. Make sure you pick out the key events and texts and explain why they are important in relation to discipleship. This means that yours is not just a general answer that presents 'a limited range of isolated facts… with mainly random and unorganised detail' or 'information presented within a structure which shows a basic awareness of the issue raised' (level 1 and 2 descriptors AO1). Remember, you are aiming for 'a coherent and well-structured account of the subject matter' (level 4 descriptor AO1).

with the message that God's love is for all people. The Gospel is offered to all but people have to respond. See Jesus' teaching about the outcasts, pages 228–9.

Just as Luke records how the first disciple (Simon Peter) was commissioned by Jesus to 'catch men' (make disciples), so he ends his Gospel with a similar commissioning: '…and repentance and forgiveness of sins will be preached in his name to all nations, beginning at Jerusalem. You are my witnesses of these things,' (24:47–8).

iii) Have faith

Luke emphasises that entry into salvation and discipleship demands faith (7:50). Though disciples must have faith, Luke records an incident where the disciples are admonished for their lack of faith. When the storm arose on the lake and they feared for their lives, thinking the boat might sink, Jesus asked them: 'Where is your faith?' (8:22–5). They should have trusted him.

In a similar way, Jesus told his disciples that they should not be anxious or worried. He reminded them that God will take care of their every need. Though they may not have been materially rich, they would not lack anything. Instead, the focus should have been on seeking God's kingdom. They should have been about God's work (12:22–34).

The story of Mary and Martha illustrates how followers should avoid being distracted by things of the world. Martha seemed worried over lots of things while Mary displayed dependence on Jesus (10:38–42).

Luke records Jesus' prayer in the garden of Gethsemane, in which he prayed that Simon Peter's faith might not fail (22:31–2).

iv) Love one another

One of the marks of a true disciple is love. The parable of the Good Samaritan (10:25–37) showed the extent of the love that followers should display. The impetus for such love is the love that God has shown to us. Compare the parables of the 'lost' (pages 229–30).

The sermon on the plain (6:20), addressed to the disciples, contains teaching about love for enemies (pages 223–6).

On two occasions in Luke's Gospel, the disciples had a dispute about greatness. Luke places each of them immediately after an occasion where Jesus had been talking about his own death (9:46; 22:24). While Jesus was thinking of others, the disciples were thinking of themselves. Discipleship required humility, not pride.

3 The demands of discipleship

a) The cost

Luke's Gospel makes clear the cost of being a disciple. A key passage is Luke 14:25–33, where Jesus addressed a crowd that had not yet become disciples and warned them to count the cost. He stressed that allegiance to him overrode that of family and even one's own life (14:26). Indeed, it overrode everything (14:33).

Jesus told two parables to illustrate the cost of discipleship. The first involved building a tower. No one should start building the tower without first being sure they can finish it. In the second parable, the king is attacked and must make a decision as to what he should do. Jesus wants followers who are serious and have considered the cost. On the one hand, a person must decide if they can afford the cost of becoming a follower

> 66 **KEY QUOTE**
> *Jesus said to the woman, 'Your faith has saved you; go in peace.'*
> (Luke 7:50)
> 99

> 66 **KEY QUOTE**
> *If anyone comes to me and does not hate his father and mother, his wife and children, his brothers and sisters – yes, even his own life – he cannot be my disciple.*
> (Luke 14:26)
> 99

TASK

Carry out some research into possible identifications of the tower that Jesus might have been referring to, in the parable of the Tower builder.
Objective: To develop 'detailed knowledge of the subject material' (level 4 descriptor AO1).

EXAM TIP

When you illustrate a point, make sure that you explain the illustration and, in particular, how it illustrates or supports the point you are making. This demonstrates selection of clear relevant knowledge and understanding through the use of examples (AO1).

TASK

Read the parable of the Sower. Why did the seed fail to grow? Attempt to relate these causes to other passages in Luke's Gospel, about the difficulties of being a disciple.
Objective: To develop 'using well-chosen evidence to support understanding of key ideas, expressed clearly and accurately' (level 4 descriptor AO1).

(tower builder). On the other hand, they must decide if they can afford not to become a follower (king at war).

b) Persecution and the world's hatred

The disciples were warned that they would face persecution. The exhortation: 'Take up (carry) his cross daily' occurs twice (9:23; 14:23). When someone carried their cross they were on the way to be crucified. Soon they would be dead and be seen no more. Jesus was saying that, in becoming a disciple, a person dies to self. A person dies to his own interests because he puts the interests and the cause of Jesus above all else.

Despite opposition, the disciple was not to be ashamed of Jesus or his words (9:26). When the Twelve and the Seventy (seventy-two) were sent out on their mission, they were warned that they would not always be welcomed by people. Their mission would be dangerous and they were described as 'lambs among wolves' (10:3).

Jesus encouraged his followers with the promise that when (not if!) they were brought before synagogues, rulers and authorities, they were not to worry about how they were to defend themselves. The Holy Spirit would give them the words to say (12:11–12). A similar promise was made again in Luke 21, when Jesus prophesied: 'All men will hate you because of me,' (21:12–19).

For other relevant material on the Beatitudes and the Woes, see pages 224–5.

c) Temptation

The word 'tempt' has two meanings. One is that of testing someone to demonstrate faithfulness. The more common usage refers to the idea of enticing someone into sin. Jesus warned his disciples of the temptations of the world that they would face. The temptation is, at root, to turn away from the ways of God and follow the ways of the world instead. Following Jesus was difficult and often the disciples were tempted to follow the ways of the world.

Such temptations can be found in the Gospel, for example:

● not to love one another
● not to trust Christ
● to rely on their own strength
● not to want to be servants.

The parable of the Sower warned how temptations of the world caused people to fall away (8:4–15).

The episode in the Garden of Gethsemane describes a two-fold request by Jesus, to his disciples, that they pray that they may not enter into temptation (22:40, 46). However, they were unaware of the events going on, so they slept rather than prayed.

Peter's denial of Jesus (22:54–62) showed Peter's fear and his lack of trust.

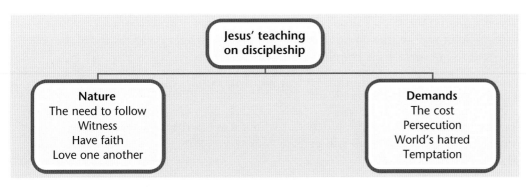

Summary diagram: Jesus' teaching on discipleship

4 The role of key people in the ministry of Jesus

a) John the Baptist

In Luke's Gospel, John the Baptist has four main roles.

i) Part of the salvation history

Scholars, such as **Conzelmann**, see in Luke's Gospel an emphasis that salvation has come with the coming of Jesus. God has intervened in human history and Jesus is the focus of all history. The time of salvation had arrived and John the Baptist is one person in this chain of salvation history.

When John was born, his father Zechariah prophesied, in what is known as *Zechariah's song* (1:67–79). This tells of how those promises made to Abraham were now being fulfilled. It was the task of John the Baptist (Zechariah's son) to prepare the way for the Messiah. The long-awaited Messiah is arriving. John's role, as the last of the prophets (the prophet of the Most High), was to prepare the way (1:76).

This idea of John as a vital part of the salvation history can be seen in Luke 16:16.

In one sense, John was also part of this central time when the good news of salvation was preached, since he also preached the Gospel (good news).

ii) Preparer for Jesus

The role of John the Baptist was to point people to Jesus. This is again made clear in *Zechariah's song*:

> …for he will go on before the Lord to prepare the way for him…
>
> (1:76)

It is even highlighted at the first mention of John in Luke's Gospel, when an angel appeared to Zechariah announcing that Elizabeth would bear a son.

> And he will go on before the Lord, in the spirit and power of Elijah…to make ready a people prepared for the Lord.
>
> (1:17)

It was believed that the prophet Elijah would return to announce the arrival of the Messiah. This seems to be based on a verse in the Old Testament book of Malachi (4:5).

KEY PERSON

Hans Conzelmann (1915–89) A German scholar who applied redaction criticism to Luke's Gospel, he concluded that Luke divides history into three periods. The first, the time of preparation, includes the Old Testament period right up to the time of John the Baptist. The second is the time of Jesus. The third is the time of the Church. Conzelmann argued that Luke's Gospel covered the second period (the middle time) and the Book of Acts covered the third period.

KEY QUOTES

And with many other words, John exhorted the people and preached the good news to them.

(Luke 3:18)

See, I will send you the prophet Elijah before that great and dreadful day of the Lord.

(Malachi 4:5)

In Luke 3, John the Baptist drew attention to the prophecy from Isaiah 40:3 which Jesus fulfilled. John was not the Messiah but he was the one whom Isaiah predicted, the one who was to prepare for the coming of the Messiah.

Later, when John was imprisoned, he sent his own disciples to ask Jesus if he was the Messiah (Luke 7:18–35).

Jesus replied that John was the prophet of whom it was written: 'I will send my messenger ahead of you, who will prepare your way before you.' This is a quote from Malachi 3:1.

iii) A witness to Jesus

Luke seems to structure his birth narratives so that the birth of John is paralleled by the birth of Jesus. However it is made clear that John was subordinate to Jesus, even though Jesus stated: 'among those born of women there is no one greater than John,' (7:28). John is depicted as the Prophet of the Most High (1:76) whilst Jesus is depicted as the Son of the Most High (1:32).

John made clear Jesus' superiority by claiming that he was not worthy even to carry his sandals (3:11). Whereas John baptised with water, the 'coming one' would baptise with the Holy Spirit and with fire.

The fortress at Machaerus, where John the Baptist was imprisoned and killed

b) The Twelve

i) The term

There seems to be a difference between being a disciple of Jesus and being one of the Twelve. There are disciples outside of the Twelve. For example, Luke refers to a large crowd of his disciples. The inner group of twelve were chosen disciples rather than volunteers. They were co-workers who travelled with Jesus, and had left all to follow him. They were also to become key leaders within the Church.

TASK

Design a diagram to show both the comparisons and contrasts between the person and work of John the Baptist and of Jesus.

Objective: To develop the skill of showing 'emphasis on significant features' and 'using well-chosen evidence' (level 4 descriptor AO1).

TASK

Carry out some research into why John the Baptist was killed and the circumstances of his death.

Objective: To develop 'detailed knowledge of the subject matter at a broad range or in significant depth' (level 4 descriptor AO1).

There seems to be a connection between the number twelve and the twelve tribes of Israel. If this is correct, then it would suggest that Jesus was establishing the true Israel, the people of God. The Twelve are not listed in John, though the other three Gospels do list them. In those lists, commentators point out that they seem to be in three groups of four with the same person at the start of each group of four (Simon Peter, Philip, James, son of Alphaeus). From this, it has been argued that each group of four had a leader.

ii) The individual people

Simon, later called Peter, was a Galilean fisherman who worked with his father and his brother, Andrew. The account of Peter's call to be a disciple involved the miraculous catch of fish and his recognition that he was sinful. He appeared to be the main spokesperson of the Twelve (12:41). He is always listed first in the list of the Twelve; in the Garden of Gethsemane Jesus prayed that Peter's faith may not fail so that he would be a strength to the other disciples (22:32).

Peter is depicted as an impulsive character. It is he who both blurted out the confession that Jesus was the Christ (9:20), and also that he would never deny Jesus (22:33). It was Peter who, on hearing the account from the women that Jesus had been resurrected, ran to the tomb and saw the strips of linen lying by themselves. He went away wondering what had happened (24:12).

Along with Peter, the two brothers James and John seem to form the inner group of disciples. Only those three witnessed the Transfiguration.

Judas is known as the one who became a traitor (6:16). Luke gives no reason why Judas acted in this way, apart from the statement: 'Then Satan entered Judas, called Iscariot, one of the Twelve,' (22:3). Judas led a band of soldiers to where Jesus was alone with his disciples, in the garden of Gethsemane. He then kissed Jesus to identify him for the soldiers.

5 The Holy Spirit

> *A shoot will come up from the stump of Jesse; from his roots a Branch will bear fruit. The Spirit of the LORD will rest on him, the Spirit of wisdom and of understanding, the Spirit of counsel and of power, the Spirit of knowledge and of the fear of the LORD and he will delight in the fear of the LORD. He will not judge by what he sees with his eyes, or decide by what he hears with his ears; but with righteousness he will judge the needy, with justice he will give decisions for the poor of the earth. He will strike the earth with the rod of his mouth; with the breath of his lips he will slay the wicked.*
>
> **(Isaiah 11:1–4)**

Judaism anticipated a Messiah who would be endowed with the Spirit. The words of Isaiah 11:1–4 reflect this expectation. According to Isaiah, the work of the Spirit would be wisdom and understanding and power.

Luke has an emphasis in his Gospel on the Holy Spirit. The birth stories in the first two chapters are full of references to people prophesying about Jesus as the Messiah (see page 280), including Mary, Zechariah and Simeon.

Luke makes clear that the virgin birth of Jesus is through the creative activity of the Holy Spirit. Luke would have seen the wisdom and understanding displayed by Jesus when, aged 12, he visited the Temple, as a demonstration of the truth of Isaiah's prophecy.

KEY IDEA

The three groups who made up the Twelve (Luke 6:13–16):
- Simon, named Peter
- Andrew, brother of Peter
- James
- John

- Philip
- Bartholomew
- Matthew
- Thomas

- James, son of Alphaeus
- Simon, called the Zealot
- Judas, son of James
- Judas Iscariot, the traitor.

66 KEY QUOTE

Jesus is not merely filled with the Spirit, like John, rather his very being is attributed to the Spirit.

(Schneider)

99

Luke records: 'Everyone who heard him was amazed at his understanding and his answers.' (2:47).

John the Baptist claimed that Jesus would baptise with the Holy Spirit and fire (3:16). At Jesus' baptism 'the Holy Spirit descended on Jesus in bodily form like a dove' (3:22). This event marked the call of Jesus to public ministry. The call was confirmed by a voice from heaven. It symbolised the Spirit remaining with Jesus to exercise his Messianic mission. Luke describes Jesus as 'full of the Spirit' (4:1) as he went into the wilderness to face the temptations. His return from this event is described as Jesus returning 'in the power of the Spirit' (4:14). This fulfils the Isaiah prophecy about the spirit of power, and so leads on to healing and the defeating of the works of the devil (13:10–15).

Jesus promised his disciples that, when they were being persecuted and brought before rulers and authorities, the Holy Spirit would teach them what they should say (12:12).

After the resurrection, the disciples were told to wait until 'you have been clothed with power from on high' (24:49). This can be seen as a reference to the coming of the Holy Spirit at Pentecost.

Reflection and assessment (AO1)

It is vital to bring together the information covered so far and recognise how it can be transformed into effective examination-style revision and answers. The best way to do this is to ask: 'How am I going to be assessed on this information?'

The first way is through assessment objective 1 (AO1). You need to be able to 'select and clearly demonstrate the relevant knowledge and understanding through the use of evidence, examples and correct language and terminology'.

Look back to pages 8–10 in the Introduction to review the level descriptors for AO1.

Use what you have so far learned about levels of response, writing frames and essay plans to do this task.

1   Split into small groups.

2   Within the group, list bullet points to create a five-level response in answer to this question.

Examine the role played by the Holy Spirit in the ministry of Jesus. (21 marks)

3   Then each person in the group should take one set of bullet points and use it to write up a paragraph.

4   Put the paragraphs together as an answer and swap with another group.

5   The receiving group comments on the work and returns it to the original group.

6   Review the comments and use them to improve the answer.

Suggestion for further application of skills

In your revision sessions, use this approach as a basis for revisiting the other topics. This does not apply to a specific focus on questions but is a way to create some good-quality summaries that demonstrate the skills relevant to AO1.

TOPIC 2: KEY EMPHASES IN THE STUDY OF THE TEACHINGS OF JESUS CHRIST

Part 2C: A critical analysis of the issues

> **This means I am expected:**
>
> **to analyse and critically evaluate:**
> - Jewish prayer at the time of Jesus
> - Jesus' use of the word 'abba'
> - the teachings of Judaism about prayer compared to Jesus' teaching on prayer
> - who does the term 'disciple' include?

1 Jewish prayer at the time of Jesus

Prayer was, and is, a major feature of Judaism (page 221). Prayers can be found throughout the literature of Judaism. In Jesus' time the Temple itself was called a house of prayer and synagogues were often referred to as prayer-houses.

Jews prayed at set times. There were set prayers such as the Eighteen Benedictions, and it was also the practice of Jews to give thanks to God before eating a meal.

There is some evidence that, at the time of Jesus, the set prayers were still developing, as different forms of them existed. Indeed, the **Mishnah** stated that a mechanical repetition of a prayer was of no real effect.

 KEY WORD

Mishnah: a written form of the Jewish oral traditions; they were collected and written down so that they would not be lost or forgotten

2 Jesus' use of the word 'abba'

> 66 **KEY QUOTE**
>
> *Going a little further, he fell to the ground and prayed that if possible the hour might pass from him. 'Abba, Father,' he said, 'everything is possible for you. Take this cup from me. Yet not what I will, but what you will.'*
>
> (Mark 14:35–6)
>
> *Because you are sons, God sent the Spirit of his Son into our hearts, the Spirit who calls out, 'Abba, Father.'*
>
> (Galatians 4:6)
> 99

? KEY QUESTION

Did Jesus address God as abba?

The word 'abba' actually only occurs once in the Gospels (Mark 14:36). It is said by Jesus in a prayer to God the Father. The word is Aramaic for father. The scholar Jeremias argued that it was a word used by children to refer to their father and so had the more intimate sense of 'daddy'.

The word also appears in Romans 8:15 and Galatians 4:6. In this context it refers to usage by the early Christians. This supports the tradition that Jesus used this word in his prayers, since they associated it with Jesus and continued to use the same word. In addition, scholars argue that 'abba' underlies the Greek *pater*, which is the usual word in the Gospels that Jesus used to address God.

3 The teachings of Judaism about prayer compared to Jesus' teaching on prayer

 KEY QUESTION

Did Jesus teach anything different to Judaism about prayer?

Is Jesus' teaching about prayer different from that of Judaism?

Yes	No
Jesus introduced the intimate prayer address of 'abba'. It was never used in Judaism.	There is evidence that individuals did address God as Father, in a context that would convey the intimate expression of 'abba' (Wisdom 14:3).
Judaism emphasised the ritual and the formality of prayer. Jesus taught that prayers should not be words of empty ritual.	Jesus attended both synagogue and Temple worship. The Mishnah stated that a mechanical repetition of a prayer was of no real effect.
Judaism stated how many times a day a person should pray. Jesus' emphasis was on persistence in prayer and prayer as part of a relationship with God.	Judaism saw prayer as an important element of a spiritual life.
Judaism required people to stand when praying. Jesus knelt to pray.	Even if true, it is of no significance.

 KEY QUOTE

...but it is thy providence, O Father, that is its pilot...
(Wisdom of Solomon 14:3)

"

4 Possible conclusions

When assessing the issues that arise from Jesus' teaching on prayer, it is important to reflect upon the arguments previously discussed and arrive at some appropriate conclusion.

It may be that you accept none of these listed here, or just one of them, or you may have a different conclusion that is not listed. However, what is important is the way that you have arrived at your conclusion – the reasoning process.

From the preceding discussions, here are some possible conclusions you could draw.

1 Jesus' teaching on prayer is very different from that of Judaism.

2 Jesus' teaching on prayer is similar to that of Judaism but has a different emphasis.

3 There are no differences between Jesus' teaching on prayer and that of Judaism.

5 Who does the term 'disciple' include?

The term 'disciple' has a wide use in Luke's Gospel. The phrase is used of:

- one of the Twelve
- the large number who believed but did not travel around with Jesus (Luke 6:13,17).

Do all disciples have to exhibit all those things listed in Part 2B?

EXAM TIP

Always refer back to the question in your answers, demonstrating that you comprehend the demand of the question.

 **EXAM TIP**

Remember that evaluation involves the process of reasoning. Good answers will display a sustained argument rather than presenting a list of points. This demonstrates justifying a point of view through reasoned argument. (AO2).

- Does discipleship demand understanding or complete realisation of who Jesus was? (Often they were confused.)
- Does discipleship require meeting the demands to love one another? (They argued.)
- Does discipleship require willingness to witness? (They ran away.)
- Does discipleship require putting faith in Jesus? (They lacked faith and Judas betrayed Jesus.)

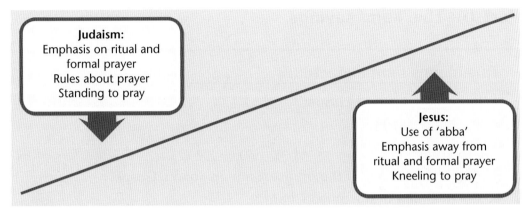

Summary diagram: Prayer differences, a comparison of the attitudes of Judaism and Jesus to prayer

Reflection and assessment (AO2)

It is vital to bring together the information that has been covered so far and recognise how it can be transformed into effective examination-style revision and answers. The best way to do this is to ask: 'How am I going to be assessed on this information?'

Look back to page 10 in the Introduction, to review the level descriptors for AO2. There is a description of the character and features for each level. The exam is marked with reference to levels.

Look at the following notes for a sample basic level 1 answer, a response to this question.

> **Comment on the importance to the ministry of Jesus of John the Baptist.**
>
> (9 marks)

A basic answer might address the question by:

- stating a role of John the Baptist, such as preparer for Jesus
- giving some basic evidence to support or illustrate this role
- drawing a simple conclusion, linking the role of John to the importance it had for Jesus' ministry.

Suggestion for further application of skills

Now try this technique to build a level 4 answer for this question.

> **Comment on the importance to the ministry of Jesus of the Holy Spirit.**
>
> (9 marks)

TASK

Look at the notes for the *basic* answer opposite. Try to work out how a *developed* answer (level 2–3) would address the question, by adding two or three more bullet points. Now develop this answer to indicate how a *higher* answer (level 4) might address the question, by adding further bullet points. Remember to keep the points focused on the question.

Objective: To develop awareness of what will constitute a very good answer, by gradually building up a response that 'clearly expresses viewpoints supported by well-deployed evidence...and a careful analysis of alternative views' (level 4 descriptor AO2).

FOUNDATIONS

Area I: New Testament – the Fourth Gospel

TOPIC 1: KEY ISSUES IN THE STUDY OF THE TEACHINGS OF JESUS CHRIST

Part 1A: The 'I am' sayings

This means I am expected:

to know about the key issue:

- the 'I am' sayings

and to study:

- the different uses of the phrase 'I am' in John's Gospel
- the meaning of the phrase 'I am'
- the 'I am' sayings and their meanings.

In this book the evidence and examples given are relevant and appropriate because this material focuses only on the content for AO1 that is given by the Edexcel specification. The evaluation materials for AO2 will be aimed at helping you 'critically evaluate and justify a point of view through the use of evidence and reasoned argument'.

It would be helpful to write your notes using the headings listed above, as it is from these areas that the examination questions will be derived.

In your studies, remember that you have to bear in mind the **two** basic assessment objectives of:

- Knowledge and Understanding (AO1)
- Evaluation (AO2).

See pages 7–8 in the Introduction to remind yourself of these objectives.

The evaluation material set out in Part 1C (page 287) can be studied either alongside the AO1 material, as you work through this unit, or as a separate unit.

This section of the unit explores various aspects and features of John's Gospel. Before starting this unit, read through John's Gospel. If one is available, watch a DVD of the Gospel. Also, read through, and refer back to, the introduction to the background to Jesus' life (see pages 220–3). In particular, the section on why the Jewish religion is important because John used much symbolism based on the Torah and the Jewish religion.

This particular part of the unit on the Fourth Gospel, explores the seven 'I am' sayings. The exam questions may specify one or more of these sayings, and the focus will be on their meaning, significance and teaching. The sayings need to be used to explain and illustrate the particular focus of the question; in particular, you need to demonstrate understanding of their background and context. You are expected to cite Old Testament

(OT) references and offer some explanation of the symbolism. It is therefore important that you know the text of the sayings so that you are able to refer to them. It is assumed that you will have the text in front of you for the notes in this section as they refer to verse numbers.

1 The different uses of the phrase 'I am' in John's Gospel

The 'I am' sayings in John can be divided into **two** main types.

a) Those with no predicate

This means there is nothing following them. (This isn't always obvious in English translations as the translator often inserts a **predicate**.)

There are ten 'I am' statements with no predicate; four of them are generally regarded as special usage where there is a claim by Jesus to be God. These four are found in John 8:24, 8:28, 8:58 and 13:19.

Each of the other six has a predicate, understood though not expressed. An example of this type is 6:20, where the Greek text has 'I am' but most commentators regard this as simply meaning 'It is I', so they insert a predicate.

b) Those in which a predicate is given

There are seven predicate versions of 'I am' statements in John's Gospel.

- 'I am the bread of life.' (6:35,51)
- 'I am the light of the world.' (8:12; 9:5)
- 'I am the (sheep) gate.' (10:7,9)
- 'I am the good shepherd.' (10:11,14)
- 'I am the resurrection and the life.' (11:25)
- 'I am the way, the truth and the life.' (14:6)
- 'I am the true vine.' (15:1,5)

2 The meaning of the phrase 'I am'

The phrase in the Greek that we are discussing is *ego eimi*, literally: I (*ego*), I am (*eimi*). As in English, the words 'I am' could be used in various ways in the ancient world.

a) Without a predicate

There was a common usage where the phrase without a predicate just meant 'It is I'. This probably explains six out of the ten, as explained above.

However the reaction given to Jesus' use of this phrase (see 8:58) indicates that, on occasions, something more is being suggested.

The key to understanding this special use, is to realise that the **LXX** (the Old Testament in Greek) uses the expression *ego eimi* when translating the Hebrew 'I Yahweh'. In particular, it occurs in the story of the burning bush, when God reveals his name as Yahweh, which means 'I am who I am,' (Exodus 3:14).

Raymond Brown argues that the phrase came to be understood as a divine name. He cites Isaiah 43:25, which can be translated 'I am "I AM" who blots out transgressions.' Further examples are in Isaiah 41:4, 43:10 and 45:18.

? KEY QUESTION

Does Jesus' use of the phrase 'I am' mean he is claiming to be God?

🔑 KEY WORD

Predicate: the part of the sentence that qualifies the subject

❝ KEY QUOTE

'I tell you the truth,' Jesus answered, 'before Abraham was born, I am!' (John 8:58) ❞

🔑 KEY WORD

LXX: an abbreviation for the Septuagint, which is the name given to the translation into Greek of the Old Testament; it is called this because tradition said that 70 people had translated it

❝ KEY QUOTES

This is what you are to say to the Israelites: 'I am has sent me to you.' (Exodus 3:14)

I, even I, am he who blots out your transgressions, for my own sake, and remember your sins no more. (Isaiah 43:25) ❞

C.H. Dodd cites rabbinic evidence from the second century CE where 'I AM' was used in the liturgy as the name for God. This would then make sense of the reaction of the crowds in John 8:58 and Mark 14:62.

b) With a predicate

There was the simple usage, equivalent to 'I am Peter.' In these instances the emphatic pronoun *ego* (I) would not usually be added. It was sometimes added for emphasis.

Most, if not all, scholars support the view that the 'I am' sayings in John express this divine claim. Indeed, the predicates of the 'I am' sayings were descriptions that were reserved for God himself, for example, light, the shepherd. By stating that he is *the* light of the world, Jesus points to himself and, by implication, away from others.

3 The 'I am' sayings and their meanings

a) I am the bread of life

i) The context

In John 6, Jesus provides bread in the feeding of the 5000. The people seek him out because of what he has done, but Jesus rebukes them because they simply want their stomachs filled (verse 26). Instead they should seek the bread that the Son of Man will give them. The people ask Jesus what sign he will do so that they may believe, as they remind him about Moses and the giving of manna in the wilderness. Jesus claims that the bread that he gives is greater than that given to Moses. The true bread from heaven is a present reality and consists of 'that which comes down from heaven and gives life to the world' (verses 32, 33). When the crowd ask for Jesus to give them such bread, he claims to be what they seek. Jesus further claims: 'This bread is my flesh, which I will give for the life of the world…whoever eats my flesh and drinks my blood has eternal life.' (verses 51, 54).

KEY IDEA

Eternal life:
The idea of eternal life is more than never-ending life. It is about quantity but it is also about quality. It is life beyond our imagined best. It refers to the life of the age to come, and therefore resurrection life. However, in John's Gospel that life can, in part, be experienced now. It involves the passing over from guilt and condemnation to forgiveness and acceptance, from death to life.

John's Gospel also links the idea of a relationship with the idea of eternal life. In 17:3 he writes: 'Now this is eternal life: that they may know you, the only true God, and Jesus Christ, whom you have sent.'

ii) The background – the symbolism of bread
● **Bread as a source of physical nourishment**
  For the ancients, bread was the principal element in the normal diet. It could stand for prosperity and was a symbol for that which supported the whole of life.

● **Manna**
  The phrase 'bread from heaven' and the comparison with manna reminded the people of the special provision of food by God for his people. Jesus contrasts himself with the manna, pointing out that, unlike the manna, he will never leave them hungry and they will have life. Jesus refers to himself as the living bread.

EXAM TIP

Do not use a Bible quotation just to repeat what you have written. You need either to allude to the quotation or to use it to draw out some further comment. This demonstrates relevant knowledge and understanding 'using well-chosen evidence to support understanding of key ideas and concepts' (level 4 descriptor AO1).

66 KEY QUOTES

I tell you the truth, whoever hears my word and believes him who sent me has eternal life and will not be condemned; he has crossed over from death to life.

(John 5:24)

On this mountain the Lord Almighty will prepare a feast of rich food for all peoples, a banquet of aged wine – the best of meats and the finest of wines.

(Isaiah 25:6)

True nourishment, which brings eternal life, is possible only for those who accept His sacrifice, who are incorporated by faith into His body…and who abide in Him.

(Tasker)

99

● **In the Old Testament**

Bread was an important part of the Jewish religion. Each Sabbath, 12 loaves of unleavened bread were baked and placed in the sanctuary. Also at Passover, there was unleavened bread. Bread had become used as a symbol for the Law. There is also the idea of a messianic banquet (see page 280), although some think the connection is fairly tenuous. The Jews always depicted the celebration of the establishing of the new kingdom by the **Messiah** in terms of a feast or banquet.

● **Metaphorical imagery**

Eating and drinking are explained by John in terms of coming to Jesus and believing in him. As verse 35 states:

> *Then Jesus declared, 'I am the bread of life. He who comes to me will never go hungry, and he who believes in me will never be thirsty.'*

● **Sacramental imagery**

John does not include any description of the Last Supper and many scholars argue that this passage is his equivalent. However, nowhere in John is there anything to suggest that Jesus refers to a meal in which bread represents his body. Instead, eating and drinking are explained in terms of coming to Jesus and believing in him (verse 35).

If he wanted to make reference to the Last Supper (Eucharist), then it is strange that he did not refer to 'this is my body' rather than 'this is my flesh'. Equally, if John's interest was **sacramental**, then would he not have included the actual events of the Last Supper?

iii) The meaning

The imagery and symbolism is rich and varied. Not surprisingly, scholars have suggested a number of meanings.

Some scholars suggest that, in claiming to be the true bread from heaven, Jesus was claiming to supersede the law of Moses. By linking himself with the food that God gave in the form of manna during the Exodus, Jesus was claiming to satisfy the spiritual hunger of the world. This was achieved by means of creating a relationship between Jesus and human beings. This relationship was symbolised by the eating of bread, which represented faith in him.

b) I am the light of the world

i) The context

In one sense, when it appears in chapter 8 the idea of Jesus as the light of the world is not new. The prologue (1:1–18) states: 'In him was life and the life was the light of men,'(1:4, 5).

John the Baptist is seen to be no more than a witness to the light. It is of Jesus that it is said: 'The true light that enlightens every man was coming into the world,' (1:9, 10).

Having been questioned by the Pharisees about the authority of his witness after the incident with the woman caught in adultery (chapter 8), Jesus takes up the theme of light again in chapter 9. He shows he has authority by healing the blind man. Light is contrasted with moral and spiritual darkness.

The statement: 'I am the light of the world,' appears twice, though its occurrence in 9:5 is without the emphatic *ego eimi*.

KEY WORDS

Messiah: the Hebrew form of the Greek word Christ, meaning 'the anointed one' and refers to one approved by God; often linked to kings, it later became associated with the hope of an ideal king, the one sent by God to restore Israel

Sacrament: a rite where symbolism is used to represent spiritual realities

KEY QUOTE

John 6 is not about the Lord's Supper; rather, the Lord's Supper is about what is described in John 6.

(Brown)

KEY QUOTE

The Lord is my light and my salvation.

(Psalm 27:1)

TASK

A number of the events described in John's Gospel take place during festivals. Many scholars argue that John shows how Jesus fulfils these festivals. Read the account of the healing of the blind man (Chapter 9) and see what parallels there are with the feast of Tabernacles.
Objective: To develop 'relevant and detailed knowledge' of the subject matter 'at a wide range or considerable depth' (level 4 descriptor AO1).

➡ EXAM TIP

Check for material that is irrelevant or material that is not explained. The answer should be organised in a sequential way so the reader follows a clear line of thought and development.

ii) The background – the symbolism of light

● **In the Old Testament**

For the Jews, light was one of the first things God created and it was seen as a mark of God's activity. It came to signify God's presence and favour, in contrast to God's judgement. Part of the Exodus tradition spoke of the pillar of light that guided the Israelites. Indeed, the imagery of light is often used in the Old Testament. In Isaiah 49:6 the Messiah is portrayed as light, bringing spiritual enlightenment to humankind. Light also conveys the idea of guidance in life: 'Thy word is a lamp to my feet and a light to my path,' (Psalm 119:105). The Rabbis spoke of the law as a light or a lamp.

● **In the Jewish religion**

The setting to this 'I am' saying in chapter 8 is the last day of the Feast of Tabernacles. Part of this festival commemorated the events of the Exodus, when the people were led by a pillar of fire. Four huge lamps were lit in the Temple's court of women. Jesus seems to see himself as fulfilling this imagery.

iii) The meaning

As in all the 'I am' sayings, Jesus makes a claim to be God. Light is an attribute of God. Rather ironically, the law was seen as a light, yet it kept them in darkness. The true light was Jesus. This light symbolism shows Jesus as giving physical light (sight to blind), moral light (moral guidance, the way to live) and spiritual light (revelation and faith). The healing of the blind man illustrates these ideas. The discussion with the Pharisees shows that those who think they see still remain blind to the light. Jesus warns of the inevitable consequences of light, for where there is light there is also judgement for those who falsely claim to be enlightened.

c) I am the gate for the sheep

i) The context

John 10 begins with a parable about the contrast between those who come to steal and the shepherd of the sheep. From this parable Jesus takes two images and applies them to himself. The first of these is the image of the gate by which both the sheep and the legitimate shepherd must pass.

The sheepfold was a roofless enclosure in an open field. It consisted of a wall built with rough stones. The shepherd would sleep across the opening to prevent sheep going out and other animals getting in.

Jesus states that he is the gate and that those who had come before him were thieves and robbers. In other words, those who had not used the legitimate means of entry into the sheepfold were imposters. Here he seems to be referring to the Pharisees.

He then states what his role as gate means to the sheep (verse 9). Those who enter by him will be saved and will go in and out to find pasture.

ii) The background – the symbolism of the gate of the sheep

● **The Old Testament**

In his Bethel experience (Genesis 28:10–23), Jacob saw a gate of heaven. A similar idea is found in Psalm 118:19, 20. Apocalyptic Judaism frequently refers to the 'gate of heaven' through which the visionary has a glimpse of heaven and whence comes salvation.

iii) The meaning

Jesus is the only means by which the sheep enter the safety of the fold and the rich pasture. Jesus is claiming that there is only one way of receiving eternal life, namely through faith in him. He is the only means of salvation.

The passage makes a contrast between Jesus, who cares for his flock and offers security and plenty, and the thieves and robbers, who have selfish motives and steal and kill the sheep. This shows Jesus as the life giver. Not only will he give life to those who enter by him, he will also give them pasture and they will have abundant life.

The nature of the personal relationship between the shepherd (Jesus) and the flock (his followers) is enhanced by an understanding of the Near East. Shepherds in that area had their own peculiar calls to which their own sheep would respond. In this passage, the shepherd actually calls them by name. He knows them.

Also, unlike Western shepherds who drive the sheep from behind, shepherds of the Near East walk in front of the flock. This gives a picture of Jesus going ahead of us, leading and protecting. The shepherd is no stranger to the sheep. They know his voice.

d) I am the good shepherd

i) The context

This is the second image taken up in the parable. Here he is contrasted with the hireling (hired hand) who leaves when danger approaches (verse 12). Jesus claims not only to know them but to have the same relationship with them as he has with the father. Jesus comes in order that his sheep might have life to the full. How this becomes possible is revealed in the fact that he lays down his life willingly for the sheep (verses 15, 17). Somehow, in laying down and taking up his life, Jesus shows, through his obedience and trust of the Father, why the Father loves and trusts him (verse 17).

ii) The background – the symbolism of the good shepherd

● **The Old Testament**

God is seen to be the shepherd of Israel. In particular, Ezekiel 34 is full of references to God as shepherd, as is Psalm 23. The word 'shepherd' was used for kingship. David is spoken of as a shepherd in Psalm 78:70–2 and his people are called sheep.

iii) The meaning

Jesus takes on the role of the good shepherd and that role was reserved for God. This may be another claim by Jesus to be God.

The previous 'I am' saying contrasted the thieves and robbers with Jesus the shepherd. In this passage, the contrast is with the hired hand. Although the hired hand is not deliberately evil, he is still more interested in his own safety. When danger arises he abandons the sheep. Jesus shows his commitment to the sheep not only by risking his life for the sheep, but actually laying down his life for them. He deliberately lays down his life, and by his death they are saved. Here there is a clear emphasis on sacrifice.

This relationship between the shepherd and the sheep is a reflection of the relationship between the Father and the Son (verse 17).

> 66 **KEY QUOTE**
>
> *This is the gate of the Lord, through which the righteous may enter.*
>
> **(Psalm 118:20)**
>
> 99

> 66 **KEY QUOTE**
>
> *I will shepherd the flock with justice… You my sheep, the sheep of my pasture, are my people, and I am your God, declares the Sovereign Lord.*
>
> **(Ezekiel 34:16, 31)**
>
> 99

> 66 **KEY QUOTE**
>
> *Jesus' sacrificial death was not an end in itself, and his resurrection an afterthought. His death was with the resurrection in view. He died in order to rise…so that others, too, might live.*
>
> **(Carson)**
>
> 99

e) I am the resurrection and the life

i) The context

The setting for this 'I am' saying is the miracle of the raising of Lazarus. Lazarus had been dead for four days before Jesus arrived. When Jesus announced to Martha that her brother Lazarus would rise again, Martha was confused. For Martha, resurrection was a reality at the end times (verses 24, 27). Jesus then explained to her that that reality is present in his person. Like the 'I am' saying about bread, this one is accompanied by a sign that points to the reality of what Jesus is saying. His authority to give eternal life is seen in the miracle of the raising of Lazarus. This miracle led to the Jewish Council (Sanhedrin) plotting to kill Jesus.

TASK

Carry out some research on the symbolism in Rembrandt's painting of the raising of Lazarus. How does it reflect Rembrandt's understanding of the meaning of the miracle story?

Objective: To recognise different ways in which the miracle of Lazarus is understood. This demonstrates 'using well-chosen evidence to support understanding of key ideas and concepts' (level 4 descriptor AO1).

KEY QUOTE

When he heard this, Jesus said, 'This sickness will not end in death. No, it is for God's glory so that God's Son may be glorified through it.'
(John 11:4)

The Raising of Lazarus (Rembrandt, 1631–2)

ii) The background – the symbolism of the resurrection and the life
● **Jewish beliefs**

Pharisaic Judaism believed in the resurrection of the dead. This resurrection would take place on the last day, as one of the features of the arrival of the messianic kingdom. It was this belief that Martha reflects. In 11:4 there is reference to God's glory and God's Son being glorified. For Jewish background on the idea of glory see pages 279–80.

The reference to Lazarus being dead for four days may reflect a Jewish belief that the soul departed from the body after three days. Hence the statement is assuring the reader that Lazarus really was dead.

iii) The meaning

A physical reality explains a spiritual truth. Jesus brings the life and resurrection of the end times into the present, within his person. He is declaring himself both Messiah and God. In 11:27 Martha actually makes that declaration of belief.

The linking of life with resurrection perhaps points to the idea that the life he brings is the life of the age to come. Not only does Jesus suggest that he is able to bring the resurrection of the end times into the present, he also brings that life that would be expected to accompany such a resurrection into the present. Indeed, Jesus promises that the people who already enjoy resurrection in life, this side of death, will in some sense never die. The life that Jesus gives never ends.

Interestingly, the ultimate proof of Jesus' claim to offer resurrection and eternal life is seen in his own resurrection, rather than in the raising of Lazarus. Perhaps this is because, though Lazarus' raising from dead foreshadows Jesus' resurrection, it was of a different nature. Lazarus rose only to die again, whereas Jesus defeated death for ever.

f) I am the way, the truth and the life

i) The context

This and the final 'I am' saying are both addressed to the disciples. In John 14, Jesus proclaims that he is going away. Instead of excluding the disciples from the place to which he is going, he is actually going to prepare a place for them (verses 2, 3). He also says that they know the way to where he is going. When Thomas expresses doubt, Jesus explains that they know the way because they know him, who is the way. But Jesus is not only the way, but also the truth and the life. Some scholars argue that by this Jesus meant 'I am the true and living way.'

ii) The background – the symbolism of the way, the truth and the life
● **The Old Testament**

Truth in the Old Testament not only refers to that which opposed to falsehood, or reality as opposed to pretence; it also refers to faithfulness, reliability, trustworthiness (Psalm 31:5; Isaiah 65:16). The Old Testament came to use the term 'way' in a more spiritual sense. God's way is described as perfect (2 Samuel 22:31). Psalm 27:11 speaks of the Lord teaching his way, and Psalm 77:13 says that his way is holy.

iii) The meaning

This 'I am' saying gives a very high image of the person of Jesus. Jesus does not have to find the way, he is the way. He does not have to learn the truth, he is the truth. He does not have to receive the life in order to pass it on, he is the life.

> 66 **KEY QUOTE**
>
> 'Yes, Lord,' she [Martha] told him, 'I believe that you are the Christ, the Son of God, who has come into the world.'
> (John 11:27)
> 99

> 66 **KEY QUOTE**
>
> Redeem me, O Lord, the God of truth.
> (Psalm 31:5)
> 99

John 14:6 is the only time that the term 'way' is used in John's Gospel. The only explanation of the term is given in part b of the verse: 'no one comes to the Father but by me.' Jesus is not only the way to his Father's house but to the Father himself.

The truth that sets men free (8:31–2) is a knowledge that Jesus is the only way to the Father, and acknowledgement that Jesus alone gives life, because he is the life.

The word 'life' is very important in John's Gospel; it occurs in three 'I am' sayings and is used 36 times in all. John's Gospel could be called the Gospel of Life (20:31). In John's Gospel, this life is the life of God himself, which the Son possesses from the Father (6:57) and he is sent to bring it to all the world (3:16). Jesus has to lay down his own earthly life before he can bring the resurrection life to others. The receiving of this life is symbolised by Jesus breathing into his disciples the Spirit of Life (20:22). This life is available to believers who come to know God in Christ (17:3) and it is a present reality (3:36).

g) I am the true vine

i)   The context
Like the previous 'I am' saying, the setting for this is the **Farewell discourse**.

Jesus is the vine and the disciples are the branches. They must remain in the vine in order to get their sustenance and thus to produce fruit. Branches that are unproductive will be pruned to make them fruitful. Completely fruitless branches will be taken away (verse 2).

The responsibility of the branches is to remain in the vine and to produce fruit.

ii) The background – the symbolism of the vine
● **The physical vine**
  The vine was an important item in the diet of the Jews so it became associated with prosperity. It also became the symbol of peace, since grapes could not be cultivated when the land was at war. They all knew that it was essential that the vine should be pruned if it was going to be fruitful.

● **The Old Testament**
  In Isaiah 5:1–7 there is a parable about the vineyard, which stood for Israel, the covenant people of God. It is described as the Lord's vine but it had consistently disappointed its owner. The vineyard had to be destroyed as it produced only bad grapes. The imagery may also have a messianic link since the vine was used to denote wisdom and the Messiah in later Judaism.

● **Sacramental image**
  Many scholars link the fruit of the vine and the wine it produces. Some scholars argue that John is making a reference here to the Last Supper and the wine refers to his blood. However, the life that Jesus gives to the branches is described in terms of abiding in his love and not in terms of drinking of his blood.

iii) The meaning
The main theme of the passage is the relationship between the vine and the branches. Just as the branches need to remain in the vine, in order to bear fruit, so the disciples need to remain in Jesus, in order to bear spiritual fruit. God the Father is depicted as the gardener who cuts off the deadwood (the branches that bear no fruit) and prunes

KEY WORD

Farewell discourse: the name given to the section in John's Gospel chapters 13–17 that contains Jesus' words to his disciples as he prepares for his death and return to the Father

KEY QUOTE

I had planted you like a choice vine of sound and reliable stock. How then did you turn against me into a corrupt, wild vine?

(Jeremiah 2:21)

those that do bear fruit. The mark of the Christian is fruitfulness and that is achieved by continuous dependence upon Jesus. Jesus' words have power to cleanse.

Jesus' claim to be the true vine is clearly in contrast to what had come before. By remaining in Jesus, the disciples can bear the fruit that Israel failed to bear.

In order to abide in Jesus' love, followers are to keep his commands. The core of these commands involves loving one another. This love is defined in terms of the love that Jesus showed in laying down his life.

Jesus makes clear his claim that without him his disciples can achieve nothing.

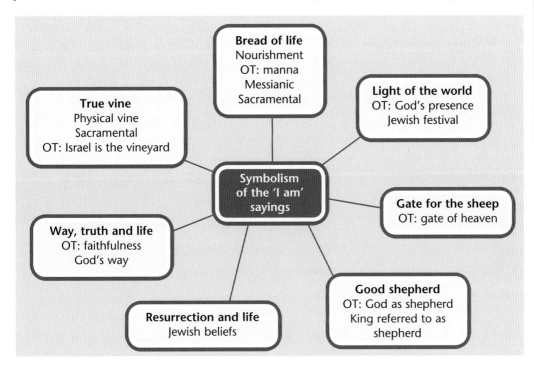

Summary diagram: The symbolism of the 'I am' sayings (OT = Old Testament)

⮕ EXAM TIP

Exam questions are expressed in words that tell you what to do in your answer. For AO1 they are:

- Compare…
- Describe…
- Examine…
- Give an account of…
- How…
- Identify…
- Illustrate…
- In what ways…
- Outline…
- Select…
- What…?

Reflection and assessment

It is now time to channel the information you have considered in a more focused way. To do this, you need to ask yourself the question: 'How am I going to be assessed on my use of this information?'

The first way is through assessment objective 1 (AO1), for which you need to be able to 'select and clearly demonstrate the relevant knowledge and understanding through the use of evidence, examples and correct language and terminology'.

As you work through each unit in this book, you will find that the amount of support in these sections will gradually be reduced, in order to encourage the development of your independence and the honing of your AO1 skills.

Use the writing frame provided below to answer this question.

> **Examine the meaning and teaching of the 'I am' saying 'I am the Good Shepherd.'** (21 marks)

a) Writing frame

The significance for Jews, of the phrase 'I am' is...

Jesus is contrasted with...

When danger approaches...

The sheep can have life to the full because...

An Old Testament reference where God is seen as shepherd is...

The good shepherd is called good because...

Christians understand this act of the good shepherd to refer to...

TASK

After completing the question, award marks out of 21. Use the AO1 level descriptors to identify reasons for the mark awarded.

Objective: To identify strengths and areas for development in each answer, by referring to the key statements found in the level descriptors.

Remember that correct technical language needs to be used where appropriate. Examining the meaning and teaching requires more than just recounting the actual text.

b) Suggestion for further application of skills

Identify strengths and areas for development in each answer. Then, as a group, collaborate to create an ideal answer that demonstrates:

● 'a coherent and well-structured response to the task at a wide range or considerable depth'
● 'selecting the most important features for emphasis and clarity', and also
● 'using evidence to explain the key ideas' (high level 4 descriptor AO1).

Now construct your own writing frame for the same question.

> **Examine the meaning and teaching of the 'I am' saying 'I am the Good Shepherd.'** (21 marks)

As a group, collaborate to create an answer that demonstrates a level 4 response. Look back to pages 8–10 in the Introduction to check the range of level descriptors for level 4.

TOPIC 1: KEY ISSUES IN THE STUDY OF THE TEACHINGS OF JESUS CHRIST

Part 1B: The meaning and significance of the miracles

> **This means I am expected:**
>
> **to know about the key issues:**
> - the meaning and significance of the miracles
>
> **and to study:**
> - how the miracles stories in John differ from those in the synoptic Gospels
> - the meaning of the word 'sign'
> - the meaning of the signs
> - the importance of the signs for the ministry of Jesus.

In this book the evidence and examples given are relevant and appropriate because this material focuses only on the content for AO1 that is given by the Edexcel specification. The evaluation materials for AO2 will be aimed at helping you 'critically evaluate and justify a point of view through the use of evidence and reasoned argument'.

It would be helpful to write your notes using the headings listed above, as it is from these areas that the examination questions will be derived.

In your studies, remember that you have to bear in mind the **two** basic assessment objectives of:

- Knowledge and Understanding (AO1)
- Evaluation (AO2).

See pages 7–8 in the Introduction to remind yourself of these objectives.

The evaluation material set out in Part 1C (page 287) can be studied either alongside the AO1 material, as you work through this unit, or as a separate unit.

This section of the unit explores four of the miracle stories (signs) in John's Gospel. The exam questions may specify one or more of the miracle stories and the focus will be on their meaning, significance or importance for the ministry of Jesus. The signs need to be used to explain and illustrate the particular focus of the question. It is therefore important that you know the accounts of the four signs so that you are able to refer to the story. Indeed, the notes in this section assume you have the text in front of you, as it refers to verse numbers.

KEY IDEA

The four signs to be studied are:
- the water into wine
- the official's son
- the healing at the pool
- walking on water.

KEY WORDS

Synoptic: literally, seeing together, identifying similarities between the first three gospels set out in parallel
Synoptic Gospels: the first three Gospels in the New Testament: Matthew, Mark and Luke

 KEY WORDS

Stoic: a Greek school of philosophy founded by Zeno; it taught that virtue and happiness are attained by submission to destiny and the natural law, the development of self-control and fortitude was a means of overcoming destructive emotions
Epicureans: a philosophy based on the teachings of Epicurus that argued that the highest good is pleasure or freedom from pain
Exodus: literally, departure; it is used to refer to the time Moses led the Israelites out of Egypt to the Promised land

 KEY IDEA

The Exodus motifs: The key themes (motifs) of the Exodus events that demonstrated to the Israelites that God was guiding and protecting them were the provision of:
● manna (food)
● light
● water.

1 How the miracle stories in John differ from those in the synoptic Gospels

Miracle stories occur both in the **synoptic Gospels** (Matthew, Mark, Luke) and John's Gospel. As a result there are a number of similarities between the accounts. For instance, all four Gospels include the feeding of the 5000. However, there are also several important differences between the synoptic Gospels and John's Gospel. In particular, John's Gospel has no account of an exorcism (casting a demon out of a person), whereas the synoptic Gospels have a number of such stories. The synoptic Gospels refer to the miracles as *mighty works*, whereas John calls them *signs*.

Hence, scholars have argued that the miracle stories in John's Gospel serve different functions from those in the synoptics. Whereas the synoptics link miracles with the destruction of the power of Satan, John sees miracles as works of revelation, showing who Jesus is. This leads the reader to faith.

2 The meaning of the word 'sign'

a) The Greek connection

In classical Greek the word for sign means a distinguishing mark, a token, a signal or a signet on a ring. With Aristotle it means a probable argument over and against a certain proof. With the **Stoics** and **Epicureans** it is an observable basis of inference to the unobserved or unobservable.

Apart from the simple meanings of mark and miracle, the word also acquired a non-miraculous meaning. When Ezekiel took a stone he drew on it a picture of Jerusalem besieged (Ezekiel 4:3). It thus becomes a special part of the prophetic activity. It was no mere illustration, but a symbolical anticipation, a showing forth of a greater reality. The idea of a sign as a pointer should not be confused with the notion that the sign is the focus. Rather, the sign points to something beyond itself. For example, when you arrive at the signpost to Worthing, you have not arrived at Worthing itself. You still have time to turn round and head back to Brighton!

By referring to them as signs, John seems to wish to indicate that the emphasis should not be on the event, or even on the idea that Jesus has the power to perform it, but instead be on the significance of the act, its meaning or meanings. That meaning may be about the person of Jesus – who he is.

b) The Exodus motifs

It is generally agreed that clues to what is understood as a sign lie in the Old Testament background. Attention is particularly drawn to motifs of the **Exodus**, especially the three events by which God showed he was their God protecting and providing for them:

● the manna from heaven
● the fire by night
● the water from the rock.

Just as God led the people from slavery in Egypt to the Promised Land, so Jesus will free people from the slavery of sin and lead them to eternal life. Just as God provided food, light and water to sustain the people escaping from slavery in Egypt, so Jesus is the 'true bread', 'living water' and 'light of the world', sustaining followers in overcoming the slavery to sin.

3 The meaning of the signs

a) Keys to understanding the meaning

i) As discussed above, the very word implies that the actual miracle itself is not the point at which the reader should end. Rather, they are to look beyond the event itself, to a deeper reality to which it is pointing. The actual physical cure is secondary in importance in the account.

ii) John 20:31 states the purpose of the signs:

> These [signs] are written that you may believe that Jesus is the Christ, the Son of God, and that by believing you may have life in his name.

According to John, the signs are pointers to Jesus as the Christ and as the Son of God. They authenticate and reveal the person and work of Jesus. In the events that are recorded, it is assumed that the reader will come to a realisation of who Jesus is.

iii) The account of the sign itself may also contain a statement about the meaning of the sign. For instance, the sign of the water into wine states:

> He thus revealed his glory, and the disciples put their faith in him.

iv) Some of the signs are linked to a discourse in which Jesus explains the sign. For example, the sign of the feeding of the 5000 has an accompanying discourse about Jesus being the bread of life. (See pages 268–9.)

b) The miracle stories (the signs)

The exam requires you to study the meaning of the following four signs. The significance and importance of the signs are clearly related to the meaning of the signs and the notes on them should be read in conjunction with these on the meaning of the signs.

i) The water into wine (John 2:1–11)

● **Revealed his glory**

> 66 **KEY QUOTES**
>
> *When my glory passes by, I will put you in a cleft in the rock and cover you with my hand until I have passed by.*
>
> **(Exodus 33:22)**
>
> *The Word became flesh and made his dwelling among us. We have seen his glory, the glory of the One and Only, who came from the Father, full of grace and truth.*
>
> **(John 1:14)**
> 99

As mentioned above, the story of the miracle of water into wine includes a reference to its meaning, namely 'he revealed his glory'. Glory is a theme found throughout John's Gospel. It first occurs in John 1:14, where it refers to God making himself known visibly: his visible presence. It is God revealing himself as God (Exodus 33:22). Indeed, Exodus 33:18 records how Moses begged God: 'Now show me your glory'; the LXX translates this as 'Show me yourself.'

Psalm 29:9 shows how the word developed into a form of praise by those in the Temple when they become aware of the presence of the Lord.

> **EXAM TIP**
>
> When you illustrate a point, make sure that you explain the illustration and, in particular, how it does illustrate the point you are making. This demonstrates selection of 'accurate and relevant knowledge, organised and presented in a clear structure' (level 3 AO1 descriptor).

> 66 **KEY QUOTE**
>
> *And in his temple all cry 'Glory!'*
>
> **(Psalm 29:9)**
> 99

EXAM TIP

Remember to explain fully each point that you make in an exam answer. Think carefully about each sentence and how it relates to the question and the previous sentence. Aim for at least three sentences to explain a point. This demonstrates 'detailed knowledge of the subject matter at a wide range or in significant depth' (level 4 descriptor AO1).

KEY QUOTES

Jesus replied, 'The hour has come for the Son of Man to be glorified.'

(John 12:23)

On this mountain the Lord Almighty will prepare a feast of rich food for all peoples, a banquet of aged wine – the best of meats and the finest of wines.

(Isaiah 25:6)

A further association with the Old Testament is in the account of the presence of God, or God's glory, linked to the appearance of a bright cloud (Exodus 24:15f). The cloud became the visible symbol of God's presence.

In John's Gospel, a New Age has arrived with God being visibly present in the form of Jesus. Right at the start of the Gospel (1:14), John refers to the Word making 'his dwelling among us'. The Word refers to Jesus and the picture describes how God has chosen to dwell amongst his people in a very personal way; the Word becomes flesh. The Word takes on human form. God becomes a human being.

The idea is of God living in his tent, among the people. God was going to be with his people in a new and personal way. The root word is the same for dwelling and for glory.

The sign of the water into wine is a pointer to who Jesus is, because John claims it reveals Jesus' glory. Not all who saw the sign perceived this glory. There is no indication that the servants put their faith in Jesus after seeing the miracle. This is in sharp contrast to the response of the disciples. They saw what the sign was pointing to.

Some scholars have seen this theme of glory as being so central to the Gospel that they divide it into two parts:

- chapters 1–11, the Book of Signs, in which Jesus reveals his glory
- chapters 12–21, the Book of Glory, in which Jesus receives his glory.

Some see pointers towards Jesus' supreme glorification (his death and resurrection, see John 12:23; 13:31–2) in some of the details of the story. For instance, verse 1 sets the timing as the third day, a phrase that was widely used in referring to the resurrection of Jesus. This could be seen as a way of drawing attention to the meaning of the sign, pointing to Jesus' glorification (the resurrection).

KEY IDEA

The Christ, the Messiah:
In the Old Testament God is recognised as King, having authority and power over all (Psalm 145:11–13), although God's authority was not accepted by all nations. Therefore, many Jews looked forward to a future kingdom. This was compared to the great kingdom at the time of David: Israel's Golden Age. Instead of David, a new ruler, a descendant of David, would come and would be called Messiah (the anointed one). In Greek, 'the anointed one' is translated as 'Christ'. The Messiah (Christ) would be God's chosen one; he was expected to be a warrior who would lead Israel to victory over her enemies. The formation of this earthly kingdom, ushered in by the Messiah, would demonstrate and establish God's authority over all nations.

● Jesus as Christ

There are several elements in the account of this miracle that could be seen as pointers to Jesus as the Christ (Messiah). The whole event is based around a wedding. The Jews always depicted the celebration of the Messiah establishing the new kingdom in terms of a feast or banquet. In particular it is depicted often as a wedding feast. This may or may not be the intended connection here.

Some see significance in the setting of the sign in Cana of Galilee. It is possible that Cana is representative of Canaan, in the Old Testament, the region that God's chosen people entered as their Promised Land. Here is the new Promised Land, into which all believers are invited.

In John 2:4, Jesus refers to the fact that his 'hour has not yet come'. John uses the word 'hour' in a technical sense, to refer to Jesus' death and resurrection. Hence, John seems to make a connection between 'the hour' and Jesus' response to his mother about providing more wine.

This emphasis on the wine is seen by some as a messianic claim. The Old Testament prophets characterised the Messianic Age as a time when wine would flow liberally (Jeremiah 31:12). Jesus could be making clear that the time for the messianic celebration has not yet arrived, since he has not yet been glorified (the means by which the New Age would be achieved).

● Jesus as the Son of God

Some scholars see in this story pointers to Jesus being the Son of God. Much has been written about the time sequence and John's interest in setting this miracle very precisely, in terms of order of days. John seems to place the miracle of the water to wine on the sixth or seventh day (depending how the time sequence is interpreted). By some, this is seen to mirror creation week, reflected in the beginning of John's Gospel (John 1:1). God is now making a new creation, through Jesus' death and resurrection.

The miracle itself shows divine power over nature. The water is turned into wine, breaking the laws of nature.

ii) The official's son (John 4:43–54)

● Revealed his glory

Some see pointers in this sign directing the reader to focus on Jesus' death and resurrection: his glorification. For example, the whole story is about a boy 'close to death' (4:47).

Jesus enables the boy to have life rather than death; that is the difference Jesus makes. Jesus' word is life to the boy.

Some scholars have seen a parallel between the earthly son (the official's son) and the heavenly son (Jesus).

It may also be deliberately symbolism to have the son's healing take place at the seventh hour. Seven is the symbol of perfection and completion. The official's son's fever left him at that exact time and he was made well (complete) by Jesus, who is himself perfect.

The fact that 'he [the official] and all his household believed' (4:53) also shows that Jesus had revealed his glory to them.

In John 11:4 Jesus links healing with God's glory. Hence all healings could be seen as glorifying Jesus.

KEY QUOTE

When he heard this, Jesus said, 'This sickness will not end in death. No, it is for God's glory so that God's Son may be glorified through it.'

(John 11:4)

KEY QUOTE

'Father, the hour has come. Glorify your Son, that your Son may glorify you.'

(John 17:1)

KEY QUOTE

...they will rejoice in the bounty of the Lord – the grain, the new wine and the oil...

(Jeremiah 31:12)

KEY QUOTE

In the beginning was the Word and the Word was with God, and the Word was God.

(John 1:1)

TASK

Many scholars have focused on symbolism in the signs. What significance might be read into the miracle happening on (a) the sixth day (b) the seventh day? Do you see any problems with interpreting possible symbolism?
Objective: To demonstrate 'a coherent and well-structured response to the task at a wide range or considerable depth' (level 4 descriptor AO1).

KEY QUOTE

Thirty-eight years passed from the time we left Kadesh Barnea until we crossed the Zered Valley. By then, that entire generation of fighting men had perished from the camp, as the Lord had sworn to them.

(Deuteronomy 2:14)

• Jesus as Christ

John links this miracle, the healing of the son of the official from a distance, with the first sign. John makes actual reference to the first sign. Jesus is in Cana (the site of the first sign) but the official's son is in Capernaum. The story is introduced by a saying that a prophet has no honour in his own country. Much debate has arisen over what John means by 'own country' here. One understanding is that John is contrasting what had recently happened a couple of days before, in Samaria (John 4), with the Jewish attitude towards Jesus. The Jewish reaction to Jesus is seen as growing opposition and controversy (John 2:18), with an expression of faith that is spurious, based on wanting miracles rather than on real faith in Jesus (John 2:23–5). In contrast, the Samaritan episode ends with the recognition that Jesus is the saviour of the world (4:42). The despised Samaritans recognise Jesus as the Messiah, while many of the Jews either oppose him or have a fascination with miracles rather than a revelation of who Jesus is.

• Jesus as the Son of God

The miraculous nature of the sign shows the supernatural power of Jesus. He had authority to declare someone healed even at a considerable distance. The word he spoke was sufficient to overrule the powers of nature. When he spoke it was done. This is akin to the power of the word of God, the creator.

iii) Healing at the pool (John 5:1–15)

• Jesus as Christ

The work of the Christ (Messiah) was to bring in the Kingdom of God. Some scholars see significance in the fact that the man had been an invalid for 38 years. This is the number of years the Israelites spent wandering in the wilderness (Deuteronomy 2:14) before they entered the Promised Land.

The passage could then be seen as an indication of how a sinful man has awaited cleansing and entry into the Promised Land. Now the Messiah has come, who cleanses and gives entry to the new kingdom.

Jesus healing the paralytic at the pool of Bethesda (Tiepolo, circa 1759)

● **Jesus as the Son of God**

This sign is followed by a long dialogue (5:16–46) about the Father and the Son. The discussion is prompted by the fact that the sign takes place on the Sabbath. This is therefore seen as a claim by Jesus that he is the Son of God.

Other pointers revealing Jesus as the Son of God include the fact that the laws of nature are broken, showing the supernatural power of Jesus.

The event happens near the Sheep Gate. Those who favour symbolism see in this detail a claim that Jesus is God, the Good Shepherd who invites his flock to enter by 'the door'. Likewise, the five pillars of the pool are sometimes seen to refer to the five law books of the Old Testament (the first five books, known as the Torah). Jesus is thus seen as replacing the Law with his life-giving word. It is through the word, not the Law, that the man is made whole. This focus on the words – 'get up' – might well anticipate the voice of the Son of God on the last day (5:28–9).

iv) Walking on water (John 6:16–21)

● **Jesus as the Son of God**

God is light. It is interesting that, though this story appears in the synoptic Gospels, only John records that 'It was now dark' (verse 17). In John's Gospel, darkness refers to the work of Satan (3:20; 13:30). The implication might be that the absence of light implies the absence of Jesus.

John also omits the introductory words of Jesus: 'Take heart,' and calms their fears by identifying himself. His account has Jesus saying: 'It is I'. This implies the usual *ego eimi* (I am), used in the 'I am' sayings of Jesus elsewhere.

The Greek phrase (*ego eimi*) is the one used in the translation of the Hebrew Old Testament into Greek for the name for God (Exodus 3:14). For fuller discussion of this phrase see pages 267–8.

Barrett believes here, and in 9:9, 'It is I' is purely for identification and not to be seen as a claim to divinity. Others, such as Carson, suggest that it is an anticipation of a later, clearer self-disclosure.

A further pointer to Jesus as Son of God is the fact that, in the Old Testament, the sea stands for chaos and disorder, and it is God who controls it and stills it.

4 The significance of the signs

a) What the signs lead to

John 20:31 states that the signs should lead to belief and that belief should lead to eternal life. In other words, the signs reveal who Jesus is (the Christ, the Son of God), and realisation of that leads to faith in Jesus. This in turn leads to salvation. The belief has a content and a consequence.

A characteristic of the signs stories is that people come to faith in Jesus. For instance, with the water into wine sign, the disciples put their faith in Jesus (2:11). In the account of the official's son, it was the official and all his household who came to believe.

The early chapters of John show the spread of faith, even to Samaritans and Gentiles (if it is true that the official was a Gentile).

➡ **EXAM TIP**

Do not answer a question about the signs simply by 'telling the story'. You should always select and make reference to the key events, that is, the appropriate information relevant to the question. This demonstrates more personal understanding or ownership of the knowledge. It is evidence of a 'coherent and well-structured response… selecting the most important features for emphasis and clarity' (level 4 descriptor AO1).

66 **KEY QUOTE**

This is what you are to say to the Israelites: 'I am has sent me to you'.

(Exodus 3:14)

99

b) What the signs reveal about the person of Jesus

As has been discussed above, the signs reveal who Jesus is. John sees in the signs pointers to the revelation that Jesus is both the Christ (Messiah) and the Son of God.

In the creation story in Genesis, God said and it was done.

There is a parallel in the signs, in that in each case Jesus gives a command and it is done. For instance, in the story of the official's son, Jesus says: 'Your son will live.'

The father realised that the son was healed at the exact time Jesus had spoken these words (4:53).

c) What the signs reveal about the work of Jesus

The signs indicate the nature of the ministry of Jesus, what his mission is. (See below for details.)

5 The importance of the signs for the ministry of Jesus

The signs help us to understand Jesus' work and ministry.

a) The signs reveal the inadequacy of Jewish purification

In the water into wine sign, some scholars see symbolism in the Jewish water pots of purification (verse 6).

Firstly there are only six water pots: 'only' because the number of completion is seen to be seven. There is something inadequate or incomplete, about Jewish purification.

The jars are stone, whereas Jesus is flesh and blood, and he sheds his blood in order to bring purification (salvation). The legalism of Jewish purification is replaced by the grace and truth of Jesus. The new is shown to be better than the old. God has kept the best, 'the good wine until now' (2:10).

Some scholars identify a similar idea in the healing by the pool. The man had been waiting 38 years yet, when Jesus spoke the word, he was immediately healed (made whole). The legalism could be indicated by the reference to the five pillars that some see as symbols of the Law.

b) Eternal life available through the death of Jesus

The mention of wine is seen by some to symbolise the blood of Jesus. It was only through the death of Jesus that eternal life (salvation) was possible.

Many of the signs pointed towards the death and resurrection of Jesus. Indeed, many scholars see the resurrection not as a signpost, but that to which all the signs point.

c) The role of signs in Jesus' ministry

The signs are depicted as one way in which Jesus revealed himself. Those who looked beyond the event itself realised that they pointed to the person of Jesus. In doing this, the signs more obviously revealed the authority, the power, the divinity, the uniqueness and the compassion of Jesus.

66 KEY QUOTE

For the law was given through Moses; grace and truth came through Jesus Christ.
(John 1:17)
99

TASK

Summarise in table form, key points that each of the signs reveals about the person and work of Jesus.

Objective: To develop skill of 'selecting the most important features for emphasis and clarity' (level 4 descriptor AO1).

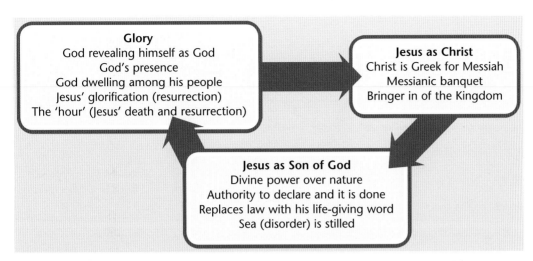

Summary diagram: The ministry of Jesus

Reflection and assessment

It is vital to bring together the information covered so far and recognise how it can be transformed into effective examination style revision and answers. The best way to do this is to ask: 'How am I going to be assessed on this information?'

The first way is through assessment objective 1 (AO1). You need to be able to 'select and clearly demonstrate the relevant knowledge and understanding, through the use of evidence, examples and correct language and terminology'.

Look back to pages 8–10 in the Introduction to review the level descriptors for AO1. There is a description of the character and features for each level. The exam is marked with reference to levels.

Look at the answer overleaf, which is a response to this question.

Examine the meaning of the healing at the Pool. (21 marks)

What is the relevance of this? The candidate needed to go on to discuss the idea of signposts which could then lead into the focus of the meaning of the sign of the healing by the pool.

Only partially discussed the significance of working on the Sabbath and what it implies about Jesus himself, and his work.

Needs to be explained further. Where is the evidence that this is taught in the sign?

The word sign comes from the word semion. The signs are miracles. It is clear that there is a deeper meaning to the signs. For instance the 38 years waiting to be cured is significant.

In this sign, Jesus was criticised for working on the Sabbath. The sign teaches us that God's work never stops, and that there is no harm in working on the Sabbath if the deed is good.

This sign also can be said to be replacing Jewish authority.

This sign reveals that it is within Jesus' nature to mix with so-called untouchables, that other people in authority would never assist. This is a continuous theme throughout all the signs.

Another thing taught in this sign is realised eschatology. The things of the world to come are in part realised now. This sign also reveals the person and work of Jesus. The man is healed by a command from Jesus and shows Jesus' links with God. The overall meaning of the sign is that Jesus is divine and is the Messiah.

Need to support this claim with some evidence.

What is its significance?

What is the justification for claiming this? What is the significance of Jesus replacing Jewish authority.

Relevance?

How does it show that?

TASK

In the light of the comments, now write a level 4 answer.

Objective: To be able to 'select accurate, relevant and detailed knowledge...used concisely to present a coherent and well-structured response.' (level 4 descriptor AO1).

a) So what does it score?

In the exam the answer will be marked according to levels (see pages 8–10 in the Introduction). Certainly this candidate has some knowledge and understanding. There is some attempt to keep to the focus of the meaning of the sign. However, statements are made without support or explanation. There is very little reference back to the actual account of the miracle to support the points made. The key meanings were not explained or developed. This would score a top level 2.

It would not take much to develop this essay into a level 4 response. The problem is that, as it stands, the candidate has left it to the examiner to work out how the meaning is demonstrated in the story of the sign.

b) Suggestion for further application of skills

Produce a spider diagram for the following question.

> **By reference to any two signs, show how the signs reveal Jesus as the Messiah (the Christ), the life giver.** (21 marks)

Your spider diagram will need to break down the essay title into its component parts, identifying the relevant material required in each part.

TOPIC 2: KEY ISSUES IN THE STUDY OF THE TEACHINGS OF JESUS CHRIST

Part 1C: A critical analysis of the issues

> **This means I am expected to:**
>
> **analyse and critically evaluate:**
> - what is a sign
> - is there a link between signs and the 'I am' sayings
> - are the sayings authentic
> - are the signs symbolic
> - are there other meanings for the signs?

1 What is a sign?

In five cases, Jesus' miracles are designated as signs: the water into wine (2:11), the official's son (4:54), the feeding of the 5000 (6:14), the man born blind (9:16) and the raising of Lazarus (12:18).

There seems a tendency for commentators to want there to be seven signs. This could then be seen as part of the symbolic structure, for example, with seven as the number representing completion, or with the seven 'I am' sayings, or even with a notional seven-week division of the material in John for use in Church. Yet it is also acknowledged that there may be as few as six or as many as nine signs.

The additional signs that are usually included, but not actually referred to as signs, in John's Gospel are:

- the healing of the crippled man at the pool (5:1–15)
- walking on the water (6:16–22)
- the resurrection (chapter 20)
- the miraculous catch of fish (21:1–14).

Some scholars exclude the case of Jesus walking on the water because it may not be a miracle if we read 'by the sea' in 6:19 rather than 'on the sea'. Others disregard the resurrection as a sign, since it is in a different category from the other signs, for either this is the supreme sign, or it is that to which all the signs point. This is now the real thing.

The miraculous catch of fish is also disregarded by many, as it is post-resurrection. If it is correct to say that all the signs point to the final great sign of the resurrection, then there would be no signs after the resurrection. However, Stephen Smalley accepts it, since it fulfils the criteria of signs. Namely, it reveals Jesus' glory in the flesh (all be it in the resurrection body) and shows him bringing life or salvation to humankind.

EXAM TIP

Exam questions are expressed in words that tell you what to do in your answer. For AO2 they are:

- Comment on...
- Consider...
- How far...
- To what extent...
- Why...?

? KEY QUESTIONS

- Do you think there are seven signs? What criteria did you apply to help you decide?
- Do all the signs have to share the same characteristics? Are there some characteristics that are necessary for it to be classed as a sign?

This list of stories that scholars refer to as signs have some common features (though not every feature may be found in every story):

- a miraculous act
- a word of command associated with the miracle
- faith results
- pointers to something about the person of Jesus
- pointers to something about the work of Jesus (salvation)
- links to the Exodus motif.

In addition, Raymond Brown, in his commentary, sees the signs linked to Jewish festivals. Jesus fulfils them.

2 Is there a link between signs and the 'I am' sayings?

Stephen Smalley considers the signs to be linked to the 'I am' sayings. Indeed, he regards the signs as the central core of a carefully constructed whole.

TASK

Copy the table, then complete it by putting the appropriate evidence from the text into the relevant box.

Objective: To develop the AO2 skill of 'careful analysis of alternative views...supported by well-deployed evidence' (level 4 descriptor AO2).

Sign – 'I am' saying	Linked	Not linked
Water into wine – True vine		
Official's son – The way, truth and life		
Crippled man – The gate of the sheep		
The 5000 fed – The bread of life		
The blind man – The light of the world		
Raising of Lazarus – The resurrection and the life		
Catch of fish – Good shepherd		

3 Are the sayings authentic?

A number of questions have been raised about the reliability of the material in John's Gospel. For instance, the material is very different from that found in the synoptic Gospels. It is very theological and some scholars argue that it represents a later theology rather than that of Jesus. In the 'I am' sayings, Jesus seems to be making a claim to be God, which some scholars reject. In particular, the 'I am the bread of life' saying has been debated. One problem is that if this saying is seen to refer to the Last Supper, then it seems strange that Jesus referred to something that could only be understood later. However, other scholars question the sacramental interpretation of this saying. **Bultmann** argued that the sacramental element had been added later, to redress the imbalance of the teaching in the Gospel on this matter.

In response, some scholars, such as Smalley, argue that Jesus was speaking to a different audience, and this will have caused differences in the form of address he used. The background to John's Gospel is now seen to be Jewish, and the background to the sayings is also predominantly Jewish.

4 Are the signs symbolic?

Not only has doubt been raised about the historical reliability of the miracle stories (signs) on grounds that they are very different from those recorded in the synoptic Gospels, but also that they appear full of symbolism and therefore suggest they have been artificially created to make a theological point. In particular, this view is supported by

KEY PERSON

Rudolph Bultmann (1884–1976)

A German theologian and a professor of New Testament, he called into question the historical reliability of the Gospels and argued for the presence of a lost Signs source. He is particularly associated with demythologising (see page 57).

those who dispute the possibility of miracles occurring. Bultmann, for instance, rejected the supernatural and saw the origin of the account of the water into wine as Hellenistic and part of the Dionysus cult.

Other scholars have defended the historicity of the accounts of the stories, arguing that the fact that elements of the story have a possible symbolic interpretation does not deny that the miracle happened. Indeed, John shows accurate knowledge, for example, archaeological excavation has uncovered the pool with five porticoes, and many of the elements of the accounts have no clear symbolic meaning.

Many historical events that actually happened can later provide useful symbols of religious truth. The fact that events can be used in this way does not diminish the reality of the original event. Nor does the fact that the event is historical lessen the effectiveness of the symbolism.

5 Possible conclusions

When assessing the issues that arise with historicity, it is important to reflect upon the arguments above and arrive at some appropriate conclusion.

It may be that you accept none of these listed below, or just one of them, or you may have a different conclusion that is not listed. However, what is important is the way that you have arrived at your conclusion: the reasoning process.

From the preceding discussions, here are some possible conclusions you could draw.

1   The sayings are not from the mouth of Jesus and the records of the signs are not historically accurate.

2   The sayings are authentic (from Jesus) but the records of the signs are not historically accurate.

3   The sayings are not authentic but the records of the signs are historically accurate.

4   The sayings are based on what Jesus said but have been developed later.

5   The records of the signs are historically accurate and lend themselves to symbolism.

6   Only some of the sayings are authentic and only some of the records of the signs are historically accurate.

7   The sayings are authentic and the records of the signs are historically accurate.

6 Are there other meanings of the signs?

a) John 20:31

In some manuscripts, there is an alternative interpretation that implies that the signs were written so that 'you may go on believing'. In other words, the purpose was not evangelistic (so that you may believe...) but encouragement (go on believing...).

b) The focus on faith

The signs do not always lead people to believe. Signs often give rise to controversy and conflict. This is demonstrated in the incidents of healing of the crippled man (John 5) and that of the blind man (John 9) performed by Jesus on the Sabbath. Equally, the authorities plot to kill Jesus, following the raising of Lazarus.

? KEY QUESTION

Are the signs accounts of actual events that happened? What criteria did you apply to help you to decide?

➡ EXAM TIP

Look at the levels (page 10) and create a brief list of essential requirements in order to access a high level of response for an argument at AO2. For example, there needs to be 'technical language that is fluent and accurately applied' (level 4 descriptor AO2).

Signs source: Bultmann argued that the author of John's Gospel used a written source that contained the miracle stories (the signs)

Particularly problematic are the statements in John's Gospel that imply a negative attitude towards the signs (2:23–5; 4:48; 6:26f; 12:37).

This led Robert Fortna, basing his work on Bultmann, to see a **signs source** in John and then argue that the compiler of John had a different view of signs from that in 20:30–1. The compiler kept the signs source, including its ending at 20:30–1, but inserted some verses that indicated his own view, which was different from that of the signs source. Hence the tension in the Gospel indicated by those verses listed above.

The theologian Raymond Brown distinguishes four reactions to the signs:

- refuse to see the signs with any faith (11:47)
- see the signs as wonders and believe in Jesus as a wonder-worker sent by God (2:23–5; 4:45–8; 7:3–7)
- see the true significance of the signs and come to believe in Jesus and to know who he is (4:53; 6:69; 9:38; 11:40)
- believe in Jesus without seeing signs (20:29).

c) Other meanings

It is possible that these include:

- sacramental teaching (Baptism and Last Supper or Eucharist)
- a consideration of the superiority of Christianity (Christ) over Judaism (Moses)
- misunderstandings as people view the earthly rather than appreciate the spiritual
- eschatology and judgement emphasis.

7 Possible conclusions

When assessing the issues that arise in determining the meaning of the signs, it is important to reflect upon the arguments above and arrive at some appropriate conclusion.

It may be that you accept none of those listed below, or just one of them, or you may have a different conclusion that is not listed. However, what is important is the way that you have arrived at your conclusion: the reasoning process.

From the preceding discussions, here are some possible conclusions you could draw.

1 The meaning of the signs is that stated in John 20:31.

2 There is no one meaning of the signs. The meaning depends on which sign it is and this meaning is found in the symbolism of the story.

3 There is a difference between Jesus' purpose of the signs and the purpose of that of the author of the Gospel.

4 We do not know the purpose of the signs.

Reflection and assessment (AO2)

Earlier in this topic you considered the assessment objective AO1 which focused on knowledge and understanding. The second way of being assessed is through assessment objective AO2. For this objective you need to be able to attempt an evaluation of the issue(s) raised, typically through a careful analysis of alternative views.

Use the writing frame provided below to help you answer this question.

To what extent can the signs be regarded as actual historical events? (9 marks)

a) Key points

Always point out the case in support of the statement and the case against.
- If appropriate, respond to and assess each point as you proceed through.
- Avoid just listing points.
- Keep relating the material back to the focus of the evaluation.
- Always give a clear weighing up, leading to an appropriate conclusion, even if the conclusion is that both sides of the debate are equally persuasive.
- Remember that the case against can include better alternatives as well as weaknesses of the case in support.

b) Writing frame

The signs are accounts of miracles involving healings...

They are events against the laws of nature, which makes some people question them as historical events because...

In addition, the signs appear to be full of symbolism. This makes their historical value questionable because...

However, many scholars have argued for the signs being historical events. In support, they point out that though they do recount miracles, nonetheless...

Also, the symbolism does not mean the story is not historical, since...

Some have pointed out that most of the signs are only in John's Gospel and so...

In reply, some scholars argue that...

In the light of the above arguments it seems best to conclude that...

This writing frame, although quite basic, does focus on analysis of alternative views. It is better to deal with three or four criticisms in some detail, than a longer list with very brief comment. It is important also to make clear in what way your criticism challenges the argument or view.

c) Suggestion for further application of skills

After completing the writing frame use the levels and AO2 descriptors to award marks out of 9. Identify strengths and areas for development in each answer.

Now construct your own writing frame for this question.

To what extent is the main teaching of the signs about faith?   (9 marks)

Now, as a group, collaborate to create an answer that demonstrates level 4. Look back to page 10 in the introduction to check the level descriptors.

TOPIC 2: KEY EMPHASES IN THE STUDY OF THE TEACHINGS OF JESUS CHRIST

Part 2A: Women

> ### This means I am expected:
>
> **to know about the key issue:**
> - women
>
> **and to study:**
> - women in the Fourth Gospel
> - the Samaritan woman
> - the woman caught in adultery
> - Mary and Martha at the raising of Lazarus
> - Mary at the tomb of Jesus
> - the social status of women within Judaism
> - the religious status of women within Judaism.

In this book the evidence and examples given are relevant and appropriate because this material focuses only on the content for AO1 that is given by the Edexcel specification. The evaluation materials for AO2 will be aimed at helping you 'critically evaluate and justify a point of view through the use of evidence and reasoned argument'.

It would be helpful to write your notes using the headings listed above, as it is from these areas that the examination questions will be derived.

In your studies, remember that you have to bear in mind the **two** basic assessment objectives of:

- Knowledge and Understanding (AO1)
- Evaluation (AO2).

See pages 7–8 in the Introduction to remind yourself of these objectives.

The evaluation material set out in Part 2C (page 310) can be studied either alongside the AO1 material, as you work through this unit, or as a separate unit.

This section of the unit explores the role of women, as revealed in the Fourth Gospel. The exam questions may single out one or more of the named woman listed above and the focus will be their role and importance in the ministry of Jesus. It is important that you know the relevant texts in the Gospel, so that you are able to refer to the relevant incidents. Indeed, the notes in this section assume you have the text in front of you, as they refer to verse numbers.

Other areas that you need to know about are the social and religious status of women within Judaism at the time of Jesus.

1 Women in the fourth Gospel

All four Gospels recall events in which Jesus has dealings with women. His attitude is positive and affirming, in contrast to the negative attitude that scholars think was normally displayed towards women, at that time and in that society.

This section of the AS course focuses on four women who feature in John's Gospel. Each is discussed below.

2 The Samaritan woman (4:1–42)

The story tells many different things about this woman.

- She came alone (4:7); women usually came in groups to fetch water.
- The woman came to the well at an unusual time, the sixth hour, when the sun was at its highest (4:6).
- She suffered public shame (4:16f), which might explain why she went to the well at this time and why she went alone.
- The woman was a **Samaritan** (see page 294) and as such was seen by Jews as ritually defiled. A later rule in the **Mishnah** stated that 'all the daughters of the Samaritans are menstruants from their cradle'. This meant that they were to be regarded as in a perpetual state of ceremonial uncleanness.
- The woman sees Jesus as a mere traveller wanting a drink. She fails to recognise who he is. She asks if he is greater than Jacob, who built the well (verse 12), clearly believing that he is not. She also misunderstands about the water Jesus refers to and assumes he is speaking about natural running water. John appears to highlight the sheer irony of this questioning.
- In John's Gospel, the woman is the first person to whom Jesus declares his Messiahship (verse 29).
- The reference to the woman leaving her water jar (verse 28) is seen by a minority of commentators as symbolic of the woman abandoning the old ceremonial forms of worship of Judaism and accepting the living water, worshipping in spirit and truth.
- She is depicted as the first real disciple who responds to the words of Jesus. She is also the first evangelist in that her testimony to the people brought them to belief in Jesus (verse 39).

The story says several things about Jesus.

- He broke social custom by asking the Samaritan woman for a drink. (Jews feared ritual defilement which would result from eating with Samaritans.) The NIV has an alternative translation of verse 9: 'For Jews do not use dishes Samaritans have used.' It seems that Jesus did not regard himself as being defiled by the touching of unclean things.
- The living water that Jesus offered was, of course, not natural water at all, but the font of God poured into the human heart, bringing to individuals the personal and permanent reality of God's gift of eternal life (verse 14).
- Jesus reveals his supernatural knowledge about the Samaritan woman's past and belief about him moves from 'a prophet' (verse 19) to 'the Messiah' (verse 29) and the 'Saviour of the world' (verse 42).

KEY WORD

Mishnah: a written form of the Jewish oral traditions; they were collected and written down so that they would not be lost or forgotten

TASK

Using the following references, draw a diagram to show the various meanings of the phrase 'living water'. Jeremiah 2:13; Ezekiel 36:25–7; Zechariah 14:8; John 7:38; 19:34
Objective: To develop the skill of 'using well-chosen evidence to support understanding of key ideas and concepts' (level 4 descriptor AO1).

TASK

Compare Jesus' encounter with the Samaritan woman with his encounter with Nicodemus (3:1–15). What does this show about John's portrayal of women?
Objective: To develop the skill of 'using well-chosen evidence to support understanding of key ideas and concepts' (level 4 descriptor AO1).

KEY PROFILE: THE SAMARITANS

At the end of Solomon's reign in 931BCE, the country of Israel divided into two kingdoms: the northern and the southern. Samaria was an area in the northern kingdom, which took its name from the capital city built by King Omri (1 Kings 16:24) in about 870BCE. The name 'Samaria' was sometimes used to designate the entire northern kingdom.

In 721BCE the Assyrians captured Samaria, deported all the Israelites of substance and settled the land with foreigners. Over the years, intermarriage took place so that, when the Jews eventually returned to what remained of the southern kingdom, many years later, they regarded the Samaritans as of mixed race, whose religion had become tainted.

In about 400BCE the Samaritans erected a rival temple on Mount Gerizim and developed their own religious traditions, accepting only the first five books of the Jewish scriptures (the **Pentateuch**). Tensions mounted between the Jews and the Samaritans so that, by Jesus' time, Jews would avoid walking through Samaria and choose to take a longer route. Jesus is called a Samaritan as a term of abuse and insult (John 8:48).

Today, there remain about 700 Samaritans, living in the Palestinian city of Nablus in the West Bank and the Israeli seaside town of Holon, south of Tel Aviv.

Samaritan priests covering with soil the oven containing their skewered Passover sacrifices, after slaughtering sheep during the ritual of Sacrifice, part of a Samaritan Passover ceremony, on Mount Gerizim

3 The woman caught in adultery (7:53–8:11)

Most scholars agree that this account of the woman caught in adultery was not part of the original John's Gospel, as the story is not found in any of the oldest Greek manuscripts of the New Testament. However, most scholars do regard it as an authentic story about Jesus, with parallels in the synoptic Gospels.

The story tells us many different things about this woman.

- The woman is unnamed.
- She is guilty of the same sin as the Samaritan woman, though the reference to stoning (verse 5) suggests she had sinned during the period of betrothal.
- The text implies that the woman was guilty because Jesus tells her to leave her life of sin (verse 11).

The story says several things about Jesus.

- Jesus realised that there were political rather than religious motives behind the question that the scribes and the Pharisees were asking (verse 6). They were trying to trap him in order to find a charge against him. Would he uphold Jewish law and risk challenging Roman authority (since only Rome could give the death sentence), or would Jesus reject the Jewish law and side with Rome?
- Scholars have argued about what Jesus may have written in the dust. T.W. Manson suggested that Jesus was imitating the practice of Roman magistrates who first wrote their sentence and then read it. Other scholars see the action as incidental.
- The words of Jesus shame the very people who had come to shame Jesus (verse 9).
- Jesus' words to the woman show him as one who came not to condemn but to save.
- Jesus does not imply, by his non-condemnation, that the sinful actions of the woman did not matter. He did tell her to sin no more. John's Gospel explains how Jesus' death makes possible forgiveness, since the penalty for sin has been paid (John 3:16).
- In his reply, Jesus is claiming the right to forgive sins.

4 Mary and Martha at the raising of Lazarus (11:1–45)

The story tells us many different things about these two women.

- Mary and Martha were sisters and they had a brother called Lazarus.
- It is because Jesus loved the Bethany family that he waited two days before setting out. The resulting clear-cut miracle of raising Lazarus from the dead would result in strengthening of the faith of the two women. It would also show them who he was. This disclosure is seen in Martha's three-fold confession: 'I believe you are the Christ, the Son of God, who was to come into the world.' Scholars draw parallels between Martha's confession and Peter's confession in Matthew 16:16.
- Martha shows that she has faith, for when Jesus arrives (verse 21–2) she is confident that, had Jesus been present earlier, he could have healed her brother. She also recognises that Jesus has a special relationship with God, but Martha does not think in terms of Jesus raising Lazarus from the dead.
- When Mary reaches Jesus, she falls at his feet, indicating confidence in Jesus and his power (verse 32).
- Martha's reaction to being asked to remove the grave stone (verse 38) indicates that she did not think that Jesus was going to raise Lazarus from the dead.

KEY QUOTES

If a man happens to meet in a town a virgin pledged to be married and he sleeps with her, you shall take both of them to the gate of that town and stone them to death…

(Deuteronomy 22:23)

For God so loved the world that he gave his one and only Son, that whoever believes in him shall not perish but have eternal life. For God did not send his Son into the world to condemn the world, but to save the world through him.

(John 3:16–17)

KEY QUOTE

'But what about you?' he [Jesus] asked, 'Who do you say I am?' Simon Peter answered, 'You are the Christ, the Son of the living God.'

(Matthew 16:16)

KEY QUOTE

Women, like Martha and Mary, were among his [Jesus'] friends, and he thought them worthy of his highest teaching. He saw in them, that is, the same spiritual worth and capacity as men.

(Bishop Gore)

> **EXAM TIP**
>
> When answering a question about the importance of women in the ministry of Jesus, make sure that you do not just recount the incident but focus on what that incident demonstrates about the importance of women in Jesus' ministry. This means that it is not just a general answer that presents 'a limited range of isolated facts… with mainly random and unorganised detail' or 'information presented within a structure which shows a basic awareness of the issue(s) raised' (level 1 and 2 descriptors AO1). Remember, you are aiming for 'a coherent and well-structured account of the subject matter,… selecting the most important features…using evidence to explain the key ideas' (level 4 descriptor AO1).

- Chapter 12 gives a picture of Mary's faith as she anoints Jesus' feet with expensive perfume and wipes it with her hair. Many scholars read into this a symbolic act of preparing Jesus' body for burial, as she realised that Jesus would soon die. Certainly the raising of Lazarus is seen in the Gospel as a turning point, where the authorities started to plot to have Jesus killed (verse 53).

The story says several things about Jesus.

- The death of Lazarus, and his subsequent being brought back to life, showed the glory of God. This means that the event would reveal Jesus. It linked the glory of God with the work of Jesus. It began to show who Jesus was. For John the supreme moment of glorification is Jesus' death. (See page 281, water into wine)
- Jesus' delay did not cause the death of Lazarus. Lazarus must have died almost as soon as the messenger left Bethany with the news of his illness. The reason for the delay seems to be to make sure that there could be no misinterpretation of the miracle as one of resuscitation.
- Jesus shows emotion (verses 33–6). Some scholars, such as Carson and Tasker, translate this emotion in terms of indignation and outrage rather than grief or effects of empathy. Carson argues that it could be understood as Jesus being angry with sin, sickness and death in a fallen world that generates so much sorrow. Alternatively, it could be anger at unbelief, where people grieve because they have no hope. Another strong possibility is that what moved Jesus so deeply was the sense that something rather wonderful was about to happen. God was about to act overwhelmingly, in power and love, and to defeat death and reveal his glory. To see God at work in this way was to see God's glory.
- In Jesus' public prayer to raise Lazarus, he clearly refers to God as 'Father' and shows his total dependence and obedience to his Father's will.

5 Mary at the tomb of Jesus (20:1–18)

This story tells us many different things about this woman.

- Mary Magdalene was the first person to see the resurrected Jesus. This is significant, since a woman's evidence was not normally admissible in court, according to the Mishnah. Here a reversal of the world's values, as God chooses to reveal first to a woman the great event of the resurrection.
- Seeing the tombstone rolled away, she concludes that tomb robbers have raided the tomb.
- Mary returns to the tomb and weeps, showing that she still thinks that the tomb has been robbed.
- She becomes aware of someone near the tomb and assumes it is the gardener. Then suddenly she recognises Jesus, when he utters her name. Anguish and despair turn to astonishment and delight.
- Mary is the first to be told to spread the news.
- Jesus refers to God as 'my Father and your Father, my God and your God' (verse 17).

This story says several things about Jesus.

- The story makes clear that Jesus was not immediately recognised by Mary. This may reflect the state of Jesus' new resurrected body, or people's lack of expectation to see Jesus again.

● Mary now believes Jesus is alive but does not yet comprehend that he must ascend and leave. Hence, Jesus tells her not to hold on to him. This is in contrast to Jesus' encounter with Thomas, where he tells Thomas to touch him, since Thomas had doubted the reality of Jesus' resurrection.

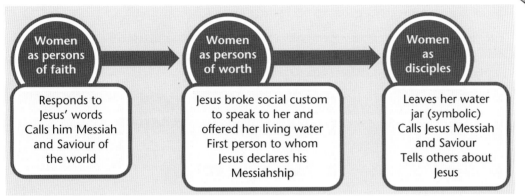

Summary diagram: The Samaritan woman

TASK

Study the summary diagram for the Samaritan woman. Now draw your own summary diagrams for:
● the woman caught in adultery
● Mary and Martha at the raising of Lazarus
● Mary at the tomb of Jesus.

6 The social status of women within Judaism

Judaism at the time of Jesus is always depicted as having a mainly negative view of women. Their social status was usually limited to the role of wife and mother and they were seen in purely domestic terms. Women were expected to be submissive, as they were seen as inferior. Philo, a first-century CE Jewish philosopher, regarded women and female traits as examples of weakness.

According to the rabbinic **Tosefta**, a Jewish man prayed three benedictions each day. One of these included thanking God that he was not made a woman. Women were not allowed to bear witness in a court of law. Men did not speak to women in public, for fear of seduction and corruption. In the story of the Samaritan woman (page 293), no mention is made of the man. This may be because the blame was clearly put on the woman alone. However, it may also be that the man had simply fled.

KEY WORD

Tosefta: literally, supplement; a supplement to the oral law in Judaism

7 The religious status of women within Judaism

In the Jerusalem Temple, women were limited to one outer court, which was five steps below the court for men. In the synagogues, the women were separated from the men and were not allowed to read aloud or take any leading part. A rabbi regarded it as beneath his dignity to speak to a woman in public.

Only boys and men were required to study the law; at age 12, a boy who attended rabbinic school graduated as bar-mitzvah. Girls were not allowed to attend the rabbinic schools.

Women were not counted and, in a meeting or an assembly, they could not be counted to form a quorum.

Reflection and assessment (AO1)

It is vital to bring together the information covered so far and recognise how it can be transformed into effective examination-style revision and answers. The best way to do this is to ask: 'How am I going to be assessed on this information?'

The first way is through assessment objective 1 (AO1). You need to be able to 'select and clearly demonstrate the relevant knowledge and understanding through the use of evidence, examples and correct language and terminology'.

Look back to pages 8–10 in the Introduction to review the level descriptors for AO1.

There is a description of the character and features for each level. The exam is marked with reference to levels.

Look at the following suggestions for a *basic* level answer, which is a level 1 response to this question.

> **Examine what the story of the Samaritan woman teaches about Jesus' attitude towards women.** (21 marks)

The *basic* answer might address the question by:

- stating the basic story
- giving a brief explanation that Jesus broke with custom by talking to the woman.

What makes this a level 1 answer? Now indicate how a developed answer (level 2–3) might answer the question, by adding two or three more bullet points.

Now go on to develop this answer to indicate how a *higher* answer (level 4) might address this question, by adding further bullet points. Remember to keep the bullet points focused on the question.

Suggestion for further application of skills

Create a plan for this question.

> **Examine what the story of the woman caught in adultery teaches about Jesus' attitude towards women.** (21 marks)

Then write up your answer, under timed conditions.

Working in a group, compare your answers. Photocopy the best answers and, still as a group, consider what makes the selected essays good.

Use this time of reflection to revisit your own work and improve it by redrafting it.

Alternatively, you may want to look at an essay that you have recently completed.

1 Underline in green what could have been omitted or was repeated.

2 Underline in blue key terms or technical words.

3 Underline in red any references back to the wording in the question.

4 Referring to the level descriptors, consider the reasons for the level awarded for your essay.

5 Use the level descriptors to identify how the essay could be improved.

EXAM TIP

Check for material that is irrelevant or material that is not explained. The answer should be organised in a sequential way so the reader follows a clear line of thought and development. This will demonstrate 'a coherent and well-structured account of the subject matter' (level 3 descriptor AO1).

TOPIC 2: KEY EMPHASES IN THE STUDY OF THE TEACHINGS OF JESUS CHRIST

Part 2B: The nature and demands of discipleship

> **This means I am expected:**
>
> **to know about the key issues:**
> - the nature and demands of discipleship
>
> **and to study:**
> - the meaning of 'discipleship'
> - the nature of discipleship
> - the demands of discipleship
> - the role of key people in the ministry of Jesus
> - the Holy Spirit.

In this book the evidence and examples given are relevant and appropriate because this material focuses only on the content for AO1 that is given by the Edexcel specification. The evaluation materials for AO2 will be aimed at helping you 'critically evaluate and justify a point of view through the use of evidence and reasoned argument'.

It would be helpful to write your notes using the headings listed above, as it is from these areas that the examination questions will be derived.

In your studies, remember that you have to bear in mind the **two** basic assessment objectives of:

- Knowledge and Understanding (AO1)
- Evaluation (AO2).

See pages 7–8 in the Introduction to remind yourself of these objectives.

The evaluation material set out in Part 2C (page 310) can be studied either alongside the AO1 material, as you work through this unit, or as a separate unit.

This part of the unit examines the teaching in John's Gospel about the nature and the demands of discipleship. The exam questions may specify one or more of the areas listed above. You should know the text sufficiently well to explain and illustrate the particular focus of the question. Indeed, the notes in this section assume you have the text in front of you, as they refer to verse numbers.

In addition, the specification also requires you to study the importance of John the Baptist, the Twelve and the Holy Spirit to the ministry of Jesus.

1 The meaning of 'discipleship'

The word 'disciple' conveys the idea of a follower or student of a great teacher. The New Testament refers to various groups of disciples. There are the disciples of Jesus, of which there was a core of twelve. Also mentioned are the disciples of the Pharisees (probably linked to a particular institution), the disciples of John the Baptist and the disciples of Moses (a self-designation by the Pharisees).

The word 'discipleship' highlights the nature of the master–disciple relationship. This section examines the features that mark out the disciple and what demands this relationship makes.

2 The nature of discipleship

The four aspects of discipleship

i) The need to follow

> *Then Nathanael declared, 'Rabbi, you are the Son of God; you are the King of Israel.'*
>
> (John 1:49)

The verb 'to follow', in the sense of following as a disciple, is used six times in John's Gospel (1:40, 43; 8:12; 12:26; 21:19, 22). It implies a decisive and continuing act of allegiance to Jesus. The first reference to Jesus inviting anyone to follow refers to Philip being called by Jesus ('Follow me…'). This act of allegiance seems to be triggered by a recognition of who Jesus is. Similarly, recognition of the true identity of Jesus results in Nathanael becoming a disciple (1:49). Indeed, in the sign of water into wine, it is when Jesus reveals his glory (2:11) that his disciples put their faith in him.

John presents the call to follow as a command by Jesus. In John 21, where the reinstatement of Peter is recounted, Jesus says to Peter: 'You must follow me,' (21:22). In choosing to follow, the disciple commits himself to certain demands (see page 302). It is not a neutral action. Discipleship caused such radical change that the external life of each disciple was seen to change.

ii) Witness

Another mark of the disciple is the natural desire to tell others. John comments: 'The first thing Andrew did was to find his brother Simon and tell him: 'We have found the Messiah,' (1:41). John then records that Andrew brought him to Jesus (verse 42). A similar reaction is shown by Philip who, after choosing to follow Jesus, immediately went and witnessed to Nathanael (verses 45–6).

The Samaritan woman told others of her meeting with Jesus the Messiah. The result was: 'Many of the Samaritans from that town believed in him because of the woman's testimony,' (4:39).

The commission to tell others occurs in Jesus' encounter with his disciples at his resurrection. He tells them: 'As the Father has sent me, I am sending you.'

iii) Have faith

Belief and faith are key themes in John's Gospel. John seems to indicate there are different qualities of belief. The scholar Raymond Brown has drawn attention to four different reactions to the signs, which illustrate this.

KEY IDEA

Aspects of discipleship:
- to follow
- to witness
- to have faith
- to love one another.

Someone reacting to the signs may:

- refuse to see the signs with any faith (11:47)
- see the signs as wonders and believe in Jesus as a wonder-worker sent by God (2:23–5; 4:45–8; 7:3–7)
- see the true significance of the signs and come to believe in Jesus and to know who he is (4:53; 6:69; 9:38; 11:40)
- believe in Jesus without seeing signs (20:29).

The first two types of reaction are seen as unsatisfactory and do not lead to a saving faith. The third type has several stages (2:11). Raymond Brown sees that the 'signs' lead to an unfolding Christology in which, if one appreciates the 'signposting', one can, through faith, grasp who Jesus is and so become a true disciple.

The fourth type of reaction suggests that, even in John's Gospel, there seems a desire for faith to be forthcoming without signs: 'Unless you see signs and wonders you will not believe,' (4:48), and later, when speaking to the previously doubting Thomas: 'blessed are those who have not seen and yet believe,' (20:29). However if it takes a sign to bring someone to belief, then so be it. It is the end product of believing, with its benefit of eternal life, that is important.

It is important to understand that John is not saying that faith is just believing that certain claims about Jesus are true. Faith, for John, clearly meant a personal trust in Jesus that led to a close relationship, as taught in the illustration of the vine (John 15).

Just as there is faith and true faith, so there are disciples and true disciples. John 6:60–6 illustrates this. John makes a distinction between the true disciples and disciples who join the group that follow Jesus from place to place, or regard him as an authoritative teacher. Being a true disciple is described as 'believing in his name' (1:12). To such, he gave the right to become children of God: children born not of natural descent, nor of human decision or a husband's will, but born of God (1:12–13).

True disciples are those who trust Jesus, are born again by the Spirit (3:4) and hold to Jesus' teaching (8:31). Such disciples, who believe and experience this new birth, will receive eternal life (3:16), are joined to Jesus as the branches are joined to the vine (John 15).

On one occasion, Jesus is asked: 'What must we do to do the works God requires?' Jesus answered: 'The work of God is this: to believe in the one he has sent,' (6:28–9).

The reaction to the first sign (2:11) suggests that the followers who were there changed, to become true disciples who recognised who Jesus was and put their faith in him.

iv) Love one another

One of the marks of a true disciple is love. In the Farewell discourse, Jesus begins to set out what he expects from his disciples, as he is soon to leave them:

> A new command I give you: Love one another. As I have loved you, so you must love one another. By this all men will know that you are my disciples, if you love one another.
>
> (John 13:34–5)

The old commandment demanded that people should love their neighbours as themselves. The new commandment demands more. It insists that we love everyone (the sphere of the love has widened); it requires us to love as Jesus loved (the incentive of the love has widened). Indeed, further on in the Farewell discourse, Jesus repeats the command:

TASK

Read John 6. Why were the disciples grumbling (see verses 14–15; 26; 30–1; 32f; 41–6; 61)? What does this reveal about a true disciple?

Objective: To develop understanding of the characteristics of a true disciple. This demonstrates the 'significant depth' required for a level 4 answer for AO1.

❝ KEY QUOTES

I tell you the truth, no one can see the Kingdom of God unless he is born again.

(John 3:4)

To the Jews who had believed him, Jesus said, 'If you hold to my teaching, you are really my disciples. Then you will know the truth and the truth will set you free.'

(John 8:31–2)

He thus revealed his glory, and his disciples put their trust in him.

(John 2:11)

❞

TASK

List the reasons why, according to John's Gospel, Jesus and his followers were persecuted.

Objective: To develop 'accurate, relevant and detailed knowledge' about persecution of disciples (level 4 descriptor AO1).

TASK

Find out how Peter died and whether the prediction was accurate.

Objective: To demonstrate 'knowledge of the subject matter at a wide range or in significant depth' (level 4 descriptor AO1).

My command is this: Love each other as I have loved you. Greater love has no one than this, that he lay down his life for his friends.

(15:12)

Here the degree of the self-sacrifice that such love demands is made clear. Our love (like that of Jesus) must be sacrificial. It must imitate the love that has been shown to us by the Father and the Son.

3 The demands of discipleship

a) Persecution

John's Gospel traces the growing persecution against Jesus as his ministry unfolds. Right at the start, John (in the Prologue) states that, though the world was made through Jesus, the world did not recognise him and his own did not receive him (1:10,11). As his ministry progressed, opposition grew. For instance, after the healing at the pool, John records that: 'the Jews persecuted him [Jesus],' (5:16). By the time of the raising of Lazarus from the dead, the persecution had become much more intense.

So from that day on they plotted to take his [Jesus'] life.

(11:53)

In the same way, Jesus' followers also suffered persecution. The Jews decided that anyone who acknowledged that Jesus was the Christ would be put out of the synagogue (9:22). The chief priests made plans to kill Lazarus, after Jesus had raised him from the dead (12:10).

Jesus makes it clear that to be a disciple will involve persecution: 'If they persecuted me, they will persecute you also,' (15:20). The reason, Jesus says, is: 'because of my name' (verse 21). The persecution of the disciples is not so much because of who they are but of who Jesus is.

The persecution is so severe that Jesus warns his disciples: 'the time is coming when anyone who kills you will think he is offering a service to God,' (16:2). The disciples were certainly aware of the danger of being associated with Jesus, as is shown by Thomas' remark to the other disciples when Jesus announces his desire to return to Judea. Thomas said to the rest of the disciples: 'Let us also go, that we may die with him,' (11:16).

A summary of what is meant by true discipleship appears in Jesus' conversation with Peter after the resurrection (21:18–19). In other words, persecution and even death were part and parcel of being a disciple.

b) The world's hatred

The cause of the persecution of both Jesus and his disciples was that 'Light has come into the world but men loved darkness instead of light because their deeds were evil. Everyone who does evil hates the light…' (3:19–20). Jesus makes clear that the created moral order has been corrupted and is in rebellion against God. When Jesus refers to 'the world', he is referring to this rebellion against God.

The deeds of humankind are evil and the world is a society of rebels. Therefore, those who expose these deeds, or swear allegiance to the rightful King, are not going to be tolerated and will be hated. The followers of Jesus should expect to be hated by the world (15:18–19). It is true that these same followers were themselves once members of this rebellious order. They have now been 'called out of the world' (15:19) and so should expect the same treatment that Jesus received. The world loves its own and hates those who are aliens: those who challenge the world and are in rebellion against God.

c) Temptation

My prayer is not that you take them out of the world but that you protect them from the evil one.

(John 17:15)

The word 'tempt' has two meanings. One is that of testing someone to demonstrate faithfulness. This is the usage in John 6:6 when Jesus asks Philip about feeding the crowd. The more common usage, though, refers to the idea of enticing someone into sin.

In the Farewell discourse, Jesus prayed that his disciples might be protected from the evil one. Jesus was warning them of the temptations of the world that they would face. The temptation is, at root, to turn away from the ways of God and follow the way of the world instead. Following Jesus was difficult and the disciples were often tempted to follow the way of the world.

Examples of such temptations can be found in the Gospel, for example:

● not to love one another
● not to trust Christ
● to rely on their own strength
● not to want to be servants.

In particular, Peter's denial of Jesus (John 18) showed Peter's fear and his lack of trust.

4 The role of key people in the ministry of Jesus

a) John the Baptist

In John's Gospel, John the Baptist has two main roles.

i) A Witness to Jesus

In the first chapter, the writer makes clear that John was sent by God to witness about Jesus (1:6–7) and that John the Baptist is subordinate to Jesus. It is Jesus who is the light, not John the Baptist. John's subordination is made even clearer when he says of Jesus: 'This was he of whom I said, "He who comes after me has surpassed me because he was before me.",' (1:15). The Baptist hints that not only was Jesus pre-existent (verses 1–2), but that his importance was far above that of the Baptist himself. He makes clear Jesus' superiority by claiming that he will not be worthy even to untie his sandals (verse 27). Many commentators note that John the Baptist's denial that he was the Christ was a positive witness to Jesus as the true Christ (verse 20).

John the Baptist points to Jesus as 'The Lamb of God who takes away the sin of the world' (verses 29, 36). He also claimed that God ordained him to baptise so 'that he [the Coming One] might be revealed to Israel,' (verse 31). John recognised Jesus by the dove at his baptism (verses 31–3). Hence he could say, with confidence: 'this is the Son of God,' (verse 34). Whereas John baptised with water, the 'coming one' would baptise with the Holy Spirit.

> **KEY QUOTE**
> *He asked this only to test him, for he already had in mind what he was going to do.*
> **(John 6:6)**

> **TASK**
> **Find examples in John's Gospel to illustrate the temptations that the disciples faced.**
> Objective: To develop 'accurate, relevant and detailed knowledge' (level 4 descriptor AO1).

> **KEY QUOTE**
> *He [John the Baptist] did not fail to confess, but confessed freely, 'I am not the Christ.'*
> **(John 1:20)**

Through John the Baptist's witness to Jesus, two of his own disciples followed Jesus (verse 37).

There are two further references (chapter 5 and chapter 10) to the testimony of John the Baptist. Jesus says that John the Baptist's witness may help people to believe. Indeed, that was its purpose. Jesus describes him as 'a lamp that burned and gave light' (5:35). He prepared the people for the Messiah, but now the time had come for the Father to be the witness to the Son.

John the Baptist's faithfulness to his mission bore fruit. The people believed in Jesus because they recognised in him all that John the Baptist had said about this Jesus (10:40–2).

The writer of the Gospel places the witness of John the Baptist at both the beginning and the end of Jesus' public ministry.

KEY IDEA

Lamb of God:

In Christian tradition, the idea of Jesus as the Lamb of God is usually linked to ideas of Jesus as the sacrificial lamb who was slaughtered in place of us (Revelation 5:9). As a result, many scholars question whether John the Baptist would ever have said this. The historical reliability of the account is then challenged. This view is strengthened by the fact that John the Baptist did not seem to view Jesus as a suffering Messiah (see Matthew 11:2–6).

Some have suggested that the imagery of the word 'lamb' refers to the warrior lamb of some Jewish texts and that the taking away of the sins of the world may have been about judgement and destruction (see Luke 3:15–17). Alternatively, it may be more natural to link this carrying away of sins with some Old Testament sacrifices for sins. For example, Leviticus 4:32–5 refers to a lamb being used as a sin offering. When the priest burns it: 'he will make atonement for him for the sin he has committed, and he will be forgiven,' (verse 35).

ii) Preparer for Jesus

He [Jesus] must become greater; I [John the Baptist] must become less.

(John 3:30)

The role of John the Baptist is to point people to Jesus. John the Baptist draws attention to the prophecy from Isaiah 40:3 that Jesus fulfils (verse 23). John is not the Messiah but he is the one that Isaiah predicted, the one who is to prepare for the coming of the Messiah.

In John 3, John the Baptist's followers raise questions about the growing popularity of Jesus. However, the Baptist uses the occasion to state his subordination to Jesus, pointing out that his own task was to be sent ahead of Jesus (verse 28). He then uses an analogy of a wedding, where the friend who attends the bridegroom gets his greatest joy from watching the ceremony. In other words, the Baptist knew that his God-given mission to prepare for the Messiah was successful. Jesus was supreme (verse 30).

b) The Twelve

i) The term

There seems to be a difference between being a disciple of Jesus and being one of the Twelve. There are disciples outside of the Twelve. For example, Joseph of Arimathea is referred to as a disciple (19:38) but was clearly not one of the Twelve. The inner group of twelve were chosen disciples rather than volunteers. They were co-workers who travelled with Jesus, and had left all to follow him. They were also to become key leaders within the Church.

There seems to be a connection between the number twelve and the twelve tribes of Israel. If this is correct, then it would suggest that Jesus was establishing the true Israel, the people of God. The twelve are not listed in John, though the other three Gospels do list them. In those lists, commentators point out that they seem to be in three groups of four with the same person at the start of each group of four (Simon Peter, Philip, James, son of Alphaeus). From this, it has been argued that each group of four had a leader. Only seven of the twelve are mentioned by name. Those not specifically mentioned are: James and John, the sons of Zebedee (see below for identifying John as the beloved disciple); Bartholomew (see below for identifying Nathanael with Bartholomew); Matthew; James, son of Alphaeus.

ii) The individual people

● Simon Peter

Simon, later called Peter, was a Galilean fisherman who worked with his father and Andrew, his brother. It was Andrew who led Simon Peter to meet Jesus (1:41). Jesus gives Simon a new name, Peter (meaning 'rock'), as a declaration of what Jesus would make him. Until then his name was Simon, son of John (21:16).

Peter's name occurs first in all the lists of the Twelve, which suggests that he was the overall leader. He often acts as spokesmen for the Twelve (6:68). He is portrayed as an impulsive character. For instance, he does not understand Jesus' washing of the disciples' feet (13:6–11) and states that Jesus will never wash his feet. Later, he confidently states that he would lay down his life for Jesus (13:37). Finally, it is Peter who impulsively reacts when Jesus is arrested, and strikes the high priest's servant with a sword (18:10). Despite Peter's denial of Jesus, it is Peter who is the first of the Twelve to enter the empty tomb, though he still did not understand the meaning of the events (20:3f).

At the end of John's Gospel is an account of Peter's reinstatement. Its public nature, where the other disciples were present, is seen as significant. After Peter's denial of Jesus it was important that he received Jesus' forgiveness and that the other disciples were a witness to his reinstatement. Without this event, Peter's return to service might have been questioned by the other disciples.

● Andrew

Andrew was the first disciple (1:40) and witnessed to Simon Peter, his brother. He appears in two other passages in John's Gospel. Firstly, he is named as the person who brings to Jesus the boy with the loaves and fish (6:8). The second incident was when, together with Philip, he brought the inquisitive Greeks to Jesus (12:22).

Andrew is mentioned as being 'tested' by Jesus when the crowd comes to Jesus for food (6:5–7). However, Andrew thinks only in earthly terms, still not having a full understanding of who Jesus is. This lack of spiritual insight is reflected again in discussion about knowing the Father (14:7–9).

● The Beloved disciple

John's Gospel alone makes reference to a disciple 'whom Jesus loved'. He is mentioned five times and it is possible that 1:40, 18:15 and 19:35 also refer to him.

> **→ EXAM TIP**
>
> Do not use a Bible quotation just to repeat what you have just written. You need either to allude to the quotation or to use it to draw out some further comment. This demonstrates 'relevant knowledge…using evidence to explain key ideas' (level 4 descriptor AO1).

> **❝ KEY QUOTE**
>
> *…in John 1, the focus is much less on what this name change means for Peter, than on the Jesus who knows people thoroughly…but so calls them that he makes them what he calls them to be.*
>
> **(Carson)** ❞

TASK

Look up the following verses in John's Gospel: 13:23; 19:26–7; 20:2; 21: 7; 20; 21:4. Then draw up a table. In one column write bullet points to support identifying the Beloved disciple with John, son of Zebedee. In the other column give bullet points against such a view.

Objective: To develop evidence that supports a point of view. This demonstrates 'using well-chosen evidence to support understanding of key ideas and concepts' (level 4 descriptor AO1).

Various identities have been suggested. The one with the strongest internal and external evidence is John, the son of Zebedee, whose brother (James) was also one of the Twelve. The Beloved disciple is also identified with the writer of the Gospel (21:24).

Alternative identifications for the Beloved disciple have included Lazarus, John Mark and a symbolic figure rather than a real person.

● Philip

Philip seems to have been a disciple of John the Baptist, before becoming a follower of Jesus (1:40). He recognised Jesus as the one about whom Moses wrote, in the Law, and to whom the prophets referred. This implies he had an understanding of Old Testament expectations about the Messiah. Showing the typical characteristic of a disciple, he was eager to bring others to Jesus, so that they too might become followers (1:46; 12:21–2).

● Bartholomew

Most commentators identify Bartholomew with Nathanael.

● Thomas

He is often known as 'doubting Thomas' because of his disbelief that Jesus had been resurrected from the dead. However, he concluded that Jesus is 'Lord and God'.

Earlier in John's Gospel, Thomas is depicted as pessimistic but loyal when he regards the journey to Judea as one that will probably result in death (11:16).

● Judas, son of James

He only has one mention in John's Gospel (14:22).

● Judas Iscariot

John tells us that Judas was the treasurer for the Twelve. However, it seems that Judas had become a thief and had taken money from the treasury funds (12:6).

Jesus knew that Judas would betray him; the text comments that when Judas took the bread at the Last Supper, Satan entered into him (13:27). Later that night, Judas led a band of soldiers to where Jesus was alone with his disciples in the garden of Gethsemane. He then kissed Jesus to identify him for the soldiers.

TASK

***The last supper**, painted by Leonardo Da Vinci, specifically portrays the reaction of each apostle when Jesus said that one of them would betray him. Carry out some research about the various characters, symbols and speculations about the painting, as well as its history.*

Objective: To understand interpretations of the relationship between the Twelve and Jesus. This demonstrates 'using evidence to show general understanding of the key ideas' (level 4 descriptor AO1).

The Last Supper (da Vinci, 1495–8)

5 The Holy Spirit

a) Terminology

There are two different Greek words used in John's Gospel to refer to the Holy Spirit:

- *pneuma*
- *paraclete*.

Pneuma is a neuter word, rather than masculine or feminine, implying a thing. Therefore, it should be referred to as 'it' rather than 'he'. This may suggest that the Spirit is impersonal. In contrast, *paraclete* is a masculine word, which seems to convey the idea that the Spirit is a person. The word *paraclete* only occurs four times in John's Gospel and these are in the Farewell discourse.

KEY WORD

Paraclete: Paraclete is really a transliteration of the Greek. Rather than translate the word into English, many decided that, because no one knew what the English equivalent was, it was better to leave it in the Greek. The Greek alphabet is different from that used in English. It has different symbols, so we just use the English equivalent symbols.

π	α	ρ	α	κ	λ	η	τ	oζ
↕	↕	↕	↕	↕	↕	↕	↕	↕
p	a	r	a	c	l	e	t	e

The root meaning is 'one who has been called to the side of another' and many see it as having a legal background in the sense of an advocate, or friend at court, or one who is called to speak in our defence.

This legal meaning fits in with John's overall setting of a trial, so perhaps this is a good translation: a legal counsellor, an advocate.

However, the functions attributed to the *paraclete* in John's Gospel are primarily teaching, revealing and interpreting Jesus to the disciples. As a result, other meanings have been sought, which include this non-legal aspect.

Another root meaning is 'to encourage'.

In 16th- and 17th-century English, 'comforter' could mean someone who strengthens or encourages. The King James Version translates *paraclete* as comforter. The RSV and NIV use counsellor, which again has a legal sense to it.

Other suggestions that go back to the legal courtroom background include the aspect of intercessor, one who stands before judges and intercedes.

b) The Holy Spirit and discipleship

i) The New Birth

In his discussion with Nicodemus, Jesus insisted that, in order to enter the Kingdom of God, we need to be born not only a first time, in a natural physical way, but a second time, of the Spirit. He went on to link this spiritual birth with personal faith in him (3:16–18). This second birth was linked to someone becoming a believer and a disciple of Jesus.

Later on, Jesus promised his disciples that 'whoever believes in me, streams of living water will flow from within him.' John comments that 'by this he meant the Spirit, whom those who believed in him were later to receive,' (7:37–9).

> ### KEY QUOTE
>
> *Jesus answered, 'I tell you the truth, no one can enter the Kingdom of God unless he is born of water and the Spirit. Flesh gives birth to flesh, but the Spirit gives birth to spirit...'*
>
> (John 3:5)

ii) The presence of Jesus

The disciples were promised that the Holy Spirit, who lives *with* them, from now on would live *in* them (14:17). Jesus made it clear that, because the Holy Spirit was living in them, he and his Father would be making their home with the disciples. Jesus was saying that he was leaving them physically but he would remain with them spiritually, and was in them through the Holy Spirit. This would mean that they were not left as orphans but, through his presence, would be left with the peace of Christ, which would overcome their fears (14:27).

It would also mean that this presence allowed the disciples to bear much fruit (15:4–5).

iii) The Spirit of Truth

The Holy Spirit is the person who teaches the disciples the truth of God and brings to their mind the things that Jesus had already taught them (14:26). The Holy Spirit doesn't just stop them forgetting, it enables them to understand what Jesus had said. Jesus' teaching and words bring life. The Spirit will bring followers to a clearer appreciation of Jesus' nature and message. The Spirit will guide them into all truth (16:13).

He will also reveal to them what is yet to come (16:13). Some see in this reference to 'tell you what is to come' an allusion to the Spirit revealing to the disciples the prophetic events at the end of time (such as the book of Revelation). Other scholars prefer to limit this to events that were in the short-term future of the disciples, and put the emphasis on revealing the relevance of, for example, Jesus' death.

iv) The Spirit and the mission of the disciples

Because the Spirit testifies about Jesus, the disciples are commanded that they, too, must testify about Jesus, for they have been with him from the beginning (15:26–7). The Holy Spirit assists the disciples in their mission to the world by convicting the world of sin, righteousness and judgement (16:8–11).

- The Holy Spirit will come to convict the world of guilt, to carry on the lawsuit with the world. The disciples will preach the truth of Jesus but their words, empowered by the Spirit, will have convicting powers. It will convict the world of sin, or unbelief in Jesus. He will convict people that Jesus was indeed the Holy One of God. This is designed to bring people of the world to recognise their need and so turn to Jesus and escape judgement.
- He will convict the world of righteousness. This phrase sounds odd. Possibly it means that the world's verdict about Jesus is wrong. Jesus was the righteous one, as shown by his resurrection and exaltation to the right hand of God. Alternatively, it could mean that the life of the believer and the way of Jesus combine to convict the world of its empty righteousness.
- Finally he will convict the world of judgement, in that the death of Jesus meant the defeat of the prince of evil. God is not ignoring evil but there will be a day of judgement, both for the prince of this world and also for the world itself!

Jesus links up his statement that the disciples are to take part in his mission with the gift of the Holy Sprit. The Holy Spirit enables them to assure people of the forgiveness of sins. Their mission is to preach the forgiveness of sins (20:21–3). Now that Jesus is going, the believers are to take on his message of salvation.

KEY IDEA

The meaning of the word 'convict' (16:8–11):
There has been much discussion about the meaning of the word 'convict' as used in John 16:8–11. In classical Greek the word can have the meaning of 'putting to shame'. Its usage in other parts of the New Testament has the idea of showing someone their sin, usually as a way to bring them to repentance. Hence, Carson argues that the verses mean that the paraclete will shame the world and convince it of its own guilt, thus calling it to repentance. The world is guilty of its sin, of its false and empty righteousness, and of its false judgement.

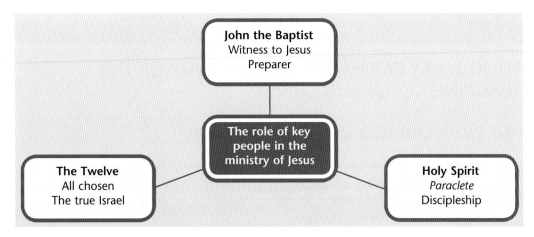

Summary diagram: The role of key people in the ministry of Jesus

Reflection and assessment (AO1)

It is vital to bring together the information covered so far and recognise how it can be transformed into effective examination-style revision and answers. The best way to do this is to ask: 'How am I going to be assessed on this information?'

The first way is through assessment objective 1 (AO1). You need to be able to 'select and clearly demonstrate the relevant knowledge and understanding through the use of evidence, examples and correct language and terminology'.

Look back to pages 8–10 in the Introduction to review the level descriptors for AO1.

Use what you have so far learned about levels of response, writing frames and essay plans to do this task.

1 Split into small groups

2 Within the group, list bullet points to create a five level response in answer to this question.

   Examine the role played by the Holy Spirit in the ministry of Jesus. (21 marks)

3 Then each person in the group should take one set of bullet points and use it to write up a paragraph.

4 Put the paragraphs together as an answer and swap with another group.

5 The receiving group comments on the work and returns it to the original group.

6 Review the comments and use them to improve the answer.

Suggestion for further application of skills

In your revision sessions, use this approach as a basis for revisiting the other topics. This does not apply to a specific focus on questions but is a way to create some good-quality summaries that demonstrate the skills relevant to AO1.

TOPIC 2: KEY EMPHASES IN THE STUDY OF THE TEACHINGS OF JESUS CHRIST

Part 2C: A critical analysis of the issues

> **This means that I am expected:**
>
> **to analyse and critically analyse:**
> - the status of women in Judaism
> - Jesus' attitude to women
> - the meaning of discipleship.

1 Is the negative portrayal of the status of women in Judaism in Jesus' time accurate?

KEY QUOTE

Her children arise and call her blessed; her husband also, and he praises her...

(Proverbs 31:28)

TASK

Find out what the New Testament says about the following women. Dorcus; Mary, the mother of Mark; Lydia; Priscilla; Phoebe; Lois and Eunice. What do these accounts suggest about the status of women?

Objective: To set out reasons for a range of views (level 3 descriptor AO2).

It was argued in Part 2A (page 297) that the male view of women was generally negative and the woman's place was seen to be in the home, secluded and serving the needs of the man. However, a number of scholars now argue that it is wrong to think that in Palestine in the time of Jesus women were regarded as second-class citizens and were not respected. Scholars such as Alfred Edersheim note that women take a significant role in the Jewish Scriptures. For instance, the rabbis referred to Sarah, Rebekah, Leah and Rachel as 'the four mothers' because of the important parts they played in patriarchal history. Likewise, the Jewish scriptures contain the Book of Ruth and the Book of Esther, and the relationship of the Jews and God is constantly compared to that of a marriage. There are positive statements about women in the Proverbs. For instance in Proverbs 31 there is an Epilogue to 'The Wife of Noble Character' (31:10–31).

There is also evidence that some women held the office of ruler or president of a synagogue. Inscriptions have been found with these titles used of women. Further evidence for a more positive view of the religious status of women is found in the *Testament of Job*, in which Job's three daughters speak the language of angels.

2 Jesus' attitude

KEY QUOTE

As for his [Jesus'] own estimation of women, is it not proven, in that before he left heaven, he chose Mary to be his mother, and after his victory over death elected another Mary to be the first herald of his resurrection?

(Bishop Gore)

Certainly, the New Testament shows that women were not seen as inferior. In Luke 1:48, Mary says '...for he [God] has been mindful of the humble state of his servant.

From now on all generations will call me blessed, for the Mighty One has done great things for me…' The stories discussed in Part 2A show that:

- Jesus spoke to women in public
- Jesus welcomed women to listen to his teaching
- Jesus showed compassion to women
- Jesus allowed women to minister to his needs
- Jesus included women amongst his followers (disciples)
- Jesus revealed his messiahship to a woman first
- Jesus revealed his resurrection to a woman first
- Jesus regarded women as persons of worth
- Jesus included women as examples of people of faith
- Jesus included women as proclaimers of the Gospel
- Jesus included women as witnesses and proclaimers of the resurrection
- Jesus showed acceptance, love, value and appreciation of women. Their encounters with Jesus left them with their dignity restored.

3 Possible conclusions

When assessing the issues that arise in determining the significance of Jesus' approach to women, it is important to reflect upon the arguments above and arrive at some appropriate conclusion.

It may be that you accept none of those listed below, or just one of them, or you may have a different conclusion that is not listed. What is important is the way to which you have arrived at your conclusion – the reasoning process.

From the preceding discussions, here are some possible conclusions you could draw.

1 Jesus had a positive view of women and Judaism had a negative view of women. Christianity offered a revolutionary change of view.

2 Jesus had a positive view of women but so did Judaism. Christianity offered no great revolutionary change.

3 It is not known for certain what view was taken of women within Judaism at the time of Jesus.

4 Who does the term 'disciple' include?

The term 'disciple' has a wide use in John's Gospel. The phrase is used of:

- one of the Twelve
- a wider group than the Twelve who were around Jesus in Jerusalem, for example, those who went to the tomb
- the large number who believed, such as Nicodemus, but did not travel around with Jesus
- those who left him, in John 6.

Do all disciples have to exhibit all those things listed in Part 2B?

- Does discipleship demand understanding or complete realisation of who Jesus was? (Often they were confused.)
- Does discipleship require meeting the demands to love one another? (They argued.)

> **EXAM TIP**
>
> Critical evaluation means reasoning and responding to a point of view, rather than just stating a view. Opinions that are unjustified do not qualify as evaluation. They are merely an expression of a personal view. This 'careful analysis of alternative views' is required for the highest level evaluation (level 4 descriptor AO2).

● Does discipleship require willingness to witness? (They ran away.)
● Does discipleship require putting faith in Jesus? (Thomas doubted and Judas betrayed Jesus.)

Negative view
Expected to be submissive
Seen as inferior to men
Jewish prayer included thanks for not being a woman
Not allowed to bear witness in court of law
Men did not speak to women in public
Not allowed to attend rabbinic schools
Limited to certain areas in Temple

Positive view
Significant role in Jewish Scriptures
Book of Ruth, Book of Esther
Relationship of Jews and God is compared to a marriage
Proverbs positive about women
Women may have held office of president of a synagogue
Job's three daughters said to speak language of angels

Summary diagram: Judaism's view of women

Reflection and assessment (AO2)

It is vital to bring together the information that has been covered so far and recognise how it can be transformed into effective examination-style revision and answers. The best way to do this is to ask: 'How am I going to be assessed on this information?'

Look back to page 10 in the Introduction, to review the level descriptors for AO2. There is a description of the character and features for each level. The exam is marked with reference to levels.

Look at the following notes for a sample basic level 1 answer, a response to this question.

> **To what extent did Jesus show a new approach in his attitude towards women compared with that of the Judaism of his time?** (9 marks)

A basic answer might address the question by:

● stating an example of Jesus' attitude towards women
● drawing a simple conclusion that this was either similar to or different from Judaism's attitude.

Suggestion for further application of skills

Now try this technique of building a level 4 answer for this question.

> **Comment on the view that both Jesus and Judaism had a negative view of women.** (9 marks)

TASK

Look at the notes for a basic answer, opposite. Try to work out how a developed answer (level 2–3) would address the question, by adding two or three more bullet points. Now develop this answer to indicate how a higher answer (level 4) might address the question, by adding further bullet points. Remember to keep the points focused on the question.

Objective: To develop awareness of what will constitute a very good answer, by gradually building up a response that 'clearly expresses viewpoints supported by well-deployed evidence...and a careful analysis of alternative views' (level 4 descriptor AO2).

UNIT 2 INVESTIGATIONS
Introduction

WHAT IS INCLUDED IN THE INVESTIGATIONS UNIT?

> **What this unit is *not* about**
>
> **This unit does *not* lead to a piece of coursework (although presentation skills are a way forward in assimilating the relevant information and practising the skills developed).**
>
> **The end product should not be a lengthy thesis.**

This Investigations unit is intended to encourage students in more independent study of particular areas of the course. There are many ways in which teachers and students may approach this. Here are some ideas.

An investigation could take the following structure.

- An area is introduced and a brief overview is given of the nature of the content of that area. Although the Edexcel specification does not require a study of the whole of an area, some idea of the context from which to select a focus could be useful.
- The student agrees with the teacher on a focus for further study, based upon the student's personal interest in a particular aspect or focus of this area.
- The student researches this through a guided study of this focus.
- The focus of study is then prepared for the examination.
- The focus is used in the examination as evidence for answering the question set.

> **What this unit does require**
>
> **The *focus* for study *does* need to be researched like a piece of coursework.**
>
> **The end product *does* need to be used in a compact, timed situation, as in the examination, in which the student will have only 75 minutes to deliver their research in response to a general question on the whole topic.**

How should investigations be approached?

In order to keep closely to the aims of the Investigations unit as a whole, we have presented a format for each **area** selected in this book. This is presented, together with a step-by-step guide that constantly refers the student back to what is to be attained, through reflection on the assessment objectives and level descriptors for the marks awarded for this Investigations unit. This leads to a refined and specific analysis as preparation for the examination.

We suggest that you use the information and guidance in this book as follows.

Note: Each area is presented with separate AO1 and AO2 elements. This serves to support the student to make a clear identification of skills and assessment objectives. The area itself can be studied piece-by-piece, maintaining an inter-relationship between the content, or progressively, one assessment objective after the other. This will be a matter of choice for both the teacher and the individual student. Likewise, for research tasks, it is important to have an overview of the whole task elements (AO1 and AO2) before starting research.

1 As a group, briefly work through the overview of the **area for study** (as recommended above).

2 In agreement with the teacher, decide upon a **focus**.

3 Work through the tasks and guidance set out in the sections that follow the general introduction to the area.

4 When completing the examination preparation section, re-group and share ideas for delivering your focus for the area studied.

The course that you are studying specifies that the key to this unit is in developing the ability to become more independent in your studies. You will achieve this through selecting an area of study in which you are interested and doing some personalised study.

Here is what the specification states

Aims

This unit provides for a balance of both teacher-directed and more independent student enquiry. It offers a choice between these methods of teaching and learning by giving students the opportunity to undertake individual research into a topic in which they are particularly interested. This will enable students to study independently and to use, and evaluate, a wide range of source material.

This specification seeks to:

- involve students as active participants
- provide possibilities for open-ended enquiry and independent learning
- identify questions, issues and problems as a starting point for enquiry
- present opportunities for enquiries, using a wide range of source material
- provide scope for an effective balance of teacher-directed and more independent student enquiry
- present opportunities for the development of a wide range of skills and abilities.

This unit facilitates a range of teaching styles. Teachers should ensure that students are:

- studying a topic suitable to their needs and interests
- fulfilling the assessment aims and objectives
- selecting and using relevant and appropriate source material
- receiving appropriate guidance and advice
- able to construct useful essay plans
- planning and structuring their work so as to structure their evidence in a coherent and logical manner
- being encouraged to develop their own ideas and views
- exploring and using a wide range of scholarly material
- able to sustain a critical line of argument and justify a point of view
- able to critically evaluate arguments
- aware of a range of viewpoints
- able to choose an appropriate and coherent structure for their answer
- able to formulate and discuss an evaluative conclusion which reflects the development of their thinking over a period of time, using religious and technical language appropriately.

SUMMARY OF PURPOSE AND AIMS FOR THE INVESTIGATIONS UNIT

The course that you are studying specifies that the key to this unit is in developing the ability to:

1 study and research on your own
2 be disciplined in terms of time management
3 plan carefully
4 listen and act upon advice
5 take the initiative with your own learning
6 claim ownership of a particular area of interest for study
7 structure your notes and express yourself coherently
8 raise questions about and identify problems in the material you study
9 develop your own ideas and views
10 arrive at an overall conclusion.

How will this book help?

As suggested above, one approach to Investigations (although not required by the specification) could be to have a brief overview available of all aspects of the area studied from which students can make an informed selection of focus. This section will then serve as a springboard for further study, or, as the specification states, a 'starting point'.

Indeed, candidates do select and begin work at a very early stage and so any overview should be completed quickly and serve the purpose only of giving a taster or 'flavour' of the context for study. This can even be read beyond allocated lesson time and used as a tool for arriving at a focus for study during a planning period.

The information covers most areas outlined in the guidance notes although, for practical reasons, not all aspects can always be covered. This book provides a context to some of these areas and within this information some of the specific details may be useful to candidates. However, the overview may stimulate the study of some focus beyond the immediate content of this book and this is perfectly reasonable and within the parameters of the specification.

It is important to remember that the value of this book for investigations is not necessarily found in the immediate content in the overview, but rather in the process of study and reflection it encourages through use of the tips and techniques suggested.

As you work through a topic you will be given assistance through suggested tasks, key words, key ideas and key quotes from different sources. You may wish to use these as a basis for your research.

In addition, there will be gentle reminders throughout to place all your work firmly within the reference frame of the assessment objectives (AO1 and AO2) and the corresponding descriptors found in the levels of response. This information is found in the *Specification sample assessment materials* document published by the examination board but, for your convenience, we include a copy in this book on pages 9–10. This will be a vital point of reference.

Final focus: the examination

At the end of each section is an Assessment and reflection section that will serve two purposes.

1 First, it will provide a basis, a structure for your work.

2 Second, and more important, it will remind you towards the end of your research of the final focus and execution of your work – preparation for the examination.

Study skills for investigations

This unit is very different from the Foundations unit. If offers much more freedom in selecting areas in which to pursue research. However, freedom, while liberating and recognising individuality, brings with it different demands:

- responsibility and ownership of your own study
- accountability for yourself to your teacher
- independence and demand for initiative in study
- discipline to plan well and maintain work ethic.

Do not:

- take lessons off
- waste time procrastinating and drawing and colouring lovely plans
- promise that you'll work later at home because you'll get more done
- rely upon your teacher to produce work and notes for you
- rely upon one book or source.

Do:

- use your time effectively
- plan effectively
- use school time effectively
- make use of your teacher – ask for advice when unsure
- use a variety of resources
- look at the tips in the margin to help you with ideas.

Assessment for learning through investigations

In many ways, this final section is the most important. Your research and hard work will be all for nothing unless it meets the assessment criteria as outlined by the examination board.

The aim of this section is to provide you with tasks that will effectively meet the assessment criteria while simultaneously encouraging you to aim for the highest levels of achievement in your work by using level 5 as a standard, contrasted with lower levels of achievement.

The principle of assessment for learning simply means that as you work through the tasks and assess your work and reflect upon it, this will inevitably inform your learning and improve your skills as you study.

RESEARCH TIPS CHECKLIST

Try some of the following.

1 Devise a clear plan of action – a diary, work book for your notes.

2 Do some preparatory reading from a variety of resources.

3 Write comprehensive notes.

4 Collect some varied, relevant and interesting quotes.

5 Find a 'buddy' or 'study partner' to talk to, bounce ideas off and with whom you can check progress.

6 Get a copy of the assessment objectives and levels of response to refer to.

This, then, is a section that will keep you focused in your research while simultaneously preparing for a timed examination.

These tasks will help give you structure and focus to your study. More important, it is vital preparation for the examination.

Assessment and reflection

AO1 A time for further investigation – some research tasks

a) Introduction

By now you will have selected your area for research in relation to 'your chosen area of study'.

The examination board states that your study should reflect an 'open-ended enquiry and independent learning'.

This section is a guided focus for your investigation. The tasks are to follow a pattern that is generic and skills based, relating directly to:

- the aims of investigations, as outlined by the Specification
- the assessment objectives AO1 and AO2 (see pages 7–10)
- the levels of response descriptors with particular attention to the highest levels for success (see pages 9–10).

b) AO1 research tasks

1 What to use
Make a checklist for the wide range of resources that you will use, including:

- specific books with a clear focus on your topic (at least three)
- general books for reference that have some focus (for example, a chapter) on your topic (at least five, for example, dictionary, general introductions, concordance)
- exploration of websites, triggered by a specific search on your topic
- any other media resources such as journals, newspapers, film, DVD, art
- any specific interest groups that are dedicated to the promotion or awareness of your topic.

This enables you to meet the level 5 AO1 criteria of the specification:

Presentation of a wide range of selected, relevant factual knowledge and understanding of the topic investigated; present opportunities for enquiries using a wide range of source material.

2 Terms to understand
It is important that, as you do your research, you extract, define and explore the meanings of the specific terminology associated with your selected focus. This might require you to compile a glossary of key words and/or a table that highlights questions and issues of interpretation and understanding.

This enables you to meet the level 5 AO1 criteria of the specification:

the proficient use of religious language, widely and skilfully deployed

(refer to mid and high level 5 descriptors AO1).

3 Selecting and organising the material

The level 5 AO1 descriptor expects you to:

- offer some analysis of issues raised by the topic
- use a variety of resources and examples
- select material to demonstrate emphasis and clarity of ideas
- carry out careful analysis of key concepts.

One way of meeting this criteria could be:

- Look back to the overview of your topic and the accompanying summary diagram. Use the focus that you have chosen and, from this, create your own spider diagram or flowchart that highlights and identifies the areas to explore in your enquiry. This will serve as a basis for your headings and sub-headings.
- Systematically work through your resources and gather the relevant information for each appropriate heading or sub-heading. There are different ways to do this; for example, using a notebook or word-processor, drawing a table, compiling a comprehensive list or using a series of diagrams.
- Make sure that you collect quotations and references to use as evidence, examples and/or illustrations.

4 Presenting the main themes of your focus (drafting notes into a coherent structure)

In reference to the AO1 level descriptors for Investigations, it is clear that the lower levels are awarded for 'a largely simplistic and unstructured framework' and 'lacking clarity and focus' (level 1).

Level 2 indicates that a piece of work has 'a limited framework' or only 'partial awareness of the issue' and makes only 'general links to the task'.

If you are to achieve a higher level, then the research will need to contain an 'explanation of key ideas/concepts supported by evidence and examples' (higher level 4). In addition, it will need to be 'a well structured response to the task in breadth or depth.'

In order to achieve the higher level you should:

- draft your notes into a coherent structure
- order your notes appropriately
- read, edit and redraft your notes
- have another person read through your notes to provide constructive criticism
- arrange to deliver a class presentation of your research, using a clear structure for delivery
- use an evaluation sheet to gather suggestions for improvements.

Assessment and reflection

AO2 A time for further investigation – some research tasks

a) Introduction

By now you will have selected your area for research in relation to your chosen focus.

The examination board states that your study should reflect an 'open-ended enquiry and independent learning'.

RESEARCH ADVICE

The specification states that for the focus on your topic you will need to 'identify questions, issues and problems as a starting point for enquiry'. Make sure that by this stage you have:

1 selected and agreed your focus with your teacher
2 clearly identified the key questions, issues and problems to do with the focus you have selected
3 clearly defined the starting point for your enquiry, for example, a question or a hypothesis you wish to test
4 a wide range of source material available.

This section is a guided focus for your investigation. The tasks are to follow a pattern that is generic and skills-based, relating directly to:

- the aims of investigations as outlined by the specification
- the assessment objectives AO1 and AO2 (see pages 7–10)
- the levels of response descriptors with particular attention to the highest levels for success (see pages 7–10).

b) AO2 research tasks

The skill of evaluation is awarded a range of marks that extends through four levels. The evaluation and reasoned argument become gradually more sophisticated, focusing more on the critical issues, as you progress to the higher levels.

Level	Descriptor	Meaning
1	'mainly descriptive response' and 'reference to a simple argument'	You are describing and stating in simple terms one argument.
2	'some attempt to set out alternative views' and 'supported by limited but appropriate evidence'	You are recognising different views but these are not fully developed or evidenced.
3	'some attempt to set out reasons for a range of views' and 'a point of view… supported by relevant evidence'	You are explaining and justifying the reasons for an argument, using evidence.
4	'a careful analysis of alternative views' and 'clearly expressed viewpoint supported by well-deployed evidence'	You are developing each line of argument in a critical manner, enabling a clear assessment of its strengths and weaknesses. This allows an appropriate conclusion to be drawn.

In the light of the above, in order for your evaluation skills to develop through to level 4 when researching your focus, remember to do the following.

1 Research alternative points of view in response to, or that arise from, your focus.

2 Present these alternative views, using quotations and references as evidence.

3 Comment on, and explain fully, the reasons that justify these alternative views.

4 Arrange or group the different views, for example, different approaches that support the same view.

5 Look at the strengths and weaknesses associated with the evidence presented.

6 Critically evaluate and challenge these strengths and weaknesses.

7 Identify further questions that need to be addressed in response to the debate presented.

It is expected that your research leads to 'a clearly expressed viewpoint supported by well-deployed evidence and reasoned argument'.

A REMINDER OF THE AO2-BASED AIMS FOR YOUR RESEARCH

Are you:

- being encouraged to develop your own ideas and views
- able to sustain a critical line of argument and justify a point of view
- able to critically evaluate arguments
- aware of a range of viewpoints
- able to formulate and discuss an evaluative conclusion which reflects the development of your thinking over a period of time, using religious and technical language appropriately?

In order to achieve this, you will need to draw an appropriate conclusion, which could be:

- one clear conclusion
- a series of possible conclusions
- a conclusion that poses further questions
- a recognition that no clear conclusion is possible
- a recognition that the strengths and weaknesses are equally weighted.

In order to achieve the higher level you should:

- write out the different views
- arrange the different views appropriately in a table or diagram
- identify the key questions arising from these views and rank them in terms of importance
- respond to these key questions through a summary of their strengths and weaknesses
- begin to outline your own response to the views presented
- have another person read through your analysis to provide constructive criticism
- arrange to deliver a class presentation of your research, using a clear structure for delivery
- use an evaluation sheet to gather suggestions for improvements.

Assessment and reflection

Using AO1 and AO2 in the examination – bringing your research together coherently and working through some revision tasks

Now that you have gathered, presented and improved your **focus** of study, it is vital that you remember that the end product **does** need to be used in a compact, timed situation.

Remember, you are taking an examination, in which you will have only 75 minutes to deliver your research in response to a general question on the whole topic.

Preparation for this aspect is vital.

It is important that you work with your teacher and fellow students in developing suitable ways to revise and focus, based upon your preferred learning styles.

Look in the Introduction about assessment for learning (page 2) and at the tasks, objectives, examination tips, reflections and suggestions contained in the features throughout this book.

These will give a good basis for a variety of revision activities that are clearly focused on examination technique, ways for improvement and the pursuit of academic excellence in your answers.

Make a plan and decide upon some collective activities to work through. Remember, collaborative learning, reflection, critical analysis and self-reflection for the purpose of improvement are the keys to building successful answers, using refined skills.

Good luck!

The specification states that for the focus on your topic you will need to:

- develop your own ideas and views
- be able to sustain a critical line of argument and justify a point of view
- be able to evaluate arguments critically
- be aware of a range of viewpoints.

As you work through your research, make sure that you use the above bullet points as a checklist of your progress.

The individual unit content outline from the specification gives three possible areas of study for a topic. The authors have chosen one area for each unit.

For this unit they have selected **1: Religion and science**.

Whichever area of the specification is chosen, one possible approach is to become familiar initially with the overall context of a whole area.

For the purposes of this book, this means the relevant part and corresponding assessment and reflections.

RESEARCH TIP

Make sure that you read through the information for the topic and, perhaps, make some preliminary background notes before you focus your attention on choosing an area of interest.

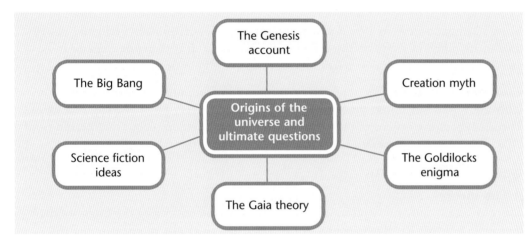

Overview: Religion and science

This diagram shows an outline of the sorts of area we are going to look at. Using this as a basis, create and extend it into your own thought-process diagram as you progress. This may help you decide on a focus. Then you can use your focus to start another chart.

Specification guidance notes (AO1)

Assessment objective 1 (Knowledge and understanding)

Select and demonstrate clearly relevant knowledge and understanding through the use of evidence, examples, and correct language and terminology appropriate to the course of study.

For this skill, you are expected to select and present relevant and appropriate information from the specification in order to answer questions on an area examined.

The examination board provides guidance notes in order to assist you with preparation for assessment.

In the notes it states:

Students may investigate the methodologies of religion and science and their possible relationship to each other, including the view that science may replace a religious account of the Universe. Students may investigate a variety of creation myths and their possible relationship with scientific cosmologies.

Here we shall study the Genesis account of creation and consider the theories of the Big Bang, evolution and intelligent design.

POSSIBLE AREAS FOR FOCUS IN THIS BOOK

- Christian creation
- Scientific explanations as to the origins of the Universe and life
- Evolution
- Intelligent design
- Other creation myths
- Science-fiction myths
- Gaia theory
- The Goldilocks enigma

Various possibilities are then included for focus, ranging from 'concepts and terms such as multiverses, intelligent design…a variety of religious traditions…specific issues such as evolution and related debates, or the Gaia hypothesis and environmental science…the relationships between religious concepts and ideas in science fiction'.

Then we shall study the different creation myths, science fiction and modern developments in cosmology.

Some of these topics are covered in depth in other areas of this book.

1 Religion and science: scientific and philosophical views on the origin of the Universe

a) Introduction

Many scientists believe in a creator and just as many do not. Similarly, religious people hold many different views on the origin of the Universe. It is therefore difficult to be precise about what science or religion says about the origins of the Universe.

Cosmology is the scientific study of the origin and nature of the Universe. The Universe is more than just our Solar System: it includes every physical thing that exists. Theories about the origins of the Universe could raise questions about the meaning and value of human life; therefore, religious belief and scientific study may overlap.

b) The Big-Bang theory

i) The theory

There are really only two options to choose from when considering the origin of the Universe. Either it has always existed, or it began at a particular moment in the past. The idea that the Universe has always existed is not now a widely held view.

The evidence points more to the Universe having a beginning. The current popular scientific theory about how the Universe began is called the Big-Bang theory. Some 13.7 billion years ago there was an event that scientists call the Big Bang. The Universe came into existence after the explosion of an infinitely small and infinitely dense ball of energy, called a space–time singularity. This should not be thought of as a fireball somewhere in space. It did not appear in space: rather, space began inside the singularity.

Before this, nothing existed, not space, time, matter, energy – nothing. What existed prior to the Big Bang is unknown. Mathematical models have attempted to describe physical processes associated with the Big Bang to within 10^{-43} seconds of its start. At that stage, infinite density is almost reached and known laws of physics cease to function.

After the initial appearance of the singularity, it inflated – this was the Big Bang. It expanded and started to cool. After some 300 000 years, the fundamental forces of physics (gravity, electromagnetism, nuclear) began to emerge. From sub-atomic particles, hydrogen and helium were formed. As the cooling continued, galaxies and stars were formed, followed by planets and the earliest life-forms.

KEY WORD

Cosmology: the scientific study of the origin and nature of the Universe

KEY QUOTES

The mathematical laws of physics underlie everything. Many physicists think they are real, and inhabit a transcendent Platonic realm.

(Davies)

The Universe has been expanding for billions of years, so there must have been a time in the ancient past when all the matter in the Universe was concentrated in a state of infinite density.

(Kaufmann)

ii) The evidence

- Galaxies appear to be moving away from us at speeds proportional to their distance from us. This is Hubble's law, named after **Edwin Hubble** who discovered this phenomenon in 1929. He noticed that galactic light is slightly distorted in colour – a phenomenon known as red shift. This suggests rapid recession, with every galaxy moving away from every other one. This is consistent with the idea of an expanding Universe.

- The idea of an expanding Universe is consistent with Albert Einstein's theories about gravity. He argued that gravity stretches or distorts space and time. The galaxies are not moving about through space. Rather, intergalactic space is being inflated. A helpful analogy is a balloon. The Big Bang is not like a balloon popping and releasing its contents, but more like a balloon being blown up and continually growing.

- Stephen Hawking, George Ellis and Roger Penrose investigated the application of Einstein's theory of relativity to notions of time and space. They concluded that time and space had a finite beginning that corresponded to the beginning of matter and energy.

- The Big-Bang theory suggests that the Universe was initially extremely hot. If that was so, we should be able to find some remnant of this heat. In 1965, Arno Penzias and Robert Wilson discovered cosmic microwave background radiation, which they thought was this remnant.

- The Big-Bang theory implies that heavy elements would have formed later than lighter elements such as hydrogen and helium. The occurrence of hydrogen and helium in the Universe supports this expectation.

The Universe is becoming more and more disordered as time passes. This is consistent with the second law of thermodynamics and so suggests that the Universe did not always exist. It had a beginning.

The original theory was suggested by George Gamow, Ralph Alpher and Robert Herman in 1948. The term 'Big Bang' was coined by Fred Hoyle in a radio interview in 1950.

> *At the moment of the Big Bang, a state of infinite density filled the Universe. Space and time throughout the Universe were completely jumbled up in a state of infinite curvature like that at the centre of a black hole. Thus, we cannot use the laws of physics to tell us what happened at the moment of the Big Bang. And we certainly cannot use science to tell us what existed before the Big Bang. These things are fundamentally unknowable. The phrases 'before the Big Bang' or 'at the moment of the Big Bang' are meaningless, because time itself did not really exist.*
>
> (Kaufmann)

KEY PERSON

Edwin Hubble (1889–1953) demonstrated the existence of other galaxies besides the Milky Way and, through investigating distances, pushed the frontiers of the Universe to hundreds of millions of light years; he also found observational proof that the Universe was expanding (the red shift).

KEY IDEA

John Gribbin refers to the idea of a singularity as at best *'a naïve image of the birth of the Universe'* and as a product of Einstein's general relativity theory. However, in *The Universe: A Biography*, Gribbin indicates that: *physicists are uncomfortable with the idea of singularities and infinities, and usually regard any theory that predicts their existence in the physical Universe as flawed*.

What exactly happened at the moment of the Big Bang will always remain unknown.

John Gribbin agrees.

This is true, even of the general theory. It can tell us how the Universe as we know it emerged from a state of nearly infinite density; but it cannot tell us actually what happened at the very beginning, the moment of the Big Bang itself.

(**Gribbin**)

Davies answers the often-asked theological question of what happened prior to the Big Bang:

As Stephen Hawking has remarked, asking what happened before the Big Bang is rather like asking what lies north of the North Pole. The answer, once again, is nothing, not because there exists a mysterious Land of Nothing there but because there is no such place as north of the North Pole. Similarly, there is no such time as 'before the Big Bang'.

? KEY QUESTION

What came before the Big Bang?

✏️ **TASK**

Find out what happens to time clocks when you move in space. How does this support the Big-Bang theory?

Objective: To improve understanding of the Big-Bang theory and to develop the 'use of evidence and examples' to 'demonstrate clearly relevant knowledge and understanding' (AO1).

c) Creationism

Creationism, as it is normally understood, is a belief that the Universe and life were created by God over a very short period of time.

The view is anti-evolutionary because it suggests a sudden and complete process rather than one that stretches for countless millions of years.

It is often associated with a very literal interpretation of religious texts, such as the creation account in Genesis.

d) The Genesis account

The main source for the Christian view of the creation of the Universe (and life) is the early chapters of Genesis.

The account in Genesis depicts God as creating the Universe (and life) in eight divine acts over a period of six days.

- Let there be light... (Genesis 1: 3)
- Let there be an expanse between the waters... (Genesis 1: 6)
- Let the waters under the sky be gathered together... (Genesis 1: 9)
- Let the land produce vegetation... (Genesis 1: 11)
- Let there be lights in the expanse of the sky... (Genesis 1: 14)
- Let the waters teem with living creatures, and let birds fly... (Genesis 1: 20)
- Let the land produce living creatures... (Genesis 1: 24)
- Let us make man in our image... (Genesis 1: 26)

It is important to note that a substantial majority of those who would call themselves Christians do not take a strictly literal view of the Genesis account of creation and would accept some kind of evolutionary process (see section 2 below).

2 Attempts at reconciling different approaches

Biblical literalists believe that the seven days in the Genesis account correspond exactly to 24-hour days of history during which God created the world. This results in understanding the creation not in terms of billions of years but rather thousands. Such a view is often referred to as Young Earth creationism. Some supporters of this view argue that, by working back through the Biblical genealogies, the actual date of creation can be established. The classic dating was calculated by Bishop James Ussher as the nightfall preceding 23 October 4004BCE.

Clearly, if a Young Earth view is taken, then it is difficult to see how the scientific account and the religious account can be reconciled. However, various other understandings and interpretations have been given to the Genesis account that make possible some reconciliation between the scientific and religious approaches. Many believe in God as the Creator without taking a strictly literal view of the whole of Genesis 1–3. Some of the various theories of such people are described here, although this list is not exhaustive.

a) Progressive creationism (Day–Age theory)

This response holds that each day of creation week represents a long age (millions or even billions of years) in which God acted upon creation. They see no reason to interpret the days in a literal sense, since God's time is not the same as our time.

b) Gap theory

Many argue that a gap should be inserted between Genesis 1:1 and Genesis 1:2. This then accommodates geological time.

c) Framework interpretation

This response sees Genesis 1 as written to provide a theology of creation opposing myths from pagans. It is not to be taken as a scientifically or historically accurate record. This is often expressed as: 'Science answers the *how* question, while religion answers the *why* question.'

TASK

Read Genesis 1:1 to 2:3 and make a list of the things created on each day. Now read Genesis 2: 4–23. Can you see any problems arising from comparing the two accounts? Can you suggest any solutions to those problems?

Objective: To develop an understanding of the problems of interpreting religious texts. To develop an understanding of the literal meanings of religious texts but also their wider non-literal interpretation and application. To demonstrate a deeper understanding of the idea of creation and the origins of life, using examples to support explanation, and demonstrating a 'coherent understanding of the task...based on selection of material to demonstrate emphasis and clarity of ideas' and also a 'careful analysis of key concepts' (higher level 5 descriptor AO1).

d) God as source of the Big Bang

The Big-Bang theory is seen as consistent with the claim that there is a God. The theory says that the Universe had a beginning, and that both time and space came from nothing. This is seen as a parallel to the beginning of Genesis. God is seen as the explanation of the Big Bang. Indeed, in 1951 Pope Pius XII declared approval for the Big-Bang theory, based on this understanding.

3 Scientific and philosophical views on the origins of life

a) The theory of evolution

Darwin's theory provided a way of understanding the natural world, in which its complex biological functions no longer required an intelligent designer to account for apparent order.

Firstly, Darwin identified that variations occur in offspring within a species. These are accidental. Secondly, he argued for natural selection, which included the theory of the survival of the fittest. This proposes that organisms that are best able to survive – for example, finding food, avoiding predators – pass on their genetic traits. The combination of variation and survival leads eventually to the emergence of organisms that are better suited to their environment. Over time, beneficial mutations accumulate and the result is an entirely different organism. This may have the appearance of design, but is the result of organisms evolving by variation and survival. God becomes an unnecessary hypothesis.

Darwin demonstrated that order was not necessarily evidence of purpose and design. Order could result from blind chance.

b) The Genesis account

This describes each species as being complete and created separately, rather than progressing and developing into different species. (For details of the order see section 1, above.) The literal interpretation of Genesis is associated with creationist theories and is particularly supported by those who take the text of scriptures literally.

In particular, human beings are seen as being made in the image of God with the faculty of having a relationship with God. This marks out human beings as different from the rest of creation.

4 Attempts at reconciling different approaches

a) Progressive creationism (Day–Age theory)

As already discussed, this belief holds that each day of creation week represents a long age (millions or even billions of years) in which God acted upon creation. There is no reason to interpret the days in a literal sense since God's time is not same as our time.

Holders of this view would accept much of what would be called micro-evolution, adaptation within a species and even some larger changes. But macro-evolutionary changes, such as a bird evolving from a fish, are not seen as a viable process. In particular, human beings are special creations and are not evolved from another species.

b) Theistic evolution

This takes the Genesis account as religious and theological rather than historical and scientific. Evolution is seen as the mechanism God used to bring about life and human beings. This therefore retains the theistic belief that the world is ultimately the result of divine creation. Some theistic evolutionists prefer to call it Evolutionary Creation. It emphasises their belief in a creator while still accepting evolution.

In 1996, Pope John Paul II made a statement about evolution. He seemingly accepted the idea although he did not identify the actual mechanism. The Pope stated that humankind was created in the image and likeness of God, and so he reinforced the Catholic teaching of earlier popes, such as Pius XII, that God infuses souls into human beings, regardless of what process he might have used to create our physical bodies.

Science, the Pope insisted, can never identify for us 'the moment of the transition into the spiritual'. He argued that such a matter was for religion, not science. More recently, in July 2007, Pope Benedict XVI said that the theory of evolution has strong scientific proof, but the theory does not answer the question: 'From where does everything come?'

Paul Davies considers the question: 'But will God go quietly? Even within the world of organised religion, the concept of "God" means many different things to different people.' He points out that the 'Cosmic Magician' is no longer a realistic or tenable argument today and certainly not compatible with a scientific approach, being 'in flagrant contradiction to the scientific view of the world' and argues:

Many people envisage God as a sort of cosmic magician who existed for all eternity and then, at some moment in the past, created the Universe in a gigantic supernatural act. Unfortunately, this scenario raises some awkward questions.

However, the God of theology, philosophy and critical scholarship 'is largely immune from scientific attack' despite arguments from some scientists.

i) From *The God Delusion* by Richard Dawkins

Darwinism teaches us to be wary of the easy assumption that design is the only alternative to chance, and to seek out graded ramps of slowly increasing complexity. Before Darwin, philosophers such as Hume understood that the improbability of life did not mean it had to be designed, but they couldn't imagine the alternative. After Darwin, we all should feel, deep in our bones, suspicious of the very idea of design. The illusion of design is a trap that has caught us before, and Darwin should have immunised us by raising our consciousness. Would that he had succeeded with all of us.

KEY QUOTE

The intention of the Holy Ghost is to teach us how one goes to heaven, not how heaven goes.

(Galileo)

KEY QUOTE

[1:]*In the beginning God created the heavens and the Earth.* [2:]*The Earth was without form and void, and darkness was upon the face of the deep; and the Spirit of God was moving over the face of the waters.* [3:]*And God said, 'Let there be light' and there was light.*

(Genesis 1:1–3)

KEY QUOTES

When it comes to actual physical phenomena, science wins hands down against gods and miracles. That is not to say that science can explain everything. There remain some pretty big gaps: for example, scientists don't know how life began, and they are almost totally baffled by consciousness.

(Davies)

So long as the Universe had a beginning, we could suppose it had a creator.

(Hawking)

ii) From *The Goldilocks Enigma* by Paul Davies

I do take life, mind and purpose seriously, and I concede that the Universe at least appears to be designed with a high level of ingenuity. I cannot accept these features as a package of marvels which just happen to be, which exist reasonlessly. It seems to me that there is a genuine scheme of things – the Universe is 'about' something. But I am equally uneasy about dumping the whole set of problems in the lap of an arbitrary god, or abandoning all further thought and declaring existence ultimately to be a mystery.

➡ EXAM TIP

Remember to explain each point that you make in an exam answer to the full. Think carefully about each sentence and how it relates to the question and the previous sentence. Aim for at least three clear sentences to explain a concept or idea, giving examples from different sources to support your point. For development of the point, bring in a variety of ways in which the application of this principle is demonstrated and introduce some contrasting scholarly views. This demonstrates that the answer is 'well-structured in depth or broad response to the task' (mid level 5 descriptor AO1) as opposed to the information being simply 'uncritical and descriptive presentation' (level 1 descriptor AO1) or 'presented within a limited framework' (level 2 descriptor AO1).

---

5 Other religious understandings of creation and how they relate (are compatible) with scientific views

a) Religious understandings of creation (examples of religious creation stories and how they are interpreted)

i) Islam

This account follows the same sort of order as the Christian story except that it is not described in days, but rather in 'periods'. Also, God did not need to rest at the end.

This story is always taken literally because the Qur'an is the word of God; it cannot be questioned and is not open to modern interpretations. Like scientists, however, Muslims believe that our understanding of how the Universe came to be is becoming more and more clear; the only difference is that in Islam this understanding is direct support for the literal truth of the Qur'an.

Yet in fact Islam, with its strong sense of creation, is exceptionally well placed to see the Universe as an unfolding revelation of God, which extends or at least provides an informative commentary on the Qur'an.

(Bowker)

ii) Hinduism

This account proposes the idea that the Universe is a continuous cycle (just like life itself, for example, the samsara cycle of life, death and reincarnation – see page 116). Brahma (four-headed God) creates the Universe; Vishnu is the preserver of the Universe and maintains order; Shiva is the angry God who performs the 'dance of death' (tandava) and destroys the Universe, only for Brahma at the last moment to step in and re-create it.

This story is believed to be an accurate description, not of what the Gods do, but rather of how the Universe works; it has the great spirit (Brahman) running through it and this gives it its energy to survive. Some Hindus, such as Fritjof Capra, see this as compatible with the ideas of modern physics.

iii) Buddhism

The account is very similar to that of Hinduism, without the idea of a divine being. It is a continuous cycle of cause and effect and of inter-changing and transforming energies:

> There comes a time, Vasettha, when, sooner or later after a long period, this world contracts…but sooner or later, after a very long period, this world begins to expand again.
>
> (Agganna Sutta)

Despite this, one could argue that this is a very 'rationalist' interpretation of the ideas behind the Buddhist creation myths. Buddhism itself is very varied, has a very complex cosmology and, although on an ultimate level it can be expressed logically, there are other more creative expressions of the cosmos that involve divine beings and share common ground with traditional Indian mythology such as those from Hinduism.

iv) Aborigine

The story begins with land and the Maker (Baiame) who creates 'dreamtime ancestors'. These 'dreamtime ancestors' take a variety of forms (animals, humans, fish and birds) and could change their shapes. They fought battles to make the land what it is today. Humans developed from these ancestors and the bones of dead ones made rocks, etc. The Sun and Moon originated from a battle between an eagle and an emu fighting (the Sun is one of the emu's eggs).

This story is obviously myth, but the Aborigines see it as containing valuable truths about how their ways developed. Despite this, there is once again a sense of 'order' to the story.

b) Classification of creation myths

In 1964, Philip Freund wrote a book entitled *Myths of Creation*. In it he presented a classification of creation myths into five different types.

1 Water myths see the cosmos as arising from some kind of misty, watery substance, as a result of the abstract nature of God and the beginning. In these myths there is initially talk of voids and the primordial principle of existence. Examples range from Hinduism, Egyptian, Southern American and also Hebrew myths.

2 In egg myths the 'birth' of the cosmos erupted from a basic physical formation and is seen as being directly related to the divine being. Hinduism, myths from China, Japan, Finland and Samoa are a few examples.

3 Dismemberment myths involve a primordial monster or creature of some kind used to carve out creation, such as Purusha in the Vedic myth or Pan Ku in Chinese thought.

4 Mating of the Gods is the fourth category of creation myth. Tibet, New Zealand, ancient Egypt and Greece all have examples of deities copulating to produce a chain of lesser deities that eventually give birth to the cosmos and human life.

5 The final category involves the idea of the spoken word. Freund called them edict myths. A divine utterance, 'the utterance of a demi urge', causes the cosmos to come into existence. The Hebrew story is a classic example but there are many more.

KEY QUOTES

For thousands of years people have looked up at the heavens and found themselves inspired to contemplate the nature of the Universe…To wonder about the nature of the Universe is one of the most characteristic of human traits.

(Kaufmann)

Buddhism and science share a fundamental reluctance to postulate a transcendent being as the origin of all things.

(The Dalai Lama)

Obviously some of the above are not absolute classifications and there are myths that share more than one of these characteristic traits; however, it is interesting to see how humanity has explained the origins of the cosmos and human life.

It is also important to establish that myths of creation are not just ancient, primitive ideas. The main thrust of writers such as Freund is to demonstrate the complexity of mythical ideas and their parity and consistency with what we know about our Universe. Freund himself, is scathing in his criticism of the idea that ancient ideas can be dispensed with in the light of modern scientific knowledge:

> *The more insignificant modern man becomes…the more arrogant he is. He feels far less humility toward the ever-vaster unknown than his forefathers did toward what was thought to be known in a flat, God-ruled, man-centred Universe.*
>
> **(Freund)**

There may be a case to answer for this; however, Freund's comment cuts very close to the bone in the ongoing debate concerning the compatibility of religion and science:

> *Science does not seem to touch man's emotions at all: he loses his religious awe and acquires in its place only a boastful complacency about himself. His intelligence grows, but not his genius.*
>
> **(Freund)**

This may well be disputed by scientists such as Paul Davies, as we shall later see, but it does underline the scorn that today's thinkers such as Dawkins may have towards an appreciation of the mythical.

Myth is not confined to the past. This argument is all the more interesting when modern mythical writings are considered. Modern writers in the genre of science-fiction present imaginative ideas connected (albeit in varying degrees of accuracy) to scientific principles. Classic examples of two such writers are Douglas Adams and Terry Pratchett.

c) Modern cosmological myths

i) Adams and the ultimate answer to the question of life, the Universe and everything

Douglas Adams, who died in 2001, offered the answer by way of a series of five novels, the first of which was entitled *The Hitchhiker's Guide to the Galaxy*. One of the most highly regarded science-fiction writers of all time and recipient of numerous prestigious awards, Adams followed the initial *Hitchhiker's Guide to the Galaxy* with a series of four more books:

- *The Restaurant at the End of the Universe* (1980)
- *Life, The Universe and Everything* (1982)
- *So Long and Thanks for all the Fish* (1984)
- *Mostly Harmless* (1992).

> *According to the books, a civilisation of extremely advanced and intelligent aliens set out one day to answer the ultimate question of Life, the Universe and Everything, by building an enormously powerful computer called Deep Thought. For millions of years the computer pondered the question before finally, and with much fanfare, revealing the answer: 42.*
>
> **(Pincock and Frary)**

KEY QUOTE

Many scientists who are struggling to construct a fully comprehensive theory of the physical Universe openly admit that part of the motivation is to finally get rid of God, whom they view as a dangerous and infantile delusion… They concede no middle ground, and regard science and religion as two implacably opposed world views.

(Davies)

Is 42 symbolic? Is it mythical? What truth does it reveal? The problem was two-fold:

- The aliens were unhappy with the answer.
- The aliens did not really know what the original question was.

As a result, another computer, the Earth – even more powerful than the first computer – is sought out to find the question and make sense of the answer. At the moment of ultimate calculation, the Earth is destroyed, apart from two remaining human survivors, one of which is Arthur Dent.

The resulting quest involves seeking out alternative Earths in space that have the ability to compute the ultimate question. Unfortunately, the ultimate question is never revealed as all alternative Earths are destroyed at the end of the last novel.

The answer remains, however, as 42!

ii) The absurd world of Terry Pratchett

Millions of readers were inspired by Douglas Adams, but even more popular today are the writings of Terry Pratchett. Pratchett's writings are about the fantasy world of Discworld. He is the second most read author in Britain today and has sold over 55 million books.

> *Fantasy isn't just about wizards and silly wands. It's about seeing the world from new directions.*
> **(acceptance speech for his Carnegie Medal)**

Pratchett has produced three books entitled *The Science of Discworld*, explaining the theoretical basis of his work. These have been written in collaboration with two scientists from Warwick University.

These books have chapters that alternate between fiction and non-fiction. Obviously, the fictional chapters are set within the Discworld and this is where the characters perform experiments on a Universe like our own and observe the results in relation to the laws of physics. Book 3 is particularly pertinent as it deals with 'Darwin's Watch' and the ideas associated with the origins and developments of life.

The opening novel of Discworld, *The Colour of Magic*, describes a kind of creation story. Discworld itself is described as a large disc resting on the backs of four giant elephants, all supported by the giant turtle 'Great A'Tuin' as it swims its way through space.

> *In a distant and second-hand set of dimensions, in an astral plane that was never meant to fly, the curling star-mists waver and part... see...Great A'Tuin the turtle comes, swimming slowly through the interstellar gulf, hydrogen frost on his ponderous limbs, his huge and ancient shell pocked with meteor craters. Through sea-sized eyes that are crusted with rheum and asteroid dust He stares fixedly at the Destination. In a brain bigger than a city, with geological Slowness, He thinks only of the Weight. Most of the weight is of course accounted for by Berilia, Tubul, Great T'Phon and Jerakeen, the four giant elephants upon whose broad and star-tanned shoulders the disc of the World rests, garlanded by the long waterfall at its vast circumference and domed by the baby-blue vault of Heaven.*
> **(Terry Pratchett)**

Where this cosmic turtle originated is a mystery ('in a distant and second-hand set of dimensions') but its presence and power call into question possible futures for the turtle's Universe:

> *Would A'Tuin keep walking until he crawled at a steady gait until he returned to the nowhere he came from? Or was he heading toward a Time of Mating, where he and all the other turtles*

KEY QUOTE

It is often said that science cannot prove the existence of God. Yet science does have value in theological debate because it gives us new concepts that sometimes make popular notions of God untenable.

(Davies)

carrying stars in the sky would briefly and passionately mate, for the first and only time, creating new turtles and a new pattern of worlds? This was known as the Big-Bang hypothesis.

(Terry Pratchett)

There is, in Pratchett, a distinctive mix of accurate, contemporary scientific cosmological theory enshrined in a mythical cloak.

66 **KEY QUOTES**

There are, of course, eight days in a disc week and eight colours in its light spectrum. Eight is a number of some considerable occult significance on the disc and must never, ever, be spoken by a wizard...

The sudden departure of several quintillion atoms from a Universe that they had no right to be in anyway caused a wild imbalance in the harmony of the Sum Totality which it tried frantically to retrieve, wiping out a number of subrealities in the process. Huge surges of raw magic boiled uncontrolled around the very foundations of the multiverse itself, welling up through every crevice into hitherto peaceful dimensions and causing novas, supernovas, stellar collisions, wild flights of geese and drowning of imaginary continents. Worlds as far away as the other end of time experienced brilliant sunsets of corruscating octarine as highly-charged magical particles roared through the atmosphere. In the cometary halo around the fabled Ice-System of Zeret a noble comet died as a prince flamed across the sky...

Precisely why all the above should be so is not clear, but goes some way to explain why, on the disc, the Gods are not so much worshipped as blamed.

(Terry Pratchett)

99

d) Recent debates in cosmology

There have been some new discussions about the nature of the Universe in recent years. The Gaia hypothesis is not totally new but it has re-emerged recently as one explanation of the nature of our Universe. A second debate centres around the re-emergence of the idea of the anthropic principle (see Unit 1 Area A, Part 1A, page 17) and has been renamed the *Goldilocks enigma*.

i) The Gaia hypothesis

In the 1960s James Lovelock proposed that the Earth is in a condition of full homeostasis. That is, the Earth's biomass alters certain conditions to make it a more hospitable environment and also functions as a single organism that maintains conditions necessary for its survival. It was seen as a way to explain the fact that combinations of chemicals, including oxygen and methane, persist in stable concentrations in the atmosphere of the Earth.

James Lovelock defined Gaia as:

...a complex entity involving the Earth's biosphere, atmosphere, oceans, and soil; the totality constituting a feedback or cybernetic system which seeks an optimal physical and chemical environment for life on this planet.

Some have interpreted this to mean that the Earth is a single organism that regulates and maintains itself. However, it is clear that this is not seen to be driven by a conscious self-awareness of the holistic picture but rather as a more 'Darwinian' quest for survival.

S.J. Gould criticised Lovelock for this 'metaphorical' description of the overall hypothesis and demanded to know more about the nitty-gritty of the mechanisms that worked the whole and led to this conclusion. The theory was then attacked by many mainstream biologists, including Richard Dawkins, and was accused of being teleological (all things have a predetermined purpose) by his critics. It was even compared to a New-Age Religion.

ii) The Goldilocks enigma

Why Goldilocks? According to the story, when Goldilocks tasted the baby bear's porridge it was 'not too hot' and 'not too cold'. In fact, it was 'just right for her' as if it had been prepared for her. Likewise, many people have argued that the Universe is just right for life, as if it had arisen with the purpose of life in mind. The key question is: 'Does the fact that the Universe is just right for life allow us to draw the conclusion that life is the purpose of the Universe?'

John Gribbin describes the question well:

> People have long been puzzled by the fact that our Universe is in many ways 'just right' for the emergence and evolution of life. Some people argue that the Universe has been designed for life…Others, though, have suggested that in an infinite number of universes every possible combination of laws of physics and forces of nature must exist somewhere, or somewhen…some, just by chance, will indeed be just right for life, in the same way that baby bear's porridge was just right for Goldilocks, even though it was not made for her.
>
> (Gribbin)

Paul Davies discusses the enigma in his book and explores a variety of explanations for the Universe. In summary, he looks at ideas of absurdity, uniqueness, multiplicity, self-explanatory and designed universes.

The basic explanations of each idea are presented below.

e) Summary of key ideas

View	Explanation	Role of religion
Absurd Universe	The Universe has no meaning or purpose.	There is definitely no God.
Unique Universe	There may be an answer to the Universe to be found in a unified theory of everything.	If there is a God, God is separate and distant from the Universe. Could we ever know God?
Multiverse	Our Universe is one of many.	The idea of a single creator God becomes irrelevant.
Intelligent design	There is the traditional idea of a creator God, from the general design argument to the idea of intelligent design.	God is necessary and very much in control.
Life-principle Universe	A development of the anthropic principle through the Goldilock's enigma.	There could be a God but the specific identity of this God is not necessarily comparable to traditional ideas. God needs re-defining into 'a more subtle, purpose-like principle' (Davies).

KEY IDEA

The name Gaia was actually suggested by the author and close friend of Lovelock, William Golding after the Greek goddess of Earth. Until 1975 the hypothesis was almost totally ignored. An article in the *New Scientist*, of 15 February 1975, began to attract scientific and critical attention to the hypothesis. In 1979 the book *Gaia: A new look at life on Earth* was published.

66 **KEY QUOTE**

Is this a cosmic fix? Many scientists say no. For them, remarking on the fact that the Universe is fit for life is a little like a puddle waking up one morning and being amazed at how perfectly the pothole fits it.

(Pincock and Frary)

99

Scientists have long been aware that the Universe seems strangely suited to life, but they mostly chose to ignore it. It was an embarrassment – it looked too much like the work of a Cosmic Designer.

It is important to distinguish between design in the law of physics and design in objects or in systems such as biological organisms. The appearance of design in organisms has a testable scientific explanation based on Darwin's theory of evolution.

(Davies)

View	Explanation	Role of religion
Self-explaining Universe	The meaning of the Universe can be found within itself in 'a closed explanatory or causal loop'. The Gaia hypothesis falls within this category.	There is no necessity for God. Indeed, the Universe becomes its own God.

Davies' own position lies between the life-principle and that of the self-explaining Universe.

The measured value of dark energy is 120 powers of ten less than its natural value, for reasons which remain completely mysterious. If it were 119 rather than 120 powers of ten less, the consequences would be lethal.

(Davies)

Specification guidance notes (AO2)

Assessment objective 2 (Critical evaluation)

Critically evaluate and justify a point of view through the use of evidence and reasoned argument.

The examination board provide guidance notes in order to assist with preparation for assessment. In the notes it states:

Students may investigate the methodologies of religion and science and their possible relationship to each other, including the view that science may replace a religious account of the Universe.

Here we shall consider the issues raised by the relationship between religion and science.

- The strengths and weaknesses of different cosmological views
- Modern cosmological views and their compatibility with religion
- The incompatibility of religion and science
- The similarities between religion and scientific method

Religion and science do have areas of compatibility but are distinctive disciplines, with the diminishing 'God of the Gaps' giving way to the superiority of science.

Religion and science do have more in common than some people think in terms of methodology and whatever is revealed through scientific investigation does not shrink the 'God of the Gaps' but simply incorporates the idea of God and enhances our understanding of what religion is

Religion and science are totally incompatible because religion is unscientific in its approach to the ultimate questions about life

There are those who consider religion and science totally incompatible because religion deals with revealed truths that cannot be challenged

Overview: Issues for debate

1 A critical evaluation of the issues (AO2)

This whole area of study has been concerned with the relationship between religion and science; any AO2 analysis and evaluation would make this relationship the central focus, whether it be with creation stories, evolution, the Gaia hypothesis, intelligent design, science fiction or modern developments in cosmology. In particular, one crucial consideration that appears to run throughout is the issue of compatibility.

There are clearly several distinctive positions taken on this issue.

- There are those who consider religion and science totally incompatible because religion is unscientific in its approach to the ultimate questions about life.
- There are those who consider religion and science totally incompatible because religion deals with revealed truths that cannot be challenged.
- There are those who argue that religion and science do have areas of compatibility but are distinctive disciplines, with the diminishing 'God of the Gaps' giving way gently to the superiority of science.
- There are those who feel that the two disciplines of religion and science do have more in common than some people think, in terms of methodology, and whatever is revealed through scientific investigation does not shrink the 'God of the Gaps' but simply incorporates the idea of God and enhances our understanding of what religion is.

In the light of all this, it is also important to point out that there is no discernible and distinctive divide between philosophers, scientists and theologians. Although most scientists may take an agnostic or atheistic position, this is by no means the position of all. Indeed, there are different reasons for the positions taken that make the whole area of debate even more complex.

In an article written for *The Observer,* on 17 September 2006, entitled 'Masters of the Universe', Tim Adams reviewed three new books from renowned scholars, two of them scientists and the other a playwright/philosopher, that were to be published that year. Adams referred to them as three 'wise men…their books could hardly be bettered'. The books were Michael Frayn's *The Human Touch: Our Part in the Creation of the Universe,* Richard Dawkin's *The God Delusion* and *The Goldilocks Enigma* by Paul Davies.

It is interesting to see that, although the books each had their own distinctive agenda and approach, as an impartial reviewer, Adams noticed: 'The consensus they reveal is often striking.' He continued:

> They agree on most elements of this picture: that in the beginning there was a Big Bang, that evolution by natural selection is irrefutable, and that Gods with white beards or other supernatural forces who concern themselves with the goings-on of human beings are a manifest absurdity (this is, in particular, the unanswerable thrust of Dawkins's book).

Frayn is philosophical and reflects the innermost depths of being human, Dawkins' familiar ground is the minute world of cells and genes and Davies' territory extends to the vastness of the Universe itself.

Despite agreeing on factual elements, it is in the interpretation of these facts, that is, with apportioning meaning, where they differ.

It is Davies' book that provides the focus of this evaluation, as it considers exactly the matters that this area of study evaluates, in particular, answers to the question as to how we

RESEARCH TIP

Why not try creating your own evaluation scales as you research your topics?
It is essential that you make a list of questions to ask in response to your studies.
For every quote, piece of evidence, proposal or argument, try to think of a counter argument that is relevant.

EXAM TIP

Do not just give a list of criticisms like some shopping list. It is far better to discuss and develop three or four criticisms, explaining and responding to them, than to give a list of seven or eight.
This demonstrates a process of reasoning and a sustained argument that is akin to 'a careful analysis of alternative views' (level 4 descriptor AO2) and the overall AO2 objective of 'critical evaluation'.

KEY QUOTE

It is inevitable that any discussion that sets out to grapple with the ultimate questions of existence will eventually slide well beyond the comfort zone of most scientists and enter a realm of speculation which may seem outlandish.

(Davies)

can explain the nature of the Universe in relation to the ultimate questions posed by both religion and science. It will be useful to refer to his discussion before attempting to outline some possible lines of argument and conclusions that can be drawn.

In his last chapter, entitled 'Ultimate Explanations', he outlines the several positions taken by thinkers in response to the issues of cosmology, considering their strengths and weaknesses.

TASK

Think of the questions you would like to ask about the topic you have chosen or about the views that scholars have presented in response to the topic you have chosen. Is there anything that is not clear? What needs further explanation? Do you wish to challenge the thinking or view of a scholar? If so, can you list your reasons or evidence?

Objective: To develop AO2 skills of questioning, considering different views, analysing arguments and responding to the material studied; to 'critically evaluate and justify a point of view through the use of evidence and reasoned argument'. It aids self-reflection and development of an argument, working towards 'some attempt to set out reasons for alternative views; a point of view expressed clearly, supported by some relevant evidence and argument' (level 3 descriptor AO2) or even an 'attempt at an evaluation of the issue(s) raised in the task, typically through a careful analysis of alternative views; leading to a clearly expressed viewpoint supported by well-deployed evidence and reasoned argument' (level 4 descriptor AO2).

Life, the Universe and Everything: a critical evaluation

Davies divides the different answers and positions taken as to the origins of the Universe and life into different categories, some of which can be considered here.

i) The absurd Universe

The Universe is '…as it is, mysteriously, and it just happens to permit life.' There is no answer to our questions that has meaning or purpose. 'It could have been otherwise, but what we see is what we get.' There is definitely, therefore, no design or purpose to our Universe.

Strengths

- It is straightforward and uncomplicated.
- It is easy to argue from the evidence.
- It voids the need for religion.
- It supports the idea of a chaotic but evolving Universe through chance.

Weaknesses

- Some see it as a cop-out and the dependence upon chance as unreasonable.
- Links between life, mind and the cosmos are removed.
- Some argue that it makes the pursuit of knowledge and understanding futile.
- It means there is no overall coherent scheme of things within which science can operate, leaving the discipline as totally enigmatic.

ii) The unique Universe

This involves the pursuit of a final unified theory of everything. The strongest version of this suggests that the Universe exists necessarily: 'There is a unique, self-consistent description of physical reality.'

The weaker version argues that there is no ultimate reason for this working and it either still remains a mystery or is absurd.

Strengths

- It offers a complete explanation of everything.
- It either had to be this way or would not exist at all.
- There are no remaining questions since answers are within the Universe, not beyond it.
- God is irrelevant for explaining existence.

Weaknesses

- The question of why 'this way' is not answered.
- An element of mystery remains.
- The bio-friendliness of the Universe is sheer coincidence.
- The bio-friendliness of the Universe is insignificant in the light of the whole.

iii) The multiverse

The 'existence of a multiplicity of cosmic domains' is just one of many, possibly an infinite number of universes. This is a minority position held by scientists but it is growing in support. Supported by string theory or M theory, it indicates that there is nothing to suggest that our particular Universe is unique or special. There are interesting parallels of multiverses with ancient Mahayana Buddhist ideas found in sources such as the Ratnagotravibhanga and associated with the interpenetration teaching of Chinese Buddhism.

Strengths

- It is a straightforward answer to the Goldilocks enigma, in that if it is possible then it will happen.
- Our Universe is not the only one suitable for sustaining life and so is not unusual.
- The extreme version explains everything because it contains everything – all possibilities for existence.

Weaknesses

- It is an 'overabundance of entities' – think of Occam's razor.
- It is difficult to test.
- It is an extravagant way to explain bio-friendliness.
- Is it 'a theory which can explain anything at all' that 'really explains nothing'?

iv) Intelligent design

See the section on Intelligent design for a recap of the more extreme version of the Design argument (see page 33) in accommodating evolution. The Universe exhibits clear patterns of order and purpose that indicate overall design and hence a designer. This is the traditional monotheistic religious view although, as stated above, it does have different degrees of application concerning the relationship between religion and science.

Strengths

- Many argue that it is a reasonable assumption, in light of the evidence.
- If one accepts God exists by faith then it makes sense to see design.
- It provides a simple explanation of the 'cosmic fine tuning and bio-friendliness'.

Weaknesses

- Is 'God did it!' an adequate enough answer?
- How did God do it?
- Why did a single creator God do it?
- These questions are not explained in the answer 'God did it'; the criticism of the Design argument can be applied here (see pages 18–21).

 EXAM TIP

Be careful when using quotes in critical assessments. Always make sure that they relate to the argument that is presented. To make sure of this, always explain the relevance of the quote in your answer. This is the difference between 'a mainly descriptive response…supported by reference to a simple argument or unstructured evidence' or 'a point of view supported by limited but appropriate evidence and/or argument' (levels 1 and 2 descriptors AO2) and that of a level 3 and above answer that clearly attempts analysis with 'some attempt to set out reasons for alternative views' (level 3 descriptor AO2) and the best answer that delivers 'a careful analysis of alternative views' (level 4 descriptor AO2).

v) The life principle

There is an underlying principle in the Universe that determines that it evolves towards life and consciousness. Rather than acknowledging a supernatural agent of traditional religious and philosophical understanding, this theory allows for a 'more subtle, purpose-like principle' and hence re-defines our understanding of 'God'. However, this principle is not essential to the theory.

Strengths

- It is a modern interpretation of the 'design' argument.
- It has scientific credibility.
- It strengthens the relationship between religion and science.

Weaknesses

- Teleology should not be part of scientific discipline.
- It does not explain why this life principle arises unless one invokes a deity.
- Does it make sense without a deity?
- 'One could just as well nominate any distinctive and complex state of matter and enshrine its emergence in a teleological principle.'

vi) The self-explaining Universe

The meaning of the Universe can be found within itself in 'a closed explanatory or causal loop'. It avoids the idea of infinite regress or 'tower of turtles' as Davies describes it. Indeed, this incorporates the idea that the Universe can create itself! The Gaia hypothesis falls within this category of understanding. There is no need for a God and, in a sense, the Universe becomes God.

Strengths

- It avoids philosophical problems of infinite regress.
- It can be understood in conjunction with other theories, for example, the idea of multiverses.

Weaknesses

- Why is this any different in principle to the cosmological idea of a necessary being?
- Why does this self-explanatory Universe exist as opposed to another?

Like Davies' study proposes, there are a variety of positions that can be taken in response to considering the nature of the Universe and the implications this may have for the relationship between religion and science.

2 Possible conclusions

When assessing religion, it is important to reflect upon the arguments previously discussed and arrive at some appropriate conclusion.

It may be that you accept none of these listed here, or just one of them, or you may have a different conclusion that is not listed. However, what is important is the way that you have arrived at your conclusion – the reasoning process.

From the previous discussions, here are some possible conclusions you could draw.

a) Possible conclusions about scientific and philosophical views on the origin of the Universe

1 It is not possible to know the cause of the beginning of the Universe as the event is beyond empirical investigation. It is an absurd Universe.

2 It is possible to know the cause of the beginning of the Universe by producing a theory that is consistent with the evidence.

3 The beginning of the Universe has a naturalistic explanation. It is a life-principle Universe or a self-explaining one.

4 The beginning of the Universe has a supernatural explanation based on God. This could be an intelligent design theory.

5 Religious texts interpreted literally are the source for finding out about the beginning of the Universe. Truth is revealed and found only in religion.

6 Any one or reasonable combination of the positions outlined by Davies.

b) Possible conclusions about scientific and philosophical views on the origin of life

1 It is not possible to know how the beginning of life came about.

2 The beginning of life has a naturalistic explanation.

3 The beginning of life is explained by evolutionary theory and is not consistent with a belief in God.

4 The beginning of life is explained by evolutionary theory and is consistent with a belief in God and a figurative interpretation of religious texts.

5 The beginning of life is explained by the theory of intelligent design.

6 The beginning of life is explained by a literal interpretation of religious texts, for example, Genesis 1–3.

RESEARCH TIP

Make sure that you read through the information for the topic and, perhaps, make some preliminary background notes before you focus your attention on choosing an area of interest.

The individual unit content outline from the specification gives three possible areas of study for a topic. The authors have chosen one area for each unit.

For this unit they have selected **4 Religious experience: meditation**.

Whichever area of the specification is chosen, it is important that you are familiar with the overall general topic.

For the purposes of this book, this means the relevant chapter and corresponding assessment and reflections.

This diagram shows an outline of the sorts of area we are going to look at. Using this as a basis, create and extend it into your own thought-process diagram as you progress. This may help you decide on a focus. Then you can use your focus to start another chart.

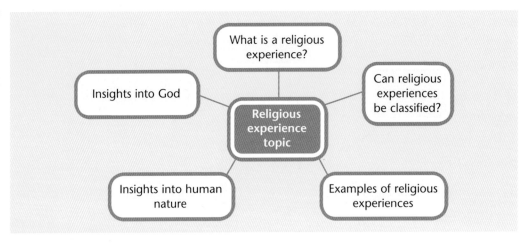

Overview of religious experience: meditation

Specification guidance notes (AO1)

Assessment objective 1 (Knowledge and understanding)

Select and demonstrate clearly relevant knowledge and understanding through the use of evidence, examples, and correct language and terminology appropriate to the course of study.

For this skill, you are expected to select and present relevant and appropriate information from the specification in order to answer questions on an area examined.

The examination board provides guidance notes in order to assist you with preparation for assessment.

In the notes it states:

Students may investigate the contributions of various scholars to an understanding of religious experience.

In addition to a number of key ideas from which the focus can be selected, students may study 'possible insights about human nature and God arising from such religious experiences'.

POSSIBLE AREAS FOR FOCUS IN THIS BOOK:

- What is meant by a religious experience
- Classifying religious experiences
- Examples of religious experience
- Insights about human nature
- Insights about God

1 What is a religious experience?

A good example of a religious experience is one that points to belief in God or some sense of being part of some ultimate reality. It is something subjective in that I can't experience your experience, since it is happening inside your mind to which I have no access. Also there are difficulties in finding language to describe it.

Research has shown the sheer breadth and variety of such experiences. When asked, many people included accounts of paranormal experiences as well as the more traditional religious experiences such as visions of the Virgin Mary and of angels. The charismatic Christian movement has also drawn attention to such experiences as speaking in tongues, prophecy and words of knowledge.

So do some features commonly occur in most religious experiences? Is there a common core? Probably the most cited list is that from Walter Stace. His eight-fold list of features of religious experiences includes:

- the unifying vision, expressed abstractly by the formula 'all is one' – all things are one, part of a whole
- timelessness and spacelessness
- sense of reality, not subjective but a valid source of knowledge
- blessedness, joy, peace and happiness
- feeling that what is apprehended is holy, or sacred, or divine – the quality that gives rise to the interpretation of the experience as being an experience of 'God'
- a sense of the presence of paradox and logic defied
- **ineffability**, cannot be described in words
- loss of the sense of self.

The experience…usually induces in the person concerned a conviction that the everyday world is not the whole of reality; there is another dimension to life…it alters behaviour and changes attitudes…[and] may be seen by an individual as life-enhancing, or he may recognise it as a special force which gives him added confidence or courage. As a result of their experiences many are led to prayer and religion.

(Hardy)

KEY WORDS

Ineffable: indefinable, defying expression or description
Theism: the belief in the existence of a God or gods
Monism: the view that there is only one basic and fundamental reality

Other definitions focus on an experience as an event that one lives through and about which one is conscious or aware. To be a religious experience, that which is experienced is either some supernatural being or God, or a being related to God, such as the Virgin Mary, or some indescribable Ultimate Reality. Hence religious experiences can be **theistic** (where God is the source and content of the experience) or monistic (where inner being or consciousness is experienced), as **monism** is the view that all reality is a unity or single substance.

Recent work on religious experience has drawn attention to their sheer breadth and variety. For instance, Jakobson (*Negative Religious Experiences*, 1999) has studied some accounts of negative experiences. Another area of growing interest is that of the paranormal and near-death experiences that are seen as having religious significance.

KEY WORDS

Transcendent: having existence outside the universe, usually depicted as an immaterial realm
Immanent: existing or remaining; in theology, it refers to God's involvement in creation

KEY QUOTES

A religious experience involves some kind of 'perception' of the invisible world, or involves a perception that some visible person or thing is a manifestation of the invisible world.

(Smart)

There is no single thing that can be bottled and neatly labelled as 'religious experience'

(Harvey)

 KEY IDEA

Features of mysticism:
- ineffability
- noetic
- transiency
- passivity
- sense of timelessness
- the oneness of everything
- the ego is not the real 'I'.

2 Can religious experiences be classified into groups?

Given the wide variety of experiences, it is not surprising that people have attempted to find some way of grouping them or trying to collate features that are common. For instance, a basic grouping is of experiences where there is contact with a **transcendent** being. The features in this case are awe and dependence. This is in contrast to those experiences that feature a more inward and **immanent** awareness.

Caroline Franks Davis has a different six-fold listing in her book *The Evidential Force of Religious Experience* (1989).

- Interpretive experience: an event that has no specifically religious characteristics is attributed to a divine source by a person with prior religious beliefs, for example, an answer to prayer.
- Quasi-sensory experience: The primary element is a physical sensation, such as a vision or hearing a voice.
- Revelatory experience: The 'enlightenment' experience in which the religious content makes it a religious experience.
- Regenerative experience: A conversion experience or an experience that renews the person's faith.
- Numinous experience: An experience of God's unapproachable holiness.
- Mystical experience: The sense of apprehending ultimate reality or a oneness with God.

The categories are not mutually exclusive, since an experience may exhibit characteristics of several categories.

3 Examples of particular types of religious experience across traditions

a) Mysticism

Mysticism can be defined as an experience that alters the state of consciousness and brings people to a new awareness of ultimate reality. For Christians, it is union and communion with God. For Buddhists, it is realisation of enlightenment.

James identified four features that an experience should have in order to justify calling it mystical.

- Ineffability: No adequate account of the experience can be given in words. They defy expression.
- Noetic quality: They are states that allow insight into the depths of truth unobtainable by the intellect alone.
- Transiency: The states cannot be maintained for long periods of time.
- Passivity: There is a sense of feeling that one is taken over by a superior power.

F.C. Happold identified another three characteristics of the mystical experience.

- Consciousness of the oneness of everything: This seems to be a sense of cosmic oneness. The usual awareness of identity, or ego, fades away and the person becomes aware of being part of a dimension much greater than themselves. This unity can be both introvertive, where external sense impressions are left behind, or extrovertive,

➡️ **EXAM TIP**

Remember to explain to the full each point that you make in an exam answer. Think carefully about each sentence, how it relates to the question and to the previous sentence. Aim for at least three clear sentences to explain a concept or idea, giving examples from different sources to support your point. For development of the point, bring in a variety of ways in which the application of this principle is demonstrated and introduce some contrasting scholarly views. This demonstrates that the answer is 'well-structured in depth or broad response to the task' (mid level 5 descriptor AO1) as opposed to the information being simply 'uncritical and descriptive presentation' (level 1 descriptor AO1) or 'presented within a limited framework' (level 2 descriptor AO1).

where the person reports that he feels a part of everything that is (for example, objects, other people, nature or the universe), or, more simply, that 'all is one'. For some this is the defining feature that serves to mark them off from other kinds of experiences. Many experiences have been recorded that lack this central feature of the consciousness of the oneness yet possess other mystical characteristics.

- Sense of timelessness: The subject feels beyond past, present and future, and beyond ordinary three-dimensional space in a realm of eternity or infinity.
- The understanding that the ego is not the real 'I': This seems to be a sense that there is an unchanging self that is immortal and that lies behind the usual experience of self (*Mysticism: A Study and Anthology*, 1963).

Hinduism has perhaps the oldest tradition of mysticism. The self (atman) in a person is identified with the supreme self (Brahman) of the universe. The apparent separateness and individuality of beings and events are held to be an illusion (maya). This illusion can be dispelled through the realisation of the essential oneness of atman and Brahman. Then a mystical state of liberation (moksha) is attained. The Hindu philosophy of Yoga is a discipline to experience union with the divine self.

Meditation is a key aspect of practice in most schools of Buddhism (see page 149). There is a range of different techniques and approaches, from quietly concentrating on your breathing to reciting mantras. The technique of mental concentration is called samatha, and its aim is to discover the real nature of the body and mind by overcoming attachments. A mantra is a short phrase and some believe that reciting the phrase in itself is sufficient to reveal enlightenment.

Zen Buddhism has a particular understanding of the idea of the dissolution of individuality, which contrasts markedly with that of Hinduism.

One of the most often-quoted Christian mystics is St Teresa of Avila (1515–82). Teresa wrote about her mystical experiences and the ineffable characteristic is prevalent, for example, in *The Collected Work of St Teresa of Avila* (1987).

> ...the soul is fully awake as regards God, but wholly asleep as regards things of this world.

Teresa's most famous book, *The Interior Castle*, describes a person's soul as a multi-chamber castle. Going deeper and deeper into your soul and facing your own fears, self-interest, ego and temptations gradually leads you to a deeper relationship with God. At the very centre chamber the soul is at complete peace and complete union with God.

✏️ **RESEARCH TASK**

Find out about the different techniques and approaches practised in Buddhism.

Objective: To develop 'wide range of selected relevant factual knowledge and understanding of the topic investigated' (level 5 descriptor AO1).

Sufism is the inner, mystical dimension of Islam. One person who made Sufism more acceptable within Islam was Al-Ghazali (CE1059–1111). He emphasised the personal, inner religious faith that should accompany the external practices of the religion. However, many Muslims and non-Muslims believe that Sufism is outside the sphere of Islam. All Muslims believe that they are on the pathway to God and will become close to Allah in Paradise, after death and the 'final judgement'. Sufis believe that it is possible to become close to God and to experience this closeness in this life now.

> *In the Presence, says the Sufi mystic [Shabistari], 'I' and 'thou' have ceased to exist, they have become one; the Quest and the Way and the Seeker are one.*
>
> **(The Mystics of Islam, 1963)**

b) Conversion

TASK

Read the poem *The Hound of Heaven* by Francis Thompson. What elements of conversion does this poem describe?

Objective: To develop 'key concepts explained by reference to evidence and examples' (level 5 descriptor AO1).

The word 'conversion' means 'to change direction' or 'to turn around'. McGuire (*Religion: The Social Context,* 1997) defined it as '…a process of religious change which transforms the way the individual perceives the rest of society and his or her personal place in it, altering one's view of the world.'

Conversion is a broad term and covers a variety of circumstances. The three possible types are:

- conversion from no religion to a faith: for example, Augustine
- conversion from one faith to another: for example, Sundar Singh
- conversion from faith (believing) to faith (trusting): for example, Martin Luther.

Religious conversions are very varied. In 1981 John Lofland and Norman Skonovd (*Journal for the Scientific Study of Religion,* 20) described six patterns (motifs) of religious conversion. The list has been summarised by Moojan Momen (*The Phenomenon of Religion,*1999).

- Intellectual: The emphasis is on intensive study with little interpersonal contact.
- Mystical: Occurs suddenly and dramatically, accompanied sometimes by dreams or visions.
- Experimental: The emphasis is on active exploration, assessing the religion over a period of time through participation.
- Affectional: Involves contact and bonding with actual members of the religion and experiencing being loved and nurtured.
- Revivalist: Occurs in a revivalist meeting. Usually involves emotional arousal.
- Coercive, through persuasion and thought programming: New religious movements are sometimes accused of this, though it is doubtful if they are guilty. Another form of this involves enticements with finance or social status.

Constantine's conversion to Christianity depicted in *The Emblem of Christ Appearing to Constantine* (Peter Paul Rubens, 1622)

TASK

Research what happened at Constantine's conversion to Christianity.

c) Visions

A vision can be defined as something seen other than by ordinary sight; it may be a supernatural or prophetic sight experienced usually in sleep or ecstasy, especially one that conveys a revelation. Hence it sometimes overlaps with mystical experiences, conversion, and revelation.

Visions are about:

- an image or event in which there is a message: for example, see Acts 10:9–16
- religious figures: for example, Joan of Arc's vision of Saint Michael
- places (heaven and hell): for example, Guru Nanak's vision of God's court
- fantastic creatures or figures: for example, see Ezekiel 1:6–10
- future (end of world or final judgement): for example, see Revelation 20:12–15.

d) Revelation

Revelation is divine self-disclosure. Through revelation, the divine becomes known to humanity. Like visions, revelation can be an aspect of any of the types of religious experience, for example, conversion. One approach to understanding what is meant by revelation is to view it as either propositional or non-propositional.

EXAM TIP

When answering a question on religious experience, make sure that you include a range of ideas – show how different concepts affect the issue you have chosen pick out the key principles and explain why they are important in relation to the issue debated and how they have been applied and interpreted by different scholars. This ensures focus is on 'a wide range of selected, relevant factual knowledge and understanding of the topic investigated; offering some analysis of issues raised by the topic, using a variety of sources, examples and/ or illustrations' (level 5 descriptor AO1) and also 'structured around, and showing clear understanding of, the main theme(s) or concept(s) of the task' (level 5 descriptor AO1). This would distinguish your work from a poorer answer that would focus simply on the general topic with an unspecific summary of ideas and with little reference to scholars meaning only 'some relevant and partially structured knowledge of the topic investigated' and evidencing only 'a limited framework…with a general link to the task' (level 2 descriptor AO1).

i) Propositional revelation

Propositional revelation is the communication of some truth by God to humans through supernatural means. The content of this revelation is a body of truths expressed in statements or propositions. Judaism, Christianity and Islam all claim instances of such revelation. For instance, Judaism cites the revelation of the Law to Moses on Mount Sinai (Exodus 19–23). In Christianity, the Bible is regarded as 'the Word of God' and in Islam the prophet Muhammad received the Qur'an.

ii) Non-propositional revelation

Non-propositional revelation is not a matter of Divinity imparting knowledge directly to humanity, but of a moment of realisation coming at the end of a period of reflection. In contrast to the propositional view that produces a body of truths about God, the non-propositional concept of revelation represents human attempts to understand the significance of revelatory events. It involves seeing or interpreting events in a special way. For instance, the prophets of the Old Testament saw events in a special way, as having spiritual significance rather than just political or sociological importance. To them the Fall of Samaria or Jerusalem were expressions of judgement on Israel and its people because of their disobedience. They saw God as actively at work in the world around them.

Buddhism contrasts with the theistic religions, in that the various Buddhist scriptures are not seen as emerging from some transcendent source but rather from within the Buddha himself. After six years of hardship and continual striving, the Buddha finally gained enlightenment. The profundity of this experience left him in no doubt that he had achieved final knowledge, that there was something beyond the cycle of old age, sickness and death, that there *was* an end to suffering. As he sat meditating under the Bodhi tree, he realised that he had been reborn many times, that all beings were reborn according to their deeds, that suffering was fuelled by craving and that there was a means of bringing this suffering to an end. What comes through in the scriptures is the Buddha's absolute certainty that he had attained ultimate realisation and that he knew the precise means by which others could attain it too.

According to Davis (*The Evidential Force of Religious Experience*, 1989), there are five distinctive features of revelation experience.

- They are sudden and of short duration.
- The alleged new knowledge is acquired immediately.
- The alleged new knowledge is from an external agent.
- The alleged new knowledge is received with utter conviction.
- The insights are often impossible to put into words (ineffability).

One of the main features listed above was acquiring new knowledge. There is a great sense of certainty and the knowing is perceived in quite a different way from intellectual knowledge.

As to what exactly it is that is known seems to vary.

- Universal truths: for example, when Guru Nanak received a universal truth revelation about the name of God.
- The future: for example, when Hildegard of Bingen seemingly foretold the Protestant Reformation.
- The present: for example, Benny Hinn, who claims God will heal people at his meetings.
- Spiritual help: for example, Martin Luther when he studied the book of Romans.

4 Insights about human nature

If religious experiences are of God, then they demonstrate that human beings can have communication with God and that human beings can experience God. God interacts with our lives and affects them. Swinburne argued that:

An omnipotent and perfectly good creator will seek to interact with his creatures and, in particular, with human persons capable of knowing him.

If the religious experiences are not of God, then it shows us something about the human psyche. Certainly many psychologists have focused on this understanding and insight.

There has also been much research into personality types and religiousness. For instance a survey carried out by Hay found that:

- women report more religious experiences than men
- the occurrence of religious experiences gradually increases with the believer's age
- educated individuals are more active in aspects of religion and report more religious experiences
- incidence is higher among upper-middle class than unskilled workers
- they occur to members of all denominations and none, and also to agnostics and atheists
- the occurrence is higher among church members.

It has long been noted that many conversions take place at the age of puberty and some commentators have therefore tried to identify some connection between the two, for instance, they may be seen either as a form of independence and rebellion against parents or as some form of sexual love.

Freud argued that it was related to the relationship with the father. God is a projected father-figure; needed as a source of protection but also a source of fear and guilt. Research claims that converts have had weaker relations with their fathers than matched unconverted people. However, even if people have need for a father figure, it does not mean that God is not one. There does still remain the possibility that such a state is a necessary requirement for the experience, but such a state would not necessarily negate acclaimed experience of God.

5 Insights about God

If religious experiences are of God, then they demonstrate that God exists since he is the cause of the experiences. If so, then it shows that God seeks to interact with his creatures. He is able to make himself known to us. It also implies that God is loving and personal.

Specification guidance notes (AO2)

Assessment objective 2 (Critical evaluation)

Critically evaluate and justify a point of view through the use of evidence and reasoned argument.

The examination board provides guidance notes in order to assist you with preparation for assessment. In the notes it states:

> **TASK**
>
> **Draw up a table with the three headings:**
> - **Definition**
> - **Meaning**
> - **Examples.**
>
> **Use the information found in your selected topic to complete the table, clearly relating the key ideas and relevant terms to the central issues.**
>
> Objective: To develop an understanding of the literal meanings, key ideas and relevant terms but also the wider application of these meanings. To demonstrate a deeper understanding of these key ideas and relevant terms, using examples to support explanation and demonstrating a 'coherent understanding of task; based on selection of material to demonstrate emphasis and clarity of ideas' and also a 'careful analysis of key concepts' (higher level 5 descriptor AO1).

Students may study the Gospel narratives, the Letters and place the context of these ideas in relation to philosophy and science.

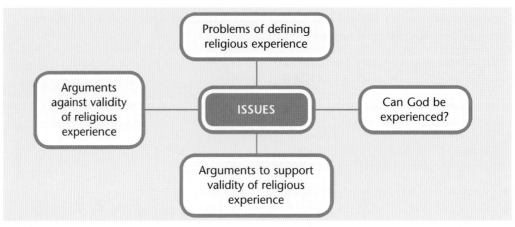

An overview of issues for debate

1 Problems of defining religious experience

Philosophy is notorious for asking awkward questions about things that most consider obvious and straightforward! Not surprisingly then, philosophers have raised questions about the meaning of the words 'religious' and 'experience'.

a) Religious

Anthony Thiselton (*A Concise Encyclopedia of the Philosophy of Religion,* 2002) highlights three factors in post-modern thought that make defining 'religion' and 'religious' a problem. Firstly, there is the awareness of diversity and pluralism and a growing reluctance to generalise. The word 'religious' can mean almost anything, but because of this it can also mean very little.

Secondly, there is the recognition that our knowledge and understanding are conditioned by our own intellectual background. They are not value-neutral. Thiselton cites Wittgenstein's criticisms of Frazer:

> *Wittgenstein criticised Frazer's* The Golden Bough *for offering 'explanations' of the beliefs and practices of other cultures and other religions as if these were practised by men who think in a similar way to himself. Frazer too readily 'explained' them in such a way as to make them seem 'stupidities', because he abstracted them from the life-context that made them intelligible.*

Thirdly he notes that the post-modern view of religions has viewed them as serving the vested interests of social power, and so has viewed them sociologically or ideologically, rather than theologically. In other words, we take the 'God' out of them.

b) Experience

One meaning of 'to experience' is to participate in or to live through. We might talk about having experience with cars. This poses no problem as the event is in the public sphere, other people can see you working on a car. The other meaning of 'experience', however, is more problematic. It is to perceive directly, be aware of or be conscious of. In this case the experience is subjective and private. It is some inner process that others cannot see. Therefore no one can refute my claim that I am experiencing something, even if the source is disputed. If I claim to hear the voice of God, there is no way of either verifying or falsifying that claim. The claimed source of the experience is beyond our powers of investigation.

Steven Katz argues that there is no experience that is unmediated by concepts and beliefs. All experience is processed through the beliefs, learned categories and conceptual frameworks of the experiencer; religious belief conditions religious experience so that persons in different religious traditions actually experience differently. There is not one religious experience but many.

2 Is the notion of 'experience of God' meaningful?

Analogies are appealed to, to justify the philosophical notion of a religious experience of God, but many argue that the analogies have weaknesses.

- It is like a sense experience: People argue that just as you can encounter a table, you can also encounter God, but the two are very different. For instance, God is not material, nor does he have a definite location. Also, claims can be checked of encounters with objects, but when the object is God, they are not checkable.
- It is similar to an experience of people: People argue that just as we are known to each other by a kind of direct apprehension rather than through our physical body; so in the same way we experience God who is non-corporeal.
- Can God be recognised? The problem arises as to how you can distinguish God from other possible objects of experience. For instance, God is said to be Creator. How would you recognise that attribute? God is said also to be omnipresent, infinite, omnipotent and eternal. But how, simply by virtue of an awareness of an object of experience, can anything be recognised to be that? To recognise omniscience, you would have to be omniscient yourself!
- Direct experience of God is impossible: Some claim that the finite cannot experience the infinite – so we cannot experience God. Others argue that to speak of a direct experience is not philosophically correct since we infer and interpret every experience. For instance, even an ordinary object is mediated and interpreted via our sense data and organs. Indeed it could be argued that the religious person interprets according to a religious framework of life, while the atheist interprets experiences as purely natural events. Hick referred to this as 'experiencing-as' and used the ambiguous figure of the 'rabbit–duck' to illustrate it.

KEY IDEA

When shown the rabbit–duck image, some see a duck and some see a rabbit. If tested on Easter Sunday many more see a rabbit. We interpret according to our framework.

TASK

Think of the questions you would like to ask about the focus you have chosen or about the views that scholars have presented in response to the focus you have chosen. Is there anything that is not clear? What needs further explanation? Do you wish to challenge the thinking or view of a scholar? If so, can you list your reasons or evidence?

Objective: To develop AO2 skills of questioning, considering different views, analysing arguments and responding to the material studied: 'critically evaluate and justify a point of view through the use of evidence and reasoned argument'. It aids self-reflection and development of an argument, working towards 'some attempt to set out reasons for alternative views; a point of view expressed clearly, supported by some relevant evidence and argument' (level 3 descriptor AO2) or even an 'attempt at an evaluation of the issue(s) raised in the task, typically through a careful analysis of alternative views; leading to a clearly expressed viewpoint supported by well-deployed evidence and reasoned argument' (level 4 descriptor AO2).

3 Arguments to support the validity of religious experience

a) Swinburne's principle of credulity

Swinburne's argument is focused on the onus of proof and put in the context of ordinary sense experiences. He argued that we are justified in accepting that an event occurs unless there are strong reasons to the contrary, for example, reasons for supposing the viewer was hallucinating. It is up to the disbeliever to show that it is unreasonable to believe the account, rather than for the believer to show that it is reasonable to believe. It is a case of religious experiences being viewed as true until proven otherwise.

To express this principle formally: 'In the absence of any special considerations, if it seems that X is present to a person, then probably X is present.' What one seems to perceive is probably the case. Swinburne points out that unless we do this we cannot know anything. We would have to be sceptical about all our sense experiences. If my experience of seeing a cat in a tree does not justify my belief that there is a cat in the tree, then it seems that I could never be justified in believing that there is a cat in the tree, nor indeed anything else for that matter.

b) Swinburne's principle of testimony

Swinburne argues that, in the absence of special considerations, it is reasonable to believe that the experiences of others are probably as they report them. We should believe other people unless we have good reason not to. Clearly he accepts the point that people can lie or be mistaken, but the significance of this approach is to put the onus on the sceptic to show that religious experience should be rejected rather than for the believer to show that it is true.

c) Circumstantial evidence

Whether religious experience is seen to be caused by God will depend to a great extent upon individual pre-suppositions. If our pre-suppositions favour particular types of experience we are more likely to be convinced of reports of them.

However, the following criteria may add weight to validity.

- It must be in keeping with the character of God as made known in different ways, for example, through natural theology, agreement with doctrine, resemblance of experience to classic cases in religious tradition as judged by spiritual authorities.
- The results of the experience should make a noticeable difference to the religious life of the person. It should lead to a new life marked by virtues such as wisdom, humility and goodness of life. It should build up the community rather than destroy it. Teresa of Avila said:

  Though the devil can give some pleasures…only God-produced experiences leave the soul in peace and tranquillity and devotion to God.

- The person should be regarded as someone who is mentally and psychologically well balanced.

It should also be noted that some argue that the origin of an experience is irrelevant. The fact that the source may be an ordinary experience doesn't mean that the experience cannot become a religious one by the interpretation of the subject.

EXAM TIP

Be careful when using quotes in critical assessments. Always make sure that they relate to the argument that is presented. To make sure of this, always explain the relevance of the quote in your answer. This is the difference between 'a mainly descriptive response…supported by reference to a simple argument or unstructured evidence' or 'a point of view supported by limited but appropriate evidence and/or argument' (levels 1 and 2 descriptors AO2) and that of a level 3 and above answer that clearly attempts analysis or 'some attempt to set out reasons for alternative views' (level 3 descriptor AO2) and the best answer that delivers 'a careful analysis of alternative views' (level 4 descriptor AO2).

4 Arguments against the validity of religious experience

Swinburne used the ordinary sense experience as a parallel to a religious experience. However, it is questionable whether it can be authenticated in the way that an ordinary sense experience can. Religious experiences are very much a private matter rather than public and it is not possible therefore to check someone's religious experience. A number of points have been discussed about this whole area.

a) The physiological

Drugs do seem to be linked to religious experiences in that, for example, the Aztecs are known to have used a drug. Likewise marihuana is used in parts of India by such groups as the Rastafarians, as was LSD among some religious groups in the US in the 1960s.

A test carried out on theological students during a Good Friday meditation (1966) involved half being given a drug and half a placebo. The result was that those on drugs had significantly more religious experiences. Such evidence implies religious experiences have a physiological explanation. Investigations into the existence of a religious gene, and the role of the temporal lobes in causing such experiences, have been the latest focuses of research.

b) The psychological

The part the mind plays in causing supposed religious experiences has long been debated. Some see conversion as meeting the psychological needs of people, whilst Freud saw religious experience as a reaction to a hostile world. We feel helpless and seek a father figure. Thus we create a God who is able to satisfy our needs.

Other psychological states suggested to account for such experiences include mental illness, sexual frustrations, adolescence, guilt and particular personality types.

c) Reasons that make it unlikely

Some people argue that if religious experience comes from God then surely certain things would be expected to follow. Several points have been put forward.

- Lack of uniformity of experience: The fact that different experiences are recounted seems to count against the argument. If God were the source of them all, surely there would be greater similarity between them. Some see Allah, some see the Virgin Mary some see Jesus. Others just experience a great power. Very few (if any) Hindus have visions of the Virgin Mary, and very few (if any) Roman Catholics have visions of Vishnu. If Hinduism is true, then Roman Catholicism is false and vice versa.
- Not all experience it: If God existed, he would want everyone to know about him and therefore we all should have religious experiences.
- There is no God: therefore the experience of God cannot be valid. The experiences must have a natural explanation.

KEY IDEA

There are at least three ways to assess a religious experience.
- **What do I think actually happened?**
- **How do I interpret it?**
- **Would I interpret it differently if the experience had happened to me rather than to someone else?**

It is said that in 1917 Mary, the mother of Jesus, appeared several times over a period of six months, to three young shepherd children, in a village called Fatima in Portugal.

5 Possible conclusions

When assessing religious experience, it is important to reflect upon the arguments previously discussed and arrive at some appropriate conclusion. It may be that you accept none of these listed here, or just one of them, or you may have a different conclusion that is not listed. However, what is important is the way that you have arrived at your conclusion – the reasoning process.

From the preceding discussions, here are some possible conclusions you could draw.

1   Religious experiences cannot be valid since there is no God.

2   The concept of a religious experience is philosophically incoherent.

3   All religious experiences can be explained naturalistically.

4   Though religious experiences have a natural explanation, they nonetheless, still result in a religious experience.

5   Some religious experiences can be explained naturalistically, some have no apparent explanation.

6   Some religious experiences can be explained naturalistically but some appear to be valid.

7   Religious experiences occur in all religions.

8   Religious experiences occur in only one religion, the claims from other religions are false.

INVESTIGATIONS
Area C: The study of ethics

The individual unit content outline from the specification gives three possible areas of study for a topic. The authors have chosen one area for each unit.

For this unit they have selected **7: Medical ethics**.

Whichever area of the specification is chosen, it is important that you are familiar with the overall general topic.

For the purposes of this book, this means the relevant chapter and corresponding assessment and reflections.

RESEARCH TIP

Make sure that you read through the information for the topic and, perhaps, make some preliminary background notes before you focus your attention on choosing an area of interest.

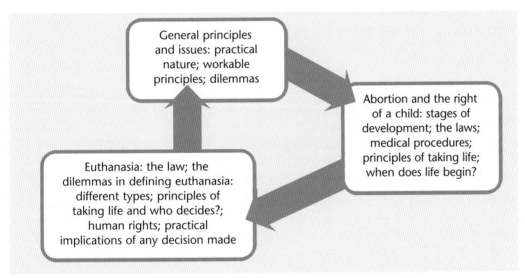

Overview: Medical ethics

This diagram shows an outline of the sorts of area we are going to look at. Using this as a basis, create and extend it into your own thought-process diagram as you progress. This may help you decide on a focus. Then you can use your focus to start another chart.

Specification guidance notes (AO1)

Assessment objective 1 (Knowledge and understanding)

Select and demonstrate clearly relevant knowledge and understanding through the use of evidence, examples, and correct language and terminology appropriate to the course of study.

For this skill, you are expected to select and present relevant and appropriate information from the specification in order to answer an area examined.

The examination board provides guidance notes in order to assist you with preparation for assessment.

In the notes it states:

Students may investigate one or more of a range of issues in medical ethics. This may focus on issues such as abortion, contraception, genetic engineering, organ transplantation, use and distribution of medical resources, euthanasia in its various forms, palliative care, fertility treatment, neo-natal care, for example, in the case of exceedingly premature births or handicapped newborns, or development of new medical treatments and procedures.

POSSIBLE AREAS FOR FOCUS IN THIS BOOK

- abortion
- euthanasia
- genetic engineering

Turn to the section on *Ethics* in the Foundation section, to find out some more information about different ethical theories and applied ethics.

Objective: To develop a 'coherent understanding of the task; based on selection of material to demonstrate emphasis and clarity of ideas' (level 5 descriptor AO1).

KEY WORDS

Fetus: the developing unborn baby from the end of the eighth week after conception (when the major structures have formed) until birth

Surrogacy: one woman carrying a baby for another woman who cannot do so herself

Zygote: a cell formed by the union of a male sex cell (a sperm) and a female sex cell (an ovum), which develops into the embryo according to information encoded in its genetic material

Blastocyst: a group of multiplying cells

Embryo: an animal in the early stage of development before birth; in humans, the embryo stage is the first three months after conception

Here we shall study abortion, euthanasia and genetic engineering.

Various possibilities are then included for applied ethics ranging from 'Students should consider the range of controversies which arise from these issues, examining them from one or more ethical perspectives, for example, utilitarian approaches, religious ethics, or deontological moral theories.' Some of these topics can be found in depth in other areas of this book.

Then we shall study some different perspectives on the selected issues.

1 Medical ethics – introduction

Before reading this section, turn to the Foundations section on Ethics and read the introduction to ethical theory and applied ethics (if you have not studied this before).

2 Abortion and the right to a child

a) Introduction

The issue of abortion is complex; debate can be very passionate and emotive. Although there is some degree of consensus, there is vagueness and lack of clarity in crucial areas. The perceptions of rights and principles, viewed from medical, legal, ethical and religious perspectives, are often conflicting. Against this complex background is the additional factor of the continual advance of science and technology; for example, rapid progress has been made in supporting a **fetus** outside the womb.

Abortion is an issue that involves conflicting rights of individuals, therefore it is vital to consider all angles and perspectives when considering a response. Another issue related to that of abortion is the right to have a child, or whether a child is a 'gift from God'. This includes the issues of infertility treatment and surrogacy.

Approximately ten per cent of marriages in the UK are infertile. There is a distinction between childlessness and infertility. Infertility is a medical condition and there are medical treatments available to assist with reproduction; childlessness, however, is a general term applied when such treatment has been unsuccessful. This introduces the concept of **surrogacy**.

b) Key facts

It is important to begin with the stages of development of a human being. The beginning of 'humanness' is debated in philosophical, ethical and legal circles but, biologically speaking, the beginning is at conception.

In its broadest terms, the development, that is, the actualisation of the potentiality to become fully human, takes the following course:

1 conception

2 **zygote** (pre-embryo, 0–5 days)

3 **blastocyst** (a group of multiplying cells, pre-embryo, 5–14 days)

4 **embryo** (14 days to 8 weeks)

5 fetus (8 weeks onwards)

6 newborn (birth, usually between 38 and 42 weeks).

It is interesting that the stage of pregnancy is calculated from the first day of the woman's last period. Despite such accuracy of science and technology, even the stage of conception is, arguably, vague and the timings given above assume normal growth rates.

Personhood may be one thing and human life another; hence it is possible to argue that, while the zygote may not be a person, there is no logical alternative to regarding it as the first stage in human life.

(Mason and Laurie)

An abortion can be defined as the termination of a pregnancy before 24 weeks. Abortions are available on the NHS but women seeking them must be referred by a doctor. According to the Brook Advisory Service:

...although the normal legal limit for abortion is 24 weeks, it is usually easiest to get an abortion on the NHS if a woman is under 12 weeks pregnant.

KEY WORDS

Medical abortion: abortion by means of the abortion pill

Surgical abortion: abortion by means of the suction method

There are two classifications of abortion: medical and surgical. **Medical abortion** is achieved by means of an abortion pill (*mifepristone*) and a tablet (*prostaglandin*) inserted into the vagina 36 to 48 hours later. It involves no surgery and, in effect, is like heavy menstruation; however, it is not available in all areas.

Surgical abortion is most common. It is achieved through vacuum aspiration or suction and is available up to the 13th week of pregnancy. Women usually recover within a few hours and can go home the same day. In later stages of pregnancy, a process of dilation and evacuation is used, which involves opening the cervix and entering the womb, then removing the contents by means of surgical instruments as well as suction.

The traditional Christian teaching, that a child is a blessing and a gift from God, is recognised many times throughout both the Old and New Testaments. The more specific biblical teachings about sexual relationships, understood at a literal level, suggest that the purpose of sexual intercourse is procreation. Indeed, this is the line taken by both the Roman Catholic Church and the theory of natural law. A child should clearly be born within a marriage.

There are, however, definite disagreements within Christianity regarding the ideas of both infertility treatments and surrogacy. This tends to be related to how the biblical text should be interpreted and understood.

From a non-religious perspective, the *Universal Declaration of Human Rights*, Article 16, cites 'the right to marry and found a family'. The crucial question, however, depends upon how this right is understood. Does this extend to and mean that any government should provide opportunities for infertile couples as a basic human right? What about single women? What about homosexual relationships?

The *Human Fertility and Embryology Act 1990* (HFEA) provides regulations on infertility treatments. Surrogacy has a separate Act or Agreement dating from 1985.

Generally, treatments for infertility are partial and involve donor insemination (the insertion of semen from either the woman's partner or another donor) or IVF, in which the egg and sperm cells (gametes) are combined outside the woman's body and then inserted into her womb, to produce what are known as test-tube babies.

TASK

Try to identify the positive and the negative aspects in relation to the issue that you choose. Record your ideas in the form of a table. Look at factors such as religious ideas, the law and practical implications.

Objective: To develop the 'presentation of a good range of well-selected material from the topic investigated, to show a coherent understanding of its significant features within the context of the issue(s) raised' and, at the same time, 'highlighting some key concepts and supported by the use of appropriate evidence and/or examples' (level 4 descriptor AO1).

There is, however, another alternative to infertility treatment as described above. This involves the complete insertion of the gametes into a third party.

> *Surrogate motherhood requires the active cooperation of an otherwise uninvolved woman in the process of pregnancy and birth. It thus introduces a third party into the reproductive process.*
> **(Mason and Laurie)**

This is often referred to as womb-leasing.

c) The legal status

The history of the law against abortion begins with the *Offences Against the Person Act 1861*, which depicts procuring a miscarriage as a criminal act. The problem was that there was no option for therapeutic activity. In 1929 the *Infant Preservation Act* allowed the preservation of the mother's life as reason for a termination.

David Steel introduced the *Abortion Act 1967* that stated:

● two doctors must agree that an abortion is necessary.

It is deemed necessary if:

● the woman's physical health is threatened by having the baby and existing children would be harmed, mentally or physically, by the woman proceeding to have the baby
● there is a high risk the baby would be handicapped.

This was clarified by the *Embryology Act 1990* (section 37):

> *...it now states that a person is not guilty of an offence under the law of abortion when termination is performed by a registered practitioner and two registered medical practitioners have formed the opinion in good faith that the continuance of the pregnancy would involve risk, greater than if the pregnancy were terminated, of injury to the physical or mental health of the pregnant woman or any existing children of her family.*
> **(Mason and Laurie)**

The legal limit was reduced from 28 weeks to 24 weeks but the 1990 Act, however, also removed time restrictions for a fetus aborted due to abnormality. This raises two issues.

> *What is to be done with a live fetus? The 1990 Act absolves the gynaecologist of destruction only and not the killing of a 'creature in being'.*

> *The dilemma of the gynaecologist who is there to relieve a woman of her fetus, however, is that 'there is now an infant who, on any interpretation, is entitled to a birth certificate, and, if necessary, a certificate as to the cause of death'.*
> **(Mason and Laurie)**

Infertility treatment is currently legal, although it is very difficult to access and is also expensive. Voluntary surrogacy is legal but, in line with the *1985 Surrogacy Agreement*, any form of surrogacy for financial gain is illegal. The illegal nature of payments relates directly to laws covering adoption, the only alternative prior to surrogacy:

> *...the rigid prohibition of commercialisation within adoption derives from a fear of exploitation of the woman concerned.*
> **(Mason and Laurie)**

66 **KEY QUOTE**

The basic argument against abortion, on which all others build, is that the unborn child is already a human being, a person, a bearer of rights, and that abortion is therefore murder.

(Mackie)

99

Because 'both the ethics and the law relating to surrogacy are still in an uncertain state' (Mason and Laurie), a review was set up to evaluate the situation. The Brazier Review, as it was known, recommended that:

- genuine expenses and reasonable costs for surrogacy need to be defined by ministers
- agencies should be overseen and arrangements established and registered by health departments that also operate under a code of practice
- current legislation be improved by the addition of a consolidated and separate surrogacy act.

At present, costs incurred through surrogacy are estimated at £10–12 000. One final complication is that surrogacy arrangements cannot be enforced by law and either party can change its mind at any time.

Is a child a precious gift, given by a divine creator, or a human right that should be afforded to a person, regardless of ability to procreate?

> **KEY QUOTE**
>
> *Whether or not abortion should be legal turns on the answer to the question of whether and at what point a fetus is a person. This is a question that cannot be answered logically or empirically. The concept of personhood is neither logical nor empirical: it is essentially a religious, or quasi-religious idea, based on one's fundamental (and therefore unverifiable) assumptions about the nature of the world.*
>
> **(Campos)**

d) Specific ethical issues and key areas of the debate

These tend to be grouped into debates concerning key ideas, as discussed below.

i) Principles

The first issue involves the principles associated with abortion and hinges on the consideration of the act of killing and the ethical questions that this raises.

> *To kill a human adult is murder, and is unhesitatingly and universally condemned. Yet there is no obvious sharp line which marks the zygote from the adult. Hence the problem.*
>
> **(Singer)**

The second and related issue involves the **sanctity of life**, which is the belief that life is in some way sacred or holy, traditionally understood as being given by God. Kant actually gives the idea of the sanctity of life a non-religious perspective based on purely ethical grounds, and philosophers such as Peter Singer have long called for a shift from talking about the sanctity of life towards a more universal discussion about the value of life.

> **KEY WORD**
>
> **Sanctity of life:** the belief that life is sacred or holy, given by God

We may take the doctrine of the sanctity of human life to be no more than a way of saying that human life has some very special value…The view that human life has unique value is deeply rooted in our society and is enshrined in our law.

(Singer)

The key debates then consider when an act can be classed as killing, or even murder, and at which point potential human life acquires such value as to make abortion an ethical injustice. This leads into more specific questions concerning the nature and status of the fetus, which is the second key area of debate.

Is this status of personhood dependent on the ability to think and reason?

ii) The beginning of life and personhood

One of the major problems with the abortion debate is that there are blurred and inaccurate definitions for the terminology. For example, those campaigning against abortion (**pro-life**), and those campaigning for the rights of women to have abortions (**pro-choice**), interpret the terms *life* and *unborn* differently. For one group the idea of a human person includes the stage of an embryo, while the other considers only that stage beyond birth.

It is important, therefore, to establish what such interested parties actually mean when they refer to a baby, a person and a life. This is intrinsic to this aspect of the debate and therefore it is important to consider some different views.

There are several arguments concerning the application of the status of personhood to the embryo, fetus or child. These tend to be based on either biological stages or related to philosophical and religious principles or concepts.

iii) Biological debates

Biological debates depend upon physical evidence to define the status of the fetus.

- **Birth**: The status of personhood is only applied at actual physical birth. This is the first true point of independence and individuality.
- **Viability**: The status of personhood is awarded at that time when the unborn can exist beyond any dependence on the mother. Obviously, with advancing technologies this stage is fluid. There is also debate about the appropriate meaning of viability. For example, how can a newly born child exist independently, in real terms?
- **Quickening**: A traditional understanding that the status of personhood can be applied when the 'child' is first felt to move, although this varies from individual to individual. The ideas of viability and live birth 'both depend upon the medical support available' and 'the diagnosis can only be made after the event' (Mason and Laurie).
- **Potential** (at conception): The possibility, from the point of fertilisation of the egg (conception), of becoming a human.

iv) Philosophical and religious debates

Philosophical or religious arguments are based on concepts or principles beyond the physical evidence, that is, the metaphysical issues.

- **Consciousness**: The status of personhood is applied at the first point of consciousness; however, is status of personhood dependent on the ability to think and reason?

KEY WORDS

Pro-life: against abortion

Pro-choice: supporting women's right to have abortions

Birth: the point at which the child is separated from the mother and becomes a separate entity

Viability: the ability to grow and develop into an adult, especially the ability of the child to exist without dependence on the mother

Quickening: traditionally, when the child is first felt to move inside the mother

Potential: the possibility, at conception, of becoming a human person

Consciousness: awareness of self

- **Ensoulment**: The status of personhood is deemed appropriate when the soul enters the body. Once again, this point is debated, proposals between 40 and 90 days have been offered, but the argument defies accuracy.
- **Continuity**: Life must begin when the potential life as an individual entity is recognisable, which is the zygote at conception. Any line drawn beyond this is arbitrary and has no justification, since life is one continuous and related process.
- **Relational factors**: All arguments are based upon the meaning of words, or what Vardy calls relational factors. That is, there are different interpretations or understandings of the same words. This is where the argument began. Until accurate definitions of key terms are agreed, the stage at which personhood status is awarded can never be universal.

Finally, there is a clear disparity in the development of individuals. During life, although there are broad timescales at which people mature, develop and grow, there is, by the very nature of individuality, a blurring of the exact moment one moves from adolescence to adulthood, from childhood through puberty and so forth. Why are the early stages of development any different?

This leads to the last key issue: when the point of life is established and the status of personhood awarded, does it follow that the rights afforded to a person are already in place when this status is established?

v) Rights

The underlying question here is the right of all those involved to life. This must include both the established personhood and the woman involved. When the rights of both are in direct conflict, for example, when the mother's life is at risk, the law is clear – but is it ethically justified? When rights have been awarded it is then appropriate to consider the relative importance of different rights. Are those of the personhood limited and restricted or basic in any way? Does the woman's right to choice supersede the basic right to life of the personhood? Although these issues are difficult to consider, they are at the heart of the untidy nature of the debate.

Related to this, among physicians is the issue of adherence to the Hippocratic oath, to preserve life at all costs, but also the right not to take part in abortion according to conscience.

This oath has been the basis of medicine for centuries. Although it has been updated for our times and transformed to suit the current aims of medicine, the principles of preservation of life still remain.

 KEY IDEA

Hippocratic oath – classical version:
...I will neither give a deadly drug to anybody who asked for it, nor will I make a suggestion to this effect. Similarly I will not give to a woman an abortive remedy. In purity and holiness I will guard my life and my art.

...What I may see or hear in the course of the treatment or even outside of the treatment in regard to the life of men, which on no account one must spread abroad, I will keep to myself, holding such things shameful to be spoken about.

If I fulfil this oath and do not violate it, may it be granted to me to enjoy life and art, being honoured with fame among all men for all time to come; if I transgress it and swear falsely, may the opposite of all this be my lot.

🔑 KEY WORDS

Ensoulment: the point when the soul enters the body
Continuity: occurs at the first point at which potential life is recognisable
Relational factors: different interpretations of the same words or terms, depending on the viewpoint of the observer

---

❝ KEY QUOTES

The only absolute in the saga is that 'life' as it is generally understood begins with the formation of the zygote; on this view, the conservative Roman Catholic view represents the only tenable option – the difficulty is that it is also the least practical solution to the question.

Definitions intended for statistical use are not, however, necessarily the same as those to be applied in practice.

The doctor's dilemma is self-evident – is he or she practising truly 'good' medicine in keeping alive a neonate who will be unable to take a place in society or who will be subject to pain and suffering throughout life?

(Mason and Laurie)
❞

TASK

Draw up a table with the three headings 'definition', 'meaning' and 'examples'. Use the information found in your selected topic to complete the table, clearly relating the key ideas and relevant terms to the central issues. Objective: To develop an understanding of the literal meanings, key ideas and relevant terms but also the wider application of these meanings. To demonstrate a deeper understanding of these key ideas and relevant terms, using examples to support explanation, and demonstrating a 'coherent understanding of the task; based on selection of material to demonstrate emphasis and clarity of ideas' and also a 'careful analysis of key concepts' (higher level 5 descriptor AO1).

66 KEY QUOTE

The massive technological advances of the last half century have increased our capabilities...we have become more and more aware that, occasionally, the preservation of life can be a negative blessing.

(Mason and Laurie)

99

In such a consideration of rights, there is also the issue of infertility and the right to have a child. If a woman has established the right to decide how to treat and deal with her own body, this has implications for the manipulation and use of advancements in both medical science and technologies associated with infertility treatment. Should bearing a child be seen as a right? Or, as some would argue from religious perspectives, is a child a divine gift?

Several awkward questions remain.

- What exactly are the rights of the third party in surrogacy?
- What are, and who protects, the rights of the fetus?
- What about the freedom to choose for non-medical reasons?
- Do the infertility technologies invade a woman's life?
- Does a woman relinquish control over her own body?
- Alternatively, is technology the opportunity to exercise the rights afforded to the status of womanhood?
- Are the infertility technologies an opportunity for women to have more power?

vi) Practical implications

Finally, whatever conclusion is drawn or line of argument taken, it is vital to consider the opening observation regarding applied ethics. One of the most crucial stages and factors for arriving at a conclusion to an argument is its workability. Each line of argument will have practical implications that affect real people in the real world.

On the pro-life side there is the practical impact of cheapening what they regard as the specific status of life. It has often been said that the Abortion Act encourages in practice a lack of responsibility and hides the real issues concerned with sexual behaviour and individual responsibilities. The final practicality here would be the devaluation and undermining of the sexual act that, according to some, is for procreation.

The issue of a right to have a child raises many questions. With IVF comes the option of choosing the gender of the child. Although posing 'a negligible effect on the distribution and status of the sexes in the UK' (Mason and Laurie), this could have devastating effects in other areas of the world. Even if there were valid medical reasons for gender selection, what are the implications of selection for non-medical reasons?

Infertility treatment is very costly and therefore its availability is restricted. The issue of infertility treatment being available, nationwide, has prompted the recent proposal to aim to offer three free cycles of treatment for all qualifying infertile couples. How far in the future is this and how is it prioritised?

On the issue of surrogacy, the right of singles or homosexuals to have a child has already been mentioned. Effectively, '...since there is no legal regulation of the matter, the practitioner acting in a private capacity will have to decide on ethical grounds alone whether or not to proceed in these circumstances.'

- Should such a crucial decision be made on personal ethical grounds alone?
- If the fetus is deformed, then can the surrogate mother request an abortion?
- Who actually owns the unborn child?

The whole nature of what it means to be a mother, whether in biological or social terms, needs consideration.

Surrogacy could, however, be used for purely selfish reasons – for example, a desire to have a child without interference with a career – although the prospect may be given exaggerated importance.

(Mason and Laurie)

Indeed, the matter is further complicated by the suggestion that to prohibit payments, despite preventing potential exploitation, could lead to another, equally unpleasant social scenario:

…the effect of prohibiting paid arrangements in the registered field must be to force the process onto the 'back streets', which would be to overturn the whole purpose of regulation.

(Mason and Laurie)

However, to tighten up on abortions or surrogacy and to restrict them would equally imply the curtailment of rights for which society has fought. There would be a clear feeling of oppression and lack of human freedom. This also leads to considerations of feminist issues.

3 Euthanasia

a) Introduction to euthanasia

The issue of **euthanasia** is equally as complex as abortion and for similar reasons. The context is the end, as opposed to the beginning, of life, yet some of the principles are the same. Certainly, the ethical issues identified progress under similar headings.

KEY WORD

Euthanasia: literally, 'good death' (Greek), ending someone's life in a painless manner, usually to relieve suffering

The first problem involves the technical difficulties surrounding the different definitions and types of euthanasia. There is a clear disparity in law both between countries and the ways in which legislation is applied. Euthanasia as an issue is as emotive as abortion, perhaps even more so, and involves a variety of principles and conflicts of interests. It is in the practicality and implementation of any decision where the most ferocious debate can be found.

b) Key facts about euthanasia

The meaning of the word derives from the Greek *eu thanatos*, interpretations of which include good, easy, gentle (*eu*) and death (*thanatos*). The key idea goes beyond the mere descriptive term and encompasses an idea of a death that is beneficial for the party involved. However, as with confusion over key terms in the debates about abortion, the actual understanding of the various types of euthanasia needs clarification.

Tony Hope, Professor for Medical Ethics at the University of Oxford and author of a key text for student doctors, *Medical Ethics and Law: The Core Curriculum*, offers the following distinctions.

- Euthanasia: One person kills another with intention or allows another's death for the other's benefit.
- Active euthanasia: One person actions another's death for the other's benefit.
- Passive euthanasia: By withholding treatment or taking away vital life-prolonging support, one person allows another to die.
- Voluntary: The request to die by the person who competently wishes it so.
- Non-voluntary: A decision that one person should be allowed to die, made by a second party, on behalf of the one who is unable to make that decision.

- Involuntary: One person decides to impose or permit the death of another even though death is against the other's wishes.
- Suicide: One person intentionally killing him or herself.
- Assisted suicide: One person helps another to commit suicide.
- Physician assisted suicide: A qualified physician helps a person to commit suicide.

c) The legal status of euthanasia

Having clarified and identified the key types of euthanasia, it is important to consider the legal status of euthanasia and again, as with applied ethics in general, to debate the workability of any change in law or viewpoint put forward.

The legal status of euthanasia varies according to geography. In the Netherlands and Belgium it is within the bounds of the law if specific criteria are met; in Switzerland physician-assisted suicide is allowed subject to specific criteria being met. In Britain, euthanasia is illegal.

In 1961 suicide was decriminalised. Despite this, the *Suicide Act 1961* was very explicit that to aid or assist suicide in any way was still a crime. Clearly this has implications for euthanasia.

d) Specific ethical issues and key areas of debate surrounding euthanasia

i) Principles

As with the debate surrounding abortion, there are two central principles at stake. The first is whether or not killing should be allowed in any circumstances. The second relates to the value that is given to life in respect of issues such as sanctity or quality, whether for religious, ethical or philosophical reasons.

ii) Life and the quality of life: where does it finish?

In the consideration of abortion, a second area for debate was the point at which it could be said that life actually begins. The problems associated with establishing the start of a life could be deemed similar to those related to the end of life.

Generally, a physical end of life can be determined medically. However, what criteria operate for a person in a prolonged state of unconsciousness or a condition known as **persistent vegetative state (PVS)**? Such a situation again calls into question the definition of life and even whether a physical definition suffices. This is a key question in the euthanasia debate.

Related to this issue are also the philosophical questions about quality of life. Is there a point at which one can conclude that life has lost its value? If so, exactly when should this be and who is going to decide?

iii) Human rights

It is interesting to note that:

> ...patients have the right to decide how much weight to attach to the benefits, burdens, risks and the overall acceptability of any treatment. They have the right to refuse treatment even where refusal may result in harm to themselves or in their own death, and doctors are legally bound to respect their decision.
>
> **(General Medical Council)**

This refers to those who are dying. They have the right not to prolong their life, by refusing treatment. They do not have the right, however, to hasten an end to their life by administering a different course of medication.

Does this pose a contradiction? If a person refuses treatment to prolong life then have they shortened their life? How, in principle, is this different from shortening life in another way?

Thus, humans have the legal right to the opportunity to extend life but not to shorten it. Where death is inevitable, humans can only stave it off and are not allowed to welcome it.

There appears to be an uncomfortable inconsistency here. Consciously refusing treatment, knowing that the consequence is death, is seen as acceptable. Consciously willing medication of which the consequence is also death, only sooner and with less pain, is unacceptable. It is this delicate dilemma – if, indeed, it is one – that is at the very heart of the euthanasia debate: namely, just how far should a person's individual rights extend over their own body, fate and destiny?

This discussion of rights is further complicated when the affected party has lost the capacity to indicate preference, the physical ability to commit suicide or the ability to reason and make an informed decision regarding treatment.

e) Practical implications

The issue of **medical futility** is crucial here. That is:

...treatment may be contra-indicated on the grounds either that it is achieving no medical effect or that continued treatment can be seen as being against the patient's best interests...

(Mason and Laurie)

- Who is to decide and how is this decision to be reached?
- Is a law that allows euthanasia workable?

Some countries legislate that, under strict conditions, it is. In support of euthanasia it could be pointed out that death might be for the person's benefit and that passive euthanasia is already widely accepted.

Ethically, perhaps people should have a duty to prevent the prolonged and meaningless suffering of others. In addition, consideration should be given to the impact that a prolonged and painful death may have on others, such as close family and friends.

Arguments against the introduction of a law that allows euthanasia point to the very real risk of abuse:

- How could such a law be effectively monitored?
- Would it be in the best interests of society as a whole?
- Would it be a workable law?
- Further, does euthanasia go against the Hippocratic oath?
- Is it interfering with the natural or divinely ordained course of events?

For medical practitioners there is no clear legal guideline other than advice given by such bodies as the British Medical Association in 2001 or the Royal College of Paediatrics and Child Health. However, such guidelines are very vague with respect to active intervention and the withholding of curative medical treatment. Even doctors are unsure and clearly vulnerable, both legally and ethically.

 EXAM TIP

It is important to be able to describe and explain the key facts relating to ethical ideas. However, it is even more important to be able to discuss the implications and questions raised by the ethical issues with use of quotes, references and development of key ideas. This demonstrates 'a wide range of selected, relevant factual knowledge and understanding of the topic investigated; offering some analysis of issues raised by the topic, using a variety of sources, examples and/ or illustrations' (level 5 descriptor AO1) and also 'structured around, and showing clear understanding of, the main theme(s) or concept(s) of the task' (level 5 descriptor AO1).

This would distinguish your work from a poorer answer that would focus simply on the general topic with an unspecific summary of ideas and with little reference to scholars, meaning only 'some relevant and partially structured knowledge of the topic investigated' and evidencing only 'a limited framework...with a general link to the task' (level 2 descriptor AO1).

 KEY WORDS

Medical futility: a situation in which treatment achieves no positive medical results, or is against the patient's best interests

Specification guidance notes (AO2)

Assessment objective 2 (Critical evaluation)

Critically evaluate and justify a point of view through the use of evidence and reasoned argument.

The examination board provides guidance notes in order to assist you with preparation for assessment. In the notes it states:

Students may consider ethical questions which are relevant to one or more issues in medical ethics, such as the principle of the sanctity of life, medical consent, rights and duties, responsibilities and choices. Students will not be disadvantaged whether they study only one issue in medical ethics or cover a range.

We shall consider the range of questions and arguments associated with the selected topics.

Abortion: in support
The mother has a human right to choose; it is a morally acceptable course of action; abolishment would mean greater suffering and injustice; there are strict guidelines to prevent misuse.

Euthanasia: in support
It is humane; it is immoral and irresponsible to deny someone a gentle death; it supports the rights of the individual; it prevents needless physical suffering, emotional pain and mental anguish; the laws as they stand do not assist medical practitioners – there is still a vagueness and uncertainty; some forms of euthanasia need introducing.

Abortion: against
The fetus has an equal right for protection; teachings concerning the sanctity of life; the beginning of life can be established as conception; it is morally irresponsible in the light of technological advancements and the new possibilities of saving lives to continue with the law as it stands.

Euthanasia: against
Against principles of not killing and the Hippocratic oath; a legalisation of euthanasia would see a 'slippery slope'; any legalisation of euthanasia is far too complex to manage and would be a unmanagable law.

Overview: Issues for debate

TASK

In groups, develop your questions to include extra arguments in support of and challenging the issues under debate. Discuss some possible conclusions and devise a flowchart or thought process diagram for each area. Include key questions for discussion.

Objective: To encourage the use of questions and counter questions in developing the skills of AO2 which serve to 'critically evaluate and justify a point of view' (AO2). Developing questions give evidence of at least 'some attempt to set out reasons for alternative views' (level 3 and above descriptor AO2).

1 Key questions

- How do you define the issue that you have chosen?
- Are the principles and arguments used in approaching your chosen topic more absolutist or more relativist?
- Are the issues and questions involved in your chosen topic 'user friendly and flexible' or 'too complex and impractical'?
- Is the promotion of human rights more important than the establishment of absolute principles?
- Can the impact of the sanctity and value of life ever really be measured?
- How simple are the solutions and arguments offered to your chosen issue?
- Is it possible to be precise in debating and defining the key questions in your topic?
- How strong are the arguments and attitudes of key scholars? Can you identify any weaknesses?

RESEARCH TIP

Try creating your own evaluation scales as you research your topics. It is essential that you make a list of questions to ask in response to your studies.

For every quote, piece of evidence, proposal or argument, try to think of a counter argument that is relevant.

2 A critical evaluation of the issues

a) Introduction

When critically evaluating the ethical issues studied, it is always useful to identify the strengths and weaknesses of each of the arguments that are put forward.

Generally, this involves highlighting the crucial points that support an issue and those that challenge it. The next stage is to decide which arguments are effective and which can be challenged. However, in terms of standardised strengths and weaknesses, there is little that can be written here because of the subjective nature of argument. Remember that what one person views as a strength of an argument may well be seen as a weakness by another.

Therefore, no official judgements are made here regarding the quality of the points put forward. That is for you to decide, after study, reflection and debate. Each topic is presented with one or two points that support and one or two that challenge an issue.

It is anticipated that classes will use these as a basis for further thought, analysis and argument.

Since the section of the specification that covers applied ethics involves many distinctive issues associated with life and death and medical ethics, it would be impossible to group them all together under issues of life and death for evaluation purposes.

Each issue that we have focused on will therefore be dealt with separately.

 EXAM TIP

Do not just give a list of criticisms like some shopping list. It is far better to discuss and develop three or four criticisms, explaining and responding to them, than to give a list of seven or eight. This demonstrates a process of reasoning and a sustained argument that is akin to 'a careful analysis of alternative views' (level 4 descriptor AO2) and the overall AO2 objective of 'critical evaluation'.

✎ **TASK**

Think of the questions you would like to ask about the topic you have chosen or about the views that scholars have presented in response to the topic you have chosen. Is there anything that is not clear? What needs further explanation? Do you wish to challenge the thinking or view of a scholar? If so, can you list your reasons or evidence?

Objective: To develop AO2 skills of questioning, considering different views, analysing arguments and responding to the material studied: 'critically evaluate and justify a point of view through the use of evidence and reasoned argument'. It aids self-reflection and development of an argument, working towards 'some attempt to set out reasons for alternative views; a point of view expressed clearly, supported by some relevant evidence and argument' (level 3 descriptor AO2) or even an 'attempt at an evaluation of the issue(s) raised in the task, typically through a careful analysis of alternative views; leading to a clearly expressed viewpoint supported by well-deployed evidence and reasoned argument' (level 4 descriptor AO2).

➡️ **EXAM TIP**

Be careful when using quotes in critical assessments. Always make sure that they relate to the argument that is presented. To make sure of this, always explain the relevance of the quote in your answer. This is the difference between 'a mainly descriptive response...supported by reference to a simple argument or unstructured evidence' or 'a point of view supported by limited but appropriate evidence and/or argument' (levels 1 and 2 descriptors AO2) and that of a level 3 and above answer that clearly attempts analysis or 'some attempt to set out reasons for alternative views' (level 3 descriptor AO2) and the best answer that delivers 'a careful analysis of alternative views' (level 4 descriptor AO2).

b) Abortion

In support	Challenges
The mother has a basic human right to choose the fate of her own body when it comes to abortion and this right supersedes the right of the fetus.	The rights of the fetus for protection are equal to those of the woman and should be protected.
The law is on the side of those that champion the right to abortion as a morally acceptable course of action.	Teachings concerning the sanctity of life are crucial for religious people. Even the non-religious appreciate the value of human life.
History suggests that if the law was abolished then greater suffering and injustice would result.	If the beginning of life can be established as conception then this has implications as to the lawfulness of abortion and the 1967 Abortion Act would need changing.
Strict guidelines are there to prevent any misuse of the law and the abortion act is grounded in medical rationale.	It would be morally irresponsible in the light of technological advancements and the new possibilities of saving lives to continue with the law as it stands.

c) Euthanasia

In support	Challenges
Euthanasia can be considered humane. It is immoral and irresponsible to deny someone a gentle death and allow needless suffering simply because of a 'principle'.	It is against the principles of not killing and the Hippocratic oath.
Euthanasia supports the rights of the individual.	Some have argued that a legalisation of euthanasia would set up a 'slippery slope', opening the situation up to abuse and sinister motives.
Euthanasia benefits both the individual and any persons involved with the individual, preventing needless physical suffering, emotional pain and mental anguish.	There is a strong argument that any legalisation for euthanasia is far too complex to manage in practical terms. It would be an unworkable law.
The laws as they stand do not assist medical practitioners. There is still vagueness and uncertainty that leads to a moral dilemma for doctors. Some forms of euthanasia need introducing.	Once again, if euthanasia is legalised it will be impossible to measure and monitor its use because the parameters are so blurred.

INVESTIGATIONS
Area D: The study of world religions (Buddhism)

The individual unit content outline from the specification gives three possible areas of study for a topic. The authors have chosen one area for each unit.

For this unit they have selected **10: A study of one or more religions concerning ethical precepts and applied ethics (Buddhism).**

Whichever area of the specification is chosen, it is important that you are familiar with the overall general topic.

For the purposes of this book, this means the relevant chapter and corresponding assessment and reflections.

RESEARCH TIP

Make sure that you read through the information for the topic and, perhaps, make some preliminary background notes before you focus your attention on choosing an area of interest.

Eight-fold path and the role of morality
- abortion – absolute aspect of karma, relative aspect of intention
- euthanasia – relative aspect of intention versus the universal absolute of rebirth governed by karma

Precepts
Abstaining from:
- killing any living being
- stealing
- unlawful sexual intercourse
- lying
- the use of intoxicants

No God
- suffering as a point of departure
- compassion and skilful means as tools to apply

Overview: Buddhist ethics

This diagram shows an outline of the sorts of area we are going to look at. Using this as a basis, create and extend it into your own thought-process diagram as you progress. This may help you decide on a focus. Then you can use your focus to start another chart.

Specification guidance notes (AO1)

Assessment objective 1 (Knowledge and understanding)

Select and demonstrate clearly relevant knowledge and understanding through the use of evidence, examples, and correct language and terminology appropriate to the course of study.

For this skill, you are expected to select and present relevant and appropriate information from the specification in order to answer an area examined.

POSSIBLE AREAS FOR FOCUS IN THIS BOOK
- The five precepts
- Karma [kamma]
- The eight-fold path
- Compassion and skilful means
- Abortion
- Euthanasia

The examination board provides guidance notes in order to assist you with preparation for assessment. In the notes it states:

Students may investigate key ethical teachings in one or more religions and/or the implications for applied ethics within these traditions…they may focus on specific ethical teachings such as the Jewish ten commandments and the Buddhist five precepts.

Here we shall study the key ethical teachings of Buddhism.

Various possibilities are then included for applied ethics ranging from '…religious fundamentalism; racial or sexual equality including arranged marriages and feminist issues; sexual ethics; justice and crime; business ethics; political issues; peace and war.' Some of these topics can be found in depth in other areas of this book.

Then we shall study the application of these ethics to the issues of abortion and euthanasia.

1 Buddhist ethics – introduction

Buddhism is often described as a philosophy or way of life rather than a religion. The emphasis in Buddhism is on practice. Questions about belief are relatively unimportant in the sense that the way of life is driven by the goal of diminishing suffering, both mental and physical. This is not dependent on any external agency or creator God. The Buddhist path is **empirical**; it involves scientific testing and a practical solution.

What does this mean for Buddhist ethics? Is there a clear ethical system? Clearly, if there is, it is not one 'given by God'. There is no **divine command theory** in Buddhism.

It should be mentioned that any external supernatural agency plays no part whatever in the moulding of the character of a Buddhist…there is no one to reward or punish. Pain or happiness are the inevitable results of one's actions.

(Thera)

However, while morality is not dependent upon God it would be wrong to say that religion and morality are not inter-twined.

Buddhism is much more than an ordinary moral teaching. Morality is only the preliminary stage on the Path of Purity, and is a means to an end, but not an end in itself. Conduct, though essential, is itself insufficient to gain one's emancipation. It should be coupled with wisdom or knowledge. The base of Buddhism is morality, and wisdom is its apex.

(Thera)

The Buddhist ethical system, then, is driven by the ideas of eliminating suffering through a proactive, empirical approach to the problem and also by developing wisdom to help a person deal with suffering.

Ethical practice is the start of the Buddhist path. This relates to the ancient Indian ideal of the **sadhu** or wandering holy man and **yoga**, the practice of meditation. In order to practise meditation one's conduct has to be moral. The idea of morality as a foundation to spiritual progress and practice is not new and is certainly not unique to Buddhism.

The ideas of conducting oneself appropriately, spiritual development, the cultivation of wisdom and the elimination of suffering are all inextricably linked. That is, one must behave ethically in order to eliminate suffering and be able to focus on becoming wise.

KEY QUOTES

Morality in Buddhism is not founded on any doubtful revelation nor is it the ingenious invention of an exceptional mind, but it is a rational and practical code based on verifiable facts and individual experience.

A Buddhist is aware of future consequences, but he refrains from evil because it retards, does good because it aids progress to Enlightenment (bodhi).

(Thera)

KEY WORDS

Bodhi: the wisdom by which one attains enlightenment
Empirical: based on evidence and experience
Divine command theory: a system of ideas or commandments given by a supreme being
Sadhu: an ascetic or practitioner of yoga who has achieved the first three Hindu goals of life
Yoga: meditation that aims to unite the Atman with Brahman

More than this, ethical conduct actually reduces the incidence of suffering and also benefits other beings.

Buddhist ethics are derived from basic observations about the world in which we live. Buddhist ethics have been referred to as a common-sense 'morality from within'. Central to this are the basic observations of the three marks of existence or characteristics of being (see the Foundation section on Buddhism).

- **Suffering:** A person who has a true understanding of the nature of suffering would appreciate that it is not the best course of action to inflict suffering upon another.
- **Impermanence:** Things change and do not last; this means a person can change and develop for the better, no matter what has been done. There is a famous Buddhist tale of a detestable character called Angulimala who changed for the better in response to an encounter with the Buddha.
- **Selflessness:** While Buddhists hold to this principle literally by denying the existence of a permanent entity known as a soul, it does encourage giving up any idea of self in terms of attachment. Therefore, the idea of selflessness and an ultimate concern for others who suffer follows from this.

TASK

Turn to the Foundation section on Buddhism, to find some more information about karma.
Objective: To develop the 'use of evidence and examples' to 'demonstrate clearly relevant knowledge and understanding' (AO1).

2 Buddhist ethical theory

The Buddhist teaching about karma has been called the Buddhist absolute ethic. Karmic influence is described as **wholesome** or unwholesome, **fruitful** or unfruitful or even **skilful** or unskilful, rather than as good and bad. In everyday use, good and bad tend to have more personal value judgements attached to them. Thus, an action is either beneficial to oneself and to others or it is not beneficial. The whole idea of Buddhist karma is related to motive.

Actions are measured by the intention associated with them, and may be:

- intentional actions
- accidental or neutral actions
- ignorant actions.

Each action has different consequences based upon the seriousness of intention. For example, an intentional action that does not benefit others is worse than an accidental or neutral action. An ignorant action that does not benefit others can sometimes be the worst type!

Harvey outlines five such principles of karmic formations, graded from least damaging to most damaging:

- an unintentional action
- an action done in a state of passion, diminished responsibility or lack of self-control
- an action of which the outcome is uncertain in terms of its beneficial nature, or about which one is genuinely mistaken with regard to its effects
- an action that is done in full knowledge that it is wrong

KEY WORDS

Suffering: the idea that life involves dissatisfaction
Impermanence: the idea that the universe is in an unstable state of flux
Selflessness: the idea that there is not a permanent essence within a person as all is impermanent

KEY QUOTES

As a moral teaching it excels all other ethical systems, but morality is only the beginning and not the end of Buddhism.

(Thera)

The law of karma is seen as a natural law inherent in things, like a law of physics.

(Harvey)

KEY WORDS

Wholesome: description of positive and beneficial actions
Fruitful: description of actions that will yield positive results
Skilful: description of intelligent or wise actions

- an action that is done when one is in full control and intends to perform it and yet is unaware that it is wrong through ignorance or a lack of compunction.

To find out more about karma refer to the Buddhism section.

3 Compassion and skilful means

KEY WORDS

Karuna: compassion; sometimes interpreted as the idea that concern for others demonstrates selflessness
Skilful means: the application of wisdom so that karmic benefits are maximised

Two other principles that impact upon Buddhist ethics are:

- **karuna** or compassion: the idea that concern and understanding for others demonstrates an attitude of not-self, that is, selflessness
- **skilful means:** basically the application of wisdom to a given situation so that the karmic benefits are maximised, both for others and self.

Skilful means is a flexible approach to ethics, involving the prioritising of principles. For example, killing a violent murderer in self-defence or in defending another is contrary to the principle of not killing but, in the long term, the outcome is skilful because it saves more lives and prevents further killing. A calculated decision may appear contrary to ethical principles in the short term, but is more in line with ethical principles in the long term. In Mahayana Buddhism, this principle has been used widely, even to justify 'compassionate killings' and to arrive at the conclusion that:

…where the motive is to help people, there is no fault in an action.

(Harvey)

In practice, the principles of karma, as determined by intention when combined with the ideas of compassion and skilful means, encourage a relativist or situationist approach to ethics. While the absolute principle once again appears to be karma, in practice it is much more complex than this.

KEY QUOTE

For Buddhism, a good society is one in which individuals act correctly together – not a society that is coerced into obedience by a set of laws or regulations.
(Vardy and Grosch)

➡ EXAM TIP

When answering a question on Buddhist ethics, make sure that you include a range of ideas – show how different religious concepts affect the issue you have chosen and pick out the key principles and explain why they are important in relation to the issue debated and how they have been applied and interpreted by different writers.

This ensures the focus is on 'a wide range of selected, relevant factual knowledge and understanding of the topic investigated; offering some analysis of issues raised by the topic, using a variety of sources, examples and/or illustrations' (level 5 descriptor AO1) and also 'structured around, and showing clear understanding of, the main theme(s) or concept(s) of the task' (level 5 descriptor AO1).

This would distinguish your work from a poorer answer that would focus simply on the general topic with an unspecific summary of ideas and with little reference to scholars, meaning only 'some relevant and partially structured knowledge of the topic investigated' and evidencing only 'a limited framework…with a general link to the task' (level 2 descriptor AO1).

4 Buddhist ethical precepts

As discussed above, Buddhists tend not to describe actions as being good or bad but rather in terms of being (un)skilful, (in)appropriate and (un)fruitful. This may be because there are no rules or 'oughts' in Buddhism that can dictate whether something is good or bad.

a) Precepts as vows

Buddhists do have some basic ethical principles to guide them, known as the **pancasila** or five precepts. They are, however, forms of guidance for moral behaviour and are taken as **vows**. The precepts are not commandments given by an outside agency or God. They encourage personal ethical responsibility. The precepts are, broadly, abstaining from:

KEY WORDS

Pancasila: the five moral precepts
Vows: personal undertakings rather than rules

- killing any living being
- stealing
- unlawful sexual intercourse
- lying
- the use of intoxicants.

The idea that the precepts are guidelines implies that they are not absolute. Indeed, although Buddhists are encouraged to take all vows, it is entirely a personal decision based upon individual spiritual and moral development.

The precepts are interpreted and applied in different ways. Some Buddhists take them very literally. For example, there is a warning from Thanissaro Bhikkhu that altering the implications and understanding of the precepts too much sets impossible standards that defeat the whole basis and idea of the precepts.

Others, for example, Harvey, give great thought and consideration to analysing each one and considering its broader implications and applications.

For the first precept, Harvey includes the idea of injury as 'clearly against the spirit of the precept' and also says that 'fraud, cheating, forgery and falsely denying that one is in debt' are embraced by the second precept. According to Harvey: 'The third precept relates primarily to the avoidance of causing suffering by one's sexual behaviour.' In addition, 'any form of lying, deception or exaggeration, either for one's own benefit or that of another' is precluded by the fourth precept. Finally, the fifth precept is really to do with states of unmindfulness. This means that anything that causes such a lack of focus should be avoided. The full implications of this precept are often debated, but its essential relationship to the other four can be stressed by a story of a Thai monk who was challenged to break a precept. Seeing the fifth as having the least direct impact, he became drunk, only to break the other four precepts while in this state!

Whatever the case may be, it can be concluded that the precepts form the basis of moral behaviour and, whichever way they are interpreted, they can be applied to real-life situations and ethical dilemmas.

b) Breaking the precepts

In relation to the workings of the principles of karma, there are also different levels of demerit (or negative karmic influence) involved in breaking a precept. This depends upon intention. Therefore, breaking a precept cannot be described as a bad action but is better described as unskilful.

EXAM TIP

Be careful when using quotes in critical assessments. Always make sure that they relate to the argument that is presented. To make sure of this, always explain the relevance of the quote in your answer. This is the difference between 'a mainly descriptive response…supported by reference to a simple argument or unstructured evidence' or 'a point of view supported by limited but appropriate evidence and/or argument' (level 1 and 2 descriptors AO2) and that of a level 3 and above answer that clearly attempts analysis 'some attempt to set out reasons for alternative views' (level 3 descriptor AO2) and the best answer that delivers 'a careful analysis of alternative views' (level 4 descriptor AO2).

Buddhist ethics are not codified into a rigid moral code; nor are they about making judgements and arousing sin and guilt.

(Snelling)

KEY WORDS

Ottappa: complete awareness of intentions and motives behind moral actions

Hiri: shame, reflecting the idea of self-responsibility and encouraging self-respect

The role of conscience in Buddhism is played by mindfulness; that is, a person is aware of their actions and the intentions or motives behind them. This ideal of complete awareness is referred to as **ottappa**.

The term **hiri** is used when breaking a precept. It means shame rather than guilt and reflects the idea of self-responsibility and, essentially, encourages self-respect and a positive approach to life. To dwell too much on oneself would be too indulgent, so Buddhists are encouraged to learn from mistakes and move on. Therefore a Buddhist is to develop from the stage of hiri or self-indulgence to that of ottappa, where there is a complete regard for consequences.

c) Emphasis on the positive side of the precepts

According to Thanissaro Bhikkhu, the precepts are part of a course of therapy for wounded minds and are aimed at curing the ailments that underlie low self-esteem.

Healthy self-esteem comes from living up to a set of standards that are practical, clear-cut, humane, and worthy of respect; the five precepts are formulated in such a way that they provide just such a set of standards.

(Thanissaro Bhikkhu)

KEY QUOTE

The Buddha was like a doctor, treating the spiritual ills of the human race. The path of practice he taught was like a course of therapy for suffering hearts and minds.

(Thanissaro Bhikkhu)

Thanissaro Bhikkhu sees the precepts as practical. If they become over complicated or their interpretation is widened, they become complex and unmanageable. Kept simple, they are workable principles. Actions are also clear-cut and either fit a precept or not. The precepts are humane in their treatment of others and their regard for self and they also command respect and are vindicated as principles in themselves. The precepts are, therefore, totally positive and set an aspiration that is reachable.

KEY IDEA

The five precepts:
- **Without killing or causing injury to any living creature, man should be kind and compassionate towards all, even to the tiniest creature that crawls at his feet.**
- **Refraining from stealing, he should be upright and honest in all his dealings.**
- **Abstaining from sexual misconduct, which debases the exalted nature of man, he should be pure.**
- **Shunning false speech, he should be truthful.**
- **Avoiding pernicious drinks that promote heedlessness, he should be sober and diligent (Thera).**

TASK

Draw up a table with the three headings 'Precept', 'Meaning' and 'Further meanings'. Use the information on Buddhist ethics to complete the table.

Objective: To develop an understanding of the literal meanings of the precepts but also the wider application of these meanings. To demonstrate a deeper understanding of the precepts, using examples to support explanation, and demonstrating a 'coherent understanding of the task; based on selection of material to demonstrate emphasis and clarity of ideas' and also a 'careful analysis of key concepts' (higher level 5 descriptor AO1).

5 The relationship between morality and religion

The relationship between morality and religion can clearly be seen in Buddhism through both karma and the moral principles discussed so far. Indeed, Nyanatiloka's *Buddhist Dictionary* states that morality is 'the acting out of positive karma'.

This becomes more evident when the ultimate teaching of Buddhism is considered; this is the **eight-fold path** (see the Foundation section on Buddhism for more information on this). In Buddhism, to follow the path is to aim towards enlightenment. On the path there is a clear section that deals with morality. One has to be ethically pure in one's actions if **nirvana** or enlightenment is to be reached. One who is unethical cannot be enlightened.

> *It is the foundation of the whole Buddhist practice, and therewith the first of the three kinds of training that form the three-fold division of the eight-fold path – morality, concentration and wisdom.*
>
> **(Nyanatiloka)**

KEY WORDS

Eight-fold path: practical measures needed to become enlightened

Nirvana (Nibbana): enlightenment

Concentration: employment of all one's powers or attention

Morality involves right speech, action and livelihood. Speech and action are integral to the idea of karma at a generic level. In terms of application of these principles, once again, karma comes into play:

> *This is making one's living in a way that does not involve the habitual breaking of the precepts by bringing harm to other beings, but which hopefully aids others and helps cultivate one's faculties and abilities.*
>
> **(Harvey)**

All these aspects are driven by intention and thus directly related to the principle of karma. The parts of the eight-fold path are:

- **panna** or wisdom
- **sila** or morality
- **samadhi** or meditation.

It is the case, however, that the whole of the eight-fold path, and not just the section designated as morality, is driven by the idea of mindfulness or awareness of intentions. The morality section is overtly ethical; the other two sections covertly link themselves to ethics.

> *These eight factors are the key to Buddhist ethics…*
>
> **(Vardy and Grosch)**

KEY WORDS

Panna: wisdom or insight

Sila: moral teachings associated with the middle section of the eight-fold path

Samadhi: meditation

Directly related to the whole idea of religion and morality is the idea of rebirth (see the Foundation section on *Buddhism* for further information). The ethical actions of an individual have consequences, not just in this life but also beyond it. Ethical activity, then, is inextricably linked to the idea of liberation, enlightenment or the Buddhist religious goal beyond this life.

> *Meditation helps the individual to pay close attention to whatever he or she is doing without being distracted – it therefore has an ethical value.*
>
> **(Vardy and Grosch)**

6 Buddhist attitudes to abortion

As with the issue of abortion itself, the debate in Buddhism begins with the question: 'At what point does life, or consciousness, begin?' Given that the idea of karma and rebirth imply a continuous cycle of existence (see the Foundation section on *Buddhism*), this is by no means a clear decision.

Most Buddhists have adopted the later classical Indian teachings that the **transmigration** of consciousness happens at conception. This includes the acceptance that this passing over of one consciousness stream into another is a sudden and not a gradual event. The true nature of this passing over, however, is still debated.

Harvey and Keown suggest that the accepted Buddhist view is that life, or consciousness, begins at fertilisation. Abortion is therefore a serious act.

It must be noted again that the language of right and wrong in Buddhism is replaced by degrees of karmic consequences. These impact upon individual access to, or regress from, the spiritual path.

The serious nature of abortion demands that if a monk is involved he can be permanently expelled from the **sangha**. Indeed, **jataka** tales refer to abortion-mongers in hell, once again reflecting the karmic seriousness of the act.

So is abortion ever an acceptable course of action for Buddhists?

Harvey identifies several grounds for abortion in Buddhism and grades them accordingly in terms of order of priority for consideration:

- the threat to mother's physical or mental health
- the threat to the health of the fetus
- socio-economic factors
- the woman's rights
- the needs of society.

Despite the apparent absolute that life or consciousness begins at conception, there is also the relative, **utilitarian** or **situationist** aspect to karma that accounts for all the complexities embracing intentions, age and development of being. In practice, as Ling has demonstrated through research in **Theravada** Buddhist countries, the seriousness of the act of abortion increases with the age of the embryo. This relates to the Buddhist ideal that destroying a more developed being generates greater consequences.

Given the above, one could argue that, in practice, the nature of karma and intention can justify different routes and therefore transforms the Buddhist approach from an absolutist one to a causistic, relativist approach.

For example, Suwanbubbha argues that therapeutic abortion '…may be considered as unsevere karma as long as this action is not based on the roots of unwholesome or bad intention.' In addition, regarding the socio-economic view, Suwanbubbha writes:

> …it is very difficult to determine absolutely what one should do…the doers…will know best what their real intentions and states of mind are.

In terms of applying karuna or compassion and skilful means, a Buddhist can argue that the karmic benefit in the long term can certainly outweigh the immediate seriousness.

KEY WORDS

Transmigration: the passing over of one consciousness stream into another

Sangha: the Buddhist monastic community

Jataka: sutras narrating the birth stories of the Buddha in past lives, and effects related to the past and the present lives

Utilitarian: ethical doctrine that the moral worth of an action is solely determined by its contribution to overall utility

Situationist: individual circumstances rather than sets of rules determine the outcome of any ethical dilemma

Theravada: literally, the way of the elders, it focuses on the devotion to and support of the sangha as the primary source of teaching and example

However, in counter-argument to this approach, one should bear in mind the words of Damien Keown:

> *The doctrine of rebirth, moreover, sees the new conceptus as not just a 'potential person' evolving from the first time from nothing, but as a continuing entity bearing the complete karmic encoding of a recently deceased individual. If we rewind the karmic tape a short way…we would typically find an adult man or woman fulfilling all the requirements of 'personhood'.*

Despite Keown's words, it is still the case that this entity is a product of previous karmic activity and should not necessarily be seen as a storehouse of karmic consequences in the same way as in the previous guise of a fully developed being.

All in all, abortion is to be avoided. If it is performed there are serious karmic consequences. The relative seriousness of these consequences is the area of debate today among Buddhists.

 EXAM TIP

Remember to explain each point that you make in an exam answer to the full. Think carefully about each sentence and how it relates to the question and the previous sentence. Aim for at least three clear sentences to explain a concept or idea, giving examples from different sources to support your point. For development of the point, bring in a variety of ways in which the application of this principle is demonstrated and introduce some contrasting scholarly views. This demonstrates that the answer is 'well-structured in depth or broad response to the task' (mid level 5 descriptor AO1) as opposed to the information being simply 'uncritical and descriptive presentation' (level 1 descriptor AO1) or 'presented within a limited framework' (level 2 descriptor AO1).

7 Buddhist attitudes to euthanasia

The Buddhist view of suicide is straightforward enough:

> *…suicide is an act which will bring grief to friends and relatives, and so, if for no other reason, is to be avoided.*

(Harvey)

Despite this, remember the nature of applied ethics – sometimes the ideal is not a workable principle. In his book, *Buddhist Ethics: A Very Short Introduction*, Damien Keown presents the powerful image of the suicide of Buddhist monk, Thich Quang Duc, in Saigon in 1963, which had a profound impact on the world. The monk calmly sat while his body was destroyed by flames in protest against the policies of a dictator.

It can be seen, then, once again that questions are raised concerning the theoretical principles and the conflicts of actual situations.

The key issue, according to Peter Harvey, is whether or not euthanasia breaks the first precept. The Buddhist stance, if there is a single approach, is very complicated. The criteria of karma, the precepts, compassion and skilful means can all have various possible responses. Generally, however, the Buddhist stance resists the idea of euthanasia, based upon the following principles.

● Killing is to be avoided.

It is clear that Buddhism sees abortion as akin to killing an adult human, but that does not mean that all such acts are equally as bad.

(Harvey)

Buddhist literature emphasises the importance of meeting death mindfully since the last moment of one life can be particularly influential in determining the quality of the next rebirth.

(Keown)

Whoever, O monks, would nurse me, he should nurse the sick.

(Buddha)

99

POSSIBLE AREAS FOR DEBATE

- The strengths and weaknesses of Buddhist ethics and their relevance today
- Their relevance in a secular society
- Their difference from other religious ethical systems
- Their similarities to other religious ethical systems

- Compassion is to be encouraged and there is greater merit in supporting the dying than helping them to die early.
- Euthanasia could have a negative impact upon rebirth.
- Life is suffering and killing is not an effective way to end suffering because life continues through rebirth.

One might think that compassion would permit euthanasia; however, this must be weighed against the principles of karma and the consequences of actions for a better rebirth in the long term.

Indeed, unlike the issue of abortion, where a life is rudimentary and karmic accumulation minimal, the ending of a fully developed human life seriously impacts upon the balance of karmic accumulation incurred by that life.

This, then, is the biggest problem for a Buddhist. The main question appears to be: 'Can killing ever be effective enough to end suffering in the ultimate context of rebirth?' It is for this reason that most Buddhist writers advise against euthanasia as a preferred course of action. Indeed, in Theravada countries, monasteries have been used as hospices, reflecting Buddhism's practical approach to dealing with the problem of suffering.

Specification guidance notes (AO2)

Assessment objective 2 (Critical evaluation)

Critically evaluate and justify a point of view through the use of evidence and reasoned argument.

The examination board provides guidance notes in order to assist you with preparation for assessment. In the notes it states:

Students may study similarities and differences between different religious traditions and may investigate issues such as whether these teachings are relevant in a secular society.

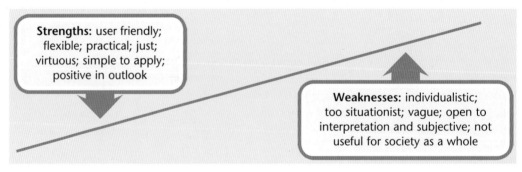

Strengths: user friendly; flexible; practical; just; virtuous; simple to apply; positive in outlook

Weaknesses: individualistic; too situationist; vague; open to interpretation and subjective; not useful for society as a whole

Overview: Issues for debate

RESEARCH TIP

- Try creating your own evaluation scales as you research your topics.
- It is essential that you make a list of questions to ask in response to your studies.
- For every quote, piece of evidence, proposal or argument, try to think of a counter argument that is relevant.

1 A critical evaluation of Buddhist ethics

It is very difficult to define Buddhist ethics as a system. In terms of the precepts and the guidance offered by the eight-fold path, it can be argued to be absolutist. In terms of the absolute principle of karma that underpins the whole ethical system, however, the approach can be argued to be more relativist.

Adding to this the flexible principles of intention, compassion and skilful means, one could argue that most actions could be in some way ethically justified.

Mel Thompson regards Buddhism as situationist; that is, individual circumstance rather than a set of rules determine the outcome of any ethical dilemma.

Damien Keown prefers to see it as a mixture of alternatives. It is both egotistical and altruistic, mainly absolutist but not exclusively so, and objective in principle in that it is related to universal impersonal laws of karma. Overall, Keown sees it as a form of virtue ethics as opposed to a deontological or teleological approach.

Whatever the case may be, it is important to bear in mind that there is diversity of opinion in Buddhism, just as in any other world religion, as to what precisely the Buddhist perspective entails.

a) Strengths of Buddhist ethics

The first key strength of Buddhist ethics is that it is clear and simple to apply. For example, the precepts are very explicit as to what should be avoided, the morality section of the eight-fold path is precise as to how to live and the ideal of selflessness combined with compassion for others can consistently be applied.

The Buddhist ethical system also has the attraction of being empirical in its approach and offers analysis of life without divine influence. It is based upon the very simple observation: things that do not cause suffering are wholesome acts; things that bring suffering are to be avoided. Where suffering cannot be avoided, the least suffering for all, a utilitarian perspective, is, in most cases, the most appropriate course of action.

It moves beyond what is right and wrong. It eliminates the idea of self-indulgence through self-pity, guilt and remorse. It frees the consciousness to speak a new language of what is appropriate and universally conducive to enlightenment for all.

The principle of karma in Buddhist ethics is easily applied at a personal level. In this sense it is accessible to all. It is almost like an individualised learning plan that equips a person to cope with the complexities of life, by reference to a few basic principles.

Positive virtues of compassion, wisdom through skilful means, selflessness and empathy with others are promoted through Buddhist ethics.

Possibly the greatest strength of Buddhist ethics is the provision of a flexible framework that can be applied to different situations, at the same time following the few central principles offered as guidance.

b) Weaknesses of Buddhist ethics

There are weaknesses to the Buddhist system. The first observation is that it is not really a universal system but much more an individualised programme. In this sense it can never be workable as a system of ethics for society as a whole. In decisions concerning

? KEY QUESTIONS

- How do we define Buddhist ethics?
- Are the principles of Buddhist ethics more absolutist or more relativist?
- Are the principles of Buddhist ethics 'user friendly and flexible' or 'too complex and impractical'?
- Is the promotion of virtues more important than the establishment of absolute principles?
- Can the impact of karma according to Buddhist ethics ever really be measured?
- How simple are the principles of Buddhist ethics?
- Are the principles of Buddhist ethics a precise science?
- How flexible is the principle of karma?

➡ **EXAM TIP**

Do not just give a list of criticisms like some shopping list. It is far better to discuss and develop three or four criticisms, explaining and responding to them, than to give a list of seven or eight. This demonstrates a process of reasoning and a sustained argument that is akin to 'a careful analysis of alternative views' (level 4 descriptor AO2) and the overall AO2 objective of 'critical evaluation'.

TASK

Think of the questions you would like to ask about the topic you have chosen or about the views that scholars have presented in response to the topic you have chosen. Is there anything that is not clear? What needs further explanation? Do you wish to challenge the thinking or view of a scholar? If so, can you list your reasons or evidence?

Objective: To develop AO2 skills of questioning, considering different views, analysing arguments and responding to the material studied: 'critically evaluate and justify a point of view through the use of evidence and reasoned argument'. It aids self-reflection and development of an argument, working towards 'some attempt to set out reasons for alternative views; a point of view expressed clearly, supported by some relevant evidence and argument' (level 3 descriptor AO2) or even an 'attempt at an evaluation of the issue(s) raised in the task, typically through a careful analysis of alternative views; leading to a clearly expressed viewpoint supported by well-deployed evidence and reasoned argument' (level 4 descriptor AO2).

matters of life and death, ethical principles need to be clearly defined and applied for the good of society as a whole.

Buddhist ethics may be seen as vague. There is clearly debate and indecision as to the applications and interpretations of the precepts.

In addition, the role of karma is unclear in that it is based entirely on the subjective nature of intention, which is really self-governing and not means-testable by an outside absolute or objective view.

Principles of Buddhist ethics are too open to interpretation and subjective views and decisions. This is the case with the precepts and their application, the role of intention behind karma, the application of skilful means and an understanding of compassion.

At best, Buddhist ethics can offer a useful guide for the individual but would be useless for society as a whole in arriving at decisions. Rather than making decisions when ethical principles conflict, the Buddhist ethical system has the beauty of avoiding the conflicts by recognising a variety of applications. This cannot, however, be considered a strength.

2 Possible conclusions

When assessing the Buddhist ethical system, it is important to reflect upon the arguments previously discussed and arrive at some appropriate conclusion. It may be that you accept none of these listed here, or just one of them, or you may have a different conclusion that is not listed. However, what is important is the way that you have arrived at your conclusion – the reasoning process.

From the preceding discussions, here are some possible conclusions you could draw.

1   The Buddhist ethical system reflects the very complex nature of the practical aspects of the dilemmas involved in applied ethics. Thus it is one of the most realistic systems.

2   When the Buddhist ethical system is kept simple and the precepts are prioritised in their purest form, it is a clear and effective guide to the dilemmas presented by applied ethics.

3   Due to the potential computations and complexities of karma, skilful means and interpretation of the precepts, the Buddhist ethical system is so flexible that it serves no useful purpose in establishing ethical parameters. It is too vague and subjective.

4   The Buddhist ethical system is simply too complicated. Might this mean that only those capable of working out the appropriate course of action would be the intelligentsia of society? In this case is it in danger of becoming an elitist and authoritarian system?

INVESTIGATIONS
Area D: The study of world religions (Islam)

The individual unit content outline from the specification gives three possible areas of study for a topic. The authors have chosen one area for each unit.

For this unit they have selected **10: A study of one or more religions concerning ethical precepts and applied ethics (Islam)**.

Whichever area of the specification is chosen, it is important that you are familiar with the overall general topic.

For the purposes of this book, this means the relevant chapter and corresponding assessment and reflections.

RESEARCH TIP

Make sure that you read through the information for the topic and, perhaps, make some preliminary background notes before you focus your attention on choosing an area of interest.

Overview: Muslim ethics

This diagram shows an outline of the sorts of area we are going to look at. Using this as a basis, create and extend it into your own thought-process diagram as you progress. This may help you decide on a focus. Then you can use your focus to start another chart.

Specification guidance notes (AO1)

Assessment objective 1 (Knowledge and understanding)

Select and demonstrate clearly relevant knowledge and understanding through the use of evidence, examples, and correct language and terminology appropriate to the course of study.

For this skill, you are expected to select and present relevant and appropriate information from the specification in order to answer an area examined.

The examination board provides guidance notes in order to assist you with preparation for assessment. In the notes it states:

Students may investigate key ethical teachings in one or more religions and/or the implications for applied ethics within these traditions…they may focus on specific ethical teachings such as the Jewish ten commandments and the Buddhist five precepts.

Here we shall study the key ethical teachings of Islam.

POSSIBLE AREAS FOR FOCUS IN THIS BOOK

- Tribal codes of morality
- The Qur'an and ethics
- The shari'ah law
- Sins and punishments in Islam
- Abortion
- Euthanasia

Various possibilities are then included for applied ethics ranging from '…religious fundamentalism; racial or sexual equality including arranged marriages and feminist issues; sexual ethics; justice and crime; business ethics; political issues; peace and war.' Some of these topics can be found in depth in other areas of this book.

Then we shall study the application of these ethics to the issues of abortion and euthanasia.

1 Muslim ethics – introduction

It is important to note that the basis of this section is grounded in the **Sunni** tradition of Islam.

To have a real understanding of Muslim ethics one needs to be familiar with the pre-Islamic context of jahiliyya or ignorance. This refers to the beliefs and practices around at the time of Muhammad.

It is important to begin with a little revision or preliminary background reading and so it will be useful to work through the task opposite. The information needed is in Part 1A of the Foundations section on Islam, on page 162.

2 The tribal code

From the Foundations section on Islam it will be apparent that, while Muhammad radically challenged and changed many immoral practices, this did not mean that all people in society at the time followed these, nor did it mean that there were no ethical codes in place at the time.

Indeed, in Islam we begin with the strong sense of what are known as 'tribal codes'.

> *Unlike Christian ethical concepts, which in many respects represent a radical departure from traditional Jewish morality, the Islamic ethical system continues to represent itself as observance of the true paths of ancestral morality, as contrasted with the 'corruption' or 'straying' of contemporary society.*
>
> (Ruthven)

To summarise, the principles of this ancestral morality were as follows.

- There was a strong sense of the extended family and clans were democratic in appointing leaders and making decisions for the benefit of the community as a whole.
- There was a sense of principle, or nobility, in terms of a code of conduct among tribes, which can be understood as **muruwa** or manliness.
- Virtue and bravery were important qualities for a tribe.
- One aspect of Arab 'paganism' was the existence of religious people, called **Hanifs**, who lived a very strict lifestyle of moral purity, almost as a reaction to the practices of the day. Hanifism was also strictly monotheistic, in line with Christianity and Judaism.
- Overall there were in fact many good qualities of tribal society such as honour, bravery, hospitality and generosity.

To repeat the quote of Colin Turner:

> *Yet the old image of the 'uncivilised **Bedouin**' is most misleading, for in fact desert life was lived to the highest of values.*

KEY WORD

Sunni: main branch of the Muslim Community consisting 85 per cent of the world's Muslim community

TASK

Turn to the Foundation section on Islam to find out some more about pre-Islamic Arabia.

Objective: To develop the 'use of evidence and examples' to 'demonstrate clearly relevant knowledge and understanding' (AO1).

 **KEY QUOTE**

The ethical system founded in the Qur'an also has its roots in the moral and social environment of a desert tribal society.

(Ruthven)

 KEY WORDS

Muruwa: the tribal term used to denote manliness or honour
Hanifs: tribal ascetics known for their moral qualities
Bedouin: nomadic peoples of the deserts of Arabia

3 The Qur'an as a basis

As well as the rich Arab tribal heritage present in Muslim ethics, there is also a familiarity and, some believe, a similarity between the basic values, as found within the Qur'an and those of other Near-Eastern regions. This rings true with that which the Qur'an identifies as either forbidden or allowed:

> *Much of this basic moral attitude reflected in the terminology of 'forbidden' and 'permitted' corresponds to that found in Near Eastern religion in general and in the Bible especially. Such parallels are sometimes seen to go further. A comparison is sometimes drawn between the biblical 'ten commandments' and sura 17 verses 22–39.*
>
> **(Rippin)**

If we are to extract certain ethical principles from the passage cited above, then it reads:

> *Your Lord has commanded that you should worship none but him, and that you be kind to your parents…Do not go anywhere near adultery…Do not take life, which God has made sacred…Honour your pledges…Give full measure when you measure, and weigh with accurate scales…*
>
> **(Sura 2:22–9)**

In line with the ten commandments of Judaism and Christianity, the following similarities can be identified:

● monotheism
● honouring parents
● avoiding adultery
● sanctity of life
● keeping your word and promises
● being honest – honour your pledges.

Sura 2, The Cow, a sura believed to originate later in Madinah, also has elements of morality:

> *Worship none but God; be good to your parents and kinsfolk, to orphans and the poor; speak good words to all people; keep up the prayer and pay the prescribed alms…Do not shed one another's blood or drive one another from your homelands.*
>
> **(Sura 2:83–4)**

Before considering Muslim ethics any further, it is important to recognise the following principles.

● There is no overall systematic presentation of ethics in Islam.
● The ethical code for living is inherently and essentially woven into the greater picture of being a Muslim.
● Therefore, Islam is a complete way of life incorporating religion, ethics, politics; there is no real ethical focus as it is inter-twined with the idea of living right in religion.
● There is great importance afforded to **niya** (intention) in any action, ethical or religious; it is the true motive of the heart that gives any good religious or ethical action its purity and worth.

 **KEY WORD**

Niya: intention

Intention (niya) is a crucial factor underlying true 'religious' actions, such as the five pillars (see page 198), but this also extends to life and the path of Islam in general. Indeed, it is often noted that there is no real distinction made in Islam between the nature of actions, religious, ethical or otherwise; all should be done with a total awareness of the greatness of God.

Sura 2 once again highlights the importance of intention for ethical action:

Goodness does not consist of turning your face towards East or West. The truly good are those who believe in God and the Last Day, in the angels, the Scripture, and the prophets; who give away some of their wealth, however much they cherish it, to their relatives, to orphans, the needy, travellers and beggars, and to liberate those in bondage; those who keep up the prayer and pay the prescribed alms; who keep pledges whenever they make them; who are steadfast in misfortune, adversity and times of danger. These are the ones who are true, and it is they who are aware of God.

(Sura 2:177)

Despite all this, Islam universally recognises that the science of ethics (**akhlaq**) sits firmly within the scheme of Islamic sciences. In terms of analysis, it is located just beneath the Qur'an, Hadith and **shari'ah** and rests alongside creed (aqida), roots and application of the law (**usul al-fiqh**) and the way of the mystic (Sufi tasawwuf).

The identification and application of the ethical code is similar to the process of extracting shari'ah; indeed, some would argue that it is inextricably linked. The Qur'an is the first source of ethics, followed by the Sunnah and Hadith, the scholars and then certain principles that are applied for understanding. In summary, the hierarchy of application is identical to that of shari'ah law:

- Qur'an
- Sunnah–Hadith
- **ulama fiqh** (scholar-defined law)
- usul al-fiqh (roots of the law)
- **istihsan** (a judge or scholar's preference), in line with public interest or agreement
- **qiyas** (analogy)
- **ijma** (consensus)
- **ijtihad** ('a **jurist**'s deduction of a point of law from the sources', literally 'effort').

As demonstrated from observing this long chain of sources, their application and interpretation, it is interesting to see how much of the body of ethical discourse in Islam actually derives from the Qur'an itself:

Of the whole melange, only the Koran [Qur'an] can claim to be divine, and even then, in comparison with the other two components, its direct contribution to the direct body of Islamic law is minimal.

(Turner)

> **KEY QUOTE**
>
> *...there is no such thing as a practice or action that is inherently sacred, religious or 'Islamic': an action is only as good, bad, sacred or profane as the intention which engenders it and the attitude which underpins it.*
>
> (Turner)

KEY WORDS

Akhlaq: ethics as a science

Shari'ah: literally, 'the way to the watering hole'; Islamic law, the rightly guided path, God's law

Usul al-fiqh: roots of the law

Ulama fiqh: scholar-defined law

Istihsan: a judge or scholar's preference; in line with public interest or agreement

Qiyas: analogy

Ijma: consensus

Ijtihad: 'a jurist's deduction of a point of law from the sources'; literally 'effort'

Jurist: a scholar of Islamic law that sits on a legal jury to make significant decisions of ethical and legal concern

> **KEY QUOTE**
>
> *The most impressive and characteristic monument in the religious culture of Islam is the shari'ah.*
>
> (Waines)

➡ EXAM TIP

When answering a question on Muslim ethics, make sure that you include a range of ideas – show how different concepts affect the issue you have chosen and pick out the key principles and explain why they are important in relation to the issue debated and how they have been applied and interpreted by different scholars.

This ensures focus is on 'a wide range of selected, relevant factual knowledge and understanding of the topic investigated; offering some analysis of issues raised by the topic, using a variety of sources, examples and/or illustrations' (level 5 descriptor AO1) and also 'structured around, and showing clear understanding of, the main theme(s) or concept(s) of the task' (level 5 descriptor AO1).

This would distinguish your work from a poorer answer that would focus simply on the general topic with an unspecific summary of ideas and with little reference to scholars, meaning only 'some relevant and partially structured knowledge of the topic investigated' and evidencing only 'a limited framework…with a general link to the task (level 2 descriptor AO1).

> **66 KEY QUOTE**
>
> *The general ethical principles it endorses are given a positive legal content. Obedience to God and His Prophet demands the observance of certain rituals and rules of social behaviour… These rules, though only sketched out in the Qur'an, were elaborated by the scholar–lawyers of the first two or three Islamic centuries to become the basis of shari'ah law.*
>
> (Ruthven)
> **99**

4 The relationship between religion and morality

In considering how religion and morality are related, there are two key areas to consider. The two aspects are basically:

- how ethical principles relate to religion
- how ethical principles are applied by humanity.

5 The relationship between God and morality

Allah is the source of all in creation. Therefore, Allah has to be the originator of ethical precepts. For Islam, however, as noted already, ethics is not divorced from religion. An ethical action not only reflects attitudes towards other human beings but also attitudes towards Allah. This relationship will unfold more when we consider briefly the notions of life after death (see below).

David Waines writes:

The law finally embraced two broad sets of relationships, the first being the spiritual relationship between Allah and humankind (ibadat) and the second, the normative relationship between one human being and another (mu'amalat). Both were believed to be governed by the guiding will of Allah.

6 The understanding and application of the ethical system

There is a definite tension in Islam between a divine–command style understanding of ethics and those of a rationalist application:

In the modern debates on social and political ethics, it is mainly the rationalist theory that is finding support among activist reformers because of the doctrine of human capacity to know right through reason.

(Oxford Dictionary of Islam)

TASK

Draw up a table identifying the different sources for Muslim ethics. Use the information here to complete the table and identify particular ethical principles.

Objective: To develop an understanding of different principles, their origins and also the wider application of these ideas. To demonstrate a deeper understanding of the basis for Muslim ethics, using examples to support explanation, and demonstrating a 'coherent understanding of the task; based on selection of material to demonstrate emphasis and clarity of ideas' and also a 'careful analysis of key concepts' (higher level 5 descriptor AO1).

KEY WORDS

Ulama: religious scholars or clerics
Mufti: legal expert in religious law
Taklif: obligation to follow divine law or ethics

Despite this trend to modernity, it will become apparent that there is a strong element of divine command underpinning some of the basic ethical principles in Islam. Such principles are seen to be eternally established by Allah.

7 The nature and formation of shari'ah

It has already been noted that there is a strong link, if not identity, between shari'ah law and ethical codes. The shari'ah law encompasses ethical codes but also much more than this. It is a complete way of life involving religious law, family law, social law, general etiquette and much more.

There is, however, a disparity in how the shari'ah is viewed, as can be seen from the following two observations:

In the west the idea of shari'ah calls up all the darkest images of Islam: repression of women, physical punishments, stoning… It has reached the extent that many Muslim intellectuals do not dare even to refer to the concept for fear of frightening people…

(Ramadan)

Far from being an unwelcome or burdensome imposition, it is considered to be the greatest of blessings and guidance for successful and individual communal life in this world, in preparation for the hereafter.

(Denny)

The shari'ah first and foremost is God's law. As noted above, it is based on the Qur'an, Hadith and Sunnah as primary sources, and reasoning, consensus and analogy as secondary sources. Shari'ah is formed through the application of these sources and the principles contained within them by certain historical law schools.

God's law has absolute primacy and timeless authority because its basis is the word of God and exemplified by the life of Muhammad. It is therefore Holy Law, leading to justice. It leads to the straight path and humanity is rewarded for following the will of Allah.

Shari'ah covers both the sacred and the secular. As God's law it is a reminder that God is omnipotent and omniscient. God's will must be obeyed.

How is God's will defined? It is extrapolated through the ruling of the **ulama** (group of religious scholars) and **muftis** (legal experts). An ulama council or group of muftis (muftiat or diyanet) have a general role of advisor to Muslim state governments, acting as points of reference for Muslim matters regarding application of the shari'ah in any given context. They are scholars who base their views solely upon precedents and the application of tried and tested Muslim principles for working out and applying Muslim law.

A mufti or ulama requires no formal qualifications but their authority is recognised by other scholars through virtue of belief, character, maturity and intellect. Although a mufti or ulama may have no official, legal authority it is common for a muftiat or ulama to influence a government. Individual muftis and scholars have also been known to contradict state proclamations that are seen to be un-Islamic.

However, the shari'ah law also operates at an individual level through ethical principles:

*Its moral order demands an ethical system which requires the Muslim to meet and fulfil the responsibility and obligation (**taklif**) of the divine trust at the individual level.*

(ibn Ally)

Esposito sees the roots of Islamic ethics in the idea of stewardship or vice-regents for Allah as illustrated by passages such as 6:165 in the Qur'an:

It is he who hath made you (his) agents, inheritors of the Earth.

Esposito writes:

It is here that we see the roots of Islamic ethics. God ordains; humankind is to implement His will. Human responsibility and mission are of cosmic proportion, and people will be judged on the cosmic consequences of their acts. As God's representatives, the measure of human actions, and indeed life, is the extent to which the Muslim contributes to the realization of God's will on Earth.

So the whole idea of individual action and community ideals are inter-twined and connected.

In the second and third centuries Muslim religious and legal scholars devised categories of actions:

1 **wajib** or **fard** (obligatory)

2 **mustahabb** (preferred, commendable) male circumcision, extra prayers, visiting friends and family, tidy room – use example of Muhammad

3 **mubah** (permissible) anything that is not the others, for example, freedom of personal choice, preference for things

4 **makruh** (discouraged, reprehensible) no prescribed punishment but not seen to be good, for example, urinating in stagnant water or sleeping late in the morning

5 **haram** (absolutely forbidden) alcohol, pork, killing innocents, adultery.

First of all, it is important to stress that the focus of Islam is on the 'straight path' according to the will of Allah. There is much in life that is encouraged and celebrated but relatively little that is forbidden:

Contrary to popular opinion there are relatively few forbidden acts in Islam, particularly when compared, say, with the long lists of the forbidden that one finds in the Old Testament.

(Turner)

In establishing ethical principles for behaviour, one of the key aspects of the primary sources is that of the behaviour of the prophets, in particular, the 'seal of the prophets', Muhammad:

The life of a prophet is a beacon light for the rest of humanity.

(ibn Ally)

Ethical principles are often established on the basis of how Muhammad behaved.

> **66 KEY QUOTES**
>
> *A dichotomy of forbidden (haram) and permitted (halal) permeates the Qur'an and provides an element of the foundation for Islamic ethics.*
>
> (Rippin)
>
> *…there is no such thing as a practice or action that is inherently sacred, religious or 'Islamic': an action is only as good, bad, sacred or profane as the intention which engenders it and the attitude which underpins it.*
>
> (Turner)

> **66 KEY QUOTE**
>
> *…the shahadah translates the idea of 'being Muslim', and the shari'ah shows us 'how to be and remain Muslim'…the shari'ah is not only the expression of the universal principles of Islam but the framework and the thinking that makes for their actualisation in human history.*
>
> (Ramadan)

> **KEY WORDS**
>
> **Wajib** or **fard:** obligatory
> **Mustahabb:** preferred, commendable
> **Mubah:** permissible
> **Makruh:** discouraged, reprehensible
> **Haram:** absolutely forbidden

> **66 KEY QUOTE**
>
> *This trusteeship (khalifah) confers both responsibility and obligation (taklif) for the whole universe; it is the basis of a Muslim's humanity.*
>
> (ibn Ally)

8 Islam and the issues of death, abortion and euthanasia

It is beneficial, before studying issues of life and death, to gain some basic background information on Islamic beliefs about what happens upon death and also the views about the value of life.

a) Islam and life after death

Muslims' beliefs concerning death and the afterlife include:

- life is a preparation ground for the afterlife
- the soul is immortal
- the soul hovers above the grave until the day of judgement
- the body stays inside the grave until the last day
- our bodies are then raised to stand before God for judgement
- our life is a test
- everyone is given a book (written by recording angels – one sits on each shoulder, to record good and bad deeds), into the right hand if the person is to go to heaven, the left if hell
- Allah is merciful and will forgive if a person has demonstrated correct and pure intention
- all non-Muslims will go to hell unless they have lived a good life
- because the body is physically raised on the last day, they never cremate bodies
- heaven is like a beautiful garden or paradise
- hell is like a place of great heat and torment or torture.

b) The value of human life

The absolute belief in the sanctity of human life is proclaimed in the Qur'an. Allah creates all and it is Allah's decision when a life is to cease.

According to the Qur'an:

> *Take not life which Allah made sacred otherwise than in the course of justice*
>
> **(Sura 6:151 and 17:33)**

The shari'ah does elaborate and identify in great detail the defining conditions when taking life is permissible, for example, in times of war; however, the conditions are rigorous. Such conditions are considered below in the issues of abortion and euthanasia.

KEY QUOTES

A Muslim, then, is not the absolute owner of his or her life. God is its owner, since in Islam, God gave it. A person has the responsibility to preserve and prolong that life, not the right to destroy it.

(ibn Ally)

On that account We ordained for the children of Israel that if anyone slay a person – unless it be for murder or spreading mischief in the land – it would be as if he slew the whole people. And if anyone saved a life, it would be as if he saved the life of the whole people.

(Sura 5:32)

EXAM TIP

Remember to explain to the full each point that you make in an exam answer. Think carefully about each sentence and how it relates to the question and the previous sentence. Aim for at least three clear sentences to explain a concept or idea, giving examples from different sources to support your point. For development of the point, bring in a variety of ways in which the application of this principle is demonstrated and introduce some contrasting scholarly views.

This demonstrates that the answer is 'well-structured in depth or broad response to the task' (mid level 5 AO1 descriptor) as opposed to the information being simply 'uncritical and descriptive presentation' (level 1 descriptor AO1) or 'presented within a limited framework' (level 2 descriptor AO1).

c) Islam and abortion

Although the sanctity of life is universally recognised within Islam, the principle is not always seen as absolutely binding in situations where there are mitigating circumstances. War has already been suggested as a reason for taking life, but this can also extend to times when there is a genuine moral dilemma.

In principle, **abortion** is a sin against Allah and is forbidden. All life is a gift from Allah and therefore human life is a loan that needs repaying to God. The sanctity of life and the recognition of the human nature of the fetus is so important in Islam that a pregnant woman cannot be executed:

> *If a pregnant woman is condemned to die, the death sentence must be postponed until after she has given birth.*
>
> *(Oxford Dictionary of Islam)*

The Qur'an does not make any explicit statements about abortion in general although the following verse is usually interpreted as referring to abortion for reasons of poverty (possibly as an alternative to female infanticide):

> *Kill not your children for fear of want. We shall provide sustenance for them as well as for you. Verily the killing of them is a great sin.*
>
> *(Sura 17:31)*

Scholars have therefore concluded that the killing of a **fetus** is not allowed, as soon as it is seen to be a child, a person whose parts are fully formed and possessing a soul.

There is no universal agreement as to abortion regulations among the four law schools; however:

- after the fetus is completely formed and has been given a soul, abortion is haram
- it is also a crime because it constitutes an offence against a complete, living human being
- the payment of **diya** or blood money is due if the baby is aborted alive and then dies, while a fine is to be paid if it is aborted dead, although this is a lesser amount.

KEY QUOTES

Allah, being omnipotent and omniscient, is the ultimate cause of both man's good and his evil actions, Whomsoever He wills he lets go astray [yudlilhuh]; and whomsoever He wills He sets him on a straight path [siratin mustaqimin]...

(Sura 6:39)

Those who are good and follow the path are destined for paradise; those who are evil are destined for hell.

(Ruthven)

KEY WORDS

Abortion: termination of a pregnancy, either spontaneously (due to complications during pregnancy) or by the removal or expulsion of an embryo or fetus from the uterus, resulting in its death; the latter is the more commonly understood usage

Fetus: the developing unborn baby from the end of the eighth week after conception (when the major structures have formed) until birth

Diya: blood money; payment for the loss of the life of a relative

Imam al-Ghazali (CE1058–1111) stated that:

Abortion is a crime against an existing being.

However, he also recognised three different phases of development.

1 The semen settles and fertilisation takes place – do not disturb it as it is a crime.

2 The fetus is 'a lump'; at this point, aborting is a 'greater crime'.

3 *When it acquires a soul and its creation is completed, the crime becomes more grievous. The crime reaches a maximum seriousness when it is committed after it (fetus) is separated from (the mother) alive.*

However, abortion is allowed if the life of the mother is threatened. It is the lesser of two evils, according to shari'ah law. If it is reliably shown that the continuation of the pregnancy would necessarily result in the death of the mother, then, in accordance with the general principle of the shari'ah, abortion must be performed. This is because:

- the mother is the origin of the fetus
- her life is well established, with duties and responsibilities
- she is also a pillar of the family
- it would not be right to sacrifice her life for the life of a fetus that has not yet acquired a personality and which has no responsibilities or obligations to fulfil.

However, abortion is not allowed after the fetus is formed (120 days). This may be for any of a number of reasons but mainly centres around the issue that before this time the fetus (unborn child) has not yet developed a human personality. It has not been ensouled.

In Turkey, the Middle East and Central Asia, abortions are generally permitted up to 120 days into the pregnancy, as it a moral transgression but not a crime. This is according to the jurists ruling in the Hanifite school of shari'ah law. However, there has to be 'good cause', including that the mother may still be nursing an infant and there are fears that her milk may run out during the new pregnancy.

In south-east Asia the Shafite school takes a similar line to the above.

For the Malikite and Hanbalite schools of Africa and Saudi Arabia respectively, an abortion is allowed, with the consent of *both* parents, up to the 40th day (Hanbalite) or up to and including the 40th day (Malikite).

Once again, exceptions are made sometimes if the life of the mother is threatened. This is based on Sura 2:233:

A mother should not be made to suffer because of her child.

As a result, it is argued by some scholars that abortion is possible for health reasons up to day 90.

d) Islam and suicide and euthanasia

i) Suicide

Euthanasia and suicide are perceived by Muslims to be morally equivalent.

(ibn Ally)

Suicide is officially 29th in the list of the 70 major sins. It is prohibited by the Qur'an:

KEY QUOTE

Muslim jurists uniformly hold abortion to be blameworthy but permissible under certain conditions. Ensoulment of the fetus is understood to occur 120 days after conception; after ensoulment, abortion constitutes homicide and requires a juridical punishment.

(*Oxford Dictionary of Islam*)

KEY WORDS

Euthanasia: literally, 'good death' (Greek), ending someone's life in a painless manner, usually to relieve suffering

Suicide: deliberately ending one's own life

Do not kill (or destroy) yourselves, for verily Allah has been to you most Merciful.

(Sura 4:29)

Islam teaches the sanctity of human life: '…it is Allah that gives life and only Allah makes the decision on when a life ends.' Allah, not the individual, is the owner of a human body. Despite this, the shari'ah does define conditions whereby taking life may be allowed but does not include suicide, which is seen as both a crime and a sin. The Hadiths, such as Bukhari, depict any form of suicide as punishable by hell. Every life is worth living; even euthanasia is encompassed by the teachings about suicide. Nonetheless, there is a sharp distinction between a martyr and suicide. Dying for the cause of Allah is rewarded by an afterlife of immediate heaven. This fine line has been exploited by terrorists and extreme aspects of Islam.

ii) Euthanasia

There is a story from the Hadith of al'Bhukhari that gives Muslims clear teachings on euthanasia:

In the time before you a man was wounded. His wounds troubled him so much that he took a knife and cut his wrist to bleed himself to death. Thereupon, Allah said, 'My slave hurried in the matter of his life, therefore he is deprived of heaven.'

There are traditional reasons for the rejection of euthanasia, summarised as follows.

- Muslims must never give up on this life.
- Euthanasia is not allowed under any circumstance.
- Life is a test and euthanasia is cheating.
- Life is always worth living as long as Allah wills it.
- The concept of a life not worth living does not exist in Islam.
- Allah decides the precise length of a person's life.
- Muslims do not own their own lives.
- Shari'ah law makes no allowance for mercy killing.
- Islam does not accept the justification of taking life to escape suffering.
- Patience and endurance are highly regarded and highly rewarded values in Islam:

Those who patiently preserve will truly receive a reward without measure.

(Sura 39:10)

The *Islamic Code of Medical Ethics*, created by the First International Conference on Islamic Medicine states:

Mercy killing, like suicide, finds no support except in the atheistic way of thinking that believes that our life on this earth is followed by void. The claim of killing for painful hopeless illness is also refuted, for there is no human pain that cannot be largely conquered by medication or by suitable neurosurgery…

and again:

…the doctor is well advised to realise his limit and not transgress it. If it is scientifically certain that life cannot be restored, then it is futile to diligently keep the patient in a vegetative state by heroic means or to preserve the patient by deep freezing or other artificial methods. It is the process of life that the doctor aims to maintain and not the process of dying. In any case, the doctor shall not take a positive measure to terminate the patient's life.

> ## KEY QUOTES
>
> *Some Muslims perceive these actions as a necessary part of active armed struggle and view the death that results as martyrdom, not suicide.*
>
> (*Oxford Dictionary of Islam* on suicidal military missions)
>
> *Euthanasia has no place in Islam, not even for the very old whose lives are just as sacred as those of the young. Death is a time allotted by God.*
>
> (ibn Ally)

Despite Islam being a 'religion of mercy', it sees the position it advocates as 'true mercy' and indicates that euthanasia is only 'mercy apparent'. The underlying reasons and principles that it may destroy in performing euthanasia offer no compensation for, or mitigating circumstances towards, justification of euthanasia.

Specification guidance notes (AO2)

Assessment objective 2 (Critical evaluation)

Critically evaluate and justify a point of view through the use of evidence and reasoned argument.

The examination board provides guidance notes in order to assist you with preparation for assessment. In the notes it states:

Students may study similarities and differences between different religious traditions and may investigate issues such as whether these teachings are relevant in a secular society.

> The relevance of shari'ah-based Muslim ethics in today's world: shari'ah has its basis in the lifetime of Muhammad, connected to articles of faith and the regulations that they postulate are beyond time; challenges cannot be made effectively against God; leads to reward from God and is linked to the afterlife; fixed as sacred law and unites all Muslims; a divine mandate; links to judgement and salvation.

> Challenges to shari'ah based Muslim ethics in today's world: the nature of any law as it unfolds reflects assimilation, for example, the law schools; an element of doubt over the reliability of its sources at a secondary level; shari'ah law is limited – some issues are not overtly considered; not all Muslims may be able to implement shari'ah law over secular law; further guidance is needed for 21st century life and challenges of secularisation; there is no unity in interpretation or practice today amongst Muslims.

Overview: Issues for debate

A critical evaluation of Muslim ethics

In terms of ethics it is suggested that there is an inherent element of conservatism within the very fabric of the Islamic ethical system that is alien to change. There is the comfort of what is known, approved and practised; then there is the uncomfortable nature of the new and undiscovered:

> *These two concepts…clearly derive from the moral order of a tribal society where the 'known' or familiar way of doing things is socially approved, while the unknown or unfamiliar is disapproved of because it falls outside the framework of established custom.*
>
> **(Ruthven)**

a) Ways in which Muslim ethics and the shari'ah law are relevant today

1 Shari'ah has its basis in the lifetime of Muhammad and the early Muslim community.

Muslims today must try to emulate its example. Ruthven uses Sura 3:110 to analyse the terms al'maruf (good, literally 'known') and al-munkar (the unknown). The Qur'anic text states:

> *[Believers] you are the best community singled out for people: you order what is right, forbid what is wrong, and believe in God.*
>
> **(translated by Haleem)**

2 The Qur'an and Sunnah are connected to articles of faith; the regulations that they postulate are beyond time.

Challenges cannot be made effectively against God. The divine nature of the Qur'an and its role as the basis of ethical regulations make the whole nature of ethics in Islam a 'closed book'.

3 Adherence to shari'ah leads to reward from God and is linked to the afterlife.

It is fixed as sacred law and unites all Muslims. It is ongoing law, categorising all behaviour. Muslims seek to implement God's law as it is a divine mandate. Following God's law is linked with judgement and salvation.

4 Shari'ah law and the ethical codes that it promotes unite the Muslim community.

Shari'ah law is universal and, on the whole, agreed. Any differences are minor and do not make a great deal of difference on the macrocosmic scale of Islam. Islam is about unity of belief and practice. Once this unity is diminished Islam is threatened.

b) Ways in which a strict interpretation of Muslim ethics and the shari'ah law can be challenged

1 The nature of any law as it unfolds reflects assimilation.

This is clearly seen with the law schools, so there is an element of doubt over the reliability of its sources at a secondary level. This does not deny the timeless relevance or authority of the Qur'an, but simply points to the humble and imperfect nature of humanity:

> *The fact that most of the laws by which Muslims have endeavoured to regulate their lives are in fact human concoctions may come as a bracing surprise to most readers... However, that 'Islamic law' is mostly 'human law' is not particularly earth-shattering. What is shocking is the fact that it has masqueraded as a sacred code for so long, its spurious provenance allowing it to avoid criticism and to act as a virtually impregnable barrier to legal, social and political reform.*
>
> **(Turner)**

2 The shari'ah law is limited.

As has been observed in the cases of abortion and euthanasia, some issues are not overtly considered and therefore not comprehensively dealt with.

? KEY QUESTIONS

- Can a law established by God ever be changed?
- How reliable and authoritative are decisions made by human beings that apply 'divine' principles?
- Why change a system that has had success for hundreds of years?
- Would a challenge to shari'ah and Muslim ethics cause disunity and challenge the very fabric of Islam itself?

TASK

Think of the questions you would like to ask about the topic you have chosen or about the views that scholars have presented in response to the topic you have chosen. Is there anything that is not clear? What needs further explanation? Do you wish to challenge the thinking or view of a scholar? If so, can you list your reasons or evidence?

Objective: To develop AO2 skills of questioning, considering different views, analysing arguments and responding to the material studied, 'critically evaluate and justify a point of view through the use of evidence and reasoned argument'. It aids self-reflection and development of an argument, working towards 'some attempt to set out reasons for alternative views; a point of view expressed clearly, supported by some relevant evidence and argument' (level 3 descriptor AO2) or even an 'attempt at an evaluation of the issue(s) raised in the task, typically through a careful analysis of alternative views; leading to a clearly expressed viewpoint supported by well-deployed evidence and reasoned argument' (level 4 descriptor AO2).

3 Not all Muslims may be able to implement shari'ah law over secular law.

There are clear conflicts between shari'ah law and some areas of secular law. What does a Muslim do? Does a Muslim break any laws that are unjust or unrighteous in their eyes? Do they follow the secular law?

4 Further guidance is needed for 21st-century life and challenges of secularisation.

It is clear that there are problems in some areas of ethics and shari'ah law in relating them to the 21st century. There is need for progression and a distinctively Muslim response to the issues raised by modernisation. But what changes, how much, when, in what areas and who actually decides? The main problem remains in defining a united approach:

> *The issue is not change. Rather, the key questions are: What change, and how much change is possible? What is the Islamic rationale for change? Whose interpretation of Islam should prevail?*
>
> (Esposito)

5 Different Muslim countries follow different law schools so there is no unity in interpretation or practice.

If there is currently no unity in interpretation and practice, then what hope is there of a future unity?

> *What Islam? What interpretation(s) of Islam is normative and appropriate?...is the implementation of Islam in state and society simply to be a process of imitation (taqlid) of the past or of reinterpretation (ijtihad) and reform of tradition? Is there one classical Islamic model, or are there many possible models for development?*
>
> (Esposito)

5 Possible conclusions

In thinking about conclusions in relation to the problems raised by Muslim ethics, we could consider the words of Ally:

> *The ethics of all prophets was one of moderation and balance (wast), therefore fanaticism...has no place in Islam. Fanaticism is an attitude of faith which arises out of fear of the unknown, and may lead to extreme behaviour.*
>
> (ibn Ally)

It is exactly this deep-rooted fear of what is unfamiliar that can be seen either as a strength in upholding the traditions and standards of Islam or, alternatively, a major obstacle against progress.

When assessing the problems raised by Muslim ethics, it is important to reflect upon the arguments previously discussed and arrive at some appropriate conclusion. It may be that you accept none of these listed here, or just one of them, or you may have a different conclusion that is not listed. However, what is important is the way that you have arrived at your conclusion – the reasoning process.

From the preceding discussions, here are some possible conclusions you could draw.

1 Shari'ah and Muslim ethics are timeless, beyond criticism and need to be maintained.

2   Muslim ethics and shari'ah law can and should be questioned, in light of today's advancement in science, technology and philosophical understandings of the world and humanity.

3   Muslim ethics and shari'ah law can and should be questioned because they are essentially 'man-made'. There is very little of Qur'anic substance in the majority of the shari'ah law.

4   God is merciful, compassionate and forgiving. Shari'ah law should not be made into a standard that is worshipped. The crucial factors in living the Muslim life are intention and purity. In the face of human suffering, is it right blindly to advocate a principle with the full knowledge of the appalling human consequences?

➡ **EXAM TIP**

Be careful when using quotes in critical assessments. Always make sure that they relate to the argument that is presented. To make sure of this, always explain the relevance of the quote in your answer. This is the difference between 'a mainly descriptive response…supported by reference to a simple argument or unstructured evidence' or 'a point of view supported by limited but appropriate evidence and/or argument' (levels 1 and 2 descriptors AO2) and that of a level 3 and above answer that clearly attempts analysis 'some attempt to set out reasons for alternative views' (level 3 descriptor AO2) and the best answer that delivers 'a careful analysis of alternative views' (level 4 descriptor AO2).

INVESTIGATIONS
Area F: The study of the New Testament

The individual unit content outline from the specification gives three possible areas of study for a topic. The authors have chosen one area for each unit.

For this unit they have selected **18: Life after death**.

Whichever area of the specification is chosen, it is important that you are familiar with the overall general topic.

For the purposes of this book, this means the relevant chapter and corresponding assessment and reflections.

This diagram shows an outline of the sort of areas we are going to look at. Using this as a basis, create and extend it into your own thought-process diagram as you progress. This may help you decide on a focus. Then you can use your focus to start another chart.

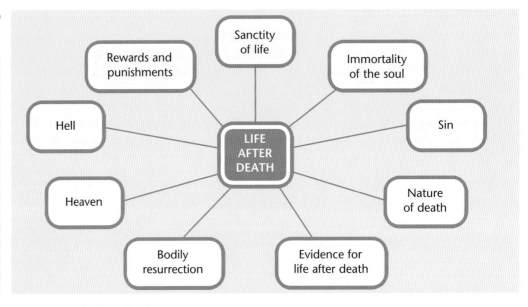

Overview: Life after death

Specification guidance notes (AO1)

Assessment objective 1 (Knowledge and understanding)

Select and demonstrate clearly relevant knowledge and understanding through the use of evidence, examples, and correct language and terminology appropriate to the course of study.

For this skill, you are expected to select and present relevant and appropriate information from the specification in order to answer an area examined.

The examination board provides guidance notes in order to assist you with preparation for assessment.

In the notes it states:

Students may investigate the textual narrative of the New Testament, probably with particular reference to the Gospels, 1 Corinthians, Paul's letters and the Book of Revelation. Students are not limited to these exemplars.

POSSIBLE AREAS FOR FOCUS IN THIS BOOK

- Sanctity of life
- The nature of death
- Sin
- Immortality of the soul
- Bodily resurrection
- Heaven
- Hell
- Reward and righteousness

In addition to a number of key ideas, from which the focus can be selected, students may study 'the context of these ideas in relation to philosophy and science'.

1 Sanctity of life

The word 'sanctity', from the Latin *sanctus*, means sacred, holy or inviolable. It involves a principle, or moral conviction that human life must be held to be sacred. Human life is said to be holy and special.

There are a variety of arguments from within Christianity, to support the sanctity of life argument.

1 Human beings are created in the 'image of God' (Genesis 1:26). This distinguishes mankind from all other life-forms. Most scholars agree that the word 'image' does not mean physical characteristics. The image of God is seen to be present in humanity through the existence of such faculties as:

- thought – rational beings
- choice – moral beings
- love – social beings
- creativity – creative beings
- prayer – spiritual beings.

In addition, God became man in Jesus. This affirmed the intrinsic value of every human life.

2 Life is a gift from God. It is God who is the author of life and it is God who determines when it ends.

3 Paul taught that, for the Christian, the body is the temple of the Holy Spirit, and this temple should be treated with great respect (1 Corinthians 3:16–17).

4 Jesus taught that human beings were valued by God very highly and much more highly than other life-forms (Matthew 10:29–31).

2 The nature of death

By physical death we usually mean the final ceasing of the bodily functions. In the past, it has been defined in terms of the heart stopping and the person no longer breathing. However, with medical advancements, death is now defined in terms of the non-functioning of the brain. An electroencephalogram can monitor the activity of the brain. When this is shown on a screen a wavy line indicates brain activity. If the trace is a flat line, this indicates that there is no brain activity. That is the moment of clinical death.

According to the New Testament, death is more than just physical. It is about our relationship with God. In one sense death is an intrusion. It is not what God had planned for us, for sin entered the world and, with it, brought death. As a result, death is not some accident of the universe, or something that we will eventually be able to overcome with medical advancement.

…man is destined (appointed) to die once, and after that to face judgement.

(Hebrews 9:27)

66 KEY QUOTES

Then God said, 'Let us make humankind in our image, in our likeness…'
(Genesis 1:26)

…the Lord God formed the man from the dust of the ground and breathed into his nostrils the breath of life, and the man became a living being.
(Genesis 2:7)

You shall not murder.
(Exodus 20:13)

Naked I came from my mother's womb, and naked I shall depart. The Lord gave and the Lord has taken away; may the name of the Lord be praised.
(Job 1:21)

99

KEY IDEA

The sanctity of life:
- **Created in the image of God**
- **Life is a gift from God**
- **Body is the temple of Holy Spirit**
- **Valued by God.**

Adam was threatened with death if he disobeyed God. He did disobey. As a result, he suffered a change of state (from possession of access to the tree of life to a state of mortality), and a change of place (from Eden to banishment), with continuity of person and character. According to many theologians, that is the biblical understanding of death. Death is about a new sphere of life, rather than 'the end'.

✎ TASK

Research what various scholars have understood by the 'tree of life'.
Why was it a sin to eat the fruit of the tree of life?

Objective: To develop a 'wide range of selected relevant factual knowledge and understanding of the topic investigated' (level 5 descriptor AO1).

---

3 Sin

The biblical account of the history of the human race tells of human beings in a state of rebellion against God and of God's plan of restoration, to bring us back to himself. The rebellion is about our failure to conform to the moral law of God, in act or attitude, which the Bible calls sin. Indeed, Ephesians 2:3 suggests that the very essence of who we are, our internal character, our very nature, can be sinful:

Like the rest, we were by nature objects of wrath.

a) The meaning of sin

A biblical definition of sin is lawlessness (1 John 3:4), the failure to conform to the moral law of God. The root of the word used has the idea of missing the mark or falling short. When Paul seeks to demonstrate the universal sinfulness of humankind, he cites the law of God and the human rebellion against it (Romans 2:15–19).

b) The origin of sin

Rebellion (sin) is depicted as first occurring, with respect to the human race, in the garden of Eden (Genesis 3:1–19). Some see certain references in scripture as evidence of a previous rebellion in the angelic world, resulting in the fall of Satan and his angels (Isaiah 14:12–15, Luke 10:18).

The story of Adam and Eve and the eating of the fruit of the tree of knowledge of good and evil portrays the essence of what sin is. They rejected God's view about:

- what is true (doubted that they would die if they ate from the tree)
- what is right (doubted that it was wrong to eat from tree)
- who they were (they wanted to be like God).

In other words, the human race resists God's rule and sets itself up as its own lord.

There is no fear of God before their eyes.

(Romans 3:10)

The characteristic feature of sin is that it is directed against God. Romans 8:7 states that 'the sinful mind is hostile to God. It does not submit to God's law…'.

c) The results of sin

- Like Adam, human beings become spiritually separated from God, unfit to stand before him and enjoy the intimacy of his presence.

- They become enslaved to sin.
- They become condemned before God.
- The separation affects the relationships between human beings.
- The separation creates inner conflicts within people.

d) God's dealing with sin

According to the New Testament, God's dealings with the problem of sin are motivated by his love and his justice. If God had done nothing, then the human race would have been eternally separated from God.

His love motivated him to do something. He loved the world. However, he could not ignore the sin. The very nature of God is **righteousness** and justice. He cannot ignore the consequences of sin. The way God has acted is expressed in different ways in the New Testament.

- **Atonement:** Jesus died for the sins of the world. 'For Christ died for our sins once for all, the righteous for the unrighteous, to bring you to God,' (1 Peter 3:18).
- Sacrifice: Jesus died as a sacrifice for us. 'But now he has appeared once for all at the end of the ages to do away with sin by the sacrifice of himself,' (Hebrews 9:26).
- Reconciliation: Jesus made it possible for us to come back into fellowship with God. 'All this is from God, who reconciled us to himself through Christ…' (2 Corinthians 5:18).
- Redemption: this has the idea of deliverance. '…all have sinned and fall short of the glory of God, and are justified freely by his grace through the redemption that came by Christ Jesus. God presented him as a sacrifice of atonement…' (Romans 3:23–5).

The result of God's actions is that 'there is now no condemnation for those who are in Christ Jesus,' (Romans 8:1).

KEY WORDS

Righteousness: right standing and right behaviour, rather than the abstract idea of justice or virtue

Atonement: to make at one; usually used to describe the work Christ did in his death, to reconcile sinners to God

> **KEY QUOTES**
>
> *Jesus replied, 'I tell you the truth, everyone who sins is a slave to sin.'*
> (John 8:34)
>
> *For God so loved the world that he gave his one and only Son, that whoever believes in him shall not perish but have eternal life.*
> (John 3:16)
>
> *Death has been followed up in victory. Where, O death, is your victory? Where, O death, is your sting?*
> (1 Corinthians 15:54–5)

EXAM TIP

Remember to explain to the full each point that you make in an exam answer. Think carefully about each sentence, how it relates to the question and to the previous sentence. Aim for at least three clear sentences to explain a concept or idea, giving examples from different sources to support your point. For development of the point, bring in a variety of ways in which the application of this principle is demonstrated and introduce some contrasting scholarly views. This demonstrates that the answer is 'well-structured in depth or broad response to the task' (mid level 5 descriptor AO1) as opposed to the information being simply 'uncritical and descriptive presentation' (level 1 descriptor AO1) or 'presented within a limited framework' (level 2 descriptor AO1).

4 Immortality of the soul

Some scholars claim that in the New Testament there is little indication that human beings are naturally immortal. Only God is described in such terms. Hence, scholars such as Oscar Cullmann argue that the afterlife is about **resurrection** rather than immortality. In other words, the emphasis is on the unity of a person. Actions we take in this life involve both body and soul. It is an act of the whole person.

However, there does seem to be clear reference in the Bible to an immaterial part of a person – a soul and/or spirit, as well as the physical body.

KEY WORD

Resurrection: rising from the dead into a new kind of life, not subject to sickness, ageing, deterioration, or death

a) References to this immaterial part

Paul refers to the spirit as something independent of our thought processes. 'For if I pray in a tongue, my spirit prays, but my mind is unfruitful,' (1 Corinthians 14:14).

He also indicates that he believed that, after death, his spirit would go into the Lord's presence: 'We are confident, I say, and would prefer to be away from the body and at home with the Lord,' (2 Corinthians 5:8).

Revelation 20:4 refers to souls: 'And I saw the souls of those who had been beheaded because of their testimony for Jesus and because of the word of God.'

b) Soul is same as spirit

The **Hebrew parallelism** of Luke 1:46–7 implies that soul and spirit are interchangeable: 'My soul glorifies the Lord and my spirit rejoices in God my Saviour.'

Jesus' reference to body and soul: 'Rather, be afraid of the One who can destroy both soul and body in hell,' (Matthew 10:28), seems equivalent to Paul's use of spirit in 1 Corinthians 5:5.

In the parable of the Rich Fool, Jesus says: 'This very night your soul will be demanded from you,' (Luke 12:20). Likewise, when referring to death, Acts records Stephen saying: 'Lord Jesus, receive my spirit,' (Acts 7:59). Thus, the two terms of soul and spirit seem interchangeable.

c) Soul and spirit are different

Examples of verses in the New Testament that seem to imply a three-part nature of human beings, body, soul and spirit include:

- 'May your whole spirit, soul and body be kept blameless at the coming of our Lord Jesus Christ,' (1 Thessalonians 5:23)
- '…it penetrates even to dividing soul and spirit…' (Hebrews 4:12)
- 'For if I pray in a tongue, my spirit prays, but my mind is unfruitful,' (1 Corinthians 14:14)
- 'But if Christ is in you, your body is dead because of sin, yet your spirit is alive because of righteousness,' (Romans 8:10).

5 Evidence for life after death

Both the Old Testament and the New Testament contain beliefs in life after death.

a) The Old Testament

In the Old Testament there are accounts of both Enoch and Elijah being translated into heaven, as well as the story of Saul and the witch of Endor (1 Samuel 28).

b) Jesus' resurrection

The strongest argument in the New Testament for belief in an afterlife is the account of the resurrection of Jesus. If it is true that Jesus was resurrected in a bodily form, then it shows that death is not final. There is the hope of resurrection for all who believe in Christ. The case for the accounts of Jesus' resurrection being historically accurate include the following evidence.

- The date of the accounts: The writings of the New Testament can be dated within

---

KEY WORD

Hebrew parallelism: a poetic device in which the same idea is repeated, using different but synonymous words

KEY QUOTE

…so that the sinful nature may be destroyed and his spirit saved on the day of the Lord

(1 Corinthians 5:5)

KEY QUOTE

Samuel said to Saul, 'Why have you disturbed me by bringing me up?'

(1 Samuel 28:15)

the lifetime of witnesses. For example, 1 Corinthians was written within 25 years of the death of Jesus. 1 Corinthians contains an account of the resurrection of Jesus, and is thought to be too close in time to the events for the story to be created by the Early Church.

- The tone of the accounts: Although written from within the Christian Church, they are written with apparent sincerity. The writers seriously claim that the events are historical and produce arguments for their historicity.

Those who argue for the resurrection of Christ as an historical event claim that, at the very least, there is an historical case to be answered for the resurrection.

c) The nature of God

To those who already believe in the existence of a God of love, there are very strong grounds for believing that his intention is not our extinction. In his book, *Holding Fast to God*, Keith Ward also argues that a Christian is committed to belief in **immortality** because of the existence of a God of love.

> *The whole life of faith is one of trusting that the love which we fitfully apprehend in this life will be clearly seen hereafter.*

> **(Ward)**

 KEY WORD

Immortality: not subject to death or decay, everlasting

KEY QUOTE

For what I received I pass on to you as of first importance; that Christ died for our sins according to the Scriptures, that he was buried, that he was raised on the third day according to the Scriptures, and that he appeared to Peter and then to the Twelve...
(1 Corinthians 15:3–5)

➡ EXAM TIP

When answering a question on life after death, make sure that you include a range of ideas to show how different concepts affect the issue you have chosen and pick out the key principles and explain why they are important in relation to the issue debated and how they have been applied and interpreted by different scholars.

This ensures focus is on 'a wide range of selected, relevant factual knowledge and understanding of the topic investigated; offering some analysis of issues raised by the topic, using a variety of sources, examples and/or illustrations' (level 5 descriptor AO1) and also 'structured around, and showing clear understanding of, the main theme(s) or concept(s) of the task' (level 5 descriptor AO1).

This would distinguish your work from a poorer answer that would focus simply on the general topic with an unspecific summary of ideas and with little reference to scholars, meaning only 'some relevant and partially structured knowledge of the topic investigated' and evidencing only 'a limited framework…with a general link to the task' (level 2 descriptor AO1).

6 Bodily resurrection

a) The Old Testament

The Old Testament says very little about the afterlife, though it does not deny its existence. The emphasis is much more on present life. Evidence for Jewish belief in an afterlife is shown in the story of Saul attempting to consult the witch of Endor (1 Samuel 28:1–25). Also, there are two Old Testament stories of people being taken up to be with God: Enoch (Genesis 5:24) and Elijah (2 Kings 2:9–11). Although there is no speculation about details of the afterlife in the Old Testament, there is a confidence that even death cannot destroy the reality of fellowship with God. Perhaps the clearest statement is to be found in Daniel 12:2–3:

Multitudes who sleep in the dust of the earth will awake: some to everlasting life, others to shame and everlasting contempt. Those who are wise will shine like the brightness of the heavens, and those who lead many to righteousness, like the stars for ever and ever.

b) The New Testament

Resurrection and the afterlife are clearly taught in the New Testament. It links the nature of our resurrected body with that of Jesus' resurrected body. Paul implies in Philippians that our resurrected body will be like Christ's glorious body:

…who by the power that enables him to bring everything under his control, will transform our lowly bodies so that they will be like his glorious body.

(Philippians 3:21)

Jesus' resurrection is seen as ensuring our resurrection: 'By his power God raised the Lord from the dead, and he will raise us also,' (1 Corinthians 6:14).

Jesus' resurrection is not just a resuscitation of a corpse, but the emergence of a new order of life.

c) Evidence for bodily resurrection

New Testament texts refer to the resurrection of the body. For example, '…he who raised Christ from the dead will also give life to your mortal bodies through his Spirit, who lives in you,' (Romans 8:11). Similarly in 1 Corinthians 15:49: 'And just as we have borne the likeness of the earthly man, so shall we bear the likeness of the man from heaven.' Philippians 3:21 again points to bodily resurrection: '…the Lord Jesus Christ, who…will transform our lowly bodies so that they will be like his glorious body.'

In 1 Corinthians 15 Paul states: '…it [the body] is sown a natural body, it is raised a spiritual body,' (verse 44). Many scholars argue that the reference to 'spiritual' does not mean 'immaterial' but rather 'suited to and responsive to the guidance of the Spirit'. In Pauline writing the word 'spiritual' never has the idea of 'non-physical'.

Given that we are to be resurrected like Jesus, then we need to examine the evidence that Jesus' resurrection was bodily.

- The tomb was empty – the body had gone.
- The grave clothes were left behind (John 20:6–8).
- He could be touched (Matthew 28:9; John 20:17, 27).
- He could be heard (John 20:16).
- He was capable of eating (Luke 24:42–3; Acts 10:41).
- He said that he was flesh and bones (Luke 24:39).

The body also had properties that set it apart from our natural bodies and suggest that it belonged to a different order of reality.

- It could appear suddenly.
- It could seemingly pass through matter (John 20:19, 26).
- It could disappear suddenly (Luke 24:31).

66 KEY QUOTES

A ghost does not have flesh and bones, as you see I have.

(Luke 24:39)

He was not seen by all the people, but by witnesses whom God had already chosen – by us who ate and drank with him after he rose from the dead.

(Acts 10:41)

99

The details of the resurrection body are not given. Our future existence and substance is not made clear.

…what we will be has not yet been made known. But we know that when he appears we shall be like him for we shall see him as he is.

(1 John 3:2)

However, the New Testament is clear that it will be 'glorious' and beyond all that we can now imagine.

7 Heaven

a) *What terms are used?*

- Heaven: although this often has the meaning of the sky, it is used to refer to the dwelling place of God (our Father in heaven).
- A more common phrase in the synoptic Gospels is 'Kingdom of God'. The word 'kingdom' implies God's ruling activity rather than indicating the place in which the ruling occurs. It can refer to the life to come (Matthew 25:34) and a present aspect.

  But if I drive out demons by the finger of God, then the Kingdom of God has come upon you.
  (Luke 11:20)

- Eternal life is cited in John. He defines eternal life: '…that they may know you, the only true God, and Jesus Christ, whom you have sent,' (John 17:3). It is defined in terms of relationship with God. Through Christ, a person can enjoy eternal life here and now. 'He who believes has everlasting life,' (John 6.47).
- However, some scholars understand eternal life to mean the life of the age to come. In his book, *St John*, John Marsh states:

  Life in that divine order that would supervene upon this when history was brought to its close by God.

  (**Marsh**)

- In John, at the raising of Lazarus, Jesus said: 'He who believes in me will live, even though he dies,' (John 1:25). Jesus is promising life beyond death.
- Paradise is a Persian word meaning 'garden' and is used of the Garden of Eden. When a Persian ruler wanted to reward one of his subjects he would make him a companion of Paradise. He was free to walk in the king's garden. In Luke 23:43, it conveys the sense of being with God. It has a similar meaning in the other occurrences in the New Testament (2 Corinthians 12:3–4; Revelation 2:7).

b) *What is it?*

Heaven is a place where God dwells: 'Our father in heaven' (Matthew 6:9). It is the place from which Jesus was sent and to which he ascended: 'No one has ever gone into heaven except the one who came from heaven – the Son of Man,' (John 3:13); 'While he was blessing them, he left them and was taken up into heaven,' (Luke 24:51).

Paul refers to it as a place (2 Corinthians 5:1) calling it a building from God, an eternal house in heaven, not built by human hands.

KEY IDEA

Wayne Grudem (*Systematic Theology*) argues that the 'spiritual body' is a physical body raised to the degree of perfection for which God originally intended it.

KEY IDEA

Matthew uses the term 'Kingdom of heaven'. However, most scholars regard this as identical to 'Kingdom of God', and Matthew avoids the word 'God' out of Jewish respect.

c) Who will go there?

- The righteous: 'Then the righteous will shine like the sun in the Kingdom of their Father,' (Matthew 13:43).
- The persecuted: Those who are persecuted for Jesus' name sake – 'Blessed are you when men hate you…because of the Son of Man. Rejoice in that day and leap for joy, because great is your reward in heaven,' Luke 6:22–3).
- The sacrificial: 'You still lack one thing. Sell everything you have and give to the poor, and you will have treasure in heaven. Then come, follow me,' (Luke 18:22).
- Jesus' disciples: 'In my Father's house are many rooms…I am going there to prepare a place for you,' (John 14:2).
- Those who believe in Jesus: '…whoever believes in him [Jesus] shall not perish but have eternal life,' (John 3:16).
- Those who have been cleansed by the blood of Christ: 'Blessed are those who wash their robes, that they may have the right to the tree of life and may go through the gates into the city,' (Revelation 22:14).
- Those whose names are written in the Lamb's book of life: (Revelation 21:27)

TASK

Draw up a table with the three headings:
'definition', 'meaning', 'examples'.
Use the information found in your selected topic to complete the table, clearly relating the key ideas and relevant terms to the central issues.
Objective: To develop an understanding of the literal meanings, key ideas and relevant terms but also the wider application of these meanings. To demonstrate 'a deeper understanding of these key ideas and relevant terms, using examples to support explanation' and demonstrating a 'coherent understanding of task; based on selection of material to demonstrate emphasis and clarity of ideas' and also a 'careful analysis of key concepts' (higher level 5 descriptor AO1).

KEY QUOTES

Then the King will say to those on his right, 'Come, you who are blessed by my Father; take your inheritance, the Kingdom prepared for you since the creation of the world.'

(Matthew 25:34)

And I know that this man – whether in the body or apart from the body, I do not know, but God knows – was caught up in paradise.

(2 Corinthians 12:3–4)

To him who overcomes, I will give the right to eat from the tree of life, which is in the paradise of God.

(Revelation 2:7)

8 Hell

a) What terms are used?

The Hebrew word *sheol* occurs in the Old Testament. It seems to refer to the place of the dead, though both the righteous and the unrighteous go there (Isaiah 38:10; Numbers 16:33). Many commentators argue that a better understanding of sheol is 'the grave'.

However, it developed in meaning to be the place reserved for the wicked.

The Greek word used in the **LXX** is Hades.

A more common word used in the New Testament is *Gehenna*. This again appears in the Old Testament and means literally 'the valley of Hinnom'. This valley, on the south slope of Jerusalem, became notorious in Old Testament times because sacrifices were burnt there, including children (2 Chronicles 28:3). This then became synonymous with the place for God's judgement. Some scholars argue that by Jesus' time Gehenna was a rubbish dump where anything not fit to be in the city was excluded. This links with Revelation 21:27: 'Nothing impure will ever enter it [the city of God].'

The New Testament also refers to places of punishment as the Abyss (Luke 8:31) and eternal fire (Matthew 25:41), as well as Hades and Gehenna. The abyss seems to refer specifically to the place of confinement for spirits, including Satan (Revelation 20:1). In

KEY WORD

LXX: an abbreviation for the Septuagint, which is the name given to the translation into Greek of the Old Testament; it is called this because tradition said that 70 people had translated it

the parable of the Rich Man and Lazarus, it seems that Hades is reserved for the wicked, since Lazarus was in a different place. What is not clear is the extent to which the details in the parable should be read as an authoritative account of what life after death will actually be like. It is, after all, a parable.

b) How is it described?

It is described in terms of being the opposite to heaven. For instance, it is always 'in depths' rather than 'in heights'. It is dark rather than light. It is a place of silence rather than joy and celebration.

It also seems to involve eternal punishment. Mark 9:47–8 has a vivid image: 'It is better for you to enter the Kingdom of God with one eye than to have two eyes and be thrown into hell [Gehenna], where their worm does not die, and the fire is not quenched.'

Another New Testament image is that of 'weeping and gnashing of teeth' (Luke 13:28). Some scholars have also argued that annihilation is implied in such passages as John 15:6, where the image is of things thrown into a fire and burnt. Revelation 21:14 also refers to a lake of fire but, in this case, the torment is said to last for ever (Revelation 20:10).

The idea of isolation and separation from God is found in 2 Thessalonians 1: '...and shut out from the presence of the Lord and from the majesty of his power...'. Indeed, many people view hell in terms of exclusion from heaven and from God rather than a literal burning and torment.

c) Who will go there?

- The devil and demons: 'And the devil, who deceived them, was thrown into the lake of burning sulphur, where the beast and the false prophets had been thrown.' (Revelation 20:10)
- Those whose name was not found written in the book of life (Revelation 20:15)
- Those who do not know God and do not obey the Gospel: According to 2 Thessalonians 1:8-9, they will be punished with everlasting destruction.
- Those who do not believe: John 3:18 states that whoever does not believe stands condemned already. When contrasted with John 3:16 ('shall not perish'), it suggests that those who do not believe will perish.

Universalists believe that, in the end, God will bring all to repentance and save all. They claim that verses such as 1 Corinthians 15:22 and 2 Peter 3:9 indicate that ultimately none will perish.

> **KEY QUOTE**
>
> *He [Ahaz] burned sacrifices in the Valley of Ben Hinnom and sacrificed his sons in the fire.*
>
> (2 Chronicles 28:3)

> **KEY WORD**
>
> Universalism: the belief that God will save all peoples

> **KEY QUOTES**
>
> *For as in Adam all die, so in Christ all will be made alive.*
>
> (1 Corinthians 15:22)
>
> *He is patient with you, not wanting anyone to perish, but everyone to come to repentance.*
>
> (2 Peter 3:9)

TASK

Compare the view of hell that this medieval illustration presents (research the illustration on the internet) with the view of hell depicted in the Bible.

Objective: To develop 'careful analysis of key concepts; supported by widely deployed evidence/arguments/ sources' (higher level 5 descriptor AO1).

Medieval illustration of hell in the *Hortus deliciarum* manuscript of Herrad of Landsberg (c1180)

9 Rewards and righteousness

The New Testament portrays a judgement day 'in the presence of God and of Christ Jesus, who will judge the living and the dead,' (2 Timothy 4:1). Both unbelievers and believers will be judged. However, for the believer, the judgement is not one of condemnation or death since: '…there is no condemnation for those who are in Christ Jesus,' (Romans 8:1). Their judgement is about bestowing various degrees of reward, for example:

- 'Blessed are you when people insult you…because great is your reward in heaven,' (Matthew 5:12)
- 'If what he has built survives, he will receive his reward,' (1 Corinthians 3:14)
- 'For if you do these things, you will never fall, and you will receive a rich welcome into the eternal kingdom…' (2 Peter 1:10–11)
- 'Now there is in store for me the crown of righteousness, which the Lord, the righteous judge, will award to me on that day…' (2 Timothy 4:8)
- 'To him who overcomes and does my will to the end, I will give him authority over the nations…I will also give him the morning star,' (Revelation 2:27–8).

The idea that people receiving different rewards would spoil heaven is possibly to misunderstand. Theologians point out that happiness is not based on the status or power that we have. For the Christian, happiness consists in delighting in God.

> **KEY QUOTE**
>
> *The 'rewards' are not a servant's wages but a son's inheritance.'*
> (Calvin)

Specification guidance notes (AO2)

Assessment objective 2 (Critical evaluation)

Critically evaluate and justify a point of view through the use of evidence and reasoned argument.

The examination board provides guidance notes in order to assist you with preparation for assessment. In the notes it states:

Students may study the Gospel narratives and the Letters and place the context of these ideas in relation to philosophy and science.

> **POSSIBLE AREAS FOR DEBATE**
>
> - Does science support or deny the New Testament ideas of life after death?
> - Does philosophy support or deny the New Testament ideas of life after death?
> - Is the evidence for Jesus' resurrection compelling?

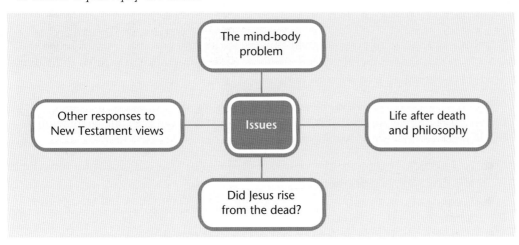

Overview: Issues for debate

1 A critical evaluation of the relationship of ideas about life after death to science and philosophy

a) Life after death and science

The mind–body problem

The belief in life after death has come under attack from various quarters. Modern advances in the sciences have seemingly supported a **monistic** and natural world view rather than a **dualistic** and supernatural one. Equally, the growth of **secularisation** has led to a rejection of traditional religious beliefs.

In particular, much debate has surrounded the relationship between the mind, the brain and consciousness.

KEY WORDS

Monistic: the view that ultimate reality is all of one kind.
Dualism: a fundamental two-fold distinction, such as mind and body
Secularisation: society no longer under the control or influence of religion

- **Dualism**

  Dualists argue that people have composite natures, namely material and non-material. This supports the idea of immortality of the soul. Although the material, the physical body, decomposes at death, there is something of a different nature that continues.

  The classic presentation of dualism is by Descartes. He argued that the body is spatial and in no sense conscious, whilst the mind is non-spatial and is conscious, having thoughts, feelings, desires, etc.

  How these two natures interact is much discussed and Descartes remained agnostic about this.

- **Materialism**

  This view argues that so-called mental events are really physical events occurring to physical objects. Gilbert Ryle rejected the idea of the mind as a different kind of thing from the body. This would reject any notion of an immaterial soul that survives through physical death.

KEY QUESTION

- What are the problems of materialism?

- **Recent challenges to materialism**

  Theories of modern quantum physics question the idea of electrons as small solid particles. Reality seems more mysterious and less 'solid' than science had previously thought. For instance, some have argued that human thoughts and feelings might ultimately be downloaded into magnetic fields.

  Science also speaks of possible multi-universes with different space–time dimensions. Such an idea might interpret Jesus' ascension as stepping out of our three-dimensional world and stepping into a fourth dimension.

  Paul Badham challenges this rejection of dualism and the mind as a function of the physical brain. He argues that it makes sense to speak about the soul, as something different from the body. Among his arguments are:

  - parapsychology supports the view that the mind or soul is different from the brain and may survive death of the brain
  - if mind = brain then human beings are physically determined and are not free agents
  - if there is no 'I' over and above our bodies, our experience is incoherent
  - science observes the 'outside'; it cannot investigate 'self' or our experiences.

TASK

Think of the questions you would like to ask about the focus you have chosen or about the views that scholars have presented in response to the focus you have chosen.
Is there anything that is not clear? What needs further explanation? Do you wish to challenge the thinking or view of a scholar? If so, can you list your reasons or evidence?
Objective: To develop AO2 skills of questioning, considering different views, analysing arguments and responding to the material studied 'critically evaluate and justify a point of view through the use of evidence and reasoned argument'. It aids self-reflection and development of an argument, working towards 'some attempt to set out reasons for alternative views; a point of view expressed clearly, supported by some relevant evidence and argument' (level 3 descriptor AO2) or even an 'attempt at an evaluation of the issue(s) raised in the task, typically through a careful analysis of alternative views; leading to a clearly expressed viewpoint supported by well-deployed evidence and reasoned argument' (level 4 descriptor AO2).

b) Life after death and philosophy

i) Is the concept meaningful?

Linguistic philosophy challenges whether it is even meaningful to talk of life after death. Flew suggested that the concept of life after death was contradictory. In his essay: 'Can a man witness his own funeral?' Flew likened the phrase 'surviving death' to 'dead survivors'. To classify the crew of a torpedoed ship into 'dead' and 'survivors' is both exhaustive and exclusive: it covers all possibilities and no one can be in both groups. Likewise with 'surviving death'; it is self-contradictory and therefore meaningless.

Science-fiction stories involving body transfer illustrate the concept of 'I' remaining 'I' though clothed with a new and different body. Reported out-of-body experiences also display the concept of selfhood being applied to something other than the body.

ii) Continuity

Advocates of materialism face a major difficulty since there is nothing that could continue through death. If nothing continues then in what sense can one say that it is the 'same' person after death? The only solution would be for the body to be recreated. The criticism then is that nothing of the original entity survives, so in what sense can it be considered the same? It would be more accurate to refer to it as a replica.

1 John Hick's 'Replica' theory

The 'Replica' theory is one that John Hick argues for, following on from his theodicy of the 'vale of soul-making'. Hick acknowledges that there is a problem about continuity, but through three examples he argues that it is meaningful to call it the same person if someone dies and appears in a new world with the same memories, etc. He uses the word 'replica' in inverted commas because he uses it in a particular sense, namely that it is not logically possible for the original and the 'replica' to exist simultaneously or for there to be more than one 'replica' of the same original.

2 Dualism

Dualism fares better since it allows for mental continuity. However, it involves isolating the 'ghost in the machine'. By definition, it is not physical and therefore elusive.

TASK

Do some research into Hick's 'Replica' theory. What are the three examples that he gives? Do you agree with his conclusions?
Objective: To develop 'a careful analysis of alternative views... supported by well-deployed evidence and reasoned argument' (level 4 descriptor AO2).

iii) Identification

Another philosophical problem involves our awareness after death of who we are and to what extent others will recognise us. Linguistic philosophy argues that the only possibility of identifying a person is to indicate some bodily criteria. However, at death the body decomposes and ceases to be. It is true that bodily criteria are necessary for identification in the conditions of the world in which we now live. Nevertheless, that does not prove that they are therefore necessary when these earthly conditions are absent. Indeed, it is difficult to understand what would be meant by 'the same body' after death. During our lifetime we all change physically: our very cells change.

Some have suggested that in the resurrection world we shall have bodies that are the outward reflection of our inner nature, but reflect it in ways quite different from that in which our present bodies reflect our personality. If so, presumably people would recognise us. Perhaps God would ensure that others recognised us.

c) Did Jesus rise from the dead?

Alternative explanations for the resurrection accounts include these theories.
- New Testament accounts are symbolic and mythological rather than literal.
- The reports are late and one-sided and events were inaccurately remembered or passed down.
- The disciples had hallucinations that convinced them that God's purposes in history would be continued despite the crucifixion.
- It was not Jesus who was crucified.
- Jesus did not die on the cross but was in a coma and later recovered.

> ## ➡ EXAM TIP
>
> Be careful when using quotes in critical assessments. Always make sure that they relate to the argument you are presenting. To make sure of this, always explain the relevance of the quote in your answer. This is the difference between 'a mainly descriptive response...supported by reference to a simple argument or unstructured evidence' or 'a point of view supported by limited but appropriate evidence and/or argument' (level 1 and 2 descriptors AO2) and that of a level 3 and above answer that clearly attempts analysis, with 'some attempt to set out reasons for alternative views' (level 3 descriptor AO2) and the best answer that delivers 'a careful analysis of alternative views' (level 4 descriptor AO2).

d) Other responses to the New Testament view about life after death

1   Theologians, such as Paul Tillich, see immortality not in terms of individual destinies but in terms of 'eternal memory'. Process theology has a similar view in which the dead will be remembered in the mind of God.

2   John Hick argued that at death we temporarily enter into a mind-dependent world similar to that described in *The Tibetan Book of the Dead*. Then we proceed to a series of embodied existences in other worlds, in our growth towards perfection. Only then do we arrive at the perfect ultimate state. This ultimate state is what Hinduism refers to as 'absorption into the infinite consciousness' and what Buddhism refers to as 'nirvana'. In the Christian tradition it is like the 'unitive state' in Christian mysticism.

TASK

Do some research into evidence about out-of-body or near-death experiences. To what extent do they help with the philosophical problems raised in this section?

Objective: To develop AO2 skills of questioning, considering different views, analysing arguments and responding to the material studied, to 'critically evaluate and justify a point of view through the use of evidence and reasoned argument' (level 3 descriptor AO2).

3 Although John Macquarrie does not support the traditional Christian view of life after death, he appealed to modern relativity theory in his discussions about time and eternity.

> *When we look at the night sky we are actually seeing it as it was some time ago. Although the whole sky and all the objects in it are simultaneously present to our senses, we are in fact looking over a wide range of times. The concept of an absolute present has been abolished.*
>
> **(Travis)**

2 Possible conclusions

When assessing life after death, it is important to reflect upon the arguments previously discussed and arrive at some appropriate conclusion. It may be that you accept none of these listed here, or just one of them, or you may have a different conclusion that is not listed. However, what is important is the way that you have arrived at your conclusion – the reasoning process.

From the preceding discussions, here are some possible conclusions you could draw.

1 There is no life after death. The concept is contradictory to our modern understanding of science.

2 There is no life after death. Philosophy shows the concept to be self-contradictory.

3 There is no life after death. The concept of the immortality of the soul is contradictory.

4 There is no evidence for life after death. The New Testament accounts are not historically reliable.

5 There is life after death but it is not to be understood in the traditional sense of the phrase.

6 There is life after death but it is does not involve the idea of the immortality of the soul.

7 There is life after death but it is disembodied existence.

8 There is life after death and it is embodied existence.

9 Life after death is consistent with modern science.

10 Life after death is consistent with modern philosophy.

TASK

In groups, develop your questions to include extra arguments in support of and challenging the issues under debate. Discuss some possible conclusions and devise a flowchart or thought-process diagram for each area. Include key questions for discussion.

Objective: To encourage the use of questions and counter-questions in developing the skills of AO2 which serve to 'critically evaluate and justify a point of view' (AO2). To develop questions to give evidence of at least 'some attempt to set out reasons for alternative views' (level 3 descriptor AO2).

GLOSSARY

A posteriori after experience, derived from observed facts

A priori the truth value can be determined without reference to any experience or investigation

Abhinnas supra-mundane powers

Abortion termination of a pregnancy, either spontaneously (due to complications during pregnancy) or by the removal or expulsion of an embryo or fetus from the uterus, resulting in its death; the latter is the more commonly understood usage

Absolutist an ethical system involving rules that are to be followed by all people at all times, in all circumstances

Act utilitarianism every new situation is different and requires a fresh calculation

Adhan the official 'call to prayer'

Aesthetic appreciation of beauty

Ahimsa non-violence

Akhlaq ethics as a science

Akirah notion of being held accountable for one's deeds before God on a final day of reckoning

Al-Allat one of Allah's daughters, whose name means 'goddess'

Allah the highest form of divinity in pre-Islamic Arabia; also used for the name of the One True God in Islam

Al-Manat one of Allah's daughters, whose name means 'fate'

Al-Marwa one of two hills between which Hagar ran to find water

Alms something given to the poor as charity, such as money, clothing or food

Al-Safa one of two hills between which Hagar ran to find water

Al-Uzza one of Allah's daughters, whose name means 'mighty'

Analogy a comparison of two or more things to show how they are similar

Anapanasati focus on breathing to aid concentration and calm in Buddhist meditation

Anatta the Buddhist observation that there is no 'soul' or that things are 'not self'

Animism belief that a soul or spirit exists in every object, animate or inanimate; from the Latin anima meaning breath or soul

Animistic worshipping objects in the belief that they contained spirits

Anthropic argument the argument that nature is planning in advance for the needs of humans

Antinomian the freedom of the individual is paramount, regardless of the rules

Anti-realism truth is relative to the community who are making the statement

Anussati bringing to mind the qualities of the Buddha to aid meditation

Apostle (Islam) messenger

Applied ethics the application of ethical theory to actual problems

Arbitrator person who negotiates between conflicting groups and decides upon a course of action to be taken

Argument a set of statements which is such that one of them (the conclusion) is supported or implied by the others (the premises)

Ariya magga noble path, from *ariya*, meaning noble or worthy, *magga* meaning path

Aryan invader from the West of India referred to by their 'pale skins'

Ascetic living a very disciplined lifestyle

Asubha a focus on impurities or ugly things, to aid detachment through meditation

Atman individual soul

Atonement to make at one; usually used to describe the work Christ did in his death, to reconcile sinners to God

Bedouin nomadic peoples of the deserts of Arabia

Begging-bowl a bowl used *not* for begging but for allowing people to display dana by offering food to the monks

Bhavana literally 'becoming' but generally translated as mental development

Bhikkhunis Buddhist nuns

Bhikkhus Buddhist monks

Big Bang theory the theory of an expanding Universe that began as an infinitely dense and hot medium at some finite time in the past; the initial instant is called the Big Bang

Birth the point at which the child is separated from the mother and becomes a separate entity

Blastocyst a group of multiplying cells

Bodhi the wisdom by which one attains enlightenment

Bodhisattva literally 'a being whose essence is wisdom', generally understood as one who is on the path to enlightenment

Brahma viharas four states of mind associated with Buddhist meditation that develop the qualities required to eliminate the hindrances

Brahman universal soul or universal spirit

Brahmin priest

Brahminism religion based upon priestly practices and sacrifice

Buddha ksetra Buddha field or Universe

Buddha enlightened one; one who possesses insight into ultimate and perfect wisdom

Buraq winged horse that took Muhammad up to heaven

Chastity freedom from human and emotional attachments

Christology ideas about Jesus Christ

Classical theism the belief in a personal deity, creator of everything that exists and who is distinct from that creation

Concentration employment of all one's powers or attention

Conclusion a statement that purports to be drawn from a set of premises

Consciousness awareness of self

Consequentialism another name for teleological ethics

Constitution of Madinah an agreement drawn up by Muhammad in Madinah

Contingent being a being that depends upon something else for its existence

Continuity occurs at the first point at which potential life is recognisable

Cosmology the scientific study of the origin and nature of the Universe

Counter-argument an argument that tries to refute another argument

Covenant agreement, promise; the idea of God bestowing his favour on the people in return for their obedience

Cullavagga second section of the Khandhaka

Dana giving, the best example of selflessness

Darwinism the theory of natural selection to account for changes in nature

Day of judgement the idea of responsibility for one's actions and consequent accountability before God on a final day

Deduction a process of reasoning by which the conclusion is shown to follow necessarily from the premises

Deontological ethics any ethical system that is concerned with the act itself rather than the consequences of the act; from the Greek, meaning 'obligation' or 'duty'

Dhamma Cakka Pavattana 'turning of the wheel of dhamma'

Dharma (Pali: **dhamma**) basis of faith; the religious doctrine

Dharmakaya (Pali: **Dhammakaya**) ultimate body of truth

Dhyana meditation, the last section of the eight-fold path, broadly understood in a variety of ways as a practice that stimulates mental development and concentration; deep state of thought

Dhyanas stages of meditation through which one passes to reach enlightenment

Digha Nikaya section of the Sutta Pitaka

Din a complete way of life

Divine command theory a system of ideas or commandments given by a supreme being

Diya blood money; payment for the loss of the life of a relative

Dropsy an old term for the swelling of soft tissues due to the accumulation of excess water

Dualism a fundamental two-fold distinction, such as mind and body

Dukkha suffering

Eid ul-Adha the celebration at the end of hajj

Eid ul-Fitr the celebration at the end of Ramadan

Eight-fold path the practical measures needed to become enlightened

Embryo an animal in the early stage of development before birth; in humans, the embryo stage is the first three months after conception

Empirical based on evidence and experience

Empiricism the view that the dominant foundation of knowledge is experience

Empiricist a person who takes the view that the dominant foundation of knowledge is experience

Enlightenment (The) an eighteenth-century philosophical movement that stressed the importance of reason

Enlightenment ultimate wisdom

Ensoulment the point when the soul enters the body

Epicureans a philosophy based on the teachings of Epicurus that argued that the highest good is pleasure or freedom from pain

Epistemic distance distance from knowledge of God – God is hidden and so this allows human beings to choose freely

Ethical and religious pacifism belief that war cannot be condoned on any grounds

Ethics a theory or system of moral values

Euthanasia literally, 'good death' (Greek), ending someone's life in a painless manner, usually to relieve suffering

Exodus literally, departure; it is used to refer to the time Moses led the Israelites out of Egypt to the Promised land

Exorcism the rite of driving out evil spirits from a person who is believed to be possessed

Fallacy unsound reasoning

Fard obligatory, compulsory, see wajib

Farewell discourse the name given to the section in John's Gospel chapters 13–17 that contains Jesus' words to his disciples as he prepares for his death and return to the Father

Fetus the developing unborn baby from the end of the eighth week after conception (when the major structures have formed) until birth

Feudal an environment of retribution and vendetta in the struggle for overall power

Four noble truths the four teachings that explain the reality of our world

Fruitful description of actions that will yield positive results

Genocide mass killing, unlawful mass murder; the intentional destruction or eradication of an entire racial, political, cultural or religious group

Hadith oral traditions relating to the words and deeds of Muhammad

Hafiz the fertile area of Arabia including Makkah and Madinah

Hagiography a spiritual or religious biography

Hajar al-aswad the black stone housed at the eastern corner of the Ka'aba

Haji one who has completed hajj

Hajj pilgrimage

Hanifs pre-Islamic non-Jewish, non-Christian Arabian monotheists; tribal ascetics known for their moral qualities

Haram absolutely forbidden

Hebrew parallelism a poetic device in which the same idea is repeated, using different but synonymous words

Hedonism an ethical theory that defines what is right in terms of pleasure

Henotheistic worshipping a single god while accepting the possible existence of others; a term coined by Max Muller and supported by recent writers such as Turner

Hijaz road key trade route

Hijra flight of Muhammad from Makkah to Madinah

Hilf tribal pact or agreement

Hiri shame, reflecting the idea of self-responsibility and encouraging self-respect

I'jaz has no equal, cannot be compared or imitated

I'tikaf a retreat to focus spiritually during the month of Ramadan

Ibadah worship

Ihram a state of purity recognised by ablutions and dress

Ijma consensus

Ijtihad 'a jurist's deduction of a point of law from the sources'; literally 'effort'

Immanent (Islam) close, immediate

Immanent (Philosophy) existing or remaining; in theology, it refers to God's involvement in creation

Immortality not subject to death or decay, everlasting

Impermanence the idea that the universe is in an unstable state of flux

Induction a process of reasoning that draws a general conclusion from specific instances

Ineffable indefinable, defying expression or description

Inoffensiveness the principle of non-harm to all living beings

Intermediary one who enables communication between God and humanity

Irreducible complexity when all parts of the system must be in place in order for the system to work. The removal of any one of the parts causes the system to stop functioning

Istihsan a judge or scholar's preference; in line with public interest or agreement

Jahiliyya ignorance, a term used to describe life at the time of Muhammad, referring to pre-Islamic Arabia

Jataka sutras narrating the birth stories of the Buddha in past lives, and effects related to the past and the present lives

Jinn spirits

Jiva Jain interpretation of, or replacement for, the idea of a soul

Jurist a scholar of Islamic law that sits on a legal jury to make significant decisions of ethical and legal concern

Jus ad bellum a set of criteria to be consulted before engaging in war, in order to determine whether entering into war is justifiable

Jus in bello laws stating acceptable practices while engaged in war, such as the Geneva Convention

Jus post bellum suggested rules about justice after a war, including peace treaties, reconstruction, war crimes trials and war reparations

Just war a specific concept of how warfare might be justified, typically in accordance with a particular situation or scenario

Ka'aba black stone of religious significance housed in the centre of Makkah (some texts use the alternative spelling Ka'ba)

Kaalam argument everything that begins to exist has a cause of its existence

Kafir unbelievers

Karma (Pali: **kamma**) actions, good or bad, bring consequences that affect the course of a person's life and future lives

Karuna compassion; sometimes interpreted as the idea that concern for others demonstrates selflessness

Kasinas visual objects for meditation

Khandhaka the section of the Vinaya Pitaka that deals with guidance on issues of organisation and discipline for the monastic life and the sangha as a whole

Kingdom of God God's rule or reign; the idea of kingdom is not necessarily one of territory, but more describing dominion

Kutubullah the revelation of the Qur'an, literally meaning 'writings, or books, of Allah'

Lakhmids Bedouin supporters of Zoroastrianism

Law of nature a generalisation based on regular happenings within nature

Legalistic set principles are applied regardless of the context

Liturgy the traditional public worship carried out by a religious group; a particular order of form of worship that is prescribed by a Church

LXX an abbreviation for the Septuagint, which is the name given to the translation into Greek of the Hebrew Old Testament; it is called this because tradition said that 70 people had translated it

Madinah city to which Muhammad fled and established Islam, second most holy city in Islam, originally known as the oasis city of Yathrib (some texts use the alternative spelling Medina)

Madrassah classes for children to learn teachings of Islam, usually held at a mosque

Maha-parinibbana Sutta story of the last days and death of the Buddha

Mahavagga first section of the Khandhaka

Makkah city of Muhammad's birth (some texts use the alternative spelling Mecca)

Makruh discouraged, reprehensible

Medical abortion abortion by means of the abortion pill

Medical futility a situation in which treatment achieves no positive medical results, or is against the patient's best interests

Meditation the specific practice of concentration that the Buddha taught

Meditative planes specific states of mind, accessed through the fourth dhyana

Messiah the Hebrew form of the Greek word Christ, meaning 'the anointed one' and refers to one approved by God; often linked to kings, it later became associated with the hope of an ideal king, the one sent by God to restore Israel

Messianic Age the time when the Messiah (the anointed one) would come and bring in an age of peace

Middle way the balance between the extremes of asceticism and a life of luxury

Minaret tower from which the call to prayer is given

Mishnah a written form of the Jewish oral traditions; they were collected and written down so that they would not be lost or forgotten

Moksha escape from the cycle of rebirth

Monism the view that there is only one basic and fundamental reality

Monistic the view that ultimate reality is all of one kind.

Monophysite heretic form of Christianity

Monotheism belief in only one God

Morality the application of an ethical theory to produce appropriate conduct

Morals concerned with the application of principles derived from ethics to work out appropriate conduct or behaviour

Mosque place of prayer or prostration, sometimes called masjid

Mu'min believers

Mubah permissible

Muezzin the one who calls prayer from the minaret

Mufti legal expert in religious law

Muruwa tribal term used to denote manliness or honour

Mustahabb preferred, commendable

Nabi or navi, the Hebrew term for prophet

Najd road key trade route

Necessary being a being which, if it exists, cannot not exist

Nicene Creed statement of belief for early Christians (ce325, amended 381)

Night journey Muhammad's ascension to heaven

Nirmanakaya transformation body

Nirvana (Pali: **nibbana**) enlightenment

Nisab the amount of property that denotes the mark below which one does not offer zakat

Niya intention

Niyati destiny

Oasis fertile area of the desert

Objective external to the mind; real or true regardless of subject and their point of view

Oral tradition the preservation and transmission of 'literature' by the spoken word

Ottappa complete awareness of intentions and motives behind moral actions

Pacifism the doctrine that all violence is unjustifiable; opposition to war or violence as a means of settling disputes

Pagan a term used describe a variety of religious traditions at the time of Muhammad

Pali Canon the Buddhist scriptures

Pancasila the five moral precepts

Paraclete literally, 'one who is called to the side of another', transliteration from Greek, see p 307

Paradigm model, example

Parinirvana (Pali: **Parinibbana**) passing over into nirvana

Parivara the final section of the Vinaya Pitaka that summarises all the Vinaya for the purpose of teaching monks and examinations

Patimokka specific rules, traditionally 227, for Buddhist monks to follow when living in a monastery

Pentateuch the first five books of the Hebrew Bible (Old Testament), said to have been written by Moses

Persistent vegetative state (PVS) a state in which body processes are maintained but the brain is functioning only at its lowest automatic levels

Personalism the view that ethical theory and morality deal with people as a priority as opposed to principles

Phonic resonance, sound

Planck constant used in quantum mechanics to describe the sizes of quanta

Polytheistic worshipping many gods or idols

Portent miracle

Positivism the theory that statements of faith precede reason

Potential the possibility, at conception, of becoming a human person

Poverty living a simple life with basic needs

Pragmatism the theory that a moral solution is only good if it is workable in practice

Pranja (Pali: **Panna**) wisdom associated with the first two sections of the eight-fold path and indicating insight into the reality of existence

Predicate the part of the sentence that qualifies the subject

Preference utilitarianism an ethical theory that sees actions as right when they allow the greatest number to live according to their own preferences, even if those preferences are not those that will make them experience the most pleasure

Pre-Islamic Arabia the time of Muhammad

Premise a statement that forms part of an argument from which a conclusion is drawn

Principle of sufficient reason there is a complete explanation for everything

Principle of utility an action is right if it maximises happiness

Privation the absence or lack of something that ought to be there; the malfunctioning of something that in itself is good

Process theodicy emphasises 'becoming' rather than 'being' – God is not seen as omnipotent but is changeable and persuasive

Pro-choice supporting women's right to have abortions

Pro-life against abortion

Protest theodicy theodicy that protests against God and puts him on trial

Qiblah niche in mosque wall indicating the direction of the ka'aba in Makkah

Qiyam first chapter of the Qur'an

Qiyas analogy

Qua a Latin word meaning 'as relating to'

Quickening traditionally, when the child is first felt to move inside the mother

Qur'an Muslim scripture

Quraysh Muhammad's tribe, dominant in the Makkah area

Rakahs prayer movement

Ramadan holy month of fasting in Islam

Rasul one who is sent

Rebirth the transfer of energies from one form to another

Relational factors different interpretations of the same words or terms, depending on the viewpoint of the observer

Relativism the theory that there is no absolute principle and every decision depends upon the situation or context

Relativist an ethical system that has no fixed rules but each action depends on the situation

Resurrection rising from the dead into a new kind of life, not subject to sickness, ageing, deterioration, or death

Right in ethical usage, a judgement made that acknowledges behaviour as morally appropriate or acceptable

Righteousness right standing and right behaviour, rather than the abstract idea of justice or virtue

Ruku bowing

Rule utilitarianism an action can only possibly be right if it follows the rules, which should never be disobeyed

Sabbath the seventh day of creation when God rested; in Judaism, it is observed from sundown on Friday to sundown on Saturday

Sacrament a rite where symbolism is used to represent spiritual realities

Sadhu an ascetic or practitioner of yoga who has achieved the first three Hindu goals of life

Sai an effort to move between two hills

Salah prayer

Samadhi meditation

Samana a group of wandering holy men or philosophers who were trying to find answers to ultimate questions

Samatha a form of meditation usually associated with concentration (samadhi)

Sambhogakaya enjoyment body

Samma right

Samma ajiva right livelihood

Samma ditthi right view

Samma kammanta right action

Samma samadhi right concentration

Samma sankappa right thought

Samma sati right mindfulness

Samma vaca right speech

Samma vayama right effort

Samma-sambodhi perfect enlightenment

Samma-sambuddhasa the perfectly self-enlightened one

Samsara cycle of life, death and reincarnation

Sanctity of life the belief that life is sacred or holy, given by God

Sangha the Buddhist monastic community

Sannyasin another term for sadhu

Saum fasting

Seal of the prophets the final prophet

Second-order good a moral good that is a response to evil

Secularisation society no longer under the control or influence of religion

Selflessness the idea that there is not a permanent essence within a person as all is impermanent

Shahadah testimony

Shari'ah literally, 'the way to the watering hole'; Islamic law, the rightly guided path, God's law

Shaykh chief or tribal ruler

Shirk associating something or someone as being on an equal basis as God

Signs source Bultmann argued that the author of John's Gospel used a written source that contained the miracle stories (the signs)

Sila moral teachings associated with the middle section of the eight-fold path

Situationist (Buddhism) individual circumstances rather than sets of rules determine the outcome of any ethical dilemma

Situationist (Ethics) each situation is considered on its merits before the principle of Christian agape love is applied

Skilful means the application of wisdom so that karmic benefits are maximised

Skilful description of intelligent or wise actions

Smriti to bring before the mind, to recollect, to reflect or remember

Soteriology a personal religious quest for salvation

Soul-making the presence of evil helps people to grow and develop

Stoic a Greek school of philosophy founded by Zeno; it taught that virtue and happiness are attained by submission to destiny and the natural law, the development of selfcontrol and fortitude was a means of overcoming destructive emotions

Study to remember and preserve the dhamma

Stupa monument built as a memorial to the Buddha and usually containing parts of his remains

Subjective having its source within the mind; a particular point of view; dependent on the subject

Suffering the idea that life involves dissatisfaction

Sufism the mystical tradition within Islam

Suicide deliberately ending one's own life

Sujud prostration

Sunnah actions of Muhammad

Sunni main branch of the Muslim Community consisting 85% of the world's Muslim community

Supramundane paranormal or extraordinary powers

Sura chapter of the Qur'an

Surgical abortion abortion by means of the suction method

Surrogacy one woman carrying a baby for another woman who cannot do so herself

Sutrah a boundary marking off a personal space for prayer

Sutta Pitaka second section of the Pali Canon

Sutta Vibhanga the commentary on the patimokka and the first part of the Vinaya Pitaka

Synoptic Gospels the first three Gospels in the New Testament: Matthew, Mark and Luke

Synoptic literally, seeing together, identifying similarities between the first three gospels set out in parallel

Takbir God is the greatest

Taklif obligation to follow divine law or ethics

Talbiyah the beginning prayer of hajj

Tarawih extra prayers during Ramadan

Tashahud and **salam** sitting up to announce a declaration of faith and greetings of peace

Tawaf processing around the Ka'aba

Tawhid Muslim teaching of absolute monotheism

Teleological explanation by reference to end, goal or purpose, derived from the Greek *telos*, meaning end, purpose or goal and *logos*, meaning reason

Teleological ethics any ethical system that is concerned with consequences of actions; from the Greek, meaning 'end' or 'purpose'

Theism the belief in the existence of a God or gods

Theodicy a justification of the righteousness of God, given the existence of evil, from the Greek *theos* meaning 'God' and *dike* meaning 'righteous'

Theravada literally, the way of the elders, it focuses on the devotion to and support of the sangha as the primary source of teaching and example

Torah usually refers to the first five books (the law books) of the Bible; the word Torah comes from a root word meaning guidance or instruction, although it is often translated as 'law'

Tosefta literally, supplement; a supplement to the oral law in Judaism

Transcendent having existence outside the universe, usually depicted as an immaterial realm

Transmigration the passing over of one consciousness stream into another

Treaty of Hudaybiya ten-year agreement to allow access for Muslims to Makkah during pilgrimage

Trikaya three bodies

Trinity belief in one God in three parts

Trustworthy title given to Muhammad to reflect his noble nature

Truth value whether a statement is actually true or false

Ulama fiqh scholar-defined law

Ulama religious scholars or clerics

Ummah community or brotherhood of Muslims

Umra extra, voluntary pilgrimage beyond hajj

Universalism the belief that God will save all peoples

Upasakas Buddhist lay-men

Upasikas Buddhist lay-women

Usul al-fiqh roots of the law

Utilitarian ethical doctrine that the moral worth of an action is solely determined by its contribution to overall utility

Utilitarianism an ethical theory that maintains that an action is right if it produces the greatest good for the greatest number; morality of actions is therefore based on consequences for human happiness

Value judgement an assessment that says more about the values of the person making it than about what is actually being assessed

Vedas written holy books in Hinduism

Viability the ability to grow and develop into an adult, especially the ability of the child to exist without dependence on the mother

Vipassana A form of meditation usually associated with insight or wisdom (panna)

Vows personal undertakings rather than rules

Wahy revelation (of the Qur'an)

Wajib obligatory

Warner key function of a prophet

Weapons of mass destruction weapons capable of killing enormous numbers of people

Wholesome description of positive and beneficial actions

Wrong in ethical usage, a judgement made that acknowledges behaviour as morally inappropriate or unacceptable

Wudu ritual washing

Wuquf literally, 'standing' before God

Yoga meditation that aims to unite the atman with Brahman

Yuktah Sanskrit term for yoga

Zakat purification through giving

Zamzam famous spring of water believed to be discovered by Hagar and provided by God

Zoroastrian Persian religion

Zoroastrianism the belief in a God of Light who is eternally battling the God of Darkness

Zygote a cell formed by the union of a male sex cell (a sperm) and a female sex cell (an ovum), which develops into the embryo according to information encoded in its genetic material

INDEX

a posteriori 14
a priori 14
abba 263
Abd Allah 174
Abhidhamma Pitaka 140
abhinnas 139
absolutist 72
aborigine, creation 329
abortion 74, 354–61, 366,
   387
   Buddhism 374–5
   Islam 387–90
absurd Universe 336
Abu Talib 174
accidental actions 369
act utilitarianism 82
action 369
active euthanasia 361
Adam and Eve 396
Adams, Douglas 330
adhan 203
adultery 106, 108
aesthetic argument 12, 17
afterlife 400
agape 76, 225
age of consent 103
ahimsa (passive resistance) 74,
   76, 118, 145
Ajivakas 118
akhlaq 382
akirah (judgement) 194–5,
   201
Al-Allat 169
Al-Kandaq 180–1
Al-Manat 169
al-Qadr 195–6, 201
Al-Uzza 169
Alara Kalama 126
Ali 174
Allah 165, 169, 185, 188–9,
   383
alms 242
analogy 13, 18, 34
Ananda 130
anapanasati 154
anatta (not-self) 119
Andrew 305
angels 190
animism 169
animistic 164
anthropic argument 13, 17,
   33
anti-realism 56
antinomian 84
Antipas 223
Anuruddha 130
anussati 154
applied ethics 73–4
aqida (creed) 382
Aquinas, Thomas
   cosmological argument
      24–6, 29
   design argument 12, 15
   Five Ways 15, 25–6
   miracles 55
arbitrator 178

Archelaus 223
argument 44
Aristotle 81, 278
ariya magga (noble path) 151
Aryan 120, 121
ascetic 117, 126
Aslan, Reza 166
assessment for learning
   316–17
assessment *see* reflection &
   assessment
assimilation 391
assisted suicide 362
asubha 154
atman 116
atonement 51, 397
Augustine 44, 47, 48, 51,
   65–6, 66

Badham, Paul 406
Badr 180
Barclay, William 88–9, 93
Bartholomew 306
beauty 18
Bedouin 164, 166, 168, 380
begging-bowl 145
Behe, Michael 33
being 26
Beloved disciple 305–6
Benedict XVI 327
The *Benedictus* 250
benefit 12
Bentham, Jeremy 80–1
bhavana 152
bhikkhus 143, 144, 146
bhikkunis 143, 144, 146
bias 61
Big Bang theory 39, 322–3
birth 358
blastocyst 354
blessed 223–4
bodhi 368
Bodhisattva 139
bodily resurrection 399–401
brahma viharas 153
Brahman 116
Brahmanism 116
Brahmins 116, 122
bread 268–9
Brown, Raymond 267, 290,
   301
Brunner, Emil 84
Buddha 115, 119, 125, 133–5,
   159
   ascetic practices 126
   death 129–30
   enlightenment 127–8
   four signs 125–6
   middle way 128–9
   status 138–9
Buddhism 115–22, 124–30,
   137–47
   abortion 374–5
   action 369
   councils 141
   creation 329

dhamma 121, 140–2
eight-fold path 128,
   151–2, 373
ethics 368–78
euthanasia 375–6
four noble truths 129, 150
four-fold sangha 143–4
mindfulness 372
pancasila 371
revelation 346
sangha 138, 142–7, 159,
   374
three refuges 138, 159
trikaya doctrine 140
war 99–100
yoga 118, 126, 153, 368
see also meditation; nirvana
Bultmann, Rudolph 57, 288
Buraq 177

Cana of Galilee 280
caste system 120–1, 134
Channa 125
chanting 155
chastity 145
Christianity 167
   abortion 355
   bodily resurrection
      399–401
   death 395–6
   Genesis 324
   Heaven 401–4
   hell 402–3
   immortality of the soul
      397–8
   life after death 398–9
   mysticism 343
   rewards 405
   sanctity of life 395
   sexual ethics 106–8
   sin 396–7
circumstantial evidence 350
classical theism 52, 60
compassion 370
concentration 373
conclusion 13
conscience 372
consciousness 358
Constitution of Madinah 179
contingency miracle 56
contingent being 26
continuity 359, 407
conversion 201, 344
convict 308
Conzelman, Hans 259
Copleston, Frederick 27–8
cosmic microwave radiation
   322
cosmological argument
   23–30, 38–40
   Aquinas 24–6, 29
   Copleston 27–8
   Craig 27
   Hume 28–9
   Kalaam 27, 40
   Leibniz 24–5, 27

reflection & assessment 31,
   41–2
   Russell 27, 29
cosmological constants 33
cosmological myths 330–1
cosmology 24, 39, 322
councils 141
counter-argument 66
Covenant 220, 241
Craig, William 27, 56
creation *ex nihilo* 189
creation myths 329–30
creationism 324
Cullavagga 142
cultural Darwinism 36
cultural evolution 21

dana 145
Darwin, Charles 20, 36, 326
Darwinism 19
Davies, Paul 327, 328, 333,
   335, 336–8
Dawkins, Richard 21, 36,
   327, 335
Day-Age theory 325, 326
death 47–8, 395–6
deduction 13
deductive arguments 13
deontological ethics 73
design argument 11–22, 32–7
   Aquinas 12, 15
   Darwin 20, 36
   Dawkins 21, 36
   Hume 18–20, 34
   Mill 20, 36
   Paley 12, 13, 15, 16
   Swinburne 17–18, 36
   Tennant 17
Dhamma Cakka Pavattana
   128
dhamma (faith) 121, 140–2,
   159
dhammakaya (dhamma body)
   140
dhyana 127, 150, 152
   see also meditation
Digha Nikaya 129
din (way of life) 199
discipleship 256–8, 264–5,
   300–6, 311–12
   Holy Spirit 307–8
dismemberment myths 329
disorder 36
divine command theory 75,
   368
divorce 104–5, 108–9
diya (blood money) 387
Docetists 168
Dodd, C.H. 268
donor insemination 355
'doubting' Thomas 306
Drake, Durant 84
dropsy 252
drugs 351
du'a (personal prayer) 202,
   204

dualism 406, 407
dukkha (suffering) 129
Dunn, James 241

edict myths 329
egg myths 329
Eid ul-Adha 212
Eid ul-Fitr 207
eight-fold path 100, 128,
   151–2, 373
Einstein, Albert 322
election 241
embryo 354
Embryology Act 1990 356
empirical 368
empiricism 28, 60, 118
enlightenment 57, 119
   see also nirvana
ensoulment 359, 388
Epicureans 278
Epicurus 44
epistemic distance 50
eternal life 268, 272
ethical dilemmas
   sexual ethics 102–11
   war 96–100, 112–13
ethical theory 71–3
   action 369
ethics 71
   applied 73–4
   Buddhism 368–78
   critical evaluation 365–6
   divine command theory
      75
   Euthyphro dilemma 75
   Muslim 380, 390–3
   Qur'an 381–3
   reflection & assessment 78
   situation 83–9, 92–3
   utilitarianism 79–83
eudaimonia 81
euthanasia 76, 361–3, 366,
   388
   Buddhism 375–6
   Islam 388–90
Euthyphro dilemma 75
evil 36, 43–52
   Augustine 44, 47, 51, 65–6
   free will 47, 50
   Irenaeus 46, 50, 51, 66–7
   logical problem 44
   moral 44
   natural 44, 65
   origins 48–9
   reflection & assessment 53
   Swinburne 47–8
   theodicy 46–52, 65–8
evolution 36, 326
examination 316
Exodus 278
exorcism 234
experience 348–9
Ezekiel 278

faith 121, 257, 283, 289, 301
fallacy 29

fallacy of composition 29
fard (obligatory) 199, 385
farewell discourse 274, 301
fasting 111, 205–7
Fatima 174
fetus 354
    rights 360
feudal 170
five pillars 199–212, 215–17
    Hajj (pilgrimage) 199,
      209–12
    salah (prayer) 199, 201–5
    saum (fasting) 199, 205–7
    shahadah (testimony) 199,
      200–1
    zakat (purification through
      giving) 199, 207–9
five ways 15, 25–6
Fletcher, Joseph 83–7, 92
followers 300
forgiveness 229–31, 243
Fortna, Robert 290
Foucault, Michel 103
four noble truths 129, 150
four signs 125–6
four-fold sangha 143–4
Fourth Gospel 266–75
    the Beloved disciple 305–6
    discipleship 300–6
    'I am' sayings 267–75, 288
    Jewish setting 221–2
    Lamb of God 304
    Mary Magdalene 296–7
    Mary and Martha 295–6
    miracles 277–85
    persecution 302
    Roman influence 223
    Samaritan woman 293
    temptation 303
    woman caught in adultery
      295
    women 292–7
framework interpretation 325
Frayn, Michael 335
free will 47, 50
freedom 66
freedom to choose 360
Freund, Philip 329
fruitful 369

Gabriel (Jibril) 175, 190
Gaia hypothesis 332–3
Gandhi, Mohandas
    Karamchand 74, 98
gap theory 325
Garden of Gethsemane 258
gender selection 360
Genesis 324, 326
genocide 96
Ghassanids 168
ghusl (washing) 203
The *Gloria* 250
Gnostics 168
God
    Big Bang 326
    cosmological argument
      23–30, 38–40
    design argument 11–22
    miracles 54–62

morality 75
Muhammad 175
    nature of 60, 399
    praise 250
    problem of evil 44
    religious experience 347,
      349
    sin 397
    tawhid 188–9, 201
    water into wine miracle
      280
    see also Jesus; The Holy
      Spirit
gods 119
Golden Rule 225
Goldilocks enigma 333
Gould, S.J. 333
gravity 322
Gribbin, John 324, 333
Griffin, David 48
guided marriage 107

Hadith 174, 192, 200
Hafiz 164
hagiography 139
Hajar al-aswad 210
haji 212
Hajj (pilgrimage) 199,
    209–12
Hamza 176
hanifs 165, 169, 380
happiness 81
Happold, F.C. 342
haram (forbidden) 385
Harvey, Peter 99
healing at the pool miracle
    282–3
healing miracles 236
Heaven 195, 401–4
    see also Kingdom of God
Hebrew parallelism 398
hedonic calculus 80–1, 91
hedonism 80
Hell 195, 402–3
henotheistic 169, 184
Herod the Great 223
HFEA *see Human Fertility and
    Embryology Act 1990*
Hick, John 46, 407, 408
Hijaz road 165
hijra 174, 177–8
hilf (tribal pact) 179
Hinduism 116, 328, 343
Hippocratic oath 359
hiri (shame) 372
Holland, Ray 55–6
Holocaust 47
The Holy Spirit 261–2,
    307–8
homosexuality 105–6, 109–
    11, 113, 360
Hope, Tony 361
Hubble, Edwin 322
*Human Fertility and
    Embryology Act 1990*
    (HFEA) 355
human nature 347
human rights 98, 355, 362
Hume, David

cosmological argument
    28–9
design argument 18–20, 34
empiricism 60
miracles 55, 57, 60–1, 67

'I am' sayings 267–75, 288
ibadah (worship) 191, 199
ID *see* intelligent design
identification 408
ignorant actions 369
ihram 211
I'jaz 193
ijima (consensus) 382
ijtihad 382
immanent 342
immortality 399
immortality of the soul
    397–8
impermanence 369
in vitro fertilisation (IVF)
    355, 360
induction 13
inductive argument 14, 32
Indus Valley civilisation 120
ineffable 119, 341
Infant Preservation Act 1929
    356
infertility treatment 355, 356
infinity 38
inoffensiveness 145
intelligent design (ID) 33–4,
    337
    see also design argument
intention 36
intentional actions 369
intermediary 191
interventionist approach
    54, 57
investigations 313–19
    assessment for learning
      316–17
    specification 314
    study skills 316
involuntary euthanasia 362
Irenaeus 46, 50, 51, 66–7
irreducible complexity 33, 34
Islam 162–71, 188–96
    abortion 387–90
    angels 190
    creation 328
    ethics 381–3
    euthanasia 388–90
    fasting 199, 205–7
    five pillars 199–212,
      215–17
    giving 199, 207–9
    God as creator 188–9
    Kalaam cosmological
      argument 27, 40
    Kutubullah 192–4
    life after death 194–5, 386
    morality 170–1
    mysticism 344
    pilgrimage 199, 209–12
    prayer 199, 201–5
    pre-Islamic Arabia 163–6
    predestination 195–6
    prophethood 191–2

Ramadan 194, 206–7
sanctity of life 386
sexual ethics 106–8
suicide 388–9
testimony 199, 200–1,
    216–17
tribal code 380
see also Muhammad;
    Qur'an
istihsan 382
i'tikaf 206
IVF *see* in vitro fertilisation
Izrail 190

jabr 201
jahiliyya (ignorance) 163,
    168–9, 380
Jainism 117–18
jataka 374
Jeremias, Joachim 247
Jesus 185, 220, 241
    abba 263
    attitude towards women
      310–11
    bread 268–9
    discipleship 256–8, 264–5,
      300–6
    eternal life 268, 272
    faith 257
    farewell discourse 274, 301
    forgiveness 229–31, 243
    healing at the pool 282–3
    'I am' sayings 267–75, 288
    Judaism 241–4
    Lamb of God 304
    light 269–70
    Lord's Prayer 247–8
    Mary Magdalene 296–7
    Mary and Martha 295–6
    miracles 234, 244, 284
    New Birth 307
    official's son 281–2
    resurrection 272–3, 398,
      399–401, 408
    Sabbath 251–2
    Samaritan woman 293
    sermon on the plain
      222–36
    sheep 270–1
    shepherd 271
    Son of God 281, 282, 283
    Son of Man 253
    teaching about outcasts
      228–9, 242
    teaching about the poor
      228
    teaching on prayer 247–9,
      264
    teaching on wealth 226–7,
      242
    violence 74
    walking on water 283
    water into wine 279–81
    witness 256–7
    woman caught in adultery
      295
jinn 169
Jiva 118
John the Baptist 234, 259–60

discipleship 300–1
    preparer 304
    signs 278–9
    witness 303–4
John Paul II 327
John's Gospel *see* Fourth
    Gospel
Joseph of Arimathea 304
Judaism 167, 220, 241–4
    forgiveness 243
    outcasts 242
    prayer 264
    resurrection 273
    wealth 242
    women 297
    see also Torah
Judas Iscariot 261, 306
Judas, son of James 306
judgement 225
judgement day 194
jurist 382
jus ad bellum 97
jus in bello 97
jus post bellum 97
just war 97
justice 86

Ka'aba 165, 166, 169, 185,
    210
kafir (unbelievers) 194
kahkahins 169
Kalaam cosmological
    argument 27, 40
kalam (theology) 195
Kant, Immanuel 357
karma 117, 119, 145, 369,
    373, 377–8
karuna (compassion) 370
kasinas 154
Katz, Steven 349
Keown, Damien 375
Khadijah 174
Khandhaka 141
khums 208
killing 74, 170, 357
Kingdom of God 223, 235,
    401
kohens (priests) 167
Kshatriyas 122
Kutubullah 192–4, 201

Lakhmids 168
Lamb of God 304
Last Supper 288, 306
laws of nature 54, 56, 59–60,
    67
Lazarus 272, 289, 295–6
legalistic 84
Leibniz, Gottfried 24–5, 27
Levi (Matthew) the tax-
    collector 256
life 98, 362
life after death 194–5, 386,
    398–9, 407
life principle 338
light 269–70, 283
linguistic philosophy 32, 407
liturgy 247
Lord's Prayer 247–8

lostness 229
Lourdes 58
love 66, 86
Lovelock, James 332
Luke's Gospel 219–53
    discipleship 256–8
    forgiveness 229–31, 243
    miracles 233–8
    Pharisees 241
    praise 250
    Sabbath controversies 251
    sermon on the plain 222–36
    Son of Man 253
    teaching about outcasts 228–9, 242
    teaching about the poor 228–9
    teaching on prayer 247–9
    teaching on wealth 226–7, 242
LXX (Septuagint) 267, 402

McGrath, Alister 36
Macquarrie, John 409
Madinah 164, 178–9
madrassah 194
The Magnificat 250
Maha-parinibbana Sutta 129
Mahavagga 142
Mahayana Buddhism 139
Makkah 164, 165–6, 181
makruh (discouraged) 385
mala in se 97
mala'ika (angels) 190, 201
manna 268
Mara 127
marriage 104, 107
martyrdom 76
Mary Magdalene 296–7
Mary and Martha 257, 295–6
materialism 406
Materialists 118
mating of the gods 329
meaning 32
Mecca see Makkah
medical abortion 355
medical ethics 354
medical futility 363
meditation 119, 150–6, 158–9
    bhavana 152
    Brahminism 116
    discipline 152–3
    eight-fold path 151–2
    four noble truths 150
    monks and nuns 146
    mysticism 343
    progression 153–4
    purposes 156
    samadhi 155, 373
    samatha 153, 155–6, 158
    three refuges 159
    vipassana 153, 155, 156, 158
meditative planes 127
memes 21
Messiah 234, 269, 280
Messianic Age 234

metaphorical imagery 269
Michael (Mikail) 190
middle way 128
Mill, John Stuart
    design argument 20, 36
    utilitarianism 81–2
minaret 203
mind-body problem 406
mindfulness 372
minority rights 91
miracles 54–62, 67–8, 244, 277–85
    Aquinas 55
    Bultman 57, 288
    calming the storm 237–8
    catch of fish 287
    healing at the pool 282–3
    healing of the paralytic 236
    Holland 55–6
    Hume 55, 57, 60–1
    interventionist approach 54, 57
    Luke's Gospel 233–8
    official's son 281–2
    Polkinghorne 58
    raising the widow's son 236
    reflection & assessment 62–4, 68–9
    Swinburne 55, 56–7, 58
    testimony 60–1, 67
    walking on water 283
    water into wine 279–81
    Wiles 62
    see also signs
Mishnah 263, 293
moksha 119
monastic possessions 144
monism 341, 406
Monophysite 165, 168
monotheism 184, 241
morality 66, 71
    Buddhism 373
    God 75
    Islam 383
    religious 76
morals 71
Moses 220
mosque 179
motives 91
mubah (permissible) 385
muezzin 203
mufti 384
Muhammad 163, 170–1, 174–82, 184–6
    battles 180–1
    Constitution of Madinah 179
    hijra 174, 177–8
    night journey 177
    Treaty of Hudaybiya 181
    upbringing 174–6
Muller, Max 169
multiverse 337
mu'min (believers) 194
muruwa (honour) 165, 380
mustahabh (preferred) 385
mysticism 342–3
myth 57

nabi (navi) 175
nabuwwa (prophethood) 191–2
nafila (extra prayers) 202, 204
Najd road 165
natural selection 36
necessary being 26, 29, 39
Nestorians 168
New Testament
    bodily resurrection 400–1
    death 395–6
    ethics 86
    Heaven 401–4
    hell 402–3
    immortality of the soul 397–8
    life after death 398–9
    rewards 405
    sanctity of life 395
    sin 396–7
Nicene Creed 168
Nicodemus 307
Niebuhr, Reinhold 84
night journey 177
nirmanakaya (transformation body) 140
nirodha 156
nirvana (enlightenment) 119, 127, 156, 159, 373
nisab 208
niyati (intention) 118, 202, 381
noetic quality 342
non–propositional revelation 346
non–voluntary euthanasia 361
The Nunc Dimitis 250

oasis 164
objective 72
Ockham's razor 35
Offences Against the Person Act 1861 356
official's son miracle 281–2
Old Testament
    bodily resurrection 399–400
    life after death 398–9
    truth 273
omnipotence 44
omniscience 44
ontological argument 39
oral tradition 164
order 12, 17, 20, 35
oscillating Universe theory 28
ottappa 372
outcasts 228–9
overview 315

pacifism 98
pagan 164
paganism 168, 380
Palestine 223
Paley, William 12, 13, 15, 16
Pali Canon 140
Palmer, M. 61
pancasila 371

panna (wisdom) 154, 155, 373
    see also prajna
parables 227, 257
    discipleship 257–8
    Good Samaritan 257
    lostness 229–30
    other son 230–1
    rich fool 398
    shepherd 270–1
    Sower 256, 258
    vineyard 274
paraclete 307
parapsychology 406
parinirvana 129
Parivara 142
passive euthanasia 361
passive resistance see ahimsa
Patimokka 141
peace 96–100
Pentateuch 294
persecution 258, 302
persistent vegetative state (PVS) 362
personalism 84
personhood 358
Pharisees 221–2, 241
Philip 223, 306
philosophical arguments 13–14
phonic 193
physician assisted suicide 362
pitakas 140
Planck constant 33
Plato, Euthyphro dilemma 75
pleasure 81, 82
pleasure calculus see hedonic calculus
pneuma 307
Polkinghorne, John 58
polygamy 107
polytheistic 164, 184
Pompey 223
portent 192
positivism 84
potential 358
potentiality 354
poverty 144, 228
POWs see prisoners of war
pragmatism 84
praise 250
prajna (wisdom) 150, 154
Pratchett, Terry 331–2
prayer
    Islam 199, 201–5
    Jesus 247–9, 264
    Judaism 264
pre-Islamic Arabia 163–6
predestination 195–6
predicate 267
preference utilitarianism 83
premises 13
principle of credulity 350
principle of sufficient reason 27, 29
principle of testimony 350
principle of utility 80–1
prisoners of war (POWs) 97
privation 48

pro-choice 358
pro-life 358, 360
probability 17
process theodicy 48, 52
progressive creationism 325, 326
Promised Land 281
prophethood 191–2
proportionality 97
propositional revelation 346
protest theodicy 47
purification 284
purpose 12
PVS see persistent vegetative state

qiblah 203
Qiyam 203
qiyas (analogy) 382
qua 16
Quaker Peace Testimony 99
quality of life 362
queer theory 103
quickening 358
Qur'an 174, 192–4, 200, 381–3, 391
Quraysh 166

Rahula 125
rakahs (prayers) 203–4
Ramadan 194, 206–7
rasul 175
rebirth 119
reconciliation 397
red shift 322
redemption 76, 397
reflection & assessment 317
    Buddhism 123, 131–2, 135–6, 148
    cosmological argument 31, 41–2
    design argument 21–2
    ethics 78
    evil 53
    examination 320
    Holy Spirit 262, 309
    Islam 196–7, 214, 217–18
    Jesus 231–2, 244–5, 253–4, 265, 275–6, 285–6, 298, 312
    meditation 157, 161
    miracles 62–4, 68–9, 238–40, 291
    Muhammad 172, 182–3, 187
    research tasks 317–20
    sexual ethics 111, 114
    situation ethics 95
    utilitarianism 90
    war 101
regularity 12

Reimarus 57
reincarnation 119
relational factors 359
relativism 85
relativist 72
reliability 61
religious experience 341–52

religious morality 76
renouncing 146
Replica theory 407
reprisals 97
research tasks 317–20
research tips 316
resurrection 58, 272, 397, 399–401
revelation 345–6
Rig-Veda 121
right 71
righteousness 397, 405
rights 359
risallah (prophethood) 191–2, 201
Robinson, John 75, 84
Roman occupation 223
ruku (bowing) 203
rule utilitarianism 82
Ruqayya 174
Russell, Bertrand 27, 29, 98

Sabbath 220
Sabbath controversies 251
sacramental imagery 269
sacrifice 76, 397
sadaqat 208
Sadducees 222
sadhu 153, 368
sai 211
St Teresa of Avila 343
salah (prayer) 199, 201–5
salam (greeting of peace) 203
salvation 284
samadhi (concentration) 155, 373
Samana 117
Samaritan woman 293
Samaritans 228, 294
samatha (calm) meditation 153, 155, 158
sambhogakaya (enjoyment body) 140
samma ajiva (right livelihood) 152
samma ditthi (right view) 151
samma kammanta (right action) 151
samma samadhi (right concentration) 152
samma-sambodhi (perfect enlightenment) 128
samma-sambuddhasa 138
samma sankappa (right thought) 151
samma vaca (right speech) 151
samma vayama (right effort) 152
samsara 116, 119
sanctity of life 357, 386, 395
sangha 138, 142–7, 159, 374
sannyasin (sadhu) 153
sarana (refuge) 138
satori 156
  see also nirvana
saum (fasting) 199, 205–7
science 58

scriptures (Kutubullah) 192–4
Seal of the prophets 191
second-order good 50
secularisation 406
self-explaining Universe 338
selflessness 369
sermon on the plain 222–36
sexual ethics 102–11, 113–14
Sexual Offences Act (2003) 103, 106
sexuality 103
shahadah (testimony) 199, 200–1, 216–17
shame 372
Shari'ah 76, 382, 384, 391
shaykh 164
sheep 270–1
shepherd 271, 283
shirk 188
Siddhartha Gotama see Buddhism
signs 55, 278–9, 283–5, 287–90
signs source 290
sila (morality) 150, 373
Simon Peter 256, 261, 305
sin 396–7
Singer, Peter
  abortion 357–8
  utilitarianism 83
situation ethics 76, 83–9, 92–3, 374
Skeptics 118
skilful 369
skilful means 370
Smalley, Stephen 287
smriti 154
Son of God 281, 282, 283
Son of Man 253
songs of praise 250
soteriology 139
soul 397–8
soul-deciding 47
soul-making 46, 51
specification 314
  Buddhism
    AO1 367–76
    AO2 376–8
  ethics
    AO1 353–63
    AO2 364, 364–6
  investigations 314
  Islam
    AO1 379–90
    AO2 390–3
  New Testament
    AO1 394–405
    AO2 405–9
  philosophy of religion
    AO1 340–7
    AO2 347–52
  research 317
  study of religion
    AO1 321–34
    AO2 334–9
specified complexities 33
Steel, David 356
Stoicism 278
study 146

study skills 316
stupa 130
subjective 72
suffering 369
Sufism 344
suicide 362, 388
Suicide Act 1961 362
suitability 12
Sujata 126
sujud (prostration) 203
Sunnah 193, 391
Sunni 380
superstition 167
Sura 193
surgical abortion 355
surrogacy 354, 356–7
  rights 360–1
Surrogacy Agreement 1985 356
sutrah 205
Sutta Pitaka 129, 140, 141
Sutta Vibhanaga 141
Swinburne, Richard
  apparent order 35–6
  design argument 17–18
  evil 47–8
  miracles 55, 56–7, 58, 67
  principle of credulity 350
  principle of testimony 350
  religious experience 347
symbolism 281, 284, 288–9
synagogue 221
synoptic Gospels 278

tahajjud (night prayers) 202, 204
takbir 203
taklif 384
talbiyah prayer 210
tarawih 206
tasbih (prayer beads) 202, 204
tashahud 203
tawaf 211
tawhid (nature of God) 188–9, 201
teleological argument 12
teleological ethics 73
The Temple 221, 241
temptation 258, 303
Tennant, design argument 17
test-tube babies 355
testimony
  Islam 199, 200–1
  miracles 60–1, 67
Thanissaro Bhikkhu 371, 372
theism 341
theistic evolution 327
theocracy 178–9
theodicy 46–52, 65–8
Theravada 374
Theravada Buddhism 139
thermodynamics 322
Thiselton, Anthony 348
Thomas 306
Thompson, Mel 377
three refuges 138, 159
ti-ratana 138
Tillich, Paul 408
Torah 220, 241
Tosefta 297

trade routes 165
transcendent 189, 342
transmigration 374
Treaty of Hudaybiya 181
tribal code 380
trikaya doctrine 140
Trinity 167
triviality 62
trustworthy 192
truth value 14
Turner, Colin 169, 380
the Twelve 260–1, 304–5

Uddaka Ramaputta 126
Uhud 180
ulama 384
ulama fiqh 382
ummah (followers) 178, 184, 212–13
umra 209
uncaused causer 26
unique Universe 336–7
Universal Declaration of Human Rights 355
universalisability 82
universalism 403
Universe origin 322
unmoved mover 25
upasakas 143
upasampada 146
upasikas 143
Ussher, Bishop James 325
usul al-fiqh 382
utilitarianism 79–83, 91–2, 374
  Bentham 80–1
  Mill 81–2
  Singer 83
  war 99

value judgement 73
Vedas 116
viability 358
Vinaya Pitaka 140, 141
violence 74
vipassana meditation 153, 155, 156, 158
visions 345
voluntary euthanasia 361
vows 371

Waines, David 383
wajib (obligatory) 385
walking on water miracle 283
war 96–100, 112–13
warner 191
water into wine miracle 279–81
water myths 329
wealth 226–7, 242
weapons of mass destruction 96
Whitehead, A.N. 48
wholesome 369
Wiesel, Elie 47
Wiles, Maurice 62, 67
wird 202, 204
witness 256–7, 300, 303–4
woes 224–5

womb-leasing 357
  see also surrogacy
women
  Fourth Gospel 292–7
  infertility technologies 360
  Islam 170
  Judaism 297, 310
wrong 71
wudu (ritual washing) 202–3

Yasodhara 125
yoga 118, 126, 153, 368
Young Earth creationism 325
yuktah (yoga) 153

Zacchaeus 227, 229, 256
zakat (purification through giving) 199, 207–9
zamzam water 211
Zen Buddhism 343
Zoroastrian 165, 168
zygote 354

The Publishers would like to thank the following for permission to reproduce copyright material:

Photo credits:

p.13 *l* Corbis, *r* SPL/Helen McArdle; **p.17** *l* Richard Gregory, *r* SPL/Fred Espenaks; **p.45** Press Association; **p.49** *both* Historical Image Partnership; **p.59** Getty Images; **p.98** *both* Corbis; **p.117** Corbis; **p.120** Corbis; **p.126** Richard Gray; **p.139** Circa Photo Library; **p.144** Corbis; **p.145** Corbis; **p.155** Alamy/James Davis; **p.162** NASA; **p.203** Alamy/Robert Harding Picture Library; **p.204** Rex Features; **p.210** Corbis; **p.222** SPL/NASA; **p.237** Scala Archives, Florence; **p.249** The Joint Church Council, St Mary's Church, Banbury; **p.260** Alamy/Dario Bajurin; **p.272** Los Angeles County Museum of Art, Gift of H. F. Ahmanson and Company, in memory of Howard F. Ahmanson. Photograph ©2009 Museum Associates/LACMA; **p.282** Tiepolo, Giandomenico (Giovanni Domenico) (1727–1804); Louvre, Paris, France/Lauros/Giraudon/The Bridgeman Art Library; **p.294** Press Association; **p.345** Philadelphia Museum of Art/Art Resources/ Scala Florence; **p.352** Mary Evans Picture Library; **p.357** Richaed Gray; **p.404** Hortus Deliciarum/ Herrad von Lansberg.

Text credits:

Aslan, Reza. from *No God But God* by Reza Aslan, 2005, published by William Heinemann Ltd. Reprinted by permission of The Random House Group Ltd. **pp. 165, 167, 168, 169, 177, 181, 189**; Childress, James. from *Situation Ethics* by James Childress, 1997, published by Westminster John Knox. **pp. 83, 85, 92, 93**; Davies, Paul. from *The Goldilocks Egnima*, 2008, © Houghton Mifflin Harcourt 2008, **pp. 322, 324, 327, 328, 330, 331, 334, 335**; Esposito, John. from *Islam: The Straight Path*, 2004, © Oxford University Press 2004, **pp. 192, 193, 202, 206, 209, 385, 392**; Fletcher, Joseph. from Situation Ethics by James Childress, 1997, published by Westminster John Knox, **pp. 83, 85, 86, 87, 88**; Gombrich, Richard Francis. from *Theravada Buddhism* Routledge 1988, © Taylor and Francis 1988, **pp. 121, 122, 142, 143, 146, 147**; Mason and McCall Smith Law, from *Medical Ethics*, © Oxford University Press, 2006, **pp. 355, 356, 359, 360, 361**; Pratchett, Terry. from *The Colour of Magic* by Terry Pratchett, 1983, reprinted by kind permission of Colin Smythe Ltd, **pp. 331, 332**; Ruthven, Malise. from *Islam in the Modern World*, © Oxford University Press 2006, **pp. 181, 380, 383, 387, 390**; Swinburne, Richard. from *The Existence of God* OUP 1979, © Oxford University Press 1979, **pp. 17, 35, 39**; Turner, Colin. from *Islam the Basics*, © Taylor and Francis 2006, **pp. 168, 169, 170, 175, 179, 189, 190, 191, 193, 195, 200, 201, 205, 210, 211, 382, 385, 386, 391**; Waines, David. from *An Introduction to Islam*, © Cambridge University Press, 2006, **pp. 181, 193, 194, 210, 382, 383**.

b = bottom, *c* = centre, *l* = left, *r* = right, *t* = top

Every effort has been made to trace all copyright holders, but if any have been inadvertently overlooked the Publishers will be pleased to make the necessary arrangements at the first opportunity.